Policy-Making in the European Union

The New European Union Series

Series Editors: John Peterson and Helen Wallace

The European Union is both the most successful modern experiment in international cooperation and a daunting analytical challenge to students of politics, economics, history, law, and the social sciences. The EU of the twenty-first century will be fundamentally different from its earlier permutations, as monetary union, eastern enlargement, a new defence role, and globalization all create pressures for a more complex, differentiated, and truly new European Union.

The New European Union series brings together the expertise of leading scholars writing on major aspects of EU politics for an international readership.

The series offers lively, accessible, reader-friendly, research-based textbooks on:

EU Policy-Making

The EU's Institutions

The History of European Integration

Theorizing Europe

The EU's Member States

The EU as a Global Actor

The European Union: How Does it Work?

Policy-Making in the European Union

Fourth Edition

Edited by

Helen Wallace
and
William Wallace

OXFORD
UNIVERSITY PRESS

OXFORD

UNIVERSITY PRESS

Great Clarendon Street, Oxford OX2 6DP

Oxford University Press is a department of the University of Oxford.
It furthers the University's objective of excellence in research, scholarship,
and education by publishing worldwide in

Oxford New York

Athens Auckland Bangkok Bogotá Buenos Aires Calcutta
Cape Town Chennai Dar es Salaam Delhi Florence Hong Kong Istanbul
Karachi Kuala Lumpur Madrid Melbourne Mexico City Mumbai
Nairobi Paris São Paulo Singapore Taipei Tokyo Toronto Warsaw
with associated companies in Berlin Ibadan

Oxford is a registered trade mark of Oxford University Press
in the UK and in certain other countries

Published in the United States
by Oxford University Press Inc., New York

British Library Cataloguing in Publication Data
Data available

Library of Congress Cataloging in Publication Data
Data available

ISBN 0-19-878242-X

3 5 7 9 10 8 6 4

Typeset by RefineCatch Limited, Bungay, Suffolk
Printed in Great Britain by
TJ International, Padstow, Cornwall

Praise for the Third Edition

'This book is the best of its kind . . . There is no more satisfactory introduction to the life of the European Union. I insist that my students use it . . .'

Ernst B. Haas, Professor of Government, University of California, Berkeley

Praise for the Fourth Edition

'More than ever, the fourth edition of Wallace and Wallace is a "must". This book nicely combines an analysis of EU sectoral policies by the best experts with the overall and systemic approach to the complex European machinery of the two editors. There is nothing equivalent on the market.'

Yves Mény, Director of the Robert Schuman Centre,
European University Institute

'Readers looking for a solid, comprehensive account of European policy-making, authored by some of the best experts in the business, need look no further than this thoroughly updated revision of the Wallaces' classic text.'

Robert D. Putnam, Professor of Government, Harvard University

'Empirical richness and deep insights into the complexity, dynamics, and varieties of policy-making in the EU make this book an invaluable guide for those who want to learn what is really happening in Europe. It is also a powerful reminder to theorists and model-builders that attempts to force the intricacies of European multi-level governance into a single analytical scheme can easily end in frustration.'

Johan P. Olsen, ARENA Programme, University of Oslo

'In a crowded market of text books, the fourth edition of *Policy-Making in the European Union* extends the lead this book enjoys over its many competitors. Comprehensive in coverage, this book offers a depth of analysis that makes students understand the complexities of Europe's emerging polity without burdening them with unnecessary detail. This text works extremely well in very different kinds of courses that cover the policy process in the European Union.'

Peter J. Katzenstein, Walter S. Carpenter, Jr. Professor
of International Studies, Cornell University

Outline contents

Part I Institutions, Process, and Analytical Approaches

Part II Policies

Part III **Conclusions**

Detailed contents

Preface

This fourth edition launches a new series of companion volumes. These will examine the institutions, theory, history, and external policies of the European Union in more depth, and analyse the experiences of member countries in coming to terms with Europeanization.

This is a new book which builds on three editions of an old one. It follows the pattern established in *Policy-Making in the European Communities* (1977), extended and developed in the second and third editions of 1983 and 1996. All of its chapters have been rewritten, many extensively, with references to the earlier versions as appropriate. Readers who wish to understand the historical development of European Union (EU) policies and policy-making in more detail are encouraged to refer back to earlier editions, to gain a broader sense of how patterns of policy-making and institutional interaction have changed over the past two decades.

A great deal has happened in the four years since the third edition was sent to press. The EU, which had expanded from twelve to fifteen in 1995, opened negotiations in 1998 for a much more radical enlargement, to take in the former socialist states of central and eastern Europe, as well as other Mediterranean countries. Another Intergovernmental Conference (IGC), in 1996–7, led to further constitutional changes in the Treaty of Amsterdam, which came into force in May 1999. A succession of critical reports from the Court of Auditors and the European Parliament led to confrontation between Parliament and college of Commissioners over the 'discharge' of the 1997 budget, culminating in the resignation of the Commission in March 1999. Political changes at national level have replaced the majority of Christian democratic and centre-right governments with a majority of social democratic governments. There have been major developments in the field of justice and home affairs, with the incorporation into the EU of the Schengen agreements on the abolition of internal frontiers, the emergence of a European judicial network, and the operationalization of Europol. A Franco-British initiative on European defence, much influenced by the bitter experiences of Bosnia and Kosovo, is gathering momentum as this volume goes to press. The euro was successfully launched as a single currency in January 1999, with eleven member states participating. Plans for a further IGC, to be held in 2000, are under way.

This is a study of policy-making, not of west European integration as such. We do not therefore plunge into discussions of the democracy deficit, of the slow evolution of a Europe-wide civil society, of the interaction between national politics and political parties at the European level. Several of the contributors have written on these issues elsewhere. Our aim here is to provide a detailed picture of the diversity of EU policy-making across a range of policy domains, to enable the student of policy analysis, as well as those primarily interested in the EU, to identify predominant patterns and characteristic styles.

The first edition was produced to fill a gap in what was then a thin academic literature on west European integration. Since then European academic research has mushroomed, contributing to a broadening flow of empirical and theoretical publications. The student of European policy-making is now well provided with a range of detailed case-studies, on which we have drawn in the chapters which follow. The consolidated References list at the end of this volume provides the reader with a guide to the recent literature in English, German, and French, as well as to some of the classical literature from the early years.

The fifteen case-studies have been chosen both to cover the most important fields of EU activity and to illustrate the range of policy domains in which EU institutions now operate. Familiar issues of distribution and redistribution, the single market, agriculture, competition, external trade, North–South relations, monetary integration, and foreign policy have been covered in each of the four editions. The expansion of the EU's policy agenda since the early 1980s is reflected in the inclusion of case-studies of environmental regulation, the social dimension, justice and home affairs, and the response to the emergence of the central and east European states from the socialist bloc. Some of the most insightful examples of how European policy is made and managed emerge from examination of developing fields of policy, or of narrowly defined sectors of established policy. Some reviewers of the third edition questioned our choice then of the banana regime as a case-study; its emergence in 1997–8 as a confrontational issue in transatlantic relations, as well as a source of divergent interests among member governments, justifies that choice. In this edition Chris Stevens has incorporated the banana regime into a broader examination of the changing balance of policies in north–south relations. Case-studies of the fisheries regime and of the attempts to develop common policies in the biotechnology sector illustrate the blend of entrenched interests, expert communities, and encapsulated regimes which characterizes much of EU policy-making.

EU policy-making has accumulated its own myths and entrenched errors. The classic apocryphal story, now repeated even in academic studies, relates to the supposedly dismissive comments made by the British official Russell Bretherton about European integration as he walked out of the Messina Conference, given widespread credence by repetition in the French press. But Bretherton was never at the Messina Conference, and so could not have delivered the speech which has been so widely attributed to him. The painful process of checking on references and quotations for this edition has uncovered another apocryphal classic in the history of west European integration. It appears that Henry Kissinger never spoke the words variously attributed to him in newspaper articles, and taken from there into books, about not knowing which phone number to call when he wanted to get Europe on the line; this developed out of journalistic licence in reporting his frustration with the Danish EU presidency in the tense weeks after the Arab–Israeli conflict in October 1973. We have done our best to ensure that no further errors or apocrypha have crept into our text; we welcome comments from anyone who wishes to challenge or correct any detail.

Sixteen of the nineteen authors of this volume contributed to the third edition. They are drawn from six of the fifteen EU member states, as well as from the United States. Janne Matlary, who contributed to the third edition, then entered the Norwegian government. Michael Hodges, a contributor to all three previous editions and a valued friend, sadly died on his way to work at the London School of Economics in the spring of 1998; we miss his advice and criticism, as well as his friendship. This volume has benefited from informal ties and friendships among contributors since the first edition, sustained through exchanges of visits and children as well as through conferences and shared research. Special thanks go to those authors who have succeeded in producing both chapters and babies at the same time. A preliminary meeting of contributors for this edition was held in London in February 1999.

We would like to thank Tim Barton and Angela Griffin at Oxford University Press for their patience and encouragement. Edward Wallace's computer skills have been deployed in designing graphs and tables, in the management of documents and files, and in allaying occasional bouts of techno-hysteria. Harriet Wallace proved a skilled and highly efficient editor of the text; both editors and contributors recognized the calibre of her queries and attention to detail, and the determination with which she pursued the responses she needed. The quality of a collected volume partly depends on the way it is put together; she has put this volume together superbly well.

H.W., W.W.

London
September 1999

Appendices

Figures

Boxes

Tables

Abbreviations

This volume uses EU as the general abbreviation for the European Union and its component parts. Occasionally it uses EC, especially for developments before the (Maastricht) Treaty on European Union of 1992, or to signify a controversy about which policy powers come within the EC and its classical procedures. Box 1.1 summarizes the elements of the EU, and the history of treaty revisions.

ACEA	European Automobile Manufacturers' Association (from the French abbrev.)
ACFM	Advisory Committee on Fishery Management
ACP	African, Caribbean, and Pacific countries
AFNOR	Association Française de Normalisation
Amcham	American Chamber of Commerce (Brussels)
ANC	African National Congress
AP	Accession Partnership
APEC	Asia-Pacific Economic Cooperation
ASEAN	Association of South East Asian Nations
AWACS	airborne warning and control system
BAT	best available technology
BATNEEC	BAT without excessive economic cost
BCC	Biotechnology Coordinating Committee
Benelux	Belgium, the Netherlands, and Luxembourg
BRIC	Biotechnology Regulations Inter-Service Committee
BSC	Biotechnology Steering Committee
BSE	bovine spongiform encephalitis
CAP	common agricultural policy
CBI	Confederation of British Industry
CCBG	Committee of Central Bank Governors
CCP	common commercial policy
CCT	Common Commercial Tariff
CEECs	countries of central and eastern Europe
CEEP	Confédération Européenne des Employeurs Publics
CEFAS	Centre for Environment, Fisheries, and Aquaculture Science
CELAD	Coordinators' Group on Drugs (from the French abbrev.)
CEN	Committee for European Norms (Standards)
CENELEC	Committee for European Electrical Norms (Standards)
CFI	Court of First Instance
CFP	common fisheries policy
CFSP	common foreign and security policy
cif	price including carriage, insurance, and freight
CIREA	Centre for Information, Discussion, and Exchange on Asylum (from the French abbrev.)
CIREFI	Centre for Information, Discussion, and Exchange on Frontiers and Immigration (from the French abbreviation)

CIS	Commonwealth of Independent States (ex-USSR)
CJTF	Combined Joint Task Forces
CMEA	Council for Mutual Economic Assistance (Comecon)
CNPEM	Comité National des Pêches Maritimes et des Élevages Marins
COPA	Confederation of Professional Agricultural Organizations
CoR	Committee of the Regions
Coreper	Committee of Permanent Representatives
Coreu	Correspondant Européen (EPC communications network)
CORINE	Coordinated Information on the Environment
COSAC	Conférence des Organes Spécialisées aux Affaires Communautaires
CP	Contracting Party
CPE	European Farmers' Coordination
CSCE	Conference on Security and Cooperation in Europe
CSF	community support framework
CSFR	Czech and Slovak Federal Republic
CTE	Committee on Trade and the Environment (WTO)
CTEU	Consolidated Treaty on European Union
CUBE	Concertation Unit for Biotechnology in Europe
DECHEMA	German Chemical Manufacturers' Association (from the German abbrev.)
DG	Directorate-General (of the European Commission)
DGB	Deutscher Gewerkschaftsbund (German Trade Union Confederation)
DIN	Deutsche Institut für Normung
DM	Deutschmark
DNA	dioxyribonucleic acid
DOM	départements d'outremer
DSB	Dispute Settlement Body
DSU	Dispute Settlement Understanding
EA	Europe Agreement
EAEC	European Atomic Energy Community (Euratom)
EAGGF	European Agricultural Guidance and Guarantee Fund
EAPC	Euro-Atlantic Partnership Council
EBRD	European Bank for Reconstruction and Development
EC	European Community
EC6	Belgium, France, Federal Republic of Germany, Italy, Luxembourg, the Netherlands
EC9	+ Denmark, Ireland, UK
EC10	+ Greece
EC12	+ Portugal, Spain
EC > EU15	+ Austria, Finland, Sweden
ECB	European Central Bank
ECHO	European Community Humanitarian Office
ECJ	European Court of Justice
ECO	European Cartel Office
Ecofin	Council of Economic and Finance Ministers
ECSC	European Coal and Steel Community
ecu	European currency unit
EDC	European Defence Community
EDF	European Development Fund

EDU	European Drugs Unit
EEA	European Economic Area
EEB	European Environmental Bureau
EEC	European Economic Community
EEZ	exclusive economic zone
EFB	European Federation of Biotechnology
EFTA	European Free Trade Association
EIB	European Investment Bank
EIONET	European Information and Observation Network
EIS	European Information System
ELV	end-of-life vehicle
EMEA	European Agency for the Evaluation of Medicinal Products
EMBO	European Molecular Biology Organization
EMI	European Monetary Institute
EMS	European Monetary System
EMU	economic and monetary union
EP	European Parliament
EPA	Environmental Protection Agency (US)
EPC	European Political Cooperation
EPP	European People's Party
ERDF	European Regional Development Fund
ERM	exchange-rate mechanism
ERT	European Round Table of Industrialists
ESA	European Space Agency
ESC	Economic and Social Committee
ESCB	European System of Central Banks
ESDI	European Security and Defence Identity
ESF	European Science Foundation
ESF	European Social Fund
ESNBA	European Secretariat of National Bio-industry Associations
ETUC	European Trade Union Confederation
EU	European Union. See also EC
EU11	The eleven member states who by Sept. 1999 had joined EMU
Euratom	European Atomic Energy Community
€ euro	name of the single currency for EMU
Eurocorps	multilateral European force, expanded from Franco-German brigade in 1991
Eurodac	European Automated Fingerprint Recognition System (from the French abbrev.)
Eurogroup	European group within Nato from 1970
EUR-OP	Office of Official Publications of the European Communities
Europol	European Police Office
FAO	Food and Agriculture Organization
FBI	Federal Bureau of Investigation (US)
FCO	Foreign and Commonwealth Office
FDA	Food and Drugs Agency (US)
FDI	foreign direct investment
FIFG	Financial Instrument for Fisheries Guidance

fob	prices free-on-board
FOC	Forum of Consultation (of WEU)
FRG	Federal Republic of Germany
FTA	Free Trade Agreement
FTAA	Free Trade Agreement of the Americas
FYROM	former Yugoslav Republic of Macedonia
G7	Group of Seven (western economic powers): Canada, France, Germany, Italy, Japan, UK, USA
G8	G7 plus Russia
G24	Group of Twenty-Four (member states of OECD)
GAC	General Affairs Council
GATS	General Agreement on Trade in Services
GATT	General Agreement on Tariffs and Trade
GDP	gross domestic product
GDR	German Democratic Republic
GILSP	good industrial large-scale practice
GMAG	Genetic Manipulation Advisory Group (UK)
GMO	genetically modified organism
GNE	Group of National Experts (on Safety and Regulation in Biotechnology)
GNP	gross national product
GSP	Generalized System of Preferences
ICC	International Chamber of Commerce
ICCAT	International Commission for the Conservation of Atlantic Tuna
ICES	International Council for the Exploration of the Sea
IDP	Integrated Development Programme
IEA	International Energy Agency
IEPG	Independent European Programme Group
Ifor	(Nato-led) Implementation Force (in Bosnia)
IFREMER	Institut Français de Recherche pour l'Exploitation de la Mer
IGC	Intergovernmental Conference
IIA	Inter-Institutional Agreement
IMF	International Monetary Fund
IMP	Integrated Mediterranean Programme
IMPEL	European Network for the Implementation and Enforcement of Environmental Law
INSERM	Institut National pour l'Enseignement et la Recherche Médicale
Interpol	International Police Association
IPC	Integrated Pollution Control (UK)
IPPC	Integrated Pollution Prevention and Control (EU)
IPR	intellectual property rights
ISO	International Standards Organization
IT	information technology
ITQ	individual transferable quota
JHA	justice and home affairs
K4	committee of senior officials for JHA (now Article 36 Committee)
LDC	less developed country
MAFF	Ministry of Agriculture, Fisheries, and Food (UK)
MAG '92	Mutual Assistance Group (for 1992)

MAGP	Multi-annual Guidance Programme
MAI	Multilateral Agreement on Investment
MCA	monetary compensatory amount
MDG	Multidisciplinary Group on Organized Crime
MEP	member of the European Parliament
Mercosur	Common Market of the Southern Cone
MFA	Multi-Fibre Arrangement
MFN	most-favoured nation (GATT)
MSC	Marine Stewardship Council
MTR	Mid-Term Review (of Uruguay Round)
NACC	North Atlantic Co-operation Council
NAFTA	North American Free Trade Area
Nato	North Atlantic Treaty Organization
NCPI	New Commercial Policy Instrument
NEAFC	North East Atlantic Fisheries Commission
NFFO	National Federation of Fishermen's Organizations
NGO	non-governmental organization
NIC	newly industrialized country
NTB	non-tariff barrier
OECD	Organization for Economic Cooperation and Development
OEEC	Organization for European Economic Cooperation
OJL	*Official Journal of the European Communities*, Law Series
OLAF	Office de la Lutte Anti-Fraude (Fraud Prevention Office; previously UCLAF)
OSCE	Organization for Security and Cooperation in Europe
Phare	Pologne–Hongrie: Assistance à la Restructuration des Économies (extended to other CEECs)
PESC	politique étrangère et de securité commune
PfP	Partnership for Peace
Piatnika	grouping of five successive Council presidencies
QMV	qualified majority voting
QR	quantitative restriction
R&D	research and development
rDNA	recombinant DNA
RDP	regional development plan
REPA	regional economic partnership agreement
REX	External Economic Relations (Committee) (of the EP, from the French abbrev.)
SAA	Stabilization and Association Agreement
SAD	Statement of Assurance
SAGB	Senior Advisory Group for Biotechnology
SBF	Save Britain's Fish
SCA	Special Committee on Agriculture
SCR	Common Service for External Relations
SEA	Single European Act
SEM	single European market
SFC	Sea Fisheries Committee
SFF	Scottish Fishermen's Federation

SG	Steering Group
SIC	Schengen Implementing Convention
SIRENE	Supplementary Information System of Schengen
SIS	Schengen Information System
SLIM	Simpler Legislation for the Internal Market
SME	small and medium-sized enterprises
SPD	single programming document
STECF	Scientific, Technical, and Economic Committee for Fisheries
T&C	textiles and clothing
TAC	total allowable catch
TACIS	Technical Assistance for the CIS Countries
TAIEX	Technical Assistance Information Exchange Office
TBR	Trade Barriers Regulation
TBT	technical barrier to trade
TCA	trade and cooperation agreements
TEC	Revised Treaty of Rome (Treaty of the European Community)
Tempus	Trans-European Mobility Programme for University Studies
TEN	Trans-European Network
TEP	Transatlantic Economic Partnership
TEU	Treaty on European Union
ToA	Treaty of Amsterdam
TOM	territoires d'outremer
Trevi	Terrorisme, Radicalisme, Extremisme, Violence, Information (agreement on internal security cooperation)
troika	grouping of three successive Council presidencies
UAPF	Union des Armateurs à la Pêche de France
UCLAF	Unité de Co-ordination de la Lutte Anti-fraude (anti-fraud unit; now OLAF)
UK	United Kingdom
UN	United Nations
UNECE	United Nations Economic Commission for Europe
UNFCCC	United Nations Framework Convention on Climate Change
UNHCR	United Nations High Commission for Refugees
UNICE	Union of Industrial and Employers' Confederations of Europe
Unprofor	United Nations Protection Force in Bosnia
UR	Uruguay Round
US, USA	United States
USSR	Union of Soviet Socialist Republics
USTR	United States' Trade Representative
VAT	value-added tax
WEU	Western European Union
WG	Working Group
WTO	World Trade Organization
WWF	World Wide Fund for Nature

List of contributors

DAVID ALLEN	*University of Loughborough*
MONICA DEN BOER	*Catholic University of Brabant (Tilburg)*
ANTHONY FORSTER	*University of Nottingham*
BRIGID LAFFAN	*University College, Dublin*
STEPHAN LEIBFRIED	*University of Bremen*
CHRISTIAN LEQUESNE	*Centre d'Études et de Recherches Internationales, Paris*
FRANCIS MCGOWAN	*University of Sussex*
LEE ANN PATTERSON	*Universities of California (San Francisco) and Pittsburgh*
PAUL PIERSON	*Harvard University*
ELMAR RIEGER	*University of Bremen*
ALBERTA M. SBRAGIA	*University of Pittsburgh*
ULRICH SEDELMEIER	*Central European University*
MICHAEL SHACKLETON	*European Parliament*
CHRISTOPHER STEVENS	*University of Sussex*
LOUKAS TSOUKALIS	*London School of Economics and Political Science*
HELEN WALLACE	*University of Sussex*
WILLIAM WALLACE	*London School of Economics and Political Science*
STEPHEN WOOLCOCK	*London School of Economics and Political Science*
ALASDAIR R. YOUNG	*University of Sussex*

Editors' note

A number of problems of dating and numbering should be noted. Treaty reforms are dated to their signature by member governments, rather than to the completion of negotiations (often the year before) or ratification (often the year after). The well-intentioned renumbering of treaty articles, agreed as an afterthought to the Treaty of Amsterdam, has created immense difficulties for all students of the European Union. We generally quote treaty articles under the numbering in the Consolidated Treaty on European Union agreed in 1997, and cross-refer to the previous numbering, still relevant for earlier periods. One section of the CTEU is confusingly the Consolidated Treaty establishing the European Community (TEC). Special care is needed to follow the two parallel sets of numbering that cover the common foreign and security policy and justice and home affairs.

Until September 1999 Directorates General (DG) of the European Commission were generally known by their numbers, e.g. DGVI for Agriculture. Numbers have been replaced by functional names only. However, in this volume the numbers have been retained, since most of the material belongs to the period in which they were relevant. The two nomenclatures are set out in Tables 1.2 and 1.3.

Part I

Institutions, Process, and Analytical Approaches

Chapter 1
The Institutional Setting
Five Variations on a Theme

Helen Wallace

Contents

Summary

This chapter sets the policy process of the European Union (EU) in its institutional context. Since the EU is part of, not separate from, the politics and policy processes of the member states, the institutions that are relevant include national (and infra-national) institutions, as well as those created by the EU treaties. Features of the national processes pervade the EU, and differences between member states pervade EU policies and the way that they are applied. The same member states take part in many other international and European organizations, another factor which shapes EU policy-making. Globalization and Europeanization are intertwined. The institutional design of the EU is explained, especially the Commission, Council, European Council, European Parliament, and the European Court of Justice. New trends include the emergence of quasi-autonomous agencies, such as the European Central Bank and Europol. EU and national institutions interact differently in different policy domains. Five variants of the EU policy process are identified: a distinctive Community method; the EU regulatory model; multi-level governance; policy coordination and benchmarking; and intensive transgovernmentalism. The last two of these are particularly strong in the new areas of active EU policy development.

Introduction

The EU is perhaps the most important agent of change in contemporary government and policy-making in western Europe. Jacques Delors, then the President of the European Commission, claimed in 1988 that about 80 per cent of socio-economic legislation in the EU member states was framed by treaty commitments, policy rules, and legislation agreed through the institutions of the EU. Whether or not the percentage is precisely accurate does not matter. What matters is the acknowledgement that EU agreements pervade the policy-making activities of individual west European countries, both the member states and their neighbours. Explaining how and why this is so is the key aim of this volume.

In Part I we sketch the broad contours of the EU policy process and the institutions through which it is articulated, and then identify some of the different ways in which the policy process can be analysed. Part II consists of a series of case-studies, which cover many of the policy domains in which the EU dimension is significant. The cases cover a wide range of policy domains, both long-established and infant regimes, both overarching complex policies and specific sectoral concerns, and both more and less formally structured policies. Two new cases on biotechnology (Chapter 12) and fisheries (Chapter 13) appear in this edition. Many of the case-studies carried over from previous editions have been extensively revised to illustrate either different dimensions of their policy domain or major changes that have occurred over the past few years. Part III offers some conclusions on the character of the process and the directions in which it is evolving.

For convenience we have mostly used the term 'European Union' in this volume. The EU is built out of three originally separate Communities, each with different powers, characteristics, and policy domains, complemented by other 'pillars' of organized cooperation. These various elements of the EU are:

- the European Coal and Steel Community (ECSC), founded in 1951 by the Treaty of Paris;
- the European Economic Community (EEC), founded in 1957 by the Treaty of Rome;
- the European Atomic Energy Community (Euratom), also founded in 1957 by another Treaty of Rome;
- these three together came to be referred to as the European Community (EC), and in a loose sense the 'first pillar', once the term EU was introduced by the (Maastricht) Treaty on European Union (TEU) of 1992;

- the 'second pillar' for developing the common foreign and security policy (CFSP), acknowledged in the Single European Act (SEA) of 1986, and put on to a more formal basis in the TEU; and

- the 'third pillar' for developing cooperation in justice and home affairs (JHA), established also by the TEU in 1992.

Membership of the EU had expanded from six countries in 1951 to fifteen by 1995, with further enlargement in prospect, as follows:

1951   Belgium, the Federal Republic of Germany, France, Italy, Luxembourg, the Netherlands
1973   + Denmark, Ireland, the United Kingdom
1981   + Greece
1986   + Portugal, Spain
1995   + Austria, Finland, Sweden.

Current candidates include: Bulgaria, Cyprus, the Czech Republic, Estonia, Hungary, Latvia, Lithuania, Malta, Poland, Romania, Slovakia, Slovenia, and Turkey.

Some preliminary observations

Four broad points need to be made clear at the outset. First, the EU policy process is based on west European experience. So far the member countries of the EU, and its various precursors, have been west European countries with market economies and liberal democratic polities, even though some, notably Greece, Portugal, and Spain, had moved quite swiftly from authoritarian regimes to EU membership in the 1980s. It is not our contention that these various countries all neatly fit into a single political and economic mould, but none the less they have some strong shared characteristics which permeate the EU policy process. However, the EU now stands on the brink of an eastwards enlargement, perhaps to embrace a number (how many and how soon remains to be seen) of central and east European countries, with very different inheritances. One important question which follows is whether this fit between country characteristics and European process will be sustainable in a larger and more diverse Union.

A second preliminary point is that the west European experience, in which the EU is embedded, is one of which dense multilateralism is a strong feature. The EU constitutes a particularly intense form of multilateralism, but western Europe is a region of countries with an apparent predisposition to engage in cross-border regime-building. In part this relates to specific features of history and geography, but it seems also to be connected to a political culture of investing in institutionalized cooperation with neighbours and partners, at least in the period since the second world war. This is part of the reason why transnational policy development has become more structured and more iterative than in most other regions of the world.

Thirdly, the EU has, since its inception, been active in a rather wide array of policy domains, and indeed has over the decades extended its policy scope. Most international or transnational regimes are more one-dimensional. Part of our contention in this volume is that this array of policy domains has generated not one, but several, modes of policy-making. Our case-studies do not reveal a single predominant mode, but rather several interestingly different modes. Moreover, the same EU institutions, and the same national policy-makers, have different characteristics, exhibit different patterns of behaviour, and produce different kinds of outcome, depending on the policy domain and depending on the period. Thus, as we shall see, there is no single and catch-all way of capturing the essence of EU policy-making. All generalizations need to be nuanced, although, as will be argued below, five main variants of the policy process can be identified.

Fourthly, this volume goes to press at a moment when important systemic changes are taking place in the EU. Not only may the EU be altered by eastern enlargement, but even with its current membership of fifteen west European countries there are major factors of change. Three in particular stand out: the establishment of economic and monetary union (EMU) (Chapter 6); the incorporation of a new societal dimension, through the 'area of freedom, security, and justice' (Chapter 18); and the rapid moves under way to construct a form of European defence autonomy (Chapter 17). As will become clear, both from the individual accounts of these topics and from Part III, the net effect may be to change in rather fundamental ways the nature of EU policy-making.

The patterns of policy-making in these three domains are not entirely clear, and it is premature to try to distil a clear assessment. However, one striking feature characterizes all of them. Each is being constructed to a large extent outside the classical Community framework. Some EU institutions, so far at least, have been on the margins of the main developments. In particular the Commission, the European Court of Justice (ECJ), and the European Parliament (EP) have been rather passive actors, while the main dynamics have been found in the intensive interactions between national policy-makers. The investments being made in new institutional arrangements in each of these areas have been designed to underpin this intensive transgovernmentalism rather than to incorporate them within the traditional Community procedures (communitarization). The case-study chapters suggest that this may be a sustained pattern, not a mere staging-post in the transition from nationally rooted policy to 'communitarization'. Tempting though it might be to see this as the triumph of 'intergovernmentalism' (a process in which traditional states predominate) over 'supranationalism' (a process in which new European institutions enjoy political autonomy and authority), we argue that a new transnational policy mode is emerging.

The European Union in context

Most studies of the EU concentrate on describing what happens in and through the special institutions of the EU, located in Brussels, Luxembourg, and Strasbourg: the European Commission; the Council of the EU; the European Council; the EP; and the ECJ.[1] However, we should be careful not to regard these EU institutions as existing in a vacuum. Most of the policy-makers who devise and operate EU rules and legislation are from the member states themselves. They are people who spend the majority

---

[1] Those new to the subject should note the existence of the entirely separate organization the Council of Europe, created in 1949, based in Strasbourg, originally with only west European members, but now with a continent-wide membership of forty countries. It has a classical intergovernmental structure, except for the rather autonomous European Court of Human Rights.

of their time as national policy-makers, for whom the European dimension is an extended policy arena, not a separate activity. Indeed much of EU policy is prepared and carried out by national policy-makers and agents who do not spend much, if any, time in Brussels. Rather what they do is consider how EU regimes might help or hinder their regular activities, and apply the results of EU agreements on the ground in their normal daily work. If we could calculate the proportions, we might well find that in practice something like 80 per cent of that normal daily life was framed by domestic preoccupations and constraints. Much the same is true of the social and economic groups, or political representatives, who seek to influence the development and content of EU policy.

On the face of it, it might appear that it cannot simultaneously be the case that 80 per cent of the member states' socio-economic legislation is shaped by the EU, while 80 per cent of the policy context of national policy-makers is framed by domestic concerns. Yet precisely what distinguishes the EU as a policy arena is that it rests on a kind of amalgam of these two levels of governance. Country-defined policy demands and policy capabilities are set in a shared European framework to generate collective regimes, most of which are then implemented back in the countries concerned. Moreover, as we shall see from several of the case-studies in this volume, how those European regimes operate varies a good deal between one EU member state and another. In other words, the EU policy process is one which has differentiated outcomes, with significant variations between countries. Hence it is just as important to understand the national institutional settings as to understand the EU-level institutions in order to get a grip on the EU policy process as a whole (H. Wallace 1973, 1999a).

This two-level picture does not, however, describe the whole story. In all EU countries there are other levels of infranational government, that is local or regional authorities, the responsibilities of which are to varying extents shaped by EU regimes. Many of these authorities have occasional direct contacts with the EU institutions. In addition, and increasingly, national policy processes in western Europe depend on other kinds of agencies and institutions, which lie between the public and the private spheres and also vary a good deal in character from one country to another. One striking feature of western Europe in the past decade or so has been the proliferation of bodies with public policy functions outside the central governments. This is especially so in the regulatory arena, perhaps the most extensive domain of EU policy activity. The shift towards more autonomous or semi-autonomous agencies, or to forms of 'self-regulation', represents a move away from the inherited heavy state version of government towards a kind of partnership model. What the EU policy process does is to add another layer, making cross-agency coordination one of its key features, as we shall see in various of our case-studies.

Even this multifaceted picture does not encompass the whole story. The EU arena is only part of a wider pattern of making policy beyond the nation state. In many areas of public policy, including those within which the EU is active, there are broader transnational consultations and regimes. These vary a great deal in their robustness and intensity, but they are part of a continuum of policy-making that spreads from the country, through the European arena, to the global level. Many of the same policy-makers are active across these levels, and policy development consists of choices between these levels or the assignment of different segments of a given policy domain to different levels. Several of our policy case-studies illustrate this phenomenon, and mostly stress its increased salience. One important question to bear in mind here is whether or not the EU institutions provide the main junction box through which connections are made between the country level and the global level.

One further preliminary point needs to be made. Most accounts of the EU policy process work from the EU treaties outwards, starting from the policy powers explicitly assigned to them, and then considering extensions of policy powers, or refusals to extend policy powers. Such accounts place the EU at the centre of the picture, and tend to make the EU appear the fulcrum of policy-making. Other European transnational policy regimes—and there are many—tend to be viewed as second-best solutions, or weaker forms of policy cooperation. This volume takes issue with this image. Instead we argue that the EU is only one, even if by far the most invasive, arena for building European policy regimes. Hence we need to compare and contrast the EU with these other policy regimes, both the highly structured (such as the North Atlantic Treaty Organization (Nato) for defence) and the relatively informal (such as in the past have enabled national police forces to develop cross-border cooperation). Then we can consider with more nuance why the EU process is especially important in some policy domains, but not in others, just as we can examine how experiences in other kinds of European policy regime might be changing the character of the EU policy process.

In short, the EU policy process needs to be viewed through several sets of spectacles. Different lenses may be needed depending on the division of powers and influences between these different levels and arenas of policy development. To be sure we then need to focus squarely on what happens in and through the EU institutions. But we need peripheral vision to take in the country-level processes (both national and infranational), the global level, and the alternative European frameworks. And we need to be aware that policy-making shifts between these in a fluid and dynamic way.

The European Union as a unique arena—or perhaps not

Most accounts of the EU policy process, as we have noted, concentrate on the EU's own institutions. Their main features and characteristics are set out in this chapter, and their roles in the policy process will be a recurrent theme in this volume. We shall observe general features that are present in most areas of EU policy, as well as features that are specific to particular sectors, issues, events, and periods.

But how far do the particular features of the EU's institutional system produce a distinctive kind of policy process? It has been commonplace for commentators on the EU to stress its distinctive features, and indeed often to argue that they result in a unique kind of politics. Whether such an assertion is warranted is a question to keep in mind in reading subsequent chapters. In forming an answer to the question it is important to reflect on what other political arrangements might be appropriately compared with the EU. Some would say loose-knit states, such as Canada or Switzerland, mostly confederal in character. Others would say some multilateral regimes, especially those which focus on the political economy, such as the Organization for Economic Cooperation and Development (OECD), or the various regional customs unions and free trade areas elsewhere in the world. Depending on which comparators are chosen, different benchmarks will be useful for evaluating the EU institutions and their performance.

As we shall see in Chapter 3, this issue has been one of the longest-running sources of controversy among political analysts of the EU. On one side of the debate are ranged those who see the EU as one example, perhaps a particularly richly developed example, of a transnational or international organization. On the other side of the debate are the proponents of the view that the EU is a kind of polity-in-the-making, and in this sense statelike. The analyses of the EU's institutions conducted in these two camps differ considerably. A third camp argues that contemporary politics in western Europe are changing anyway, with traditional forms of politics and government being transformed in quite radical ways. The net result, it is argued, is that it is more appropriate to talk of 'governance' than of 'government'. The EU has, according to this view, emerged as part of a reconfigured pattern of European governance, with an evolution of institutional arrangements and associated processes that have interestingly novel characteristics.

This volume starts out closer to the third camp than to either of the first two. However, subsequent chapters will reveal some policy sectors in which the EU has powers as extensive as those normally associated with country-level governance, while other chapters will describe much lighter and more fragile European regimes. The institutional patterns vary between these two kinds of cases. This chapter provides an anatomical overview, while the subsequent case-studies identify many of the variations of institutional patterns that are observable in specific areas of policy, along with the organic features of the institutional processes. These variations make the EU policy process a challenging one to characterize and hence the subject of lively argument for both practitioners and analysts.

However distinctive and unusual the EU institutions might be argued to be, we should not forget that the people, groups, and organizations which are active within these institutions are for the most part going about their 'normal' business in seeking policy and political outcomes. There is no reason to suppose that their activities have different purposes simply because the institutional arena is different from the others in which they are involved. The politics of the EU are just that, normal politics, with whatever one thinks the normal features are of domestic politics—and by extension policy-making—in west European countries. None the less, we need to be alert to differences in behaviour, in opportunities, and in constraints that arise from being involved in a multi-level and multi-layered process. It is around this feature of the EU that much of the most interesting analytical debate takes place, a point to which we return in Chapter 3.

The institutional design of the European Union

The EU has grown out of three originally separate Communities (ECSC, EEC, and Euratom), each with its own institutions. These were formally merged in 1967. The main elements originally consisted of: a collective executive of sorts—the European Commission; a collective forum for representatives of member governments—the Council (of Ministers); a mechanism for binding arbitration and legal interpretation—the European Court of Justice; and a parliamentary chamber—the European Parliament (originally 'Assembly')—with members drawn from the political classes of the member states, later by direct election. In addition the Economic and Social Committee provided a forum for consulting other sectors of society. The powers and responsibilities are set out in the treaties, and have been periodically revised (see Table 1.1). As this volume went to press plans were in hand for a further IGC to be held during 2000. Romano Prodi asked for a report (Dehaene *et al.* 1999) from a group of three 'wise men' as an early contribution to this discussion.

Table 1.1 The main treaties and treaty reforms

Year	Treaty	Outcome
1951	Treaty of Paris	European Coal and Steel Community (ECSC) (signed by Belgium, the Federal Republic of Germany, France, Italy, Luxembourg and Netherlands)
1957	Treaty of Rome	European Economic Community (EEC)
1957	Treaty of Rome	European Atomic Energy Community (Euratom)
1965-6	Luxembourg crisis and compromise block reforms	
1965	Merger Treaty	Combines institutions into single set
1970	Budgetary Treaty	'Own resources' (i.e. revenue) created; some budgetary powers for European Parliament (EP)
1972	Act of Accession	Admits Denmark, Ireland, and UK
1975	Budgetary Treaty	More powers to EP; new Court of Auditors
1978	Treaty revision	For direct elections to EP
1980	Act of Accession	Admits Greece
1985	Act of Accession	Admits Portugal and Spain
1986	Single European Act (SEA)	More qualified majority voting (QMV) in Council; some legislative power for EP; new Court of First Instance; introduces cohesion; expands policy scope
1992	Treaty on European Union (Maastricht) (TEU)	Three-pillar structure of European Union (common foreign and security policy (CFSP) and justice and home affairs (JHA)); more QMV in Council; formalizes European Council; some co-decision for EP; new Committee of Regions; expands policy scope, especially for economic and monetary union (EMU); introduces subsidiarity and citizenship; Social Protocol (UK opt-out)
1994	Act of Accession	Admits Austria, Finland, and Sweden
1997	Treaty of Amsterdam (ToA)	More legislative powers to EP, and stronger requirement for its 'assent' on (e.g.) enlargement and Commission appointments; introduces 'flexibility' (some member states cooperating without others); modest extra QMV in Council; incorporates Schengen
1997	Consolidated Treaty on European Union (CTEU)	'Simplifies' the treaties by combining into a single set, and therefore renumbering, the provisions of earlier treaties

In the 1990s the EC was turned into what is now generally called the European Union, a term which serves two quite different purposes. One is to imply a stronger binding together of the member states. The other is to embrace within one broad framework the different Communities and also the other arenas of cooperation that have emerged, in particular the two 'pillars' of so-called intergovernmental cooperation: the 'second pillar' for CFSP (see Chapter 17); and the 'third pillar' for JHA (see Chapter 18). We summarize here some key elements of the institutional arrangements (readers already familiar with these can move on to the section dealing with the five policy modes in the EU policy process (p. 28).

The European Commission

The Commission was designated as both secretariat and proto-executive in the EU's institutional system. In its earliest version, as the High Authority of the European Coal and Steel Community (agreed in 1951), it leaned more towards being executive in nature, with considerable autonomy. It is from this experiment that the term 'supranational' was coined. When the EEC was created in 1958, some member governments had second thoughts about the consequences of creating a strong autonomous institution. Thereafter the Commission had an ambiguous remit, with strong

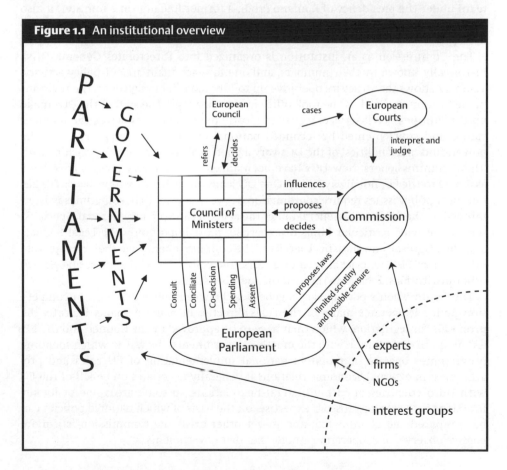

Figure 1.1 An institutional overview

powers in some fields (notably competition policy—see Chapter 5), and weaker powers in most others. The onus was left to the Commission itself to develop credibility, expertise, and the bases for a political power of its own.

The Commission exercises its responsibilities collectively. The Commissioners themselves, two from each of the 'larger' member states, and one from each of the others, constitute a 'college' of high officials, currently twenty in the EU of fifteen. Their decisions and proposals to the Council and EP have to be agreed by the whole college, voting, if necessary, by simple majority, at its weekly meetings. The Commission is chaired by a President, chosen with other colleagues, by 'common accord' in the Council, with two other commissioners as Vice-Presidents, initially for a term of four years. Those chosen are senior politicians or high officials from member states, but they swear an oath of independence on taking office. Under the TEU the term of office was extended to five years, to coincide with that of the EP, and nominations were made subject to consultation with the EP; the Treaty of Amsterdam (ToA) gave the EP the stronger power to confirm commissioners in office.

Commissioners are accountable to the EP, which has the power to censure the college with a two-thirds vote. In March 1999 the college, presided over by Jacques Santer, was forced into resignation by the EP on a charge of financial mismanagement. This prompted a decision by the European Council to nominate a stronger team under the presidency of Romano Prodi, a former Italian prime minister. It also led to a particularly intense and public scrutiny of the new team by the EP in September 1999.

The Commission as an institution is organized into Directorates General (DGs), historically known by their numbers, and one for each main area of policy activity. Table 1.2 shows the structure operative up to July 1999. Table 1.3 shows the revisions made by Romano Prodi, as he took office in summer 1999. The staff of the DGs make up the European civil service, recruited mostly in competitions across the member states, and supplemented by seconded national experts and temporary staff. The powers and 'personalities' of the DGs vary a good deal, as do their relationships with 'their' commissioners. New DGs have been added as new policy powers have been assigned to the EU, not always tidily. One DG leads on each policy topic, as *chef de file*, but most policy issues require coordination between several DGs, sometimes masterminded by the Secretariat-General under the aegis of the Secretary-General. Specialist services provide particular kinds of expertise, most importantly the Legal Service, and the linguistic and statistical services. The commissioners have their own private offices, or *cabinets*, who act as their eyes, ears, and voices, inside the house and *vis-à-vis* other institutions, including those of the member states.

The Commission's powers vary a good deal between policy domains. In competition policy it operates many of the rules directly; in many domains it drafts the proposals for legislation, which then have to be approved by the Council and the EP; it defines, in consultation with the member governments, the way in which spending programmes operate; it monitors national implementation of EU rules and programmes; in external economic relations it generally negotiates on behalf of the EU with third countries or in multilateral negotiations; in some areas one of its key functions is to develop cross-EU expertise, on the basis of which national policies can be compared and coordinated; and in yet other areas the Commission is a more passive observer of cooperation among member governments.

Table 1.2 The structure of the European Commission, July 1999

Directorate-General	Policy area
DG I	External relations: trade policy and relations with most of the developed countries
DG IA	External relations: Europe and CIS, and CFSP
DG IB	External relations: Mediterranean, Middle East, Latin America
DG II	Economic and financial affairs
DG III	Industry
DG IV	Competition
DG V	Employment, industrial relations, and social affairs
DG VI	Agriculture
DG VII	Transport
DG VIII	Development (and Joint Service for Community Aid)
DG IX	Personnel and administration
DG X	Information, communication, culture, and audiovisual
DG XI	Environment, nuclear safety, and civil protection
DG XII	Science, research and development (and Joint Research Centre)
DG XIII	Telecommunications, information market, and exploitation of research
DG XIV	Fisheries
DG XV	Internal market and financial services
DG XVI	Regional policy and cohesion
DG XVII	Energy
DG XIX	Budget
DG XX	Financial control
DG XXI	Taxation and customs union
DG XXII	Education, training, and youth
DG XXIII	Enterprise policy, distributive trades, tourism, and cooperatives
DG XXIV	Consumer policy and health protection

Responsible to the President
Secretariat-General
■ Task force for cooperation in justice and home affairs
■ Task force for coordination of fraud prevention
■ Institutional matters
Legal Service
Security Office
Forward Studies Unit
Inspectorate-General
Joint Interpreting and Conference Service
Spokesman's Service

Other services/agencies
Statistical Office (Eurostat)
European Community Humanitarian Office (ECHO)
Euratom Supply Agency
Office for Official Publications of the European Communities (EUR-OP)
Translation Service

Table 1.3 The proposed reorganization of the European Commission, September 1999

Commissioner	Area of responsibility
President	Secretariat-General Forward Studies Unit Legal Service Media and Communication Service
Vice-President for Administrative Reform	Personnel and Administration DG Inspectorate-General Joint Interpreting and Conference Service Translation Service
Vice-President for Relations with the European Parliament and for Transport and Energy	Secretariat-General, relations with the EP Transport DG Energy DG Euratom Supply Agency
Commissioner for Competition	Competition DG
Commissioner for Agriculture and Fisheries	Agriculture DG Fisheries DG
Commissioner for Enterprise and Information Society	Enterprise DG Information DG
Commissioner for Internal Market	Internal Market DG Customs and Taxation DG
Commissioner for Research	Research DG Joint Research Centre
Commissioner for Economic and Monetary Affairs	Economic and Financial Affairs DG Statistical Office (Eurostat)
Commissioner for External Relations	External Relations DG Common Service for External Relations overall coordination with other commissioners dealing with external relations
Commissioner for Development and Humanitarian Aid	Development DG European Community Humanitarian Office (ECHO)
Commissioner for Enlargement	Enlargement Service
Commissioner for Trade	Trade DG
Commissioner for Health and Consumer Protection	Health and Consumer Protection DG
Commissioner for Regional Policy	Regional Policy DG *ad personam* deals with Intergovernmental Conference
Commissioner for Education and Culture	Education and Culture DG Publications Office
Commissioner for Budget	Budget DG Financial Control DG Fraud Prevention Office (OLAF)
Commissioner for Environment	Environment DG Nuclear Control Office
Commissioner for Justice and Home Affairs	Justice and Home Affairs DG
Commissioner for Employment and Social Affairs	Employment and Social Affairs DG

Broadly, within the classical areas of Community cooperation the Commission has a jealously guarded power of initiative, which gives it the opportunity to be the agenda-setter. For this reason it is a target for everyone who wants to influence the content of policy. One of the key questions therefore to be asked about the Commission is how it exploits the opportunities available to it. Some of the resources available to it include: the capability to build up expertise; the potential for developing policy networks and coalitions; the scope for acquiring grateful or dependent clients; and the chance to help member governments to resolve their own policy predicaments. Versions of all of these are the subject of debate in the theoretical literature, and are addressed throughout our case-studies.

However, as we shall see, in many areas of policy the Commission has a less entrepreneurial role, either because it is not able to exploit the opportunities available to it, or because the nature of the policy regime allows less room for the Commission to play a central role. In addition we should note that there is a broader problem of capacity. The Commission is quite a small institution, with only some 20,000 staff—not very many to develop or implement policies across fifteen different countries. Hence a great deal depends on how the Commission works with the national institutions, which in practice operate most Community rules and programmes. Over the years this feature of the policy process has become more explicit. Indeed, as several of our case-studies illustrate (see, for example, Chapters 5, 9, and 13), if anything the balance is tilting towards recognizing much more systematically the role of national (or local) agencies in operating Community policies.

Hence partnership between the national and the European levels of governance has become one of the marked features of EU policy-making. One key mechanism for this is the clumsily named system of 'comitology'. In essence it is very straightforward. Both to prepare policy proposals and to implement agreed policies the Commission needs regular channels for discussion with relevant national officials. Over the years a dense network of advisory, regulatory, and management committees has grown up to provide these channels, much as happens in individual countries. In the case of the EU these committees are the subject of procedural, legal, and political debate. Most of the committees are governed by legally specified arrangements, which vary according to the policy, and which strike different balances of influence between national representatives and the Commission. Some insights into the workings of these committees appear in several of our case-studies.

The Commission has had several high points of political impact, especially in the early 1960s and the mid-1980s, under the presidencies of respectively Walter Hallstein and Jacques Delors. It has also had low points, after the 1965–6 Luxembourg crisis (when President de Gaulle withdrew French ministers from Council meetings), in the late 1970s, and the late 1990s. In this most recent period the problems have partly been the result of weak internal management and coordination, overstretched staff, and lacklustre leadership. But there also seems to have been an underlying shift of influence away from the Commission towards other EU institutions and the member governments.

The Council of the European Union

The Council of the EU is both an institution with collective EU functions and the creature of the member governments. In principle and in law there is only one Council, empowered to take decisions on any topic. Its usual members are ministers from incumbent governments in the member states, but which ministers attend meetings depends on the subjects under discussion and on how individual governments choose to be represented. Time and practice have sorted this out by the Council developing specialized formations according to policy domains. Figure 1.2 summarizes how these have developed. Highly specialized groupings have evolved, each with its own policy domain, and each developing its own culture of cooperation.

To the extent that there is a hierarchy among these groupings the General Affairs Council (GAC), composed of foreign ministers, is supposed to be the senior Council.

Figure 1.2   The structures of the Council

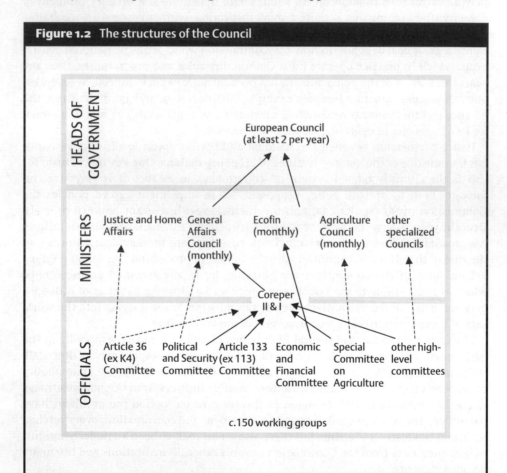

Notes: The Article 36 Committee deals with justice and home affairs; the Political and Security Committee deals with common foreign and security policy; the Economic and Financial Committee deals with EMU; Coreper II (Ambassadors) prepares Councils and topics that are more political; Coreper I (Deputies) prepares the more technical and financial issues; the Article 133 Committee deals with trade issues.

Its seniority rests on the presumption that foreign ministers have an overarching and coordinating role inside the member governments. It is partly because in practice foreign ministers cannot always arbitrate that prime ministers have become more involved, but on some cross-cutting issues foreign ministers remain leading decision-makers (see Chapters 8, 9, 14, and* 16). The proliferation of foreign policy issues in recent years has meant that GAC meetings have been increasingly dominated by foreign policy and external affairs, leaving less time or inclination to coordinate on other subjects (see Chapter 17). As EMU has taken shape, so the Council of Economic and Finance Ministers (Ecofin) has grown in importance (see Chapter 6). As other new policy areas become active, so corresponding formations of the Council emerge—JHA is a striking recent example (see Chapter 18), and defence policy may well be the next. Table 1.4 summarizes the frequency of Council meetings.

Meetings of ministers are prepared by national officials in the committees and working groups of the Council. Traditionally the most important of these has been the Committee of Permanent Representatives (Coreper), composed of the heads (Coreper II) and deputies (Coreper I) of the member states' permanent representations in Brussels. These each meet at least weekly to agree items on the Council agenda, and to identify those that need to be discussed (and not merely endorsed) by ministers. In some other policy domains (trade policy, agriculture, EMU, JHA, CFSP) similar senior committees of national officials prepare many of the ministerial meetings; often they act as the main decision-makers.

Table 1.4 Sessions of the Council (no.)

Session	1975	1980	1990	1994	1997
General Affairs	16	13	13	16	15
Agriculture	15	14	16	13	11
Ecofin	8	9	10	11	10
Internal Market	—	—	7	3	3
Budget	2	3	2	2	2
Environment	2	2	5	4	4
Research	2	—	2	4	2
Industry	—	—	4	4	2
Transport	2	2	4	4	4
Development	3	1	4	2	2
Social Affairs	2	2	3	4	5
Fisheries	—	7	3	5	3
Energy	2	2	3	2	3
Education	1	1	2	2	2
Telecommunications	—	—	2	2	3
Consumer Affairs	—	—	2	2	2
Health	—	—	2	3	2
Culture	—	—	2	2	2
Catastrophe Protection	—	—	1	1	0
Tourism	—	—	1	—	1
Trade	—	—	1	—	—
Justice and Home Affairs	—	1	1	4	3
Others	2	4	1	2	2
Total	57	60	91	92	83

The permanent representations contain a range of national officials whose job is to follow the main subjects being negotiated in the Council, to maintain links with all of the other EU institutions, and to keep in close touch with national capitals. Numerous (150 or so) working groups provide the backbone of the Council and do the detailed negotiation of policy. Their members come from the permanent representations or national capitals—practice varies. Something like 70 per cent of Council texts are agreed in working groups, another 10–15 per cent in Coreper or other senior committees, leaving 10–15 per cent to the ministers themselves. These proportions are pretty close to the normal practice in a national government.

National governments work in parallel to the Council. National officials follow each level of Council discussion and each area of Council debate, preparing ministerial positions and coordinating national positions. National ministers are involved in much of this work—how and when depends on national practices and on the degree of political interest in each subject within individual countries. Much of this involvement is at the level of individual ministries, where the relevant officials in turn consult the other branches of central, regional, or local government, public agencies, and relevant private sector or non-governmental organizations. Aggregating national positions is the responsibility of the coordinating units in each member government. Again practices vary between countries, some more centralized and some more decentralized in their approaches. Thus a comprehensive view of how the deliberations of the Council proceed needs to include that part that emanates from the continuous engagement of national administrations.

What does the Council do? Mostly it negotiates over detailed proposals for EU action, and very often it does so on the basis of a draft from the Commission. Sometimes the Council will earlier have indicated to the Commission that it would welcome a draft on a particular subject. On most of the topics where the Commission has been the primary drafter, the EP is now co-legislator with the Council (see below). In these areas of policy the decision-making outcome depends on the interactions between these three institutions. The dynamics of the process rest on the way in which coalitions emerge within the Council and between the Council members and the other EU institutions.

In some other areas the Commission and the EP play more marginal roles, and the Council itself is more in charge of its own agenda—CFSP and JHA are apt examples. Here more reliance has to be placed on the Council's own General Secretariat. This has not historically been an organ of policy-making, but rather a facilitator of collective decision-making. However, the growth of work under the second and third pillars (CFSP and JHA) has prompted the expansion of the Council Secretariat. Successive treaty reforms over the past decade have accepted that the CFSP needs administrative underpinning. Member governments have therefore chosen to expand the relevant sections of the Council Secretariat (see Chapter 17). Following the ToA a section of the Council Secretariat has been strengthened to deal with JHA (see Chapter 18). As a result we now need to consider the Council Secretariat as much more of an actor in the policy process than hitherto.

The proceedings of the Council are managed by its presidency. This rotates between member governments every six months. The Council presidency chairs meetings at all levels of ministers and officials, except for a small number of committees which have elected chairs. This involves the preparation of agendas, as well as the conduct of meetings. The presidency speaks on behalf of the Council in discussions with other EU institutions and with outside partners. Often the Council and the Commission presidencies have to work closely together, for example in external negotiations where policy powers are divided between the EU and the national levels. In the legislative field it is the Council and EP presidencies that have to work together to reconcile Council and parliamentary views on legislative amendments. A recurrent question is how far individual governments try to impose their national preferences during the presidency or whether the experience pushes them towards identifying with collective EU interests. As EU policy cooperation has developed directly between governments, rather than at the promptings of the Commission and through formal procedures, so it has fallen to successive presidencies to act as the main coordinators. This has been a particular feature of CFSP and JHA.

The important point to bear in mind is that the Council is the EU institution that belongs to the member governments. It works the way it works, because that is the way that the member governments prefer to manage their negotiations with each other. Regularity of contact and a pattern of socialization mean that the Council, and especially its specialist formations, develop a kind of insider amity. Sometimes clubs of ministers—in agriculture, or dealing with the environment, and so forth—are able to use agreements in Brussels to force on to their own governments commitments that might not have been accepted at the national level. None the less the ministers and officials who meet in the Council are servants of their governments, affiliated to national political parties, and accountable to national electorates. Thus their first priority is generally to pursue whatever seems to be the preferred objective of national policy.

The Council spends much of its time acting as the forum for discussion on the member governments' responses to the Commission's proposals. It does so through continuous negotiation, mostly by trying to establish a consensus. The formal rules of decision vary according to policy domain and over time—sometimes unanimity, sometimes qualified majority voting (QMV), sometimes simple majority. The decision rules are a subject of controversy and have been altered in successive treaty reforms. Broadly QMV has become the rule in areas where Community regimes are fairly well established, while unanimity is a requirement either in areas in which EU regimes are embryonic or in those domains where governments have tenaciously retained more control of the process. There is a great deal of misunderstanding about how the process works in practice. Habits of consensus-seeking are deeply ingrained, and actual votes relatively rare, even when technically possible. Under QMV the knowledge that votes may be called often makes doubting governments focus on seeking amendments to meet their concerns rather than on blocking progress altogether. Under unanimity rules reluctant governments are generally much more likely to delay or obstruct agreements.

The Council used to be the main legislator on EU policies. However, as the EP has acquired powers over legislation, the system has become more bicameral. Thus the Council now reaches 'common positions' which have to be frequently reconciled with amendments to legislation proposed by MEPs in a 'conciliation' procedure. This has meant that the Council is now more explicitly required to justify publicly its collective preferences, an important change in the process.

In some policy domains the Council remains the decision-maker of last resort.

Interestingly this includes some established areas, such as agriculture, where the EP still has little opportunity to intervene (see Chapter 7), and some new policy domains, where the member governments, through the Council, retain the main control of policy. JHA and CFSP are the main examples. EMU provides a different contrast: here the main control of the single currency has been assigned to the European Central Bank, leaving Ecofin and the new Euro-11 Council (including ministers only from member governments with currencies inside EMU) pushing to gain influence over decision-making (see Chapter 6).

The European Council

The European Council started its existence in the occasional 'summit' meetings of heads of state (France and Finland have presidents with some policy powers) or government (i.e. prime ministers). Two especially important meetings, in The Hague in 1969 and Paris in 1972, were agenda-setters and package-makers for several succeeding years. From 1974 onwards, under the prompting of Giscard d'Estaing, then French President, European Councils were put on to a regular footing, meeting at least twice a year. Successive treaty reforms have put the European Council on to a more formal basis. It remains, however, the case that the European Council operates to an extent outside the main institutional structure. The location and preparation of its meetings, as well as the drafting of its conclusions, depend essentially on the presidency-in-office of the Council, and the agenda of its sessions is much influenced by the preferences of the government in the chair. By custom and practice national delegations in the room are restricted to the president or prime minister and the foreign ministers. Increasingly large cohorts of other ministers and officials have parallel meetings, the topics depending on the preoccupations of the moment.

Over the years the role of the European Council has varied. Conceived of initially as an informal 'fireside chat', it became in the 1970s and 1980s a forum for resolving issues that departmental ministers could not agree, or that were subjects of disagreement within the member governments. By tradition it is the European Council that has been left to resolve the periodic major arguments about EU revenue and expenditure, as Chapter 8 explains in general, and Chapter 9 illustrates in relation to the structural funds. In addition the European Council became, from the negotiations over the SEA in 1985, the key forum for determining treaty reforms. Views have varied as to whether the shifting of decision-making to so senior a political level marked a failure of the 'normal' institutional arrangements or rather a sign of success for the EU, as its agenda has risen up the ladder of political salience.

From the late 1980s and during the 1990s the role and behaviour of the European Council have changed. It has increasingly become the venue for addressing what J. Peterson (1995a) calls the 'history-making decisions' in the EU, namely the big and more strategic questions to do with the core new tasks of the EU and those that define its 'identity' as an arena for collective action. Some of our case-studies, especially Chapter 6 on EMU, Chapter 16 on eastern enlargement, Chapter 17 on CFSP, and Chapter 18 on JHA, record European Council pronouncements as the main staging-posts in the development of policy. The level of activity has expanded, with four sessions in 1999, and what seems to be a sharply increasing concern on the part of the most senior national politicians to take control of the direction of the EU. Their offices now have a direct electronic link (Primenet), and within their national settings it seems that they are more strongly engaged in framing national European policies. One obvious issue for future treaty reformers is whether or not to encapsulate this increasing role within the 'constitutional arrangements' of the EU.

The European Parliament

The EP now consists of 626 members (MEPs) elected directly on a basis of proportional representation from across the member states. Originally it was composed of national parliamentarians, but in 1978 a treaty amendment provided for direct elections. Its location, for reasons of member state sensitivities, is divided between Luxembourg, Strasbourg, and Brussels. MEPs vary in their backgrounds, some having been national politicians, others bringing different professional experience, and a few having made the EP their primary career. The EP is organized into party groupings, of which by far the most important are the European People's Party and the European Socialists. These groupings have gained in importance over time. Much of the work of the EP is carried out in its specialist committees, which have become increasingly adept at probing particular policy issues in detail, more so than in many national parliaments.

In the early years of the EU the EP had only a marginal role in the policy process, with only consultative powers, apart from its power to dismiss the Commission in a censure motion. During the 1970s the EP gained important powers *vis-à-vis* the EU budget, and especially over some areas of expenditure (although significantly not over most agricultural expenditure) (see Chapter 8). In the 1980s and 1990s the role of the EP has been transformed, as it has acquired legislative powers in successive treaty reforms. These have been rationalized in the ToA into *co-decision* with the Council across a wide range of policy domains; *cooperation* with the Council in some other domains, especially on EMU-related questions; and *consultation* in those areas where member governments have been chary of letting MEPs into the process, including agriculture, and JHA. In addition the EP must now give its formal *assent* on some issues: these include certain agreements with third countries and enlargement. Box 1.1 summarizes the powers of the EP.

The net result of these changes is that the EP is now a force to be reckoned with across a wide range of policy domains. It is in important respects a necessary partner for the Council, although one with a contested electoral authority, because of the rather low participation rate in European elections (in some member states). On many areas of detailed rule-setting the EP has a real impact, as various of our case-studies show, and therefore it too is the target of those outside the institutions who seek to influence legislation (see, for example, Chapter 12). However, there are other areas—JHA, CFSP, and oddly the common agricultural policy (CAP)—where its voice is muted. In 1999 the EP acquired greater political prominence as a result of its role in provoking the resignation of the European Commission on the issue of financial mismanagement. The signs are that this may have increased the political standing of the EP such that it may influence the policy process as a whole rather more in the future.

Box 1.1 Powers of the European Parliament

Consultation

> Commission proposals to Council are passed to EP for an Opinion. EP may suggest alterations, or delay passing a resolution to formalize its Opinion, or refer a matter back to its relevant committee(s).
> *Applies* to: agriculture, and those (few) justice and home affairs topics that fall within the 'Community' framework.

Cooperation

> Commission proposals passed to Council for a 'common position' and to EP for a first reading, in which it may propose amendments. The EP may at its second reading seek to amend the Council's common position, or by an absolute majority reject it. Council can override the EP's rejection only by unanimity. Alternatively the EP and Council try to negotiate agreement in a conciliation procedure.
> *Applies* to: limited aspects of economic and monetary union.

Co-decision

> Council and EP may both agree a proposal at first reading. If they disagree at second reading, the EP may by an absolute majority reject the proposal, which then falls. Or the EP may amend the Council's common position by an absolute majority, in which case conciliation takes place between the Council and the EP. The results of conciliation must be approved in third reading by both Council (QMV) and EP (majority of votes cast). Proposal falls if not agreed.
> *Applies* since Treaty of Amsterdam to: most areas of legislation, unless otherwise specified as exempted, or falling under one of the other procedures.

Assent

> On certain issues the EP must, in a single vote, give its assent by an absolute majority of its members.
> *Applies* to: certain international agreements, enlargement treaties, and framework agreements on the structural funds.

Budget

> EP may try to modify 'compulsory' expenditure, or to amend 'non-compulsory' expenditure. It must approve the budget as a whole, and subsequently 'discharge' the accounts of previous years' actual expenditure. Box 8.1 has details.

Installation of the college of commissioners

> EP holds individual hearings with nominated commissioners and passes a vote to approve the whole college.

Censure of Commission

> EP may censure the college of commissioners by a two-thirds majority of its members.

The European Court of Justice

From early on it became clear to close observers of the EU that the role and rule of law were going to be critical in anchoring EU policy regimes. If the legal system could ensure a high rate of compliance, a way of giving authoritative interpretation to disputed texts, and a means of redress for those for whom the law was created, then the EU process as a whole would gain a solidity and a predictability that would help it to be sustained. The ECJ was established in the first treaty texts; these have been virtually unchanged since then, except to cater for the increasing workload and successive enlargements of the EU membership.

The ECJ, sited in Luxembourg, is now composed of fifteen judges, as well as the nine advocates-general who deliver preliminary opinions on cases. The SEA in 1986 established a second Court of First Instance, composed now of fifteen judges, to help in handling the heavy flow of cases. The EU has thus something like a supreme court, able to provide an overarching framework of jurisprudence, as well as to deal with litigation, both in cases referred via the national courts and in those that are brought directly before it. The Courts' sanctions are mostly the force of their own rulings, backed up in some instances by the ability to impose fines on those (usually companies) found to have broken EU law. The TEU gave the ECJ power to fine member governments for non-application of European law. Also, as a result of its own rulings (especially one of the *Factortame* cases on fisheries—see Chapter 13), damages can be claimed against governments that fail to implement European law correctly. The Courts take their cases in public, but reach their judgments in private by, if necessary, majority votes; the results of their votes are not made public, and minority opinions are not issued.

A series of key cases has, since the early 1960s, established important principles of European law, such as: its supremacy over the law of the member states, its direct effect, a doctrine of proportionality, and another of non-discrimination. In doing so the ECJ has gone further in clarifying the rule and the role of law than had specifically been laid down in the treaties. In some policy domains court cases have been one of the key forces in developing EU policy regimes (see Chapters 4, 5, 10, and 13). Tables 1.5 and 1.6 summarize the pattern and volume of cases before the two Courts.

This strong legal dimension has a large influence on the policy process. Policymakers pay great attention to the legal meaning of the texts that they devise; policy advocates look for legal rules to achieve their objectives, because they know that these are favoured by the institutional system; policy reformers can sometimes use cases to alter the impact of EU policies; and in general there is a presumption that rules will be more or less obeyed. Hence policy-makers have to choose carefully between treaty articles in determining which legal base to use, and to consider carefully which kind of legislation to make.

Regulations are directly applicable within the member states once promulgated by the EU institutions. Directives have to be transposed into national law, which allows some flexibility to member governments, but within limits set by the ECJ. Decisions are more limited legal instruments applied to specific circumstances or specific addressees, as in competition policy (see Chapter 5). All three kinds of law may be made either by the Commission (under delegated powers), or by the Council, or jointly by the Council and EP (under co-decision). And all are subject to challenge through the national and European courts.

The vigour of the European legal system is one of the most distinctive features of the EU. It has helped to reinforce the powers and reach of the EU process, although in recent years the ECJ has become a bit more cautious in its judgments. We should note also that in some policy domains member governments have gone to considerable lengths to keep the ECJ out of the picture. Part of the reason for the three-pillar

Table 1.5 New cases at the European Court of Justice, 1972–1997 (no.) (five-year periods, since 1972; last five-year period 1992–1997; each year given)

Subject-matter	Cases until 1971	1972	1977	1982	1987	1992	1993	1994	1995	1996	1997
Agriculture and fisheries	99	36	61	83	81	198	210	65	70	60	66
Transport	3	—	2	4	5	14	10	11	5	3	11
Taxation	27	1	2	9	35	20	21	25	36	33	61
Free movement of goods and customs	53	3	25	56	45	33	58	86	79	50	61
Competition and state aids	38	6	10	42	34	54	35	20	35	28	45
Freedom of establishment and to provide services	3	—	2	4	12	12	20	47	34	46	39
Free movement for workers and social policy	37	11	19	17	35	49	59	44	54	70	51
Environment	—	—	—	—	—	15	11	11	42	59	47
Rest[a]	—	2	16	21	44	23	43	29	26	54	34
Staff of EU institutions[b]	268	23	25	85	77	9	10	5	15	13	14
Other (ECSC, EAEC, privileges and immunities)	—	—	—	25	27	11	9	4	13	4	15
All	895	82	162	348	395[d]	438	486[c]	347	409	420	444

[a] Inc. common commercial policy and cases under agreements with third countries.
[b] These are contract and 'social security' cases of EU 'civil servants', mostly dealt with by Court of First Instance created in 1989, except for appeals to ECJ.
[c] 186 cases were handed over to the Court of First Instance.
[d] Calculation by Stephen Leibfried.

Source: Compiled by Stephan Leibfried, with advice from Josef Falke, from Commission (1972–).

structure of the TEU was to keep both CFSP and JHA well away from the reach of the European legal system. Even though the ToA goes some way towards incorporating parts of JHA and Schengen more fully within the system, it remains contested how far they will be brought within the jurisdiction of the ECJ. One issue which floats in the debate is how far the other European legal order, based on the European Convention of Human Rights attached to the Council of Europe, is to be linked to the EU, and whether the EU should adopt its own Charter on Fundamental Rights.

The wider institutional setting

The EU institutional system includes in addition a number of additional organizations that have an impact on, or provide instruments for, EU policies. Some are

Table 1.6 New cases at the Court of First Instance, 1992–1997 (no.) (each year given)

Subject-matter	1992	1993	1994	1995	1996	1997
Agriculture and fisheries	—	425	223	49	35	75
Transport	—	1	1	—	—	1
Taxation	—	—	3	—	—	—
Free movement of goods and customs	—	2	2	2	9	18
Competition and state aids	36	41	71	87	53	50
Freedom of establishment and to provide services	—	1	—	3	1	3
Free movement for workers and social policy	—	14	2	3	9	4
Environment	—	3	2	3	—	—
Rest[a]	—	16	38	19	20	324
Staff of EU institutions[b]	79	84	85	19	107	155
Other (ECSC, EAEC, privileges, and immunities)	—	2	23	7	7	6
All	115	589[d]	460[c]	102	237	636

Notes:
[a] Incl. common commercial policy.
[b] These are contract and 'social security' cases of EU 'civil servants'; the large volume of these was part of the reason for creating this new court.
[c] The ECJ handed fourteen cases to the Court of First Instance.
[d] The ECJ handed 452 cases to the Court of First Instance.

Source: Compiled by Stephan Leibfried, with advice from Josef Falke, from Commission *Annual Reports*.

consultative. Some provide control mechanisms. Some provide autonomous operating arms.

Consultation and lobbying

The founding treaties established the Economic and Social Committee (and the Consultative Committee for the ECSC) as a point of access to the policy process for socio-economic groups. Its creation borrowed from the corporatist traditions in some of the founder member countries. It has not, however, become an influential body in the policy process. Instead socio-economic groups have found their own more direct points of access since the 1960s, both through EU-level federal associations and through sector-specific trade and producer organizations. These became even more active in the period around the development of the single European market. Individual large firms have also taken pains to develop links with the EU institutions, again some since the 1960s, but many more and with more vigour since the early 1980s. A more recent development has been the increased activity of groups and lobbies representing societal interests, the consumers, the environmentalists, women's groups, and increasingly a range of other advocacy groups and non-governmental organizations (NGOs). Illustrations of the activities of these different kinds of groups can be found in many of our case-studies.

The TEU introduced a second consultative body, the Committee of the Regions, in response to the extensive involvement of local and regional authorities in seeking to influence those EU policies that impacted on them. The Committee provides regional and local politicians from the member states with a multilateral forum, and an opportunity to enhance their local political credibility. At least as important, however, is the direct lobbying by infranational (local and regional) authorities, many with their own offices in Brussels. These same infranational authorities also engage in efforts to influence national policy positions and the implementation of Community programmes. Chapters 9 and 13 comment on this in relation to the structural funds and the common fisheries policy.

Control and scrutiny

In the mid-1970s concern started to be voiced that the EU policy process was subject to few external controls. The EP at the time had few powers, and national parliaments paid rather little attention to EU legislation and programmes. It was the growing scale and scope of the EU budget and spending programmes that led the arguments about the inadequacy of scrutiny. This led to the creation of the European Court of Auditors by the 1975 Budget Treaty. Since 1978 it has, from its seat in Luxembourg, endeavoured to evaluate systematically both revenue-raising and spending. Both in its Annual Reports and in specific reports it has drawn attention to various weaknesses in the budgetary process, as handled by the Commission and national agencies. Here we should note that about four-fifths of EU budgetary expenditure is disbursed by national agencies. Chapter 8 describes some of the Court of Auditors' activities and impact. We note here that many of its criticisms fell for many years on deaf ears—member governments that were reluctant to face up to some of the issues, an EP that had other preoccupations, and a Commission which repeatedly undervalued the importance of sound financial management. In late 1998 this situation was reversed by the row over alleged financial mismanagement by the Commission.

Another new instrument of *post hoc* control is provided by the Ombudsman attached to the EP under the provisions of the TEU. The aim is to provide a channel for dealing with cases of maladminstration *vis-à-vis* individuals. Thus far the existence of this office has not had a large impact, although it may have contributed to making the policy process a little more open than hitherto.

Some control and scrutiny of policy depends on national institutions, both parliamentary and financial. National parliaments had no official recognition in the institutional system until the early 1990s. Each member state had developed its own, mostly rather limited, procedures for national parliamentary scrutiny of EU policy. The same discontent that had led to some strengthening of European procedures started to provoke a debate on national scrutiny. Both the TEU and the ToA mention the importance of encouraging this, although there is little likelihood of standardized procedures emerging. Instead it seems likely that EU-level policy-makers, especially in the Commission, will pay more attention to national parliamentary discussions and appear more readily before national parliamentary committees of inquiry. This heightened sensitivity to country-level preoccupations is becoming a more marked feature of the EU policy process. It may well be emphasized by the establishment of national parliamentary offices in Brussels (by September 1999 from Denmark, Finland, France, and the UK).

Operations

The longest-established autonomous agency is the European Investment Bank (EIB), established by the Treaty of Rome (EEC). Its task was, and is, to generate loans for agreed investments in support of EU objectives, both within the EU and in associated third countries. It operates like a private bank, with triple-A credit rating in money markets. Its work is to varying degrees coordinated with programmes directly administered by the Commission, such as the structural funds. Its big moment might have come in the early 1990s after the breakdown of the communist system in central and eastern Europe. However, a decision was taken to establish a new and separate European Bank for Reconstruction and Development, with the reforming post-communist countries and other western states as stakeholders.

One other phenomenon should be noted. Especially during the past decade there has been a trend in the EU to contract out some policy implementation activities, mirroring practice that was becoming more common in many of the member states. One group of agencies has been set up, or contracted, to administer programmes for which the Commission lacked either the staff or the inclination; for example, the European Community Humanitarian Office (ECHO), and the office which administers the Socrates programme for educational interchange. Another group of agencies handles regulatory functions, such as the European Agency for the Evaluation of Medicinal Products. Europol is another example. A third group provides direct services for the EU institutions, such as the translation centre. There has been some discussion of whether this process could be taken even further, for example by setting up a European Competition Office clearly separate from the Commission (see Chapter 5), or perhaps a European Food Standards Agency.

The most important example of a new and autonomous operating agency is the European Central Bank (ECB) in Frankfurt (see Chapter 6). The battle in 1998 over who should be its first president was an indication of the expected importance of an agency that was to exercise considerable independence in a crucial policy domain with high political salience. Quite what the extent of the ECB's autonomy will be in the longer term remains to be seen; several finance ministers have already made it clear that they want their own hands on the tiller.

Overall we should note the proliferation of agencies for operating EU policy regimes and programmes. This diffuseness of arrangements for policy operation and programme delivery has increased over the past decade. It seems set to be a persistent feature of the policy process, especially as regards policy implementation, and thus likely to fragment the institutional structures. This should lead us to modify the notion of the Commission as a centralized and centralizing policy executive.

National institutions

I have summarized above some key points about the EU's own institutions and agencies. However, I stress that those institutions are in a real sense the property of the member states which comprise the EU. In addition, the institutions in the member states are also fundamental elements in the EU institutional architecture and partners in the EU policy process. The European dimension is not just an add-on to the work of national governments; in a real and tangible sense national governments, and other authorities and agencies, provide much of the operating life-blood of the

EU. After all, in some senses what the EU system does is to extend the policy resources available to the member states. Our case-studies illustrate a variety of ways in which this is so. As a result, learning how to manage this extra dimension to national public policy has been one of the most important challenges faced by national governments in the past fifty years.

Much of that challenge has had to be faced by the central governments in each member state, and the patterns of response have varied a good deal from one to another. As a broad generalization we note that the experience has been somewhat different from what many commentators had expected. The trend has been not so much a defensive adjustment to the loss of policy-making powers, but rather in most member states an increasingly nuanced approach to incorporating and encapsulating the European dimension. This has not, however, meant that central governments can operate as gatekeepers between the national and the EU levels. The points of cross-border access and opportunities for building cross-national networks and coalitions have steadily proliferated for both public agencies and private actors. National actors play important and influential roles at all stages of the EU policy process.

Opportunities for access and influence are, however, not evenly distributed within member states. Economic agents and NGOs seem the most flexible in operating at both EU and national levels. Infranational authorities have become more adept, though how much influence they exert is debated. National parliaments have been much slower to adapt, and indeed are among the national institutions most displaced by the emergence of a strong European dimension to policy-making.

One Community method—or several policy modes?

This section sets out five variants of the EU policy process:

- a distinctive Community method;
- the EU regulatory model;
- multi-level governance;
- policy coordination and benchmarking; and
- intensive transgovernmentalism.

A distinctive Community method

For a long time much of the literature on west European integration and the EU took as its starting-point that a single predominant Community method of policy-making was emerging. Because of its early priority on the agenda of the original EEC, the CAP set the template. This was defined by the late 1960s roughly as follows:

- a strong role for the European Commission in policy design, policy-brokering, and policy execution;
- an empowering role for the Council of Ministers through strategic bargaining and package deals;

- a locking-in of agricultural interests, through a form of cooption in a European process which offered them better rewards than national politics;

- an engagement of national agencies as the subordinated operating arms of the agreed common regime;

- a distancing from the process of elected representatives at the national level, and only limited opportunities for the primitive EP to impinge;

- an occasional, but defining, intrusion by the ECJ to reinforce the legal authority of the Community regime; and

- the resourcing of the policy on a collective basis, as an expression of sustained 'solidarity'.

The template constituted a form of 'supranational' policy-making, in which powers were transferred from the national to the EU level. It was structured by a kind of functionalist logic, in which those concerned with a particular policy sector could build cross-national allegiances, but mediated by a form of politics in which political and economic élites colluded to further their various, often different, interests.

How far this template accorded with reality, even in the case of agriculture, is a matter for debate. In Chapter 7 Rieger suggests that the real story may be different, and one in which national politics determined rather more of the outcomes. Interestingly, the fisheries regime, which was intended to imitate the CAP regime, does not fit the template very well either, as Chapter 13 shows. None the less this version of the Community model came to set many of the reference points for both practitioners and commentators. However, by the mid-1980s two other versions of a distinctive Community model became current: the EU regulatory model; and the multi-level governance model.

The EU regulatory model

As the single European market developed (see Chapter 4), so an alternative policy model emerged. Its roots went back to the ambition of the Treaty of Rome to remove barriers between the national economies of the member states. But much of its driving force came from changes in the international economy, which had made the search for competitiveness in both domestic and international markets critical to the ability of firms to adjust and to prosper. Public policy-makers across the industrialized 'western' world found themselves subject to demands for different kinds of regulation that would facilitate that adjustment. Within the USA there were already traditions of both public regulation and private self-regulation that showed an alternative approach to market management (see Chapter 5). A version of this regulatory approach started to develop in western Europe, although in varied formats in individual countries.

It turned out that the EU arena was especially amenable to the further development of a regulatory model of policy-making. The strength of the European legal process, the machinery for promoting technical cooperation, and the distance from parliamentary interference were all factors that encouraged this further. In addition the bargaining process, in and through the European Commission and Council of Ministers, helped national policy-makers to escape some of the constraints of politics that had built rigidities into national policy-making. The EU was particularly well-fitted for generating an overarching regulatory framework that could combine transnational standards with country differences. Indeed so successful has been its implantation that this European model has begun to be promoted as a model for the development of broader global regulation.

This regulatory model provides the framework for numerous micro-level decisions and rules, as well as for the shape of relationships with member governments and economic actors. It has been characterized by:

- the Commission as the architect and defender of regulatory objectives and rules, increasingly by reference to economic criteria;

- the Council as a forum for agreeing minimum standards and the direction of harmonization (mostly upwards towards higher standards), to be complemented by mutual recognition of national preferences and controls, operated differentially in individual countries;

- the ECJ as the means of ensuring that the rules are applied reasonably evenly, backed by the national courts for local application, and enabling individual entrepreneurs to have access to redress in case of non-application or discrimination;

- the EP as one of several means for prompting the consideration of non-economic factors (environmental, regional, social, and so forth), with increasing impact as its legislative powers have grown; and

- extensive opportunities for economic actors, and sometimes other societal actors, to be consulted about, and to influence, the shape and content of European market rules.

This regulatory model has been applied most obviously in the development of a single market without internal barriers (Chapter 4), and it has been buttressed by the reinvigoration of EU competition policy (Chapter 5). To the extent that the EU has an industrial policy, it is mostly by using regulatory prompts and the competition regime to leverage industrial adjustment, one example of which—biotechnology—is explained in Chapter 12. In so far as the EU has a social policy (see Chapter 10), it is mainly constructed through legal regulation and market-making. Much of what the EU has done in the environmental domain (see Chapter 11) has been by regulating industrial processes. Moreover, the EU's interactions with the rest of the world are an external reflection of its internal approach to regulation and industrial adjustment, as is made evident in Chapter 14 on trade policy, Chapter 15 as regards policy towards developing countries, and Chapter 16 in relation to central and eastern Europe.

The strength of this regulatory model is considerable. Efforts to analyse it account for a good deal of the contemporary literature on west European integration. During the 1990s regulation displaced the CAP as the predominant policy paradigm among many EU policy practitioners. It had the advantage of reflecting an approach focused on a modernization trajectory, through which the rigidities of the 'old' west European political economy would be replaced by more flexible instruments of market encouragement, and through which a different, and less corporatist, relationship could be struck with socio-economic actors. The literature on this regulatory model has been marked by an emphasis on the role of interest groups, lobbying, and corporate actors (firms rather than trade associations), by approaches based on the networks, coalitions, and alliances that they form, and by a much increased interest in the rule of law as an instrument of policy-making.

Multi-level governance

Yet regulation was not the only new feature of the EU landscape. Persistently over the years the EU policy process had been caught up in distributional policy-making, that is the allocation of resources to different groups, sectors, regions, and countries, whether intentionally or unintentionally. The framers of the original treaties included some elements of distribution in the policy repertoire to be exploited. The CAP was funded from a collective base and for a long time accounted for the lion's share of the EU budget. Farmers became the clients of European funding. It is to the early years of the EEC that the language of 'financial solidarity' owes its origins. From the early 1970s efforts were made to develop a similar common fisheries policy (Chapter 13). In both of these cases the European arena was used to protect social groups that were being marginalized in the domestic economy and rendered uncompetitive by global markets.

When the arguments came to be joined over the distribution of burdens and benefits of participation in the EU, notably in the period following British accession in 1973, it was on the budget as a measure of the impacts of EU membership that attention was focused. As Laffan and Shackleton point out in Chapter 8 (and as previous editions of this volume have shown in more detail), EU policy-makers had to confront some difficult choices about how to establish financial arrangements, for both revenue and expenditure, that would be equitable. This persists as a contentious issue in the EU.

When the single market was being pushed forward in the mid-1980s, the debate about the distributional impacts of integration was joined again, but this time more explicitly couched in the language of relative wealth and poverty. The term 'cohesion' was added to the policy-makers' vocabulary; it connoted a commitment to pay attention to economic and social divergence, and the needs of the more backward regions and social groups. This appeared to signal a shift from haphazard distribution of resources (especially from the EU budget) to a more planned redistribution through designed resource transfers. The main spending mechanism was through the 'structural funds', as explained in Chapter 9, which involved programmes and projects for, on the one hand, agencies dealing with training and employment creation, and, on the other hand, regional and local authorities. While most of the spending was concentrated in the main 'cohesion' countries—Greece, Ireland, Portugal, and Spain—some of the programmes were also open to some clients in the other member states.

It was this opening for more direct contacts between the European and the infranational levels of government, and the politics that developed around them, that provoked the term 'multi-level governance' to characterize this new policy mode. It rested on two essential points: first, that national central governments could no longer monopolize the contacts between the country and the EU levels of policy-making; and, secondly, that engagement at the European level created an opportunity to reinforce a phenomenon of regionalization. The implication was that the domestic polities of the member states were being partially reshaped as a consequence of EU policy-making, in which financial incentives could leverage new political relationships.

This multi-level governance model thus comprised:

- the Commission as the deviser of programmes, in partnership with local and regional authorities, and using financial incentives to gain attention;

- member governments in the Council, under pressure from local and regional authorities, agreeing to an enlarging and redistributive budget;

- an EP in which the MEPs would often constitute an additional source of pressure from territorial politics in the regions;

- local and regional authorities benefiting from policy empowerment as a result of engaging in the European arena, with, from 1993 onwards, a new embryonic institution, the Committee of the Regions, to represent their concerns, and many of them with their own offices in Brussels; and

- a recasting of the EU budget to spend quite large sums of money on cohesion.

The multi-level governance model inverted much of the discussion on how the EU worked by its emphasis on politics on the ground, and by shifting attention away from the Brussels-centred and entrepreneur-oriented images of, respectively, the Community method and the regulatory model. The approach is, however, not without its critics. Allen suggests in Chapter 9 of this volume that the evidence does not add up to support the argument, in that infranational activity should not be confused with impact. Central governments from the member states have, he suggests, remained in the driving seat of the bargains about EU spending. The debate on the analytics of this phenomenon will continue; and it serves to remind us that much depends on which pair of spectacles the observer is wearing.

Policy coordination and benchmarking

An old contrast in the study of European collaboration has been drawn between versions of the Community method outlined above and what in shorthand might be described as the 'OECD technique'. The OECD, the Paris-based club of western industrialized countries, has since the early 1960s provided a forum within which its members could appraise and compare each other's ways of developing public policies.

In its early years the Commission used this technique to develop light cooperation and coordination in order to make the case for direct policy powers. Thus, for example, in the 1970s the Commission promoted increasingly systematic consultations among member governments on environmental issues, and eventually made a persuasive case for the SEA to give the EU formal legislative powers. Some similar efforts were made in domains such as research and development or aspects of education policy. Policy coordination served as a mechanism of transition from nationally rooted policy-making to a collective regime. As Chapter 13 shows cogently, this approach has been one of the key elements in the efforts to address the conservation of fish stocks. For the advocates of a strong EU, policy coordination might be a useful starting-point, but it was seen as very much a second-best resting-point.

The approach rests a great deal on expertise and the accumulation of technical arguments in favour of developing a shared approach. It also relies on efforts to use expertise to promote modernization and innovation. The typical features are:

- the Commission as the developer of networks of experts or epistemic communities;
- the involvement of 'independent' experts as promoters of ideas and techniques;
- the convening of high-level groups in the Council, in brainstorming rather than negotiating mode; and
- dialogue (sometimes) with specialist committees in the EP, as the advocates of particular approaches (drawing on the greater willingness of MEPs than their national counterparts to probe some policy predicaments in depth).

Latterly we can see that this approach of coordination, strengthened by the contemporary fashion for 'benchmarking', is being developed not as a transitional mechanism, but as a policy mode in its own right. The employment policy domain, not addressed directly in this volume, is one such instance. Here the main thrust of EU involvement is to compare national, local, and sectoral experiences of labour market adaptation. The object is not to establish a single common framework, but rather to share experience and to encourage the spread of best practice. There are some grounds for expecting this to be a typical mode in future EU policy-making, as an alternative to the formal reassignment of policy powers from national to EU level.

Intensive transgovernmentalism

Throughout the history of the EU there have been examples of policy cooperation which have depended mainly on interaction between the relevant national policy-makers, and with relatively little involvement by the EU institutions. This has been especially so in domains that touch sensitive issues of state sovereignty. Generally such cooperation has been described as 'intergovernmentalism'—by both practitioners and commentators. Generally it has been regarded as a weaker and much less constraining form of policy development. In the early 1960s General de Gaulle was instrumental in promoting the controversial Fouchet Plans, which aimed to shift delicate areas of cooperation well away from the then EEC into a firmly intergovernmental framework. This was vigorously resisted by some of the more integration-minded governments. None the less, in the early 1970s policy cooperation did develop in two domains in particular—money and foreign policy—largely outside the EU institutional framework. In both domains heads of state or government were important actors, and often their preferences were developed in groupings smaller than the whole EU membership. Franco-German bilateral cooperation was at some moments an important catalyst of policy advancement.

The term 'intergovernmental' does not, however, really capture the character of this policy mode in the EU. It resonates too much of cooperation between governments in many other international organizations, in which the intensity of cooperation is quite limited. We therefore prefer the term 'transgovernmental', to connote the greater intensity of some of our examples, where EU member governments have been prepared cumulatively to commit themselves to rather extensive engagement and disciplines, but have judged the full EU institutional framework to be inappropriate or unacceptable.

Intensive transgovernmentalism is characterized by:

- the active involvement of the European Council in setting the overall direction of policy;

- the predominance of the Council of Ministers (or an equivalent forum of national ministers), in consolidating cooperation;

- the limited or marginal role of the Commission;

- the exclusion of the EP and the ECJ from the circle of involvement;

- the involvement of a distinct circle of key national policy-makers;

- the adoption of special arrangements for managing cooperation;

- the opaqueness of the process, to national parliaments and publics; but

- the capacity on occasion to deliver substantive joint policy.

It might be tempting to dismiss this intensive transgovernmentalism as simply a weak form of cooperation. However, two factors challenge such a conclusion. First, this is the preferred policy mode in some other strong European regimes. Nato is one obvious example; the European Space Agency is another, and very different, case. In both of these instances quite extensive and sustained policy collaboration has been achieved. Secondly, within the EU this mode has in practice been a vehicle for developing extensive and cumulative cooperation, gradually with elements of a treaty foundation, but one which has made arrangements aside from most of the main EU institutions.

In the case of EMU (Chapter 6), the European Council, national finance ministers and officials, and central bankers between them produced such sustained intensity of cooperation that a single currency became acceptable. Moreover, it is based on a strong collective regime. In the sphere of foreign policy (Chapter 17), first European Political Cooperation from 1970, then from 1993 onwards CFSP, were built up. Initially defence cooperation was left within two separate frameworks, Nato and Western European Union (WEU), with clear competition between these alternative frameworks. However, since 1998 these frameworks have gradually been drawn together, with the Nato mode of policy cooperation setting the parameters of the way in which defence is being pulled into the EU setting. In JHA (Chapter 18), two processes have converged. On the one hand, informal policy consultations, both bilateral and multilateral, have bred habits of increasingly intense cooperation since the early 1970s. On the other hand, a wittingly separate treaty framework was constructed under the Schengen agreements, apart from the EU. These two different processes of cooperation are now being drawn into a single framework.

These three domains were among the most dynamic areas of EU policy development at the end of the 1990s. In each case the EU framework has become in a broad sense more accepted, but the detailed institutional arrangements are untypical. In the case of EMU, a European Central Bank, a network of national banks, and a privileged committee of national finance officials are at the heart of the process. In the case of foreign and defence policy, the European Council, flanked by defence and foreign ministry officials, is at the heart, with a secretariat now located in the Council of Ministers (not the Commission). In the case of JHA, policy is mainly being developed among the relevant national ministries and executive agencies, with a new secretariat in the Council, some shared agencies, such as Europol, some legal agreements based on conventions, and others through classical EU law.

These three cases suggest that an important systemic change may be under way within the EU policy process. New areas of sensitive public policy are being assigned by EU member governments to collective regimes, but using an institutional format over which they retain considerable control. These regimes have 'soft' institutions, though the arrangements for EMU have gone the furthest in hardening the institutional arrangements. Yet these soft institutions seem to be capable of developing 'hard' policy, or at least to be aimed at creating the capacity to deliver 'hard' policy.

Politics and policy-making

The focus of this volume is on policy-making in the EU, not the politics of the EU, and hence we deliberately do not deal with some topics, such as the electoral politics of the EU and its member states. Nor do we deal directly with the 'constitution-making' episodes in the development of the EU, especially through Intergovernmental Conferences (IGCs) and treaty reforms, except in so far as treaty changes are relevant to the particular policy cases that we cover. None the less, policy-making is part of a wider political process, and politics pervades the way that EU policies are made.

Some aspects of the EU as a policy arena make an important difference to its politics. In an ideal-type, or traditional, state public policy-making is located in and around the same territory as the politics that produces authoritative forms of government. Governmental bodies are then responsible for devising and delivering appropriate public policies, and are held to account through the electoral process for what they have achieved, or failed to achieve. In contemporary western Europe political and policy-making processes do not coincide quite so neatly. The main locus of politics, political debate and argument, the formulation of programmatic alternatives, patterns of mobilization, affiliation and representation, and so forth remain concentrated within individual countries. In contrast, the provision of public policy is diffused between country and transnational levels of activity, in the EU case with very specific and extensive public policy powers attributed to EU institutions. But the normal channels of political accountability are not present, or at least in only an attenuated form. Thus there is a kind of disjunction between politics and public policy.

Of course within most European countries this political arena encompasses different levels and layers of politics; and, increasingly, that arena is invaded by cross-boundary influences and interactions; yet the heart of the political process is still country-based. At the same time those who exercise political power, or who seek to influence those with political power, often have to seek their policy instruments from outside the political territory in which they are mainly located. Meanwhile, the transnational public policy processes are embedded in political institutions that are less clearly defined, and much less authoritative, than those of a traditional state. An important point to note here is that some political actors have more easy access to the transnational policy processes than others. In other words there is a kind of imbalance of participation and access, which in turn has consequences for the conduct of politics inside European states. This too is a theme to which we shall return throughout this volume.

One further geographical clarification needs to be made. What do we include in our definition of Europe, when assessing the impact of EU institutions and policies? The simple answer would be the territories of those west European countries that are full members of the EU, where the local political authorities have accepted the obligations of membership. Yet this is a clearly inadequate answer. Many, perhaps most, other European countries have, one way or another, connections with the EU institutions and policy process. Both those countries where EU membership has not been accepted and those in the long queue of candidates are deeply affected by EU policies, whether willingly or unwillingly. Much of their domestic legislation is defined by reference to EU rules and practice. Political actors from these other countries are involved in institutionalized forms of association with the EU and its full members. Hence the 'extra-territorial' impact of the EU needs to be taken into account.

One other feature of the EU political environment needs to be mentioned here. In the member countries political parties have programmatic characteristics; they develop programmes for government, and try to pursue them if elected. Electors have the chance to choose between programmes. This is not how politics has traditionally worked as regards EU policy development, partly because of its technocratic features, partly because of its opaqueness, and partly because the main institutions through which policy has been formulated (the Commission and the Council) have not been composed on a programmatic basis. This seems to be changing. Over the past couple of years or so programmatic positions have been more explicitly articulated within the EU, and the question of which transnational political family is in the ascendance is now more directly discussed as a potential influence on the policy agenda and policy substance. Interestingly in summer 1999 the composition of the new college of commissioners, to be presided over by Romano Prodi, was to an extent determined by party political affiliations, and more so than on previous occasions. The emergence of a stronger programmatic dimension to EU politics would presumably exert significant influence over the policy process as well.

The EU institutions as a junction-box

One way of understanding the policy process of the EU is as the junction-box, that is as a concentrated point of intersection, interaction, and filtering, between country-based institutions and processes, and the wider international context. Thus the institutions of the EU provide the interface between the many policy inputs and demands from across the member states of the EU, and from the global arena, in those areas of policy where it has been agreed to involve the EU—or where the EU can capture a policy role. Here again there are opposing camps of analysts. One argues that the main impulses remain country-based, with the EU providing a supplementary and complementary arena. The other argues that increasingly the main pressures stem from the global arena, in so far as globalization has changed the direction of the pressures that bear on national policy-makers and politicians. We shall return to this debate in Chapters 2, 3, and 19, building on the evidence laid out in the case-study chapters from particular policy domains.

Further reading

There is a huge literature on the institutions of the EU and their development. J. Peterson and Bomberg (1999) provide a dynamic analysis, as well as detailed illustrations of policy cases. Scharpf (1999) offers an excellent and critical overview, linking national and European processes. Hix (1999) stresses the politics of the process. Nugent (1999) gives a thorough catalogue of the EU institutions, while Dinan (1999) sets them into their historical context. Among the many studies of the Commission, Cram (1997), Edwards and Spence (1994), and Page (1997) provide valuable explanation and insights. For the Council and European Council, see Hayes-Renshaw and Wallace (1997) and Westlake (1995). Corbett *et al.* (1995; new edn. forthcoming) provide a comprehensive account of the European Parliament, which can be supplemented by Westlake (1995) and J. Smith (1999). The ECJ and the European legal system are covered by Dehousse (1998a), Mattli and Slaughter (1998), and Weiler (1993). On the national dimension, see Mény *et al.* (1996) and Rometsch and Wessels (1996). These academic texts should be supplemented by primary sources, including the extensive material available on the website of the EU institutions, for which the point of access is <http:// www.europa.eu.int>.

Corbett, R., Jacobs, F., and Shackleton, M. (1995), *The European Parliament*, 3rd edn. (London: Cartermill).

Cram, L. (1997), *Policy-Making in the European Union: Conceptual Lenses and the Integration Process* (London: Macmillan).

Dehousse, R. (1998a), *The European Court of Justice* (London: Macmillan).

Dinan, D. (1999), *Ever-Closer Union: An Introduction to the European Union*, 2nd edn. (London: Macmillan).

Edwards, G., and Spence, D. (1994) (eds.), *The European Commission* (London: Longman).

Hayes-Renshaw, F., and Wallace, H. (1997), *The Council of Ministers of the European Union* (London: Macmillan).

Hix, S. (1999), *The Political System of the European Union* (London: Macmillan).

Mattli, W., and Slaughter, A.-M., (1998), 'The ECJ, Governments, and Legal Integration in the EU', *International Organization*, 52/1: 177–210.

Mény, Y., Muller, P., and Quermonne, J.-L. (1996) (eds.), *Adjusting to Europe: The Impact of the European Union on National Institutions and Policies* (London: Routledge).

Nugent, N. (1999), *The Government and Politics of the European Union*, 4th edn. (London: Macmillan).

Page, E. (1997), *People who Run Europe* (Oxford: Clarendon Press).

Peterson, J., and Bomberg, E. (1999), *Decision-Making in the European Union* (London: Macmillan).

Rometsch, D., and Wessels, W. (1996) (eds.), *The European Union and the Member States: Towards Institutional Fusion?* (Manchester: Manchester University Press).

Scharpf, F. W. (1999), *Governing in Europe: Effective and Democratic?* (Oxford: Oxford University Press).

Smith, J. (1999), *Europe's Elected Parliament* (Sheffield: Sheffield Academic Press for UACES).

Wallace, H. (1999a), *The Domestication of Europe: Contrasting Experiences of EU Membership and Non-membership*, 6th Daalder Lecture (Leiden: Leiden University), 13 Mar.

Weiler J. (1993), 'Journey to an Unknown Destination: A Retrospective and Prospective of the European Court of Justice in the Arena of Political Integration', *Journal of Common Market Studies*, 31/4: 417–46.

Westlake, M. (1994), *A Modern Guide to the European Parliament* (London: Pinter).

—— (1995), *The Council of the European Union* (London: Cartermill).

Chapter 2
The Policy Process
A Moving Pendulum

Helen Wallace

Contents

Summary

Western Europe is marked by its propensity for cross-border exchanges and cooperation, and its long experience of transnational regimes. Yet many differences persist between countries, and these can obstruct or undermine cooperation. Whether or not the European Union (EU) emerges as the preferred arena for collective policy-making depends on the movements of a *policy pendulum* between the magnetic field of the domestic arena and the magnetic field of the transnational arena. Wider global frameworks, other European fora, and smaller groupings of neighbours recurrently offer alternative channels of cooperation. Which arena predominates in any given policy domain depends on the context, the functional needs, the motives of those involved, and the institutional arrangements. The context includes: the inadequacy of the individual states; globalization; and the specificity of western Europe, not only in its history and geography, but also in regard to its political and societal attributes. The relevant functions include not only socio-economic adjustment, but also geopolitical stabilization and political symbolism. In most areas there is competition between the EU and other possible arenas. Motives for cooperation include interests, but also ideas. Changing economic doctrines have been very influential in shaping (and constraining) EU policy regimes. Prevailing ideas about society, environment, and security have also been important. Particular issues or events also define the policy challenges and illustrate the capacity of the EU policy process to respond.

Introduction

This chapter charts the landscape in which the policy process of the EU is situated, and sets out some of the specific elements that frame and shape it. Underlying what follows are three defining assumptions. The first is that western Europe has several embedded features, which generate a propensity for cross-border cooperation. The second is that recent experiences have strengthened that propensity. The third is that, none the less differences between west European countries make their participation in cross-border policy cooperation uneven, and in some cases erratic.

First, then, the *embedded propensity to cooperate* is a strong part of west European history. The consolidation of the nation state from the seventeenth century onwards did not erase the habits of exchanges across borders, or the spread of ideas and norms to frame those exchanges. The long-established contours of Roman law, for example, have re-emerged and been reinforced over the centuries. They find contemporary expression in the strong shared legal regimes of today's Europe. The widespread sense that the role and rule of law are a fundamental shared inheritance is a striking characteristic. Common understandings of that living legal tradition shape political and economic exchanges.

Similarly, there are shared societal traditions. It is typical across western Europe for market-making to be accompanied by social buffers, to soften the impacts of markets and entrepreneurship on society. The forms of social market vary between countries and have changed over time, but mostly they juxtapose social responsibility with entrepreneurship. Social actors typically have access to the political domain, frequently as partners in the policy process. The Weberian legacy colours the approach to bureaucracy, with its codes of responsible behaviour, doctrines of administrative neutrality, and respect for expertise.

These common 'currencies', in terms of political and social institutions and norms, are not always used. As Mark Mazower (1998) so cogently points out, embedded liberalism is also sometimes weakened or discarded. But it forms a reservoir from which west European policy-makers in different countries have been able periodically and recurrently to draw.

The second assumption is that west European *experience has strengthened the propensity to cooperate*. It is common for analysts to describe the transaction costs of international cooperation as a disincentive to cooperate. But Europeans have strong and recent memories of the transaction costs of fragmentation and national uni-lateralism. This has left its traces in the sense that the costs—and benefits—of cooperation are often judged over the medium to long term, and often for robustly pragmatic reasons. To put it rather simply: wolves in the pack may bite each other, but they also protect each other.

One result is the frequent use of the term 'stabilization' as a virtuous objective in the political discourse of the EU: geopolitical stabilization, but also stabilization of markets, or of currencies, or of trade, and stabilization of resources and of ecology. This experience, with its reflections in west European political discourse, does not make cooperation automatic, but it does make cooperation to achieve stabilization a typical option for cross-border arrangements.

Yet, thirdly, *persistent differences between countries* remain an enduring feature as well. Cooperation as a strategy has repeatedly to contend with egoistic and unilateral pre-ferences among and within countries. Indeed cooperation is often a means to manage differences, rather than an instrument of convergence. It is this combination that brings much of the dynamic to policy-making across borders in western Europe, a dynamic that can intensify cooperation, but which also can interrupt it.

The policy pendulum

We have adopted the metaphor of a *pendulum* to convey both the sense of movement in the EU policy process and a kind of uncertainty about its outcomes. The policy pendulum swings between the national political arenas of the participating member states, on the one hand, and the transnational arena, with its European and global dimensions, on the other hand. Each of these arenas has a kind of magnetic field which attracts—or repels—the policy-makers, the claimants of policy, and would-be policy-influencers. The relative strength of these magnetic fields varies across policy domains, over time, and between countries, with some strong forces of attraction, and some forces of resistance. Sometimes the forces of magnetism are so strong that they create a propensity to settle policy at the transnational level, while at other times the country-based forces of magnetism keep policy-making located at the coun-try level. In some instances no magnetic field is strong enough to provide a firm resting-point for policy-making and the pendulum sways uncertainly. The case-studies in this volume illustrate these different possible outcomes. Also, it should be noted, the transnational arena is not necessarily only European, as we shall see below. 'European' does not necessarily mean via the EU.

Our pendulum metaphor is only one of several ways of characterizing the push–pull between these different arenas. Another way of expressing it is to define the EU policy process as the product of a *competition* between the national and the trans-national arenas to provide effective or authoritative results. Here the word 'results' is important; the EU arena gathers much of its strength from the extent to which it can deliver solid outcomes, or more solid outcomes than alternative arenas of public policy. Sometimes no arena can deliver effective results. This volume illus-trates the kinds of results that emerge from the EU process, commenting on policy implementation as well as on policy formulation, and providing examples of non-decision as well as of decision.

The choice of a mobile metaphor is deliberate. It aims to encourage the observer to think carefully about what factors are likely to encourage policy-making to develop, and to be sustained, at the European rather than at the national level, or to be addressed via the EU, rather than through some other transnational framework. In this chapter I set out what some of those factors are and how they might operate, building on the institutional anatomy that was described in Chapter 1. In later chapters we examine how in practice they bear on particular kinds of policy. Our choice of metaphor also suggests that a kind of agnosticism is useful in approaching the phenomenon of EU policy-making. This agnosticism is in deliberate contrast to two of the most well-known and opposing schools of analysts of west European integration. Realists, and more recently liberal intergovernmentalists, have argued that the state remains the basic and most important locus of policy-making, to which the EU provides various supplementary capabilities. Neofunctionalists, federalists, and fusionists, on the other hand, suggest that the state has been displaced by the emergence of a new form of European governance, even perhaps a polity-in-the-making. Here I deliberately avoid this 'either–or' question, though I shall return to it in Chapter 3. In the rest of this chapter I set out some of the factors that influence the movements of the pendulum—and make it hard for it to find a stationary position.

Policy-making beyond the state

The transnational arena consists of both European and broader global or multilateral frameworks, which provide opportunities for the resolution of policy problems beyond the state. Specifically the EU arena has built up policy capabilities—and institutionalized them—in ways that have endowed the EU with sophisticated means to provide an alternative to the country level of policy-making. It is widely argued (a point to which I shall return) that it is the way that the EU has become institutionalized which has made it a particularly attractive alternative to either country-level policy-making or other transnational fora. But of course the European policy process is not hermetically sealed off from the broader global arena, in which the USA plays an especially important part.

The range of policy cases surveyed in this volume provide examples that span these competing arenas of governance. In some fields of policy, competition policy (Chapter 5) is perhaps the clearest example, policy assignment to the European level of governance has been extensive, and the EU institutions seem to enjoy considerable autonomy. On the surface the single market (Chapter 4) looks thoroughly Europeanized, yet it depends on political and economic agents from the member states. Agriculture (Chapter 7) illustrates a period of intense investment in a common regime, now followed by a period of efforts at disinvestment, with a planned reversion to a more country-based approach. The common fisheries policy (Chapter 13) has similar elements of both European and local constituents. Cohesion policy (Chapter 9) is a case where the commentators are divided between those who view the EU's achievements as the foundations for a new form of multi-level governance and those who assert that they are based on a more limited cost–benefit calculation by governments. These features recur in the general development of the EU budget (Chapter 8).

In the fields of EU policy dealing with other countries and the rest of the world, the patterns are varied. The management of trade with both developed (Chapter 14) and developing countries (Chapter 15) has been much influenced by the relatively extensive internal regime for intra-EU trade. This has generated pressures for strengthening the corollary external regimes. But this has not been a linear process; from time to time member governments pull back from assigning more powers to the EU, even in the trade field. As Chapter 16 shows in relation to the eastern neighbours, the EU club has difficulties in putting together the internal and external dimensions of policy. The common foreign and security policy (Chapter 17) has been one of the main cases of a domain where member governments historically accepted only modest collective consultation through the EU, although many of them accepted a strong alternative defence regime via the North Atlantic Treaty Organization (Nato). This seems to be changing fast, mirroring perhaps the switch from a national to a collective regime for money (Chapter 6).

In yet other cases, the question is whether the EU is the appropriate arena for policy or a wider international framework. For example, in the instance of new developments in environmental protection (Chapter 11) or in biotechnology (Chapter 12), those concerned have to consider whether to establish appropriate rules globally (for example, through the World Trade Organization (WTO) or the Organization for Economic Cooperation and Development (OECD) or the United Nations (UN)) or within the EU. Often the practice is to use the EU arena as a stepping-stone to a broader international regime.

In some policy domains we can observe that neither the country arena nor the EU arena seems to have the capabilities to deliver coherent and consistent policy outcomes. Both social policy (Chapter 10) and justice and home affairs (Chapter 18) illustrate this. Policy responsibilities in these domains are not neatly divided between country and European arenas, but rather they waver between the two. In both instances, interestingly, there are treaty articles specifically excluding EU policy powers on some aspects of policy.

However, I am not quite so agnostic and open-ended as the paragraphs above suggest. There is a specificity to the EU and to the way in which it has developed and come to exercise its policy powers. As the cases in this volume demonstrate, there has been a particular intensity of institutional and substantive experience in building EU-level policy regimes. This has endowed the EU with capabilities beyond those of most other transnational organizations. Hence there is some plausibility in the argument that policy-makers from EU member countries will tend to prefer the EU to other international organizations, or will prefer to experiment first at the EU level before proceeding to build broader transnational regimes.

Choices about where to assign policy responsibilities

The pendulum of European policy-making oscillates between the country and the transnational arenas, because choices have to be made about the level to which to assign, and to put into effect, public policy responsibilities. Different kinds of factors influence those choices, in particular: the contextual—when and where; the functional—what; the motivational—why; and the institutional—how.

- *Contextual factors* derive from the broad circumstances in western Europe over the decades since the second world war. We stress in what follows: the *inadequacy* of the state; the development of *globalization*; and the *specificity of western Europe* as a region.

- *Functional factors* derive from some of the core functions of politics which recur across west European countries as generating demands to be met. We stress again three: *geopolitics*; *socio-economic adjustment*; and *political symbolism*. Our case-studies deliberately spread wider than the areas of socio-economic adjustment.

- *Motivational factors* are to do with the rationales of the actors involved in the EU process. Its policy regimes have been created and sustained by political actors, acting purposively to achieve specific goals or to resolve specific problems. We highlight three sets of motives: specific *interests*; prevailing *ideas*; and contingent *issues*. Although, as we shall see in Chapter 3, some schools of analysis focus on only one of these, our case-studies investigate which mixture of these three elements is important in individual policy areas.

- *Instititutional factors* comprise our fourth group. Chapter 1 summarized the particular pattern of institutions, both formal and informal, political, but also judicial, which has grown up around the EU. Much of what makes the EU so interesting as a transnational arena is the density of institutions and the evidence of institutional creativity. EU institutions provide both opportunities and constraints, and they serve to channel and to structure the behaviour of political actors from the participating countries. It has become increasingly common for analysts of the process to concentrate on institutional factors as the key to understanding EU policy regimes, both those that succeed and those that fail. Our case-studies suggest that these institutions operate in some significantly different ways in different policy domains. In this we echo much of the received wisdom of comparative politics and comparative policy analysis at the country level. This volume provides material which can be looked at through different sets of analytical spectacles.

Variations over time—and between countries

The EU policy process varies over time. At some periods we can observe a greater willingness to invest in EU-level policy-making than at others. Hence we ask why some periods have generated more investment in EU policy regimes than others. To take three examples: the single market (Chapter 4) gained credibility as a goal in a particular historical moment; so did EMU (Chapter 6); so perhaps has the notion of involving the EU in defence policy (Chapter 17), unacceptable from 1954 onwards, and apparently acceptable in 1999. The cold war, and its termination in 1989, prompted particular policy reappraisals (see Chapter 16), as did the unwinding of European colonialism (Chapter 15). But some of our cases indicate retractions from EU policy regimes at particular moments; agriculture is an example (Chapter 7). The variations over time lead us to question the notion that there has been a linear trend towards assigning more and more policy responsibilities at the EU level. History matters.

As for *country variations*, we should expect to find important and persistent differences in the way in which different countries have responded to, and engaged in, EU policy-making. This process does not exist in a vacuum, as I stressed in Chapter 1. Policy-making continues within the member states of the EU, involving many of the same actors as those who engage in the EU process, but also engaging different actors, whose contacts with the European arena may be limited or non-existent. The context, core preoccupations, and characteristics of the individual member countries vary considerably. Perhaps involvement in EU-level policy-making induces *convergence* among these different country processes—perhaps. Much of the literature implies that this is so, and much of the practitioners' discourse is about how to generate convergence between countries and between national policies.

We start from a different assumption, namely that to achieve a shared EU policy regime requires only that compatible approaches are evident. Many of our cases indicate quite wide-ranging preferences and practices among countries, not only, as in the environmental domain (Chapter 11), when policy is being first considered, but also, as in the case of agriculture (Chapter 7), long after the creation of an ostensibly 'common' policy. Hence we should distinguish firmly between the evidence of *congruence* among national policies as a requirement of common policy development, and evidence of *convergence*, as either a prompt—or a consequence—of involvement in the EU process. We need to explain why responses in some countries seem to be more or less convergent than those in some other countries, and why some countries utilize the same EU policy regimes domestically in different ways, as Chapter 13 illustrates in relation to fisheries.

One important footnote here: this question is pertinent not only for countries that are already members of the EU. One of the most interesting features of the experience of EU policy-making is its extraterritorial impact on other European countries, some of which have moved into membership of the EU through formal enlargement, and most of the rest of which are currently engaged in efforts to join the EU. The magnetic attraction of the EU policy arena does not end at the explicit political boundaries of those countries that are officially full members.

The moving pendulum in summary

To summarize so far: the EU policy process depends on the swing of a pendulum between the country arena and the transnational. Its movements are shaped by the context in western Europe, by the array of policy functions needing attention, and by the purposes and predicaments of political actors. EU institutions provide the means for devising collective policy responses. How they operate is influenced by the interests, and the ideas, that shape their preferences, and by the issues that turn up on their agendas. The development of policy varies over time and between countries.

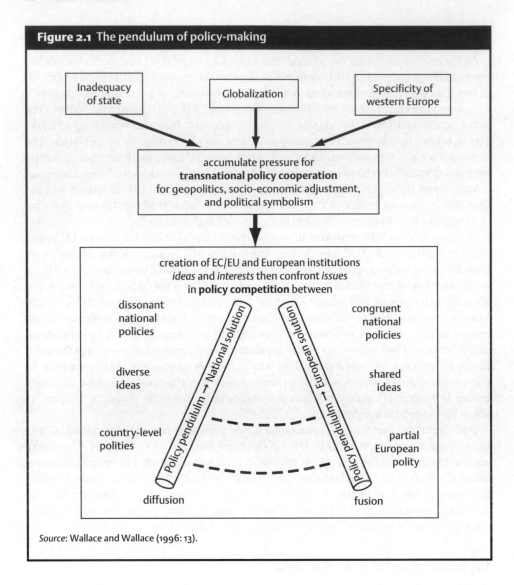

Figure 2.1 The pendulum of policy-making

Inadequacy of state

Globalization

Specificity of western Europe

accumulate pressure for
transnational policy cooperation
for geopolitics, socio-economic adjustment,
and political symbolism

creation of EC/EU and European institutions
ideas and *interests* then confront *issues*
in **policy competition** between

dissonant national policies

congruent national policies

diverse ideas

shared ideas

country-level polities

partial European polity

Policy pendulum ↑ National solution

Policy pendulum ↑ European solution

diffusion

fusion

Source: Wallace and Wallace (1996: 13).

The context in western Europe

The scope for developing collective EU policies is shaped by several contextual factors. The history of transnational policy cooperation suggests that it is in western Europe that we have seen the most far-reaching and apparently most durable such experiments. We recognize, of course, that there is a danger here of being over-impressed by this special history, and it is important to avoid the trap of circular arguments about western Europe being *sui generis*. None the less, there is a clustering of contextual features that seems to have yielded a more fertile ground for cross-border policy regimes than in most other parts of the world.

The inadequacy of the state

I start here from a simple premiss that no one set of political authorities can command sufficient political and economic resources to develop effective policy across all the main domains of public policy. The period following the second world war saw first reconstruction, then a vast extension of the powers of the west European state and in its provision of public goods. Thus the functions of government proliferated, and more and more of the life of the economy and of the citizen became subject to public policy regimes. As functions increased, so governing élites found themselves under pressures of increasing demands and expectations, and extended their ambitions to respond.

One means of responding was to draw resources from transnational cooperation as instruments of domestic policy. Indeed the scope for doing this may well have served to disguise the inadequacy of the individual state and paradoxically to preserve the notion that the state could remain effective as the primary source of most public goods, as well as the primary point of political affiliation. I note also that individual states were 'inadequate' in different ways and that EU policy cooperation may have served quite different purposes for different countries, depending on which gap in local policy provision was being addressed. Thus, to take a concrete example, EU structural funds (Chapter 9) have been used by the UK to cover part of its deficit under the EU budget, and by British local authorities later to compensate for reduced central government funding; in Ireland they contributed to a strategy of infrastructural and industrial investment; in the southern 'cohesion' countries they provided an offset for the impact of the single market on less advanced economies (A. Smith 1995).

Milward (1992) has argued that the development of the EU served to help the weakened post-war west European states to recover their policy powers, by providing them with supplementary instruments and resources. Scharpf (1999) has expressed it differently by arguing that states have lost powers progressively, without collectively managing to develop additional powers. Lindberg (1963) suggested that there was a division of labour in which some policy powers, but only some, were assigned to the European level, whereas others were retained at the country level and protected from transnational interference.

The 1950s and 1960s saw cumulative extensions of public policy, more public involvement in the economy, and the expansion of publicly provided welfare, all giving rise subsequently to a conventional wisdom about the overstretched state and overloaded government. At least historically, therefore, it can be argued that the development of European policy cooperation was one means of dealing with this proliferation of public policy activities. Thus, for example, Wessels (1997) argues that the EU has played a particularly important additional part in underpinning and empowering the west European welfare state.

However, since the mid-1980s the trend has been in a different direction, namely for the state to withdraw from parts of the economy, to retract from the provision of certain public goods, and to reduce the powers of government. This happened partly because of the costs of public provision, partly because of the pressures of international competition, and partly because ideas changed about the appropriate functions to assign to the state. In their differing adjustments to these changes west

European states found themselves losing—and in some cases deliberately renouncing—certain public policy powers.

On the one hand, EU-level policy regimes provided an alternative way of recouping a kind of control, as partly happened through the consolidation of the single market (Chapter 4), or the reinvigoration of competition policy (Chapter 5). However, the nature of the EU as a policy arena made it more effective in providing regulatory responses than in offering distributive instruments (Chapter 10). On the other hand, the waning of some state powers made national politicians more tenacious about protecting their remaining policy powers. We can see this reflex in the increasing emphasis on 'subsidiarity' from the late 1980s, with its reassertion that policy powers should be located at the lowest practicable level of governance. Environmental (Chapter 11), social (Chapter 10), agricultural (Chapter 7), and fisheries (Chapter 13) policies all illustrate this tension, as, perhaps more surprisingly, does competition policy (Chapter 5).

Globalization

It has become something of a commonplace to argue that globalization is one of the main stimuli of cross-border policy-making, and not only in Europe. Definitions abound of globalization as a phenomenon, its constituent features, its novelty (or old roots), and its consequences. It is not our task here to espouse one definition or characterization of globalization rather than another. Rather we draw attention to three points: first, that we need some consistency between our definitions of globalization and Europeanization; secondly, we need to ask if globalization takes a particular form in western Europe; and, thirdly, we need to consider what the relationship is between the two phenomena.

Common to most definitions of globalization is the increasingly free flow across borders of goods, services, money and people, technology, and ideas. Interestingly these coincide with targets early identified as arenas of policy development within the EU. The four freedoms of movement (goods, services, capital, and labour) were laid out in the Treaty of Rome in 1957. Since the late 1970s the EU has started to develop research and development programmes, as well as common standards, in new technologies. The point here is simply that these features associated with globalization have been flagged up as ones where west European countries (and not only EU members) aim to cooperate.

Another focus of the debate about globalization is on the enhanced opportunities for non-state (both economic and societal) actors to develop cross-border activities. This too is a recurrent theme of studies of European integration. Three recent emphases in studies of both globalization and Europeanization have been on: the changing character and role of the firm; the freeing up of cross-border financial flows (increasingly electronically); and the new role of transnational non-governmental organizations (NGOs). Western Europe provides a useful laboratory for testing empirically some of the assertions being made about globalization.

This brings us to the second point, whether globalization takes a particular form in western Europe. On the one hand, the phenomenon may have distinctive characteristics in the geographically concentrated area of western Europe, a proposition that can be tested empirically. On the other hand, the phenomenon may have different outcomes in western Europe from elsewhere. In particular the availability of highly institutionalized channels for managing globalization, and the EU's rich cross-border legal and judicial mechanisms, may give west Europeans more opportunities than others to control some of the consequences of globalization.

This leads us to the third dimension, namely what is the relationship between the two phenomena? Here there is something of a chicken and egg debate. Is the EU a reaction to globalization, or is it an agent of globalization? Perhaps the important pressures are global, and the Europeanization of certain policy activities is in essence a response to globalization. On the other hand, perhaps the existence of the EU has produced a different form of globalization in western Europe from that in other parts of the world. Just to give one indication of evidence relevant to this argument, the EU countries generate an enormous volume of cross-border economic transactions—but mostly with each other rather than with the rest of the world (the patterns are very similar to those *within* the USA). The collective policy regimes of the EU (single market, common trade policy, discrimination in favour of domestic producers and service providers, common currency) have, arguably, enabled west European countries to function as a more self-sufficient economic entity than might otherwise have been the case. Thereby west European vulnerability to the broader phenomenon of globalization may have been reduced.

Globalization does not, however, impact only on socio-economic policy domains. Security concerns have been redefined by the impacts of globalization, especially the so-called 'soft' security concerns of environmental and societal security (Waever *et al.* 1993). In particular it has become increasingly difficult for individual states to exercise monopoly power over who resides on their territory, or over the movements of persons (migrants, refugees, and asylum-seekers) across state borders, or over unlawful cross-border movements of, for example, criminals. International migration and cross-border crime, both major societal issues, have become the subjects of transnational regime-building. Our case-study on EU policy in relation to justice and home affairs (Chapter 18) illustrates some of the EU responses, and the limits to their effectiveness against a broader global anarchy.

The specificity of western Europe

Neither the inadequacy of the state nor the phenomenon of globalization is peculiar to western Europe. However, there is an unusual intensity to the impact of both in western Europe, a region of the world with long traditions of transnational interaction and cooperation interspersed periodically with severe conflict. Experiences of transnational cooperation date back over centuries, with a variety of regimes, going back to the Romans (see on this Rokkan's writings, collected in Flora 1999). The breakdowns of transnational cooperation in Europe have produced wars and tensions still close enough in the collective memory to be a primary factor in inducing a profound commitment to finding stabilizing frameworks. These have included the devising of regimes specifically to promote collective security, and the security of individual countries. Both neutrality and military alignment have contributed to a jigsaw of security arrangements, in turn a precondition for the guarantees of safety needed for socio-economic exchanges to take place, and thus promote prosperity.

Since the second world war this preoccupation with collective security and geopolitical stabilization has had specific outcomes in western Europe. These include: the efforts to consolidate relationships within western Europe, notably *vis-à-vis* Germany; the protection of western against eastern Europe (until 1989); and the impact of superpower confrontation (Herbst *et al.* 1990). This security setting has had profound impacts on how cross-border regimes have been shaped to promote political and economic exchanges as a means of embedding cooperative behaviour.

A second specificity of Europe has to do with geography and territory, both political and economic. Western Europe is an overcrowded region in terms of both population and the number of distinct states. The connections between populations in adjacent states have deep roots in history, then overlaid by the newer impacts of globalization. Unilateralist policies in western Europe, in tension with immediate neighbours, have not been very successful, given the character and history of interdependence. The recourse to efforts to manage that interdependence has been a recurrent feature of west European history, an experience, we note, at variance with the history of central and eastern Europe. Neighbouring states have developed local frameworks for cooperation, both to regulate their borders with each other, and to develop particular forms of practical cooperation.

A third specificity of western Europe has been the prevalent commitment to forms of liberal democracy, not as a monopoly of west Europeans, but as a strongly to be preferred system to be defended against competing models in the immediate neighbourhood. Thus both those Europeans from long-democratic states and those who had memories of recent non-democratic experience have retained an active commitment to embedding liberal democratic values across as much of the continent as possible. This 'vocation' became part of the widely understood political culture of western Europe, and a key part of the rationale for engaging Germany in particular, and Italy as well, in solid transnational regimes. It provided reasons for using transnational regimes as a means of rescuing Greece, Portugal, and Spain from authoritarianism. During the cold war it defined the boundary between those included in and those excluded from those regimes. Since the cold war ended, it has become part of the backcloth to the debate on eastern enlargement of the EU (see Chapter 16).

The fifty years of competition with state socialism in Europe had thus a particular intensity of impact on the way in which Europeanization was construed, so much so that within the EU it became commonplace to elide Europe with the EU in political discourse. The EU had resonance as the embodiment of regimes for (most of) those (west) European countries that were liberal democracies and hence able to be fully signed up members of the EU club. It is impossible to understand the history, policies, and politics of the EU, or its institutional characteristics, without taking this dimension into account. The EC and later the EU were in part devised to contribute to democratic stabilization as the club of European liberal democracies, characterized also by their functioning market economies. Hence the EU was bound to be preoccupied with enlargement as a challenge, each time that newly democratic neighbours wanted to join this club (Lepsius 1991).

A fourth characteristic of western Europe has been the development of the welfare state model, based around a kind of consensus between Christian and social democrats. In spite of important variations between countries, as many have pointed out, there are a number of common threads. These have enabled a range of societal and welfare preoccupations to be drawn into the debate about European policy regimes.

The socio-political and the socio-economic sides to market integration are crucial dimensions of EU policy experimentation, as is illustrated in Chapters 7, 10, and 13.

These have taken different forms over the past fifty years or so. On the one hand, west European countries developed particular kinds of welfare states as their way of addressing the challenges of socio-economic adjustment and 'modernization' (Kaelble 1990; Flora 1993). The linking of the EC, later EU, to the trajectory of modernization has been an important element in the domestic politics of members and aspirant member states. The interaction between domestic adjustment and wider global constraints gave a particular opening to European cooperation as a means of mediating domestic conflicts. On the other hand, the more recent pressures to reform—even to retract—the welfare state have also been situated within the orbit of EU policy cooperation. As Leibfried and Pierson argue, both elsewhere (1995*b*) and in this volume (Chapter 10), this constrained process has both produced interesting policy experiments in the EU and foreclosed other options.

To pull these threads together, preoccupations with security, crowded geography, liberal democratic systems, and the similarities of the welfare models have endowed western Europe with an array of factors that have framed the understandings of transnational cooperation. They have combined to shape the development of market integration. They have also brought into play political and societal factors relevant to the modalities and corollaries of managing integration.

It is against this configuration of features that we need to interpret the institutionalization of policy cooperation within the EU. The attachment of political and societal correlates to economic cooperation provides part of the explanation for the development of the polity-like features of EU policy regimes. Because in a country setting economic policy is linked to political and societal elements, it is hardly surprising that some of this mixture should have permeated the EU arena as well.

None the less, there are limits to this. We can observe, on the one hand, EU policy cooperation being embedded in a set of institutions that have polity-like characteristics. Yet, on the other hand, we can observe resilient differences between west European countries (Schulze 1994). In the early period of European integration these differences had a relatively small impact at the transnational level. More recently the differences seem to have been magnified, or perhaps made more vivid. In particular, we note the pressures from many EU countries to delineate more firmly the boundary between EU regimes and the domestic political space through which societal concerns are addressed. Ireland and the Netherlands illustrate this; both have developed distinct domestic models of social partnership, in spite of extensions to the scope of integration. At any rate we can observe two developments. One is the sharper variation between countries' responses to integration, which suggests that we should probe beyond generalizations about western Europe to examine country idiosyncrasies. The other development is the apparent increase in lines of resistance to integration, even in some cases efforts to return to the member states policy responsibilities that had been assigned to the European institutions. The case-studies in this volume allow some opportunity to establish country profiles across policy domains, and hence some comparisons between countries.

Core policy functions and the agenda of cooperation

EU policy-making embraces a broad agenda of cooperation, with almost no policy domain untouched, either directly or indirectly. Although the EU has not monopolized west European transnational policy-making, it has spread its tentacles into more and more domains as the years have passed, as policy tasks have been redefined, and as treaty reforms have specifically assigned new tasks to this common framework. There have been three main prompts to this process, in terms of functional requirements and of claimants for policy: *geopolitical stabilization*; *socio-economic adjustment*; and *political symbolism*. Each is briefly explained below.

However, we must note the parallel existence of other transnational frameworks for European policy cooperation. Alongside the EU there are also: a set of institutions dealing with security issues; a range of single function regimes; and narrower arrangements between immediate neighbours. The EU is better understood not in isolation, but as part of this broader patchwork of transnational regimes. This plurality of regimes has several consequences: first, it provides choices between frameworks in some policy domains, defence being the clearest example; secondly, competing frameworks constrain the scope for EU policy development, as, for example, Nato has done; thirdly, smaller subsets of countries have been the relevant grouping for some policy domains, as between France and Germany, the Benelux countries, or the Nordic countries; and, fourthly, the different memberships of these different organizations have enabled some non-EU member countries to be involved in some of the other European policy regimes. The European standards organizations are one example of the latter. The Council of Europe, with a new, much enlarged membership, is another.

Thus we always need to keep in mind the question why, if transnational cooperation is sought, the EU has been the chosen arena in some domains and not in others. We also have to consider whether there are intended complementarities between different institutional frameworks. One of the complications in the EU story is that it has so frequently been the subject of specific and focused debate about the formal extensions of its policy scope. This is much less of a feature of Europe's other transnational institutions. None of our case-studies address as such the episodes of constitutional, or quasi-constitutional, settlements in the development of the EU. However, several touch on ways in which the treaty-reforming episodes of Intergovernmental Conferences (IGCs) have altered the powers of the EU *vis-à-vis* other frameworks, in particular policy domains. Money (Chapter 6), foreign and security policy (Chapter 17), and justice and home affairs (Chapter 18) are recent examples.

Geopolitical stabilization

Geopolitical stabilization has from the second world war onwards been a core subject for transnational regime-building in western Europe. We use the term to connote: external security; safe borders; and the embedding of 'safe' democracy. This is a deliberately broad formulation, reflecting both preoccupations relevant to the early period following the second world war and more recent public policy concerns about security and geopolitics. Some of these concerns have specifically been addressed through other frameworks than the EU.

Irrespective of whether the EU becomes an explicit security framework, as is beginning to seem probable, some of the EU's activities have been driven by concerns relating to geopolitical stabilization in the terms that we have defined it. The way that the EU has developed was influenced by the fact that it was nested in a wider setting which included a plurality of other institutional frameworks. This is not a universally accepted view, as we shall see in Chapter 3.

The provision of external and military security for western Europe was from the late 1940s locked into a security-specific set of institutions: the Brussels Treaty Organization; Nato; and the Western European Union (WEU). These were in turn linked to a set of understandings about the neutral or non-aligned countries which stayed outside these organizations, notably Austria, Finland, Sweden, and Switzerland (the Irish case is a bit different). In each of these countries their special security status was for a long time held also to preclude membership of the EU, because its security 'shadow' was viewed as troublesome until the late 1980s. The security institutions also included some countries excluded for one reason or another from the EU. Thus countries such as Greece or Portugal were members of Nato, while governed by authoritarian regimes, but they were outside the then EC. Similarly, Turkey is a long-time member of Nato, but until recently was not allowed to activate its bid for full EU membership, partly because of doubts about its domestic political attributes. Iceland and Norway were Nato members, but not EU members.

The main points to note here are two. First, the twin-track arrangement, special security frameworks on the one hand, and a political economy framework on the other, allowed for some elasticity about which west European countries were involved in which policy regimes. Secondly, however, the complementarity of the twin tracks did not preclude discussion of changes to the division of labour between the two. Thus the objective of an EU-linked responsibility for European defence has been part of the debate since the mid-1950s, always controversial, and until the early 1990s more or less entirely resisted. As Chapter 17 shows, the adoption at Maastricht in 1991 of the goal of a common foreign *and security* policy reflected the changing parameters of debate. From 1998 onwards this has been extended to include defence within the explicit orbit of the EU.

Our second concern relating to geopolitical stabilization has to do with the maintenance of safe borders. Part of the experience of building transnational policy regimes in Europe has been about discriminating between the included and the excluded. This concern spans the range from safe in general defence terms, safe in terms of access to markets, through safe in the sense of which individuals are allowed to cross the borders, and safe as regards legal and illegal cross-border transactions and movements.

The core function of the EU in defining free movement within its borders and the shared responsibility for a shared external border has always been important, and has become much more important, for political as well as economic reasons. It was less important for geopolitical purposes during the cold war, because the central division of Europe into east and west was policed from the east, thus relieving west Europeans of the need to think about how to manage that sensitive eastern external border. Managing the southern and south-eastern borders has been a more explicit preoccupation for rather longer, and indeed has played into the way in which policy regimes have been established with southern and south-eastern countries before, during, and after their accession to the EU. Chapter 18 on justice and home affairs picks up part of this story. Traces of the story can also be found in Chapter 10 and Chapter 15.

The third component of geopolitical stabilization has to do with making democracy safe in western Europe. The inclusion of Germany in the privileged circle of EU cooperation as a founder member was a way of addressing this concern. The economic weight of Germany kept alive concerns about the linkage between relative economic power and the potential political corollaries. To harness that economic power was a security objective for Germany's neighbours. West European policymakers have, however, found it harder to figure out how to link political and economic cooperation to security cooperation in central and eastern Europe, as Chapters 16 and 17 show from different standpoints.

Socio-economic adjustment

Here we come to the heart of the EU policy agenda. Whatever the varying attractions of the EU arena for other policy functions, it is in the core concerns of managing economic interdependence that the EU has made the largest achievements. The main treaties founding the EU and its precursors assign distinct socio-economic or economic tasks to, in turn, the European Coal and Steel Community (ECSC), the European Economic Community (EEC), and Euratom. The bulk of the legislation and jurisprudence of the EU has developed in these policy domains. In the early years of these initially separate communities, most of these functions had to do with post-war reconstruction and the embedding of multilateralism as the mode for managing interdependencies. The importance of these functions may now seem distant memories as regards west European countries; their relevance persists as regards the countries of central and eastern Europe (CEECs).

The three Communities laid down at the outset some agreed common principles for shared regimes; these included the liberalization of markets, free movement for the factors of production (goods, services, capital, and labour), and Community preference for member countries (thus necessarily discrimination against non-members). These principles were laid down in a period when their achievement could not be taken for granted. From the early period advocates of the policies implied by these principles hoped to use European regimes in order to ratchet policy developments in their own countries and in neighbouring fellow member states.

The treaties also defined policy domains to be developed: strong competition rules; and several sectoral policies (coal, steel, agriculture, and transport), identified as economically important and subject to various forms of national protection. Internal liberalization was to be within a customs union, which required a corollary external trade policy. This in turn meant that ways had to be found to incorporate the historically special economic relations of EU member countries with overseas dependencies and former colonies. Many of our case-studies deal with policy regimes that owe their origins to the early agreements in the treaties: Chapter 7 on agriculture; Chapter 4 on the single market; Chapter 5 on competition; Chapter 14 on external trade; and Chapter 15 on the legacy of colonialism.

In those early years some policy domains were deliberately excluded, and others not even contemplated. Broadly speaking a kind of division of labour was agreed between the country and the European levels of policy assignment. Responsibility for trade-related exchanges was assigned to the European level, while the more social parts of the socio-economic agenda were retained at the country level. This sounds much more neat and tidy than it was to prove. Some social measures were included in the original ECSC and EEC treaties relating to conditions of employment and retraining, including a provision on equal pay for men and women. Grey areas persisted and have been contested over the years. Indeed the social policy domain is one of the most volatile in terms of competition between the country and European levels, as Chapter 10 shows.

Much depends on definitions. Rieger argues in Chapter 7 that one way of interpreting the development of the CAP is as the assignment of the welfare policy for farmers to the European level rather than the country level. Not only did the CAP provide the means to liberalize intra-EU agricultural trade, it insulated farmers from the competition for funding within individual countries. Some similar mechanisms were present in the arrangements for the coal and steel sectors, but not emulated in other industrial sectors. Agricultural policy also illustrates the erosion of commitment to a shared regime, as circumstances have changed both within the EU and globally. Fisheries policy (Chapter 13) is another telling illustration of contested assignment to the European level for a mix of social and trade-related reasons.

The original treaties were a product of the period in which they were written and hence excluded policy domains that have become a great deal more important over the years. Two of our case-studies—Chapter 12 on biotechnology and Chapter 11 on the environment—address important subjects that have subsequently been Europeanized, up to a point. Both are domains in which transnational policy networks (Héritier 1993) and cross-border entrepreneurship (Cowles 1994) have been important stimuli of European-level regulation. In both cases formal assignment to the EU of at least some policy functions was incorporated in the treaties after, not before, the development of some collective policy instruments. But in both cases differences of approach persist between member countries, such that it remains hard to say that policy convergence has taken place. And in both cases we can observe efforts to renege on EU policy commitments in response to country preferences and prejudices. These two domains also usefully illustrate the difficulty of deciding whether the European or some other international forum is more appropriate for dealing with policy issues that spread beyond the capacities of the individual state.

Part of the apparent logic of economic integration is that one thing leads to another, thus that policy commitments in one economic domain build up pressures for policy engagement in related areas. In the early neofunctionalist literature this phenomenon was identified as spill-over, a point to which we shall return in Chapter 3. For the moment we identify two ways in which economic policy regimes developed in the EU have built up demands for policy extension. Both relate to money: one is money in the sense of the single currency; and the other is money in the sense of distributive and redistributive resource transfers.

Each edition of this volume has included a chapter on economic and monetary union (EMU), commenting on the debate since the late 1960s about whether, when, and how economic integration might move from internal market to EMU. In this edition Chapter 6 shows the arrival of EMU as a functioning reality. One part of this story is about economic ideas and interests, another is about the political and societal impacts of EMU.

Distribution and redistribution are also important themes in the development of the European policy agenda. At the outset the various treaties provided for limited common funds to provide specified common instruments, especially to fund the common agricultural policy (CAP). None of these early funds was based on specific and planned criteria for resource allocation or transfers, though it became clear rather early on that the CAP produced some rather perverse financial flows. The decisions from the early 1970s to move to a system of independent—or quasi-independent—revenue and to proliferate spending programmes changed the situation by building up a notion of a common budget, and by generating expectations of resource transfers (especially from richer to poorer). The subsequent highlighting of the net contributions of individual member states changed the politics of bargaining. Many of these issues are addressed in Chapter 8 on the budget as a whole, and Chapter 9 on cohesion and the richer–poorer transfers. These show the tensions between economic logics and political expectations, and the difficulty of explaining the process in narrowly economic terms.

To summarize this section, the EU policy agenda is focused on socio-economic adjustment measures. The definition of what these include has expanded remarkably over the years, and changed in character. EU measures have encroached on the societal dimension to economic integration, but how far and potentially how much further are contested. The expansion of the economic agenda has also been accompanied by its greater politicization, in relation to both the kind of bargaining that takes place and the salience of issues included in the EU policy arena.

Political symbolism

Part of the specificity of western Europe as a site for the development of transnational regimes consisted of its 'embedded liberalism', the shared commitments to liberal democracy, a form of welfare state, and the general provision of security. The agenda of cooperation has expanded to include the development of forms of political symbolism, with some measures or programmes that were intended to construct political symbols. The inclusion of a form of 'European citizenship' is an obvious example. Another is the presence at ports of entry of signs separating EU citizens from others, the 'sheep' from the 'goats'. In addition this dimension to the process has permeated the way in which the EU institutions have developed, the special role of the rule of law, and the iterated debates on which applicant countries might be acceptable as full members.

This symbolic dimension to integration has become much more widely studied in recent years. The politico-sociological literature and discursive analyses have burgeoned, of which more in Chapter 3. Empirical studies are also proliferating, in particular on topics such as the creation of a form of European citizenship. From these we can see evidence of considerable activity at the level of political leaderships and élites, increased involvement of civic groups of one kind or another in the EU policy process, and valuable insights into wider public attitudes to the development of EU policies. Among other factors we can see the beginnings of the emergence of an affective dimension (not always positive) to integration, alongside the cognitive dimension, which historically has been rather stronger.

Several of our case-studies deal with domains where political symbolism is rather important, or where political symbolism seems to be becoming a more pressing element. Thus, Chapters 10 and 18 touch on questions of entitlements for citizens and residents of the EU, as well as for those wishing to enter the territory of the EU. Chapter 16 on enlargement touches on the questions of identity-building and democracy-building as relevant elements of policy. Chapter 17 touches on the question of European identity and values as prompts to the development of a common foreign and security policy, both in form and in substance. Chapter 6 raises the issue of control over the currency as a symbol of political identity. We have also included cases where wider public preoccupations to do with cultural and societal values bear on the policy process: Chapter 11 on environmental concerns; Chapter 12 on biotechnology and its impacts on both the environment and human well-being; Chapter 14 on trade policy; and Chapter 15 on the public furore over bananas.

In evaluating quite what function European political symbolism plays in these various cases, we note also the competition between European and national symbolisms. Often national symbolisms are part of the explanation for resistance to European regimes (Schnapper 1992), and differences in the resonance or interpretation of particular symbols between member states account for arguments about whether or how to proceed with a particular policy initiative.

Motives for cooperation

Both the contextual factors and the functional requirements that we have identified are necessary elements for the development of EU policies, but neither provides a sufficient explanation for them. To complete the picture we need to examine the incentives to cooperate, which induce policy-makers to attach their own goal satisfaction to the creation and sustaining of EU policy regimes. In this section I focus mainly on *interests*, *ideas*, and *issues*, as espoused by the range of policy actors identified in Chapter 1. I then mention some of the ways in which the institutional setting of the EU has shaped the ways in which these various goals are pursued.

Rational choice analysis reminds us that we must assume that policy actors behave purposefully, rationally, and strategically (Scharpf 1997). They have purposes, whether explicit or implicit, which guide their choices of how to behave. Our case-studies seek to identify who the relevant actors are, instance by instance, and to explain what their main purposes are. These are articulated in terms of a rationale or line of reasoning that calculates the relationship between those purposes and the possible means available to achieve them, at whatever level of governance might be thinkable (infranational, national, European, or broader international). Generally those involved in the policy process behave strategically, in the sense that they try to assess in advance the likely consequences of choosing one framework rather than another, and thus do not usually behave randomly. Chapter 3 notes the explosion of studies that draw on the rational choice literature and methodologies.

Much of the literature about EU policy integration and much of the discourse of practitioners, and indeed the formal EU texts, talk about policy *convergence* as either a prerequisite for agreement or a desired outcome of agreement. In this volume we do not assume that convergence is necessary, although we are interested in identifying policy domains where it can be demonstrated. Instead we emphasize the importance of *congruence*, that is to say the compatibility of the policy actors' preferences as the basis for establishing a shared policy regime. Different policy actors may have different preferences, but none the less choose the same collective action. Congruent preferences imply conditional commitments to collective regimes. Convergence of preferences may produce longer-term stability of policy regimes. Our case-studies include examples of both convergence and congruence. Persistently different, but congruent, preferences, should alert us to look for differences between one member state and another in the way that collective regimes are implemented.

Purposes and preferences—but based on what? *Interests* define some purposes and preferences, but, in our view, are not enough to explain why EU policies have emerged in some domains, but not others. *Ideas* play a part as well, and indeed there is a growing literature which points to the impact of ideas on the process of EU policy-making. One vivid example is the importance in the mid-1980s of the idea that market liberalization, combined with the privatization of more of the economy and a different mode of economic regulation, would facilitate west European firms' competitiveness in broader international markets (see Chapters 4 and 5). Our case-studies seek to identify not only when and how a particular set of congruent interests favour a collective EU policy, but also the impacts of particular ideas or doctrines in fostering EU policy cooperation.

The emphasis on interests and ideas implies that there is time for thinking, that interests can be considered and calculated, and that ideas have time to develop and to become embedded. But the world of public policy is not always so amenable to mature reflection. Public policy-makers have to react to issues as they arise and to events as they happen. Issues and events cannot always be neatly defined in terms of pre-existing interests or ideas. Contingent issues are sometimes the prompt to policy-makers. The settlement of Agenda 2000, the new financial package agreed in Berlin in March 1999, owed much to the press of events. It is covered from different angles in Chapters 7, 8, 9, and 16.

Interests

It is broadly agreed that interests and self-interests have repeatedly played a crucial part in determining the outcomes of EU policy-making. In each area of policy debate it is important, therefore, to establish where the different interests of the different participants set the parameters for the agreements that may be struck—or resisted. Interests inform the calculated reasoning of the policy actors in relation to particular policy predicaments, in relation to the costs and benefits of the available courses of action, and as regards the nature of the institutional arrangements as well.

So far so good. But it is harder in practice to define interests than this summary implies. It is tempting to suggest that interests have a kind of objective status, in that if you have enough information about the situation and attributes of a particular policy actor, then you can ascertain where that actor might calculate the costs and benefits to lie, and hence define the relevant preferences. Reality is a little more complicated. The sequencing of action and the consequences of a particular course of action may be hard to establish, and may depend on more subjective or more uncertain judgements, or on other kinds of motivation.

Five assumptions follow about the kinds of interests that bear on European policy-making.

- Interest satisfaction is a crucial feature of the process. The development and sustainability of European policies require the satisfaction of multiple interests, given the range of actors involved. Positive cost–benefit analyses of particular policies—and their achievement—tend to generate a willingness to develop the policy regime further.

- National interests or state interests are present in the process, necessarily because the governments of the member states are powerful participants, and it is among the functions of governments to articulate the interests of the member states that they represent. However, governments are also the incumbent power-holders, and have more partisan concerns, utilizing the EU arena sometimes for narrow ends of domestic party competition. And it is not always easy to establish within countries where *the* national interest lies.

- A plurality of organized interests is engaged in efforts to influence the EU policy process, some of which have easier access to the process than others. This variation in access may bias the process towards the recognition of some interests rather than others. However, we should be careful not to confuse activism with influence or impact.

- Nested games play an important part in the process, because the same actors are often involved in bargaining at different locations for political action, i.e. positions in EU discussion may be designed to influence outcomes in national discussion. The interests which are relevant in one location of political action may be different from those relevant in a different one. A particular course of action may be rational at one level, yet irrational at another level.

- Actors in the EU policy process often seem to settle for satisficing, rather than optimizing, strategies, suggesting a fluidity to their definitions of interests, partly because bargaining is iterated, partly because factors other than calculus of interest may influence their choices of action. In particular, calculations of benefits and costs seem to be spread over time and across policy domains in a form of assumed diffuse reciprocity, and not specific reciprocity.

The case-studies in the rest of this volume reveal the interplay of governmental and other interests. But they mostly adduce evidence that suggests that the calculation of interests by those involved does not provide a sufficient explanation of the outcomes.

Ideas

Part of the reason that we resist accepting interests as a sufficient explanation for EU policy-making outcomes is that ideas have had an important influence. This is not a novel observation. The early neofunctionalist studies pointed to the relevance of shared bodies of ideas in structuring policy debate. For example, the role of the EU in its early days as an agent of modernization and the embedding in the EU of a kind of cross-class compact between Christian and social democrats emerged from prevailing ideas which shaped policy. These ideas defined the range of thinkable policy regimes and tilted the policy agenda in particular directions.

Over the years different ideas have taken hold and been pursued through the EU policy process. An important example was the shift in the 1980s towards the widespread acceptance of a form of neo-liberalism as the basis for pushing market integration forwards (see Chapters 4 and 5), although this never entirely banished the contending doctrine of social responsibility as a guide for policy. Similarly, there has been a persistent competition between free traders and protectionists in the debates over internal and external EU policies (see Chapters 7, 14, and 15). The trend has been in an economically liberal direction, but not unequivocally so. In the deliberations of the Spaak Committee that had drafted the Treaty of Rome (EEC) the liberals and the more interventionist had reached a compromise that incorporated key tenets of liberalism, but softened them with a few instruments of intervention and some social buffers, notably in relation to agriculture (Chapter 7).

As time passed, it proved easier to strengthen the liberal economic doctrines than to reinforce the instruments of intervention. This suggests that the way that the bargaining process developed was more amenable to the former than to the latter, as McGowan argues in Chapter 5. None the less, traces of interventionism and social protection persisted, and have done up to the contemporary period. This is evident not only in the case of agriculture (Chapter 7), but also in the fisheries sector (Chapter 13). Social concerns stayed an object of policy debate throughout but, as Leibfried and Pierson argue (Chapter 10), became increasingly encapsulated in market-making language and methodologies.

From the mid-1980s this body of neo-liberal doctrine has been pervasive, and has found additional expression and influence in the debate about 'sound money' (Chapter 6). Indeed it can be argued that the rooting of this new prevailing idea, and its application to monetary policy, was one of the key factors in unblocking the arguments that had bedevilled the debate over EMU since the early 1970s. Reinforced economic liberalism has not completely dispatched protection in the trade policy field. As Woolcock shows in Chapter 14 and Stevens in Chapter 15, instruments of commercial protection have survived, as have some policies that discriminate in favour of EU suppliers or privileged partners. None the less, it seems to be becoming harder to gain credibility for the protectionist line of reasoning.

Neo-liberalism has not entirely banished the contending doctrine of social responsibility as a guide for policy. Rather it has meant that the proponents of social protection have had to adapt the arguments they make and the instruments that they propose, as is clear from Chapter 10. Similarly, economic and social cohesion was introduced as a formal principle of policy in the 1980s, as is discussed in Chapters 8 and 9. What is striking here too is that it seems to be increasingly hard to make the argument of principle about redistribution, although the bargaining process may produce some agreements on specific resource transfers.

More recently we have begun to see the emergence of a new variant of European social democracy being articulated through the EU institutions. It remains to be seen whether and how this might generate a new 'prevailing idea', or a softer version of neo-liberalism. One alternative possibility is that the EU policy process may be acquiring the more programmatic features associated with the policy and political processes inside the member states. The socio-economic ideas that have been summarized here have a bearing on particular policy decisions, and they have also shaped approaches to policy-making more generally, not least in terms of the emergence of a distinctive EU approach to market regulation.

Similarly, we can observe in other policy areas the impact of ideas in shaping policy preferences. Thus, for example, the environmental policy regime (Chapter 11) that has emerged has been much influenced by particular views about ecological factors and by particular interpretations of science. Some traces of this can be found in the common fisheries policy and its conservation dimension (Chapter 13). In areas involving new technologies—biotechnology is the extended case in this volume (Chapter 12)—industry-supporting preferences have had to contend with judgements about societal and environmental preferences. Ideas and paradigms have been in contention in the debates and controversies about which policy to pursue, sometimes subjected to scientific tests and the weight of expertise, and at other times held to ransom by political judgements and even political prejudices.

We shall see in Chapter 3 some of the ways in which the analytical debate about the role of ideas in the policy process has developed. It has given rise to a range of organizing concepts, including policy networks, advocacy coalitions, epistemic communities, the role of paradigms and so forth. Ideas, beliefs, values, and worldviews have permeated the EU policy process, even if their impact has often been implicit rather than explicit.

Issues

It is the issues of policy, and the impact of events, that test the capacities and reveal many of the key features of the European policy process. It is only when faced with choices over specific issues that policy-makers and policy-influencers are forced to consider whether the European policy arena is likely to be more or less productive and more or less acceptable than the available possible alternatives. As issues develop, or as events unfold, policy-makers and policy-influencers draw on their prevailing ideas and paradigms, assess their interests, define the range of possible responses, and begin to formulate their preferences about where and how to set policy.

Neither the previous policy nor the existing stock of ideas, or the prevailing paradigms, will necessarily provide a useful guide to action. Chapter 16 on eastern enlargement reveals some of the difficulties of the EU in responding to issues where the prevailing paradigm had been shattered. Chapter 17 touches on some of the difficulties of the EU in responding to events in the former Yugoslavia during the 1990s. Chapter 18 shows some of the problems of developing policy cooperation in response to events ahead of the refinement of a shared set of governing ideas. Issues may produce 'knee-jerk' responses, or be the pretext for a reappraisal of ideas or of interests.

The case-studies in this volume deal with specific issues or clusters of issues. They deliberately illustrate the range of policy domains which crowd the EU agenda, and they illustrate the variety of policy responses from the European policy process. They aim to show just how important it is to grasp the substantive policy content of each set of issues, and reveal great differences in the way in which issues get on to the agenda for possible European-level resolution. Some issues have been driven from the European arena itself, others by the emergence of a body of ideas, some by specific constellations of interests, or member governments, some by events, some by external pressures, and some by a combination of several impulses. It is by examining a variety of issues that we can start to specify the ways in which interests and ideas generate preferences, or to assess the varying ways in which different issues are channelled through the EU institutions.

Institutions

We already saw in Chapter 1 the broad anatomy of EU institutions and the ways in which those institutions connect to institutions within the member states. Institutional settings make a significant difference to the ways in which EU policies develop or fail to develop. The institutional dynamics have varied over time and they work in different ways for different member countries. These dynamics facilitate certain kinds of policy modes or substantive outcomes rather than others. The EU has acquired a number of specific institutional configurations that set the parameters for how interests are defined, ideas are propagated, and issues are addressed. Students of the EU have always been fascinated by its institutions, sometimes overly so and at the expense of paying attention to the substance of policy. None the less, the institutional inertias and dynamics play a critical part in shaping the policy process. Indeed, as we shall see in Chapter 3, the rediscovery of institutions as a focus of analysis has changed much of the discussion about the EU policy process.

Each of the case-studies in this volume deals to some extent with the particular institutional features of the policy domains that they address. It will be evident from these accounts that the institutional structures vary a good deal from case to case, both in the narrow sense that, for example, the Commission is heavily engaged in some domains and not others, and in the broader sense that the same institutional structures operate differently or have different impacts according to the case. These variations are, as we suggested in Chapter 1, associated with the five different policy modes that we identified. Students of the EU therefore need to look for, and try to explain, theses variations. One possible explanation may lie in the mix of institutions and functions that is found in any given policy domain. Another may be related to the differences between the actors who are involved in the domain under investigation. Often accounts of the EU are presented as a kind of competition between different institutional approaches. Our cases seem to suggest instead that different institutional approaches rest on—or generate—different logics of appropriateness in relation to the policy dilemmas for which they provide the settings.

These variations notwithstanding, several features run in and out of the cases that the volume covers.

- *Both procedures and practice matter.* Formal procedures, often underpinned by legal pronouncements and precedent, are very important in structuring behaviour, opening some opportunites, and closing off other options. However, informal practice accumulates, and adds other dimensions to the process, sometimes ahead of formal procedures being established, sometimes running against an apparently entrenched formal procedure.

■ *Segmentation often divides different groups of policy-makers.* The institutional evolution has been towards separated institutional settings for individual policy domains. Within and across the various institutions (both EU and national) we can identify different circles of cooperation, with different forms of behaviour, different patterns of socialization, different approaches to bargaining, different styles, and different instruments. Segmentation often shades into fragmentation, making policy coordination difficult, as we see from many of our case-studies. It also puts obstacles in the way of the development of strategies, especially in policy domains which are a composite of several sectoral policies (see Chapter 16).

■ *Consensus-building is the most frequent way of developing agreement.* Across most policy domains, across the range of policy modes, and whatever the formal institutional rules and procedures, the participants in the EU policy process tend to base cooperation on consensus, and to eschew cooperation when there is more than short-term dissensus. There is a strong impulse to find ways of accommodating dissenting voices. The ways of achieving consensus, however, differ across domains and over time. So far at least there is little evidence of majoritarian methods emerging to resolve disagreements. However, the EU may have reached a critical juncture in its development. EMU provides a striking example of a policy regime which explicitly separates the 'yes-sayers' from the 'no-' or 'not-yet-sayers'. Further enlargement might shift more of the policy process in a similar direction.

■ *Institutional loyalties depend more on cognitive attachment than on affective commitment.* Most of those involved in the institutional structures are members of one kind of élite or another. The process operates at a distance from raw politics and the wider population. Legitimation is achieved mainly through the impacts of policy in satisfying policy demands or resolving policy dilemmas. Many of the outcomes of policy have produced a kind of clientelism around the EU policy process and its country-based components. How sustainable this pattern is has become a subject of lively debate, given the evidence of public questioning of the EU across its member states.

How robust is the EU policy process?

To return to the pendulum metaphor: part of the underlying argument of this chapter is that the EU policy process is not entirely robust and not entirely stable. A great deal depends on institutional capabilities and on institutional performance. Much hangs on whether the outcomes actually deliver results that meet the context, the functional demands, and the purposes of those involved. Legitimation cannot be taken for granted and other arenas for cooperation are available. The EU policy process has different modes of operating, engages countries with some persistently different characteristics, and is vulnerable to changing expectations and ideas about the role of governance in western Europe.

Further reading

A good understanding of the recent history of western Europe is a valuable starting-point. Dinan (1999) provides a straightforward overview of the development of the EU. Milward (1992) offers a robust critique of much of the orthodoxy surrounding interpretations of the EU. Moravcsik (1998) submits the history to fine-grained political analysis. For insights into the deeper history Mazower (1998) is an excellent and provoking volume, usefully complemented by the more social scientific insights of Stein Rokkan, whose collected writings are drawn together by Flora (1999). Esping-Andersen (1990) launched a lively debate on different models of welfare state. Scharpf (1999) draws together very succinctly many of the contemporary challenges to governance in western Europe, some of which are also interestingly surveyed by Kapteyn (1995). For an attempt to situate European integration in both its global and its domestic contexts, see Laffan *et al.* (1999). For the link to 'pan-Europe', see also H. Wallace, (1999*b*).

Dinan, D. (1999), *Ever-Closer Union: An Introduction to European Integration*, 2nd edn. (London: Macmillan).

Esping-Andersen, G. (1990), *The Three Worlds of Welfare Capitalism* (Cambridge: Polity Press).

Flora, P. (1999) (ed.), *State Formation, Nation-Building and Mass Politics in Europe: The Theory of Stein Rokkan* (Oxford: Oxford University Press).

Kapteyn, P. (1995), *The Stateless Market: The European Dilemma of Integration and Civilization* (London: Routledge).

Laffan, B., O'Donnell, R., and Smith, M. (1999), *Europe's Experimental Union: Rethinking Integration* (London: Routledge).

Mazower, M. (1998), *Dark Continent* (London: Penguin).

Milward, A. S. (1992), *The European Rescue of the Nation-State* (Berkeley: University of California Press).

Moravcsik, A. (1998), *The Choice for Europe: Social Purpose and State Power from Messina to Maastricht* (Ithaca, NY: Cornell University Press).

Scharpf, F. W. (1999), *Governing in Europe: Effective and Democratic?* (Oxford: Oxford University Press).

Wallace, H. (1999*b*), 'Whose Europe is it Anyway?', *European Journal of Political Research*, 35/3: 1–20.

Chapter 3
Analysing and Explaining Policies

Helen Wallace

Contents

Summary

This chapter provides a concise overview of the range of theories and analytical approaches currently being deployed to improve our understanding of European integration and the policy process of the European Union (EU). An important development has been the 'mainstreaming' of EU scholarship, thus extending the range of approaches from across international relations and comparative politics. This opens up opportunities for more extended comparisons between the EU process and other kinds of transnational policy-making. In parallel the renewed vigour of the analytical debate is putting more pressure on students of the EU to make their analytical arguments sharper and the scrutiny of their empirical evidence more rigorous. As regards studies of the policy process, a wide array of analytical pathways is available. Some of these explore vertical segments of EU policy-making and are most helpful in characterizing one or other of the several policy modes of the EU. Other approaches provide horizontal pathways that can be used across a wide cross-section of policy domains and facilitate useful comparative explanation. Not all the ground has, however, yet been covered. Some policy domains are as yet inadequately analysed; other fora for European collaboration are often ignored; and much remains to be done to generate useful cross-country comparisons.

Introduction

This chapter locates the study of policy-making in the EU in the broader context of the search for explanations that reach further than commentaries on individual episodes in the EU or observations about particular sectors of policy-making. Readers of this volume will come from many different backgrounds and disciplines, some of them mainly interested in only part of what the EU does, for example its external relations, or its market-shaping activities. There is of course a danger of generalizing from the particular part of the beast that one encounters, as Puchala (1972) observed so acutely long ago. One key aim of this volume is to warn against generalizing from specific instances of policy-making.

A second key aim is to warn against regarding the EU as very idiosyncratic. Yes, its policy process and procedures are complex and intricate, and of course an investment of effort has to be made in understanding the complexity and intricacy. But British politics and policy-making are complex and intricate. So are those in other European countries. Any multi-level and multi-layered system of politics and policy-making is a bit more complex and yet more intricate. The US system is pretty hard to understand for the novice observer from Europe. All such 'social constructions' bear the marks of complicated histories and are vulnerable to misleading simplification. Our general guidance throughout this volume is to interpret the EU as having more features of normality than of abnormality—politics like any other, and policy-making like any other, *except* when strikingly distinctive patterns are observed. This is a good starting point for any social scientist keen to avoid the charge of generalizing from the particular or being trapped by the $n = 1$ problem.

A third aim is to be ecumenical and to encourage argument about what concepts or approaches most usefully shed light on the underlying process. Hence anyone starting out to understand EU policy-making should experiment by testing different approaches. This is not to advise intellectual promiscuity, but rather to stress that— *depending on what the objective of the enquiry is* —some exploration of alternative possible approaches should be undertaken.

A fourth aim is to make explicit the difference between the study of European integration as a broad phenomenon and the process of policy-making within the EU. Just as it is possible to study the US policy process without trying to explain what makes America tick, so it is possible to get to grips with the EU policy process without taking on board all of the debate about European integration—at least up to a point. In the case of the EU, it is perhaps more difficult to separate the policy process from its broader context because the EU is an incomplete polity. It is not a state, and there are few areas of policy in which it is the exclusive location for generating collective action or solving policy dilemmas. The EU policy process permanently and persistently coexists with other overlapping policy processes. Thus some attention has to be paid to the ways in which the broad integration issues impinge on policy-making. But not all of the discussion of the policy process has simultaneously to address the big issues of integration.

A fifth aim of this volume is to stress that the EU policy process evolves. There are some constants, but also many factors of change. As Webb (1983) argued, good theorizing about the EU needs to address its transformational features. As many of our cases in this volume suggest, the EU arena enables policy-makers to change the ways in which they address their dilemmas from what might otherwise have been the case. The EU process both constrains and multiplies the options available for collective action. Much of the contemporary analytical literature on the EU is beginning to focus on this evolutionary dimension.

The need for theoretical literacy

For the student of policy-making the main fields in which to search for helpful theories are international relations, comparative politics, and policy analysis. We deliberately mention this range, and thus side with those who resist trapping the study of the EU within only one branch of theory. Here we note the intervention of Hix (1994) to advocate comparative politics as the best approach, and the riposte from Hurrell and Menon (1996), as well as Risse-Kappen's (1996) advocacy of bridge-building between international relations and comparative politics.

We should, however, also note in passing that other areas of social science also have important contributions to make. The powerful role of law in the EU means that we can draw useful insights from legal interpretations, such as those of Weiler (1993, 1997) or Mattli and Slaughter (1998). New work on socio-legal studies is also beginning to impact on our understanding of the legal dimension (Shaw 1997). The impact of changing doctrines about the workings of the economy has been one of the factors that has changed the prevailing ideas of policy-makers, as Tsoukalis (1997) explains. We may be at a point at which we need to rethink the relationship between political integration and economic integration. Also, as has been stressed in the previous two chapters, historians, who have the benefit of being able to combine hindsight with extensive primary evidence, remind us that we should be wary of being over-impressed by the topical, the ephemeral, and the gaps between publicly stated rhetorics and underlying rationales (Milward 1992; Mazower 1998). Moravcsik (1998) demonstrates the utility of combining historical method with social scientific theorizing. The point here is that many branches of intellectual enquiry can provide us with ways of improving our understanding of the EU.

But what do we want from the theorists and from the exercise of theorizing? As Rosamond (2000) cogently argues in his new survey of theories of integration, theorizing is a necessary way of making assumptions explicit. Too many of the studies of the EU bury their assumptions in the commentary. A core objective of theory is to clarify explanatory concepts, and to separate out the 'dependent variable' to be explained from the 'independent variables' that may be relevant. Not all theorizing is concerned, or need be concerned, with empirical proof. However, for the student of the EU policy process the empirics are of central importance. Theorizing is the necessary prompt to identify the propositions that are to be tested, the methodology to be adopted, and the investigative tools to be used. Here Moravcsik (1998) is right to remind us of the importance of being rigorous at all of these stages.

We might have chosen in this volume to make a more systematic link between theorizing and the empirical evidence of our case-studies. A single theoretical approach could have been chosen, and then each case-study might have been used to test the validity and value of that approach, in much the same way that Evans *et al.* (1993) tests Putnam's (1988) propositions about 'two-level games'. Our purpose is different, namely to generate a deliberately wide range of examples of the EU policy process, and to indicate what some of the studies of those examples seem to reveal. In this sense much of the volume is 'thick description', with guides to further sources and commentary on the areas that are covered. The material on each case is filtered to make it more accessible and accompanied by suggestive commentary on, and analysis of, the cases described. Of course we recognize that the filtering in each case (and our authors do not all come from the same theoretical stable) makes some choices about what factors are relevant. But we are deliberately suggesting that some knowledge of the empirical material is a good starting-point, and that after that one should go to the theoretical literature for help and rigour in looking for explanations.

Mainstreaming the study of the EU

Perhaps the biggest change that has taken place over the past decade in the theoretical debate about the EU is that it has been brought into the mainstream of intellectual enquiry. A brief observation is needed here on the history of the subject. In the late 1950s and the 1960s a rich theoretical literature and lively debate was joined on competing approaches. The neofunctionalists, notably E. B. Haas (1958) and Lindberg (1963), in magisterial studies laid out the arguments for understanding the EU as a novel process of supranationalism. However, both the rebuttals, from scholars such as Hoffmann (1966), and the downturn in the momentum of 'real world' integration led to a disenchantment with grand theory among students of the EU. Intergovernmentalism seemed to have won its case for providing the predominant paradigm. This debate was explained in Webb (1983), with a reprise by Cram (1996), and is taken up again in Rosamond (2000). In the period that followed, there was a bifurcation between EU scholars and 'mainstream' scholarship in international relations and political science. The latter, at least implicitly, regarded the EU as not intellectually exciting, while the former concentrated mainly on more empirical work, although there was always an accompanying stream of more normative commentary. This is not to say that there were no interesting writings in the 1970s— on the contrary—but such as there were passed largely unnoticed by those in the 'mainstreams'.

Things changed in the late 1980s, mostly in response to the '1992' phenomenon set out in Chapter 4, an interesting reflection of the way in which intellectual fashions and events intertwine. A new literature emerged addressing both the macro and the meso levels of analysis. Sandholtz and Zysman (1989), Moravcsik (1991), and Sbragia (1992*b*) are examples of new American contributions. A new European literature also began to emerge, including Scharpf (1988, 1991), Majone (1991, 1992), and W. Wallace (1990*b*), much of it focused on the market-shaping and regulatory dimensions of the EU. Since then it has become almost impossible to keep up with the literature flowing from the presses on both sides of the Atlantic.

The richness of the new literature, the sharp intellectual debates that it provoked, and the continuing press of interesting 'real world' events combined to make theorizing about the EU much more stimulating to wider communities of scholars. In this sense the study of the EU came in from the cold, just as Europe itself did (H. Wallace 1991). In intellectual terms scholarship on the EU had been mainstreamed. One important consequence was that the study came to be colonized by other branches of theory.

Four main strands of 'new' theorizing need thereafter to be taken into account, summarized here in no intended order of importance. One came from work on the international political economy. Keohane and Hoffmann (1990) built some bridges with studies of interdependence. Evans *et al.* (1993) took up Putnam's (1988) two-level games. W. Wallace (1994*b*) took up the issue of the EU as an example of 'regional' integration. Running across these studies was the notion that EU integration could, and should, be compared with other efforts at cooperation between groups of countries or in other international fora. This remains fertile ground for discussion.

A second strand had to do with the rehabilitation of the study of political and social institutions. March and Olsen (1989) opened up a new wave of interest in the study of institutions, which has had a wide-ranging impact on EU scholarship. Hall and Taylor (1996) helpfully lay out the distinctive lines of analysis that characterize different approaches to institutional analysis. Specific applications to the EU include Bulmer (1994*b*) and Pierson (1996*b*). The result has been to bring a breath of fresh air into scholarship of the EU. Paradoxically this had always had institutional issues among its main concerns, but too much had been focused on procedural aspects and its static features. The assertion that institutions should be understood more broadly (rules, norms, and practices as well as organizations), and that they might shape behaviour in various ways has generated a rich vein of studies. These usefully help in the understanding of the phenomenon of integration as a whole and in the dissection of the policy process.

A third strand is rational choice analysis, now firmly in the saddle as a key school in the social sciences. This focuses on the rationales of the agent or actor, and the ways in which choices are made between different possible courses of action. Scharpf (1997) provides an accessible way into a literature which can be daunting to those not familiar with the methodologies and conventions. His study is especially valuable because it includes illustration from the experience of the EU. Tsebelis (1990) offers a route to explaining the interconnection between bargaining at different levels in terms of 'nested games', an interesting contrast to Putnam (1988). Garrett (1992) applies some of the argumentation to the single market bargains. This branch of writing has the great merit of forcing us to be much more systematic in the way we think about dissecting the motives and the behaviour patterns of those involved in the EU process. One health warning is, however, needed. Some of the literature is stronger on the stylized analysis than on its empirical accuracy.

A fourth strand is social constructivism. The starting-point here is that the political world is socially constructed, with structures that depend on social behaviour. This leads to a line of analysis that does not say either that structures determine action, or that action determines structure. Rather it is the processes of social interaction that are important, and interests are endogenous to the process. Much more attention therefore needs to be given to the role of beliefs and ideas in shaping behaviour and in underpinning the way that institutions develop. Much more weight has to be attached to dominant discourses and to social communication. Risse-Kappen (1996) has argued vigorously that this approach is especially promising as regards the study of the EU, partly because it removes a false distinction between international relations and comparative politics, and partly because it opens up more space for the study of non-governmental actors.

These strands of analysis are by no means the only ones in which there are active and interesting theoretical debates. However, they provide a good starting repertoire for those who want to go beyond the more empirical literature. Each also allows some scope for speculating about the relationship between Europeanization and globalization, a subject fast emerging as a core fulcrum of debate.

Categories of analysis

A distinction is made widely in political science between the 'macro', 'meso', and 'micro' categories of analysis. Macro explanations seek to explain at the broadest level of analysis, and in aggregate and all-embracing terms. The theoretical approaches outlined in the previous section share a primary focus on the macro level. Meso explanations focus rather on specific domains or arenas of activity, and may not be relevant to others, and indeed tend to emphasize factors that are specifically relevant to the domains or arenas under examination. Micro explanations deal with very specific or local political activities. Most of this volume is concerned with meso analysis. Thus, for example, as we shall see later, studies of regulation or of distributional issues fall into this meso category. The reader should, however, be wary. Some authors writing about the meso category in the EU suggest (implicitly or explicitly) that their meso explanation holds good for the EU process as a whole.

This volume provides many illustrations of meso policy-making. Many chapters comment on the relationship between the macro and the meso, and Chapter 16 offers particular insights into this relationship. Several chapters (especially 6, 17, and 18) place particular emphasis on the way that macro considerations have shaped the particular policy domain that they cover. However, this volume deliberately excludes chapters on the most macro issues of constitutional or quasi-constitutional design and redesign. Thus it does not cover much of the ground that informs Moravcsik's (1998) ambitious attempt to use these issues as the basis for theorizing about the European integration process as a whole. Chapter 19, however, addresses some of the issues relating to the impacts of constitutional design on the EU policy process.

Once we move to the meso level we can draw on a different kind of literature, which is more empirically rooted and more precise, though less ambitious, in its attempts at explanation. To help set these in context we set out here some basic distinctions about the EU policy process.

Degrees of salience

A first distinction is drawn from J. Peterson (1995a), further explained in J. Peterson and Bomberg (1999). He argues that there are different kinds of decision in the EU, each with different types of politics. With examples drawn from our volume these are: history-making—e.g. agreeing to economic and monetary union (EMU); policy-setting—e.g. agreeing to create an internal market in biotechnology products; and policy-shaping, or the more day-to-day—e.g. applying the regime for limiting fishing catches. Behaviour, practices, participants, and procedures vary between these different types of decision, although there are connections between them.

Note that Peterson's set of distinctions is made horizontally, essentially relating to the relative salience, and/or controversiality, of different types of decision. He characterizes his three types as, respectively (in summary), political, technocratic, and administrative.

Different policy modes

This contrasts with our five policy modes, set out in Chapter 1 (p. 28 ff.) as: a distinct Community method; regulation; multi-level governance (especially as regards distributional issues); policy coordination and benchmarking; and intensive transgovernmentalism. These modes are best understood vertically, distinguishing between domains and approaches to particular policy predicaments. Put together Peterson's horizontal distinctions and our vertical distinctions would produce a grid such as appears in Figure 3.1.

Particular periods of policy-making or episodes of decision-making can be fitted into individual boxes in the grid. Some policy domains may fit into a single vertical column. Broadly, for example, the single market (Chapter 4) and competition policy (Chapter 5) fit into the vertical column on regulation. Similarly EMU (Chapter 6) and the common foreign and security policy (CFSP) fit into the column on intensive transgovernmentalism. Other domains straddle the columns; thus cohesion and the structural funds (according to Allen's interpretation in Chapter 9) should be seen as intensive transgovernmentalism at the level of history-making bargains, though it then passes across to the mode of multi-level distributional policy-making. Similarly some efforts to construct an environmental policy are pursued by regulatory methods, while others are addressed by techniques of coordination and benchmarking.

The stylized version of the grid set out here is intended to provoke careful examination of the ways in which policies emerge and are put into operation. The grid echoes Lowi's (1972) famous four categories of policy, but adds to them. Our observation that the same policy domain may shift between modes, *as well as* between levels, is intended to emphasize the fluidity of the policy process, as is the aim of our metaphor of the moving policy pendulum (see Chapter 2).

Figure 3.1 Policy modes and decision types in European Union

Type of decision	Community method	Regulation	Multi-level (distribution)	Coordination and benchmarking	Intensive transgovernmentalism
			Modes		
History-making					
Policy-setting					
Day-to-day					

Source: Author, leaning heavily on J. Peterson (1995a).

Phases of policy

Conventional accounts of how public policies are made divide the process into essentially three phases: policy proposals; policy decision; and policy implementation. These three phases can be viewed as a sequence, one which neatly separates the three phases. This policy process is set in a broader political, economic, and social context from which demands for policy are generated. As policy is produced, so it has impacts on that political, economic, and social context, and these impacts lead to other demands for policy or claims for different policy and so on. Quite how this works in practice varies from one specific policy setting to another, and may vary between policy domains.

This three-phase distinction is helpful as a starting-point, in that it identifies different kinds of activities and different kinds of actors are involved at the three phases. Our case-studies indicate developments across the three phases. Chapter 4 (on the single market) describes the evolution of regulation across these three phases. Chapter 18 illustrates the sequence of policy development in justice and home affairs (JHA) over time.

However, as we shall see, life in practice is not quite so tidy, and often the phases blur into each other. Chapters 6 and 13 (on respectively agriculture and fisheries) illustrate the development, but then the contesting, of common policy regimes. Chapter 10 (on social policy) illustrates the emergence of much of the policy regime not through planned political policy-making, but rather by the judicial processes of the courts.

Locations of policy-making

The EU policy process is frequently described as a multi-level process. One of my policy modes is identified as multi-level governance, referring in particular to distributional policy-making within the EU. Here, however, I make a more extended observation about different *locations* of policy-making. In western Europe we can observe policies being made in many different locations. Please note that here I deliberately avoid the term 'level', which implies a hierarchy. Instead I suggest, in a more open-ended way, that European policies are constructed in locations that vary between, at one extreme, the local, and, at the other extreme, the global. Thus, to list more or less the range of possible locations, European policies emerge from: local politics; regional politics (in Spain or the UK these might involve sub-state nations, such as Scotland); the individual state; groups of neighbouring countries (e.g. Benelux, or the Nordic family, or the original Schengen group (see Chapter 18)); the EU; or other European frameworks; the transatlantic (notably the North Atlantic Treaty Organization (Nato)); the 'western' industrialized countries; one or two embryonic 'pan-European' regimes (such as the Council of Europe); and global organizations (such as the General Agreement on Tariffs and Trade (GATT) and the World Trade Organization (WTO), or other parts of the United Nations family).

This is an extraordinary array of locations. It provides those demanding and supplying policy with a multiplicity of options for pursuing their objectives and for developing capabilities. Nor does one location clearly separate itself from others. On the contrary, they overlap. Much of the French debate on this point is expressed in a discussion of 'public policy spaces', to signal the often ambiguously defined boundaries of public policy regimes. Many policy actors are active in a number of different locations, and able to exploit the different resources available in different locations (Bartolini 1998). Other policy actors are confined to a single location.

There is an extensive literature on the way in which bargaining and regime-formation across locations empower certain policy actors rather than others. One such literature is about what Putnam (1988) defined as two-level games, essentially focusing on the country level and the global level as his frame of reference. His approach has been further elaborated in Evans *et al.* (1993) and much taken up in studies of the EU as a way of understanding the interaction between the EU and the country levels of policy-making. This literature presumes the resilience of the state as the predominant political unit, and suggests that central executives have been strengthened by their ability to manipulate the international or European arena in order to achieve particular domestic purposes.

In contrast the literature on multi-level governance within the EU (Marks 1993; Marks *et al.* 1996) suggests that the direct linkages between the EU process and local or regional politics has squeezed and reduced the political powers of the state. How much and how far is actively debated in the literature.

My preference here for the term 'location' rather than 'level' invites a more intricate approach. Many of our case-studies illustrate the pursuit of collective policy regimes to deal with the same issue in different locations, sometimes simultaneously, and sometimes sequentially. The European process is distinctive in the extent to which it combines the infranational and the transnational, often in the same policy domain. This suggests that a Venn diagram, or a scatter diagram, might be a more appropriate way of illustrating the parallel existence of these multiple locations. Figure 3.2 provides a schematic illustration for this, taking environment as an example. Figure 3.3 does the same for foreign and security policy.

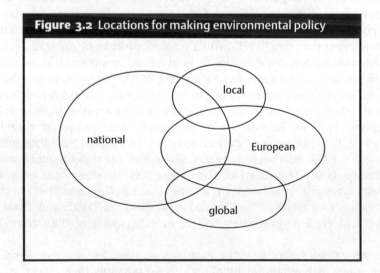

Figure 3.2 Locations for making environmental policy

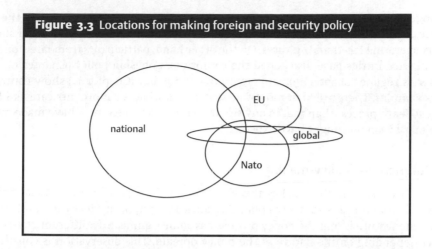

Figure 3.3 Locations for making foreign and security policy

Multinational policy-making

It is a necessary statement of the obvious that the EU policy process is multinational or multilateral in character. It is a composite of features derived from the different traditions of the participating countries. It is not just that the participants are numerous, but that they bring to the forum different languages, different discourses, different cultures, and different habits of work. To the extent that a predominant style of behaviour has emerged, it rests on an amalgam of these various features. This provides the participants with some different ways of building opportunities for policy influence; but it also makes for a more complex process, for which some special skills have to be developed. As we shall observe from the case-studies, this encourages certains kinds of behaviour and constrains others.

We do now have some evidence from anthropological studies of the process which suggest that out of this amalgam some new shared characteristics have been created—up to a point (Abélès 1996). That shared process depends on various forms of socialization, which have developed differently within the different EU institutions. Thus within the Commission, for example, it is argued that a predominant style of working seems to have emerged which is 'European' in the sense of locking Commission officials into a pattern of loyalty to their transnational or 'denationalized' functions. A slightly different pattern can be observed in Coreper (Lewis 1998*a*,*b*), where national officials have over time acquired habits of cooperation that enable them to construct bridges between the European and the country levels of governance.

None the less, we should be wary of overstating the shared European style, since these same studies also suggest that the patterns of shared policy styles vary between policy domains. In some policy domains a clustering of prime actors from one or another nationality may produce a particular orientation to policy. Some evidence for this may be found in the common fisheries regime (Chapter 13). But nationality is not the only factor. Competition policy (Chapter 5) was a domain in which lawyers used to predominate; latterly there has been a shift to involve more economists, as views about the role of policy in relation to the economy have altered. To the extent that a broad 'European' approach can be discerned it is not entirely stable in so far as changes in the membership of the EU also have an impact. On the one hand, the EU process still bears the traces of the stronger influences from the early member states in its operating facets and cultures. On the other hand, participants from later-joining member countries have also added their imprints. Cohesion policy (Chapter 9), the fisheries regime (Chapter 13), and environmental policy (Chapter 11) show contrasting examples. There are 'first-mover' advantages in what is a more intricate and less easy to learn process than that in any single country. Yet latecomers have made more of a mark than one might have expected.

Multifunctional policy-making

One of the features that makes the EU different from other transnational policy arenas is that it spans so many policy domains. Two important features result from this. One feature is that the policy process has some significantly different characteristics depending on the nature of the policy domain. This observation is consistent with our reference earlier to Lowi's (1972) seminal account of different categories. The other consequence of the multifunctional character of EU policy-making is that some of the bargaining involves cross-sectoral trade-offs. How much and in what kinds of instances has to be explored empirically. In practice cross-sectoral trade-offs are not quite as frequent as some of the literature on the EU suggest. Within-sector trade-offs are much more common. Aggregating—and mediating between—different interests and concerns across different policy domains is rather difficult in practice, especially in the EU institutional setting. As we saw in Chapter 1, the EU institutions tend to segment rather than to aggregate issues across sectors.

In each successive edition of this text we have pointed out the considerable variations in the policy process depending on the policy domain under consideration. In part this stems from the extent to which policy domains are held within the segmentation (or sectoral compartments) which has become a characteristic of the EU institutional structures, as I pointed out in Chapter 1. The institutions of the EU, and their national counterparts, tend to entrap particular policy domains in the *chasses gardées* of particular policy communities. Thus agricultural policy-making is different from trade policy-making, and different again from environmental policy-making. Each of these domains involves different kinds of societal actors, different ways of viewing the relationships between the market forces and the special interests to be satisfied, different kinds of governmental behaviour, and different kinds of electoral resonance.

But it is not only a question of who is engaged, but also a question of what kinds of considerations are relevant. In some policy domains expertise has a strong impact, while in others relative political power may be more important. Sometimes doctrines may drive policy, while on other occasions interest satisfaction may be determining. On some issues economic impacts may be critical, while on others financial costs and benefits may be crucial. Moreover, the hierarchy of pertinent factors may change within a given policy domain over time, as seems to be the case with agricultural policy and the efforts to reform it.

So, on the one hand, the multifunctional policy scope of the EU encourages distinctive policy communities to develop, and distinctive policy methodologies. On the other hand, it allows some opportunities for developing cross-sectoral trade-offs and calculations of the relative costs and benefits of cooperation. EU experience suggests a rather disparate range of consequences in this regard. There are subjects which invite cross-sectoral trade-offs—major rounds of budgetary negotiations are perhaps the clearest examples of this. There are levels of policy-making at which cross-sectoral trade-offs are more likely, perhaps most significantly sessions of the European Council. Here there is an argument for supposing that complex calculations of diffuse reciprocity weigh in the discussion and that many participants judge the potential outcomes over medium- to long-term timescales, linking assumptions of immediate costs and benefits to longer-term expected gains and losses. Yet we can also see resistance to such cross-sectoral bargains, not least because to deliver them at the European level presupposes that cross-sectoral bargains can also be delivered at the country level, where relative costs and benefits have also to be calculated. Hence we need to look very carefully at the actual evidence case by case.

Analytical pathways

We have jumped in this chapter from the abstract level of macro theorizing to the 'nuts and bolts' of the empirical setting of EU policy-making and some of its features. The question that follows is how to span this divide. One way of doing this is by reverting to a mixture of vertical and horizontal pathways for layering the analysis. Two particular ways of doing this stand out from the literature. One of these is to probe more deeply into particular policy modes and to examine how they operate. The other is to look for horizontal concepts that might be relevant across policy modes.

Vertical pathways

As regards the first, namely how to characterize particular policy modes, we have three established literatures. One goes back to the neofunctionalists and attempts to characterize what we earlier called the 'distinctive Community method'. Here a collection of features are argued to accrue so as to produce a supranational policy process. Sandholtz and Stone Sweet (1998) provide a recent effort to revive the debate on 'supranational governance'. Their claim is that this is promising as an overarching approach. Our contention is that it may fit some policy arenas, but by no means all.

Another, perhaps more convincing, literature addresses the regulatory mode of policy-making, benefiting from the wealth of empirical material and data available to sharpen the argument. Majone (1996*b*) is a major exponent of this approach. He goes so far as to suggest that the EU is especially well fitted to perform in regulatory mode, and even that regulation is overtaking and displacing many of the other functions of government. Armstrong and Bulmer (1998) have added a valuable underpinning to the regulatory analysis, backed up by detailed case-study material. Young and Wallace (forthcoming) add further illustration. McGowan and Wallace (1996) place European regulation in a comparative perspective, the EU regulatory model against (especially) the American.

Yet another set of studies addresses the distributional policy domain, especially writings that pursue the approach of multi-level governance. Here the suggestion is that the combination of competition for enlarged resources with scope for a particularly pluralist form of bargaining has empowered some actors at the expense of others. Marks (1992, 1993) and Hooghe (1996) lay out the range of the approach, to which many others have contributed. A particular emphasis is put on the opportunity structure for infranational political actors to engage influentially in shaping EU policies. The argument is not universally accepted. Allen (Chapter 6), backed by Pollack (1995) and A. Smith (1995) among others, argue that the clearly expanded level of activity of infranational actors should not be confused with real influence. Or to take up J. Peterson's (1995a) categories, presence at the day-to-day level should not be confused with impact at the systemic level.

These literatures cover three of the policy modes into which this volume categorizes EU policy-making. Proponents of each approach tend to want to go further and suggest that 'supranational governance' (their term), or regulation, or multi-level governance should be understood as the predominant analytical pathway. It will be clear that we have some doubts about this. The other two policy modes—policy coordination and benchmarking, and intensive transgovernmentalism—have as yet less well-established literatures addressing the generic features of their policy domains. We have studies in particular areas, such as Dyson (1994) on EMU, but none that compare across to foreign policy or justice and home afffairs, which, we suggest, have many similar features. So there is work here waiting to be done.

Horizontal pathways

Cutting across policy domains we have three horizontal pathways. One is about the role of ideas, a second is about how actors behave, and a third is about institutional performance. We have separated them out here for convenience of exposition, although in reality they run into each other. All of these are to some extent also ways of arguing that factors other than interests explain the process, or at least partly explain it. Our volume is deliberately ambiguous on this point. Our case-study authors were asked to look for both ideational and instrumental features relevant to their stories.

A growing field in the literature concerns the role of ideas, norms, beliefs, knowledge, doctrines, and expertise in the development of policy. Jachtenfuchs (1995) provides a strong defence of the importance of the ideational, an approach which has gathered considerable support elsewhere. A number of substantive policy domains show traces of the impact of ideas and other ideational factors. Some of these are commented on in other chapters in this volume, with references to some of the more detailed literatures that take this approach. Chapters 4, 5, and 6 mention changing economic doctrines, and Chapter 10 addresses some of the ways in which these have intruded on understandings of the welfare state. Chapters 14 and 15 comment on the free trade versus protection debate. Chapters 11, 12, and 13 adduce evidence on the role of expertise and scientific knowledge in promoting particular approaches to policy, and on particular ways of justifying policy through the EU arena. Chapter 16 speculates about the relevance of self-definition for the EU in framing policy responses to central and eastern Europe, a theme which recurs in Chapter 17.

A second horizontal pathway consists of studies that emphasize transnational groupings of policy influentials and efforts to mobilize opinion. Different authors have different ways of formulating this. Policy networks (Héritier 1993; J. Peterson and Bomberg 1999) are well established as a route to describing empirically and characterizing analytically one of the strongest features of the EU policy process at the meso and micro levels. By and large the definitions of relevant networks suggest that they have an open and inclusive nature, thus admitting access to those who can find an entry-point. The growth of rather more closed policy communities in the fields of monetary, foreign, and home affairs may need some adjustment of the argument about policy networks.

Some similar ground is covered by the literatures on advocacy coalitions (Sabatier 1998) and epistemic communities (P. M. Haas 1992). These introduce factors such as, respectively, shared beliefs and common expertise as the binding elements in creating and sustaining coalitions and collusion. Both approaches, like policy network analysis, encourage us to deconstruct governments, and to look for linkages between public and private actors, as well as with a variety of non-governmental actors.

A third horizontal pathway concentrates on institutional performance, and how the pattern of institutions impacts on the ways in which policy is developed. One important strand of the argument here is about path-dependency and the accumulation of historical commitments as defining future behaviour (Pierson 1996b). Another strand goes back to a point made earlier, and is developed in J. Peterson and Bomberg (1999), namely that institutional performance and characteristics show distinct features depending on the salience and scope of decisions. Practically all of our case-studies show the impacts of informal, as well as formal, institutions. Several bear out the argument that history-making decisions can make crucial differences to institutional behaviour, though there is also illustration of policies being built from the bottom up. The law and the *acquis communautaire* also appear as influential institutional features. But institutional limits also crop up in several areas, especially those where big policy reform is in principle on the table (see Chapters 8 and 16).

Each of these horizontal pathways has a kind of durability in that each allows for a comparative approach between policy domains, or within policy domains over time or according to the issues being addressed.

Three gaps in the literature should, however, be mentioned, each of which would be amenable to horizontal analysis and comparison. One has to do with comparing the EU as a policy location with other European or multilateral regimes. It is an interesting semantic point that 'collaboration' tends to be the chosen term for cooperation in several other European regimes—defence procurement collaboration, space collaboration, and so forth. The literature on these other subjects remains very separate from that on the EU policy process, and mostly in the hands of the technicians rather than the policy analysts. A second gap relates to the domain of defence and security policy—as distinct from foreign and security policy. The historical capture of parts of what are related policy arenas by different institutions has been echoed by the policy analysts. As the EU becomes more engaged in defence issues (if indeed this happens), so we shall need to extend our comparative grasp of these related processes. A third gap relates to the country level of analysis. In spite of the strictures of authors such as Hix (1994, 1999) that the EU is a prime field for comparative politics specialists, the literature comparing different country experiences of, and in, EU policy-making is remarkably thin (H. Wallace 1999a).

Conclusions

Scholarship on the EU in its early years benefited from pioneering theorists, and then faltered in terms of its intellectual ambition. The proliferation of theoretically informed new studies has reversed that decline, and opened the field to a range of theoretical provocations and a vigorous competition between contending approaches. Part of the test for this new wave of theorizing, as for the pioneers, is how well the theoretical studies and analytical approaches measure up against the empirical evidence. The case-studies that follow in Part II provide much material for pursuing this endeavour.

Further reading

There is a fast-growing literature on theories and analytical approaches relevant to the EU and its policy process. Rosamond (forthcoming) provides a wide-ranging and accessible overview, with an excellent guide to the various writers in the field. For earlier accounts of 'classical' integration theories, see Webb (1983) and for the links to the policy process, Cram (1996). Much of the debate is picked up and reformulated in Moravcsik's (1998) fine study of liberal intergovernmentalism. Alternative approaches can be found in Marks et al. (1996) on multi-level governance, Grieco (1995) on neo-realism, and Wessels (1997) on fusion theory. See Hix (1994) and Hurrell and Menon (1996) for the debate between comparative politics and international relations. For a starting-point on institutional theories and rational choice, see Hall and Taylor (1996). More specifically, see Scharpf (1997) for an excellent account of actor rationality, well informed by his work on the EU, March and Olsen (1989, 1998) on why and how institutions matter, and Pierson (1996b) on historical institutionalism. Majone's

various writings lay out a regulatory approach, for which Majone (1996b) is a good starting-point. For insights into negotiation and bargaining, see Putnam (1988) on two-level games, further developed in Evans et al. (1993), Keohane (1986) on reciprocity, and Tsebelis (1990) on nested games. For a sense of the analytical debate about the operations of the policy process, see Héritier (1995) on policy networks, P. M. Haas (1992) on epistemic communities, Sabatier (1998) on advocacy coalitions, and J. Peterson (1995a) for his typology of different levels of decision. Risse-Kappen (1996) opens up the discussion on social constructivism, and Jachtenfuchs (1995) sets out the arguments on why ideas matter. Kohler-Koch and Eising develop 'governance' as a unifying approach.

Cram, L. (1996) 'Integration Theory and the Study of the EU Policy Process', in J. Richardson (ed.), *European Union: Power and Policy-Making* (London: Routledge), 40–58.

Evans, P. B., Jacobson, H. K., and Putnam, R. D. (1993), *Double-Edged Diplomacy: International Bargaining and Domestic Politics* (Berkeley: University of California Press).

Grieco, J. M. (1995), 'The Maastricht Treaty, Economic and Monetary Union and the Neo-realist Research Programme', *Review of International Studies*, 21/1: 21–40.

Haas, P. M. (1992), 'Introduction: Epistemic Communities and International Policy Coordination', *International Organization*, 46/1: 1–35.

Hall, P., and Taylor, R. C. R. (1996), 'Political Science and the Three New Institutionalisms', *Political Studies*, 44/5: 936–57.

Héritier, A. (1993) (ed.), *Policy-Analyse. Kritik und Neuorientierung* (Opladen: Westdeutscherverlag).

Hix, S. (1994), 'The Study of the European Community: The Challenge to Comparative Politics', *West European Politics*, 19/4: 1–30.

Hurrell, A., and Menon, A. (1996), 'Politics Like any Other? Comparative Politics, International Relations, and the Study of the EU', *West European Politics*, 21/4: 802–4.

Jachtenfuchs, M. (1995), 'Theoretical Perspectives on European Governance', *European Law Journal*, 1/2: 115–33.

Keohane, R. O. (1986), 'Reciprocity in International Relations', *International Organization*, 40/1: 11–28.

Kohler-Koch, B., and Eising, R. (eds.) (1999), *The Transformation of Governance in the European Union* (London: Routledge).

Majone, G. (1996*b*), *Regulating Europe* (London: Routledge).

March, J. G., and Olsen, J. P. (1989) *Rediscovering Institutions* (New York, NY: Free Press).

—— —— (1998), *The Institutional Dynamics of International Political Orders*, ARENA Working Paper (Oslo: ARENA).

Marks, G., Hooghe, L., and Blank, K. (1996), 'European Integration from the 1980s: State-Centric v. Multi-level Governance', *Journal of Common Market Studies*, 34/3: 341–78.

Moravcsik, A. (1998), *The Choice for Europe: Social Purpose and State Power from Messina to Maastricht* (Ithaca, NY: Cornell University Press).

Peterson, J. (1995*a*), 'Decision-Making in the European Union: Towards a Framework for an Analysis', *Journal of European Public Policy*, 2/1: 69–93.

Pierson, P. (1996*b*), 'The Path to European Integration: A Historical Institutionalist Analysis', *Comparative Political Studies*, 29/2: 123–63.

Risse-Kappen, T. (1996), 'Exploring the Nature of the Beast: International Relations Theory Meets the European Union', *Journal of Common Market Studies*, 34/1: 53–80.

Rosamond, B. (forthcoming), *Theories of Integration* (London: Macmillan).

Sabatier, P. A. (1998), 'The Advocacy Coalition Framework: Revisions and Relevance for Europe', *Journal of European Public Policy*, 5/1: 98–130.

Scharpf, F. W. (1997), *Games Real Actors Play: Actor-Centred Institutionalism in Policy Research* (Boulder, Colo.: Westview Press).

Tsebelis, G. (1990), *Nested Games* (Berkeley: University of California Press).

Webb, C. (1983), 'Theoretical Perspectives and Problems', in H. Wallace, W. Wallace and C. Webb (eds), *Policy-Making in the European Community*, 2nd.edn. (Chichester: John Wiley), 1–42.

Wessels, W. (1997), 'An Ever Closer Fusion? A Dynamic Macropolitical View on Integration Processes', *Journal of Common Market Studies*, 35/2: 267–99.

Part II

Policies

Chapter 4

The Single Market

A New Approach to Policy

Alasdair R. Young and Helen Wallace

Contents

Summary

The single market and the Single European Act (SEA) marked a turning-point in European integration, the roots of which, however, stretch back well before 1985. Heavy harmonization had proved a frustrating approach to common standards, especially as the pressures of external competition bore down on European industry. New ideas about market regulation permeated the European Union (EU) policy process and, supported by European Court of Justice (ECJ) judgments and Commission entrepreneurship, facilitated legislative activism and important changes in the policy-implementing processes. Their longer-term impact is harder to assess, and the task of 'completing' the internal market remains unfinished. None the less, the single market has drawn other European countries towards EU membership and changed the context in which many other policies are shaped.

Introduction

The plans to complete the single market induced an explosion of academic interest in the EU. Before 1985 the theoretical debate on political integration was stalled, studies of EU policy-making were sparse, and few mainstream economists devoted themselves to the analysis of European economic integration. In the late 1980s that all changed, as competing analyses proliferated and the nooks and crannies of the new legislative programme and its economic consequences were examined. Indeed many new theoretical approaches to the study of European integration have taken the single market as their main point of reference, just as many earlier theorists had taken agricultural policy as their stimulus. The single market has been elevated so much that for many it is taken to constitute the critical turning-point between stagnation and dynamism, between the 'old' politics of European integration and the 'new' politics of European regulation.

Our task in this chapter is to re-examine the renewal of the single market as a major turning-point in European policy-making. We draw on the study by Alan Dashwood (1977, 1983) in the first two editions of this volume, a salutary reminder that the single market programme had roots that were overlooked in much of the commentary that focused on developments in the late 1980s. Essentially we argue that many of the analyses that proliferated in response to the SEA and the 1992 programme overstated their novelty and understated some of the surrounding factors that helped to induce their 'success'. We also suggest that some elements of the policy process around the single market contributed to the subsequent public disquiet about European integration.

None the less, we also believe that the embedding of the 1992 programme represents a very significant redefinition of the ends and means of policy. It enabled the European integration process to adapt to new constellations of ideas and interests and to produce a different policy mode of regulation that has permeated many other areas of policy (Majone 1994b). Other chapters in this volume illustrate the consequences, both direct and indirect, of giving so definite an emphasis to market liberalization and different forms of policy regulation, as Majone (1993) argues. Hence we situate these developments in the broader context of structural shifts in the (west) European political economy, in the expectations and behaviour of entrepreneurs, and in the debate about adapting the European welfare state.

These developments are therefore as important for their impacts on the European public policy model *within* the member states as they are for their repercussions at the transnational level. We can observe market regulation, heavily based on a transnational level of European governance, jostling, often uneasily, with other issues on the political and economic agendas evident within the EU member states. We can also see the bifurcation between transnational regulation for transnational markets, engaging transnational regulators and large market operators, and encapsulated intranational politics, engaging those charged with and dependent on the reduced domestic political space, smaller-scale entrepreneurs, local regulators, and national or regional politicians.

Nor have these ricochets been confined to the member states that accepted the SEA and '1992'. The extraterritorial impact on neighbours, partners, and competitors has been powerful. The alignment of the European Free Trade Association (EFTA) countries to the single market, first through the Luxembourg process, then through the European Economic Area (EEA)[1] and for some eventually by full accession, reveals the soft boundaries of a European economy that never did coincide with the political boundary of the EU. But the costs, social and political as well as economic, of adjustment within the single market have also generated rearguard action, sometimes focused on other intra-EU policies that might provide compensation, and sometimes by displacement to external competitors.

Several themes thus run through the story of the single market:

- the impact of new ideas, as views about the European 'welfare state' altered and Keynesianism was forced to compete with neo-liberalism as an alternative and potentially predominant paradigm in economic policy;

- the mobilization of industrial opinion and pressure in novel ways as a transnational phenomenon and a stimulus to policy change;

- the critical conjunction of changes to EU decision rules with alterations in the relationships between the business community and policy-makers and in business responses to global markets;

- evidence of policy 'entrepreneurship', especially by the Commission, backed by a new coalition of supporters of change and the recasting of the old argument about 'Community preference';

- the impact of 'statecraft' by and 'collusion' between top policy-makers from key member states;

- the pervasive impact of European law and rulings from the ECJ on the ways in which policy options were defined;

- the external dynamic of third-country competition and technological innovation; and

- the external projection of EU policy.

Un peu d'histoire

The aim to establish a single market started with the Treaty of Rome. This set targets for creating a customs union and the progressive approximation of legislation, as well as for establishing the 'four freedoms' of movement for goods, services, capital, and labour, all within a single regime of competition rules. In this it followed Bela Balassa's steps towards full economic union (see Table 4.1), though the path was more clearly defined for the customs union than for the single market (Balassa 1975; Pelkmans 1984). The policy-makers of the 1950s were more concerned about tariffs and quotas than technical barriers to trade (TBTs), a preoccupation and 'set of ideas' also reflected in the General Agreement on Tariffs and Trade (GATT).

But entrepreneurial ingenuity to segment markets combined with the activism of governments, under pressure from domestic firms, to circumscribe production, sales, and consumption by product, safety, and process standards. Thus, as tariffs came down, other barriers were revealed, even reinforced. With the new technologies and new products of the 1960s and 1970s came new standards, which, whether so

Table 4.1 Stages of economic integration

Stage	Features
Free trade area	No visible trade restrictions between members
Customs union	Free trade area plus common external trade regime
Internal commodity market	Customs union plus free movement of goods (no invisible trade restrictions)
Common market	Internal commodity market plus free movement of services, capital, and labour
Monetary union	Common market plus a common currency
Economic union	Monetary union plus a common economic policy

Source: Adapted from Balassa (1975).

intended or not, were a frequent source of protection. Local market preferences, as well as national policy and industrial cultures, were divisive. Market fragmentation was often buttressed by operating rules, such as those for public procurement, that promoted local suppliers.

Harmonization and its increasing frustration

The harmonization of national legislation, especially for standards and market management, was one important policy instrument for moving towards the common market goal. We do not argue that standards as such were the be-all and end-all of policy. But we do argue that the impact of the initial efforts at harmonizing standards played an important part in testing policy methods that proved inadequate during the 1960s and 1970s. Frustrated, Commission officials, with some allies from the member states, sought a new regulatory approach, which was then more broadly applied.

The principal instrument of the original European Economic Community (EEC) for advancing the four freedoms was the directive, in principle setting the essential framework of policy at the European level and leaving the 'scope and method' to the member states. In the case of TBTs, harmonization was based on Articles 28 (ex 30) and 94 (ex 100). Other articles provided the legal foundation for the freedoms of movement for services, capital, and labour and for aligning many other national regulations. The Commission began to tackle the negative impact on trade of divergent national standards and differing national legislation in the early 1960s. These efforts gathered pace after the complete elimination of customs duties between member states on 1 July 1968 (Dashwood 1977: 278–89). Initially the Commission tended to regard uniform or 'total' harmonization as a means of driving forward the general process of integration. After the first enlargement, however, the Commission adopted a more pragmatic approach and pursued harmonization only where it could be specifically justified. It insisted on uniform rules only when an overriding interest, such as the protection of consumers or the environment, demanded it, using 'optional' rather than 'total' harmonization.

Harmonization measures were drafted by the Commission in cooperation with working groups, one for each industrial sector, composed of experts nominated by member governments. Advice from independent specialists supplemented the Commission's resources and provided a depth and range of expertise comparable to that of the much larger national bureaucracies. The Commission also regularly invited comments on their drafts from European-level pressure groups (Dashwood 1977: 291–2). Beginning in 1973 with the 'low-voltage directive' the Commission, where possible, incorporated the work of private standard-making bodies into Community measures by 'reference to standards' (Schreiber 1991: 99). The two principal European-level standards bodies—the Committee for European Norms (Standards) (CEN) and the Committee for European Electrical Norms (Standards) (CENELEC)—did not, however, provide adequate technical assistance (Dashwood 1977: 292). Thus the complex and highly technical process produced very uneven results.

Progress was also greatly impeded by the need for unanimity in the Council of Ministers. Different national approaches to regulation and the pressures on governments from domestic groups with an interest in preserving the status quo made delays and obstructions frequent (Dashwood 1977: 296). The Commission exacerbated this problem by over-emphasizing the details and paying too little attention to the genuine attachment of people to familiar ways (Dashwood 1977: 297). Technicians and special interests often further constrained the opportunities for decision. As a result, only 270 directives were adopted between 1969 and 1985 (Schreiber 1991: 98).

ECJ jurisprudence, however, began to bite at the heels of the policy-makers. In 1974 the *Dashonville* ruling established a legal basis for challenging the validity of national legislation that introduced new TBTs. The famous *Cassis de Dijon* judgment of 1979 insisted that under certain specified conditions member states should accept in their own markets products approved for sale by other member states (Alter and Meunier-Aitsahalia 1994: 540–1; Dashwood 1983: 186). None the less, there was cumulative frustration in the Commission and in the business community at the slow pace of progress and the uncertainties of reliance on the ECJ, since its impact depends on application to cases lodged. European firms kept encountering other countries' regulatory barriers in the knowledge that the international regime offered by the International Standards Organization (ISO) was weak, as was its affiliate in the United States (Woolcock 1991). Stronger European standards would have provided a basis for negotiating more effectively for multilateral standards.

Pressures for reform

The governments of western Europe confronted an economic crisis in the early 1980s. The poor competitiveness of European firms relative to those of their main trading partners in the USA and, particularly, Japan contributed to large trade deficits

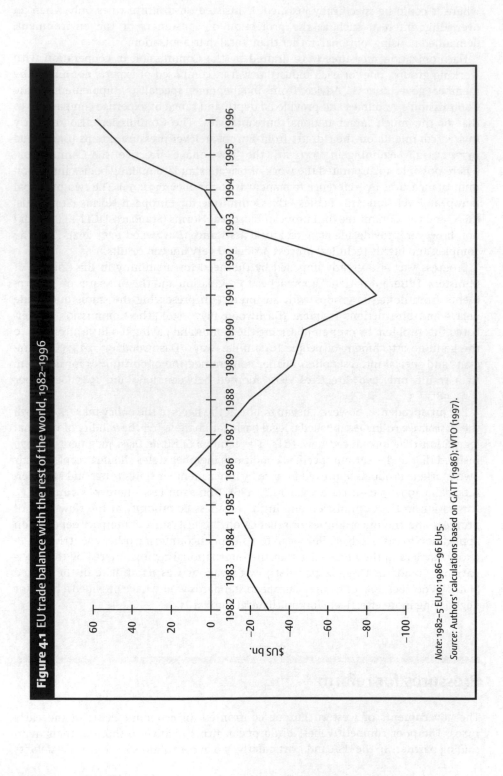

Figure 4.1 EU trade balance with the rest of the world, 1982–1996

Note: 1982–5 EU10; 1986–96 EU15.

Source: Authors' calculations based on GATT (1986); WTO (1997).

(Pelkmans and Winters 1988: 6; and see Fig. 4.1). Transnational companies proliferated, producing and selling in multiple markets, and often squeezed the profit margins and markets of firms confined to national markets. The sharp increase in oil prices following the Iranian Revolution in 1979 contributed to the trade deficit and helped to push the west European economies into recession. Inflation and unemployment both soared during the early years of the 1980s (see Fig. 4.2). Business confidence was low, and international corporations began to turn away from the Community (Pelkmans and Winters 1988: 6). American direct investment began to flow out of the Community, and European companies sought destinations outside the Community for their investments and production facilities.

During the late 1970s and early 1980s the member states increasingly used economic regulations as TBTs to protect their industries (Commission 1985*a*; Dashwood 1983; Geroski and Jacquemin 1985). This undid some of the earlier progress in harmonization, contributed to a decline of intra-EU imports relative to total imports (Buigues and Sheehy 1994: 18), and sharply increased the number of ECJ cases concerning the free movement of goods (see Fig. 4.3). The high level of economic interdependence within the EU made these TBTs costly and visible (Cecchini *et al.* 1988; Pelkmans 1984).

While the crisis was clear, the response was not (see e.g. Tugendhat 1985). Large trade deficits and high inflation constrained the ability of member governments to use expansionary economic policies to bring down unemployment. Economic interdependence further reduced the efficacy of national responses to the crisis and

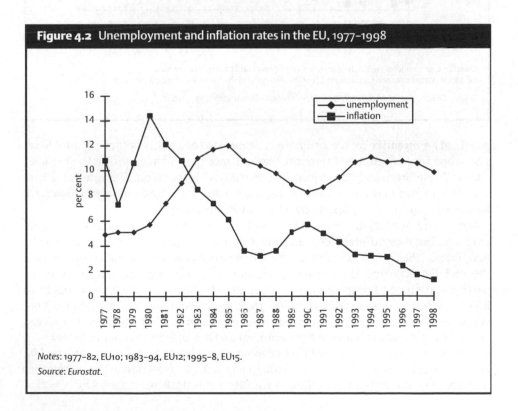

Figure 4.2 Unemployment and inflation rates in the EU, 1977–1998

Notes: 1977–82, EU10; 1983–94, EU12; 1995–8, EU15.

Source: Eurostat.

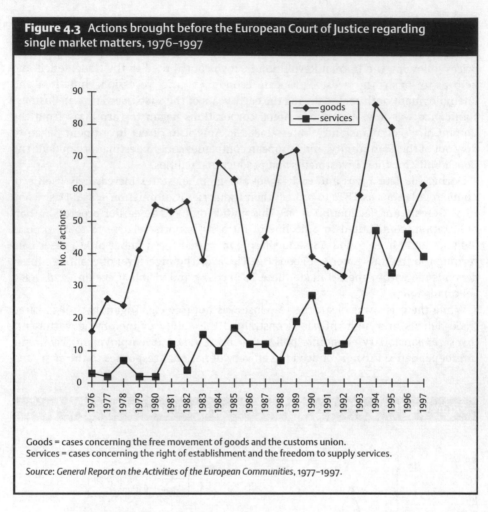

Figure 4.3 Actions brought before the European Court of Justice regarding single market matters, 1976–1997

Goods = cases concerning the free movement of goods and the customs union.
Services = cases concerning the right of establishment and the freedom to supply services.

Source: General Report on the Activities of the European Communities, 1977–1997.

provided an incentive for a coordinated response to the region's economic problems. The scope for a coordinated response was enhanced by changes within the member states. These are widely described in the political integration literature as a convergence of national policy preferences during the early 1980s (Cameron 1992: 56; Moravcsik 1991: 21; 1998; Sandholtz and Zysman 1989: 111).

But a note of caution should be added here: new government policies certainly emerged, but they differed between countries. The British government was radically neo-liberal. The French government switched policy after a factional contest within the socialist majority. The German government's policy was the product of cross-party coalition and European market strength. The Spanish government sought to link socialist modernization at home to transnational market disciplines. Convergence is thus something of a misnomer: European market liberalization served quite different purposes for each government and for different economic actors.

Parties that advocated neo-liberal economic policies came to power in the UK, Belgium, the Netherlands, and Denmark, in part due to a rejection of the parties that had overseen the economic decline of the late 1970s (Hall 1986: 100). The rejection was less marked in Germany, where the underlying strength of its economy pre-served an attachment to the established 'social market' framework. Elsewhere the Keynesian policies of the past attracted much of the blame. In France the 'policy learning' was explicit. Expansionary fiscal policies had led to increased inflation and unemployment, exacerbated the trade deficit, and swelled the public debt (Hall 1986: 199). By 1983 the French government had started to look for European solutions, reversing its threat of autumn 1982 to obstruct the Community market. The threat had been prompted by the trade deficit with Germany, attributed by some ministers to the impact of German product standards (H. Wallace 1984; Woolcock 1994).

New ideas about markets and competition thus started to be floated in response to the problems of the European economy, as the label of Eurosclerosis started to stick. Some transnational firms started to voice criticisms. The shape of an emerging policy consensus was influenced by the wave of deregulation in the United States in the late 1970s and early 1980s (Hancher and Moran 1989: 133; Majone 1991: 81; Sandholtz and Zysman 1989: 112). The ECJ's 1979 *Cassis de Dijon* judgment, although not deregu-latory, advanced the concept of mutual recognition of national standards. This pro-vided the Commission with a lever with which to pursue greater market integration (Dashwood 1983).

From the early 1980s European Council communiqués reflected a concern about the poor state of the single market. The European Council in December 1982 dis-cussed a Commission communication that recommended the removal of TBTs, sim-plification of frontier formalities, liberalization of public procurement, and closer alignment of taxes (*Bulletin of the European Communities* (December 1982)). The Euro-pean Council responded by creating an Internal Market Council to meet regularly to consider such issues.

During 1983 support for revitalizing the single market continued to grow. In April 1983 the heads of some of Europe's leading multinational corporations formed the European Round Table of Industrialists (ERT) to advocate the completion of the single market (Cowles 1994). In July 1983 the Spinelli Report linked the costs of conflicting national regulations to the need for institutional reforms (Spinelli *et al.* 1983). In September the French government circulated a memorandum advocating the development of a Community industrial 'space', the reduction of TBTs *within* the EU, and compensating external trade protection. The proposals were a response to the realization that France (or any other member state) could not on its own redress the basic problems of industry and that reinforced EU measures were needed (Pearce and Sutton 1985: 68). A month later the Union of Industrial and Employers' Confeder-ations of Europe (UNICE) added its voice to calls for greater market integration. In February 1984, with its adoption of a draft treaty on European Union, the European Parliament sought to focus attention on institutional reform, calling *inter alia* for increased parliamentary powers and greater use of qualified majority voting (QMV) in the Council of Ministers (European Parliament 1984)

Meanwhile the Commission also began to sharpen its focus on these issues. Karl-heinz Narjes, the responsible Commissioner, and his staff started to look for ways of attacking market barriers, both by systematically identifying them and by exploring ways of relaxing the constraints on policy change. They suggested the 'new approach' to standards harmonization, which advanced 'mutual recognition' of validated national rules and restricted much of harmonization to agreeing only essential requirements. Towards the end of 1983 Commission officials were able privately to persuade key officials from Britain, France, and Germany to accept the new approach, which was endorsed in July 1984, but not formally adopted until May 1985 (*Bulletin of the European Communities* (May 1985)). This built on earlier British efforts to argue the deregulation case and on bilateral exchanges between the French and Germans to coordinate the activities of their standard-setting bodies, Association Française de Normalisation (AFNOR) and the Deutsche Institut für Normung (DIN) (H. Wallace 1984). Also in this period concern to mitigate the impact of border controls led the French and Germans in 1984 to agree the Moselle Treaty, later converted at the insistence of the Benelux governments into the first Schengen Agreement of 1985 (see Chapter 18).

The new approach to harmonization developed the principle of reference to standards and built on the jurisprudence of the ECJ, notably the definition in *Cassis de Dijon* of essential safety requirements (Schreiber 1991). It was to be paralleled by 'home country control' for financial services. The new approach limits legislative harmonization to minimum essential requirements and explicitly leaves scope for variations in national legislation (subject to mutual recognition). It delegates the maximum possible responsibility for detailed technical standards to CEN and CENELEC, the private European standard-setting bodies, subject to Commission mandates, with deadlines and financial provisions. We can see here three important developments: first, a greater reliance on national definitions of acceptable standards, albeit bounded by some collective requirements; secondly, a devolution of greater responsibility to the private sector and to external agencies for taking policy forwards; and, thirdly, the involvement of standards bodies from the EFTA countries.[2]

The European Council's Fontainebleau meeting in June 1984 marked a renewed commitment to accelerate European integration. It resolved the question of Britain's budget rebate and the outstanding issues of the Iberian enlargement, thereby clearing the way for serious consideration of revision of the treaties. At this meeting Commissioner Narjes presented his plan to consolidate the single market, and the British government tabled a memorandum that called *inter alia* for the creation of a 'genuine common market' in goods and services (Thatcher 1984). The meeting also established the Ad Hoc Committee on Institutional Reform (Dooge Committee) to consider reforms to the Community's decision-making procedures, with a worrying southern enlargement in prospect.

The remaining piece of the puzzle was put in place in January 1985 with the arrival of the new Commission, with Jacques Delors at its head and Lord Cockfield as Commissioner responsible for the single market (Cockfield 1994). Delors's preliminary discussions in national capitals convinced him that a drive to 'complete the single market' was perhaps the only strategic policy objective that would find a consensus. In his inaugural speech to the European Parliament Delors committed himself to completing the single market by 1992. The Milan European Council in June 1985 endorsed the White Paper (Commission 1985*a*) drawn up by Cockfield, containing 300 (later reduced to 282) measures that would complete the single market by 1992 (for the main features of the programme, see Table 4.2).

By December 1985 a remarkably tight Intergovernmental Conference (IGC) had completed the political relay by agreeing the terms of treaty reform which became the SEA. Apart from its important focus on accommodating enlargement, it specific-ally endorsed the single market and altered the main decision rule for single market measures (taxation excepted) from unanimity to qualified majority voting (QMV) in the Council. Thus a strategic policy change and institutional reform were linked symbiotically and symbolically.

Three points should be emphasized about the SEA. First, it locked together insti-tutional change and substantive policy goals. Secondly, the agreement to proceed with the single market was embedded in a set of wider agreements, in particular the accommodation of new members and budgetary redistribution. Thirdly, it met rela-tively little resistance at the point of ratification in the member states, except in Ireland, for special reasons to do with neutrality, and in Denmark, where the Schlüter government escaped domestic censure only by calling a consultative referendum on the SEA.[3]

The theoretical debate about how the single market programme and the SEA came about can be simplified as between two main approaches: one that emphasizes the role of supranational actors, the other that stresses the importance of the member governments. Comparisons of the two views are complicated by the fact that some observers focus on the '1992' programme, while others also concentrate on the SEA. It is quite possible that different actors exerted different levels of influence in pro-cesses shaping the two linked, but different, policy areas (Cowles 1994; J. Peterson 1995a). Cowles (1994) stresses the importance of supranational business interests in shaping the EU agenda in favour of completing the single market. Sandholtz and Zysman (1989) also give pride of place to supranational actors, though they cast the Commission in the leading role, with big business lending its support. Moravcsik (1991, 1998), on the other hand, argues that the SEA was the product of interstate bargaining between the British, French, and German governments in particular, and that traditional tools of international statecraft, such as threats of exclusion and side payments, explain the final composition of the '1992' programme and the SEA. Gar-rett (1992) and Cameron (1992) also stress the role of the member governments. Garrett argues that the member states were willing to constrain their sovereignty because they were engaged in an iterated prisoners' dilemma game and wanted to avoid the high transaction costs of monitoring compliance with agreements. Cam-eron concludes that ultimately the member governments, particularly in the context of the European Council, were the crucial actors, although he concedes that supra-national actors, such as the Commission, ECJ, and big business, may have influenced their preferences.

As the theoretical debate implies and our history shows, a wide array of influences came to bear on the redefinition of market regulation (the impacts of the inter-national economy, the inadequacies of national policies during the 1970s, the redefinition of interests and the emergence of new ideas, helped by 'policy learning'). The story also shows the involvement of a plurality of public and private actors in the redefinition and the channelling of their activities within the EU institutional process over a period of years before 1985, as well as afterwards. We are therefore reluctant to endorse any interpretation of events in 1985 that seeks to offer monocausal explan-ation: the striking feature is the clustering of factors (Scharpf 1994a).

The oddity of what happened is that an array of individually dull, technical, and everyday items were combined into an overarching programme that attracted such

Table 4.2 The White Paper on the single market: a taxonomy

Markets for: Measures to regulate	Products	Services	Persons and labour	Capital
Market access	▪ Abolition of intra-EC frontier controls ▪ Approximation of: 　—technical regulations 　—VAT rates and excises ▪ Unspecified implications for trade policy	▪ Mutual recognition and 'home country control', removal of licensing restrictions (in banking and insurance) ▪ Dismantling of quotas and freedom of cabotage (road haulage) ▪ Access to inter-regional air travel markets ▪ Multiple designation in bilaterals (air transport)	▪ Abolition of intra-EC frontier checks on persons ▪ Relaxation of residence requirements for EC persons ▪ Right of establishment for various highly educated workers	▪ Abolition of exchange controls ▪ Admission of securities listed in one member state to another ▪ Measures to facilitate industrial cooperation and migration of firms
Competitive conditions	▪ Promise of special paper on state aid to industry ▪ Liberalization of public procurement ▪ Merger control	▪ Introduction of competition policy in air transport ▪ Approximation of fiscal and/ or regulatory aspects in various services markets	▪ European 'vocational training card'	▪ Proposals on takeovers and holdings ▪ Approximation of: 　—double taxation 　—security taxes 　—parent–subsidiary links

Market functioning	■ Specific proposals on R&D in telecoms and IT ■ Proposals on standards, trade marks, corporate law, etc.	■ Approximation of —market and firm regulation in banking —consumer protection in insurance ■ EC system of permits for road haulage ■ EC standard for payment cards	■ Approximation of: —income tax provisions for migrants —various training provisions ■ Mutual recognition of diplomas	■ European economic interest grouping ■ European company statute ■ Harmonization of industrial and commercial property laws ■ Common bankruptcy provisions
Sectoral policy	■ CAP proposals: —abolition of frontiers —approximation and mutual recognition in veterinary and phytosanitary policies ■ Steel: —call to reduce subsidies	■ Common crisis regime in road transport ■ Common air transport policy on access, capacity and prices ■ Common rules on mass risks insurance	■ Largely silent on labour market provisions	■ Call to strengthen the European Monetary System

Source: Pelkmans and Winters (1988: 12); reproduced with kind permission of the publisher.

high-profile attention. The congruence of preferences of governments in power around the instrumentality of European market liberalization for both domestic and external purposes partly explains this. That these preferences could be expressed as embodying new ideas as well as satisfying specific interests was in our view crucial. The EU institutions, having experimented with a different and heavier approach to policy cooperation and failed to produce results in the 1970s, were able to engineer an alternative and to fashion it into a convincing joint programme. But that programme engaged some political and economic actors more intensively than others, an imbalance for which a price was to be paid subsequently as the immediate excitement of 1992 gave way to more sober assessments, compounded by the pressures of economic recession in the early 1990s.

The 1992 programme and the ratchets of institutional change

With the formulation of the 1992 programme, drafted by Narjes and crafted by Cockfield, the EU institutions moved into top gear to drive forward an extraordinarily ambitious programme of legislation. The Commission set to producing draft directives speedily, and the Internal Market Council, meeting at ministerial and official levels, kept up a remarkable rate of legislative endorsement. QMV became an established procedure, though more by implication than by observance, in that small minorities often tolerated decisions that they could not obstruct rather than press for formal votes. The rather few decisions, ninety-one out of 233 during 1989–93 (*Financial Times*, 13 September 1994), adopted by qualified majority perversely sometimes isolated member states that had a substantive interest in the outcome. The German government, for example, was outvoted on a directive that permitted road hauliers from one member state to transport loads entirely within another (*cabotage*).

The SEA also increased the European Parliament's role in policies concerning the single market, among others, by giving it the power, under the cooperation procedure, to reject or amend proposals. This power was, however, significantly constrained. The Parliament had to vote to amend or reject a proposal by an absolute majority of its members; the Commission could choose not to integrate parliamentary amendments into its revised proposal to the Council; and the Council could overturn the Parliament's amendments or rejection by a unanimous vote. Consequently, the Parliament only very rarely rejected proposals under the cooperation procedure and only about 40 per cent of its amendments, many of which are only minor changes to the substance of the text, ended up in directives (European Parliament 1993).

The introduction of the co-decision procedure under the (Maastricht) Treaty on European Union (TEU), however, augmented the Parliament's importance in single market matters, particularly strengthening its ability to reject proposals. This has led to an apparently marked increase in the number of parliamentary amendments accepted by the Commission and Council at the second reading as well as by the

Council in the conciliation committee (Hix 1999: 96). The increased influence of the Parliament formally in decision-making and informally in proposal-shaping has had an impact on policy outcomes by enhancing the representation of civic interests, such as consumers (J. Peterson and Bomberg 1999; Young and Wallace 2000).

Evidence was compiled to demonstrate to the doubters the benefits of agreeing the measures in the White Paper. The 'Cecchini studies' of the 'cost of non-Europe' produced chapter and verse of justification for sectoral and horizontal policy change (Cecchini *et al.* 1988; Commission 1988*a*). The overall static gains from full integration were estimated at 4.3–6.4 per cent of Community gross domestic product (GDP) (Emerson *et al.* 1988: 203), deliberately not differentiated too explicitly by region. The argument focused on the overall, long-term welfare gains, thus downplaying the estimated costs of adjustment. In the wake of the Cecchini studies, the interest of economists in the single market was aroused. The spate of expert economic studies, such as those by the Centre for Economic Policy Research (CEPR), that followed helped to shift the debate cross-nationally on to the gains from market liberalization.

The institutional process gained huge new credibility as the transmission belt for delivering policy effectiveness, perhaps most sharply demonstrated by reactions from outside the EU. The neuralgic debate in the USA and Japan about 'fortress Europe' and the increased urgency of the EU–EFTA dialogue, started in Luxembourg in 1984, bore witness to the policy impact of the EU. Statistics were accumulated to show the strike-rate of achievement in legislating and to maintain momentum and later to demonstrate the relative rates of implementation by member states (see Table 4.3). This exercise gained renewed energy in the late 1990s as part of the drive to secure the promised benefits of the single market in time for the launch of the euro (see more below). Piloted by the Commission, it was to carry governments, business, and wider opinion along with the notion that legislative success would breed economic gains all round.

National institutions were conscripted as additional endorsers of the programme. National parliaments had to implement the directives, a necessary but not very visible process, since in most cases they are enacted by subordinate legislation and not much debated. Here it should be noted that subsequent criticisms of 'Brussels bureaucracy' often relate to rules that had been transposed into national law without debate and with little attention from national parliamentarians, but then 'Brussels' is always an easy scapegoat for unpopular changes. In most member states there were public relations campaigns around the 1992 theme. In the UK the Department of Trade and Industry set up a new 1992 unit and hotline. In France Édith Cresson spearheaded large public colloquia. It was the first time in the history of the EU that its policy process had engaged so wide a span of attention and engagement, remarkably so given the obscure and technical character of most of the legislation.

The hyperactivism of public policy institutions was matched by an extraordinary engagement of private sector bodies. Indeed the change in business attitudes and business behaviour, much of it anticipating legislation, is probably the most important direct 'output' of the 1992 programme (Jacquemin and Wright 1993*a*). 'Brussels' had for a long while attracted pressure groups and lobbyists from the *cognoscenti* among the would-be influencers of Community legislation; 1992 took this phenomenon to unforeseen levels and forms of activism. In part this was the simple result of the range and quantity of sectors and products affected by the single market

Table 4.3 Completion of the single market

Member state	Percentage of single market directives not transposed (May 1999)	Reasoned opinions (no.) (1 Mar. 1998– 1 Mar. 1999)[a]	Cases of infringements of mutual recognition in goods (no.) (1996–8)	Pending cases of alleged failure to comply with ECJ judgment concerning the single market (no.) (1 Mar. 1999)[b]
Portugal	5.7	19	7	2
Italy	5.5	41	23	1
Greece	5.2	11	10	7
Luxembourg	4.8	11	0	1
France	4.8	42	52	2
Austria	4.5	11	16	
Ireland	3.9	5	1	1
Belgium	3.5	30	15	3
UK	3.3	12	10	
Germany	2.4	21	33	1
Netherlands	2.4	8	12	
Sweden	2.1	4	17	
Spain	1.8	13	19	1
Denmark	1.4	3	8	
Finland	1.3	5	6	
EU 15	12.8[c]	236	228	19

Notes:
[a] For failure to apply single market rules (not incl. failure to implement directives).
[b] Letters of formal notice and reasoned opinions.
[c] Directives not transposed in all member states.

Source: Commission (1999b)

programme and the speed with which they were being addressed. Organizations (pressure groups, firms, local and regional governments, and non-govenmental organizations (NGOs)) which had previously relied on occasional trips to Brussels, reasonably so given the slow pace of earlier harmonization, started to prefer to establish their own offices or to hire lobbyists on retainers. The Commission, pressed for staff and expertise, opened its doors readily and even took some of the outsiders on to the inside on consultancy or expert contracts.

But other factors began to alter the character of the policy-influencing process. The previous quasi-monopoly of conventional peak and trade associations in the formal consultative processes was challenged by more direct lobbying from individual firms and by the emergence of the ERT. This is perhaps not so startling a phenomenon as some have argued. Firms had been players within member countries, some more than others, and some, like Fiat and Philips, had long been established in Brussels. As early as 1979 the Davignon Round Table had established a direct partnership between key information technology (IT) firms and the Commission.

Another change in style came with greater reliance on consultancy (an import from the USA), which started to erode the old distinctions between public policy-making and private interest representation. The Commission, member governments, and firms found themselves relying increasingly on consultants to inject interpretative and facilitating 'expertise' through both public and private contracts. It is an interesting question just what kind of groupings were developing around the single market programme, whether or not they warrant description as an epistemic community (P. M. Haas 1992), and whether the clusters of policy activists formed policy networks (Atkinson and Coleman 1989) or 'advocacy coalitions' (Sabatier 1988, 1998). It might be more accurate to characterize them as 'advocacy alliances' to capture the often tactical nature of often loose groupings of proponents of particular policies (Young and Wallace 2000). Overlapping groups of consultants worked for the Commission, member governments, and firms. Some were providing expertise on the economy, markets, and business opportunities; others advised on procedures, legislation, and litigation. Thus the conventional delineation of public policy-makers and private influencers became blurred.

Consumer and other 'civic interest' groups also put their feet in the door, though they found it much harder to exercise effective political muscle. The consumer and the purchaser had been intended beneficiaries of the 1992 programme, and the 'minimum essential requirements' of harmonizing and liberalizing directives were often to help them or their assumed interests. But it is easier to discern consumers as objects of policy than as partners in the process, although they are often sporadic participants (Young 1997; Young and Wallace 2000). The point is important when we compare the favourable attitude of business opinion across the EU towards 1992 with the waning of wider public expectations of benefits from 1990 onwards (Reif 1994; Franklin *et al.* 1994) or with the subsequent emergence of public antipathies to the apparent efforts of 'Brussels' to remove differences of local taste (food standards being a particularly emotive issue). The Commission's 'Citizens First' initiative was an attempt to counter this opinion by making citizens aware of their rights and of the opportunities presented by the single market. This has been transformed at the 1998 Cardiff European Summit into the 'Dialogue with Citizens and Business' and Europe Direct, which provides information by telephone and internet.

Until the mid-1990s, however, the bulk of the activity to achieve the goals of 1992 was focused on the legislative programme rather than on the follow-through, on designing rather than implementing policy rules. Its impact on economic sectors also differed: the early breakthrough on freeing capital movements was crucial in opening up opportunities for cross-border investment; the repeated obstacles to progress on food, veterinary, and phytosanitary standards were a barely heard signal of problems to come; the stubborn resistance to tax harmonization was more predictable.

Movement towards single markets in the utility sectors has also been rather belated. Given favourable circumstances (technological change, and support from users and from within the industry as well as from member governments), the Commission was able to use its competition powers under Article 86 (ex 90) of the Treaty of Rome to force the liberalization of telecommunications equipment and services (Sandholtz 1998; Schmidt 1998). Full liberalization of voice telephony was agreed in 1996 and introduced at the beginning of 1998, with some derogations for countries with less developed networks. The liberalization of the electricity market has proceeded more slowly due to a lack of such favourable conditions (Schmidt 1998). The 1996 directive aimed to liberalize only 25 per cent of member states' electricity markets by February 1999. Although a number of member governments, including those of Sweden and the UK, have gone further faster than required, others, including those of Austria, France, Germany, and the Netherlands, missed the deadline.

More than just a market

As 'flanking' policies were developed, especially the cohesion programmes for social and regional spending, other layers of governance became engaged, especially at the regional level. Traditions of local political territory jostled with adjustment to transnational markets. EU institutional links to regional and local authorities and cohesion programmes to some extent filled the policy gaps at the regional level (Marks 1993). But, as A. Smith (1995) points out so convincingly, the policy gaps were different in different member states. These issues are discussed further by Allen in Chapter 9 of this volume.

In the social arena a big push was made by the Commission, in coalition with the old social market protagonists, to buttress the single market with the reassurance that it would also deliver social progress for the labour force. This effort was a logical extension of the analysis of earlier experience of European integration and national policy adjustments, but it was to prove much harder to embed, as Leibfried and Pierson show in Chapter 10. The shared new doctrine of market liberalization and the new approach to regulation had a narrower political base than the old social market doctrine used to have. Indeed it began to emerge that regulatory instruments and competition, the mode for liberalizing movements of products and services, were beginning to define the scope for collective social policy (Majone 1993).

Policy implementation

The single market was not complete by the 1992 deadline. Although much of the legislative agenda was in place, crucial elements (including in utilities, taxation, and corporate law) were still missing. In addition, the transposition of directives into national law has been slow, and national measures continue to contravene EU law (see Table 4.3). Non-implementation of directives is particularly a problem with respect to telecommunications, transport, intellectual and industrial property, and public procurement (Commission 1999c). In addition, although some businesses see benefits, many have seen little change (see Fig. 4.4).

Attempts to ensure that the single market had its intended effects began even before the 1992 deadline. In March 1992 the Commission established the High-Level Group on the Operation of the Internal Market, under the chairmanship of Peter Sutherland, a former Commissioner, to assess ways of realizing the full potential of the single market. The Sutherland Report (Sutherland *et al.* 1992) focused on only those aspects of the single market concerned with goods and services. It called for improved consultation with the actors affected by new regulations, greater accessibility of the Community's laws, and better cooperation between the Commission and the member governments to ensure that uneven implementation of directives did

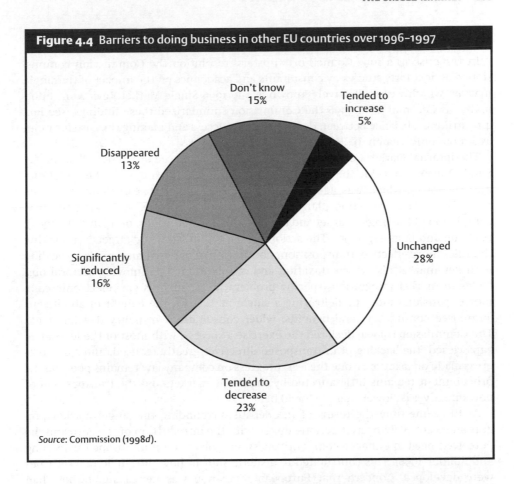

Figure 4.4 Barriers to doing business in other EU countries over 1996–1997

Don't know
15%

Tended to
increase
5%

Disappeared
13%

Unchanged
28%

Significantly
reduced
16%

Tended to
decrease
23%

Source: Commission (1998*d*).

not create trade barriers (Previdi 1997). The Commission (1992*d*) largely accepted these proposals, though it made clear that the onus for implementation lay with the member states. It also argued that additional funding would be required in order to oversee and coordinate the member states' implementation of directives.

In spite of the manifest importance of effective implementation of the 1992 programme, the Sutherland Report has received a relatively low-key response. Or at least it has been difficult to give the hard grind of implementation an exciting public face and even to rally the many relevant national agencies in the member states. Architects (Cockfield 1994) of the single market had often signalled that the real test of success would lie in thorough implementation, and critics (Metcalfe 1992) had warned of the obstacles. The Commission has taken some steps to improve implementation. An Internal Market Advisory Committee, chaired by the Director-General responsible for the single market, was formalized in 1992, and networks of national and Commission officials dealing with individual areas of regulation have been established. In addition, the first subject on the agenda of an informal meeting of the Internal Market Council in March 1995 was the effective application of Community law, including the issues of reducing the disparity between national sanctions for violations of Community law, and of increasing the transparency. The French presidency also asked the Commission for proposals for a model clause on sanctions that could be introduced into all future European directives (Lamassoure 1995).

In response to a 1992 Council of Ministers' resolution the Commission commissioned almost forty studies by consultants and academics on the impact of the single market, which were collectively known as the 1996 Single Market Review or, informally, as Cecchini II. In 1996 the Commission summarized these findings (see Box 4.1), striking a balance between demonstrating success and making the case for more assiduous enforcement (J. Peterson and Bomberg 1999).

The Internal Market Commissioner Mario Monti advanced an 'Action Plan for the Single Market' to tackle the outstanding problems identified by this exercise (Commission 1997j), which was adopted by the Amsterdam European Council in June 1997. The rather dry action plan was given political impetus by linking the true completion of the single market and the introduction of the euro on 1 January 1999 (J. Peterson and Bomberg 1999). The action plan sets four 'strategic targets': (1) making the rules more effective (transposition, notification of national measures); (2) dealing with key market distortions (taxation and competition); (3) removing sectoral obstacles to market integration (specific problem areas, such as gas, electronic commerce, pension funds); (4) delivering a single market for the benefit of all citizens (employee consultation and benefits; wider consultations in policy development). The Commission (1999a) declared the exercise a success, with most of the legislative gaps closed, the backlog of untransposed directives greatly reduced, and some progress made on taxation. None the less, progress on company law remains poor, public procurement remains little affected by the single market, and the transposition of new directives is slower than it should be.

At the same time the terms of the debate surrounding the single market programme were evolving as it became linked with the introduction of the euro and the perceived need to enhance competitiveness and job creation in Europe (Armstrong and Bulmer 1998). This contributed to a subtle shift in how the single market rules were developed. Concern that European regulation was increasing, rather than decreasing, the burden on business, particularly small and medium-sized enterprises

---

Box 4.1 The economic impact of the single market programme

- 300,000 to 900,000 jobs that would not have existed in the absence of the single market
- An extra increase in EU income of 1.1–1.5 per cent over 1987–93
- Inflation rates which are 1.0–1.5 per cent lower than they would have been in the absence of the single market programme
- Economic convergence and cohesion between different EU regions
- Investment boosted by 1–3 per cent
- Increased trade volume between member states (20–30 per cent in manufacturing products)
- Increased foreign direct investment (in the early 1990s the EU attracted 44 per cent of global foreign investment compared to 28 per cent in the mid-1980s)

Source: Commission (1996b).

(SMEs), contributed to the establishment of the Molitor Group in 1994 to work on the simplification and lightening of EU and national implementing legislation. This led, as part of the Action Plan, to the Simpler Legislation for the Internal Market (SLIM) exercise, a rolling programme of simplification and improvement of single market legislation, and the Business Test Panel, a pilot exercise to consult business on draft Commission proposals.

The European standards bodies are also struggling to adopt all of the voluntary industry standards required by the new approach directives. Although the output of European standards bodies has increased, during April 1998 and May 1999 they ratified only 40 per cent of the mandated standards (Commission 1999c). In addition, the number of standards that the member governments notify to the Commission has remained high (nearly five times more than the European standards bodies adopted in 1998) and was higher in 1998 than in 1989, although less than in 1997 (Commission 1999c).

Winners and losers

Who has gained and who has lost from the single market programme is a politically charged issue. As yet there have been no serious empirical studies that attempt to provide comprehensive answers. One study (Commission 1996a) has identified that between 1987 and 1993 per capita income in the less favoured (Objective 1) regions of the Community grew faster than in the Community as a whole. Much of this differential appears to be due to increased investment. Whether that investment was in response to the single market programme or to Greece, Portugal, and Spain (which account for a large share of Objective 1 regions) joining the EU, however, is unclear.[4]

A 1990 Commission study (Buigues *et al.* 1990: 4), which was targeted at member governments, predicted that completion of the single market should 'neither upset the mix of sectoral specialisations across member states nor lead to massive transfers of economic activities between geographic zones'. The study acknowledged that the processes in question were too complex to allow predictions of which regions or sectors would gain or lose from the single market (1990, p. vii).

While such analysis is relevant for governments and political parties wishing to draw up balance sheets, it is not satisfying in that 'national economies' may not be helpful units of analysis. Indeed, as the Cecchini studies had tried to argue, the single market was designed to improve the competitiveness of firms, not of countries as such.

Although all businesses are supposed to benefit from greater market access, large corporations are better placed than SMEs to take advantage of new market opportunities and economies of scale. None the less, even some large corporations do not view the single market with enthusiasm (Coutu *et al.* 1993). The less competitive ones, in particular, fear increased competition. Although these fears appear exaggerated, bigger companies have tended to see more of the benefits (see Table 4.4).

Consumers were also supposed to benefit from a wider choice of goods and services. As yet there has not been a systematic study of the impact of the single market

Table 4.4 The impact of the single market on company performance, 1996–1997 (per cent)

Effect	Large companies (>250 employees)	Medium-sized companies (50–250 employees)	Small companies (<50 employees)
Positive	41	28	23
Negative	3	7	8

Source: Commission (1998*d*)

on consumer welfare. Some surveys indicate that consumers do not fully appreciate their rights (Commission 1999*c*). Theoretically, the single market programme should lead to increased competition, which brings greater choice and lower prices, without compromising consumer protection. Although there is the potential, and in some cases the reality (Millstone 1991), that the single market might erode consumer protection, evidence indicates that this is not the general case; rather consumer protection appears to have been enhanced (Young 1997).

In addition to improving the competitiveness of firms and increasing consumer choice, the single market programme was also expected to increase employment in the long run (Emerson *et al*. 1988: 213–17). In the short term, however, some jobs would likely be lost as firms fail or restructure in the face of increased competition. In addition, the absence of internal frontiers and the guarantee of the right of establishment could increase the likelihood that workers in different locations might be forced to compete with each other to attract investment.

It is possible that the overselling of the benefits of the single market programme has contributed to business and public disappointment with its achievements.

Policy-making results

What have been the main results of SEA–1992 as conceived for the single market? Our concern here is with the results in terms of the policy process rather than with the economic impact of liberalizing the single market. None the less, we note that policy substance and policy process interact. For the Community level of governance, with its fragile sources of direct legitimation and dependence on support from within the member states, evidence of policy effectiveness and tangible gains are of particular relevance in establishing policy and political credibility (Reif 1994; Schmitter 1992; H. Wallace 1993; Weale 1997).

Several yardsticks can be proffered of the impact of the single market programme:

Legislative output

By the end of May 1999, 1,405 single market directives were in effect (the White Paper's 282 measures, having been greatly augmented by amendments and separation into more focused packets). With the adoption in the late 1990s of measures on intellectual and industrial property and progress on corporate taxation, company law stands out as the most significant remaining lacuna.

Judicial support

Cases lodged with the ECJ related to the single market increased during the late 1980s, but tapered off in the early 1990s before surging again in the mid-1990s (see Fig. 4.3). The *Frankovitch* ruling and the addition of Article 228 (ex 171) to the TEU (which introduced fines for member governments that fail to implement Community legislation) suggest a readiness by the both the ECJ and the Council to tighten judicial enforcement (see Table 4.2 for such cases). However, some cases have also limited the definition of those national variations of rules or practice that can be successfully contested.[5] None the less, overall the ECJ's jurisprudence has accelerated the application of the single market programme (Armstrong and Bulmer 1998).

Policy development by the Commission

Under the two Delors Commissions there was an emphasis on policy innovation rather than implementation. Other policy areas claimed attention, and responsibilities for different aspects of the single market have been uneasily divided between different DGs: III for industry; XIII for high-technology sectors; XV for financial services; and in parallel DG IV for competition. In the mid-1990s DG XV became the main coordinator. The Santer Commission, which took office in 1995, included strict enforcement of existing single market rules among its priorities (Commission 1995a: 7). This approach meshed well with the concerns of the European business community, which wanted to see the gains of the single market consolidated before the EU launched any new endeavours (Coutu *et al.* 1993). With the Action Plan, the Commission did much to deliver on this intention. Romano Prodi (1999), in his first speech to the European Parliament, flagged the need to move beyond a single market and single currency towards 'a single economy and single politics'. The single market is perceived as a key contributor to the Community's objectives of growth, competitiveness, and job creation (Commission 1999c). As a result, in the mid-1999 reorganization of the Commission services, DG XV, renamed the Internal Market DG, is retained largely unchanged.

Policy 'performance' and implementation by Commission and member governments

As noted above, the Commission has belatedly begun to address the deficiencies in implementation. Transposition of EU directives into national laws is still incomplete, although the 'fragmentation factor', which reflects the measures not transposed in all member states, has fallen sharply from 18.2 per cent in May 1998 to 12.8 per cent in May 1999 (Commission 1999c). Differences in the pace of national compliance with EU legislation pose serious problems for business, as do persisting barriers to trade, particularly in the form of state subsidies and public procurement procedures, and new barriers, such as environmental regulations (Commission 1998d, 1999a). In addition, some firms encounter difficulties in understanding the new rules of the game. Not only is the regulatory environment in which they operate in flux, but they sometimes have to cope with conflicting national and EU regulations (hence the sub-theme of deregulation as a corrective).

Industrial behaviour

Despite its shortcomings, the single market programme has had a significant impact on business behaviour. Following the programme's adoption, there was a dramatic increase in transnational investment within and into the EU. Although this has tapered off slightly since 1991, both intra-EU and inward extra-EU foreign direct investment (FDI) remain significantly above pre-single market levels (see Fig. 4.5). There has also been a substantial degree of consolidation of business activities, as businesses seek to capitalize on economies of scale (Commission 1996a; Jacquemin and Wright 1993a). This trend has progressed faster in retailing than manufacturing (Bayliss *et al.* 1994). During 1993–5 restructuring, in the form of mergers and acquisitions, in services outstripped that in manufacturing (Commission 1996a). Significantly much of the restructuring has taken place within member states. In addition, firms in various industries have collectively adopted voluntary codes of conduct as means of implementing or deferring new regulations (Matthews and Mayes 1995).

Public reception

Public perception of the single market programme was strongly positive in the late 1980s, but began to decline in the run-up to the 1992 deadline, although it remained generally favourable throughout (*Eurobarometer*, 41, 1994). In addition, the momentum of the late 1980s has proved difficult to maintain (as the problems experienced during the Maastricht Treaty ratification process demonstrated), as popular support for integration has been undermined by poor economic conditions (Eichenberg and Dalton 1993; J. Peterson and Bomberg 1999). Whatever the reasons, public perception of the benefits of membership have declined sharply since 1990, although overall more still perceive benefits than not (Hix 1999; *Eurobarometer*, 51, 1999).

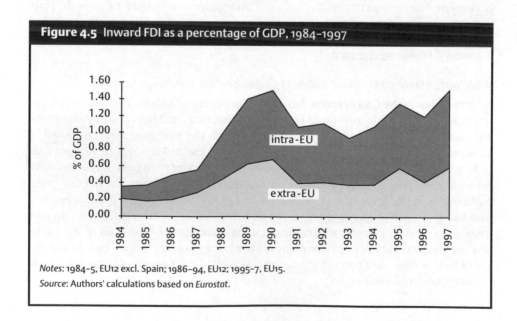

Figure 4.5 Inward FDI as a percentage of GDP, 1984–1997

Notes: 1984–5, EU12 excl. Spain; 1986–94, EU12; 1995–7, EU15.

Source: Authors' calculations based on *Eurostat.*

External impacts

Through promoting policy collaboration among the member governments, the single market programme has enhanced the EU's effectiveness in international trade negotiations (see Chapter 14). European industries, such as chemicals, that are affected by other countries' regulations recognize the advantage that common EU policies provide in international negotiations regarding the mutual recognition of standards or market access arrangements (Paterson 1991).

In addition, as a result of the ECJ's doctrine of implied powers, which implies that as internal rules increase and expand, external competences are also enhanced and extended (M. Smith 1994). Thus there is a degree of 'spill-over' from the internal to the external. As a result, the EU, as such, has authority across a wider array of policy, including important aspects of trade in services (see Chapter 14).

The single market programme, although directed at removing internal barriers, has had significant implications for other countries as well. For the most part these have been positive (Commission 1997c; WTO 1995) as third-country firms have also benefited from regulatory approximation and the application of the mutual recognition principle (within the EU). There have, however, been some high-profile cases, most notably concerning bananas (see Chapter 15) and beef hormones, in which the single market programme has led to clashes with trading partners, particularly the USA. The US government's preference for imposing punitive sanctions rather than accepting compensation indicates its desire to overturn EU regulations that impede access to the EU market for particular US firms.

The success of the single market programme has led to it being considered as a model for aspects of international trade. The General Agreement on Trade in Services (GATS) (see Chapter 14) provides opportunities for countries to conclude agreements on the mutual recognition of qualifications, licences, regulations, and other requirements concerning the provision of services. In addition, the GATS agreements on basic telecommunications built on some aspects of the EU's internal liberalization (Holmes *et al.* 1996).

Extraterritoriality

The creation of the EEA extended the single market beyond the EU to the members of EFTA, save Switzerland. This had the logic of a closer fit between the patterns of production and markets for goods and services and the emerging regulatory regimes. The EEA experience made the accession negotiations with Austria, Finland, Sweden, and Norway simpler. The other EEA countries and even Switzerland still have their regulatory arrangements framed by the single market. Extending the single market to developed and relatively small economies was relatively easy; extending it to the reforming economies of central and eastern Europe will prove more challenging for both sides (see Chapter 16).

In early 1995 a policy debate opened on how to align US and EU regulation, building on the EEA experience. Although this initiative has subsequently been tempered, the Transatlantic Economic Partnership (TEP) has provided a framework for closer coordination and for the conclusion of mutual recognition agreements, under which foreign authorities are authorized to certify products to domestic standards. Similar agreements have been concluded with a number of other trading partners, including Australia, Canada, and New Zealand.

Policy blockages

Shortcomings in national transposition and enforcement of EU legislation persist. Stubborn 'differences of taste' inhibit uniform implementation and generate controversy. Under the label of 'subsidiarity' some member governments have sought to enhance their freedom of action in 'flanking policies', especially social and environmental. Differences in both social and environmental standards allow different regions or countries to compete with each other to attract investment. These factors highlight the issue of whether a single market implies similar standards for production processes, as well as for products, and the consequences for who sets which rules.

Policy linkages

The drive to complete the single market has pervaded the policy agenda of the EU. The single market and its associated thousands of pages of *acquis communautaire* took the central place in defining the EU that the common agricultural policy had once occupied. Its scope was much greater, in that it included not only vertical measures for particular products or sectors, but horizontal measures, such as the right of establishment, that impacted across the economy. Its impact depended on the corollary availability of a tough competition policy (see Chapter 5). Its political acceptability was buttressed by the development of cohesion programmes and was argued to require an active social dimension. As products came to move more easily, attention also focused on the processes and conditions under which goods and services were produced and provided. Irrespective of other arguments for European policies on environmental and social issues (see Chapters 11 and 7 respectively), the preoccupation of entrepreneurs with operating on a 'level playing-field' turned attention to the relevance of these other factors for costs, competition, and profitability. Necessarily the change of internal policy also had to be followed through into the projection of external policy, both on trade issues in general and as regards particular economic partners (see Chapters 14, 15, and 16). The abolition of border controls within the EU meant that national trade regimes with third countries in products such as cars, bananas, and textiles had to be replaced by EU trade agreements.

In addition the single market was prayed in aid of the two big policy initiatives that followed it: the plans for economic and monetary union (EMU); and the goal of removing internal borders for people. In the case of EMU it became commonly argued that a single market logically implied a single currency. In the case of borders between member states two arguments were made: first, that the increase in cross-border economic transactions would facilitate illicit and illegal transactions, drugs, fraud, arms trade, and suchlike, which would in turn require European-level responses; and, secondly, it was asserted that border controls on persons would have to be removed lest they be used as substitute controls for economic purposes. These subjects are covered in Chapters 6 and 18.

A new approach to policy

The new policy ideas of liberalization and regulatory governance that underpinned the single market continue to resonate in Community parlance. The White Paper of December 1993 on competitiveness (Commission 1993d) and the pre-accession strategy for the (eastern) Europe associates (Commission 1995b) both reveal the embedding of these ideas, albeit with persistent echoes of other policy perspectives. The Santer Commission was quick to signal its commitment to continue in the same broad line (Santer 1995). Commission President Prodi, understandably, has been preoccupied with reforming and restructuring the Commission. None the less, the single market has been clearly flagged as one area that will help to achieve the objective of making the Community more relevant to its citizens through job creation and facilitating cross-border consumption.

A new policy mode pervades much of the work of the EU institutions and their outputs of policy and legislation. Majone's (1996b) general line of argument on this seems well substantiated, even though some of the consequences for policy management remain ambiguous. It would appear, for instance, that the move towards establishing independent regulatory agencies has receded, with the European Medicines Evaluation Agency as its high-water mark. It is harder to tell how far the management of public policy within the member states has also changed or whether any such changes have been induced by European policy, as distinct from having been the parallel product of the factors that helped to induce European policy changes. Competition among national rules had been envisaged as one possible outcome, but several key factors militate against this kind of competition. Woolcock (1994) argues that some of the basic preconditions (notably transparency of national regulations and certainty about the effects of specific regulations) for regulatory competition to occur are absent. Sun and Pelkmans (1995) contend that, even if those conditions existed, the impact of regulatory competition would be restricted. First, some factors of production are less than completely mobile, and so producers are unable to take full advantage of differences between regulatory regimes. Secondly, when capital investment decisions are made, the regulatory environment is just one among many considerations. In addition, all note that local market characteristics, particularly 'differences of taste', might make adhering to foreign regulations an unattractive option for firms.

New relationships have been established by the business community with the policy process, as is argued by Cowles (1994) and McLaughlin et al. (1993). Although it is widely accepted that the process is pluralist rather than corporatist (Streeck and Schmitter 1991), there are significant opportunities for policy capture at the European level (Cawson 1992). The continued segmentation of EU policy-making contributes to skewed access to influence. Bigger firms have and take more opportunities than SMEs. Other kinds of organized interests can less easily gain a foothold than the producers or the providers of services (Young 1995).

None the less, the danger of producer capture should not be overstated. Producer interests, even within industries, are far from homogeneous, particularly given the different regulatory traditions of the member states. The different political constellations within the member states frequently produce at least some governments interested in championing 'civic interests' in the European policy process. In addition, the Commission and European Parliament often perceive their legitimacy as tied to addressing broader constituencies. As a consequence, the EU regulatory model is sensitive to societal and political considerations and not just to corporate interests (Young and Wallace 2000).

The dependency of many economic actors on national policy has also been reduced. The scope for national policy-makers to control economic transactions on their territories has become more limited and will stay so as long as the transnational legal regime of the EU holds together. But this is not to say that the political turf has been won by EU-level policy-makers, since the new regulatory mode involves a diffusion of policy authority rather than its concentration elsewhere. Though the Commission has been heavily engaged in promoting the single market, its own net gain in authority is open to debate, not least since it has also become the butt of residual criticism about the downside effects of market liberalization. Moreover, the member governments—as the enforcers of most EU legislation, the guardians of 'home country controls', and the proponents of subsidiarity—retain important footholds in the regulatory process. In particular, member governments are forced into the position of defending the losers from the single market against the incursions of European regulation. Hence the single market programme has to be seen as an important element in the legitimacy test faced by the EU since the early 1990s. It is, moreover, a paradox that this test has been most severe in member states that have had governments strongly committed to market liberalization (the UK is a clear case in point).

The discussion continues on how far the European regulatory model can be applied more broadly. Other Europeans and immediate neighbours have become increasingly drawn within the regulatory scope of the EU by direct membership or close association or as free-riders. Indeed the closeness of the association seems increasingly to depend on how much of the single market *acquis* can be absorbed by the third country. The creation of the single market also limited the scope of derogations, particularly with respect to product regulations, that can be granted to new members to ease their transitions. In this sense the threshold for full membership has been raised much higher by the single market, though the dependence on EU markets may in any event force unilateral alignment to many EU rules—at least as far as products are concerned. Issues such as the impact of competition, environmental, and social policies on trade that became increasingly important in the EU are pushing their way into the wider international discussions in the World Trade Organization (WTO) and Organization for Economic Cooperation and Development (OECD) (Devos *et al.* 1993).

The adoption of the single market thus in many senses marks a critical change in the European policy process as well as a different choice of policy content. But its prominence and predominance in the late 1980s must also be seen in proportion, given that the follow-through to implementing the programme remains patchy and it now has to jostle with several other big subjects for the prime attention of strategic policy-makers at both European and national levels.

The 1992 programme probably would not have become such a relative success story had not policy and industrial entrepreneurs been able to talk up the importance of what they were seeking to do and thus to give political sex appeal to what otherwise consisted of a rather dreary list of separate and very technical proposals. Politicians found it convenient for a variety—we stress a variety—of reasons to use the single market and the constraints from 'Brussels' as cover for changes in domestic policies and as explanation for both inaction and action at home. Commission officials were delighted to have found a theme that had such wide resonance and to play it for all it was worth in developing the symbolism of European integration and its impacts on citizens as well as on firms. Sustaining political integration on the back of a programme of market liberalization has, however, proved elusive. Modernizing or adapting the European welfare state to the exigencies of external competition and the pressures of a changing industrial society at home is a much taller order.

Notes

1 The Luxembourg process well preceded the official recommitment of the EU to the single market. After preliminary discussion it was launched with the Luxembourg Declaration of Apr. 1984. It was when the limits of this were reached that the moves began which led to the EEA debate from Jan. 1989 onwards.

2 CEN and CENELEC then took decisions by qualified majority votes, weighted as in the Council, allowing assenting EFTA members to implement, but not allowing EFTA dissent to prevent an EU majority from agreeing a standard.

3 The issues raised were specifically focused on security policy but also revealed the split between the bourgeois parties and the 'alternative majority' (N. Petersen 1993).

4 For a detailed analysis of the impact of EU policies, including the single market, on social and economic cohesion, see Tsoukalis *et al.* (forthcoming).

5 The two most prominent examples of this are the cases concerning *Danish Bottles* (302/86) and *Keck* (267 & 268/91). In the former, the ECJ ruled that the Danish government could require the recycling of beverage containers, even though it might impede imports. In the latter, the court held that national laws restricting or prohibiting certain selling arrangements do not infringe the Treaty of Rome's rules on the free movement of goods, provided that the laws are not aimed at imports and that they have the same effect on commercial freedom to market domestic products as on imports.

Further reading

On the original development of the 1992 programme, see Cecchini (1988), Cockfield (1994), and Pelkmans and Winters (1988). For early economic evaluations, see Jacquemin and Sapir (1991) and Siebert (1990b). For more recent work, see Commission (1996b) and its biennial *Single* *Market Scoreboard* and web site <http://www.europa.eu.int/com/dgs internal market_market/index_en.htm>. The introduction to Commission (1995b) summarizes the programme and its development (in identifying a 'pre-accession strategy' for the Europe associates to adapt to the single market). For the theoretical debate, see Armstrong and Bulmer (1998), Cowles (1997), Majone (1996b), Moravcsik (1991), and Sandholtz and Zysman (1989).

Armstrong, K., and Bulmer, S. (1998), *The Governance of the Single European Market* (Manchester: Manchester University Press).

Cecchini, P., with Catinat, M., and Jacquemin, A. (1988), *The European Challenge 1992: The Benefits of a Single Market* (Aldershot: Wildwood House).

Cockfield, Lord (1994), *The European Union: Creating the Single Market* (London: Wiley Chancery Law).

Commission (1995b), *Preparation of the Associated Countries of Central and Eastern Europe for Integration into the Internal Market of the Union*, COM (95) 163 final, 3 May.

—— (1996b), *The Impact and Effectiveness of the Single Market*, COM (96) 520 final, 30 Oct.

Cowles, M. G. (1997), 'Organizing Industrial Coalitions: A Challenge for the Future?', in H. Wallace and Young (1997), 116–40.

Jacquemin, A., and Sapir, A. (1991) (eds.), *The European Internal Market: Trade and Competition* (Oxford: Oxford University Press).

Majone, G. (1996b), *Regulating Europe* (London: Routledge).

Moravcsik, A. (1991), 'Negotiating the Single European Act: National Interests and Conventional Statecraft in the European Community', *International Organization*, 45/1: 19–56.

Pelkmans, J., and Winters, L. A., with Wallace, H. (1988), *Europe's Domestic Market* (London: Royal Institute of International Affairs).

Sandholtz, W., and Zysman, J. (1989), '1992: Recasting the European Bargain', *World Politics*, 42/1: 95–128.

Siebert, H. (1990b) (ed.), *The Completion of the Internal Market* (Tübingen: J. C. B. Mohr).

Chapter 5

Competition Policy

The Limits of the
European Regulatory State

Francis McGowan

Contents

Summary

Competition policy has a strong treaty basis, enabling the Commission to investigate, decide, and enforce with few constraints from other actors. Directorate-General (DG) IV has established a high degree of autonomy, helped by the prevalence of a liberal market doctrine, backed by an epistemic community of expert lawyers and economists. The European Court of Justice (ECJ) has supported the Commission's approach in most cases. Policy-making follows a regulatory model, with limited roles for the Council of Ministers and the European Parliament. Yet the activities of the DG for Competition have been constrained in some areas, and it has had to work cautiously in employing its policy remit. European Union (EU) controls over mergers have been agreed by member governments. The Commission has made some headway as regards the utilities, and also in regulating state aids, which involves challenging national governments. Recent convergence among national approaches has allowed for closer co-operation between EU and national authorities. Indeed there is a strong pattern of decentralization emerging in the operation of EU competition policy. The regulation of competition is increasingly a matter of wider international action. A multi-level pattern is emerging in which Commission officials engage with third-country authorities and international institutions, as well as delegate to national bodies.

Introduction

European competition policy is one of the most developed and successful areas of policy-making in the EU, in terms of both its practical significance for governments, firms and consumers, and its analytical significance for students of European integration. Its principles seek to tackle distortions—both public and private—in the market-place, underpinning and to some extent defining a liberal economic orientation for the EU. Its system of rules constitutes one of the most extensive and effective cornerstones of European law. A strong treaty basis, with extensive enabling powers, allows the Commission to investigate, to decide, and to enforce policy with minimal constraint from other institutions. Thus competition policy offers a prime example of how European integration has been driven by a regulatory dynamic from a powerful and autonomous bureaucracy, utilizing a supranational legal order.

Yet one should not push too far the image of an effective and centralized regulator informed by an avowedly liberal outlook. European competition policy is not conducted in a vacuum, and the European Commission's Directorate-General for Competition (formerly DGIV) is subject to pressures (direct and indirect) from member governments, private firm lobbying and disagreements within the Commission. For all its powers to regulate the conduct of firms and governments, DGIV is constrained by them, a factor perhaps reflected in the very large number of mergers, state aids, and cooperative actions which it approves. Moreover, although competition policy is heavily informed by legal and economic principles, there is a vigorous debate on its precise orientations. The epistemic community of lawyers, academics, and consultants who occupy the grey area between analysis and practice provides a rigorous critique of policy and practice.

Indeed, while DGIV's public image as a successful and competent bureaucracy is largely justified, aspects of its performance have been criticized, not least by those on the receiving end. Frustration over the pace of decisions—in some areas decisions can be subject to extreme delays—indicate an imbalance between workload and resources (*Financial Times*, 11 February 1998). More fundamental are criticisms regarding the informal system of decision-making which characterizes much of the

Commission's work: the Commission has too much discretion and does not reveal the underlying legal and economic reasoning behind decisions (Korah 1997; Neven *et al.* 1998). Such lack of transparency and accountability has also been highlighted by those who feel the Commission is too ideological in its pursuit of competition, imposing deregulation without regard to the social consequences. Yet others argue that the Commission is too sensitive to political pressures, undermining the credibility of competition policy as an independent and impartial regulatory system.

While the many criticisms have been accompanied by a variety of reform proposals, it has been the Commission itself which has taken the initiative in proposing a radical restructuring of the way it operates competition policy. This aims to decentralize much of the conduct of policy, devolving many of the day-to-day decisions to national competition authorities and courts. The Commission would thus be left free to define the strategic orientation of EU policy and to focus on gross anticompetitive behaviour. By retaining the Commission at the core of European competition policy, the reforms also reflect the Commission's defence against attempts to reduce its role and to dilute the principles upon which the policy is based. Thus it retains its powerful institutional basis and doctrinal principles, while a pragmatic approach prevails in day-to-day decision-making, although not immune from criticism.

The evolution and conduct of European competition policy give some support to regulatory and institutionalist approaches to understanding policy-making. The importance of law, in defining and reinforcing the 'relative' autonomy of the authorities, suggests that the regime can be analysed as essentially 'regulatory' in nature (Majone 1996b). The ways in which officials have been able to use forty-year-old treaty provisions and enabling legislation to expand their competence suggest that concepts such as 'lock-in' and 'unintended consequences' (Pierson 1996b) help us to understand the process. Moreover, the current proposals to decentralize competition policy, combined with increased cooperation with non-member states' authorities and the Commission's enthusiasm for a multilateral anti-trust regime, render it an interesting case-study of multi-level governance (Marks *et al.* 1996). The shifts in both the profile and priorities of competition policy—particularly since the 1980s—suggest that 'ideational' approaches are also relevant. In particular, an 'epistemic community' has helped to foster the development of the policy, and policy learning and transfer have played a role by developing national capabilities, thus shaping the overall doctrinal orientation of competition policy (P. M. Haas 1992; C. Bennett and Howlett 1992).

It is almost tempting to see this area of policy-making as a prime example of neofunctionalism, not only as a case-study in its own right (as an instance of a supranational bureaucracy expanding its responsibilities), but also as one of the drivers of spill-over in economic integration as a whole. However, the limits to European competition policy seem to reflect the limitations of the neofunctionalist version of European integration. This chapter deals with the practical shortcomings, as well as the successes, of the policy. Its analytical focus on the institutional and regulatory aspects of competition policy will touch on those other elements of the policy process which qualify our institutionalist approach. In particular it will address the role of bargaining within and between Community institutions, member governments, and firms, and the importance of political leadership in pushing forward and defending the policy.

The chapter begins by reviewing the evolution of European competition policy, and outlining the institutional dynamics of decision-making. The four main elements of policy are then discussed, highlighting the contrast between the potential endowed in the Commission and its practical limitations. The chapter then turns to the interplay between European competition policy and national policies, on the one hand, and extra-EU policies, on the other, considering whether these interactions constitute a new dimension of multi-level governance. The chapter also looks at how competition policy sits with the multiple objectives of European integration. The conclusions consider some of the criticisms made of competition policy in the EU and, in this light, the nature of regulatory policy-making in the EU.

The development of European competition policy

Establishing European competition policy: a break with tradition?

European competition policy is possibly unique in EU policy-making in that it developed almost in tandem with national policies. More so than in other areas, there was a mutual reinforcement between the two levels of policy, in that the work of officials in Brussels gave a higher profile to issues of anti-competitive conduct at the national level, while national officials generally supported the development of a European dimension to their work. That is not to say that there were no rules on these issues prior to the creation of the European Coal and Steel Community (ECSC). There was legislation in some member states, and economists, lawyers, and some officials recognized the need for the rigorous application of such rules. However, the traditional priorities of economic governance in much of western Europe were at odds with the principles of anti-trust. Before (and to a large extent after) the second world war cartels and inter-firm cooperation were the norm across much of the continent. While they had their critics, such practices enjoyed considerable legitimacy (on the basis that they protected jobs, fostered innovation, and prevented wasteful or damaging competition), being defended by much of industry and endorsed by governments (Asbeek Brusse and Griffiths 1997; Tiratsoo and Tomlinson 1997).

The pro-competition tradition was much weaker in Europe than in the USA (where legislation had been introduced at the end of the nineteenth century)—indeed with nearly a half-century's experience of applying anti-trust, US economists and lawyers were highly critical of European practices (Mason 1946). As part of their post-war attempts to redesign multilateral, regional, and national rules on economic management, US officials pressured European governments to accept competition as a fundamental principle of market operation and competition policy as its guarantor. Removing barriers to free trade also required that private restrictions be prohibited. Multilateral efforts in the International Trade Organization (the precursor to the General Agreement on Tariffs and Trade (GATT)) ultimately came to nothing. There was more success at the national and regional levels—indeed the development of anti-trust policy in western Europe could be regarded as one of the successes of US diplomatic attempts to restructure European economic governance.[1] American economists and lawyers encouraged the development of national competition policies in the UK, France, and Germany, though in each case the details were hedged, owing to countervailing resistance from business (Dumez and Jeunemaître 1996; Mercer 1995; Howson and Moggridge 1990; Berghahn 1986; Hardach 1980). These Americans also promoted a dialogue within the Organization for European Economic Cooperation (OEEC) to enable national officials to discuss how to develop their national policies.[2] Their most important contribution, however, was in ensuring that the proposed ECSC incorporated strong anti-trust provisions.

Conceptions of economic governance and productivity, however, were secondary to the question of German economic power in the development of competition rules in the ECSC. Monnet's overall proposals in the Schuman Plan were largely designed to address the question of German reconstruction, and a key consideration in that process was the question of German cartels and concentrations. In the negotiations Monnet drew heavily upon US expertise to draw up anti-trust provisions for the Treaty of Paris (1951) which would rein in cartel-like behaviour (even though other provisions effectively endorsed collusive practices) and be administered on a supra-national basis (Duchêne 1994; Diebold 1959). Although the proposals met with opposition from German, and some other, national trade associations, the Treaty was agreed with the proposed anti-trust measures largely intact (Gillingham 1991).

The provisions of the ECSC covered the principal issues of competition policy, reflecting heavily the content of US anti-trust (Monnet 1976; Majone 1991). Articles 65 and 66 of the Treaty of Paris were particularly restrictive towards cartels and concentrations (reflecting the concerns of the post-war period). While application of the rules was not as rigorous as it could have been (Spierenburg and Poidevin 1994), they became an established part of the infrastructure of integration, likely to shape any further cooperation. The competition rules for the coal and steel industry therefore paved the way for their application to the European Economic Community (EEC) six years later. The experience of their operation and more positive approach of the German authorities (which had been struggling—ultimately successfully—to establish their own anti-trust law) ensured the inclusion of the rules in the Treaty of Rome (MacLachan and Swann 1967; Majone 1991). While the EEC provisions were not as supranational as those in the ECSC, and had a narrower scope (mergers were not explicitly included in the Treaty of Rome), they were still strongly pro-competition, and arguably more liberal in some respects.

Policy since 1958

The subsequent fortunes of European competition policy can be attributed to the strength of the rules and the willingess of the Commission to apply them. Article 3(f) (EEC) sets the objective of ensuring that competition in a common market is not distorted. This objective is implemented through the rules on competition contained in Articles 85 to 94 of the original Treaty of Rome (now 81 to 89), particularly 85 and 86 (now 81 and 82) on respectively anti-trust and abuse of dominant position, 90 (now 86) on public undertakings, and 92 (now 87) on state aids. The other provisions largely cover implementation and transitional measures. These articles set out what constitutes anti-competitive conduct and also the conditions whereby exemptions might be granted. They provide scope for firms and governments to negotiate with the Commission, and for other principles of integration to inform decisions. It is a measure of the role of competition policy in making the Community work, and of the importance which the architects of the Treaty attached to it, that it should be so rooted in the Treaty and that those provisions should have driven policy ever since. As a result, the policy has a strong legal basis, and competition policy and European law have ever since been intertwined.

The responsibility for administering these rules was granted to the Commission by the Council in a series of regulations (most importantly the implementing Regulation 17/1962). Operationally the task falls to DGIV and the Commissioner responsible for competition policy. Regulation 17/1962 provided the Commission with a number of powers, including: a notification process; consultation procedures with member states; and investigative and fining powers. The most dramatic are the so-called 'dawn raids' powers. Although few such raids occur, the Commission possesses a number of key powers, such as the right to examine company records and accounts, to enter any premises and seek explanations, and to levy fines for infringement. The Regulation was, and remains, one of the most powerful in the repertoire of the Commission.

Why did the Commission obtain such powerful weapons? Did member governments see a significant delegation of power as necessary to keep the Community honest, a motive which some have judged as characteristic of a broader delegation to the supranational level (Garrett 1995; Gatsios and Seabright 1989)? Or was it because the expectations of how the powers would be used were low and thus subsequent outcomes 'unintended' (Pierson 1996b)? The latter may have been so for member governments—understandably, given their limited experience of competition policy in domestic settings—yet there was a greater awareness of the potential role of the rules amongst Community officials. They took a very clear position on the central role of competition policy in underpinning the common market (MacLachan and Swann 1967). This determination may have been shared by national officials, who may have recognized the value of European competition policy in reinforcing the status of competition policy more generally. There is evidence that they certainly shared a similar outlook, and had extensive contacts with one another, meeting in official fora such as the OEEC and unofficial fora such as the Ligue Contre la Concurrence Déloyale (a think-tank which primarily comprised academic lawyers and economists, but with many members also holding official or advisory positions at national and EU levels).[3]

The full potential of the Regulation—and of the competition rules as a whole—was not exploited for some time, however. The fortunes of European competition policy have in many ways reflected those of European integration. Thus the years following Regulation 17 were marked by a slow consolidation of the Commission's role; much as elsewhere, the period was one of incremental accumulation of responsibilities and the tentative pursuit of common policies. If progress was slow, however, it was mainly because of the consequences of Regulation 17 itself. In the wake of its implementation by the mid-1960s over 35,000 notifications were made to the Commission, forcing it to adopt 'coping strategies', a mixture of block exemptions and informal procedures (Jong 1975). The 1960s were also a period when the ECJ was finding its feet, though its emerging jurisprudence was to be of considerable importance for competition policy (notably that of direct effect). Other aspects of competition policy were scarcely developed.

Over the 1970s the conduct of competition policy was rather stifled by resistance from member governments both to the exercise of existing Treaty powers (the state aids rules) and to the new policy assignments (mergers). In large part this resistance reflected the broader economic problems of a period when many felt that competition policy should be only lightly applied, that the rules should not be fully enforced, and that 'crisis cartels' were necessary in many of the heavy industries hit by recession and international competition (Swann 1983). The (non-)application of some parts of competition policy reflected the wider institutional sclerosis besetting the Community at this time, though in other respects (not least in terms of Court activism) there was a growing body of case law and Commission decisions, which underpinned the credibility of the policy in those areas where it was able to function.

The full assertion of competition policy was to be one of the hallmarks of the relaunch of the Community in the 1980s. Indeed the intensification of European policy-making in the 1980s was in part driven by the more activist anti-trust stance of the Commission, broadly reinforced by ECJ judgments. A more dynamic Commission gave greater emphasis to economic policies, which were in tune with the underlying philosophy of competition policy; this was no longer at odds with the thrust of other Community policies and in some respects was in the vanguard. More particularly, from 1985 onwards successive Commissioners provided aggressive political leadership, empowering their officials to make more use of their powers: first Frans Andriessen, then Peter Sutherland, then Leon Brittan. DGIV's work was shaped and endorsed by these Commissioners, willing to exploit the Treaty and the enabling legislation, and to push for more powers where needed.

The history of European integration in the 1990s is to an extent marked by the consequences of an overambitious agenda, with competition policy one of the targets of the subsequent backlash. Even before the public reaction to Maastricht and the Treaty on European Union (TEU), there were calls for reining in, or hollowing out, the European competition powers. Yet competition policy had become so central to European integration and so locked in to a particular model of economic development that it survived largely intact. Continued strong leadership from Commissioner van Miert was also a factor. The tone of policy became more pragmatic, and the focus shifted to reforming the processes rather than embarking on new adventures, as was demonstrated in a series of controversial decisions.

The institutional process

Over the past forty years the application of European competition policy has broadened partly as a result of new competences (granted by member governments in the Council) and partly through the skilful application of existing powers by the Commission, broadly endorsed by the courts. The process has been largely cumulative—a mixture of 'learning by doing', incremental and phased reforms, and, above all, bargaining within the Commission, and between it and other actors.

Institutionally, there are few areas of European policy-making where the Commission is more central or more autonomous than in competition policy. In addition to playing its traditional roles of treaty guardian and policy initiator to the full, it has, particularly since the 1980s, exercised a strong regulatory role as well. Regulation 17/1962 gave the Commission extensive powers to investigate, to adjudicate, to enforce, and to punish, while other regulations (for example Regulation 19/1965) fleshed out its role in regulating the conduct of the private sector. The Merger Regulation, eventually adopted in 1989, provided the basis for scrutiny and enforcement of concentrations, though not perhaps the same degree of discretion. In other areas the Commission has relied mainly on the treaty provisions to carry out its role. Article 86.3 (ex 90.3) allows the Commission to apply the competition rules to sectors 'of general economic interest' (broadly state enterprises and public utilities), without requiring the approval of member governments. The state aids rules were developed without recourse to member government approval until the Commission decided to seek procedural rules in 1997.

The Commission is at the core of competition policy, and DGIV is at the core of the Commission's activities. Responsible for administering the policy (handling individual cases, drafting policy initiatives, and liaising with officials in member governments and beyond), DGIV is widely regarded as one of the most coherent and 'driven' of the Commission services. It is organized into a series of directorates dealing with either discrete regulatory tasks (mergers and state aids) or economic sectors (services, basic industries, information technology), with Directorate A coordinating policy. The Director-General is responsible for the overall direction of policy and liaises with the Competition Commissioner. Longevity is a feature of DGIV; many of the officials spend in excess of ten years there, and there have only been six Directors-General. Such continuity contributes to the strong ethos which pervades DGIV, a mixture of economic liberalism (though officials are not the doctrinaire 'Ayatollahs' portrayed by some critics) and commitment to the law as a vehicle for integration. Needless to say, lawyers and economists make up the bulk of the policy staff (with the traditional dominance of the former gradually being eroded). With 150 policy officials out of a total directorate staff of 400, DGIV is quite substantial, but many believe that, even with modest increases in staffing in recent years, the numbers are low compared with the range of responsibilities and workload (Cini and McGowan 1998).

The bulk of DGIV's work is case-based, comprising specific complaints and notifications, as well as 'own initiative' investigations, in each area of competition policy. Officials take the lead in handling such cases, liaising with national officials (either bilaterally or through the Advisory Committees for restrictive practices, concentrations, and state aids), Legal Services, the Commissioner's *cabinet*, and other interested DGs. The final decision rests with the college of commissioners. While most such decisions are relatively straightforward, there are instances where disagreements emerge either within the college itself (on national, ideological or sectoral grounds) or at inter-service level. Inter-service rivalries do exist: DGIII (industry) and the 'sectoral' directorates (e.g. DGVII (transport), DGXIII (telecommunications), DGXVII (energy)) have been the most likely to challenge the positions of DGIV (just as DGIV has often pushed for more liberal policies when it is consulted by other DGs). From DGIV's perspective other DGs may seem so close to incumbent producer interests as to be 'captured' by them. Some such disagreements have spilled over into the public domain.[4] The interplay between the Competition Commissioner and DGIV, on the one hand, and the rest of the Commission, on the other, limits the autonomy of the officials concerned. However, their role and room for manœuvre is still considerable, not least since many of its decisions are carried out on an informal basis. Given the volume of cases for the Commission, it has chosen to settle many without recourse to a formal decision, thus exploiting the degree of discretion available.

However, it would be wrong to suggest that the Commission is a law unto itself in making competition policy. As in other areas it is subject to legal challenge. The ECJ adjudicates on the basis of complaints from the Commission, member governments, or firms, or in response to a referral from a national court. In a policy domain where legal powers are crucial, the ECJ's role has been especially important in setting out the limits of the Commission's powers. Overall, however, the trend in the jurisprudence has been to strengthen the role of the Commission. The ECJ has generally found in the Commission's favour, and in some landmark cases (such as *Continental Can* in 1972 and *Philip Morris* in 1987) has extended the scope of its responsibilities. In a few instances it has circumscribed and criticized the Commission, mainly on procedural grounds. Since 1989 an additional Court of First Instance has been responsible for the bulk of cases relating to competition policy, its creation reflecting the volume of competition cases. The main ECJ can still be involved when the Commission seeks to appeal against a judgment (Bellamy and Child 1996).

Thus the centre of gravity lies with the bureaucratic and judicial institutions of the EU rather than the political and representative institutions. As analysts and advocates of the regulatory state might expect, the roles of the European Parliament (EP), Council of Ministers, and European Council are relatively limited. Legislation in the Council has of course been required to establish regulatory powers and to extend competences (though it has not always been necessary in the latter). Yet the amount of legislation required has been fairly small by comparison with other areas of policy-making, and correspondingly the Council and EP have had few opportunities to shape the contours and content of competition policy. The bulk of day-to-day activities, and even strategic initiatives, are carried out without formal recourse to the Council.

That is not to say that there are not extensive contacts with member governments, however; clearly national authorities have been (and will be increasingly) involved in both individual cases and broader policy definition, while more informally ministries and ministers will lobby at both the administrative and political levels (not least when, as in state aids and public enterprises, they are the targets of the policy). But the Commission does not need to embark on the same sort of negotiations which it must do in almost every other area of policy in order to get things done. The possibility for member states to clip the wings of European competition policy arises when the Intergovernmental Conferences (IGCs) take place. Some member states have floated ideas for institutional and substantive changes to competition policy in the past, for example the German and French governments in the negotiations leading to the Treaty of Amsterdam. However, no changes (beyond renumbering and attendant minor editorial amendments) have been imposed. The weight of the original treaty provisions and the inability or unwillingness of member governments to force the issue has protected them. The minimal role of the EP in competition policy might raise fears of a democratic deficit in the conduct of anti-trust. The EP has only a consultative role in legislation on competition policy. Yet it does play a scrutiny role in obliging the Commission to respond to its concerns through its opinion on the *Annual Report on Competition Policy*, and at its regular Question Time. Commissioners also regularly appear before the Parliament to explain and defend their actions.

The limited scope for political control means that some of the most usual avenues for lobbying the Commission (through member governments and MEPs) are more limited than in other areas of policy-making. Some national influence is exercised via the representatives on the Advisory Committees, which meet periodically with the Commission. Occasionally individual Commissioners argue in the College on the basis of national loyalties (the *de Havilland* case being a particularly blatant example[5]). Yet the role of interest groups is rather different in this area from that in most other policy areas. Some lobbying rests on broadly based attempts by trade associations to shape the contours of policy on the few occasions where opinions are invited and legislation under consideration. German and French employers' organizations were actively involved in the debate over the ECSC anti-trust provisions, while the International Chamber of Commerce sought to influence the implementation of the EEC competition rules in the early 1960s (Gillingham 1991; ICC 1958).

More recently the Confederation of British Industry (CBI) and Union of Industrial and Employers' Confederations of Europe (UNICE) have argued for major changes in how European competition policy operates (*Financial Times*, 13 June 1995; *European Report*, no. 2095, 23 December 1995). Such lobbying is broadly welcomed by the Commission, which in recent years has actively sought the opinions of business and consumers by issuing consultation documents to frame changes in policy. Case-specific lobbying takes place on a day-to-day basis, with firms and/or their lawyers engaging with Commission officials and, in high-profile cases, the Director-General or even the Commissioner. Somewhere in between these two extremes is the continuing debate on competition policy by the epistemic community of economic and legal experts. Their influence can be seen in the way in which the approach to competition policy has become more rooted in economic reasoning in the past ten years.

The conduct of competition policy

Anti-trust—the core of competition policy

Articles 81 and 82 (ex 85 and 86) deal with those activities which are usually regarded as the core of anti-trust policy: the range of private business practices which can be construed as anti-competitive. As noted, the legislation which implemented the provisions—Council Regulation 17/1962—provided the Commission with extremely wide-ranging powers for the task. However, the way in which these powers have been defined and exercised has placed a serious burden upon the Commission, one which has largely been managed through an informal process of negotiation between it, national authorities, private firms, and their lawyers. While this informal system has helped the Commission to 'cope' with the demands placed upon it, there is a widespread belief—inside and outside the Commission—that the powers bestowed in the early 1960s may no longer be appropriate to a modern globalizing economy and an EU of more than twenty states.

The bulk of the Commission's workload has revolved around Article 81 (ex 85), which covers the classic areas of market-sharing and price-fixing activities, cartels

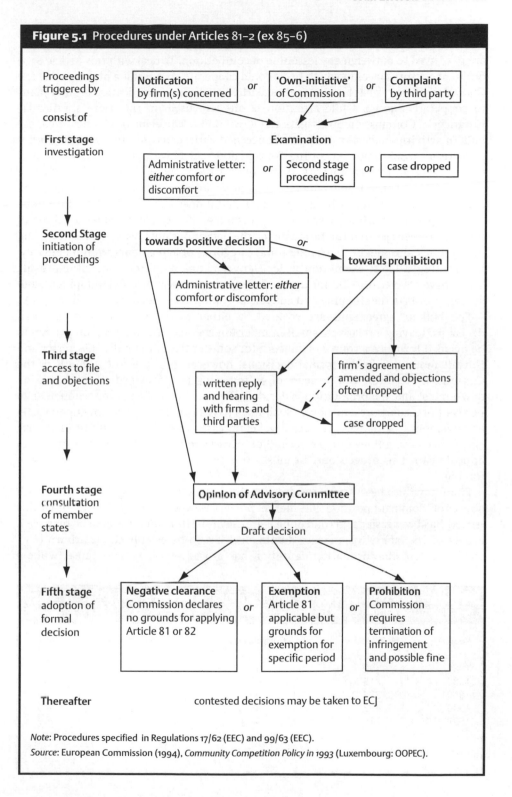

Figure 5.1 Procedures under Articles 81–2 (ex 85–6)

Proceedings triggered by

| Notification by firm(s) concerned | or | 'Own-initiative' of Commission | or | Complaint by third party |

consist of

First stage investigation

Examination

| Administrative letter: *either* comfort *or* discomfort | or | Second stage proceedings | or | case dropped |

Second Stage initiation of proceedings

| towards positive decision | *or* | towards prohibition |

Administrative letter: *either* comfort *or* discomfort

Third stage access to file and objections

written reply and hearing with firms and third parties

firm's agreement amended and objections often dropped

case dropped

Fourth stage consultation of member states

Opinion of Advisory Committee

Draft decision

Fifth stage adoption of formal decision

| **Negative clearance** Commission declares no grounds for applying Article 81 or 82 | or | **Exemption** Article 81 applicable but grounds for exemption for specific period | or | **Prohibition** Commission requires termination of infringement and possible fine |

Thereafter   contested decisions may be taken to ECJ

Note: Procedures specified in Regulations 17/62 (EEC) and 99/63 (EEC).

Source: European Commission (1994), *Community Competition Policy in 1993* (Luxembourg: OOPEC).

and other forms of collusion. Indeed the Article covers most forms of cooperation between firms, including many legitimate activities, or activities where the benefits are perceived to outweigh any lessening of competition. To deal with this Article 81(3) outlined circumstances in which firms could cooperate. As a result a major part of the Commission's work has been in dealing with firms seeking clarification of their plans to cooperate. Indeed, while attention is often focused on the more spectacular instances of Commission investigations ('dawn raids', 'cartel-busting', fines, etc.), the bulk of activities under Article 81 are concerned with such cases (though many other cases result from complaints or the Commission's own investigations). The extent of these cases—and the complexity of the investigations themselves—is such that the Commission has had to introduce various procedures to handle the workload, notably the 'comfort letter', where it indicates that it does not consider a venture to be anti-competitive. Such a letter does not have legal force, but provides a degree of security to firms (even if the rationale for the decision is not always clear). The Commission has also sought to exclude some categories of agreements from its purview by granting a block exemption (a legislative matter requiring Council approval). These have covered distribution agreements, patents, research and development, and arrangements in the shipping and air transport industries (Bellamy and Child 1996).

The bulk of agreements are covered by either block exemptions or informal decisions, leaving a relatively small number (on average fifteen a year since 1962) to be decided formally, a source of concern for some critics of the policy (Forrester and Norrall 1996). It is in the formal decisions, however, that the full strength of the Commission's powers can be seen, often involving full investigations (on occasion dawn raids) and, if a prohibition is decided, the possibility of fines for as much as 10 per cent of a company's turnover. Such fines have been imposed mainly upon cartel arrangements, particularly in recent years (in cases such as the 1998 *District Heating Pipe Cartel*, where fines of over 90 million ecus were imposed). Although firms can appeal against such decisions, in most cases the Commission's actions have been upheld.

Fines have also been levied in cases involving Article 82 (ex 86), which deals with abuses of 'dominant position' (i.e. market power). However, pursuing cases under this Article has been easier said than done, because of the difficult criteria to be met: each aspect of the 'abuse' of 'market dominance' has to be established (Fairburn *et al.* 1986). The question of market definition has proved problematic because, while a

Table 5.1 New cases before the Commission under Articles 81 and 82 (ex 85 and 86) and 65 and 66 (ECSC) (no.)

Year	Notification	Complaints	Own initiative	Total
1980	190	58	51	299
1985	213	66	25	304
1990	294	104	81	479
1995	403	146	46	595
1998	216	92	101	509

Source: Commission (1981–)

Table 5.2 Decisions under Articles 81 and 82 (ex 85 and 86 (EEC)) and 65 and 66 (ECSC) (no.)

Year	Formal	Informal	Cases pending
1980	25	183	4,203
1985	23	1,185	3,313
1990	46	928	2,772
1995	21	456	1,185
1998	42	539	1,204

Source: Commission (1981–).

firm may have a large market share inside the Community, this may reflect the scale of operations necessary to compete internationally. There may also be problems in identifying the nature of the market, especially as regards the availability of substitutes. The definition of 'dominance' can embrace not only market share but also other factors, such as the degree of vertical integration, or the structure of the market. Moreover, the possession of such a dominant position may not be in itself illegal; the act of abuse also has to be identified. Given these problems, it is perhaps not surprising that the mechanism has been used in relatively few cases (the first of which, *Gema*, was not brought until 1971). However, a sufficiently large number of cases has been decided upon to indicate some aspects of the Commission's approach, such as use of fidelity arrangements, discriminatory pricing, and access to technology. The burden of proof and the scope for imaginative interpretation of both the law and economics of market dominance mean that the Commission has fully pursued relatively few cases on the basis of this Article. A number of cases are settled by consent, obviating the need for a formal Commission decision and highlighting again the importance of informal negotiations.

Reform of the application of these two key Articles has been under discussion for some time, driven by the burden of workload, by criticisms of the Commission's own procedures, and by the prospect of enlargement (Commission 1999*d*). Yet the very powers enjoyed by the Commission are such that it has adopted a cautious approach towards reform, seeking to maintain the initiative as far as possible: it does not want to surrender its autonomy and discretion for the sake of procedural simplifications. Thus the Commission has sought to guide the reform process itself, having fended off attempts to create a European Cartel Office on the German model at the 1996–7 IGC. As Alex Schaub, the current Director-General, has argued, reforms did not need 'to be a matter for an Intergovernmental Conference but for the competent community institutions to propose and to decide' (Schaub 1998*b*). Since 1997 the Commission has pursued reform through a mix of amendments to secondary legislation, revised interpretative guidelines, and closer cooperation with national authorities. The first steps included a revised *de minimis* rule (excluding cases of minor importance), a notice of cooperation with national authorities (see below), and procedural reforms (Commission 1981–*28th Annual Report*, 1999)

Although the final shape of these core reforms was not settled at the time of writing, the priorities and the likely orientation of change seems clear. The first step, a change in the treatment of vertical (or distributive) agreements, covers one of the most common forms of inter-firm cooperation. Rules currently exist for exempting the bulk of such arrangements, via a series of block exemptions and sectoral rules, which impose a highly legalistic and form-based process. However, they are regarded as administratively cumbersome, placing a straitjacket on business. In a 1997 Green Paper the Commission outlined plans to adopt a principle more firmly based on economic effects, which would extend across the economy as a whole, reduce the compliance costs for firms, and eliminate the need for notification (Commission 1997e). The system would centre on a block exemption which stated what was not exempted, a system of thresholds under which cases would not be investigated, as well as other measures to streamline cooperation which was not anti-competitive. The measures required procedural amendments to Regulations 17/1962 and 19/1965. These were agreed by the Council in May 1999, paving the way for more substantive measures to follow in 2000 (Council Regulations 1215–16/1999).

The most radical part of the reform process is an overhaul of Regulation 17/1962 itself. A White Paper (really a Green Paper, since it was intended to serve as the basis for consultations) was published by the Commission in early 1999; any changes are likely to enter into force around 2001 (Commission 1999d). The Commission suggests a refocusing and a redistribution of responsibilities, partly with the prospect of an enlarged EU in mind. The measures include a simplification of scrutinizing procedures and an abolition of the notification system. The changes would remove much of the burden of compliance for firms and of processing for the Commission. Instead the intention is to leave much of the application of rules to national courts and national authorities. Such decentralization will be facilitated by plans to make the whole of Article 81 (ex 85) directly applicable, including the provisions on exemptions, which hitherto had been an exclusively Commission competence. There will be a new system of review and pre-emption by the Commission to ensure coherence and to prevent divergences in the application of competition policy across the Union. The final reform would be a more rigorous enforcement of the rules, establishing a swifter procedure for handling complaints. Indeed, one of the aims of the reform is to enable the Commission to concentrate on serious abuses of competition rules, for example cartels.[6]

State aids: controlling or condoning subsidies?

European competition policy has been as much directed at governments as it has been at private firms, and a central concern has been the regulation of state aids. These have been one of the ways in which governments have sought to steer their economies, and a multiplicity of objectives have been invoked to justify public intervention to support industry: the development of new industries or industrial capabilities (the latter through support for skills and research); the reduction of regional imbalances; the attraction of foreign investment; the maintenance of employment; and so forth. While such interventions are inconsistent with the principle of a free market, some types of subsidy are more justifiable than others. There is, for example, a difference between government funds aimed at the provision of public goods (such as the enhancement of skills or the development of infrastructures), and aid which is essentially mercantilist or protectionist in intent (such as the subsidizing of firms operating in internationally competitive markets which would otherwise go bankrupt).[7]

Differentiating between such purposes and minimizing the extent to which aid distorts the European economy are key tasks for EU policy. But the underlying rationale for an EU role is the need to monitor and, if necessary, prohibit member governments' actions. As the providers of support, it is unlikely that governments will be willing to regulate themselves. Yet, the fact that governments are so closely involved, as subsidizers and the main decision-makers within the EU, has made the development of a collective state aids policy difficult. While the regulation of private business is essentially a private matter, entailing behind-the-scenes negotiations and lobbying, the regulation of state aids has been prone to highly public conflicts between the Commission and member governments in particular cases. The development of an effective system of rules has emerged only since the 1980s, and even now the Commission's capacity has been weakened as a result of internal differences (inter-service and inter-Commissioner disagreements), and by the need to negotiate with governments and firms over the terms and conditions of aid. While such features are characteristic of other aspects of the competition policy process, in this area of policy the balance of power probably rests with the member states. Although there are cases where the Commission has challenged member governments' support for an industry, these instances are very much the exception: in most cases the Commission approves the aid.

The provisions of Article 87(1) (ex 92) set out a tough control on these aids which distort or threaten to distort competition. While this strongly worded prohibition is moderated by a series of provisions which permit aid to be given, explicit permission has to be given by the Commission. The process is achieved through the following mechanisms: a requirement that member governments give the Commission prior notification of any plan to provide aid; a system of review carried out by the Commission; and a procedure whereby the Commission can modify or suppress an aid. As in other areas of competition policy, the Commission has sought to develop streamlining measures, whereby it establishes principles for broad areas of aid, examines national programmes, and then leaves member governments to subsidize within that system. These cover: regional aid; horizontal aids (for research and development, small and medium enterprises (SMEs), environmental protection, employment, and restructuring firms in difficulty); and sectoral aids (for steel, coal, shipbuilding, air transport, banking, etc.). The Commission remains free to scrutinize particular programmes or instances of public support (Commission 1998f).

For much of the EU's history the Commission applied its state aid rules with a very light touch. As far back as the early days of the ECSC it was clear that major programmes of subsidy were in place for the coal industry, yet the High Authority did little to enforce the rules. In the decades after the creation of the EEC the Commission played a very modest role in state aid control. During the economic problems of the 1970s and early 1980s subsidies were to some extent approved as part of a process of industrial adjustment (Gilchrist and Deacon 1990). This pragmatic neglect has to be seen in the context of the overall status of European integration and the European economy at the time. Moreover, when the Commission did attempt to assert itself (as with its efforts to find out about state aid to public enterprises), it encountered such a

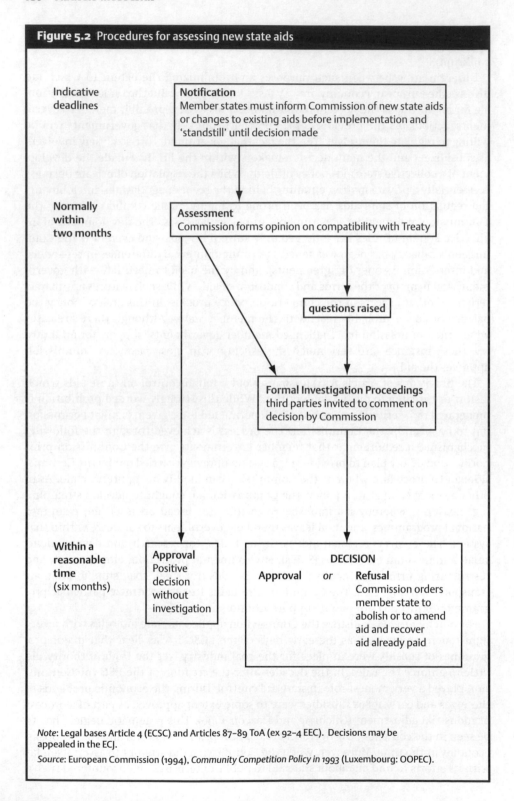

Figure 5.2 Procedures for assessing new state aids

Indicative deadlines

Notification
Member states must inform Commission of new state aids or changes to existing aids before implementation and 'standstill' until decision made

Normally within two months

Assessment
Commission forms opinion on compatibility with Treaty

questions raised

Formal Investigation Proceedings
third parties invited to comment on decision by Commission

Within a reasonable time (six months)

Approval
Positive decision without investigation

DECISION
Approval   or   **Refusal**
Commission orders member state to abolish or to amend aid and recover aid already paid

Note: Legal bases Article 4 (ECSC) and Articles 87–89 ToA (ex 92–4 EEC). Decisions may be appealed in the ECJ.

Source: European Commission (1994), *Community Competition Policy in 1993* (Luxembourg: OOPEC).

lack of cooperation that it was obliged to use Article 90 to enforce some transparency (see next section). A more active line by the Commission emerged in the 1980s, particularly in the wake of the single market programme (see Chapter 4). The White Paper programme was largely aimed at removing various distortions, many of them the result of government policies, in order to create a single market. The continued, and possibly increased, use of another government measure—subsidies—would jeopardize the single market. Some commentators even warned that, without controls, the Community members might resort to a subsidy war to support national industries (Pelkmans and Winters 1988).

Whether it was a result of the single market programme or a function of aggressive leadership by Commissioners Sutherland and Brittan, the Commission began to take a much more rigorous line towards subsidies from the mid-1980s onwards. A key element was an attempt to increase the transparency of public subsidies. In 1989 Brittan launched the first in a series of studies highlighting the degree of state aid granted to industry, services, and other economic sectors. Since then there have been seven surveys, tracking the levels of financial support given by different member states (Commission 1989–). The general impression over time was of a gradual decline in the levels of aid, but with big discrepancies in the levels offered in some of the richer member states. These surveys have played a dual role, highlighting to governments and citizens the cost of subsidy programmes in their own country and enabling them to compare, and helping the Commission to pinpoint, the greatest excesses (Brittan 1992).

This latter objective ties in with the other element in the Commission's policy—a refocusing of the rules on aid. Whereas hitherto the state aids policy had evolved on the basis of notices and guidelines issued by the Commission itself, the need to streamline some procedures and to obtain new powers required legislation. In May 1998 the Council approved a Regulation 994/1998. This allows the Commission to exempt *en bloc* aid through the various horizontal and regional programmes. Government subsidies within these schemes are almost always approved, and hence the exemption allows the Commission to concentrate on more serious cases. In November 1998 the Council also agreed to a procedural Regulation 83/1999, to streamline, codify, and strengthen the Commission's procedures for monitoring state aid. This provides a greater degree of legal certainty for member governments and gives the Commission not only a stronger legal basis for its actions but also some new powers (including the right to inspect offices). The Commission also hopes that national authorities will play a bigger role in dealing with cases, though here the expectation is that plaintiffs will challenge government actions in national courts, rather than that national authorities will challenge their fellow officials (Commission 1999e).

The need for new rules is supported by a glance at the Commission's workload. If anything, the Commission has been more active than in recent years. Yet for all its efforts (and the tone of policy statements) the proportion of cases where the Commission reaches a decision to ban aid is very small. Indeed, while the Commission seems willing to confront governments on the principles, in practice its bark is worse than its bite. Although there are exceptions, such as the 1991 *Renault* decision, in most major aid cases—airlines (at various times Air France, Alitalia, Iberia, Olympic, Aer Lingus, and Sabena), coal (the German and Spanish industries in particular), banking (notoriously Crédit Lyonnais)—the Commission has agreed weak compromises with

Table 5.3 Commission state aid activity, 1990–1998 (no.)

Year	1990	1992	1994	1996	1998
Total decisions	492	552	527	474	460
No objection after preliminary examination	415	473	440	373	308
Proceedings initiated	34	30	40	43	66
Positive final decisions	20	25	15	14	16
Negative final decisions	14	8	3	23	31
Conditional	0	7	2	3	8
New cases					
Measures notified	429	459	526	553	714
Measures not notified	105	102	68	91	135

Notes: The figures do not necessarily tally; some proceedings are not decided in the year that they are started.

Source: Commission (1981–).

the relevant member governments, approving the aid subject to relatively modest conditions. Of course such decisions can be, and increasingly are, challenged in the Courts (along with some of the few negative decisions) but the record so far has been one where the Courts have generally backed the Commission.

Article 86 (ex 90): regulating state ownership and liberalizing monopolies

The higher profile of competition policy has been only partly due to increased activism on anti-trust and state aids matters. In an increasingly integrated European economy, a vigorous policy has been needed to prevent private and public distortions of competition from undermining the single market. Competition policy has, however, also been an important mechanism for extending the scope of the single market.[8] It has been instrumental in spreading its reach to areas of the European economy which were hitherto not only shielded from competition, but also widely perceived to be best organized as monopolies. Key examples are the public utilities of energy, communications, and transport, as well as other sectors such as insurance, banking, sport, and media. Making and monitoring markets in these sectors has been a very visible part of the Commission's work programme since the mid-1980s. This has also been a highly controversial development, leading to many criticisms of the 'deregulatory' thrust of the Commission, as it challenged national champions and their governmental supporters (Stoffaes 1995).

The process should be viewed more accurately as one of regulatory reform than deregulation, moving away from monopolies towards competition. In pursuing such changes the Commission was to the fore—though not alone—in shifting the balance: the UK had already begun this process in the 1980s, as had some other north European states, then outside the EU, at that time. The US authorities had been engaged in similar reforms from the 1970s in some industries. These national policies constituted important precedents for the Commission in making the case for reform and, in the case of the reformist members, provided an important source of support in negotiating changes with the less enthusiastic member governments.

The liberalization process was facilitated by the use—or the threat of use—of the hitherto dormant Article 86 (ex 90). This Article addresses sectors of 'a general economic interest' and requires that the competition rules be applied to these sectors, as long as they do not prevent the fulfilment of the general interest. To the extent that the rules could be applied, Article 86.3 allowed for them to be imposed directly by the Commission without reference to the Council. Sectors of general economic interest were interpreted as publicly owned firms and natural monopolies, and infrastructural and utility industries. What is surprising is why such an Article found its way into the Treaty of Rome in the late 1950s and why it was not employed for more than twenty years. The case of Article 86 illustrates not so much institutional lock-in, as 'lock-up'—the incorporation of powers, which, for various reasons, were not used in the immediate aftermath of agreement, but were available to be deployed in later years. This had not been the intention of the treaty negotiators—they primarily wanted to address the problem of large state-owned enterprises in competitive sectors, a concern of smaller member states, faced by the large nationalized enterprises of Italy and France (Papaconstantinou 1988; Marenco 1983; Schindler 1970; Deringer 1964). This original objective of the provisions has been largely by-passed in the wake of extensive privatization in recent years (though it was initially used in the the late 1970s to make more transparent government relations with public enterprises).[9] Instead it has been its use as a way of liberalizing utility markets that has rendered it controversial.

The actual use of Article 86 as a means of prising open utility markets has been confined to the telecoms sector. From 1988 onwards the Commission employed this Article to introduce competition into the key telecoms services. While the opposition of member governments to this strategy receded, not least in the face of Court rulings in favour of the Commission, the direct imposition of such rules has remained controversial. The Commission had acquired a credible instrument for bringing about liberalization, but one which risked alienating some member governments. As a result Article 86 has been threatened as a lever in the gradual liberalization of other utility markets, rather than directly employed. Instead the Commission has preferred to use other treaty provisions, notably Article 95 (ex 100A), in harmonization of legislation, as the basis for several proposals. Competition policy has, however, been important in opening up the energy and transport sectors (Argyris 1989, 1993; Brittan 1992).

Even so this experience of Article 86, including the jurisprudential struggles between supporters and opponents of the provision, demonstrates how treaty provisions can resonate and empower in ways scarcely anticipated forty years ago. Indeed, for all the rhetoric about utility liberalization, the Commission has proved remarkably amenable to an incremental and drawn-out process of reform. Most of the reforms have been phased in over periods of about ten years, giving national champions and governments plenty of time to adjust (even though such opportunities were not always exploited). The telecoms reforms have been in place since the beginning of 1998, followed later that year by air transport, and energy liberalization began a phased introduction in early 1999. The major remaining targets of postal services and railways appear to be too sensitive for the Commission to tackle by anything other than the most gradualist strategies, and it may be that these remain liberalizations too far. The Commission's strategy here is partly a result of practical politics, in particular the concern not to alienate too many member governments (its previous initiatives having provoked some member governments to seek a reining-in of its powers; see below). DGIV has also had to strike compromises with other DGs, especially since it is often not *chef de file* in these cases. The economic uncertainties associated with such radical reforms have also played a part. Yet the momentum for change exists, as some governments embark on reforms in advance of EU rules, and as consumers and new entrants press for greater market access. Hence reform may prove irresistible in the medium term.

In any case, in both liberalized and unliberalized markets there is a greater will-ingness on the part of the Commission to apply the competition rules. This has been clearest in sectors where liberalization is already under way, and where the need to address the transition from monopoly to competition has been pressing. A particular problem relates to the position of incumbent firms and how to ensure that new entrants are treated fairly, not least in terms of access to the networks which are at the core of many of these industries. As competition begins to bite, another problem has been how to treat state aids in these sectors, particularly where established players have not restructured and in some cases face bankruptcy.

However, the biggest challenge has been how to deal with the corporate realign-ments which seem to accompany structural change. Former national champions seek to develop new ties so as to ensure global competitiveness, while consumers and others fear a *de facto* cartelization and consolidation under the guise of joint ventures and mergers. The Commission has been reluctant to establish itself as the sole Euro-pean regulator, though it has been keen to ensure that independent regulation emerges within the member states. Yet in many respects the problems that need to be tackled mean that it is being drawn into such a role.[10]

Merger regulation: worth the wait?

I have drawn attention to the way in which the Commission has been able to build upon the treaty provisions to establish new policy orientations. Yet widening the responsibilities of competition policy does present problems for the Commission. This can be clearly seen in the case of merger control, excluded from the original purview of the EEC (though not the ECSC). The Commission's attempts to develop an explicit competence took seventeen years, punctuated by attempts (largely supported by the Court) to reinterpret its existing powers to cover the issue.

The failure to include a merger control provision in the Treaty of Rome seems less surprising from the vantage-point of the 1950s. Such provisions were not found in national competition legislation, and their inclusion in the ECSC might be attributed to the special nature of the industries covered and the influence of the USA on the drafting of those rules. Indeed, if anything, the primary concern within Europe at that time was to encourage concentration in order to build up larger firms capable of competing in world markets (Frazer 1992). Although by the 1970s the Commission shared this view of the need for European champions, it sought to control those concentrations which might be deemed anti-competitive. It proposed a regulation on merger control in 1973, but this was opposed by a number of member governments.

The Commission, to the extent that it intervened on mergers, used its general powers under the competition rules of the Treaty, both Articles 81 and 82, and support from decisions of the ECJ. An intervention by the Commission, in the *Continental Can* case, forbidding a merger on the grounds of abuse of dominant position, was upheld by the Court in 1973. Article 81 has been used primarily *vis-à-vis* merger-type arrangements, such as joint ventures and minority shareholdings. With regard to the latter, the Court upheld in 1987 another Commission action, the *Philip Morris* case (K. George and Jacquemin 1990).

Although the special circumstances surrounding these cases meant that such actions were relatively novel, the prospect of the Commission intervening in a series of mergers on the basis of a Court ruling prompted the Council finally to agree to a Mergers Regulation (Bulmer 1994*b*; Montagnon 1990). The prospect of the Commission exercising its discretion, particularly in the light of the increased activism of DGIV under Commissioners Sutherland and Brittan, persuaded the member governments to opt for a more predictable set of rules. However, it was also clear that, in the context of intensifying economic integration, there would be more corporate consolidation across the EU. Firms themselves came to see the advantages of a 'one-stop-shop' for reviewing their mergers.

The Merger Regulation 4064/1989, which entered into force in September 1990, covers mergers where the global turnover of the firms involved is 5 billion ecus and the EU turnover of each firm is 250 million ecus. Mergers which involve firms the turnover of which is concentrated in a single member state are not covered by the Regulation. The Regulation also sets out a number of criteria which should be taken into account, including market structure, consumer interests, and technical and economic progress. A task force was established inside DGIV to apply the regulation, although, as with other areas of competition policy, other DGs are consulted, and the final decision is taken by the College of Commissioners.

The Commission has been anxious to tackle a wider range of cases than that originally agreed in the Regulation, seeking to lower the thresholds at which mergers are referred to Brussels, but it has faced considerable opposition from some member governments, notably that of the UK. Following a review of the guidelines in 1996 (Commission 1996*d*), the general thresholds remained in place, but the rules were changed under Council Regulation 1310/1997 to cover cases involving lower turnovers, but more firms. For mergers involving three or more member states, the Commission will have authority if their combined global turnover is 2.5 billion ecus, where their turnover was 100 million ecus in at least three member states, and where in each member state involved at least two of the firms have a turnover of 25 million ecus or more.

How have the rules been implemented? Although there has been a rapid increase in the number of mergers notified to the Commission, 235 in 1998 compared with sixty-three in 1991, the system of scrutiny has worked well: 238 decisions were taken in 1998. What has perhaps been surprising is the relatively low number of cases where the mergers have been disallowed outright, where changes have been required, or even where a deeper scrutiny was required. Given that the Regulation operates on the basis of relatively transparent criteria, one part of the explanation might be the 'soundness' of the proposed mergers, and another might be the ability of firms to second-guess the Commission in putting forward their plans. However,

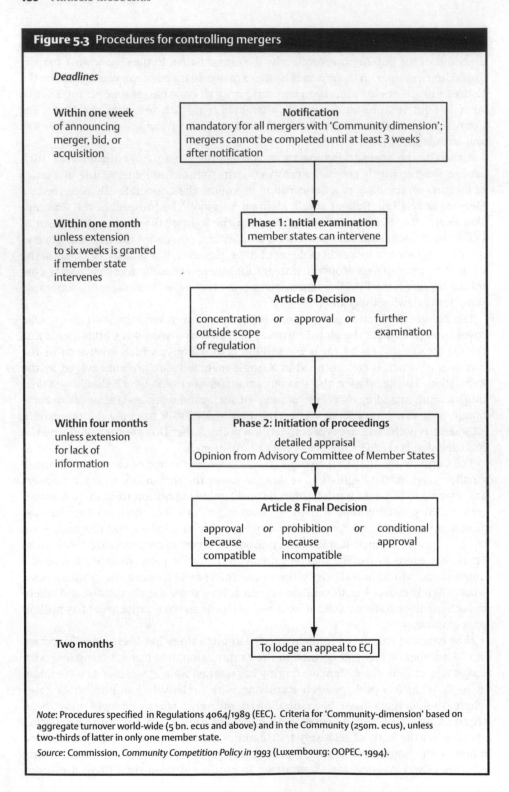

Figure 5.3 Procedures for controlling mergers

Deadlines

Within one week
of announcing
merger, bid, or
acquisition

Notification
mandatory for all mergers with 'Community dimension';
mergers cannot be completed until at least 3 weeks
after notification

Within one month
unless extension
to six weeks is granted
if member state
intervenes

Phase 1: Initial examination
member states can intervene

Article 6 Decision

concentration	*or*	approval	*or*	further
outside scope				examination
of regulation				

Within four months
unless extension
for lack of
information

Phase 2: Initiation of proceedings
detailed appraisal
Opinion from Advisory Committee of Member States

Article 8 Final Decision

approval	*or*	prohibition	*or*	conditional
because		because		approval
compatible		incompatible		

Two months

To lodge an appeal to ECJ

Note: Procedures specified in Regulations 4064/1989 (EEC). Criteria for 'Community-dimension' based on aggregate turnover world-wide (5 bn. ecus and above) and in the Community (250m. ecus), unless two-thirds of latter in only one member state.

Source: Commission, *Community Competition Policy in 1993* (Luxembourg: OOPEC, 1994).

Table 5.4 Merger regulation cases, 1990–1998 (no.)

Year	New notifications	First phase (no.)		Second phase initiated				
		Approved	Outside scope of regulation	Approved without conditions	Approved with conditions	Refused	Withdrawals	Referred to member states
1990	12	5	2	0	0	0	0	0
1991	63	50	5	1	3	1	0	0
1992	60	47	9	1	3	0	3	1
1993	58	49	4	1	0	0	2	1
1994	95	80	5	2	2	1	6	1
1995	110	93	9	2	2	2	4	0
1996	131	109	6	1	3	3	6	3
1997	172	120	4	1	7	1	9	7
1998	235	219	6	2	5	2	9	4
Total	936	772	50	11	25	10	39	16

Notes: The figures do not necessarily tally: some proceedings are not decided in the year they are started.

Source: Commission (1981–).

the relatively smooth passage of most cases may owe something to the early controversy which attended the first rejection of a merger. In that case two aircraft manufacturers, Alenia and Aerospatiale, sought to take over a third, the Canadian firm de
Havilland. The Commission rejected this in 1991 on the grounds that it would lead to
too much concentration in the commuter-aircraft market. The decision proved to be
highly controversial, with considerable opposition from France and some other governments (and apparently much dispute within the Commission itself). Although the
Commission held to its position, the case exposed the twin issues of how such politically sensitive cases would be handled, and whether the Commission should have
complete discretion in such cases. Although the Commission has held on to its
powers, it has been less aggressive in other cases, for fear of subsequent reprisals by
the member governments.

The interplay of EU competition policy with national and global regimes

Competition policy increasingly faces the challenge of subsidiarity, the need to
match the level of regulation with the scope of markets, and the operations of firms.
DGIV is approaching this challenge by, on the one hand, decentralizing responsibilities down to the national regulatory authorities and coordinating between them,
and, on the other hand, cooperating with regulatory authorities outside the EU, in
response to an increasingly globalized economy.

Decentralization

In the core activities of Articles 81 and 82 (ex 85 and 86), but also as regards state aids,
mergers, and liberalization, the Commission is increasingly encouraging the application of subsidiarity and allowing national authorities to play a greater role. The workload of the Commission has partly prompted this shift. However, developments at the
national level have rendered it possible: the convergence of national preferences
about how to conduct competition policy; and, increasingly, the alignment of
national legislation with EU law (Maher 1997). In a sense, the original rationale for
regulation at the EU level—the need to overcome problems of coordination, consistency and credibility in national policies and practices—has become redundant, as
national authorities have become more 'trustworthy'. The 'culture of competition'
which is referred to in the White Paper on modernizing competition policy (Commission 1999a) is rather a shared policy culture. Officials in the Commission now expect
that the rules will be applied in similar ways, with similar degrees of commitment,
and with similar outcomes across the member states (McGowan and Seabright 1995).
   Attempts to give a bigger role to national authorities and courts are not new.
The competition rules have always been directly applicable in the member states and
national authorities have always been involved in specific cases. But for many years
there was only a very limited application of the rules by domestic competition

agencies, which were in any case often finding their feet. Moreover, there were important differences in domestic legislation in terms of content, as well as in terms of procedure and enforcement. In some cases, not only did national competition rules not embody the principles of European anti-trust, but they allowed many exemptions (Martin 1998). As the Commission recognized in its proposals on national application of the competition rules in 1983, the scope for relying on national implementation of European competition rules was limited by persistent differences in domestic legislation and in their procedural and enforcement traditions (Commission 1981–, *13th Annual Report*, 1984). In some cases, not only did national competition rules not embody the principles of European anti-trust, but they provided many exemptions. Such differences were not really a problem when a competition issue had only domestic ramifications. However, the different approaches to policy cast doubt on how far national authorities could actively buttress a collective EU policy.

That role could have been played more easily by the national courts. European jurisprudence left open the possibility of individuals seeking redress in national courts. Yet, although some cases were brought in national courts, the number was small in relation to the volume of possible cases. This may have been due to the lack of Community case law for national courts to draw upon, but just as important was the lack of experience of national courts in applying the competition rules. To remedy this the Commission sought to enhance expertise and capabilities at the national level. After years of consultation, in 1987 it produced a guide to encourage greater take-up of the rules, liaised with national professionals to increase the profile of European rules and eventually published a notice on cooperation with national courts in 1993 (Commission 1994d). The notice set out a system of prioritization, highlighting which cases would be handled at the EU level and which could be handled nationally. The notice also stressed the advantages of such a system, in particular the procedural opportunities for individuals in taking a case in a national setting, not least the possibility of compensation. It also stressed the scope it provided to the Commission for concentrating on more important cases.

Following this notice the Commission sought to increase the involvement of national authorities. A draft notice published in 1996 argued that national agencies were better placed to monitor local developments, and that the principle of subsidiarity therefore required that these agencies be more closely involved. However, it should be noted that their sharing of responsibilities is intended to facilitate an effective application of a collective European competition policy, with which national approaches are aligned. A recent survey by the Commission showed that among the fifteen member states, nine have incorporated Articles 81 and 82 into their national law, whereas six have not. However, more important than these procedural issues may be the extent to which the priorities of national policies have converged in recent years.

During the 1990s a number of governments embarked on reforms of their national competition policy, in most cases with the objective of aligning it with EU rules. At the beginning of 1999 the German government updated the country's cartel legislation, partly with this in mind. German and EU competition policy have much in common, given that the German law and the Treaty of Rome were both finalized in 1957, and, many argue, key aspects of the EU rules draw upon German practice. However, the German government recognized the need for an explicit updating of its national law. The changes include: a prohibition of cartel agreements; fines on any abuse of dominant market position; the regulation of mergers before, rather than after, their completion; and an opening up of access to key infrastructures, such as ports and airports (other network industries, such as telecommunications and energy, are dealt with by separate legislation). The reform of British competition policy, to enter into force in 2000, was largely designed to align it with EU rules, and incorporated much of Articles 81 and 82 (ex 85 and 86).

The impact of adopting EU policy in domestic legislation has been demonstrated in Italian competition policy. Since legislation in 1990 incorporated EU principles and created an independent competition agency, the Italian economy has been subject to much more rigorous regulation. As well as monitoring anti-competitive behaviour, the Italian competition agency has been particularly active in tackling the Italian government's programme of privatization. It has, for example, lobbied for structural changes of major state monopolies before they are privatized. Although this advocacy role should not be overstated, since the government can ignore much of the authority's advice, in some areas there has been effective application of the rules. Indeed there has been a more general robustness on the part of national authorities, an essential prerequisite for any devolution of EU policy.

It would be too much to argue that all national models have converged, or even are converging, upon a single model of competition policy. There remain many differences particularly on matters of procedure and enforcement (Martin 1998; Cayseele *et al.*, forthcoming). However, there does seem to be a trend towards greater assertiveness on the part of national regulators, and for their priorities to mirror those of the broader European debate. There seems to be a deepening of the mutual support noted in our historical overview of competition policy. This reciprocity is observable in the realm of European law more generally, in the degree to which national courts have not only accepted the supranational nature of European law, but also reinforced it (Weiler 1994; Volcanseck 1992). In the case of competition policy, however, there is a crossover from the purely legal realm of courts to the wider policy-making community. It may also be that national anti-trust authorities, seeking to defend or even establish their autonomy in the domestic setting, have generally been happy to line up with European competition policy.

European competition policy and the global competition policy debate

It is scarcely surprising that the operation of the EU rules should impinge on the conduct of national competition policies. What is more surprising is their impact beyond the borders. It is worth stressing that the EU is the first example of an effective international competition policy. It contrasts both with the failure of multilateral negotiations in the 1940s and 1950s and with the very limited outcomes achieved more recently in settings such as the UN Conference on Trade and Development and the Organization for Economic Cooperation and Development (OECD). The relative success of this regional EU regime has not been accompanied by an introspective stance. On the contrary, over the past ten years in particular the Commission has been a protagonist in tackling activities which raise international competition concerns, in fostering cooperation with third countries in competition policy matters, and in advocating a multilateral anti-trust regime.

During the 1990s, especially, the Commission has sought to intervene in specific cases which impact upon not only the EU, but other parts of the world as well. This activism has been most clearly seen in a series of high-profile interventions in international merger cases. The Commission has been able to use its powers to regulate the effects of such mergers within the EU. Moreover, it has done so on the basis of cooperation with other anti-trust authorities, though in some instances (notably the Boeing–MacDonnell Douglas merger in 1997) there has been serious disagreement between the Commission and its counterpart in the USA, the Department of Justice. However, such conflicts could strengthen the case for more cooperation between authorities and even for some system of arbitration.

The Commission has been active in promoting international approaches to competition policy. Association agreements with third countries have included provisions on competition policy: both the European Economic Area (EEA), with other west European countries, and Europe agreements, with the countries of central and eastern Europe, have incorporated the core features of the policy. As a result the principles of European competition policy extend well beyond the boundaries of the EU to the rest of Europe, east and west. At the same time the Commission has been engaged in dialogue with its major trading partners to ensure greater cooperation in cases involving their jurisdictions. The Commission secured bilateral agreements with the USA and Canada, as well as deeper dialogues with other industrialized states, and has fostered the role of competition policy in developing countries.

The Commission itself recognizes that extensive bilateral cooperation is insufficient, and it has therefore pushed for the multilateral debate to be revived. In the wake of the last GATT Round the question of the relationship between trade and competition policy was reopened. The Commission has been keen to be at the fore of this debate. In July 1995 a group of experts, mostly, but not all, Commission officials, published a set of recommendations on international competition policy, subsequently adopted by the Commission (1996e). This outlines a step-by-step process which could ultimately lead to some form of global anti-trust rules. The Commission's enthusiasm undoubtedly helped to maintain the profile of the issue in the face of considerable opposition (not least from the USA) and the Commission wanted to push for its inclusion in the negotiations for the Millennium Round of the World Trade Organization (Brittan 1999).

It will be some time before we know whether the Commission's advocacy of global competition policy can translate into multilateral rules, but its profile in dealing with extra-EU competition problems is likely to remain high. It could be argued that the EU is at the hub of a network of competition policy cooperation. A similar, but much more intense, pattern of networking seems to be driving the internal reform of EU competition policy. A tiered system of regulatory cooperation appears to be emerging, although it is very different from the pattern characteristically described as multi-level governance. Instead of a subnational–national–EU interaction, we are dealing with a national–EU–global interplay. Moreover the 'squeezing of the middleman', identified in conventional accounts of multi-level processes, is not replicated in this case: on the contrary, there seems to be an enhancing of the EU's roles as a gatekeeper between the other tiers of governance. In other respects, however, notably the importance of networking and coordination, it may be a useful way of explaining the process at work.

Competition policy and other policies: reconciling conflicting objectives

Just as we need to consider competition policy as operating at different levels of governance, so we have to consider its interaction with other EU policies: it is the multiple objectives, as well as multiple levels, that characterize the overall process of EU governance. We have already touched upon the intra-Commission negotiations within which DGIV and the competition Commissioner have to operate. As in any other area of policy-making, EU and elsewhere, they will fight their corner, but in the end will seek to get the best compromise available. Competition policy is only one strand in European integration. Although it enjoys a strong legal base, it has to coexist with other EU policies and objectives.

Coexistence is easier with some policies than with others. There is a very real sense in which competition policy is at one with (and contributes to) the fundamentally liberal orientation of the EU integration project. I have already noted how the originators of the policy were adamant that this should be so. More recently competition policy has been an important complement to the single market programme, helping to bring about change, and disciplining conduct thereafter. The microeconomic effects of economic and monetary union (EMU) will probably reinforce (and be reinforced by) the role of competition policy.

However, there are many other areas of EU policy where the fit is less than perfect. Just as competition policy has been constructed around a set of norms and values, so have other policies, both sectoral and horizontal. These different values and objectives, and their priorities and mechanisms, may not always be compatible. I have already noted how DGIV has been at odds with other, so to speak 'captured', DGs (e.g. those dealing with transport or industrial affairs). These policy conflicts and the institutional antagonisms may have been transitory. However, there may be circumstances where fundamental treaty objectives are at odds with one another, and can be resolved only by one prevailing over the other.

Much depends on how the objectives, not only of competition policy itself but also of the EU, are interpreted and ranked as a whole. The goals of competition policy are surprisingly wide-ranging, and the emphasis given to them has strengthened over time (Neven *et al.* 1998). Originally primarily concerned with the promotion of 'effective competition', the common market, and consumer protection, the goals have since been broadened to include the facilitation of industrial restructuring, the promotion of technical innovation, international competitiveness, and the development of SMEs. Such a variety of objectives may not always be compatible with one another, though those concerning SMEs and research and development are largely recognized through various exemptions and derogations in the application of anti-trust and state aid rules. Reconciling the basic thrust of competition policy with broader EU objectives is even more of a challenge.

Yet in other cases it is clear that the limits to competition policy have been recognized. In a wide variety of cases dealing with the environment, for example, DGIV has been prepared to countenance state aids (for the promotion of energy efficiency and renewable energy) and collusive agreements (the AutoOil scheme amongst car producers). Here the balance of costs and benefits has been interpreted as one where significant environmental goods are achieved at the expense of relatively minor distortions of the market. Another case in point is that of economic and social cohesion.

The provision of financial support to foster regional development can be considered to be at odds with competition policy. The evidence is not unambiguous in that the bulk of such support improves infrastructure, which can then be exploited not only by those in the region, but also by those selling into the region. Yet it has been argued over the years that regional policy goals be given priority of competition concerns, and state aids policy has taken this into account. Since the Single European Act added cohesion as a primary objective (see Chapter 9), strengthened by Maastricht, the goals of competition policy have been subordinated (Frazer 1994). This tension had probably not been considered at the time that cohesion acquired so important a status.

In other instances, however, it is clear that some member governments have hoped to trump competition policy by seeking the inclusion of new treaty provisions, though with only limited success. A case in point was the addition of an industrial policy article in the TEU. This was driven by the Belgian and French governments. Their conflicts with the Commission over a number of competition cases had convinced them that a formal recognition of the legitimacy of industrial policy was required to counter such decisions. It became clear that their aims were not widely shared, either in the Commission or amongst other governments. A Commission statement on industrial policy in 1990 was very far from *dirigiste*, taking a relatively light approach (Commission 1990g). The provision that was finally agreed (Article 130, now Article 157) very explicitly hedged a rather weak commitment to industrial policy with the proviso that competition policy prevail (*Agence Europe*, no. 5611, 18 November 1991; no. 5627, 11 December 1991). In the 1996–7 IGC the French government again attempted to rein in competition policy, this time as it affected the public utilities. Initial threats to call for an amending of Article 86 (ex 90) and to include a public service charter were scaled down. After much debate the Commission published a report on services of general economic interest (Commission 1996i), which recognized the importance of the principle without surrendering any changes to competition rules. Eventually a much more limited commitment was included in the amended Treaty (under the new Article 7), though it could be argued that the campaign had had its effect by obliging the Commission to tread carefully in its programme of utility liberalization.

A critique of European competition policy

Although the Commission can legitimately claim that, in terms of its overall impact, competition policy has been one of the successes of European integration, the conduct—and, to a lesser extent, the substance—of policy has come in for serious criticism. Both the epistemic community of academics and practitioners, and the business community, which, as supplicants or targets, is the most affected by the workings of the policy, have highlighted a series of shortcomings in the procedures of competition policy. These focus on the slow pace of decision-making, as well as the content of those decisions, but also raise broader questions about the regulatory role of the Commission. How much discretion does the Commission need? Where should the balance be struck between accountability and effectiveness?

Perhaps the strongest criticism levelled at EU competition policy is that of a lack of legal certainty and transparency. The decisions taken by officials are said to be opaque, not founded on a consistent analytical approach, and, as a result, are unpredictable (Neven *et al.* 1998). The lack of rigour—or even a clear justification—in Commission decisions is contrasted by some with the work of the Court and some national authorities (Korah 1997). Such shortcomings are reinforced by the mix of informality and discretion which attends the decision-making procedure (Jong 1975). The Commission counters that these problems are largely due to limited resources. The Commission, it is argued, is a victim of its success—expanding responsibilities, an ever-increasing stream of complaints, and requests for clearance have all added to the workload of the EU authorities, but without an equivalent increase in staffing. The effect of this is a backlog of cases, which both prevents the Commission from responding rapidly to challenges to competition and prevents firms from being able to adjust to market challenges. The solution—more staff—is blocked both by budgetary constraints and by the turf sensitivities of other DGs. Instead the Commission has to resort to the system of regulation by negotiation, which depends upon discretion and flexibility.

However, it is not clear that resources are the only difficulty. While more staff might increase the throughput of decisions and thereby obviate the need for behind-the-scenes and informal settlements, there is no guarantee that a larger cohort of officials would necessarily be willing to dispense with its discretionary powers, or with the relatively opaque processes of decision-making. The lack of accountability means that inconsistencies flourish, and behind-the-scenes deals are concocted according to the strength of the interests being represented.

Yet others argue that the Commission's problem is too little, rather than too much, autonomy. For these critics, the Commission is too politically sensitive, unwilling to challenge firms or governments in anything but the most blatant anti-competitive cases. In the 1996–7 IGC the German government was anxious to see the establishment of an independent European Cartel Office which would enjoy even more autonomy than the Commission and be insulated from political pressures. The scheme was rejected both by governments less keen to see competition policy take on a more independent existence and by the Commission itself, and DGIV in particular (Miert 1996). However, the debate on the proposal raises the question of just how far the conduct of European competition policy is subject to political pressures.

Reconciling the need for accountability (i.e. responsibility for decisions taken to political representatives and/or those affected by the decisions) and effectiveness (i.e. some room for manœuvre in applying the rules) is a classic dilemma in competition policy, as it is in all regulatory decisions (McGowan and Wallace 1996). A pessimistic caricature of European competition policy would see the worst of both worlds at work: politically constrained, or arbitrary decision-makers, taking advantage of a degree of autonomy to protect themselves, but unwilling to act independently for fear of alienating political masters. Such an assessment may be belied by those cases where the Commission does assert its powers—turning down mergers, forcing through Article 86 (ex 90) regulations, fining companies, prohibiting subsidies. Yet it does contain some grains of truth, making the need for reform all the more necessary. While the reforms currently under discussion are not designed with this in mind, they may be of some help (Schaub 1998*b*; Commission 1999*b*). Greater reliance on decision rules based on economic effects would ensure greater consistency. The removal of routine cases and greater decentralization to national authorities would allow the Commission to tackle the more blatant examples of anti-competitive conduct. It would reinforce the competition policy culture at the expense of intra-Commission struggles and government and corporate lobbying. Much will depend, however, on how effective national authorities will be in dealing with cases (in terms both of administrative capacities and independence of spirit) and how prepared the Commission will be to coordinate and, if necessary, to reclaim responsibility for cases. Critics are not convinced that the reforms will ensure effective and consistent application of the rules across the EU.

Conclusions

These reforms should not just be seen as addressing shortcomings in the status quo. They also indicate that European competition policy is entering a new phase—one of multi-level regulation, characterized by a shared agenda between national and European authorities. The fact that the Commission is prepared to share the responsibility indicates its confidence both in domestic agencies (reflecting the degree to which the orthodoxy of competition policy is itself shared) and in itself as the leading force in the field. The dynamic between national and European levels is also suggestive of a strong self-confidence in the relative autonomy of agencies at both levels from the political processes. Perhaps there is even a reciprocal reinforcement in this sense: DGIV is able to rely on national agencies, which follow a broadly similar approach, while it is also able to promulgate pro-competitive doctrines, which in turn strengthen the position of national regulators *vis-à-vis* their domestic rivals.

I began by noting that the conduct of European competition policy offered one of the best examples of European policy-making as regulation, and perhaps of regulation as the most effective mode of European policy-making. The strong basis in law, through treaty provisions, enabling legislation, and court cases, and the existence of a set of technical (economic) principles underlie the policy. We have, however, seen that this picture needs to be qualified. Lack of resources, informal and negotiated processes of decision-making, pressures from other parts of the EU and of the Commission, and contending policy claims all seem to undermine the image of a supranational technocracy applying the rules consistently and without political contamination. However, such imperfections should not make our regulatory metaphor any less compelling—real-world regulation is imperfect and constrained in its operation. It cannot (and some would argue should not) be closed off from political considerations. The institutional bases and doctrinal roots provide the regulators with a certain relative autonomy which renders European competition policy a distinctive instance of policy-making in the EU.

Notes

1 In this sense competition policy can be seen as an example of 'embedded liberalism' (see Ruggie 1982). On the interaction between regional and multilateral diplomacy see Ikenberry (1989) and Lovett (1996).

2 Much of the OEEC's work focused on improving productivity and emphasis was placed on learning from each other and from the USA (see Griffiths 1997). The OEEC's work on restrictive business practices was continued in the OECD.

3 The Ligue appears to have been active as a regular forum for discussions, occasionally publishing its surveys of some aspect of European competition policy.

4 Note, for example, the public disagreement between Commissioners Sutherland and Clinton Davies over the pace of air transport liberalization in 1986 and 1987 (see *Agence Europe*, 4342, 19 June 1986; 4405, 9 Oct. 1986; 4511, 18 Mar. 1987; 4564, 6 June 1987).

5 On this occasion the Commission divided after a bitter debate. Although there was a vehement disagreement between Brittan and Delors, ultimately Delors abstained not least because he recognized that he would be outvoted (see Ross 1994).

6 To this end the Commission established a new unit within DGIV to tackle cartels at the end of 1998 (Commission 1998*f*).

7 On the rationale and critique of state aids, see Besley and Seabright (1999) and Martin (forthcoming).

8 See e.g. the discussion in Commission (1981– , *24th Annual Report*, 1995 15–16).

9 Commission attempts to find out about state ownership began in the early 1970s. The *Annual Reports* of that decade record the lack of cooperation provided by governments and the Commission's recourse to Article 90 (see McGowan 1993).

10 See e.g. CEPS (1998).

Further reading

The best guide to the evolution of European Competition Policy is the Commission's own annual report: as well as providing a review of Commission and Court activities over the previous year, it highlights the strategic priorities of policy, the Commission's own rationale, and, to some extent, the debates surrounding new initiatives. These latter aspects are also covered in some detail in the quarterly *Competition Policy Newsletter*, published by DGIV. Both publications are available from the DGIV web page on Europa (as are a plethora of policy papers and speeches).

More critical accounts of European policy (both EU and member state) can be found in the *European Competition Law Review*, a journal which embraces economic as well as legal analysis. A good introduction to the issue is provided in Cini and McGowan's (1998) comprehensive overview, while Neven *et al.*'s (1993, 1998) analyses of the EU's policies on mergers and anti-trust offer constructive economic critiques of these core aspects of EU competition policy. Historically, the accounts of the negotiations in Duchêne (1994) and Gillingham (1991) give a flavour of the pressures for and against the policy, while Swann (1983) provides a view of the conduct of policy up to the early 1980s, and Brittan (1992) is useful in outlining the activism of competition policy in the 1990s. Chapters by David Allen in previous editions of this volume also chart the earlier development of European competition policy.

Brittan, L. (1992), *European Competition Policy: Keeping the Playing Field Level* (London: Brassey).

Cini, M., and McGowan, L. (1998), *Competition Policy in the European Union* (London: Macmillan).

Commission (1981–), Annual Reports on Competition Policy (Luxembourg: Office for Official Publications of the European Communities, 1999).

Duchêne, F. (1994), *Jean Monnet: First Statesman of Interdependence* (New York: Norton).

Gillingham, J. (1991), *Coal, Steel and the Rebirth of Europe, 1945–1955: The Germans and the French from Ruhr Conflict to Economic Community* (Cambridge: Cambridge University Press).

Neven, D., Nuttall, R., and Seabright, P. (1993), *Merger in Daylight: The Economics and Politics of European Merger Control* (London: Centre for Economic Policy Research).

—— Papandropoulos, P., and Seabright, P. (1998), *Trawling for Minnows: European Competition Policy and Agreements between Firms* (London: Centre for Economic Policy Research).

Swann, D. (1983), *Competition and Industrial Policy in the European Community* (London: Methuen).

Chapter 6
Economic and Monetary Union
Political Conviction and Economic Uncertainty

Loukas Tsoukalis

Contents

Summary

Political arguments have been as important as economic arguments in driving demands for economic and monetary union (EMU), from the first commitment at The Hague Summit in 1969 to the successful launch of the single currency in 1999. The intervening history of proposals, and of the halfway house of the European Monetary System (EMS), have demonstrated the difficulty of linking divergent economies, and the asymmetries within the European economy. Political coalition-building in 1990–1 overcame the scepticism of many economists and the caution of central bankers to embed EMU in the

Treaty of European Union (TEU). Economic recession and monetary turbulence, in the years which followed, failed to blunt the political commitment of core European Union (EU) governments. What has emerged is basically a currency regime managed by the new European Central Bank and national central bankers. This is in turn intimately linked to prevailing economic orthodoxy. Questions of political accountability, and of the links between monetary union and broader macroeconomic and fiscal policies, remain unresolved.

Introduction

The final stage of EMU started with eleven countries on 1 January 1999, and it should lead in 2002 to the replacement of national currencies by the euro.[1] EMU promises to be one of the most important events—arguably, the most important—in the history of European integration, with extensive economic and political ramifications. It is therefore not easily comparable to other EU policies. If anything, it could, perhaps, be compared to the common foreign and security policy (CFSP)—money and defence being the two main attributes of national sovereignty. And we would then need to explain why monetary integration has reached the final (and irreversible?) stage, while CFSP is still moving from procedure to substantial policy.

This chapter traces the chequered history of EMU, starting with the extremely cautious handling of monetary matters by the authors of the Treaty of Rome and ending with the likely effects of EMU on European integration in general. Hardly surprisingly, there is already a vast and rapidly growing literature on the subject. The process of setting up a currency union, which will bring together some of the most advanced national economies, provides a real-world laboratory for the testing of modern economic theories. Economists have, indeed, risen to the challenge. However, most writings on the subject are of a technical nature. Thus, the initiated are separated by high fences and impenetrable jargon from the ordinary folk. This has not always helped economic arguments to enter the political debate, although in recent years efforts have been made by an increasing number of social scientists to bring down those fences.

EMU is such an important economic subject, and with such major political implications, that it can be argued that developments in this area will hugely influence the shape of the new European architecture. Money has frequently been used as an instrument of wider political objectives, even though markets and economic fundamentals have not always obliged by adjusting themselves to the exigencies of high politics.

Policy outcomes are the product of political preferences and market forces. This chapter focuses on the policy process in the context of the EU, trying to draw some conclusions about the factors determining the pendulum swings between the national and transnational levels of policy-making in the macroeconomic field. The chapter will be divided in five main parts: the first sketches the early history of monetary cooperation in western Europe until the end of the 1970s; the second examines the experience of the EMS before the decision to proceed with a complete

EMU; the third concentrates on the negotiations leading to the Maastricht revision of the treaties; the fourth traces the main developments in the long transition to the final stage; and the fifth addresses the main outstanding issues in a post-EMU Europe.

The early history: much ado about nothing

The first twenty years after the establishment of the European Economic Community (EEC) in 1958 were characterized by much talk and little action as regards monetary policy. The debate did, however, help to prepare the ground for the more substantial phase of monetary integration, which started with the setting-up of the EMS in 1979. This chapter uses the common abbreviation EC for the period from 1958 to the signature of the TEU in 1992, when EMU became a realistic target.

The Treaty of Rome contained very little in terms of binding constraints in the field of macroeconomic policy: some wishful thinking as regards the coordination of policies; provisions for balance of payments assistance; and considerable caution with respect to the elimination of exchange controls. Articles 104–9 (now much expanded as 102–30) were included in a section entitled 'Balance of Payments' and created the Monetary Committee 'to keep under review the monetary and financial situation'. It was composed of two representatives from each member state and the Commission, its secretariat provided by the Commission, and its chair elected from the membership. Interestingly, Articles 108 and 109 from the outset made provision for the Council to reach decisions by qualified majority voting.

There was clearly no intention to set up a regional currency bloc. The Bretton Woods system provided the international framework and the US dollar the undisputed monetary standard. Moreover, Keynesianism was still at its peak. This meant that national governments were zealous in retaining the independence of their monetary and fiscal policies for the pursuit of domestic economic objectives, and a heavy armoury of capital controls was considered as an acceptable price to pay for this independence (Tsoukalis 1977).

Interest in monetary integration grew during the 1960s, largely in response to the increasing instability in the international system and the perceived need to insulate Europe from the vagaries of the US dollar. The French were more sensitive to those problems than the other west Europeans, who were not keen on a confrontation with the USA. This complicated matters and helped to confine notions of a shared European interest to a general debate which remained far short of any kind of serious action by the EEC Six. In any case the EEC lived under the illusion of having a *de facto* monetary union, during a relatively long period of unchanged exchange rates. The illusion was further strengthened by the setting up of the common agricultural policy (CAP), which was predicated on common prices across the EEC (see Chapter 7). This was a typical example of trying to put the cart before the horse.

The situation seemed to change in December 1969, when at The Hague Summit the political leaders of the Six adopted for the first time the target of full EMU. It was a political decision reached at the highest level, and it was directly linked to the first enlargement of the Community and the further deepening of integration. It was also the first important example of a Franco-German initiative as the lever for a major policy development, involving President Pompidou and Chancellor Brandt, although the common basis of this initiative proved subsequently to be very fragile. The negotiations which followed revealed the existence of a broad, even though superficial, agreement about the contents of the third and final stage of EMU, and little agreement about how to get there. The Werner Report (Werner *et al.* 1970), issued by a high-level committee of central bankers and national finance officials, chaired by the Prime Minister of Luxembourg, made a valiant attempt to conceal those differences behind the thin cloak of the so-called strategy of parallelism. This presumed the complementary development of monetary alignment and macroeconomic policy coordination.

Solemn decisions were then taken at the highest level. They did not, however, prove strong enough to survive the adverse economic conditions of the 1970s. EMU became the biggest non-event of the decade. The collapse of the Bretton Woods system in 1971 brought down with it the fragile European edifice. Fixed exchange rates, with narrow margins of fluctuation, which had been seen as the most concrete manifestation of the first stage of EMU, proved incompatible with increasingly divergent economic policies and inflation rates. Very senior west European politicians had made political commitments but had not by and large translated them into the appropriate economic policies. Finally they gave way under market pressure.

After 1974 what was left of the ambitious plan for EMU was only a mutilated snake (the term used for the first system of linked exchange rates) wriggling its way in the chaotic zoo of international exchange markets. Many EC currencies had been forced to leave the system, thus turning a Community arrangement into a *de facto* German or Deutschmark (DM) bloc, in which the currencies of some small European countries (including non-EC members) were tied to the DM, and so were their monetary policies. Those left in the snake were the DM, the Dutch guilder, the Belgian and Luxembourg francs, and the Danish krone, and those pegged to it were the Austrian Schilling and the Swiss franc. This was a clear manifestation of the growing importance of Germany in the Community and Europe more generally; and also the most significant example so far of a two-tier Europe. There was something else too: the snake was a decisive step in the process of ever closer cooperation among European central bankers, thus laying the ground for more ambitious initiatives to come. The Committee of Central Bank Governors (CCBG) had been created by Council decision in May 1964 to manage collaboration among the central bankers of the EC countries. Operating independently of the EC institutions, with its own secretariat in Basle, and with monthly meetings, the CCBG emerged from this difficult period as a tight-knit circle for transnational policy coordination.

The EMS: coordination and asymmetry

Despite the serious set-backs suffered in the attempt to move towards EMU in the 1970s, interest in the subject never disappeared. The mini-snake was generally considered as only a temporary arrangement, which would be improved and extended when the economic conditions became more favourable. Hence a whole series of proposals was put forward during the 1970s, which aimed at the relaunching of monetary integration (Tsoukalis 1977).

The EMS was established in March 1979. It was the product of an initiative taken by Chancellor Schmidt, very much against the advice of his central bank, in collaboration with the then President of the Commission, Roy Jenkins. This was later developed in informal negotiations as a joint Franco-German initiative, which brought President Giscard d'Estaing on to the centre-stage. It could have been an arrangement among the 'Big Three', which the other EC countries would have been invited to join. However, the British government, once again, withdrew from the negotiations and decided not to take part in the eventual regime (Ludlow 1982).

The EMS was a renewed attempt to establish a system of fixed, but periodically adjustable, exchange rates between EC currencies, operating within relatively narrow margins of fluctuation. Unlike many academic economists, who have long remained agnostic about the costs of a floating system, the large majority of European policy-makers and businessmen have stressed the advantages of fixed (but not necessarily irrevocably fixed) exchange rates. The experience of the 1970s was read as a confirmation of this long-held belief, which had been temporarily shaken by new ideas about the alleged efficiency and stability of financial and exchange markets, ideas which were mainly imported from the other side of the Atlantic. Concern about the proper functioning of the common market was combined with the desire to preserve common agricultural prices, and thus do away with the system of monetary compensatory amounts. On the other hand, the initiative for the creation of the EMS was linked to the expectation that there would be no substantial reform of the international monetary system, and hence no prospect of a return to some wider form of exchange-rate stability in the future.

Exchange-rate stability was to be backed by an increased convergence between national economies, with the emphasis clearly placed on inflation rates. The EMS was considered as an important instrument in the fight against inflation, and its creation meant an implicit acceptance by the other EC governments of German policy priorities. The experience of the 1970s was seen as validating the German combination of an uncompromising anti-inflationary stance with a strong currency option. The EMS was also intended as a defensive mechanism against US 'benign neglect' as regards the dollar. It was also a means of strengthening Europe economically and politically through closer cooperation, at a time when US leadership was seen as waning. Once again, monetary integration was partly—and in a rather vague manner—used by its supporters as an instrument for political ends.

The EMS was built on the existing snake, but with some important novel features intended to foster the enlargement of its membership, as well as the smoother functioning of the exchange-rate mechanism (ERM). The novel features included: the European currency unit (ecu), consisting of fixed amounts of each EC currency; and the divergence indicator, intended to provide a certain degree of symmetry in the burden of adjustment between appreciating and depreciating currencies. This latter was the product of long and difficult negotiations, and implied that average behaviour should constitute good behaviour, although this did not square well with another implicit feature of the EMS, namely a general alignment to Germany's anti-inflation policy. The contradiction was soon to become apparent, and the result was that the divergence indicator was never put into effect.

In political terms, the EMS was a compromise. On the one hand, the German government feared the effects of prolonged international monetary instability and an excessive revaluation of the DM, resulting from the continuous sinking of the dollar in exchange markets. On the other hand, the governments of France and, to a lesser extent, Italy saw their participation in the EMS as an integral part of an anti-inflation strategy. All three also shared the broader political objectives associated with the EMS. The other members of the old snake, countries with small and highly open economies, were only too happy to see an extension of the area in which stable exchange rate relations applied. For Ireland, economic side-payments (through assistance for convergence) were combined with a gesture of political independence from Britain. The British government, led by Jim Callaghan, decided not to join the ERM (the cornerstone of EMS), because it shared neither the economic logic behind the EMS nor the political ambitions associated with it.

In the negotiations leading to the adoption of the final package, the strings were held rather tightly by a small number of policy-makers at the highest level. However, the final package also had to be sold to central bankers, who would later be called upon to administer the system. What was needed was both an intergovernmental bargain and a compromise between the German government and the Bundesbank (Dyson 1994).

The period between 1979 and 1992, when hell broke loose in exchange markets, was characterized by an increasing stability of exchange rates (see also Gros and Thygesen 1998). Greater stability in nominal intra-ERM exchange rates was achieved largely through a gradually accelerating convergence of inflation rates downwards. Figure 6.1 shows for the period between 1979 and 1998 the weighted average and standard deviation of inflation for the eleven countries (EU11) which joined the final stage of EMU. The early years of the EMS were marked by high inflation rates and persisting divergence between countries, which in turn explains the frequent realignments of exchange rates and the tension experienced during this early phase. The turning-point came in 1983, when the French socialist government finally decided to abandon its earlier expansionary policies. French pursuit of a *franc fort* policy, seeking 'competitiveness through disinflation', underpinned the ERM from then on (Blanchard and Muet 1993). The convergence of inflation rates downwards became even more pronounced during the 1990s. Although impossible to prove econometrically, there are strong signs to suggest that participation in the ERM acted as an external constraint on domestic monetary policies.

Price convergence and intra-ERM exchange rate stability relied basically on monetary policies and the almost exclusive use of short-term interest rates for the purposes of exchange rate stabilization. Price convergence, coupled with the growing credibility of stability-oriented policies, brought about the gradual convergence of nominal long-term interest rates. During the later part of the period there was also a gradual extension of ERM membership. Spain joined in June 1989. It was followed by the UK in October 1990, and Portugal in April 1992. Thus, only a few months before the big exchange crisis broke out, the EMS had looked stronger than ever; and only Greece still remained outside the ERM because of its high inflation.

The ERM operated for many years as a system of fixed, but adjustable, exchange

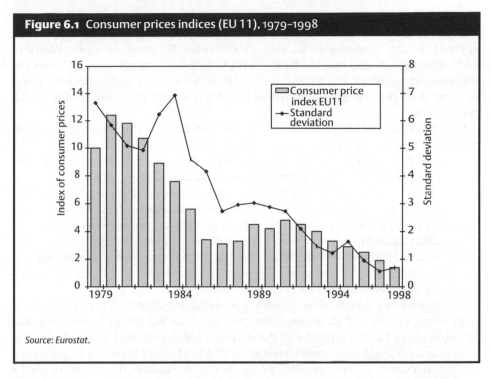

Figure 6.1 Consumer prices indices (EU 11), 1979–1998

Source: Eurostat.

rates. Adjustments, soon the product of collective decisions, became smaller and less frequent as price convergence grew. Central banks made use of a combination of different instruments whenever bilateral exchange rates came under attack. Those instruments included changes in short-term interest rates, foreign exchange interventions, and capital controls, especially in countries such as France and Italy, which were later to abandon this policy instrument in the context of liberalization (see below). Realignments were usually considered as an instrument of last resort. The everyday management of the system was left to central bankers, relying as much on informal networks as on established EC institutions and committees, and most notably the CCBG. The Monetary Committee also played a crucial role. It was the central arena for negotiation among member countries on realignment and the fixing of parities, as well as on which currencies would join or leave the system. It acted as the main preparatory body for the Council of Economic and Finance Ministers (Ecofin). It was a breeding-ground for peer group solidarity and the growth of shared orthodoxies (Westlake 1995; Hanny and Wessels 1998).

Monetary stability was, however, also directly linked to the asymmetrical nature of the EMS. Despite special provisions, such as the creation of the divergence indicator intended precisely to prevent this, the EMS operated all along in an asymmetrical fashion, thus following the earlier example of the snake. Structural factors proved in the end to be more powerful than negotiated rules. The degree and nature of the asymmetry, however, changed over time. This was reflected in the way economists assessed the effects of EMS, a function of the economic paradigm used to analyse those effects.

The asymmetry of the EMS related to the central role of the DM, and the source of it was dual: Germany had a low propensity to inflate, and the DM had acquired an international role, and both in turn were directly linked to the high reputation enjoyed by the Bundesbank. As long as the other EC partners gave priority to exchange rate stability and the fight against inflation, Germany was able to set the monetary standard for the other countries. In other words, German leadership was premissed on the new economic orthodoxy; and it was hardly based on any formal rules.

No realignment of ERM central parities ever involved a depreciation of the DM in relation to any other currency. Figure 6.2 shows the evolution of bilateral rates of the ERM currencies against the DM between March 1979 and August 1993, when the narrow margins of fluctuation in the ERM were abandoned. It thus gives an indication of the margin of manœuvre used by other members *vis-à-vis* Germany, ranging from the Netherlands on the one extreme, with an almost complete alignment to German monetary policy, to Italy on the other, which had repeatedly resorted to devaluations (and capital controls), without even being able to compensate fully for its higher inflation rates. Furthermore, the role of the DM as an international reserve currency placed the German central bank in a key position with respect to the external monetary policy of the EMS as a whole.

Asymmetry in a system of fixed (even if periodically adjustable) exchange rates is manifested in terms of an unequal distribution of the burden of intervention and adjustment, and also of influence in the setting of policy priorities. The Basle–Nyborg Agreement (among finance ministers and central bankers) of September 1987 was an attempt to correct, at least partially, the asymmetrical nature of the system. It was the result of a French initiative, following the realignment of January 1987. In subsequent years the EMS became less asymmetrical, but also more rigid, until it finally exploded during the exchange crisis of 1992–3. One thing, however, hardly changed during the whole period, namely the leadership role of the Bundesbank. This was repeatedly confirmed, until the European Central Bank (ECB) came on to the scene, since interest-rate changes initiated by the former were immediately followed by central banks in the other European countries. There was clearly little doubt among central bankers as to who was the leader in the European game.

Is asymmetry necessarily bad, at least from an economic point of view? On the one hand, it can be argued that countries with a higher propensity to inflation, such as Italy, borrowed credibility by pegging their currencies to the DM and they consequently reduced the output lost resulting from disinflationary policies. This is the alleged advantage of 'tying one's hands' to the DM mast, as Ulysses had done to protect himself from the Sirens (Giavazzi and Pagano 1988). Participation in the ERM also seems to have reinforced the commitment of national authorities to non-inflationary policies by introducing an external discipline. It thus also strengthened the hand of institutions and interest groups inside the country fighting for less inflationary policies. This largely explains the popularity of the system with most central bankers, contrary to their earlier expectations.

But, as with most arguments in economics, there is also the other hand. The asymmetry of the EMS was also seen as leading to a deflationary bias in the system, which became particularly important in times of recession and growing unemployment (De Grauwe 1994). This was evident in the early and mid-1980s and again, painfully so, in the early 1990s, when economic adversity and growing social pres-

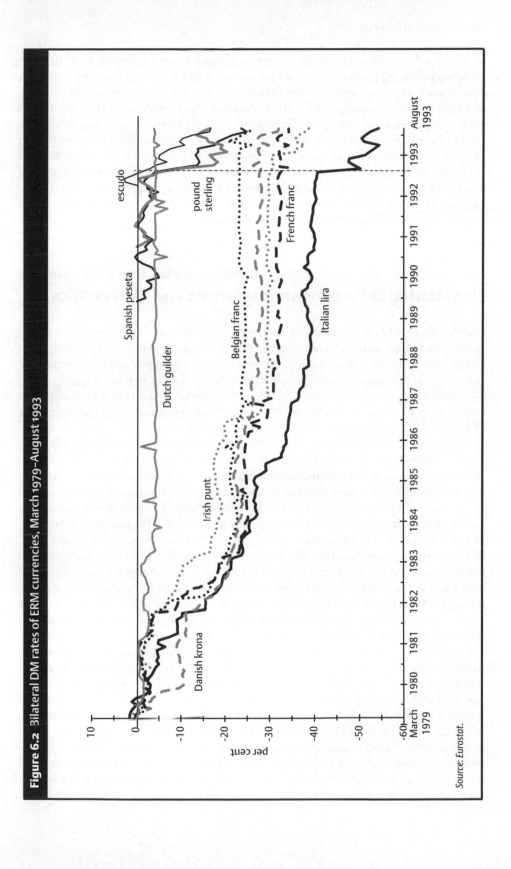

Figure 6.2 Bilateral DM rates of ERM currencies, March 1979–August 1993

escudo

Spanish peseta

pound sterling

Dutch guilder

Belgian franc

French franc

Irish punt

Italian lira

Danish krona

per cent

10

0

-10

-20

-30

-40

-50

-60

March 1979

1980

1981

1982

1983

1984

1985

1986

1987

1988

1989

1990

1991

1992

1993

August 1993

Source: Eurostat.

sures forced the other European countries to take a less benign view of German leadership. The alleged deflationary bias refers, of course, to the one-way impact of coordinated monetary policies, since there was precious little evidence of effective coordination and convergence between national fiscal policies. To the extent that such convergence did take place during the earlier phases of the EMS, it was the result of autonomous decisions in several member countries, leading to the reduction of public deficits, and not the product of an effective coordination of fiscal policies at EC level. Unlike monetary policy, which has come progressively under the exclusive control of central bankers, fiscal policy is not only less flexible, but also much more exposed to internal political pressures. It does not, therefore, lend itself easily to coordination at the European or international level.

Negotiating EMU: economic interests and high politics

The debate on EMU was initially revived by the single market, although no binding commitment had been undertaken in the Single European Act (SEA). An attempt was made, mostly by the Commission, to present EMU as the logical continuation of the single market programme, with exchange rates as another non-tariff barrier to be eliminated. In the late 1980s the EMS was still remarkably stable and Euro-euphoria was at its peak. Thus, it was urgent to win political commitment to the next stage of integration while the conditions remained favourable.

Monetary union would be the final and irrevocable confirmation of the reality of the single European market, and of a unified European economy. A common currency was seen as the means of welding national economies together, and also the means of accelerating the movement towards political union. And then came the breakdown of the old political division of the European continent, bringing down with it the communist regimes in central and eastern Europe, as well as the disintegration of the Soviet Union. It also brought with it the unification of Germany, which finally acted as a powerful driving force for EMU. For many people in Paris and Brussels in particular, the change of the European political scene called for a stronger Community, and also a Community which would provide a stable and secure framework for a larger Germany. Money once again served as the main instrument. Wider balance of power considerations were thus added to what used to be an old and deep French concern with the asymmetrical character of the existing EMS.

Earlier initiatives in the field of European monetary integration had been largely motivated by external preoccupations; the instability of the dollar and US policies of 'unbenign neglect' had served as powerful federalizing factors in Europe. This was not true of the various initiatives which finally led to the new treaty provisions adopted at Maastricht for the establishment of EMU—or, at least, not to the same extent as in the past. True, the reform of the monetary system was not on the cards and the lack of unity among European countries remained an important factor behind the asymmetry in the international system. But this asymmetry was now less evident, the US Administration did not adopt the aggressive stance of its predecessors, and intra-ERM exchange rates appeared at the time less vulnerable to the gyrations of the dollar. Perhaps a lesser preoccupation with external factors was also a sign of the new collective confidence of the Europeans.

The decision to liberalize capital movements, taken in 1988 as part of the single market programme and also a long-established German precondition for any progress towards EMU, provided the catalyst. Padoa-Schioppa (1994, ch. 6), later to become a member of the executive board of the ECB, talked about the 'inconsistent quartet' of economic objectives. This comprised free trade, free capital movements, fixed exchange rates, and monetary autonomy. His conclusion was simple and straightforward: since the EC countries had already committed themselves to the first three objectives, through the single market, the EMS, and the decision to liberalize capital movements, monetary autonomy would have to give way, moving gradually from an extensive coordination of national policies to the centralization of monetary policy at EC level. This is also the main argument on which the Commission's strategy was later based, another example of the Commission trying to make full use of functional spill-over.

The Delors Report

A French government initiative quickly turned into another joint Franco-German initiative, with strong support from Italy and the Commission. In June 1988 the European Council in Hanover set up the Committee for the Study of Economic and Monetary Union, under the chairmanship of the President of the Commission, Jacques Delors. This decision was taken only a few months after the adoption of the directive on capital liberalization, and the two were directly linked. The committee included all governors or presidents of EC central banks, an additional member of the Commission, plus a small number of independent experts. Thus, the Delors Committee was also meant as a way of incorporating central bankers into a project which had been initiated at the highest political level. It had to steer a difficult course between Scylla and Charybdis, which were represented respectively by the Bundesbank President, Karl-Otto Pöhl, and the Governor of the Bank of England, Robin Leigh-Pemberton. Neither of them was really interested in EMU, and both were keen on setting almost impossible conditions.

Thanks to Delors's skilful chairmanship, Pöhl and Leigh-Pemberton were persuaded to sign a unanimous report in April 1989 (Delors *et al.* 1989). There were many similarities with the Werner Report, which had appeared almost twenty years earlier, something which should come as no surprise since the briefs of the two committees were virtually identical. The Delors Report was, however, more explicit about the necessary transfer of powers to the level of the Union at the final stage, and put more emphasis on the institutional changes required. In fact, the central bankers, constituting a large majority in the committee, appeared only too keen to stress the full economic and institutional implications of EMU to their political masters. Much emphasis was placed on the independence of the new institution which would be in charge of monetary policy for the Union. This consensus on the question of the independence of the future ECB reflected not only the composition of the committee, but also the leadership and prestige enjoyed by the Bundesbank, which had provided the role model and the guiding influence. It was, of course, very much consistent with the prevailing economic orthodoxy. The Delors Report also called for a system of binding rules, governing the size and the financing of national budget deficits, and referred to the need to determine the overall stance of fiscal policy at the EC level, with decisions taken on a majority basis. The disciplinary influence of market forces on national budgetary policies was not deemed to be sufficient on its own.

The Delors Report set the EMU ball rolling; and it did roll very fast indeed. On the basis of the report, a decision was taken at the Madrid European Council of June 1989 to proceed to the first stage of EMU on 1 July 1990, which coincided with the complete liberalization of capital movements in eight members of the Community. This was followed by the decision reached at the European Council in Strasbourg in December of the same year to call for a new Intergovernmental Conference (IGC) to prepare the treaty revisions necessary for a complete EMU. Both decisions were taken unanimously, despite the expressed opposition of the UK, as well as the persisting differences on important aspects of EMU and the nature of the transitional period among the other members.

The Rome European Council, in October 1990, fixed the date for the second stage of EMU for January 1994, that is, one year after the expected completion of the single market. Giulio Andreotti as Council President and Helmut Kohl drove this through, successfully ambushing both Margaret Thatcher and Kohl's more reluctant colleagues Theo Waigel (German finance minister) and Karl-Otto Pöhl (Dyson 1994: 144). Before the official opening of the new IGC in December 1990 a great deal of the preparatory work had already been done by the CCBG and the Monetary Committee, following closely in the steps of the Delors Committee. This included the draft statutes of the ECB. The Commission had also published a major study of the potential costs and benefits of EMU (Commission 1990e), very much along the lines of the Cecchini Report (Cecchini et al. (1988)). Dyson writes (1994: 255): 'One Market, One Money [the name of the study] was a clear illustration of the role of economic ideas as legitimator of policy. Like the earlier Cecchini Report on the single European market, it was an example of economic research after the decision of political principle had already been taken.' The majority of academic economists had always been rather sceptical about the advantages of EMU.

Thus, money was once again at the centre of European high politics. Commitment to monetary union was almost indistinguishable from the more general commitment to European unification. The second IGC on political union, called in June 1990, was seen by the French government as an adjunct to the EMU project, and by the German government as the trade-off and counterweight to monetary union. During the negotiations the economic and political desirability of EMU was not seriously put in question. This matter was supposed to have been already settled. The political decision had been taken at the highest political level, and only British representatives were ready to express their doubts in public. The other doubters, and they did exist in significant numbers in the other countries, kept a low profile. They preferred to concentrate on specific problems instead of challenging the main principles and objectives. After all, much of the work had already been done by committees of experts. There was very little public debate on the subject of EMU prior to the signing of the Treaty, and one important reason was that it was still considered a matter for the *cognoscenti*.

The treaty rules on EMU

The articles of the new Treaty and the related protocols attached to it made provisions for the centralization of monetary and exchange-rate policy at the final stage. The European System of Central Banks (ESCB) would be based on a federal structure, composed of the ECB and the national central banks, although the precise relationship between the ECB and national central banks was not very clearly defined. The latter would operate in accordance with the guidelines and instructions of the ECB. The primary objective of the new institution would be to maintain price stability, and it would take no instructions from political authorities. Arrangements for accountability to EU institutions were made, but they were accompanied by strict guarantees of independence from political interference.

The ESCB would define and implement monetary policy for the Union as a whole, it would conduct foreign exchange operations, and it would hold and manage the official foreign reserves of member countries. As regards the exchange-rate policy of the Union, the Treaty allowed Ecofin a role, notably in the negotiation of international agreements and the formulation of 'general orientations', thus leaving the formulation of exchange-rate policy and the division of responsibilities between the ECB and Ecofin somewhat unclear. The ECB would have the exclusive right to authorize the issue of money. It would not be permitted to lend to governments: any form of 'monetary financing' of governments would be prohibited, and so would any 'bailing out' of indebted governments and other public institutions. Provision was also made for a future role of the ECB with respect to the prudential supervision of financial institutions, although this would have to be authorized eventually by the Council.

The ECB would be governed by: a six-member executive board, including a president and a vice-president, appointed for an eight-year, non-renewable term by the European Council; and a governing council, consisting of the members of the executive board and the governors of the national central banks. In order further to ensure the independence of the ESCB, national legislation regulating the operation of national central banks would have to be changed accordingly. Thus, entry into the third and final stage of EMU would imply not only the transfer of monetary powers from the national to the European level, but also a very significant change in relations between political authorities and central banks. The Bundesbank had provided the example to follow.

The Maastricht Treaty on European Union (TEU) did not create any new institution for the conduct of fiscal policies, which would remain a national responsibility, nor was there any mention of fiscal federalism which might lead to the creation of a much bigger EU budget. The TEU did, however, make provisions for the strengthening of existing mechanisms of multilateral surveillance, while also attempting to define in some detail what constituted 'economically correct' behaviour. On the basis of a recommendation made by the Commission, Ecofin would draft each year 'the broad guidelines of the economic policies of the Member States and of the Community' (Article 103, now 99); but these guidelines could easily remain a list of pious wishes. There are, however, much stricter provisions for the profligate members, which are introduced through the so-called excessive deficit procedure (Article 104c, now 104, and the attached protocol). The ceilings of 3 per cent for public deficits and 60 per cent for public debt in terms of gross domestic product (GDP), adopted as part of the convergence criteria for admission to the final stage of EMU (see below), would also be used as reference values for the assessment of national budgetary policies.

On the basis of reports prepared by the Commission, which was thereby given the role of a watchdog, Ecofin would decide by qualified majority whether a situation of excessive deficit existed in a member country. A whole range of measures would then be available to the Council, from public recommendations to the imposition of fines. In between, the Council could resort to other measures, such as requiring the European Investment Bank (EIB) to reconsider its lending policy to the particular member country and asking the latter to make non-interest-bearing deposits with the Community. This was certainly not meant to be 'soft' coordination; but was it politically realistic?

The TEU provided for the establishment of EMU in three stages. The first stage, which had already started in July 1990, was meant as a consolidation of the status quo. It was supposed to include the liberalization of capital movements and the inclusion of all currencies in the narrow band of the ERM. Unfortunately, markets did not share this view; thus, instead of consolidation, there was a breakdown of the old ERM during the first stage. The second stage would start on 1 January 1994. The main purpose of this intermediate stage was to secure the economic convergence of member countries in preparation for the complete EMU. During the second stage the CCBG would be replaced by the European Monetary Institute (EMI), which would make mostly technical preparations before the setting up of the ECB at the beginning of the third stage.

The most crucial part of the transitional arrangements related to the conditions to be fulfilled at the beginning of the third and final stage. The latter would start with the irrevocable fixity of the exchange rates of those currencies participating in it, to be followed by the 'rapid introduction' of the single currency, which would thus replace national currencies. The definition of speed, moving from irrevocably fixed exchange rates to a single currency, was to be decided later. According to the Treaty, the European Council would decide, on the basis of reports from the Commission and the EMI, whether each individual country fulfilled the conditions for admission to the final stage.

The third stage would begin on 1 January 1997 only if a simple majority of member countries were found to fulfil those conditions. Otherwise, the third stage would start on 1 January 1999 at the latest, irrespective of how many member countries were found to fulfil the necessary conditions at the time. Again the European Council was to decide on each case on the basis of qualified majority. Those failing the test would remain in 'derogation': to all intents and purposes, they would be excluded from the new institutional framework. Their case would, however, be examined at least every two years. Voluntary 'opt-outs' were added to provisions for temporary derogations, thus turning EMU into a new kind of experiment with variable speed and multi-tier forms of integration. Because the UK refused to commit itself in advance to participating in the final stage of EMU, it secured an 'opt-out' protocol which left the decision for a future government and parliament. Denmark chose a softer version of 'opting out': in this case, the relevant protocol referred to the possibility of a referendum prior to Denmark's participation in the final stage.

Conditions for entry and the convergence criteria

The conditions for admission to the final stage, otherwise known as convergence criteria, are quite explicit and they concentrate exclusively on monetary variables. The first convergence criterion refers to a sustainable price performance, defined in the attached protocol as a rate of inflation which does not exceed that of the three best-performing member countries by more than 1.5 percentage points. The second relates to the sustainability of the government financial position: the actual or planned deficit should not exceed 3 per cent of GDP, while the accumulated public debt should not be above 60 per cent of GDP. With respect to this criterion, the wording of Article 104c (new 104) of the Treaty leaves some margin for manoeuvre: it allows for higher deficits as long as they have been declining 'substantially and continuously', or are considered to be 'exceptional and temporary'; and it also allows for higher government debt on the condition that the latter is 'sufficiently diminishing and approaching the reference value at a satisfactory pace'. The wording is thus vague enough to allow room for interpretation.

Exchange-rate stability is the third criterion: the national currency must have remained within the 'normal' fluctuation margins of the ERM for at least two years prior to the decision about the final stage, without any devaluation and without any severe tension. 'Normal' has been generally understood to take account of the widening of the bands agreed for the ERM in August 1993. The fourth criterion refers to the durability of the convergence: the average nominal interest rate on long-term government bonds has been chosen as the appropriate indicator and it should not exceed that of the three best-performing member states by more than two percentage points.

The convergence criteria can be criticized on many grounds. They are mechanistic, some of them arbitrary and, perhaps, also superfluous. In economic terms, they could be viewed at best as a very rough (and also ephemeral) indicator of the stability orientation of countries to be admitted into the final stage. This could, arguably, influence the credibility of EMU and the ECB. Economic convergence as a precondition for EMU reflects an old 'economist' argument (i.e. that fixed exchange rates should not precede convergence of economic policy), which also happened to receive wide support in countries like Germany. And, of course, the criteria were meant (by the Germans) to restrict, at least for some time, the number of countries allowed into the final stage. There were those who wanted to exclude Italy from joining unless its government cut back its large budget deficit and ever-rising public debt. Economics is an inexact science, and politics the art of the possible; hence the very imperfect product of Maastricht.

The new Treaty went into considerable detail (indeed excessive detail for a document which serves as the constitution of the emerging European political system) in describing the final stage of EMU and the criteria for what should constitute 'economically correct' behaviour as a precondition for entry; the rest was more flexible and less precise. It was a typical Community compromise. The French got a clear commitment enshrined in the Treaty as well as a specific date. The Germans made sure that the date would be distant, with little happening in between, and that the new European model would be as close as possible to their own. Having tried, without success, a variety of diversionary tactics, the British secured an 'opt-out' for themselves, followed by the Danes, while the poor countries obtained a more or less explicit link with redistribution through the cohesion fund (see Chapter 9).

The momentum behind agreement on EMU

The driving force for the relaunching of monetary union came from Paris and, to a lesser extent, Rome and Brussels. French governments had always been in favour of fixed exchange rates. They had never believed in the stability or efficiency of financial markets, which were often caricatured as a den of Anglo-Saxon speculators. For France, the move towards a complete EMU would help to end the asymmetrical nature of the existing system, and would therefore secure for the country a stronger say in the conduct of European monetary policy. Last but not least, money provided the instrument for integrating the German giant more tightly into the Community system. Those objectives were largely shared by the Italians. As for the Commission, under the Presidency of Delors, it saw in EMU the consolidation of the internal market and the further strengthening of European political construction. It was the inevitable next step in the process of integration. The Commission provided valuable support, even though it played only a very limited role during the actual negotiations.

Initially, the Germans showed very little enthusiasm: the government and the central bank were happy with the status quo and any move towards monetary union was perceived, quite rightly, as leading to the erosion of Germany's independence in the monetary field. In purely economic terms, there was precious little advantage for the Germans in a monetary union, assuming, of course, that some kind of a regional currency arrangement which helps to contain the overvaluation of the DM can be taken for granted. For most of the period of the EMS the main gain for the Germans had been the stability of exchange rates for approximately half of the country's external trade and the consequential gain in competitiveness. This has always been a very important consideration, clearly more important for politicians and industrialists than for central bankers (CEPR 1995). On the other hand, there is no doubt that an EMS in which Germany set the monetary standard was infinitely better for the Germans than a monetary union in which they would have to share with others the power to run monetary policy.

What finally tipped the balance was the perceived need to reaffirm the country's commitment to European integration in the wake of German unification. This is how the matter was presented in Paris. Thus, the German decision (Chancellor Kohl's to be precise) to proceed with EMU was highly political (see also Garrett 1994; Woolley 1994). Helmut Kohl spoke of economic and monetary integration as a matter 'of war and peace in the 21st century' (*Financial Times*, 19 October 1995); and this statement is indicative of his approach to the subject. The combination of different factors, namely the relative weight of the country, its high reputation in terms of monetary stability, especially among European central bankers, and its strong preference for the status quo, strengthened enormously the negotiating power of Germany, thus enabling it in most cases to impose its own terms with respect to the transition and the contents of the final stage of EMU (Dyson 1994).

Although Moravcsik tends to underestimate the geopolitical dimension in the Maastricht negotiations (and in the shaping of German policy), he is right in arguing that 'the outcomes of distributive conflict . . . consistently reflected the preferences of

Germany—the country with the tightest domestic win-set and the most to give up in the monetary negotiations'. And he continues: 'the choice of institutions reflected above all the need for credible commitments, in particular Germany's desire to "lock in" a guarantee of low inflation by creating an autonomous ECB' (1998: 386). The monetary area is where German power has been most pronounced. This should change after the entry into the final phase, hence the attempt made by the Germans to exact as high a price as possible for allowing this to happen. They argued that they wanted only to make sure that the new European currency would be at least as stable and strong as the DM, and the German public seemed to support this argument wholeheartedly.

Once a Franco-German agreement had been reached on the subject of EMU, the process appeared almost unstoppable, thus repeating earlier patterns of European decision-making. Italy was supportive, and provided much of the intellectual input. The Dutch shared much of the economic scepticism of the Germans, but their margin of manœuvre was extremely limited. Belgium and Luxembourg were fervent supporters, although Belgium was at the same time extremely concerned that a strict application of the convergence criteria might keep it outside the privileged group, because of its very high public debt. Denmark felt almost like a natural member of the European currency area, although its politicians were not at all sure whether they would be able to carry the population with them into a monetary union, hence the 'opt-out' protocol.

The main concern of the other southern countries was to link EMU to more substantial budgetary transfers and also to avoid an institutionalization of two or more tiers in the Community. They were only partially successful, more with the former than with the latter. Ireland benefited from the transfers and felt more secure than its southern brethren that it would be among the first to obtain an entry ticket into the final stage. It would, however, have preferred that the other island separating it from the continent would also join since so much of its trade is still done with the UK.

As for Britain, it remained the only country where the government, itself internally divided, expressed grave doubts about the desirability and feasibility of EMU, on both economic and political grounds. The situation had apparently changed little since 1979. Realizing its isolation, the Conservative government made a conscious effort to remain at the negotiating table, and it sacrificed Mrs Thatcher in the process. It made alternative proposals, such as the 'hard ecu', which, however, failed to make much of an impression on the other partners. In the end, it reconciled itself with an 'opt-out' provision in the treaty.

Central bankers, who are absolutely crucial for the successful implementation of the EMU project, had been closely involved from an early stage, notably through their participation in the Delors Committee and subsequently in the drafting of the ECB statutes. They were also responsible for the everyday running of the EMS. In contrast, domestic interest groups, parliaments, and the wider public played hardly any role during the negotiations. Britain was an exception to this rule, and this can be largely explained in terms of the deep divisions created in the country by EMU. For the large majority of the other European countries, EMU became a political issue only after the signing of the Treaty; and popular reactions then came as an unpleasant surprise to most politicians.

The long transition: governments, markets, and societies

Market pressures

The Maastricht Treaty met with little applause from European societies and international markets alike. What proved to be an agonizing process of ratification of the Treaty coincided with the turmoil in the exchange markets, and the two became mutually reinforcing. The long period of exchange rate stability came to an end in 1992, under strong market pressure, partly responding to rising German borrowing to fund the costs of unification. Speculation against the existing bilateral rates began during that year; it rapidly gathered momentum, leading to unprecedented transfers of funds across frontiers and currencies. Repeated changes in interest rates and heavy central bank intervention in exchange markets proved grossly inadequate to deal with the problem. The result was a series of realignments, the withdrawal of two currencies from the ERM, and finally the abandonment of the old narrow bands of fluctuation in August 1993. Big losses were incurred by central banks, and most notably the Bank of England, and there were negative effects as well for the real economy and the process of European integration (Gros and Thygesen 1998).

It was highly unfortunate, although not unrelated, that all this happened at a time when member countries were going through the process of ratifying the TEU, the most important element of which was precisely the construction of a complete EMU with deadlines and detailed provisions. The small 'no' majority in the first Danish referendum in June 1992 acted as a catalyst for a new wave of 'Euro-scepticism', and the ratification process became both long and painful. This in turn added fuel to speculative attacks against the existing central rates in the ERM. European societies and international markets clearly took a very sceptical view of commitments solemnly undertaken by government leaders.

The entry into a new phase for the EMS, which happened violently and was forced upon unwilling governments, was caused by a combination of different factors. One such factor was the progressive overvaluation of some currencies. The crisis of September 1992 was largely a crisis of confidence affecting the weaker currencies which were widely perceived as being overvalued. The governments concerned were soon forced to concede defeat: sterling and the lira withdrew from the ERM, while the peseta and the escudo went through a series of devaluations in order to remain inside.

Market instability did, however, continue, and more currencies came under attack. Credibility had gone out with a bang, and the herd instinct (of Anglo-Saxon speculators as repeatedly denounced by French politicians!) led to ever-growing market pressure. According to an IMF study published at the time: 'The discipline exerted by capital markets is neither infallible nor is it always applied smoothly and consistently. Nevertheless, the markets eventually decide on what are unsustainable situations, and when they do, their size alone increasingly allows them to force adjustments' (IMF 1993).

National authorities had deprived themselves of a policy instrument to which they had frequently resorted in the past in the defence of exchange rates. Capital controls were no longer available when the massive transfers of funds began to take place, although they were temporarily reintroduced in some countries after the September 1992 crisis. Reacting to the crisis, some economists called for the introduction of measures which would be intended to 'throw sand in the wheels of international finance': a tax on foreign exchange transactions or non-interest-bearing deposit requirements on banks taking open positions in foreign exchange (see, for example, Eichengreen and Wyplosz 1993). But such proposals went against the trend. It was not always clear whether people objected to such measures because they were undesirable (market-distorting), or impractical (in the name of globalization), or perhaps both. The role of international financial markets seemed to be accepted as a fact of life, even though not always a pleasant one. But going against it was generally considered as politically incorrect.

Differing policy preoccupations

There were also serious problems of policy coordination in an asymmetrical system. During the crisis markets increasingly challenged the sustainability of restrictive monetary policies in a period of deep economic recession and rapidly growing unemployment. Following German unification, the burden of the stabilization effort fell almost entirely on monetary policy, while budget deficits kept on growing. The Bundesbank drove short-term interest rates upwards and kept them high, while unemployment was rising fast in the whole of western Europe.

What was good (perhaps unavoidable under the circumstances) for Germany was not good for the rest of Europe. The system of fixed exchange rates, combined with the continuing central role of the DM, meant that other countries could not lower their own interest rates, unless, of course, they were ready to opt for a more general realignment of central rates or leave the system. The resistance to a general realignment—basically a euphemism for a devaluation of the other currencies against the DM—was justified in terms of the so-called economic fundamentals (after all, several countries participating in the narrow band of the ERM were running lower inflation rates than Germany). There was, in fact, much more at stake, namely the prestige and credibility of governments. This was apparently felt particularly strongly in France, where the pursuit of 'competitiveness through disinflation' had exacted a high cost in terms of unemployment (Blanchard and Muet 1993).

There was a clear policy conflict between Germany and the other countries, and there was no mechanism in the EMS to resolve it. German (and European) interest rates remained too high in a period of recession, domestic opposition to deflationary policies kept on growing in several countries, while market operators placed ever larger bets on a general realignment of currencies, thus questioning the sustainability of existing exchange rates and/or policies. The problem was part and parcel of the fundamental asymmetry in the EMS (Tsoukalis 1997).

In August 1993 EU governments announced the widening of the margins of fluctuation of the ERM to 15 per cent, with the old 2.25 per cent margin being kept only between the DM and the guilder. This device was an ingenious way of conceding defeat to the enemy (in this case, the market). Markets had won, because they had become more powerful and also because governments had shown themselves unable to make use of the flexibility offered by the system which they had themselves designed. During the crisis of 1992–3 policy coordination at the European level showed its limitations.

Those events certainly did not augur well for the success of the EMU project. Hardly anybody would have dared to predict at the time that the final stage of EMU would in fact begin on 1 January 1999, with eleven countries participating. This became possible due to a dramatic transformation of the political and economic climate. The road leading to EMU was shaped by the continuous interaction between governments, markets, and societies. Governments operate at both the national and the European level (the sub-national level being hardly relevant in the case of monetary policy), while financial markets are international and societies stubbornly national.

Political commitment and convergence

During the transition to EMU most governments, acting separately or through European institutions, showed a remarkable commitment to this goal, not only in words but also in deeds. A number of important decisions were taken by successive European Councils, including most notably the plan for the changeover to the single currency, following the introduction of the final stage. According to this plan, the euro and those national currencies participating in the final stage will coexist until July 2002, when the euro is planned to become the only legal tender. Banknotes and coins in euros will begin to circulate in January of the same year. In the meantime, private economic agents will be able to use the euro in their financial transactions, while public authorities will gradually shift from national currencies to the new European currency in the issuing of new public debt. During the second stage the EMI, whose lifespan was limited to the second stage of EMU, undertook much of the analytical work and the technical preparations for the ECB and the single currency.

Following strong pressure from Germany, the European Council adopted a Stability and Growth Pact at its meeting in Amsterdam in June 1997. This was meant to give real teeth to the excessive deficit procedure agreed earlier at Maastricht, while also making it much more stringent. True, it also contained the appropriate references to growth and employment, but they were non-binding. The Stability and Growth Pact was and remains highly controversial, although fully consistent with the economic orthodoxy prevailing at the time and the strong emphasis on fiscal consolidation (Allsopp and Vines 1998).

Activity at the European level was continuously backed by political statements pointing to the inevitability of EMU and the appropriate macroeconomic policies, which aimed to satisfy the convergence criteria. In this respect, the role played by Chancellor Kohl was absolutely decisive. The transition to EMU survived important changes of government in different member countries. This in itself says very much about the degree and cross-party nature of the political commitment in most EU countries, and hence about the solidity of the project. Inflation rates continued to converge downwards, thus reaching levels which had not been experienced for several decades (see Fig. 6.1).

Budget deficits were also cut substantially, most remarkably in Italy, and in several countries, with the helping hand of creative accountants, the relevant convergence criterion was met on time. Figure 6.3 shows the evolution of government deficit and

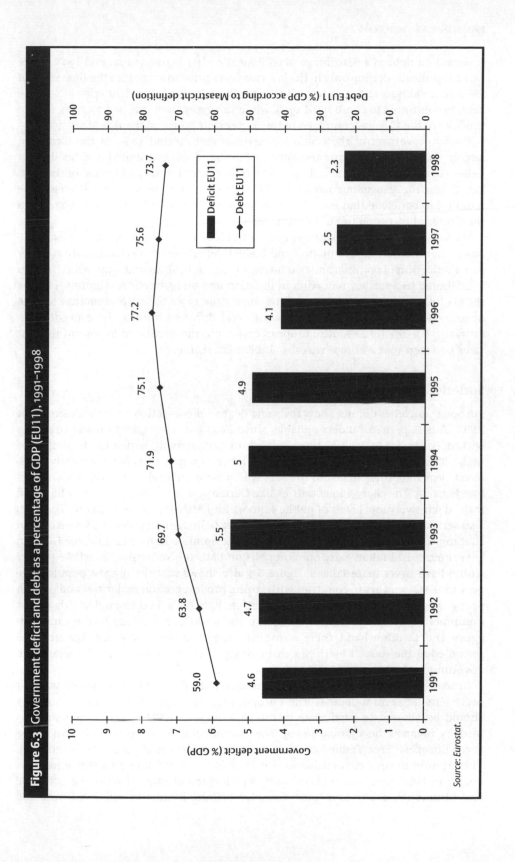

Figure 6.3 Government deficit and debt as a percentage of GDP (EU11), 1991-1998

Debt EU11 (% GDP according to Maastricht definition)

Government deficit (% GDP)

- ■ Deficit EU11
- ◆ Debt EU11

Year	Deficit	Debt
1991	4.6	59.0
1992	4.7	63.8
1993	5.5	69.7
1994	5	71.9
1995	4.9	75.1
1996	4.1	77.2
1997	2.5	75.6
1998	2.3	73.7

Source: Eurostat.

government debt as a percentage of GDP for the EU11 between 1991 and 1998. There was a significant decline only in the last two years prior to entry into the final stage of EMU, in an almost last-minute rush to meet the relevant Maastricht criterion. As for debt, it continued to climb until 1996, when in aggregate it reached 77.2 per cent of the GDP of the EU11 (as compared to the 60 per cent figure adopted at Maastricht).

The improvement of the economic environment around 1995, in the form of a largely export-led economic recovery in Europe, also contributed a great deal: it helped to reduce government deficits and to appease the 'animal spirits' of the market. Given the exogenous nature of the recovery, some people may therefore be tempted to conclude that even God was in favour of EMU, at least until 1998, when the clouds of recession began to gather again.

Markets thus gradually began to believe in EMU, and this helped to create a virtuous circle: the decline in inflation and budget deficits led to exchange rate stability and a reduction in nominal and real interest rates, both short and long, which in turn contributed to a further reduction in inflation and budget deficits. Figure 6.4 shows the evolution of long-term interest rates during the 1990s for a representative sample of countries from the EU11, countries with very different histories in terms of interest rates. For the three south European countries, the decline in long-term interest rates between 1991 and 1998 was absolutely remarkable.

Societies follow?

European societies did not show the same degree of conviction or enthusiasm about EMU. This is perhaps understandable, since EMU was identified in many countries with deflationary policies at times of high unemployment, which hardly helped to make it an object of love for European citizens. Opinion polls have regularly registered clear majorities in favour of EMU, which were increasing as D-Day approached (see Fig. 6.5). The change in countries like Germany and the Netherlands, which had started with very low levels of public support for EMU, was quite dramatic. This may also serve as an interesting lesson as to whether politicians can sometimes succeed in shaping, as opposed to simply following, public opinion. If, for example, the German government had taken early opinion polls on EMU too seriously, the whole project would have never materialized. Figure 6.5 also shows that the highest popular support for EMU appears in countries with strong pro-integration majorities and/or high propensity to inflation and debt accumulation. Italy is the best example, with almost unanimous popular support for EMU. Ireland and Greece belong to the same category. On the other hand, there were still some countries where negative attitudes prevailed at the start of EMU. Not surprisingly, these were the countries where the governments had chosen to stay out.

In May 1998, following a period of monetary stability and convergence without precedent for several decades, the European Council agreed that eleven countries should be allowed to participate in the final stage of EMU, which would start, as initially planned, on 1 January 1999. They included Austria and Finland, two of the three European Free Trade Association countries which had joined the EU in 1995. The attempt to restrict participation, at least in the beginning, to a small group of countries belonging to the old core of Europe had manifestly failed (see e.g. Schäuble and Lamers 1994). The four 'outs' included Britain, Denmark, and Sweden, in the

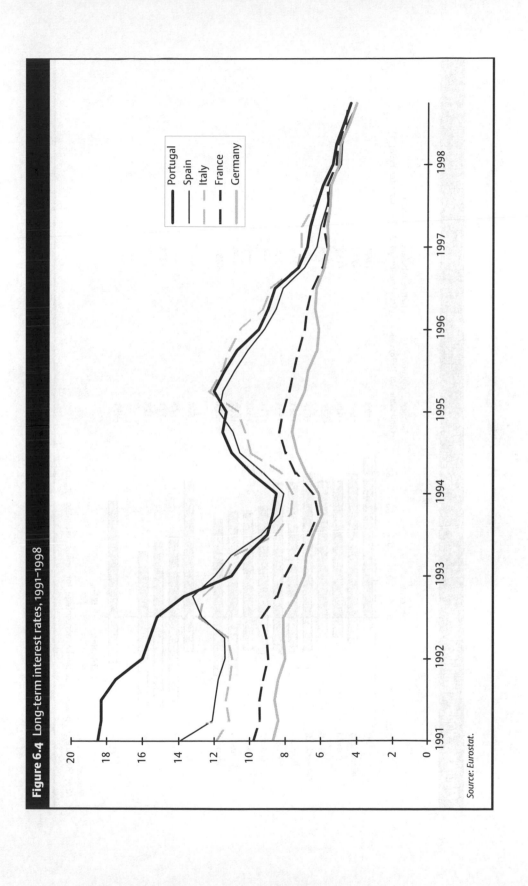

Figure 6.4 Long-term interest rates, 1991–1998

Portugal
Spain
Italy
France
Germany

Source: Eurostat.

Figure 6.5 Popular support for EMU

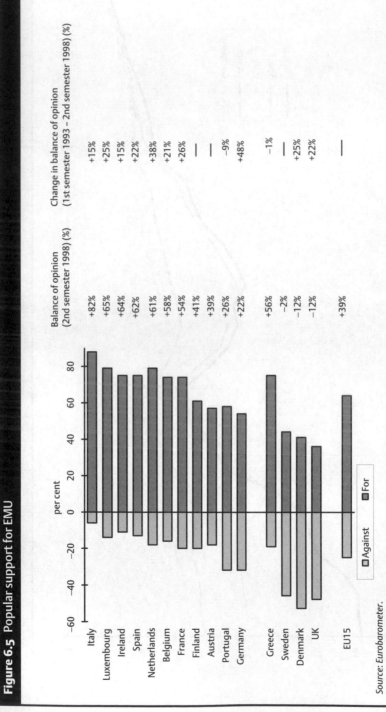

	Balance of opinion (2nd semester 1998) (%)	Change in balance of opinion (1st semester 1993 – 2nd semester 1998) (%)
Italy	+82%	+15%
Luxembourg	+65%	+25%
Ireland	+64%	+15%
Spain	+62%	+22%
Netherlands	+61%	+38%
Belgium	+58%	+21%
France	+54%	+26%
Finland	+41%	—
Austria	+39%	—
Portugal	+26%	–9%
Germany	+22%	+48%
Greece	+56%	–1%
Sweden	–2%	—
Denmark	–12%	+25%
UK	–12%	+22%
EU15	+39%	—

Source: Eurobarometer.
Note: 'Balance of Opinion' is defined as percentage 'for' minus percentage 'against'.

category of 'able but unwilling', and Greece, which was willing but still unable. This division between 'ins' and 'outs' had prompted a painful argument over the need to establish a forum for ministers from the 'ins', without causing a dangerous rupture from the 'outs'. A Euro-11 Council grouping has been set up for this purpose, meeting separately from Ecofin.

The European Council agreed on conversion rates for all the currencies participating in the final stage. It also nominated the members of the executive board of the ECB, after a long and rather embarrassing public row between the French and the others concerning the nomination of the first President of the ECB. Wim Duisenberg, the former Governor of the Dutch Central Bank, was finally appointed to this post. Incredible though it may have been a few years earlier, EMU was a reality in January 1999, with the euro and the ECB joining (with a bang?) the world of international finance.

Europe with the euro: what kind of integration?

The detailed provisions of the treaty, and the meticulous preparations which preceded the entry into the final stage of EMU, nevertheless left some fundamental questions unanswered. The Maastricht package was a political bargain, which deliberately left for later negotiation many of the wider ramifications of monetary union. The EU is not an optimal currency area; far from it. There are no adequate adjustment mechanisms, such as labour flexibility and large budgetary transfers, to act as effective substitutes for the exchange rate. The architects of EMU have produced a structure of arguably post-modern inspiration: a centralized monetary policy which operates against the background of a highly decentralized fiscal policy and an even more decentralized political system. This combination has no historical precedent, and it is also, arguably, unsustainable in the long run.

In the conduct of a centralized monetary policy, it is unavoidable that the ECB will give much greater weight to economic trends in Germany or France, rather than to those in Ireland or Portugal. In the early years of EMU, as this new institution seeks to establish its own reputation, it may be tempted to outdo the Bundesbank in countering inflation, especially in times of high unemployment. If economic cycles remain unsynchronized among individual economies within the euro zone, the costs of the 'one-size-fits-all' monetary policy will be very uneven. Yet the question of parallel measures to coordinate economic policies, or to provide compensatory budgetary transfers, has been sidestepped. The link between monetary and economic union has long been debated among economists. The MacDougall Report in 1977, reflecting the continuing influence of Keynesianism, suggested that a larger common budget would be needed; the Padoa-Schioppa Report of 1987, working within the constraints of a monetarist consensus, was more cautious on this issue. The EU budget remains very small, and with no provision for a stabilization function. Nor is there much support in most member states for a larger common budget (see Chapter 8).

In a monetary union there are strong arguments for greater flexibility of fiscal policy, to serve as an instrument of adjustment at the national and regional level.

On the other hand, there is a risk of free-riding by national, or even regional, governments operating under the shield of the Union, assuming, of course, that markets cannot be relied upon to provide an effective restraint on government overspending (and undertaxing). The treaty provisions, and the Stability and Growth Pact which followed, were aimed essentially against 'free-riders' in the future monetary union. Their effectiveness and political feasibility, however, remain to be tested.

Behind the institutional structure established to manage the single currency lies the political issue of who is to determine macroeconomic priorities for the EU as a whole, and how (Allsopp and Vines 1998; Eichengreen 1998). There is as yet no mechanism for this. The broad guidelines for the coordination of national policies, which Ecofin adopts each year, are too broad to have any noticeable effect on national economic strategies.

The existence of a large majority of centre-left governments may eventually strengthen the pressure for a more effective coordination at the EU level of fiscal policies, and macroeconomic policies more generally. This would, first of all, require the strengthening of the Euro-11 Council of Economics and Finance Ministers to provide a political counterweight to the bankers, on which French governments have placed so many expectations; and a real dialogue between this Council and the ECB. EMU could then end up being Europe's answer to the globalization and inherent instability of financial markets by restoring some of the effectiveness of macro-economic policy, which has been irretrievably lost at the national level (see also Tsoukalis 1998).

After all, the EU is still a relatively closed economy in trade terms, very similar to the United States. The external trade of the EU15 in goods (excluding trade between the members of the Union) is still virtually the same as it used to be about thirty-five years ago, namely below 10 per cent of GDP. Some elements of Keynesianism could therefore be resurrected in the context of EMU. This is certainly something not envisaged by the authors of the TEU, nor is it very compatible with current economic orthodoxy—*la pensée unique*, as denounced by its French critics (Fitoussi 1995).

The Monetary Affairs Committee of the European Parliament was attempting in 1998–9 to establish a regular dialogue with the ECB, in order to provide an element of political accountability and some political debate about the underlying macro-economic choices. But, as the single currency was launched, such questions of accountability and of political counterweight to the technocratic central bankers were still under early discussion.

Holding the two IGCs in parallel in 1990–1 was meant to stress the link between EMU and political union. The TEU, however, delivered little of substance on political union; and the Treaty of Amsterdam did little to strengthen central political authority in the EU. The emergence of a central bank without a corresponding political authority has led some analysts to portray catastrophe scenarios not only for EMU but for the EU as a whole, if there is a recession in one or more of the big countries of the euro zone, and if the ECB is perceived as not responding adequately to popular demands for more expansionary policy (Feldstein 1997). European policy-makers have left it to a future recession to test whether EMU will act as the catalyst for further political union, or whether monetary policy has been decoupled from political authority.

Monetary union carries implications for a wide range of other policy domains, some not yet drawn into the EU framework, others already subject to EU regimes. The regulation of financial markets is one field for potential spill-over, especially given the rapid restructuring in this sector, partly a consequence of the move towards a single currency. Questions of tax harmonization, or of the prevention of harmful tax competition, are creeping on to the EU agenda. Taxes on capital, which is more mobile than labour across frontiers, are a particular concern to the German government. Fiscal incentives for investment are also a focus for controversy between advocates of harmonization and defenders of national fiscal autonomy. The likelihood of further Europe-wide corporate and financial mergers, as the single currency becomes established, has implications for EU competition policy (see Chapter 5). The loss of the exchange rate as a policy instrument at the national level, and the lack of any sizeable inter-country budgetary transfers to act as shock absorbers, will place the burden of adjustment on labour markets. Hence the emphasis has shifted to promoting greater flexibility in labour markets and social policies, even though definitions of flexibility differ widely.

The international dimension of EMU and the euro, another significant political and institutional issue, had also been left to one side until a late stage in the move towards a single currency. Monetary union implies a single external representative, but finance ministers of the major EU states are accustomed to playing a role on the international stage. The European Council has so far decided that the President of the Euro-11 Council will, together with the President of the ECB, represent the countries of the euro zone in meetings of the Group of Seven (Eight, when Russia takes part), alongside—not instead of—colleagues from the larger member governments. Logically, the separate national representations of EU countries in international financial organizations, such as the International Monetary Fund (IMF), should in time give way to a single European representation. But the weak legitimacy of the EU, and the national sensitivities of the larger members, may make this a long-term prospect. The issue of common representation begs the question of what the external policy of EMU would be and how that might be defined. Until the beginning of the final stage the policy debate had been largely focused on the impact of a single currency within the EMU itself. The euro will be an international currency, operating as an international vehicle and as a reserve currency, but there had been little discussion of what this would imply (Portes and Rey 1998; Bergsten 1999).

The launch of EMU opens up the prospect of a multi-tier EU. Three groups of countries have emerged: the Eleven, which had tied their exchange rates irrevocably to the euro; Greece and Denmark, their currencies within the new ERM, and thus formally linked to the euro; and Britain and Sweden, which opted for an independent float. The Greek government hoped to fulfil the convergence criteria on the basis of 1999 figures, and to be able to join in 2001. If EMU proves successful, it will be very difficult for any member of the Union to stay outside this most important manifestation of economic integration for long. The shadow of eastern enlargement also hangs over the further development of monetary union. The DM already operates as a parallel currency in some parts of eastern Europe, including most of ex-Yugoslavia. From 1992 the Estonians pegged the kroon to the DM, with their Central Bank acting as a currency board. From 1994 the Lithuanians pegged the litas to the US dollar. The Latvians opted in 1993 to link the lats (without a currency board) to the Special

Drawing Rights in the IMF. In 1997 Bulgaria adopted a currency board, linking its currency to the DM. Such approaches might conceivably move applicant states faster towards the single currency than most EU policy-makers either expect or wish. Those in Germany and France who had hoped to start EMU with a small and homogeneous core of countries may find a lengthening queue of applicants pressing for inclusion.

Conclusions

EMU represents a major step forward in European integration. The key decisions have been taken by heads of government, through successive European Councils and through the Maastricht IGC. These recognizably historic decisions were taken largely on political grounds, often overriding the more cautious advice of finance ministries and central banks. Yet the decisions taken have been partial: immensely detailed on the convergence criteria, deliberately imprecise on other important aspects. Implementation has been passed to the central banks, beyond the reach of direct political accountability. High politics and technical expertise have interacted, without a broader debate on the long-term implications or the links to other policy domains.

European monetary integration already has a long history. Early proposals in the 1950s and 1960s, and in the 1970s (Werner Report), sketched out a broader programme of parallel policies and institutional development than that which the EU accepted in the 1990s. The narrower agenda set out in the TEU in some ways made agreement easier, but at the cost of leaving to be settled later a large number of politically sensitive issues—some potentially explosive. Political control and accountability have in some ways been deliberately reduced, by entrenching the independence of the ECB. For most national governments this has involved a double transfer of power with respect to monetary policy: from finance ministries to more autonomous central banks; and from the national to the European level.

The economic and political interests of individual countries, above all of France and Germany, have played a central role. The Franco-German relationship, with its constant attempts to reconcile the very different interests of the two governments, drove monetary integration from 1969 onwards. Germans have been concerned to embed the economy and state within a wider European framework. The French have been propelled by fears that their economy would fail to compete with Germany, a determination to maintain a political and economic balance, and concern that international monetary turbulence might threaten established EU policies. German fears that the appreciation of the DM would render their industry uncompetitive have been matched by French concerns to hold down domestic inflationary pressures. The policies of Italy, the Netherlands, and Belgium, each for different reasons, have been firmly tied to the EMU project. By the late 1980s concerns about economic and political relations within Europe, as well as domestic considerations, had replaced the external preoccupations which predominated in the EMU discussions of the 1970s. German unification provided an additional motivation for its neighbours to commit themselves to a single currency.

Given the political importance of EMU, it is hardly surprising that the crucial decisions and initiatives were taken at the highest political level. Negotiations over the rules governing the EMS and EMU brought together finance ministers, central bankers, and diplomats. Much of the key work has been done by the Monetary Committee, now retitled the Economic and Financial Committee, and set to operate at the heart of the process. Everyday management has been generally left in the safe hands of the corporate world of central bankers. The intensive transgovernmental network which had grown up among central banks since the 1960s provided a foundation for a shared commitment and a shared perspective. The Commission has been an intermittent player, with first Roy Jenkins, and then Jacques Delors, making crucial contributions at key points. But it has had little influence on the actual negotiations, and little involvement in the implementation of EMU, although an extension of macroeconomic coordination would provide some opportunity for it to be a source of expertise. The European Parliament, similarly, has so far established only a marginal role. The European Court of Justice is scarcely involved. Close links between private financial institutions and central banks constitute a narrow policy community, hard of access for others. National parliaments, and national publics, have been little engaged, except in those countries where EMU remains controversial and where referenda on participation are pending (Denmark, Sweden, and the UK).

The role of ideas in this policy domain has been particularly significant. The TEU, and subsequent developments through the 1990s, have been strongly influenced by prevailing economic ideas, most notably the belief that there is no trade-off between inflation and unemployment. If economic conventional wisdom changes, treaties and institutions will have to face a difficult test of flexibility and endurance. The ECB, at the centre of the new institutional architecture, will be tested most severely. It remains to be seen whether it will by then have found a credible political interlocutor in the form of a revamped Ecofin. Debate about macroeconomic choices, and about the balance between the instruments of economic policy, has been at the heart of national politics since the second world war. Some of those choices and instruments have now been transferred to the EU level, without the parallel institutions for generating a Europe-wide debate.

EMU is indeed a high-risk strategy. There is a serious economic risk involved in the irrevocable fixing of exchange rates, while other adjustment mechanisms are still very weak and economic divergence persists. There is also a political risk linked to the legitimacy deficit of the Union. And there is no easy exit option if things go wrong. There is, however, the other side of the coin. If EMU is successful, it will most likely bring with it a much stronger and more integrated EU, in both economic and political terms.

Notes

1 Thanks are due to Carmen Suárez for preparing the graphs.

Further reading

There is a vast literature on European monetary integration and especially the various issues associated with the functioning of EMU. It is dominated by economists, although there are also an increasing number of works from a political economy angle. For a comprehensive analysis of the EMS and monetary integration in general, see Gros and Thygesen (1998). For the politics of the EMS and EMU, see Dyson (1994), Dyson and Featherstone (1999), and Moravscik (1998). This chapter draws heavily on Tsoukalis (forthcoming), which contains a more comprehensive study of European economic integration, as well as on successive editions of Tsoukalis (1997). Previous editions of the present volume deal with earlier periods in more detail. On the creation of the EMS, see Ludlow (1982).

Dyson, K. H. F. (1994), *Elusive Union: The Process of Economic and Monetary Union in Europe* (London: Longman).

Dyson, K., and Featherstone, K. (1999), *The Road to Maastricht: Negotiating Economic and Monetary Union* (Oxford: Oxford University Press).

Gros, D., and Thygesen, N. (1998), *European Monetary Integration: From the European Monetary System towards Monetary Union*, 2nd edn. (London: Longman).

Ludlow, P. (1982), *The Making of the European Monetary System* (London: Butterworth).

Moravscik, A. (1998), *The Choice for Europe: Social Purpose and State Power from Messina to Maastricht* (Ithaca, NY: Cornell University Press).

Tsoukalis, L. (1997), *The New European Economy Revisited*, 3rd edn. (Oxford: Oxford University Press).

—— (forthcoming), *European Political Economy*, 2nd edn. (Oxford: Oxford University Press).

Wallace, H., and Wallace, W. (1996), *Policy-Making in the European Union*, 3rd edn. (Oxford: Oxford University Press).

Chapter 7

The Common Agricultural Policy

Politics Against Markets

Elmar Rieger

Contents

In the future as in the past it will be the 'interests' of individuals rather than the 'ideas' of an economic administration which will rule the world.

(Max Weber, *Economy and Society*)

Summary

The Common Agricultural Policy (CAP) in the 1960s represented a striking example of the evolution of European policy. Yet its establishment reflected defensive, essentially anti-market, national strategies of economic modernization, attaching small farmers' loyalty to rebuilt democracies, with welfare state functions transferred to the European level and farming organizations as monopolistic intermediaries. It served to insulate agricultural policy both from competing domestic political constituencies and from American demands for trade liberalization. A highly segmented system of governance developed, operating through both national and supranational mechanisms. The agricultural sector of the Union became, in both form and substance, a planned economy. Changes in exchange rates, transformations of farm structures triggered by the CAP itself, and diverging national priorities led in the 1970s and 1980s to regulatory complexity and partial, *de facto* renationalization. Rising costs forced reform in the early 1990s, with the General Agreement on Tariffs and Trade (GATT) regime and US trade policies becoming major factors affecting the timing and the agenda of internal reforms. The 1999 reform finally acknowledged renationalization by giving member states a legal basis for varying direct aids according to their own criteria. Despite some changes in the institutional structure of the CAP, and notwithstanding the inclusion of agriculture in the more liberal GATT regulatory framework, now attached to the World Trade Organization (WTO), the CAP remains a bureaucratic system of economic regulation, characterized by negative redistribution, and constantly in danger of triggering trade disputes of major proportions.

Introduction

Agricultural policy-making in the European Union (EU), despite the much acclaimed economic breakdown of the socialist countries of eastern Europe and the Soviet Union, and in defiance of global market capitalism, consists of essentially politics against markets. The stated goal of the CAP is the preservation of an economic sector with supposedly distinctive institutional and social features—socially and economically heterogeneous, 'multi-functional', and family farmed—which seem to forbid the introduction of the principles of industrial production and competitive markets. But the outcome is a costly and conflict-ridden preservation of economic and social features at odds both with the usual economic structure of an industrial society, and with the idea of traditional rural communities. This policy choice was made by the majority of the continental west European countries in the second half of the nineteenth century, and became entrenched in the wake of the Great Depression of the 1930s and the autarchic policies of the second world war. The resulting systems of economic regulation were never dismantled; as a result the agricultural sector of all the bigger west European countries is not integrated into the overall economic and political system. Instead, an elaborate and technically complex agricultural policy mediates between the agricultural sector and the wider economy. Traditionally prices were raised to a level which guaranteed even small-scale farmers a lifestyle compatible with general standards, thereby compensating for inter-sectoral imbalances. The core elements of the CAP, all-embracing regulation of markets insulated from import competition, were not invented by Brussels bureaucrats. They derive from nation states' interests.

The choice made to follow explicitly non-economic objectives in agricultural policy-making gives the CAP a rationale all of its own. Not only is it costly, but it also brings about unintended consequences, including major problems for international agricultural markets. European market organizations have grown, and their interdependence has become more pronounced as farmers have reacted in their own ways to the regulatory environment. Often the outcomes of policy have been very different from those intended by policy-makers, an endemic feature of the CAP. The variety of production systems found in Europe, and the number of farms, have made it hard to evaluate policy alternatives and their outcomes with precision. An unusual mix of European institutional structures, nationally distinctive social values, and cross-cutting economic rationales of legitimacy has made the CAP into a regime with dubious results for both producers and consumers.

Between negative and positive integration

In the early years of the EU the distinctive features of the CAP were seen as laying the ground for intensified European integration. The creation of the European common market was based on the elimination of national barriers, but in the case of agriculture this required the coordination and the fusion of six highly developed systems of state intervention (Pinder 1968).[1] Supranational organizations and agencies replaced most of the national systems of agricultural support, thereby establishing direct links between the farming population of the member states and the EU. Slowly, but persistently, elaborate and increasingly complex forms of supranational political governance evolved around the CAP, making it a positive 'story of action and success' (Lindberg and Scheingold 1970: 41). The remarkable rise of the Confederation of Professional Agricultural Organisations (COPA) as the major organization of European farmers seemed to indicate a quantum leap towards a supranational political system. Many of the general principles of European law were formed in the context of agricultural disputes (Snyder 1985; Usher 1988). Because of its size, sources, and format, the European Agricultural Guidance and Guarantee Fund (EAGGF) is closely intertwined with the Community budget as a whole.

These particular features of the CAP are mostly due to a fundamental asymmetry in the policy-making capacities of the EU. Only with regard to agriculture did the scale of political governance reach proportions resembling those of a federal government:

Here the Community institutions have the power to legislate for the Union as a whole, without being required to refer back to the national parliaments. The progress made in agriculture will be of definite importance for the integrative potential of the EEC. It represents the Union's first effort to develop a common policy in a major economic sphere. Such common policies are central to the successful implementation of the broader goal of economic union as well as the efficient operation of the customs union. (Lindberg 1963: 219–20)

Contrary to the hopes of the first generation of Europeanists, the CAP 'as a proxy for European integration' remained 'an isolated relic for the ambitions of the founding fathers of the European Community' (Duchêne et al. 1985: 1).

But one has to be careful with the notion of an institutional asymmetry. It is because the CAP is a policy of central importance, and institutionally a highly isolated one, that the major social and political forces which underlie and sustain it remain largely invisible. There is a widespread view that the CAP is, in the words of *The*

Economist (29 September 1990), the 'single most idiotic system of economic mis-management that the rich western countries have ever devised'.[2] This view of the CAP is in some way deserved, but it is not based on an analysis of the real forces shaping the agricultural policies of western Europe in the post-war era. It is too simplistic to analyse the CAP in terms of 'stupidity' or 'mistakes'. The more interesting part is its resilience in the face of widespread hostility, even from those whom the system was designed to help, i.e. the farmers. What begs for an explanation is not only the continuance, but the growth, of an expensive, and politically quite troublesome, policy in an increasingly insignificant sector, since employment in agriculture continues to shrink and its share of the gross domestic product (GDP) of the Union is now only 0.6 per cent.

To understand the CAP requires us to see it as an entity in its own right, and not as the key to something else (be it integration theory, the dangers of supranationalism, a general theory of interest group behaviour, of rent-seeking, or of joint-decision-making traps). The CAP follows its own logic;[3] despite the economic revolution in the countryside, and the ups and downs of European integration, the CAP, in its essence, has stayed the same. This is true in a narrow sense, since 'all of the changes were implemented through partial adjustments and corrections of policies in place' (Anania *et al.* 1994a: 12), and it is true in a broader sense, since the CAP has remained relatively untouched by the shifts in the debates about the wider politics of European integration. Indeed, the growing tensions in EC–US agricultural trade relations have served to remind the member states of their attachment to this 'common' policy, which has relieved them of the task of both satisfying the farm lobby and managing agricultural trade relations in an international environment dominated by liberal multilateralism (Vaubel 1994: 174).

The key to understanding this policy domain is to see the CAP as an integral part of the west European welfare state and its particular 'moral' economy.[4] In other words, it has a *political* rationale. Unlike other welfare state institutions, however, agricultural policies typically fuse production, that is output-increasing, with income-related goals, making it hard to separate the distributive and regulatory dimensions. As a consequence, the political and economic dimensions are international in ways that defy the application of normal economic efficiency criteria, a feature which has been deplored by agricultural economists since the first inception of modern, welfare-oriented agricultural price policies (Schultz 1943).

The political effects of this fusion of price and income support functions in the CAP can be summed up as follows:

- It facilitates the operation of an income-securing policy *vis-à-vis* a large and quite heterogeneous group, without requiring direct and costly contacts with individual farmers.

- It releases individual governments from having to decide on the needs of different farming groups or of individual farmers.

- It provides the farming sector with an overwhelming interest in maintaining the policy regime, since it improves the situation of all farmers, albeit the larger more so than the smaller.

- The use of comprehensive and product-specific prices has enabled governments to balance the heterogeneous needs of a highly differentiated farming sector.

- Both the governments of the member states and national interest groups have acquired a shared purpose in sustaining a supranational policy.

Hence the CAP can be seen as a politically driven and defensive strategy to modernize west European agriculture against both the internal threat of the industrial society and the external threat of American trade competition. This helps to explain three problems. First, it clarifies why the governance of the CAP is so complex, neither pure intergovernmentalism nor real supranationalism. The CAP represents an *addition* to, and not an subtraction from, the powers of the national political systems of the member states. Secondly, it explains why the CAP distributes benefits rather perversely despite its explicit social orientation. The creation of a single agricultural price support system has produced an increase in social and economic inequalities, from which big farmers, with considerable political clout, have profited. Thirdly, we have had some clues to why and how agriculture was quite surprisingly included in the Uruguay Round of GATT negotiations, and subsequently incorporated at least partially in the framework of the GATT and the WTO, namely to find a way of reinforcing political control in this sector.

Defensive modernization: the CAP as a welfare state institution

Like the welfare state institutions that deal with labour, the CAP is both an economic and a political mechanism; it seeks to integrate the national farming population into both the transnational and the national polity. Agricultural protectionism, reflected in domestic food prices often more than twice as high as world prices, is its basic instrument. This feature is by no means unique to the CAP; it continues the agricultural policies of the founder member states, and is a common feature of economic modernization. 'Cross-sectional evidence suggests that as economies grow they tend to change from taxing to assisting or protecting agriculture relative to other sectors, and this change occurs at an earlier stage of economic growth the weaker the country's comparative advantage in agriculture' (Anderson and Hayami 1986: 1). Thus in the period 1955–9 agricultural prices in Korea were 15 per cent and in Taiwan 21 per cent below world prices, in the period 1980–2, 166 per cent (Korea) and 55 per cent (Taiwan) above world prices (Anderson and Hayami 1986, Table 2.3). In these countries plebiscitarian party politics and the absence of a competitive party system have induced autocratic rulers to seek mass legitimacy with exactly the same kinds of agricultural sector policies as those which we find in democratic parliamentarian regimes.

What was at stake in the immediate post-war years in west European countries was the challenge of securing the political and social participation of severely disadvantaged and politically isolated social groups. The CAP, like its national forerunners, represents a compromise to this end; it was not a policy designed to increase food production (Milward 1981). Moreover, the much-repeated assertion that there was a political bargain between the industrial interests of Germany and the agricultural interests of France should be laid to rest. The record provides no evidence for this, nor would it have made much sense economically (Willgerodt 1983: 111–14; Milward 1992: 283–4; Vaubel 1994: 174). Much more relevantly, all of the bigger countries had sizeable farming populations which they did not want to exclude from the European Economic Community (EEC), and similarly Dutch agriculture was an integral and important part of the national export economy (Lindberg 1963: 220–5).

This integration of the agriculture sector had two consequences. First, farmers did not block European integration, which was no small achievement, given the weight of the agricultural sector both as a proportion of the labour force and as a share of the economy in the late 1950s (see Table 7.1).[5] The second was that the CAP provided political protection *vis-à-vis* overseas agricultural exporters, most notably in the United States. It seems unlikely that EU members would otherwise have been able to resist pressure from the USA. In sum, the CAP is not only a striking illustration of a major political function being Europeanized, but also a structure designed to strengthen the political governance of agriculture at the national level.

The history and features of the CAP are thus more the product of how west European societies were being transformed after the second world war than of the formulations of the Treaty of Rome. The welfare state dimension had far-reaching implications for the functioning of the CAP and its external trade relations, the role of interest groups, and the 'moral economy' accompanying its governance.

Table 7.1 Changing shares of agriculture in GDP and total civilian employment

Member state	Percentage of GDP		Percentage of total civilian employment	
	1955	1997	1955	1997
Belgium	7.9	1.1	7.2	2.7
France	11.4	1.9	27.2[a]	4.6
Germany	8.0	0.8	13.5	2.9
Italy	20.2	2.5	28.2	6.5
Netherlands	11.4	2.6	10.7[b]	3.7

[a] Figure for 1954.
[b] Figure for 1960.

Source: Commission, *The Agricultural Situation in the European Union*, appears annually.

Income maintenance and income security for farmers

The Treaty of Rome was remarkably brief on agriculture (see Box 7.1). The essence of Articles 38–46 (now 32–8) was basically an 'agreement to agree'; they gave little indication of the concrete terms for integrating agriculture within the common market (Dam 1967: 219). This imprecision was an early indication that agriculture would be controversial.

> **Box 7.1** Objectives of the common agricultural policy
>
> Article 33 (ex 38) of the EEC Treaty set out five objectives for the common agricultural policy:
>
> - to increase agricultural production by promoting technical progress and by ensuring the rational development of agricultural production and optimum utilization of the factors of production, in particular labour;
> - thus to ensure a fair standard of living for the agricultural community, in particular by increasing the individual earnings of persons engaged in agriculture;
> - to stabilize markets;
> - to assure availability of supplies; and
> - to ensure that supplies reach consumers at reasonable prices

The prior national policies were well established, wide-ranging, and highly protective, thus setting the frame for the basic instruments of the CAP in several respects (Lindberg 1963: 223–5). First, market organizations, with fixed prices, were believed to reduce the risk and the uncertainty associated with large variations in commodity prices and in the volume of production. Secondly, market organizations redistribute incomes. Since the Great Depression of the early 1930s, which hit agriculture even harder than industry, 'equity' and 'parity' concerns have been central to the farm policies of all developed societies. Income redistribution to financially stressed or low-income farmers became a major feature of farm policies (Schiller 1939; Schultz 1943). The European market organizations were, at least at the outset, expressly designed to foster small- and medium-scale family farms. Thirdly, market organizations, with fixed and guaranteed prices, were an effective means to provide farmers with higher incomes. This was of particular importance in the 1950s and 1960s in western Europe, when the farming population consisted of millions of smallholders quite remote from the normal apparatus of the state bureaucracy.

The parliamentary political process, egged on by the agrarian interest groups, has operated to bring agriculture within the mechanisms of the welfare state, rather than push towards a liberal market order. The social status and the consumption needs of farmers took precedence over the market, and decisively so in the national context. Historically the role of the European Parliament (EP) was very limited. Parties were absent as mediators of interests at the European level. Both national and transnational farm groups became the basic channels for mediating between the farmers and their needs, on the one hand, and the supranational political system, on the other hand, a form of political power which was a function of the CAP—and indeed of agricultural policies in the developed countries in general. The essence of the argument is hence not that the agrarian interest groups defined the CAP, but that the decision of governments to frame agricultural policy as an intrinsic element of their welfare states endowed these groups with a critical political influence.

At the core of the CAP is the regulation of agricultural markets and agricultural trade. Regulation leaves markets intact, but alters the constraints on the agents up to the point where their autonomy is zero. The form of regulation is not primarily concerned with maximizing the opportunities of the participants in the market themselves, but is often in direct conflict with them. Farmers have little autonomy in the price-fixing process or in economic competition. Of utmost importance in the European context is the inability of those farmers more favourably situated for production to underbid their rivals. In sharp contrast to a free market, the agricultural policy of the EU uses political power to offset or to modify the operations of the market in order to achieve results which the market supposedly would not achieve on its own; in doing so the policy is guided by values other than those determined by open market forces.[6] The principal aim of the regulation is to affect directly the *distribution* of income, the very opposite of a market function. As in all planned economies, so in the CAP: the prices governing farmers' decision-making do not balance supply and demand, but depend on political decisions. In order to stay in business farmers have to comply with directions issued in Brussels, and not with the signals of market forces or the wishes of consumers.[7] The question of the demand to be satisfied by production is not dependent on the profitability of production in the market, but on the mechanisms of the CAP. Not surprisingly, therefore, the basic economic orientation of farmers is not profit-making, in terms of income generated by markets, but rent-seeking, through exploitation of economic opportunities based on political relationships. Under these circumstances, such a strategy is not wrong-headed, but rational choice.

The CAP as a safe haven

One of the most basic features of the welfare state is its systematic disregard for its international consequences, with national borders transformed into social and therefore highly exclusionary frontiers, protected by tariff walls. Citizenship rights now extended to the lower classes and took on a social dimension, thereby transforming the moral economy as well as the basic politics of the post-war developed world (Marshall 1963). These social policy functions were not an invention of the CAP, but came into being in the early 1950s in all west European countries, not only those that founded the original EEC. The need to increase agricultural production was widespread, there was a special need to integrate farmers into the newly founded democracies, and there was the wish to keep the countryside peopled. In the inter-war period major sections of the agrarian population turned to radical right-wing parties to protest against governments that had tolerated the collapse of agricultural prices. This experience created a dramatic change in agricultural policies (Milward 1992). Gunnar Myrdal (1957) described the agricultural policies of the developed world as the most striking illustration of the importance of the democratic welfare state. As national integration, both economic and political, proceeded, it promoted a form of international economic disintegration, hence jeopardizing other forms of international economic integration, as Krugman (1995) and Henderson (1999) have argued.

Most west European countries ran into serious trouble with the USA because it too had protectionist agricultural policies. The USA had a highly efficient agricultural sector which was, due to the second world war, directed towards exports. The welfare of American farmers depended on access to foreign markets. However, in the 1950s the USA tried to use the GATT, first, successfully to get a waiver for their own programmes of agricultural subsidies, and then to force west European countries to open their agricultural markets.[8]

The protectionist policies of Germany, Belgium, and Luxembourg were explicitly denied a legitimate position in the GATT, while France, Italy, and most other west European countries had already been targeted by the US Tariff Commission, because of the protectionist impact of their agricultural import restrictions (Dam 1970: 263).[9] This situation made the inclusion of agriculture in the EEC a last resort for the agricultural protectionism of the original six member countries.[10] It was no coincidence that in 1962, when the market organization for cereals was introduced as the first step in building the CAP, after heavy conflicts with the USA in particular about agricultural policies, *The Economist* (15 December 1962) called the CAP a '*deus ex machina* which looks to most agricultural exporters in the GATT to be pretty diabolic', 'as a system of protection . . . about as watertight a system as could have been devised'. In particular the system of variable levies guaranteed that no imports would disturb the workings of the CAP's market organizations.

The normal rules of the GATT do not apply to custom unions and other forms of regional economic integration, which are exempted from the most-favoured-nation principle. Notwithstanding the general commitment in the GATT to eliminate non-tariff barriers to trade, it contains a specific exception for agricultural import quotas and similar measures, if they are deemed necessary for the functioning of measures to control domestic supply. This special exemption of agriculture has been a major source of disputes in international agricultural trade, particularly between the USA and the EU in the various GATT rounds (D.G. Johnson 1991; J. Scott 1996). Since US governments supported European integration for other, mostly non-economic, reasons, they had to swallow the closing of western Europe's agricultural markets.[11] Despite the problems created for world markets by systemic overproduction and export subsidies in the EU, the exclusion of agriculture from the GATT regime and from the rounds of tariff cuts survived until the Uruguay round. The CAP was heavily criticized by many Americans, although some dismissed this as hypocrisy, in that the USA had its own systems of protection (Dam 1970: 260–1).

The social and political dynamics of the CAP

Piecemeal reform became increasingly necessary because of developments which the CAP itself triggered and shaped. The international environment, changing world markets, and political pressure from outside, especially by the USA, were of secondary importance. Insulating the farming sector had been the *raison d'être* of the CAP, for which a really supranational policy was a precondition. Import competition played little role in shaping the agricultural sector of the Union. More important were the intra-European dynamics; the system of price support benefited bigger farmers the most, triggered concentration processes, and encouraged industrial production methods on a large scale. High prices were institutionally guaranteed; farmers were protected against the consequences of overproduction, i.e. falling prices; and import competition was offset by the subsidization of exports. Structural measures, aimed at compensating for regional disadvantages and to help small farmers, had little impact. The survival of regional production systems and of small farmers probably owes more to the in-built flexibilities of family farming,[12] and less to the mechanisms of the CAP. In particular, the smaller farms are able to survive because of two elements more important than the CAP: first, the rapid increase in other economic activities opened up new sources of income for agricultural households; secondly, welfare state payments, mostly child allowances and pension payments, formed a cushion (Arkleton Trust 1992).[13] The overall effect is the persistent lag in the transformation of west European agriculture. Notwithstanding the rhetoric of a 'European model' of agriculture, or of Commissioner Fischler's renunciation of 'industrial agriculture'—or 'American-style agriculture'—all signs point towards more industrializiation of agricultural production.

This European phenomenon, in which the economic modernization of the countryside has been retarded, need not have required either heavy regulation, or extensive supranationalism at the expense of the autonomy of the member states, although it can be claimed that the collective market organizations established in the 1960s seriously reduced the freedom of the member governments to pursue nationally defined agricultural policies. The picture of strong supranationalism is wrong. What actually emerged was a peculiar system of governance, with both national and supranational elements, in order to secure national interests.[14] On the other hand, this unique and highly segmented system of governance developed a dynamic of its own, built around a series of contradictions. The combination of price support and direct income payments to compensate for falling prices has produced persistent distortions and made reform harder to achieve. It has also made it more difficult to accommodate in a national way other policy objectives, such as environmental protection. The same features which helped the member states to maintain the integrity of their agricultural communities created a situation in which it became increasingly difficult to achieve a balance between supranationalism and national control. This governance gap hindered budgetary controls, generated perverse distributional effects, and created scope for fraud.

Political control of supranationalism

In the early negotiations over the regimes for common agricultural markets, the member governments took pains to retain a number of powers. Firstly, they hold the power to fix prices for individual commodities. The Commission had tried to link market organization to proposals for structural and social policy (Lindberg 1963: 238), but without success. Secondly, the main power to agree substantive legislation was retained by the Council of Ministers. Thirdly, although the responsibilities and powers of the EP increased substantially over time, its actual impact as regards agriculture has been particularly limited; it was not until the bovine spongiform encephalitis (BSE) crisis in 1996 that the EP came into the spotlight. A fourth element was the creation of the Special Committee on Agriculture; this body of senior national civil servants prepares most of the meetings of the Council of Agriculture Ministers (in contrast to the role of the Committee of Permanent Representatives on most issues). This has helped to preserve the pre-eminence of national interests in the policy process on agricultural matters, with its characteristic segmentation. A fifth element is the vertical integration of national and supranational decision-making through the management committee system. The Council delegated most powers for implementing the market organizations to the Commission, but required it to consult committees representing national interests. Each market organization has its own management committee, with a Commission official as chair and representatives from member governments, who vote according to qualified majority rules (Article 148(2) (EEC), now Article 205(2) (ToA)). Under this procedure the Commission proposes measures to the committee for endorsement. If the measure receives a favourable opinion by a qualified majority, the Commission can put it into operation (Usher 1988: 147–9). If there is a qualified majority against, the issue goes to the Council. The same system is applied to the Guidance Section of the European Agricultural Guidance and Guarantee Fund (EAGGF) (Weatherhill and Beaumont 1993: 53–6).

To sum up, policy has been vertically integrated through national and Community mechanisms, limiting the autonomy of the Commission and retaining key functions in the Council. The thick web of committees ensures the prominence of national interests in this apparently supranational process. In addition, the European Council has since 1974 circumscribed the function of the Commission as the sole initiator of Community legislation. At both the preparatory and the executive stages the national elements prevail. The Commission, in mapping out basic strategies and in sketching available alternatives, has little choice but to anticipate both the wishes and the possible reactions of the members of the Council of Ministers. This structural feature of the process accounts for much of the content of agricultural policy, and this biases the substance of the CAP. It helps to explain why some policy actors seem to lack effective voices in this system. Policy outcomes in this distinctive institutional context often emerge without the underlying choices being debated or without wider public scrutiny beyond the immediate interests involved in the regulatory or management committees. The CAP relies heavily on representational monopolies. The formal structures for channelling organized functional interests into the policy process provide legitimacy for their results, and thereby invite policy capture, since it is the results, rather than procedures, which provide legitimacy. The classical instruments of public accountability, including judicial review, are virtually absent in the CAP, a style more normally typical of 'high' politics. The essentially managerial and technocratic mode of policy-making creates the illusion that all problems can be resolved on the basis of technical considerations, assuming that the goals of policy are settled. The process makes it virtually impossible to develop truly redistributive policies, or to address normative issues.

The renationalization of west European agriculture

Over the years a policy process already marked by strong national influences has been brought even further back under national controls. The introduction of monetary compensatory amounts (MCAs) brought into the open the creeping renationalization of the agricultural common market. MCAs are payments made to compensate for exchange-rate changes and have an effect equivalent to a customs duty. They became necessary when the system of fixed exchange rates collapsed in 1971. MCAs emerged as a mechanism to maintain a form of common pricing for the agricultural products, while insulating national markets from the repercussions of monetary volatility. Over the years the agri-monetary system developed a 'byzantine complexity that almost defeats rational exposition even by those expert in the system' (Neville-Brown

1981: 509). Worse, however, from the point of view of a common market, was the scope for member governments to use MCAs as side-payments to offset compromises in the Council, thereby politically sustaining the CAP, but damaging both its economic and its European rationales.

MCAs had the merit of allowing countries considerable freedom to determine the level of their domestic farm prices, and in general brought about inter-country transfers which were politically acceptable and economically reasonable. But in contrast to traditional, uncoordinated national pricing, the MCA system placed (some) limits on price divergences and allowed common financing to be retained, which would not be possible if countries were free to choose their own price levels (Heidhues *et al.* 1979: 48–9). The completion of the single market and the abolition of border controls were accompanied by a decision to phase out MCAs. Because of the persistent volatility of exchange rates within the EU MCAs were retained until the adoption of economic and monetary union (EMU).

MCAs had played a significant role in the high politics of the CAP, and hence it was interesting to see what instrument would replace it as an essential element in the brokering of the deals necessary for policy reform. The Berlin European Council of 9 March 1999, which reached a decision on Agenda 2000, invented 'national envelopes'. For both the beef and milk sectors there are now financial 'envelopes' for each member state. 'This will allow member states flexibility to compensate for regional differences in production practices and agronomic conditions which might make restructuring difficult . . .' (Commission, DG VI 1999). The Council now has a new and tailor-made discretionary instrument at hand to buy off resistance to policy changes and to facilitate decision-making.

There have been other elements of renationalization. The CAP was increasingly redesigned to allow member governments—and those regions with some autonomy and appropriate political and financial resources—to make use of the CAP's instruments in their own way and for their own purposes. Two examples suffice to describe this development. First, some member governments tailor the CAP's structural programmes to discriminate against part-time farmers, particularly in southern Europe. Other member governments, however, use the same structural programmes to make part-time farming more viable, for example in Germany, where over half the farmers are part-timers (Arkleton Trust 1992).[15] A second example is the introduction of milk quotas, ostensibly to protect small milk producers. The British government, however, allowed the sale of quotas and thus the evolution of a market for them, which has resulted in considerable concentration in the dairy sector. Thus, the member governments can use the CAP for quite different purposes; they can structure and influence their national farming sectors with the help of supranational instruments, thereby eliminating, or at least weakening, the role of national parliaments. The example of the CAP shows how the EU could become a source of hidden political power for the participating governments.

The continuous strengthening of these national elements in the institutional arrangements of the CAPs, however, poses a dilemma. On the one hand, governments want to make use of the CAP for thoroughly national purposes. On the other hand, they need the CAP to have enough supranational autonomy to fulfil its basic functions of insulating west European agriculture both from its international environment and from efforts to undermine its welfare function.

Permutations of the CAP

The peculiar institutional format of the CAP entitled it to evolve into the most important agent for transforming west European agriculture. It changed the original socio-structural foundations from which it had emerged, and which had given it legitimacy and rationality. This development alone presents a formidable challenge to the CAP, since increasingly it has had to deal with the consequences of its own creation, which here led to demands for ever more corrections and interventions. Undesired and unintended consequences became common, with negative spill-over from one regulatory area to another, resulting in a continual multiplication of policy instruments.

Although the CAP has provided European legislators with a formidable legal armoury, the power of law over economic conduct has arguably grown weaker rather than stronger. After all, the ultimate source of the economic actions lies in the preferences of individual economic agents, particularly in a context where the determinants of decisions about production and consumption are far from transparent and not directly manipulable. Those who actually operate in the market regularly have a much greater knowledge of the opportunities available than do the policy-makers. Many of the repercussions of a legal measure cannot be foreseen by the legislator (M. Weber 1978: 334–7). Whatever the systems of surveillance, and they too have multiplied, farmers will often be in a position to use a measure in a quite different way from what was intended, a recurrent feature in the history of the CAP.[16]

The Commission acknowledged this problem not by revising the fundamentals of the CAP, but by further intensifying its regulatory mechanisms. The number of agricultural products covered by centralized market organizations steadily increased, even though other instruments were technically available. Existing inequalities have been aggravated by uniform price policies and led to the introduction of so-called structural measures to offset them. The workload of the Commission became heavier, presenting more and more difficult choices. At the same time the system of agricultural decision-making became increasingly hampered by the *de facto* requirement of unanimity in the Council of Ministers, although explicit vetoes of decisions have been rather rare (Vasey 1988: 731). The increased heterogeneity of the agricultural sector as a consequence of successive enlargements generated extra problems, and made the CAP dependent on even more complicated decisions.

Three institutional factors contribute to the endogenous problems of agricultural policy-making in the EU. First, the CAP's policy arrangements require annual decisions on the prices of farm products, otherwise either existing levels will continue or the Commission can use its emergency powers to intervene, as it did in 1985 and 1988 (Vasey 1988: 731). The Council has a strong incentive to avoid this happening. Secondly, the Council meets usually only as ministers of agriculture, a forum with a distinctive and homogeneous character. Such restraints as there are on their capture of decision-making operate at the national rather than EU level, where national policies are coordinated (Swinbank 1989: 304). Thirdly, since the EU has very little administrative capacity of its own, and since the CAP needs legitimacy with farmers, the agrarian interest groups from early on became an integral part of the policy process (Averyt 1977).[17] Thus there are powerful tendencies in the system to generate price agreements which side-step the pressing budgetary and distributional demands on the CAP.

This inability to control CAP expenditure or to limit its more perverse distributional effects has been a striking feature of the process. Instead, the EU budget depends on import levies and, much more importantly, revenue contributions from the member states. Originally the CAP was expected to be self-financing; since the EU at the time of its inception was still dependent on agricultural imports, levies, so the argument ran, would easily cover the costs of the CAP. However, the rapid increase in agricultural productivity in western Europe, induced by high institutional prices, turned the EU into a major exporter. From the late 1950s to the early 1970s the degree of self-sufficiency of the Community of then six members rose from 90 to 111 per cent in the case of wheat, and from 101 to 116 per cent in the case of butter. As a French negotiator stated:

It is true that in the future the Common Market may no longer have such large import deficits; overall surpluses may even appear for sugar and milk. But the Community, whose agricultural policy would by then be defined by common decision, would quite naturally have to bear the consequences of that common definition; a common policy calls for common financing. (Tracy 1989: 258)

Export subsidies, along with storage, became the biggest spending category of the CAP, rising from $740 million in 1974 to $11,137 million in 1993, with one-third going to cereals alone (Preeg 1995: 95), in contrast to 9 per cent of US agricultural export subsidies.

Despite early warnings by agricultural economists regarding the costly consequences of an output-geared system of price support, until the end of the 1970s the CAP could be characterized as a textbook case of an income-oriented policy (Rosenblatt *et al.* 1988; Tracy 1989; Anania *et al.* 1994*b*). Agricultural prices increased as the costs of agricultural production advanced, and the growth of average agricultural incomes per capita corresponded closely to general income growth. The years between 1979 and the mid-1980s saw the beginning of a more cautious price policy and the introduction of 'producer co-responsibility', with farmers bearing part of the costs of disposing of surplus production. In particular, the Commission acknowledged, through its price proposals, the need for a change in the CAP, although these bore little fruit.

The years between 1984 and 1987 brought more serious changes: the introduction of milk quotas, and restrictive price policies for most other agricultural products, so as to reduce surpluses. High budgetary costs started the push for a policy change; this reduced agricultural incomes and forced some small producers out of business, but the price reductions overall had little effect on production growth. In 1988 budget ceilings and stabilizers were introduced to control expenditure (see Chapter 8): first, by binding it to the level of the general budget of the Community through the 'agricultural guideline'; and, secondly, by introducing production thresholds, which automatically trigger price cuts. This meant a further reduction in real agricultural prices.

The agreement on the MacSharry reforms of the CAP in summer 1992, implemented from 1993, marked the beginning of a new phase. Its basic aim was to decouple the income problem of west European agriculture from price policy: price policy would be more oriented towards the efficient functioning of agricultural markets; direct income payments would help to improve the incomes of farmers; and a system of mandatory set-aside and other production controls at the level of the individual farm would depress production. But, as we shall see, much of the impetus for these reforms came from pressures external to the agricultural sector, both budgetary and international trade.

This short historical account gives only a limited view of the complex issues and conflicts accompanying the development of the CAP (Usher 1988, p. vii; Fennell 1997). It gives us some clues to why the CAP proved so resistant to major changes. Two factors, as we have seen, are of particular importance. First, the dominant feature is an institutional apparatus of supranational policy-making, married to national and sectoral interests; this brings considerable inertia into the governing of the CAP. Secondly, the distinctive 'moral economy' of the CAP has been welfare-oriented, results-oriented, and inward-looking, making it difficult to use economic and budgetary criteria to legitimate reforms.

This led to the paradox which has characterized the CAP, particularly in the past two decades: exploding costs, combined with a shrinking farming population and a diminished role for agriculture in the economy. The most revealing indicator of this is CAP expenditure per head of the population, which rose from 64.2 ecus in 1987 to 104.6 ecus in 1992 (see Table 7.2). More important than the absolute figures, however, is the manner in which CAP money is spent. Up to 1993 most CAP expenditure went on storage and export subsidization, benefiting the farmers in an indirect way. Price support in parallel helped the bigger farms much more than smaller and medium-size farms, such that, according to the Commission estimates, 80 per cent of CAP expenditure went to 20 per cent of farmers. This negative redistribution proved immensely hard to alter. The system of undifferentiated price support survived the introduction of quotas, stabilizers, and budget ceilings. The return of problems for the EU budget as a whole was the main reason for the Commission in late 1991 to formulate the concepts which became the cornerstone of the 1992 reform, in particular the reduction of the intervention price for wheat by one-third, and the introduction of direct income payments to all farmers to compensate for price cuts.

GATT and the politics of agriculture

The CAP had developed in tension with international trade and been a recurrent source of argument between the EU and its international trading partners. Necessarily, therefore, the opening of the Uruguay Round of the GATT provoked a struggle over whether and how agriculture would be drawn into the agenda for the Round (see Chapter 14; Woolcock and Hodges 1996). In the final analysis the German government helped the French to hold out against extensive liberalization, while at the same time placating the USA by pointing to the bigger issues at stake (Wood 1995: 228–31). The Agreement on Agriculture, the core document of the inclusion of agriculture into the GATT framework, provided a kind of international ratification of the MacSharry reforms of the CAP, thus changing the nature of the bargaining for the future in a fundamental way. Nevertheless, it was neither the state of international

Table 7.2 Budgetary expenditure on the common agricultural policy (m. ecus)

Area of expenditure	1987	1988	1989	1990	1991	1992	1993	1994	1995	1996	1997	1998
EU Budget	35,469	41,121	40,918	44,379	53,823	58,857	65,269	59,909	65,498	80,457	80,880	81,434
EAGGF (Guarantee)	22,968	27,687	25,873	26,454	32,386	32,108	34,748	32,970	34,503	39,108	40,423	40,437
EAGGF (Guidance)	907	1,143	1,352	1,847	2,128	2,715	3,386	2,586	3,609	3,935	4,240	4,385
Other agricultural expenditure	—	—	71	102	127	177	204	127	106	109.8	159	124
Charges under the CAP												
ordinary levies	1,626	1,505	1,283	1,173	1,621	1,207	1,029	922	844	810	873	693
sugar levies	1,472	1,391	1,382	911	1,142	1,002	1,115	1,382	1,316	1,213	1,366	1,163
Net cost of the CAP	20,777	25,935	24,561	26,318	31,878	32,791	36,194	33,378	36,057	41,128	42,583	43,090
as % of GDP	0.6	0.6	0.6	0.7	0.8	0.6	0.7	0.5	0.5	—	—	—
per head in the EU	64.2	79.9	75.4	76.6	92.2	94.7	104.6	95.9	93.9	—	—	—

Sources: Commission, *The Agricultural Situation in the European Union*, appears annually.

agricultural markets nor the pressure applied by the US government that convinced European policy-makers to take the inclusion of agriculture in the Uruguay Round more seriously. To be sure, grave international problems resulted from the CAP because of its substantial subsidies for export. But this development was not sufficient to prompt fundamental reform, despite recurrent trade wars between the EU and the USA and their disturbing impacts on transatlantic trade relationships. As we have seen, there were other critical factors, notably the difficulties of controlling expenditure and the social welfare function of the CAP. From an international trade perspective neither the MacSharry reforms nor the GATT Agreement on Agriculture solved the fundamental tensions between the EU and the agricultural exporting countries who had constituted themselves as the Cairns Group and the USA, nor did it mitigate the damage done by the CAP through EU protection *vis-à-vis* many underdeveloped countries and, increasingly, in central and eastern Europe (see also Scott 1996).

The primacy of domestic welfare

West European countries have strong domestic features that impact on the way that they trade with the rest of the world. Both their typical welfare states and the analogous CAP lead them to behave with a strongly autarchic character. What this means in practice is more or less total disregard for the international consequences of their domestic preferences, despite the obvious interdependencies of agricultural and other product markets. In Eurospeak this is called 'Community preference', namely the principle that no trade agreement should result in injury to domestic producers. This provides a mirror image to the US waiver of 1955 *vis-à-vis* the GATT, which enabled the USA to use protective devices at the frontier to prevent the undermining of domestic support arrangements (Fennell 1997: 32). The waiver was granted by GATT because Section 22 of the US Agricultural Adjustment Act of 1935 required the President to impose restrictions on imports which might harm domestic farm support programmes. In 1951 a rider was added, stipulating that no trade agreement be applied in a manner which is inconsistent with this section (Goldstein 1993: 154–8).

External relations took second place to domestic concerns in the governance of the CAP:

In international negotiations, the Community has insisted that the CAP is an internal policy: exports are a means of disposing of internal production when it exceeds internal requirements, imports serve to satisfy internal requirements when they exceed internal production ... The Community declines to admit any responsibility for the instability of world trade but uses it to justify protecting the internal market. (Pearce 1983: 148–9)

Until the late 1980s this approach held firm, but then the context in which 'Community preference' was situated changed quite dramatically (Villain and Arnold 1990; Denza 1996). First, politically it became more difficult to shelter agriculture, but no other economic sector, from the consequences of open markets and intensified competition. Secondly, structural policies for agriculture achieved a new prominence within the EU by being removed from the segmented agricultural policy-making process and drawn into a more coordinated approach to structural problems (see Chapter 9). Thirdly, environmental concerns further complicated the picture by bringing in extra demands on agriculture and a new set of players, as well as new sources of public funding. Fourthly, as the number of those employed in agriculture shrank, it became more obvious that frontier protection was a very costly way of providing income maintenance to farmers. In so far as other forms of welfare payments were available, for example for retraining or job creation, trade protection became dispensable (Corden 1997: 74–80). These other sources of funding to farmers provide adjustment assistance; compared with frontier protection they do not slow down, or prevent, change, but do provide some compensation to the individuals concerned.

Thus the real change in the agricultural policy-making arena of both the EU and the USA was brought about by the decision to allow domestic agricultural support systems—and not just agricultural tariffs and export subsidization—to become a topic of high priority in the Uruguay Round. This change came to the fore slowly and tortuously, as is characteristic of the EU. Much more important than the international consequences of overproduction, or ideological pressures, or political pressure from the USA, were the mounting budget costs of the CAP, and, even more so, the way that market support mechanisms had perversely redistributed incomes to farmers. Despite the huge increases in spending, CAP expenditure produced fewer and fewer benefits for the farming sector itself, in terms of incomes comparable to the rest of society, since so much of the expenditure was eaten up by the costs of storage and export subsidization. For this reason, the Uruguay Round, launched in September 1966, opened a 'window of opportunity' for CAP reform. An extra set of players, with clearly marked preferences, was able to intervene and to feed its views into the internal arguments over the future course of the CAP. At the same time, however, internal disagreements, linked to segmentation of the farming sector and the European market organizations for separate products, sharpened national profiles and raised the stakes for national politicians. Only by deliberately upgrading the external pressure, rather than pushing it aside, as in former GATT Rounds, could the member governments convince themselves that they were better off with a reformed than an unreformed CAP. Box 7.2 summarizes the results of the CAP reforms of 1992 and the Agreement on Agriculture reached in the Uruguay Round in April 1994. The long-standing fight against export subsidies, the *bête noire* of the GATT, was used to give an extra twist of urgency to the move within the EU to direct income payments, as the means to give markets more saliency.

The move to direct income payments

The experience of the 1980s showed that limits on the budget alone, in the form of stabilizers and thresholds to trigger price cuts, would not reduce expenditure in the long term. The main problem was the direct connection between the institutional prices set by the market organizations and the income of farmers, since the price policy had increasingly bolstered the incomes of trading and exporting companies, rather than those of farmers. The annual price settlements had become a highly unsatisfactory means of guaranteeing either adequate income levels, or income growth compared to that found in other sectors. The basic idea of the Commission was to decouple prices from income, an old problem for agricultural policy in industrialized countries (Schultz 1943: 6–19). The argument of the Commission was straightforward and focused directly on the efficiency issue: 80 per cent of the

---

Box 7.2 The 1992 common agricultural policy reforms and the Uruguay Round

The parameters of CAP reform in summer 1992	Summary of the final agreement on agriculture in the Uruguay Round
■ Reduction of grain prices by 30% within three years and beef prices by 15% ■ Introduction of compensatory direct income payments, although not production-neutral: farmers can obtain the payments only if they grow eligible produce (grain, pulses, oilseed, feed maize) ■ Introduction of a compulsory set-aside scheme: all farmers with farms above a certain size are required to set aside 15% of their arable land in order to be eligible for transfer payments ■ So-called small producers are exempt from the set-aside requirement	■ Reduction of domestic interventions in agriculture, measured by an aggregate degree of support over a six-year implementation period, starting in 1995 and taking 1986–8 as base period ■ Direct payments to farmers under production-limiting programmes are not to be subject to the commitment to reduce support, as long as they are based on fixed area and yields or on livestock numbers ■ All non-tariff barriers (quotas and other import restraints) are to be subject to tariffication ■ A reduction of the average tariff by 36% over the implementation period; each tariff line will be reduced by at least 15% ■ A reduction of export subsidy expenditures by 36% and a reduction of the volume of subsidized exports by 24% over the implementation period ■ An introduction of safeguard clauses specifying the circumstances under which countries are allowed to impose additional duties to prevent undesired market and price distortions due to imports ■ A guarantee of minimum market access equal to 3% of average domestic consumption in the base period

---

expenditure of the CAP went to 20 per cent of farmers. Direct income payments promised a more equitable means of distributing CAP money.

None the less, the battles around agricultural issues in the Uruguay Round proved extremely difficult to settle (Woolcock and Hodges 1996). In December 1991 the then Director-General of the GATT, Arthur Dunkel, presented a Final Draft for the GATT Agreement in Agriculture, which at least in some respects acknowledged the new course the Commission tried to follow. In May 1992 the CAP reform was finally agreed within the EU. In November 1992 the so-called Blair House Agreement settled the remaining differences between the Dunkel Text and the CAP reform, with all major EU objections to the Dunkel Text apparently accommodated (Anania *et al.* 1994*a*: 30). However, in autumn 1993 the French government was able to force the EU to reopen negotiations on the Blair House Agreement, and then succeeded in getting even more concessions from the USA. Despite this hiccup, the overall result, i.e. the formal inclusion of agriculture into the GATT (later WTO) framework, was a watershed in that a formal link has been made between the protectionist CAP and the much more liberal international trade regime. This formal linkage is, however, by no means a guarantee that further changes will be made to the CAP to remove its persistent elements of protection. As we shall see later, the Agenda 2000 proposals of the Commission tried to use the GATT–WTO lever to pursue rationalization of the CAP, but encountered strong forces of resistance from national interests. It should be noted here that the sum of the distinct interests of member states may not add up to the collective interest of the Union.

The role of agrarian interest groups: policy-makers or policy-takers?

The Commission had tried not to introduce social criteria into the calculation of compensation payments, nor to discriminate between the bigger—and supposedly more competitive—and the smaller farms. None the less, the reaction of the agrarian interest groups was unanimously negative. Direct income payments foreshadowed a change in the institutional structure which would, in the eyes of the farming lobby, enable the EU to rationalize the CAP in ways not previously possible. Since such payments were funded originally from national budgets, they were more transparent and easier to scrutinize than EU price supports, which are hidden in higher consumer prices (Legg 1993–4: 26). Also, they opened up the debate about 'who, where, what, and how much?' The difficult issue of which farmers were eligible for which payments could easily fragment the interest base of agriculture, particularly if direct income payments were structured to provide minimum incomes according to personal need, as is characteristic for other schemes of social welfare. Moreover, the farming lobby strongly opposed such a shift on the grounds that it would increase economic insecurity and sharpen political dependence. Budgetary constraints, agrarian interest groups argued, would have a much more direct impact on agricultural policy-making.

However, the agrarian interest groups did not have the power or the means to influence the terms of the 1992 CAP reforms significantly, at either national or European level. Their representational monopoly enabled them to shape some aspects of agricultural policy-making by pointing out the likely economic and social consequences of decisions, but they have found it harder to influence the overall parameters of policy or to formulate their own alternative proposals. National elections have been much more important and have pushed agricultural interests also to work through national channels, by focusing on individual members of the Council of Ministers. Therefore, the role and the power of COPA was more as a vector of the original CAP than as a channel for reform, despite its crucial importance in securing the acceptance of the CAP in the 1960s. The Commission had used its close relationships with COPA to bolster its—supranational—position *vis-à-vis* the Council of Ministers (Averyt 1977). But once the CAP had turned into a weight-bearing test for European integration, and once the Commission had reversed gears and tried to apply brakes on the development of the CAP, the politics of COPA became heavily constrained (Buksti 1983). Therefore, the much more important problem for the

Commission was how to deal with the disagreement over CAP reform in the Council of Ministers.

The new politics of agriculture

The GATT negotiations promised to provide the binding external constraint needed to bring about the necessary price cuts and the transition to a more transparent and a more liberal economic order in the agricultural support system. Without this political pressure it seems unlikely that the Council of Agriculture Ministers would have been able to agree. The tying of the CAP reform to the Uruguay Round compromise helped to ensure that it would survive. As the social and economic effects of the new CAP on individual farmers became more transparent, there would be more chance of political control over CAP expenditure and of a less regulated market. In this sense the details of tariffs or percentages of cuts in export subsidies are much less important than the multilateral commitment to open up the domestic systems of agricultural support to international scrutiny. None the less, we should note two important elements of the Uruguay Round Agreement. First the Agreement on Subsidies and Countervailing Measures unambiguously prohibits export subsidies and other subsidies contingent upon the use of domestic as opposed to imported goods. The second novelty is the Annexe 1A Agreement on Sanitary and Phytosanitary Measures, which tries to prevent any arbitrary, i.e. protectionist, discrimination against imports, by insisting on consultation, independent fact-finding, and conflict mediation.

As for the USA, the Uruguay Round was a major factor in bringing about the Freedom to Farm Act of 1996, which will eventually phase out the traditional systems of deficiency payments, originating in 1935. It attempts to rationalize American agriculture further, and to enable it to exploit its comparative and competitive advantages in more liberal world markets. The government has promised farmers increased prices through expanded demand for their products abroad, against the backlash of a strong trade surplus in the agricultural sector in contrast to the general trade deficit. Since the US Administration will not want to jeopardize this, further confrontations with the EU seem unavoidable, especially as regards EU export subsidies. Because the Freedom to Farm Act liberates the US from the waiver of 1955, its bargaining position *vis-à-vis* the EU has become much stronger.

As for the EU, this new international context shaped the Agenda 2000 proposals of the Commission, which sought to bring together both the reforms of 1992 and the GATT Agreement on Agriculture. The aim was to deepen the reforms, as well as to prepare the EU both for enlargement to central and eastern Europe and for the expected Millennium Round of trade negotiations, scheduled to open in 2000 (see Chapter 14). The prospects included further price cuts, the decoupling of income support from production, ceilings on direct income payments, and 'degressivity', that is phased reductions in income payments. In addition, to bring prices down more forcefully, thus eliminating the need for export subsidies, the Commission proposed to end mandatory set-aside, which could encourage market forces to operate as a discipline. The intervention systems of the market organizations would be reduced to safety nets, a change aimed not only at assuaging US concerns, but also at preparing for EU enlargement. Given the size, the character, and the overall role of agriculture in central and eastern Europe, it was obvious that to continue the CAP in its current form would be prohibitively costly (see Table 7.3).

The 1992 reforms did achieve some of the intended changes—a major shift towards direct income payment, and a slowing down in the growth of expenditure—but they did not force down prices enough to eliminate export subsidization altogether. Table 7.4 shows the changes in the distribution of spending categories, and Table 7.5 gives a picture of the contrasting movements of institutional prices *vis-à-vis* producer and consumer prices. But it was clear that further efforts were necessary to keep CAP reform moving towards more extensive deregulation.

The GATT Agreement on Agriculture thus brought what had been a highly regulated sector into the orbit of an international economic regime which is, basically, market-oriented, but without fully integrating agriculture into a liberal trading order. The Agreement on Agriculture is still crucially and explicitly set apart from the rest of the Uruguay Round Agreement (GATT 1994*a*), which clarifies its status as follows: 'In the event of a conflict between a provision of the General Agreement on Tariffs and Trade 1994 and of another Agreement in Annex 1A, the provision of the other agreement shall take precedence to the extent of the conflict.' This means that the Agreement is hierarchically superior to GATT (1994*a*), reflecting the failure to settle fully the question of what types of domestic support would be regarded as legitimate. For this reason the direct income payments introduced with the 1992 CAP reforms, like the 'deficiency payments' practised in the USA, were placed in a so-called 'blue box', because they are fixed in relation to former levels of output, and are not production-neutral, which would have been necessary to include them in the 'green box'.[18] In other words, the USA gave the EU credit for the 1992 CAP reforms, but with a clear signal that these were far from satisfactory, and would have to be dealt with in the future. This understanding found expression in the 'due restraint' or 'peace' clause in Article 13 of the Agreement. It stipulates that domestic support measures and export subsidies maintained in conformity with the Agreement and Uruguay Protocol will be largely non-actionable under GATT (1994*a*) and Annexe 1A of the Subsidies Agreement. As for measures that remain actionable, due restraint will be shown in initiating any countervailing duty investigations. The 'peace' provisions are to apply for nine years, and give a kind of acceptance to the support measures already in place.

An agreement was reached on Agenda 2000 at the Berlin European Council in March 1999. It was 'slightly less ambitious than the Commission's proposals', although in the words of the Commission, it 'nevertheless amounts to the most radical reform since the CAP was first established in the early 1960s. Indeed, seldom has a Commission proposal come through such a long and difficult negotiating process and remained so intact as these proposals on CAP reform' (Commission, DG VI 1999). *The Economist* begged to differ: 'Well, if the agreement reached in Berlin . . . was a "success", then the world could be forgiven for wondering quite what a failure would have looked like' (3 April 1999: 10). For a cross-tabulation of the Agenda proposals and the specifics of the agreement in Berlin, see Table 7.6.

Looking at these results one can argue that the Commission severely miscalculated both the timing of its new attempt at CAP reform, and the forces it could muster. The

Table 7.3 The importance of agriculture in central and eastern Europe, 1996

| Applicant state | Agricultural area | | Agricultural production[a] | | Agricultural employment | | Agrifood trade | | Food expenditure[b] (% household income) |
	000 hectares	% total area	Bn. ecus	% GDP	000	% total employment	% total exports	% total imports	
Poland	18,474	59.1	6.5	6.0	4,130	26.7	11.0	11.0	35
Hungary	6,184	66.5	2.1	5.8	298	8.2	17.5	5.1	24
Czech Republic	4,279	54.3	1.2	2.9	211	4.1	5.7	7.5	31
Slovenia	785	38.7	0.7	4.4	61	6.3	4.2	7.8	23
Estonia	1,450	32.1	0.3	8.0	74	9.2	15.7	16.6	30
CEEC (A)	31,172	56.7	10.6	5.3	4,774	18.4	–	–	–
Romania	14,789	62.0	5.3	19.0	3,975	37.3	8.8	7.6	58
Bulgaria	6,164	55.5	0.9	12.8	769	23.4	18.8	8.0	54
Slovakia	2,445	49.9	0.7	4.6	169	6.0	5.4	8.6	35
Lithuania	3,151	48.5	0.5	10.2	398	24.0	13.1	17.1	52
Latvia	2,521	39.0	0.3	7.6	208	13.3	16.8	13.4	39
CEEC (B)	29,070	55.0	7.8	13.1	5,519	27.9	–	–	–
CEEC10	60,242	55.9	18.4	7.0	10,293	22.5	–	–	–
EU15	135,260	41.8	117.5	1.7	7,514	5.1	7.4	9.6	18

Notes: CEEC (A) = countries of central and eastern Europe first engaged in accession negotiations; CEEC (B) = those to be engaged in accession negotiations in 2000.
[a] As measured by Gross Agricultural Product.
[b] Food expenditure for Poland, Hungary, and the Czech Republic incl. beverages and tobacco.

Source: Commission, DG VI (1998).

Table 7.4 Breakdown of agricultural expenditure from EAGGF (Guarantee), according to its economic character

Purpose	1991		1997	
	m. ecus	%	m. ecus	%
Total	30,551	100.0	40,423	100.0
Market support	20,471	67.0	32,704	30.6
Export refunds[a]	10,080	33.0	5,884	14.6
Storage	5,602	18.3	1,597	4.0
Direct aid[b]	13,293	43.5	28,681	71.0

Notes:
  [a] In 1991 export refunds is a category outside market support; in 1997 it is part of market support.
  [b] In 1991 direct aid is a part of market support; in 1997 it is a separate category.

Source: Commission, *The Agricultural Situation in the European Union, Annual Report* (1992, 1997).

Table 7.5 Changing prices for agricultural products

Member state	Annual % change		Guaranteed prices under the CAP (in national currencies; 1990/1 = 100)	
	Consumer prices for foodstuffs and beverages (1997/1990)	Producer prices for agricultural products (1997/1990)	(1994/95)	(1998/99)
Austria[a]	2.3	−3.8	—	—
Belgium	1.1	−1.1	78.1	70.0
Denmark	1.7	−1.9	82.4	70.3
Finland[a]	0.4	−7.0	—	—
France	1.4	−1.4	83.8	76.1
Germany	1.7	−1.2	76.5	70.9
Greece	10.4	9.5	78.5	68.3
Ireland	1.5	−0.5	83.1	71.9
Italy	4.0	2.4	100.5	90.3
Luxembourg	1.3	−2.4	82.6	72.2
Netherlands	1.2	0.7	80.8	73.7
Portugal	3.5	−0.7	67.1	61.1
Spain	3.3	2.0	93.6	82.3
Sweden[a]	−0.2	−1.2	—	—
UK	2.3	−0.2	90.9	66.4
EU		0.6	86.9	77.6

Note: Consumer prices are for foodstuffs and beverages, producer prices for agricultural products.
Institutional prices are in national currency, expressed as indices in real terms for all agricultural products.
  [a] These countries joined the EU only in 1995, so comparison of CAP prices is not possible.

Source: Commission, *The Agricultural Situation in the European Union, Annual Report* (1997).

dynamics of double-edged diplomacy could not be used to induce the Council to agree to a more far-reaching liberalization of the CAP, since the new trade round had not yet opened, and there was no chance to make use of the probable momentum US agricultural interests would have brought to the table. The Santer Commission was in an exceptionally weak position after its forced resignation. The war in Kosovo also increased the pressure to avoid a protracted argument. Therefore, not unexpectedly, it was a version of the status quo which prevailed, including (on 1997 figures) Germany financing 28.2 per cent of the total EU budget, but getting 14.2 per cent of CAP expenditures, and France paying 17.5 per cent of the total EU budget, and getting 22.5 per cent of the CAP.

The new attempt to decouple income support from production in a more serious way, by introducing ceilings and (some) degressivity of payments, and by making member governments responsible for some co-financing of direct income payments, did not survive the Council. In the period preceding Berlin a variety of formulas were tested in negotiations. Pressures from Germany to reduce the net national contribution had for a while made 'co-financing' seem an attractive proposition, especially with the other net payers (see Chapter 8). The French government countered with a proposal for 'degressivity', which would have preserved common financing but reduced the levels of that financing over the coming years. In the event, the more difficult decisions were deferred until 2002–3. The task of 'modulating' direct income payments according to economic, social, and environmental criteria has been left to member states, and in that respect represents a *de jure* renationalization. The attempt to introduce market forces, by reducing set-aside to zero and reducing institutional prices to those prevailing in world markets, came to naught. Moreover, it is doubtful whether the new instruments for greening the CAP, or the payments for extensification, provide enough incentive to change the production methods of those farmers who damage the environment the most, namely the 20 per cent responsible for 80 per cent of output.

Perhaps most seriously, the Berlin Agreement prolongs the present structure of the CAP well beyond the reach of the new WTO Round, scheduled for 2000, as Franz Fischler, the responsible member of the European Commission, has observed (Fischler 1999). For the moment it is the dispute settlement system of the WTO which is bearing the strain of trying to keep order in agricultural trade. The battle about the EU banana regime (see Chapter 15) is one case in point. Another arises as a result of biotechnology, where very different regulatory approaches to consumer safety are practised on the two sides of the Atlantic, as explained in Chapter 12, differences for which the legalism of the WTO is clearly not designed. Two key issues are genetically modified foods and the use of growth hormones in the dairy and beef industries. On the first, the EU approach is to require labelling of novel foods, which many Americans view as just an excuse for protectionism. As for the second, the EU not only bans imports of meat treated with growth hormones, but forbids their use in the EU at all, whereas in the USA hormones are used in roughly 90 per cent of beef cattle. Both issues have given rise to tense arguments and the activation of the WTO dispute settlement procedures, with each side calling on its own scientific evidence. It is far from clear that the WTO procedures will be robust enough to provide solutions to these problems, which are not only about scientific evidence or consumer acceptability, but crucially about competition for large markets (see also Chapter 14).

Table 7.6 The Agenda 2000 proposals and the Berlin compromise

Situation in 1999	Agenda 2000 proposal	Berlin compromise
Cereals, oilseeds, and protein crops		
These account for c.11% of agricultural output, c.21% of aggregate farm income, and 42% of CAP expenditure (1996). Since 1992 single intervention price for all cereals, and institutional prices for oilseeds and protein crops, abolished	Cut intervention price in one step (2000) from 119.19 to 95.35 ecus/ton (−20% 'safety net level')	Cut intervention price by 15%, in two steps, starting 2000–1, to €101.35/ton
Compensation via crop-specific per hectare payments, based on historic regional yields	Raise compensation from 54 to 66 €/ton (+22%), though lower if market prices rise higher than foreseen	Increase compensation in two steps to €63/ton (+16.7%)
Supply management by defining strictly land eligible for compensatory payments, and obliging producers to set some land aside. Set-aside rate adapted each marketing year in response to the market situation	Base rate for set-aside of 17.5%, and payment of €68.83/ton; reference rate for compulsory set-aside of 0%; voluntary set-aside allowed; 'extraordinary' set-aside abolished; set-aside areas get non-crop specific payments	Retain compulsory set-aside; base rate at 10% from 2000–1 to 2006–7; voluntary set-aside to increase (in particular for environmental reasons); payment of €58.67/ton from 2000, and €63/ton from 2001 to 2006 (to increase if intervention price drops)
Cultivated areas of oilseeds cannot exceed the 'maximum guaranteed areas'	Cease payments for silage cereals	Maize silage eligible for payment; where maize silage is not a traditional crop, grass silage may be eligible for payments
NB. The rate of self-sufficiency in the EU is estimated at 118% for cereals, 44% for oilseeds, and 80% for protein crops. The EU produces 18% of world exports of wheat and 11% of coarse grain	Oilseeds premium of 94.24 ecus/ton. Yields expected to increase very modestly. The area cultivated is strictly limited by the Uruguay Round Agreement	Oilseeds premium of €81.74/ton in 2000, €72.37 in 2001, and €63 from 2002 to 2006 (may vary if intervention price drops)
	Protein crops receive premium of 78.49 ecus/ton; a supplementary aid of 6.5 €/ton	Protein crops receive premium payment (i.e. total aid of €72.5/ton in 2000)
	Minimum price for potato starch of 209.78 €/ton; compensation of 86.94 €/ton	Minimum price for potato starch from 2001 €178.31/ton (−15%) for manufacturers; compensation for producers at €110.54/ton (+27%) subject to changes in the intervention price
Beef regime		
Beef and veal account for c.11.9% of total value of agricultural output; and c.14% of CAP expenditure. Number of farms with cattle declining rapidly, except for suckler cows	Beef intervention price of 2,780 ecus/ton, to be gradually lowered to 1,950 ecus/ton over the period 2000–2 (−30%); private storage to replace market intervention	Cut basic beef price to €2,224/ton (−20%) in three equal steps; aid for private storage, when average. Community market price less than 103% of basic price; a 'safety net' intervention system from July

Beef regime of support: with border protection, intervention buying, and export refunds; and direct payments as headage premiums for male bovines and suckler cows	Increase direct payment; for suckler cows from 145 to 215 ecus (+48 %); for male bovines from 135 to 310 ecus (+130 %); and for steers from 109 to 232 ecus (+113 %). New direct payment for dairy cows of 70 ecus per annum	2002, to guarantee market price of €1,560/ton for bulls or steers
Premiums for sucklers and male bovines, subject to limits on stock density; to control supply and for environmental reasons		Increase direct payment for suckler cows to €200 in 2002; increase additional national premium to €50; premium (up to max. 20% of suckler cow premium) can be claimed for heifers; direct payment for male bovines €210 (+56%), for steers €300 (+172%)
From 1996 short-term measures because of BSE (controls on calf-processing and early marketing of veal calves; elimination of adult cattle over 30 months in the UK). Drop in production much less than drop in consumption, resulting in intervention buying	Regional ceilings for bulls and steers, national ceilings for suckler cows; special premiums subject to ceilings: 2 animals per hectare, additional payments for a density of less than 1:4	Slaughter premium of €80 for bulls, steers, dairy cows, suckler cows, and heifers (over 8 months old), €50 for calves (1–6 months old); financial envelope for each member state for top-up payments
		Extensification premiums to rise
		Quantitative limits: for slaughter premiums based on 1995 numbers; regional for special male premium; individual for suckler cows
Dairy regime		
Milk production accounts for 18.4% of agricultural output; and 9.2% of total CAP expenditure (41% in 1980). The bulk of milk is produced in France, UK, Germany	Extension of quota regime to 2006	Quota regime extended until 2006, with review in 2003 to shape regime after 2006
Since 1984 quota system and declining milk output; continuing structural surplus has to be exported or stocked	Decrease support prices gradually, to average of 10% in total over the period	Quotas of most member states to increase by 1.5% in three steps from 2003, with specific quota increases for others (overall increase of 2.39%)
		Cut intervention prices for butter and skimmed milk powder by 15% in three equal steps from 2005
Quota system based on individual reference quantities	New yearly payment for dairy cows of 145 ecus (bringing total premium to 215 ecus); also new payment for dairy cows linked to beef context)	Introduction of a system of aids (in three equal steps) to €17.24/ton in 2007, supplemented by payments from national 'financial envelopes'
Ceilings and differentiation for direct payments		
	Different mechanisms to govern headage payments and to favour extensification (density factors, individual and regional ceilings) to take account of the termination of the maize silage regime	'Horizontal regulation' to encourage environmental protection (penalties for infringements)
	Degressive cuts to direct payments: 25% for payments of 200,000 ecus and more, 20% for payments between 100,000 and 200,000 ecus	Member states may, within limits, modulate direct payments to farmers, taking account of employment on the farm, overall wealth of the holding, total amount of aid available to it (i.e. income-related criteria)
		Individual member governments may use these to supplement Community support, subject to common rules

Conclusions

The CAP has thus reached a critical juncture. There are several reasons for arguing that its supranational features, combined with the new WTO regime, have—perversely—strengthened agricultural nationalism in the member states of the EU. Both the 1992 CAP reforms and the GATT Agreement on Agriculture have in some ways pushed west European governments towards measures which aim to block or to avert the potentially disturbing influences of international trade on the economic and social situation at home. The supranational features of the CAP have helped to achieve this goal, in so far as they have increased the autonomy of governments to escape from many of the pressures from national parliaments and interest organizations, at the expense of the interests of agricultural exporting countries. With the end of the cold war, and with the EU economically better placed to challenge the USA more forcefully, especially given EMU (see Chapter 6), there is a new context for the relationship between the USA and the EU, in which trade policy may be regarded as a zero-sum game. Economically this may be nonsense, but there is a political reality here which impinges on both domestic and international politics (Krugman 1997). In addition, in the context of the fiscal austerity which accompanies EMU, distributional conflicts between EU member states about the costs and benefits of membership have gained an extra salience. The Berlin European Council of March 1999 made it very clear that the member governments are much preoccupied with their own financial and economic circumstances. They have so far failed to make the agricultural policy changes necessary to facilitate either eastern enlargement or the next WTO Round.

Hence the CAP still sits in a kind of a half-way house between the nation state and the truly supranational, marked by limitations, and fundamental contradictions. Yet contrary to many expectations, both the member governments and the Commission have exploited this contradiction for their own purposes. In a sense, the political paradoxes of the CAP are the main source of its stability, since it provides the means for member governments to defend nationally defined agricultural policies, with their persistent elements of protection, welfare, and electoral preoccupations. After all, the most powerful organ of the EU, the Council of Ministers, is comprised of politicians with exclusively national constituents. Its reliance on forms of unanimity gives a very effective guarantee to the status quo, while at the same time promoting compromises, which have secured continued commitment to European integration.

The CAP thus helped to take agricultural policies out of divisive domestic distributional conflicts by creating a functionally segmented and politically insulated policy arena. *Not* to have any spill-over is a core rationale of the policy. Decision-making in the EU is on the face of it highly complicated and quite cumbersome, but these features have made it very effective in defending national interests. Still, every few years one can observe the spectacle of farmers demonstrating with tractors, attacking the police, blocking roads, and burning public buildings, but farmers are aware that it has become harder and harder in a national democratic polity to win the votes to support an extremely expensive transfer system especially when the social, economic, and environmental consequences are so contested. Interestingly, the agriculture groups retain their representational monopolies in the low politics of agricultural policy-making, but find it hard to make themselves heard in the high politics of decision-making. In the final analysis supranational policy-making provides a dense veil of ignorance, which has made it possible to spread the costs of the CAP to 371 million consumers and taxpayers. The small political costs to consumers and taxpayers, because they are spread diffusely, mean that it still pays the national politician to woo farmers with anti-market policies, and to disregard their blatant inefficiency.

Notes

1 Because of the agreement on the basic institutions of the CAP in 1961, Walter Hallstein, then President of the Commission of the EEC, did not see the Treaty of Rome as a step back from the supranationalism of the ECSC to a much more restricted intergovernmentalism (Hallstein 1962: 19).

2 Agricultural economists tend to agree: 'Save for that of Japan, the Common Agricultural Policy of the EC is perhaps the most distortionary agricultural intervention in the world' (Rausser and Irwin 1988: 355).

3 See Rosenblatt *et al.* (1988: 19): 'The issues facing policy-makers and the arguments put forward in the discussion of policy have remained largely unchanged since the inception of the CAP.' Surplus production and its budgetary and international implications were discussed at the Stresa Conference.

4 To avoid possible misunderstandings I stress that this is intended to be a positive, i.e. explanatory, and not a normative statement. To explain the CAP in terms of social politics is in no means intended to justify its development, nor to imply that it is without alternative.

5 Ernst B. Haas (1958: 296) identified farmers as 'finding it difficult if not impossible to reconcile their aims with the supranational economic and political organization of Europe. Spokesmen for agricultural associations . . . stress that a common market for agricultural commodities would ruin the tariff-protected and nationally subsidized peasantry in most ECSC countries.'

6 This definition of market regulation, or social policy, follows M. Weber (1978: 82–6) and Marshall (1985: 15).

7 Since a clear understanding of the distinction between market and regulation, or planning, is of crucial importance for any explanation of the *politics* of agricultural policy-making, and its peculiar distributive results, it is important to note the behavioural differences. In a market economy the individuals are independent, and their action is autonomously orientated. The basis of their orientation is anticipated money income, or the probability of market gain. 'In a planned economy, all economic action, so far as "planning" is really carried through, is oriented heteronomously and in a strictly "budgetary" manner, to rules which enjoin certain modes of action and forbid others, and which establish a system of rewards and punishments. When, in a planned economy, the prospect of additional individual income is used as a means of stimulating self-interest, the type and direction of the action thus rewarded is substantively heteronomously

determined. It is possible for the same thing to be true of a market economy, though in a formally voluntary way' (M. Weber 1978: 109). This difference helps to explain both why agricultural policy-making is an 'ugly business', and why the governments of member states (including parties) had a strong incentive to shift (formal) responsibility to Brussels. It creates a very convenient structural split, enabling politicians in the national context to claim credit for the positive effects, and to avoid the blame for the negative effects, of the distributive policies so pervasive in agriculture. And farmers can always point to public officials when there is a loss in income, and ask for compensation, whereas in case of gains it is their shrewd behaviour in the market-place which makes all the difference.

8 See the telling comment by an American legal scholar: 'The breadth of this waiver, coupled with the fact that the waiver was granted to the contracting party that was at the same time the world's largest trading nation and the most vocal proponent of freer international trade, constituted a grave blow to the GATT's prestige' (Dam 1970: 260).

9 The position of the USA in the GATT Round at the time pressed the west European countries to consider extreme measures: 'The Austrians reportedly said that if the GATT gave them too much trouble on agriculture, they were indeed ready to put all agricultural products under state trading' (Richter 1964: 14).

10 Ernst Haas saw in the international dimension a major impetus for the supranational integration of the EEC: 'The practical need for cooperation in other inter-national economic organizations is especially striking. The six countries had to act in unison in being recognized as a single contracting party in the GATT and in being exempted from extending liberalization requirements in OEEC. Had GATT permissions been denied, the six countries would automatically have been compelled to pass their tariff relaxations to third countries under the most-favoured-nation clause, thus possibly eliminating any special benefit to the integrated sectors' (E. B. Haas 1958: 297–8).

11 For the details of the capitulation of the USA in the critical 1961–2 GATT negotiation see Richter (1964: 14–15).

12 'Family farming' evolved on the European continent in the last century in parallel to the Industrial Revolution. Farms tend to be owner-operated and rely on family labour. There is no division of labour between home and work, or household and enterprise; ownership is widespread and production is diversified to reduce dependence on a single market for income and to ensure year-round use of labour. In contrast, an industrial agri-business is based on a sharp differentiation between economic roles: 'Some people work for wages, others invest for profits, and yet others manage the affairs of both workers and owners' (Strange 1988: 36). These two models of farming systems represent the opposite ends of a continuum (see Cochrane 1965).

13 The proportion of waged labour, as a proportion of the agricultural work-force, is rising sharply; for example, in France rising from 17.9% in 1970 to 28.6% in 1997, and in Germany from 18.8% to 53%. UK figures, in contrast, show a drop from 63.3% in 1980 to 44.4% in 1997. In the USA the proportion exceeds 50%. In the EU as a whole, in 1997, 27.8% of the agriculture workforce was aged 55 or over, compared with 10% in industry and 10.7% in services (data compiled from Eurostat Labour Force Survey).

14 Among the first who argued against the stereotype of agriculture as the only

economic sector in which the Community approached 'the full powers of a federal government' (still repeated by Scharpf 1988: 251) were Feld (1980) and Pearce (1983). They pointed to the substantial (and formal) control of the CAP by the member states, and stressed that agriculture yields policies which hardly deserve to be called 'common'.

15 The inclusion of the eastern *Länder*, with their larger landholdings, reintroduced a major split in the structure of German agriculture. Unlike the situation in the 1930s, this has so far had little impact on domestic agricultural politics in Germany, mainly because the Deutsche Bauernverband (the German Farmers' Federation), with its virtual monopoly in representing farming interests, has prevented the eastern *Länder* from gaining a voice of its own in agricultural matters.

16 For example, the decision to shift from price support to direct payments included provisions for each member state to set up a computerized, integrated administration and control system. There is a new system to identify land and animals, as well as a record of the details of every beneficiary's application for aid. The Commission has co-financed aerial photographs, and has purchased satellite images and provides them free of charge to the member states, becoming in this way the largest civil customer for satellite images of land surfaces.

17 The recent revival of interest in European interest groups does not extend to agriculture. Mazey and Richardson (1993*a*), for example, mention it only in passing.

18 The 'amber box' contains the measures which distort markets particularly severely, most importantly export subsidies, on which cuts were agreed. 'Green box' measures are outlined in Annex 2 of the Agreement and constitute subsidies 'exempt' from commitments to reduce export subsidization because they have minimal or no impact on trade. The most important in this respect are: (1) direct payments for producers provided through a publicly funded programme, not in the form of price support, and which are not related to either volume of production or the factors of production employed; (2) decoupled income support; (3) investment aids; (4) assistance provided for persons or land retirement programmes; and (5) payments under environmental programmes which do not exceed the extra costs or loss of income incurred in the course of complying with such a programme.

Further reading

For a more detailed political history of the CAP, see Tracy (1989). Milward (1992, ch. 5) provides the best account of the prehistory. Fennell (1997) offers the most detailed, historically oriented policy analysis of the CAP. For the social consequences, Bowler (1985) is still useful. For a view of US agricultural politics and policies, see Gardner (1995). Those interested in current developments should consult *The*

Agricultural Situation in the Union, published annually by the European Commission.

Bowler, I. R. (1985), *Agriculture under the Common Agricultural Policy: A Geography* (Manchester: Manchester University Press).

Fennell, R. (1997), *The Common Agricultural Policy: Continuity and Change* (Oxford: Clarendon Press).

Gardner, B. D. (1995), *Plowing Ground in Washington: The Political Economy of US Agriculture* (San Francisco: Pacific Research Institute for Public Policy).

Milward, A. S. (1992), *The European Rescue of the Nation-State* (Berkeley: University of California Press).

Tracy, M. (1989), *Government and Agriculture in Western Europe* (New York: Harvester Wheatsheaf).

Chapter 8
The Budget
Who Gets What, When, and How

Brigid Laffan and Michael Shackleton

Contents

> Community budgetary procedure poses a challenge of logic to any Cartesian mind, one which it is more sensible to bypass.
>
> (Jean Pierre Cot, MEP, 'The Fine Art of Community Budgeting Procedure')

Summary

The budget is a focus for repeated negotiation among the major European Union (EU) institutions, now following firmly established rules. In 1988, after several years of bruising annual negotiations, the EU moved to five- to seven-year 'financial perspectives', or package deals, for which the Commission makes proposals and the 'Budgetary Authority'—the Council and the European Parliament (EP)—negotiates agreement. This has concentrated budgetary politics into strategic bargains, linking national costs and benefits, reform of the common agricultural policy (CAP), regional imbalances, and enlargement. The 1992 Delors-2 package closely followed the Treaty on European Union(TEU); the 1999 Berlin package responded to the Commission's Agenda 2000, launched at the end of the 1996–7 Intergovernmental Conference (IGC). The capture of compulsory spending by the CAP strengthened national resistance in the early 1980s to further increases in the overall size of the budget. Mediterranean enlargement brought pressures for more progressive budgetary transfers; the Delors-1 package in 1988 agreed a substantial increase in structural funds. Problems of fraud in budgetary implementation have led from the creation of the Court of Auditors in 1975 to the EP's 'Wise Men' report and the resignation of the Commission, in March 1999. The emergence of a 'net contributors' club', with Germany and the UK now joined by the Netherlands and other northern members, meant that the Berlin package limited the ceiling for anticipated expenditure to 1.13 per cent of EU gross domestic product (GDP) until 2006.

Introduction

Historically budgets have been of immense importance in the evolution of the modern state, and they remain fundamental to contemporary government. This chapter enters the labyrinth of EU budgetary procedures so as to unravel the characteristics of budgetary politics and policy-making in this evolving political order. Where EU money comes from, how it is spent, and the processes by which it is distributed are the subject of intensive political bargaining. Budgets matter politically, because money represents the commitment of resources to the provision of public goods. Making budgets necessarily involves political choices about the allocation and distribution of scarce resources among the member states, and to regions and social groups within those states.

The politics of making and managing budgets have had considerable salience in the evolution of the EU, for a number of reasons. First, the search for an autonomous source of public finance for the original European Community (EC) was critical in building a Community that went beyond a traditional international organization. Secondly, budgetary issues have inevitably become entangled with debates about the role and competence of individual EU institutions and the balance between the European and the national levels of governance. Thirdly, budgetary flows to the member states are highly visible; 'winners' and 'losers' can be calculated with relative ease. Hence budgetary politics are more likely than rule-making to become embroiled in national politics and national electoral competition. Fifthly, questions about the purpose of the budget and the principles that govern the use of public finance in the Union are linked to wider questions about the nature of the EU and its evolution as a polity. Changing ideas about the role of public finance in integration shape the policy agenda in areas such as economic and monetary union (EMU), regional policy, and social policy. The budget has played an important role in consolidating market integration, in easing the path towards agreement in many policy fields, and in the political dynamic of integration. Yet the budget has been and remains the subject of considerable conflict among the member states and EU institutions.

Analysis of budgetary politics casts light on the relationship between political and economic integration. Financial resources are an important means of applying political cement to market integration. Put another way, the budget is a useful yardstick by which to measure positive integration. The size and distribution of the EU budget have implications for the operation of a vast range of policies. The process of managing and not just making budgets also raises questions about the management capacity of EU institutions, particularly the Commission. All the institutions, and in particular the Court of Auditors, are paying increasing attention to fraud against the budget and searching for better ways to protect the financial interests of the EU.

A thumbnail sketch of the budget

In the early years of the Community the budget was a financial instrument akin to those found in traditional international organizations. The budget treaties of 1970 and 1975 led to a fundamental change in the framework of budgetary politics and policy-making. These treaties established the constitutional framework for the finances of the Union in a number of important respects (see Box 8.1).[1] The treaties created a system of 'own resources' which gave the EC an autonomous source of revenue, consisting of three elements: customs duties; agricultural levies; and a proportion of the base used for assessing value-added tax (VAT) in the member states, up to a ceiling of 1 per cent. The 1970 agreement on own resources was subsequently altered a number of times. One basic principle was that this revenue base should apply to all member states, regardless of their size, wealth, the pattern of EC expenditure, or their ability to pay. This was to cause increasing difficulty in the years ahead.[2] The budget treaties altered the institutional framework for reaching decisions on the budget. The EP was granted significant budgetary powers, including the rights: to increase, to reduce, or to redistribute expenditure in areas classified as 'non-compulsory' expenditure; to adopt or reject the budget; and to give annual discharge, through a vote of approval, to the Commission for its implementation of the budget. The 'power of the purse' gave the EP leverage in its institutional battles with the Council of Ministers and allowed it to promote its autonomous policy preferences. The Council was no longer the sole budgetary authority, although it retained the last word in the legislative field. The 1975 Treaty provided for the creation of the independent Court of Auditors to enhance accountability in the budgetary process and the management of expenditure. Treaty provisions, together with the Financial Regulation and regulations on own resources, establish the legal rules of the budgetary game.

After 1970 the emergence of the budget as a real instrument of European public policy was constrained by a basic factor which still shapes EU finances. The EU budget was and remains small in relation to Community gross national product (GNP) and to the level of public expenditure in the member states. In 1997 it was equivalent to no more than between 2 and 4 per cent of the combined national budgets and it accounted for 1.2 per cent of Community GNP (Commission 1997a). However, although the budget has little macroeconomic significance for the Union as a whole, it is very important for those of the member states that receive extensive transfers

Box 8.1 The budgetary cycle and rules

Articles 268 to 280 (ex 199 to 209) lay down the financial provisions governing the EEC Treaty, with Article 272 (ex 203) establishing the precise timetable and procedure for making the budget each year:

The Commission initiates the budgetary cycle by presenting the Preliminary Draft Budget to the Council

The Council adopts a Draft Budget by 5 October of the year preceding its implementation. (The financial year starts in January.) The Council meets with the EP in a conciliation meeting before actually adopting the Draft Budget.

The EP has forty-five days to complete its first reading of the Draft. It is entitled to propose modifications to compulsory expenditure, expenditure needed to fulfil the Community's legal commitments (essentially agriculture guarantee spending), and amendments to non-compulsory expenditure. Its control over non-compulsory expenditure is limited to increases within a 'margin of manœuvre', which is equal to half the 'maximum rate of increase', a percentage determined each year by the Commission on the basis of the level of economic growth, inflation, and government spending.

The Council has fifteen days to complete its second reading of the Draft Budget. The Council has the final word on compulsory expenditure but returns the Draft to the EP, indicating its position on the EP amendments to non-compulsory expenditure.

At its second reading the EP has the final word on non-compulsory spending within the limits of an agreed maximum rate of increase. After its second reading of fifteen days the EP adopts or rejects the budget. If it is adopted, the EP President signs it into law.

If there is no agreement on the budget by the beginning of January, the Community operates on the basis of a system of month-to-month financing, known as 'provisional twelfths', until agreement is reached between the two arms of the budgetary authority.

The Commission then has the responsibility for implementing the budget. The Court of Auditors draws up an annual report covering the year in question, and on the basis of that report the EP decides whether or not to give a discharge to the Commission in respect of the implementation of the budget. The discharge is normally given in the second year after the year in question.

from the structural funds. In the 1994–9 period EU transfers accounted for 3.67 per cent of Greek GDP, 2.8 per cent of Irish GDP, 4 per cent of Portuguese GDP, and 1.7 per cent of Spanish GDP (Commission 1997*a*). The small overall size of the budget masked impressive increases in financial resources in the Delors-1 (1988–92) and Delors-2 (1993–9) budgetary agreements. An expanded budget was accompanied by a very significant extension of the Community's policy range (see Fig. 8.1). The Berlin Agreement (1999–2006) did not include increases of a similar magnitude to Delors-1 and 2.

The slenderness of EU budgetary resources highlights an important feature of the emerging European polity, namely, the significance of regulation as the main instrument of public power in the Union. The expansion of regulatory policies was an alternative to establishing extensive fiscal resources at EU level, and reflected a view which limited the role of public finance in integration. This view has not always been dominant. In the 1970s the acquisition of sizeable financial resources for the budget, a form of fiscal federalism, was widely seen as essential to integration, especially to EMU. It was anticipated that a larger budget would be necessary to deal with external

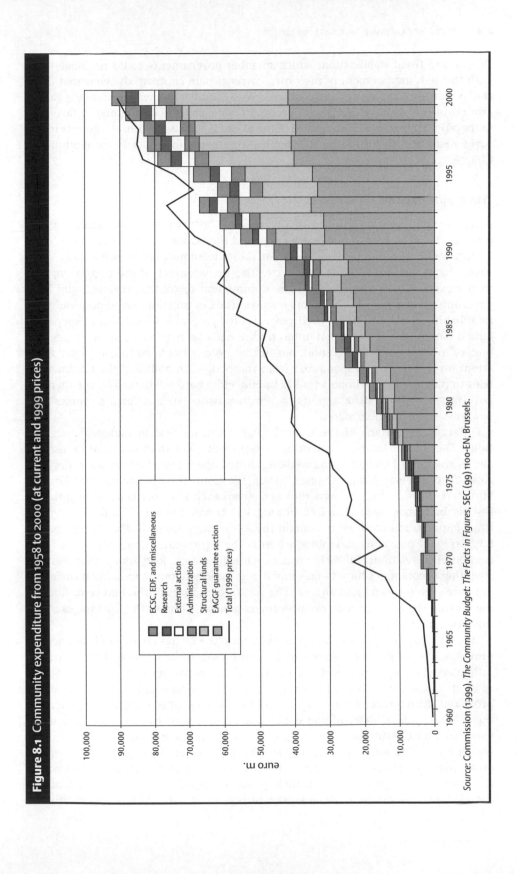

Figure 8.1 Community expenditure from 1958 to 2000 (at current and 1999 prices)

Legend:
- ECSC, EDF, and miscellaneous
- Research
- External action
- Administration
- Structural funds
- EAGGF guarantee section
- Total (1999 prices)

euro m.

Source: Commission (1999), *The Community Budget: The Facts in Figures*, SEC (99) 1100-EN, Brussels.

shocks and fiscal stabilization, which member governments could no longer deal with through management of their own currencies. In contrast, the view that there can be strong Community government, with limited financial resources, gained ground in the 1980s, as Keynesian economic policies were discredited in favour of monetarist approaches. The capture of the EU budget by agricultural interests in the 1970s made it difficult for fiscal federalist arguments to win political ground (see Chapter 7).

The major players

Budgetary policy-making in the Union rests on 'history-making decisions', i.e. big package deals, an annual budgetary cycle, and thousands of management decisions within each expenditure area. 'History-making decisions', taken periodically since 1988, shape the annual budgetary cycle. The management of the budget engages many layers of government, from the Commission to central, regional, and local governmental agencies in the member states. The Commission has responsibility for establishing the draft budget each year, and for proposals which aim to shape the 'grand bargains'. The Commission has traditionally been an advocate of a bigger EU budget to fund policy integration, but in the 1990s it has been forced to pay more attention to managing expenditure from the budget. In addition, the Commission tries to play the role of honest broker in budgetary battles, charged by the member governments with drafting reports on sensitive issues, such as 'own resources' and net flows to the member states.

Different formations of the Council play a central role in budgetary negotiations. The Budget Council, consisting of representatives from financial ministries, agrees the annual budget, using well-established operating procedures and decision rules. The General Affairs Council (GAC), the Council of Economic and Finance Ministers (Ecofin), and the Agricultural Council each play key roles in negotiating the big budgetary deals. The GAC attempts to coordinate across different negotiating chapters, and not least to contain the Agricultural Council. The Ecofin Council tries to exert budgetary discipline, whereas the Agricultural Council is locked into a clientelist relationship with farmers. Other Council formations that develop spending programmes have to face tough negotiations about money when their programmes are reviewed and altered. The increased impact of the European Council means that the heads of state or government generally broker the final stages of the 'history-making' bargains.

Since it was granted budgetary powers in 1975, the EP has regarded EU finances as providing one of its key channels of influence *vis-à-vis* the Council. The EP tries to influence what happens at both the macro and the micro levels. As we saw in March 1999, it was an intervention from the EP, criticizing financial management, which provoked the unprecedented resignation of the whole college of Commissioners. In the annual cycle of determining detailed appropriations, the EP frequently intervenes to alter the sums assigned to specific programmes and projects. For member governments, the budget is a crucial element of EU policy. Their preferences depend on a variety of factors, notably: their net position in relation to budgetary flows; the fit between EU expenditure and their preferred policies; and the importance of the EU budget to different social groups or regions at national level. Inevitably the electoral cycle and the composition of coalition governments impinge on budgetary politics at the EU level.

Budgetary politics over time

Budgetary politics and policy-making in the EU have gone through a number of different phases since the first enlargement in 1973. The first phase (1973–84) was characterized by intense conflict about the size and distribution of EU monies, and in addition by institutional battles between the Council and the EP. The second phase (1985–98) was a period of relative budgetary calm as the member governments succeeded in negotiating the two big budgetary bargains known as Delors-1 and Delors-2. The third phase since 1998 consists of the negotiation and implementation of the Agenda 2000 package, agreed by the European Council in Berlin (24–25 March 1999).

Phase 1: Budgetary battles following the first enlargement

The first enlargement disturbed the budgetary bargain between the founder member governments. In particular, between 1979 and 1984 the member governments and EU institutions were locked into a protracted dispute about both revenue and expenditure which contributed in no small way to a wider malaise in the early 1980s. The 1970 Treaty, stemming from a critical European summit at The Hague in December 1969, was designed to fix the rules before the UK became a member. The revenue sources suited the six founder countries, and the main spending would flow 'automatically' to support the CAP (see Chapter 7). The package was essentially a French achievement, won in return for the opening of accession negotiations with the UK and the other applicants. The rules of the budgetary game were fixed to the advantage of the incumbents, above all France, making confrontation with the UK more or less inevitable. The shape of the bargain structurally disadvantaged the UK on both the revenue and the expenditure sides. After accession British governments struggled to get the budget issue on to the agenda and slowly to alter the terms of the debate to ensure that distributional issues were taken seriously. The first enlargement had disturbed the cosy budgetary compact among the Six by highlighting problems of burden-sharing, redistribution, and the regressive nature of the EC budget. These issues remain central to the budgetary politics of the Union.

By the late 1970s the EU also had a serious revenue problem. The 1 per cent ceiling on VAT revenue, set by the 1970 Treaty, seemed increasingly inadequate to meet expenditure demands. In 1982 the VAT rate reached 0.92 per cent and was virtually breached the following year. The pattern and structure of expenditure also gave rise to problems. Agricultural expenditure represented 70 per cent of total spending in 1979, limiting the development of other policies. At the same time, the automatic nature of the CAP price regime made it difficult both to plan and to control agricultural expenditure in any one year, and gave rise to growing inefficiencies with the growth of 'butter and beef mountains' and 'wine lakes'.

The predominance of CAP expenditure also accentuated the 'UK problem'.

Although not directly addressed in the UK accession negotiations, it had become apparent that the UK would end up as a major net contributor to the EC budget, in the absence of changed expenditure policies. The UK had won recognition that action would be necessary to deal with an 'inequitable situation'. The British governments pressed for reform of the CAP, budgetary discipline, and the development of other spending policies. The new Labour government renegotiated the terms of accession in 1974–5 and won agreement at the Dublin European Council to a complex financial mechanism, designed to allow for rebates from the budget in the case of heavy gross contributions. However, this mechanism failed to work, bringing the question of distributional equity to the forefront of Community politics. The problem was seen to be structural rather than the result of chance consequences. Despite being one of the 'less prosperous' member states, the UK became the second-largest contributor after Germany. Hence in 1979 the new British Prime Minister, Margaret Thatcher, began to demand a structured rebate system, which would guarantee the UK a better balance between contributions and receipts. The Commission and the other member governments were loath to concede the British case at the outset. The Commission had always been reluctant to engage in discussion of the net financial flows to the individual member states, lest this encourage too narrow a calculation of the benefits of Community membership, and lead states to seek *juste retour*, i.e. to extract from the Community budget more or less what they put in. The key 'orthodoxy' about the budget at this time was that receipts flowed from EU policies and were thus automatic. This orthodoxy was challenged by the problem of UK contributions.

Although Mrs Thatcher's confrontational approach was regarded as non-*communautaire*, the essence of the British case was conceded in the form of *ad hoc* spending programmes from 1980 onwards. The interlinked budgetary issues came to a head at the Fontainebleau European Council in June 1984 during the French presidency of the Council. President Mitterrand wanted to use this six-month presidency to revitalize the Community. As part of this process, he sought to remove the contentious budgetary issues from centre-stage. At Fontainebleau agreement was reached to increase the VAT ceiling from 1 per cent to 1.4 per cent in 1986, and to establish an 'abatement' mechanism for dealing with excessive British contributions on a longer-term basis. The agreement ameliorated, but did not solve, the financial crisis in the Community. The limits of the new VAT ceiling were reached in 1986, its first year of operation. The 1987 budget was balanced by the artificial device of delaying CAP payments. Resource shortage now replaced the UK problem as the main budgetary challenge.

While the member governments were engaged in restructuring the budget, the EP and the Council were involved in a continuing struggle over their respective powers on budgetary matters. The EP rejected the 1980 and 1985 draft budgets, and the annual budgetary cycle was characterized by persistent struggle between the two institutions, the 'twin arms' of the budgetary authority. In 1982, and again in 1986, the Council of Ministers brought an action in the European Court of Justice (ECJ) for the annulment of the budget that the President of the Parliament had signed. The Council sought to limit the level of power-sharing with the EP as far as it legally could.

The Parliament, on the other hand, was determined to use the budgetary powers which it had acquired in 1975 to enhance its position in the Community's institutional landscape and to further its policy preferences. This was done in three ways. First, the Parliament attempted to use its budgetary powers to gain some leverage in the legislative field. Although the EP had gained budgetary powers, its role in legislation continued to be severely circumscribed. MEPs took the view that the budget itself was a sufficient legal basis for using appropriations entered in the budget. Consequently, it inserted additional budgetary lines designed to promote new Community actions, for example in relation to aid to Latin America and Asia, which both the Council and the Commission resisted strongly. The Council of Ministers, on the other hand, argued that budgetary appropriations had to be underpinned by a separate legal basis over which it had exclusive control. Secondly, the Parliament used its amending power to increase expenditure so as to promote Community policies of interest to it, notably, regional policy, transport, social policy, and education. Thirdly, the Parliament used the annual budgetary cycle to expand the areas falling under what is termed non-compulsory expenditure, and hence to have a larger volume of expenditure where it could use the margin for manœuvre available to it under Article 272 (ex 203) of the Treaty (see Box 8.1). In view of these priorities, the EP tended to pay more attention to authorizing expenditure than to monitoring how it was spent, a priority reflected in the importance of the EP's budget committee, and the assignment of budgetary control to only a sub-committee. This was despite the fact that its new powers over expenditure were granted in the same year as it was given the sole right of discharge in relation to the Commission's implementation of the budget, which also coincided with the establishment of the Court of Auditors.

The sharing of budgetary authority revealed a divergence of views between the EP and the Council on issues like the classification of expenditure and the maximum rate allowable for increases in spending, making the annual budgetary cycle prone to conflict. The two institutions were forced to find ways of improving their collaboration. From 1970 onwards various devices were developed to enable representatives of both institutions to meet to seek agreement. In June 1982, for example, the Council, the EP, and the Commission issued a joint political declaration laying down an agreed classification of expenditure between compulsory and non-compulsory categories. Despite the declaration, budgetary wrangles continued, with a basic absence of trust prevailing until a broader agreement on the future financing of the Community was reached in 1988.

Phase 2: Changing the rules of the game

Delors-1

The Mediterranean enlargements in 1981 and 1986 changed the constellation of forces on budgetary issues and heightened the salience of redistribution as an issue. The ratification of the Single European Act (SEA) in 1987 marked a relaunching of integration after the 'doldrums period' of the mid-1970s and early 1980s. Although the SEA appeared not to have overt implications for the budget, the new articles on 'economic and social cohesion' (Article 130 (SEA)), promoted by the Commission and the poorer member states, proved a powerful peg for the Commission to develop a strategy on redistribution. The Commission established a clear connection between the internal market process and the budget by launching two sets of proposals on budgetary reform: *Making a Success of the Single Act* (Commission 1987a); and *Report on Financing of the Community Budget* (Commission 1987b). The proposals, known in common parlance as the 'Delors Package' (later Delors-1), were negotiated at the highest political level between June 1987 and February 1988. The less prosperous states (Greece, Ireland, Portugal, and Spain) successfully linked the completion of the internal market to an increase in structural funds, designed to reinforce 'economic and social cohesion'.

The budgetary agreement reached in February 1988 was a classical EC package deal; it transformed budgetary politics by embedding the annual budgetary cycle in a medium-term financial perspective. It combined measures for reinforced budgetary discipline, additional own resources, an expansion of the structural funds, and the maintenance of the UK budget rebate. The main elements were:

- an increase in the financial resources available to the Community, rising to a ceiling of 1.2 per cent of GNP by 1992;

- an extension of the system of 'own resources' to include a new fourth resource based on the relative wealth of the member states as measured by GNP;

- tighter and binding budgetary discipline to contain agricultural expenditure at not more than 74 per cent of the growth in Community GNP;

- a continuation of the complex Fontainebleau rebate system whereby the UK receives a reduction in its contribution to Community revenue equivalent to 66 per cent of the difference between its share of revenue provided and of total allocated expenditure; and

- a doubling of the financial resources available to the less prosperous areas of the Community as between 1988 and 1993.

The arguments on Delors-1 waxed and waned during the Danish presidency of the Council in the latter half of 1987. There were tense arguments on the overall size of the budget, the commitment of resources to the poorer regions, and the need to discipline CAP expenditure. The major split was between the poorer states, fighting for a larger budget, and the paymasters, who sought to restrain the level of any such increases. At the same time the divergence between finance and agriculture ministers came into the open, with the latter doing their best to limit the extent of CAP reform. For a time, it looked as if no agreement would be found. At the Copenhagen meeting in December 1987, the European Council failed to find a solution and instead agreed to convene a special meeting in Brussels in February 1988 under the German presidency in order to overcome the deadlock. At that meeting Chancellor Kohl succeeded in brokering a deal which avoided the collapse of the Community's financial structure. In the end, Mrs Thatcher's assumption that Article 130 (SEA), promoting cohesion, was merely symbolic did not prevail, not least because Chancellor Kohl wanted to secure agreement and was willing to push for it, even though it meant a significant increase in German net contributions to the budget. The German government wanted to maintain the consensus on the internal market programme.

The Delors-1 package was accompanied by an Inter-Institutional Agreement (IIA) between the Commission, the Council of Ministers, and the EP, which entered into force in July 1988. It was based on agreement to a five-year financial perspective involving six categories of expenditure. Its purpose was to ensure that the Brussels decisions were not undone by a continued conflict between the two arms of the budgetary authority. The three institutions agreed to respect the figures contained in each category of the financial perspective for all the years up to 1992. In return, the EP saw a substantial increase in non-compulsory expenditure, underlined by a major commitment to the structural funds. Moreover, the agreement laid down that the figures for compulsory expenditure would not be revised in such a way as to lead to a reduction in the amount available for non-compulsory expenditure.

A number of features of the Delors-1 package illustrate just how far Community budgetary politics had shifted from the zero-sum bargaining of the early 1980s. The Community's policy process proved robust enough to produce a major agreement on what was traditionally a highly contentious issue on its agenda. The Brussels decisions represented a significant increase in EC expenditure: commitment appropriations were to increase by 16 per cent over the period of the agreement, rising from 44.1 to 52.8 billion ecus (in 1988 prices). The agreement to make decisions on budgetary discipline legally binding was part of the continuous search for CAP reform. The doubling of the structural funds for the poorer regions of the Community acknowledged that the benefits of market integration would be felt unevenly. Solidarity between the richer and poorer parts of the Community was affirmed as a 'value' in the political process. Spanish and Portuguese accession to the Community had clearly transformed the cohesion countries' bargaining power and the balance of budgetary priorities. The new fourth resource, based on the relative GNP figures for the member states, began to relate contributions to capacity to pay, contrary to what had been agreed in 1969–70.

The package was a major negotiating success for Jacques Delors and the Commission; the Commission claimed with some justification that they had got 90 per cent of what they wanted. Moreover, the deal heralded a period of relative budgetary calm in the Community. The annual struggle to agree a budget was replaced by reasonable cooperation between the two arms of the budgetary authority. The consequence of the IIA was to make it possible for Council and Parliament to reach agreement on the extent of the annual increase in non-compulsory expenditure. (See Box 8.1.) This removed a major source of budgetary conflict. Between 1988 and 1992 the President of the Parliament signed the budget into law each year on time and in accordance with the established procedure (Commission 1989a). Significantly, during the same period the two arms of the budgetary authority managed to agree five revisions to the financial perspective to take account of new demands arising from events in central and eastern Europe, the Gulf War, and German unification. The normalization of relations was in stark contrast to the pervasive conflict before 1988. The package had changed the dynamic of budgetary negotiations by linking the financial perspective to an inter-institutional agreement.

Delors-2

The pattern established by Delors-1 was replicated in the negotiations on Delors-2. When the next treaty change was negotiated, it was once again accompanied by a new budgetary settlement. The political link between the SEA and Delors-1 was followed by a similar link between the TEU and the Delors-2 package. The Commission launched its Delors-2 proposals in the EP in February 1992, just five days after the TEU was formally signed, with its document *From the Single Act to Maastricht and Beyond: The*

Means to Match our Ambitions (Commission 1992*a*). The Commission followed the formula successfully adopted for Delors-1 by proposing a medium-term financial perspective organized around a number of categories of expenditure. It envisaged that total spending would increase by some 20 billion ecus from 1992 to 1997, rising to a ceiling of 1.37 per cent of Community GNP. Particular increases were earmarked for structural expenditure, further strengthening the commitment to redistribution, and for a new and separate category of external expenditure, reflecting the dramatic changes in central and eastern Europe and the former Soviet Union. Expenditure in this latter area was to grow from 3.6 billion ecus to 6.3 billion ecus by 1999.

The debate on Delors-2 was just as tortuous and controversial as the earlier debate on Delors-1. The member governments grappled with their desire to reach agreement, on the one hand, and with their determination that the terms of the agreement be as favourable as possible to their viewpoint, on the other. During 1992 the budgetary issue also became entangled in wider political issues. The heads of government met in Edinburgh in December 1992 against the backdrop of the TEU ratification crisis. The Danish 'no' of June 1992 was followed by turbulence in the exchange-rate mechanism (ERM) and the pressing demands from members of the European Free Trade Association (EFTA) for accession negotiations, which added to the salience of the budgetary debate. Failure to agree to the Delors-2 package at Edinburgh would have heightened the sense of drift in the Community. The UK government, having been forced to withdraw from the ERM in September, did not want a failure at the European Council in Edinburgh, which would have reflected badly on its already troubled presidency.

The budgetary negotiations raised a number of tricky issues for the British presidency. The British government wanted both to protect the system of budgetary rebates and to contain expenditure at the lowest possible level. Its strategy was to conduct the negotiations on the future financing of the Community within the framework of Ecofin, because it felt that finance ministers would be more sympathetic than foreign ministers to its attempts to limit the growth of spending. This strategy did not work. In the lead-up to the Edinburgh meeting the Delors-2 package was dealt with by a General Affairs Council (foreign ministers) on 9 November, by the finance ministers on November 23, by a 'jumbo' meeting of both on 27 November, with a General Affairs meeting on 7 December just before the European Council. Ultimately, it required the political authority of heads of government in Edinburgh to agree the major elements of the package. In particular:

■ maximum levels of revenue and expenditure were established up to 1999, with the revenue ceiling maintained at 1.2 per cent of GNP for 1993 and 1994, but set to rise to 1.27 by 1999;

■ expenditure was divided into six categories, with specific financial allocations for each year in all six categories (unlike in 1988, when these details were settled after the Brussels European Council);

■ the system of revenue-raising was slightly revised to take more account of 'contributive capacity'; and

■ the UK secured the maintenance of its abatement mechanism (A. Scott 1993).

The negotiations were dominated by the perennial conflicts about revenue and expenditure and their likely consequences for member state contributions and receipts. The key issues revolved around the question of how much money, how it should be spent and over what timescale. The Commission was less successful during this round of negotiations in retaining the broad elements of its proposals in that it failed to get the agreement of the member governments to the budgetary increases it sought. The Commission's proposal for revenue, for a ceiling of 1.37 per cent of GNP by 1997 (five years), was reduced to 1.27 per cent of GNP over a longer timescale of seven years. The Commission's case was weakened by the fact that expenditure in 1992 represented 1.15 per cent of GNP, well within the 1.2 per cent established in the Delors-1 package. The UK presidency, in line with its well-established policy of austerity, argued that the existing GNP ceiling gave the Commission ample scope for the development of new policies. The presidency drafted a compromise document for the 'jumbo' Council meeting of 27 November which sought to restrict budgetary growth to 1.25 per cent of GNP by 1999, and freezing the GNP ceiling at 1.2 per cent between 1993 and 1995. President Delors reacted angrily to the UK proposals by issuing a letter to the member governments because he felt that the presidency compromise diluted the Commission's proposals in an unacceptable manner.

Two issues were most keenly fought over in respect of expenditure, namely: the extent of financial transfers to the poorer states; and the acceptability of measures designed to improve the Community's competitiveness. During the implementation of the Delors-1 package up to 1992 all of the member states, with the exception of Greece, Spain, Portugal, and Ireland, saw their level of net contribution go up, with France joining Germany and the UK as a net contributor to the budget. A rise in the number of net contributors in the Union, at a time of fiscal squeeze at national level, enhanced the austerity camp in the Council. However, the four cohesion countries continued to press for more money for redistribution, particularly in view of the prospective move to EMU. The Spanish Prime Minister, Felipe Gonzales, led the cohesion countries in very tough negotiations during the Edinburgh Council. He threatened to veto other agreements reached in Edinburgh, such as that on Denmark's special situation, unless a deal was achieved on the budget. In the closing stages of the Council, at a breakfast meeting, Chancellor Kohl and President Mitterrand agreed to endorse increases in the budget that went beyond the UK presidency compromise of November. This left the British prime minister with little option but to accept an agreement that allowed for higher spending than he would have wished. However, Mr Major managed to protect the British rebate, which had been questioned during the earlier negotiations. Six member governments, including the German and the French, had opposed the principle and substance of the UK refund in November. Those opposing the rebate were unwilling to press their case at Edinburgh, as they recognized the importance of a budgetary agreement and the potential impact of the issue on the Maastricht ratification debate, due to resume in the House of Commons in the New Year.

The cohesion countries had reason to be very satisfied with the terms secured in Edinburgh (see Chapter 9). The agreement envisaged a 41 per cent increase in expenditure on 'structural operations', with an effective doubling in financial flows to the poorer parts of the Community. Furthermore, it was agreed to finance a new instrument, the Cohesion Fund, to help the four cohesion countries to meet the convergence criteria for EMU. Apart from the structural funds, the Commission had limited success in getting agreement to additional internal expenditure, although it had proposed that expenditure on internal policies grow at a faster pace than external expenditure. However, the member governments were unwilling to see a substantial growth of expenditure in areas like research and development, transport networks, and telecommunications. Agriculture, by contrast, proved far less contentious than it had been in 1988. It was readily agreed to continue to apply the general guideline established in 1988, whereby CAP expenditure would increase at a rate not exceeding 74 per cent of the rate of growth of Community GNP. Agreement on additional expenditure for external actions was also arrived at with relative ease, since the member governments were committed to enhancing the Union's role in post-cold-war Europe.

There was no major change in the method of raising revenue. A radical proposal from Belgium for a new Community tax fell on fallow ground. Instead, there was some rebalancing between the third and fourth resources, aimed at strengthening the link between contributions to the budget and capacity to pay. The Commission had been a long-standing advocate of a progressive revenue base that would take account of the 'relative economic capacity' of the member states. It proposed that the fourth resource, based on GNP, should weigh more heavily than the third resource, based on VAT, which tends to be regressive. Despite strong objections from the Italian government in particular, which stood to lose most from the change, agreement was reached gradually to increase the fourth resource. The existing 1.4 per cent of VAT was retained until 1995, but would be progressively reduced to 1 per cent between 1995 and 1999.

Overall, the Edinburgh Agreement highlighted a commitment by the member governments to relative budgetary peace in the Union and to a medium-term framework for the financing of the Community. Delors-2 built on the Brussels Agreement of February 1988, emphasizing once more a pragmatic and incremental style of bargaining. Once again, the Commission played a crucial role in designing a package that found the agreement of the member governments and the EP.

Phase 3: Agenda 2000 and the pressures for change

The dynamic of budgetary politics and the balance of forces in the Union on budgetary matters began to change radically once the Edinburgh Agreement was in place. First, the sizeable expansion in the size of the budget led to the emergence of a 'net contributors' club', which composed an austerity camp concerned about the level of their financial commitments to the EU budget. Whereas before Delors-1 Germany and the UK were the only major net contributors, by the 1990s the majority of states were (see Fig. 8.2). The 1988 and 1992 budgetary deals were secured in large measure by the willingness of Chancellor Kohl and the German government to bear so much of the burden of the budget. Successive German governments had accepted that Germany would be a substantial contributor to the EU budget but were always concerned lest this be treated by the other member governments as an open-ended financial commitment. In 1984 the German negotiators had drawn attention to the growing financial burden on themselves, and as a consequence their contributions to the UK rebate were proportionately lower than for other member states. Following German unification in 1991, Germany fell from second to sixth place in the league table of per capita incomes, but remained the budget's main paymaster. The shock of

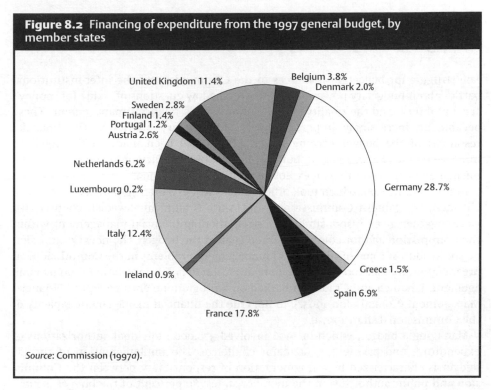

Figure 8.2 Financing of expenditure from the 1997 general budget, by member states

United Kingdom 11.4%
Belgium 3.8%
Denmark 2.0%
Sweden 2.8%
Finland 1.4%
Portugal 1.2%
Austria 2.6%
Netherlands 6.2%
Germany 28.7%
Luxembourg 0.2%
Italy 12.4%
Greece 1.5%
Ireland 0.9%
Spain 6.9%
France 17.8%

Source: Commission (1997*a*).

paying for unification had a major influence on German attitudes to the EU budget; from then on the Germans began to raise their concerns at every opportunity about financial burden-sharing. The Dutch government also raised equity considerations when they found themselves transformed from a net beneficiary to a significant net contributor, especially when measured in per capita terms. The 1995 enlargement added Sweden, Finland, and Austria to the growing net contributors' club.

Second, at the Copenhagen European Council in 1993, the member governments accepted the principle of an eastward enlargement of the Union. Like all previous enlargements, this would alter the existing budgetary bargains and necessitate considerable changes in the policy *acquis*. In addition, the accession of so many more relatively poor states would generate pressures for more redistribution and a larger budget. These had been simmering for some time, and increasingly in the period following Maastricht, when the legitimacy of the EU was contested. The management issue exploded with dramatic effect in March 1999, when the entire Commission, presided over by Jacques Santer, was forced to resign, as a result of a report that was highly critical of its financial management. This episode framed the final round of negotiations over Agenda 2000.

Managing a larger budget

The struggle for budgetary resources in the Community and the inter-institutional battles about budgetary power tended to overshadow questions of 'value for money', accountability, and the quality of the Commission's financial management. These became an increasingly important focus of budgetary politics as the financial resources of the budget became larger. Efforts had been made in the 1990s to improve financial management, but they had proved insufficient to prevent financial mismanagement becoming an explosive political issue in 1999.

In the Commission, which took office under Jacques Santer in January 1995, Erkki Liikanen, the Finnish Commissioner, and Anita Gradin, his Swedish counterpart, were together given responsibility for strengthening financial management within the Commission and for combating fraud against the budget. The new Commission began to address some of the internal management problems in the Commission, an organization that for too long paid more attention to policy innovation than its management. Liikanen and Gradin embarked on a programme entitled Sound Financial Management (Commission 1995e), to upgrade the financial management capacity of the Commission (Laffan 1997a).

Managing a budget, which in 1996 involved 370,000 individual authorizations of expenditure and payment, is a major challenge. The implementation of the EU budget is characterized by a fragmentation of responsibility between the Commission and public authorities in the member states: 80 per cent of the budget is managed on behalf of the Union by the member states. The Commission relies to a large extent on the delivery and enforcement capacity of national authorities. At the same time, the complexity of European rules, particularly in agriculture and regional policy, creates loopholes which can be exploited by those intent on defrauding the EU budget. The sheer number of agricultural subsidy payments and export refunds creates considerable opportunities for abuse. Reports of fraud in olive oil, beef, wine, and fish, running in some cases to millions of ecus, undermine the credibility of the Community's policies. Press reports have highlighted various scams involving the forging of customs documents in order to claim export refunds, switching labels on various foodstuffs to claim higher refunds, claiming headage payments for non-existent animals, and putting non-existent food into intervention storage. No one knows with any degree of certainty the level of fraud against the EU budget: estimates of between 7 and 10 per cent of the budget are often cited, but have never been convincingly proven. Investigations of fraud suggest that some member states are dilatory in following up cases of fraud against the EU budget, as this would involve devoting additional national resources to getting less money out of the Union budget.

The 1975 agreement to create the Court of Auditors (it began work in Luxembourg in 1977) enhanced the institutional commitment to more systematic accountability. In its first report (European Court of Auditors 1978) the Court raised the issue of fraud and it has continued to do so in all subsequent reports. The Court's reports have been consistently highly critical of the Commission's financial management. In Article 188c of the TEU the Court of Auditors was given additional responsibilities in relation to financial management, notably the need to make a Statement of Assurance (SAD) each year to the Council and the EP to demonstrate that the financial transactions underlying the budget are legal and regular. Aware that continuing reports on fraud would undermine public confidence in European integration, the Commission, the Council, the European Council, and the ECJ began to address the issue. In 1988 the Commission established an anti-fraud unit, Unité de Co-ordination de la Lutte Anti-Fraude (UCLAF), and in 1989 produced a forty-five-point programme. The ECJ has also become involved, underlining the legal responsibilities of the member states in combating irregularities in the use of EU funds. For example, in a 1989 case of fraud concerning maize supposedly grown in Greece, but in fact imported from Yugoslavia, it held that the member states were legally obliged under a 'loyalty clause' (Article 5 (EEC), now Article 10) to deal with EC fraud cases in a manner similar to fraud against their national exchequers.

The European Council added its authority to the fight against fraud with a declaration at its Copenhagen meeting of June 1993. This underlined 'the importance of fully implementing the provisions of the TEU (Article 209a, now 280), according to which member states are to take the same measures to counter fraud affecting the financial interests of the Community as they take to counter fraud against their own financial interests'. The inclusion of this principle arose from a widespread feeling that national authorities probe cases of fraud involving national money with greater alacrity than those against the Community budget. The Commission became more involved in monitoring and directing national enforcement of EU programmes. In December 1994 the Council (dealing with justice and home affairs) reached an outline agreement on a system of 'penal sanctions' that would allow the member states to impose fines on companies and individuals who have misappropriated EU monies. This made fraud against the EC budget a criminal offence in all but name.

The growing number of policy instruments financed by the EU raises issues not just of accountability but also of performance. Are the Community taxpayers getting 'value for money' from expenditure on regional policy, training, education, and research and development? Views differ among politicians and academic experts about the rationale behind different types of public expenditure and about benefits accruing from direct intervention. The Commission has endeavoured to increase the effectiveness of the various budgetary instruments, mindful that increases in resources would need to be justified by positive assessments of the usefulness of current expenditure. In the past the small size of the funds, slender staff resources, the multi-level nature of the delivery system, and lack of information and expertise hampered the Commission in its evaluation of how EU monies were spent. The new focus on financial management requires a growing commitment to more systematic evaluation.

Although the Commission's efforts to improve management and evaluation moved well beyond the symbolic during the 1994–9 financial period, there was still a widespread perception that EU finances were badly managed. This criticism relates not only to the Commission, but also, more importantly, throws into question national management of EU finances. The 1997 Court of Auditors' Annual Report included various references to this problem:

In the member states the fight against fraud is usually synonymous with an absence of any integrated strategy and tends to give priority to the national framework. Differences in the legal and administrative frameworks of the various member states are further risk factors that are likely to be fraudulently exploited. (European Court of Auditors 1998: 5)

A large number of inaccuracies and irregularities occur in the declarations of expenditure made by member states, which reduces their reliability. (European Court of Auditors 1998: 10)

The Commission has been working with a group of personal representatives, representing national finance ministers, to improve national management of EU finances. The Commission signed financial protocols with the member states on their respective responsibilities with regard to the management of EU monies. These efforts have also to be seen in the context of EMU, and its added discipline over national budgets.

In January 1999 political attention was drawn again to the Commission's own management of EU finances. The battleground was a classic parliamentary–executive conflict about accountability. It was prompted in part by allegations, in both the EP and the media, of mismanagement of the EU budget and of financial irregularities. A motion of censure against the Commission was tabled in the EP, but was voted down by the MEPs in January 1999 in return for a commitment from the Commission that it would co-operate with a special inquiry. A group of five 'Wise Men' (lawyers and auditors) was established by the EP with a remit to review the allegations of mismanagement and fraud in the Commission's services. Their report (Committee of Independent Experts 1999), which was presented to the Commission in March 1999, highlighted problems in relation to tourism, the Mediterranean programme, educational programmes, and the European Community's Humanitarian Office (ECHO). The report concluded that mismanagement in the Commission 'was tantamount to an admission of a loss of control by the political authorities over the administration they are supposed to be running. The loss of control implies at the outset a heavy responsibility for both the commissioners individually and the Commission as a whole.' It went on to say that 'it was becoming difficult to find anyone who has even the slightest sense of responsibility' (Committee of Independent Experts 1999: 142). The political context in which the report was drafted and its tone left the Commission, after a night of dramas, with little option but to resign. It had become clear that otherwise the EP would have passed a motion of censure and forced the college's resignation at the next plenary. The college continued as 'acting' commissioners, until the Prodi Commission was designated in September, with a remit to put the Commission's house in order.

The Agenda 2000 negotiations

The Commission followed the pattern of the Delors-1 and Delors-2 negotiations on the future financing of the Union by trying to link a new financial perspective to treaty changes. It launched its Agenda 2000 proposals in July 1997 (Commission 1997i) just after the agreement on the Treaty of Amsterdam. The proposals were the outcome of intensive work in the Commission by a range of inter-service committees, with one overall coordination committee, chaired by Carlo Trojan, Secretary-General of the Commission. The Commission established in broad outline a set of proposals with three elements: the financial perspective for the period from 2000 to 2006; the reform of Union policies, notably the CAP and structural funds, in the light of enlargement; and a detailed commentary on how to proceed with enlargement. Detailed proposals on each chapter of the reforms were presented by the Commission on 18 March 1998. The Cardiff European Council (15–16 June 1998) set March 1999 as the deadline for political agreement on the overall package in time for the EP elections in June, concentrating minds during the Austrian presidency (latter half of 1998) and the German presidency (first half of 1999). A very intensive schedule of meetings at all levels was arranged in the first three months of 1999, including two European Councils, to force the pace of the negotiations.

The issues at stake were viewed with great seriousness in all of the national capitals and by EU institutions, because they had reached a critical juncture in the development of the Union, at which relative benefits and costs might alter and the rules of the game might change. Moreover, the outcomes would have implications for the overall dynamic of integration. The dangers of an acrimonious budgetary battle were sharply stated:

> It could unleash a bruising debate on burden-sharing, reminiscent of the debilitating battle fought by Baroness Thatcher, which brought most other decision-making to a standstill for several years. It could pit the rich countries against the poor, the farm producers against the rest, and even divide Germany and France, the duo at the heart of the community. It could also delay the whole process of enlargement, to bring the new democracies of central and eastern Europe into the EU. (Quentin Peel, *Financial Times*, 20 October 1998)

The Commission's proposals

The Commission's detailed proposals of March 1998 formed the substance around which the core issues and conflicts were debated and resolved (see Table 8.1). The key elements covered future funding, structural spending, and agriculture:

- *Future funding for the period 2000–6*: the financial resources ceiling would remain at 1.27 per cent of Community GNP (the level set in Delors-2 for 1999), while any increases in real terms would depend on growth in GNP, and there would be a commitments budget of €105 billion by 2006.

- *Structural spending*: a level of 0.46 per cent of Community GNP (as envisaged by Delors-2 for 1999) would be maintained for the period 2000–6, to include €247 billion for the existing member states as well as €47 billion for the candidate countries (both before and after accession). Objective One regions would continue to receive about two-thirds of the total structural funds; the number of objectives would be reduced from six to three; 10 per cent of the structural funds spending would be a performance reserve for those regions that were using the funds in an innovative manner; and the Cohesion Fund would continue to operate with a mid-term review of which countries were eligible (see Chapter 9).

- Agriculture: CAP reform would continue along the lines established by the 1992 MacSharry reforms, with lower price support, compensation to farmers in the form of direct payments, and an emphasis on rural development and

Table 8.1 Commission proposals for the financial perspective, 2000–2006 (euro bn., 1999 prices)

Appropriations for commitments	1999	2000	2001	2002	2003	2004	2005	2006
Agriculture (guidance)	45.2	46.1	46.9	47.8	48.7	49.7	50.6	51.6
Structural operations	39.0	36.6	37.5	36.6	35.6	34.5	33.4	32.5
Internal policies	6.4	6.4	6.7	6.9	7.1	7.2	7.4	7.6
External action	6.9	6.9	7.1	7.3	7.4	7.6	7.8	7.9
Administration	4.7	4.7	4.8	4.9	5.0	5.1	5.2	5.3
Reserves	1.1	0.9	0.9	0.6	0.4	0.4	0.4	0.4
Total appropriations for commitments	103.4	101.5	103.8	104.1	104.2	104.4	104.8	105.2
Total appropriations for payments	96.4	98.8	101.7	102.9	103.5	103.8	104.2	104.6
Appropriations for payments as % of GNP	1.23	1.24	1.24	1.22	1.20	1.18	1.15	1.13
Margin (%)	0.04	0.03	0.03	0.05	0.07	0.09	0.12	0.14
Own resources ceiling (%)	1.27	1.27	1.27	1.27	1.27	1.27	1.27	1.27

Source: Commission (1998a), Agenda 2000: Financing the European Union.

environmental protection (see Chapter 7). These proposals marked a serious attempt to contain agricultural expenditure.

The Commission chose not to propose to increase the 'own resources' ceiling which would have required ratification by national parliaments and might have prompted acrimonious domestic debates on future financing. Its proposals on the structural funds and the CAP were designed to enable these policies to adjust to both enlargement and the forthcoming international trade negotiations. In contrast to its more radical proposals in 1987 and 1991, the Commission adopted a cautious strategy of incremental adjustment, rather than a bid for greatly increased resources and new sources of funding. This reflected the changing political climate following German unification, fears about the potential costs of enlargement, and the impact of the EMU convergence criteria on national budgets.

Managing the Agenda 2000 negotiations, as a set of interlocking negotiations across a broad spectrum, was a real test for the EU institutions. A key role was played by successive Council presidencies, particularly the German presidency. The GAC had an overall coordinating role; Ecofin had special responsibility for the financial aspects of the future finances; and the Agricultural Council dealt with the CAP. Given the sensitivity of the issues, the GAC became the essential filter to the European Council, where all of the crucial decisions were taken. The Council substructure— Coreper II and I, the Special Agricultural Committee, and all of the relevant Council working parties were intensively involved. In addition to the formal Council apparatus, a number of *ad hoc* high-level groups worked on the technical elements of different parts of the proposals. These included a 'Friends of the Presidency' Group, a Structural Actions Group, and a high-level group dealing with the reform of the

Table 8.2 Financial perspective for the EU15, 2000–2006 (€ bn., 1999 prices)

Appropriations for commitments	2000	2001	2002	2003	2004	2005	2006
Agriculture	40.920	42.800	43.900	43.770	42.760	41.930	41.660
CAP expenditure (excluding rural development)	36.620	38.480	39.470	39.430	38.410	37.570	37.290
Rural development and accompanying measures	4.300	4.320	4.330	4.340	4.350	4.360	4.370
Structural operations	32.045	31.455	30.865	30.285	29.595	29.595	29.170
Structural Funds	29.430	28.840	28.250	27.670	27.080	27.080	26.660
Cohesion Fund	2.615	2.615	2.615	2.615	2.515	2.515	2.510
Internal policies	5.900	5.950	6.000	6.050	6.100	6.150	6.200
External action	4.550	4.560	4.570	4.580	4.590	4.600	4.610
Administration	4.560	4.600	4.700	4.800	4.900	5.000	5.100
Reserves	0.900	0.900	0.650	0.400	0.400	0.400	0.400
Monetary reserve	0.500	0.500	0.250	0	0	0	0
Emergency aid reserve	0.200	0.200	0.200	0.200	0.200	0.200	0.200
Guarantee reserve	0.200	0.200	0.200	0.200	0.200	0.200	0.200
Pre-accession aid	3.120	3.120	3.120	3.120	3.120	3.120	3.120
Agriculture	0.520	0.520	0.520	0.520	0.520	0.520	0.520
Pre-accession structural instrument	1.040	1.040	1.040	1.040	1.040	1.040	1.040
Phare (applicant countries)	1.560	1.560	1.560	1.560	1.560	1.560	1.560
Total appropriations for commitments	91.995	93.385	93.805	93.005	91.465	90.795	90.260
Total appropriations for payments	89.590	91.070	94.130	94.740	91.720	89.910	89.310
Appropriations for payments as % of GNP	1.13	1.12	1.13	1.11	1.05	1.00	0.97
Available for accession (appropriations for payments)			4.140	6.710	8.890	11.440	14.220
Agriculture			1.600	2.030	2.450	2.930	3.400
Other expenditure			2.540	4.680	6.640	8.510	10.820
Ceiling on appropriations for payments	89.590	91.070	98.270	101.450	100.610	101.350	103.530
Ceiling on appropriations for payments as % of GNP	1.13	1.12	1.18	1.19	1.15	1.13	1.13
Margin (%)	0.14	0.15	0.09	0.08	0.12	0.14	0.14
Own resources ceiling (%)	1.27	1.27	1.27	1.27	1.27	1.27	1.27

Source: European Council (1999).

CAP. Thus very senior officials from national ministries were formally brought into the negotiations, in addition to those servicing the regular Council committees. These elements enhanced the capacity of the system to negotiate across a broad range of dossiers in a short period. The negotiations were broken down into three negotiating chapters: the future financial perspective, the structural funds, and the CAP were subsumed into what the German presidency called 'negotiating boxes' in January 1999. The key task of the German presidency was to fill the boxes with agreed text in time to deliver agreement at the European Council in Berlin in March 1999.

The Berlin Outcome

In January 1999 few would have predicted that agreement on the financial perspective would be reached by March, given the outstanding issues in the negotiations. The German presidency, particularly the new German Chancellor, Gerhard Schröder, was determined to conclude the negotiations. The need to reach agreement became more, not less important, to the German government as the presidency proceeded for a number of reasons. First, Oskar Lafontaine, the German Finance Minister, resigned in early March, an event which strengthened the German Chancellor's control of his government. Secondly, the resignation of the Commission in early March, just before the Berlin meeting, confronted the European Council with a political and institutional crisis which, if unresolved, might have an adverse impact on the new single currency. Thirdly, as the Union's leaders gathered in Berlin, the crisis in Kosovo exploded into war. It was imperative, therefore, that the Union should find agreement on the financial perspective.

The agreement, hammered out in the early hours of the morning in Berlin, fell well short of the budgetary figures proposed by the Commission. The Commission's projected commitments budget for 2006 of €105.2 billion was reduced to €90.2 billion. The ceiling on appropriations for payment was set at 1.13 per cent of GNP, which included the monies available for accession, and fell well short of the 1.27 per cent ceiling under the existing 'own resources'. The Berlin agreement amounted to a consolidation of the Union's budgetary resources, in sharp contrast to the significant increases recorded in 1988 and 1992 (see Table 8.2). The Commission's proposed expenditure was reduced under all headings: its 2006 provision for agriculture was reduced from €51.6 billion to €41.6 billion; the structural funds fell from €32.5 billion to €29.1 billion; and internal policies would receive not €7.6 billion but €6.2 billion. This represented a tight budget strategy rather than an expansionary one. The outcome must be seen in the light of the Commission's proposals, which had already taken on board the need for budgetary austerity.

The key cleavages and core issues

The key cleavages among the member states on the package had been well signalled in the lead-up to the negotiations. There were divisions: between the net contributors and net beneficiaries; between the major contributors and those who contributed proportionately less; between those who wanted to push for deep reform in the CAP and those who wanted to protect the existing regime; and between the UK, with its budgetary rebate, and those who wanted to replace the rebate mechanism.[3] These cleavages translated especially into divisions between the Mediterranean states and their northern partners, and another between France and Germany on agriculture. The core issues revolved around the traditional budgetary issues of burden-sharing and the manner in which the pattern of EU expenditure and revenue-raising impacted on net financial flows. The constellation of forces on these issues had, however, changed, and the shadow of future enlargements added force to those who wished to control and to contain EU expenditure.

The growing 'net contributors' club' became extremely vocal in its demands for a fairer system of burden-sharing. The outgoing German government of Chancellor Kohl and the new German government under Chancellor Schröder both made it clear that they wanted a reduction in their net contribution of €10 billion, or 58 per cent of the annual total. There was agreement across the political spectrum in Germany that the previous level was too onerous. The Dutch argued that in 1996 they had become proportionately the Union's largest contributor; their Finance Minister, Gerrit Zalm, demanded 'an improvement of our net position, and we want a net limiter which should be general and not just a rebate for Britain' (*Financial Times*, 16 October 1998). Sweden and Austria, two other significant net contributors, added to the chorus arguing for austerity and changes to the system of burden-sharing. The British Labour government found itself in an increasingly difficult position in that the rebate, negotiated by the Conservative government in 1984, appeared less justified; its key goal of maintaining its rebate placed it somewhat at odds with the other members of the net contributors' club. France and, to a lesser extent, Italy were marginal net contributors, and clearly identified as states that might carry a heavier financial burden, a prospect which neither government welcomed. Through successive rounds of budgetary negotiations France had successfully protected its receipts from the CAP and would not yield its entrenched position easily.

The main beneficiaries of the EU budget, particularly the Mediterranean states, found their position under threat. They continued to argue, with considerable force, the case for greater redistribution in the Union, and were unwilling to see an eastern enlargement financed by reductions in their own budgetary flows. Spanish representatives were trenchant in their defence of cohesion policy and refused to countenance any significant reductions. The governments from the two smaller Mediterranean states, Greece and Portugal, were largely supportive of the Spanish position, although less strident in the expression of these views. Ireland found itself in the uneasy position of being a net contributor-in-waiting. High growth rates in the 1990s had pushed Ireland well above the threshold for Objective One status for the purposes of the structural funds. The Commission's CAP proposals were also deeply unpopular with Ireland's vocal farming lobby. For the Irish government, a key goal was to ensure that the reduction in receipts from the budget would be phased so as to provide a soft landing for the Irish exchequer.

The re-emergence of a burden-sharing debate led the member governments to request the Commission to undertake a study of the system of 'own resources' and its impact on the member states, so that there would be an objective basis for the discussion. The Commission began its examination with some reservations, because it had never entirely overcome its traditional reluctance to calculate 'net balances'. Nevertheless, the Commission concluded that it was better that the debate be based on its calculations rather than incorrect national figures. In addition, the Fontainebleau

Agreement in 1984 on the UK rebate had concluded that 'any member state sustaining a budgetary burden which is excessive in relation to its relative prosperity may benefit from a correction at the appropriate time' (European Council 1984). Net contributors, other than the UK, began to claim an 'excessive burden' as a consequence of the Delors-2 agreement. In October 1998 the Commission (1998a) published the 'own resources' report; it established, in a comprehensive and carefully argued text, who paid what and who benefited from the EU budget. Although some governments, notably from Luxembourg, queried the categorization of different kinds of expenditure, the report provided a more or less objective account of the net financial flows. The report confirmed that Germany, Sweden, Austria, the Netherlands, and Britain were the main contributors, thus adding weight to their arguments about burden-sharing, and suggested three ways of addressing budgetary imbalances at the appropriate time (see Table 8.3).

Burden-sharing became the key dynamic in the negotiations. Faced with a reopening of the burden-sharing debate and the shadow of enlargement, the challenge was to craft a unanimous agreement from the very diverse starting preferences of the member states. This search for an agreement involved debate about what the Union spent, the balance between different policy areas, and how monies were raised for the budget.

As regards agricultural expenditure, the Commission's preference was to reduce price support from the EAGGF from 100 per cent to 75 per cent of aid, with the remainder falling on national budgets. This proposal for 'co-financing' found considerable support in Germany, since it would cut the German contribution significantly. This brought the German government directly into conflict with the French, which led the opposition to what they saw as a fundamental attack on the principles

Table 8.3 Member states' shares in EU financing and in EU15 GNP (per cent of total, data for 1997, incl. UK correction)

Country	Share in EU GNP	Share in the financing of EU budget
Austria	2.6	2.8
Belgium	3.1	3.9
Denmark	1.9	2.0
Finland	1.4	1.4
France	17.2	17.5
Germany	26.0	28.2
Greece	1.5	1.6
Ireland	0.8	0.9
Italy	14.2	11.5
Luxembourg	0.2	0.2
Netherlands	4.5	6.4
Portugal	1.2	1.4
Spain	6.6	7.1
Sweden	2.7	3.1
UK	16.1	11.9

Source: Commission (1998a).

of the CAP. Politically, the French did not want a tax-payer–farmer cleavage to emerge in domestic politics, hence their suggestion of 'degressivity' (a mechanism for reducing common prices) as an alternative approach. Its vehement opposition ensured that co-financing would not fly.

The concept of 'budgetary stabilization' gained momentum in the latter half of 1998. The Austrian presidency, in a report circulated in late November 1998, argued that the EU budget should be stabilized at 1999 figures, with allowance only for inflation up to 2006. According to this scenario, overall payment appropriations would be capped at about €85 billion per annum for the period 2000–6 and agricultural expenditure would stabilize at a constant annual level of €40 billion. The net contributors' club strongly supported this proposal. The French government, in an attempt to avert co-financing in agriculture, preferred to address the burden-sharing issue by restricting budgetary spending in general.

The proposed stabilization would represent a marked reduction in the size of the budget from the €105 billion, or 1.13 per cent of GNP in 2006, originally proposed by the Commission. The Commission opposed the concept of stabilization because of the implications for its proposals on agriculture and regional spending. Not unexpectedly, the cohesion states—Spain, Greece, Portugal, and Ireland—opposed a freeze. A middle group of states, notably Finland, Luxembourg, and Belgium, were warned that 'zero growth' might undermine the ability of the Union to meet its obligations.

As the concept of stabilization gained support, the search was on for agreement on what the Austrian presidency called a 'model of reasonable stabilization' which would not compromise the Union's aims and commitments (*Agence Europe*, 7–8 December 1998). Even Spanish policy-makers, characterized as coming from the 'no, no, no state' by a diplomat from one of the other member governments, began to use the term 'stabilization', but with the following preconditions: 1999 must be the year used for subsequent budgetary calculations; stabilization should not include monies earmarked for enlargement; and EU policies must not be compromised (*Agence Europe*, 7–8 December 1998). In the run-up to the Berlin meeting negotiators moved towards a classical EU compromise between the 'zero growth' school, on the one hand, and those governments that wanted a larger budget, on the other.

In the final phase of negotiations (March 1999) the core issues revolved around expenditure on agriculture and structural policy. The German presidency, supported by the net contributors' club, was a strong advocate of setting an annual ceiling of €40.5 billion on agricultural spending throughout the period of the new financial perspective. The Presidency Conclusions from the Berlin European Council (European Council 1999: 5) specifically requested that the Commission and the Council pursue savings to ensure that total expenditure in the 2000–6 period would not overshoot an average annual expenditure of €40.5 billion. Yet the figures entered in the financial perspective for spending already overshoot an average €40.5 billion ceiling (see Table 8.2). A meeting of the Agricultural Council in early March had agreed a set of reforms to the CAP which were far less stringent than proposed by the Commission. Under pressure from President Chirac, the reforms were further diluted at Berlin. Critically, the Commission's proposed cut in cereal prices of 20 per cent in 2000 was diluted to a reduction of 15 per cent, in two stages in the marketing years 2000–1 and 2001–2, while reform of the dairy regime, including price cuts, was postponed to the marketing year 2005–6.

This leaves serious question marks over the outcome on agriculture. Estimates of agricultural expenditure are of necessity 'soft', because so much depends on market forces and world prices. It is not evident that the commitment to stabilize expenditure can be met. Moreover, the compatibility of the agreement on the CAP with the direction of World Trade Organization (WTO) policy is being questioned (see Chapters 7 and 14). A Commission official has conceded that the EU's position at the WTO was not 'as strong as it would have been had the Commission's proposals been approved' (*Financial Times*, 30 March 1999). It may be hard to avoid pressures for compensation payments in the light of enlargement. French proposals on 'degressivity' would have involved sizeable reductions in the direct payments (compensation) to farmers over time, and would have imposed a tougher discipline on expenditure, but they did not form part of the final agreement.

The Berlin Presidency Conclusions (European Council 1999: 5) contain a number of review clauses that will impact on the operation of the CAP proposals and may lead to deeper reforms. The following are envisaged:

■ a review of the financial guideline before the first enlargement;

■ a decision on the final intervention price for cereals in 2002–3 in the light of market developments;

■ a report on oilseeds within two years of the implementation of the new arrangements;

■ a review at any time of the beef sector, if market conditions require; and

■ a Commission report in 2002 on the development of agricultural expenditure.

It remains to be seen how these will impact on the package agreed at Berlin for spending up to 2006, especially in the context of further WTO negotiations on the liberalization of agricultural trade.

The negotiations on the structural funds were no less contentious than those on agriculture (see Chapter 9). The key cleavage was between the cohesion states, led by Spain, and the other member states. However, proposals to change the status of areas such as the Highlands and Islands, Lisbon, and Hainaut in Belgium also mobilized defensive responses from individual governments. Throughout the negotiations the Spanish government had maintained that the minimum it would accept was the original Commission proposal of €239 billion for the seven-year period of the financial perspective. The net contributors wanted to limit structural funds to €200 billion. As Chapter 9 shows, a compromise was found at €213 billion, the largest proportion of this money (69.7 per cent) going to Objective One regions. The existing beneficiaries of the Cohesion Fund (the four cohesion states) would continue to receive funding, subject to a mid-term review in 2003.

As for the revenue side of the budget, there has been strong pressure for change. The Berlin Conclusions (European Council 1999: 15) underlined the key principles to govern the system of 'own resources' by stating that they should be 'equitable, transparent, cost-effective and simple'. Agreement was reached to make 'own resources' more progressive and based on 'ability to contribute'; this reduced the maximum rate of call on the VAT resource to 0.75 per cent in 2002 and 0.50 per cent in 2004, as this element of revenue had been clearly identified as regressive for the least prosperous member states. As a consequence, the GNP resource became more significant. Provision was made for a review of the system by 2006.

The other highly contentious issue concerned calls for a 'generalized corrective mechanism' or a 'net limiter', which would establish a threshold for contributions, above which member states would get a rebate. The demand for a net limiter was supported by German, Dutch, Austrian, and Swedish governments. The debate inevitably drew attention to the UK rebate mechanism, which was regarded as unfair by the other large net contributors. The British government, adamant from the outset that its rebate was non-negotiable, succeeded in protecting its position at Berlin, although it agreed to minor changes to the mechanism. The Berlin Conclusions on the rebate were designed so that payments by Germany, the Netherlands, Sweden, and Austria would be limited to 25 per cent of their notional GNP share. These states were most opposed to the continuation of the UK rebate. The question of a 'net limiter' is likely to reappear on the agenda when the budgetary consequences of enlargement are felt. It can be argued that the British escaped more lightly than might otherwise have been the case, because of the pressures of the Kosovo crisis.

The ghosts at the table: the candidate countries

The budgetary costs of future enlargements had provided the context for these negotiations on the budget. The 'net contributors' were concerned not just with the outlook up to 2006, but also about future financing arrangements once the candidate countries became members. Initial estimates of the costs of enlargement in the early 1990s led to a series of alarmist newspaper headlines about the end of the CAP and expensive transfers to the cohesion states in western Europe. Early calculations of the costs had been highly speculative, because it was unclear what the timing of enlargement would be and how internal EU policy regimes would be transformed prior to enlargement. One 1992 report concluded: 'The EU faces a stark dilemma: either it must abandon for the foreseeable future any ambition to admit the indisputably European CEECs, or their admission must be accompanied by a change in the budgetary rules' (CEPR 1992: 73).

In 1993, a Commission document (1993b: 112–14) on future finances analysed the budgetary costs of enlargement and extrapolated from the flow of EU finances to the two poorer states, Greece and Portugal. According to their estimates, Greece and Portugal would benefit from a flow of 400 ecus per capita by 1999. Based on this figure, the Commission concluded that flows to the 'Visegrád Four' (the Czech and Slovak Republics, Hungary, and Poland) would amount to 26 billion ecus, with the added inclusion of the Baltic states, Bulgaria, and Romania, costing 54 billion ecus. Between 1990 and 1992 budgetary flows to central and eastern Europe already amounted to 3.5 billion ecus. The Essen European Council of 1994 requested the Commission to prepare reports on the consequences of enlargement for the CAP and structural policy. Subsequent Commission reports sought to reassure the existing member states that the costs of enlargement would be incremental and manageable, rather than a shock to the system of financing.

The Agenda 2000 proposals on financing EU enlargement were formally based on the premiss that some candidate countries would join in 2002, with a package of pre-accession aid for broad structural adjustment and agricultural restructuring. The Commission's proposals of March 1998 envisaged spending €1 billion for structural policies and €500 million for agriculture. Pre-accession aid would merge with EU budgetary flows after accession, when, according to Commission estimates (1998a: 15), total expenditure on the new members could rise from €6.45 billion in 2002 to €16.78 billion in 2006. The tone and intent of the Commission's proposals was to suggest that the costs of pre-accession aid and enlargement could be borne within the tight limits envisaged for the overall EU budget. The member governments agreed in Berlin that this proposed expenditure on the candidate countries would be ring-fenced in a special enlargement reserve (see Table 8.4). If accession takes place over a longer period, the money allocated for the candidate countries cannot be used to finance policies in the existing member states.

The applicants have little chance to influence the internal EU debate on its future financing. They have to accept the broad parameters of what is being offered until they become members and are in a position to influence the internal debate (see Chapter 16). The Berlin Agreement on Agenda 2000 remains in essence a pre-enlargement approach. Its provisions suggest that the candidate countries cannot expect transfers on the scale of the existing poorer member states or levels of agricultural support comparable to that of the historical CAP. The applicants, once members, will want to change this when they gain voice and representation in the system.

Conclusions

Budgetary politics in the EU is marked by both elements of continuity and factors of change. Since 1988 multi-annual bargains have become the norm, in the form of an agreed financial perspective, and are now part of the *acquis*. Although difficult and protracted negotiations have characterized all three budgetary bargains outlined in this chapter, the political process demonstrated a capacity to frame an outcome that could be widely agreed. Thus the Union's annual budgetary cycle became successfully locked into a medium-term financial perspective, which reduced the dangers of acrimonious arguments and inter-institutional conflicts. The influence of the Commission on the eventual outcome was, however, much stronger in relation to Delors-1 than in relation to the two subsequent packages. That said, the broad parameters established in the 1988 proposals—a multi-annual financial perspective, CAP reform, and an emphasis on structural spending—run through all subsequent agreements.

The capture of the EU budget in the 1960s by agricultural interests has proved relatively enduring. France, the main defender of the CAP, has been successful in preserving its interests in this policy domain. However, agricultural support in the 1990s moved decisively from market measures to compensation payments, and the funding has started to shift from consumers to taxpayers. The relative weight of agricultural support in the budget has declined from a high of 80 per cent in the 1980s to 50 per cent in 1997. Changes as fundamental as a renationalization of a proportion of agricultural spending have been avoided, at least for the time being. Yet

Table 8.4 Financial framework for the EU21, 2000–2006 (€bn., 1999 prices)

Appropriations for commitments	2000	2001	2002	2003	2004	2005	2006
Agriculture	40.920	42.800	43.900	43.770	42.760	41.930	41.660
CAP expenditure (excluding rural development)	36.620	38.480	39.570	39.430	38.410	37.570	37.290
Rural development and accompanying measures	4.300	4.320	4.330	4.340	4.350	4.360	4.370
Structural operat ons	32.045	31.455	30.865	30.285	29.595	29.595	29.170
Structural Funcs	29.430	28.840	28.250	27.670	27.080	27.080	26.660
Cohesion Fund	2.615	2.615	2.615	2.615	2.515	2.515	2.510
Internal policies	5.900	5.950	6.000	6.050	6.100	6.150	6.200
External action	4.550	4.560	4.570	4.580	4.590	4.600	4.610
Administration	4.560	4.600	4.700	4.800	4.900	5.000	5.100
Reserves	0.900	0.900	0.650	0.400	0.400	0.400	0.400
Monetary reserve	0.500	0.500	0.250	0	0	0	0
Emergency aid reserve	0.200	0.200	0.200	0.200	0.200	0.200	0.200
Guarantee reserve	0.200	0.200	0.200	0.200	0.200	0.200	0.200
Pre-accession aid	3.120	3.120	3.120	3.120	3.120	3.120	3.120
Agriculture	0.520	0.520	0.520	0.520	0.520	0.520	0.520
Pre-accession structural instrument	1.040	1.040	1.040	1.040	1.040	1.040	1.040
Phare (applicant countries)	1.560	1.560	1.560	1.560	1.560	1.560	1.560
Enlargement			6.450	9.030	11.610	14.200	16.780
Agriculture			1.600	2.030	2.450	2.930	3.400
Structural operat ons			3.750	5.830	7.920	10.000	12.080
Internal policies			0.730	0.760	0.790	0.820	0.850
Administration			0.370	0.410	0.450	0.450	0.450
Total appropriations for commitments	91.995	93.385	100.255	102.035	103.075	104.995	107.040
Total appropriations for payments	89.590	91.070	98.270	101.450	100.610	101.350	103.530
Of which, enlargement			4.140	6.710	8.890	11.440	14.220
Appropriations for payments as % of GNP	1.13	1.12	1.14	1.15	1.11	1.09	1.09
Margin (%)	0.14	0.15	0.13	0.12	0.16	0.18	0.18
Own resources ceiling (%)	1.27	1.27	1.27	1.27	1.27	1.27	1.27

Source: European Council (1999).

the pressures on the CAP remain in the form of WTO disciplines and the forthcoming enlargement to the east.

Cohesion funding assumed a central role in budgetary politics in the late 1980s with the arrival of the Iberian states. At about 30 per cent of total expenditure under the Berlin Agreement, structural funds remain an entrenched part of the budgetary *acquis* and for the time being persist as a core element of the Union's finances, prompted by the continuing differentials in per capita incomes between different parts of the EU. The applicant states will have a key interest in maintaining this area of EU expenditure well into the future. That said, the funds are unlikely to approach the level of transfers found in traditional federal systems.

The Union budget does not conform to the principles of fiscal federalism and is unlikely to do so in future, notwithstanding the arrival of EMU. Fiscal federalism would require far larger budgetary resources than can be envisaged given the constellation of political forces in the Union. The increases accepted in 1988 and 1992, linked to the resurgence of integration, were followed by the stabilization debate in 1998–9. The net contributors' club is very resistant to endowing the Union with significantly larger financial resources. Many of them, including Germany, would like to reduce the current level of spending. There are limits to EU solidarity and to potential transfers to the east. The debate about how to set limits on national net contributions—and not only for the UK—is likely to continue, since Germany, in particular, was unhappy with the Berlin outcome from a national perspective. In Berlin, burdened with the presidency, the German government placed a higher premium on agreement than on getting a reduction in its contributions. The debate on burden-sharing, introduced by the UK in the 1970s and 1980s, will continue to resonate in EU budgetary debates.

As for the broad institutional process, we should note three features of recent developments. First, the Commission is under intense pressure to improve the quality of its financial management. Secondly, in spite of the rising influence of finance ministers from member governments in the Council, within the budgetary arena both foreign ministers and heads of state or government remain at the centre of the bargaining process on the budget. Thirdly, the EP has exploited its role in the budget to lever more influence for itself within the EU more generally.

Notes

1 For the most comprehensive and detailed treatment of the development of the EC budget and the rules that govern it, see Laffan (1997*b*).

2 This chapter draws heavily on the analysis of Laffan (1997*b*) and Shackleton (1990; 1993*a, b*).

3 For a detailed analysis of the UK issue see H. Wallace (1983).

Further reading

For an analysis of budgetary politics in the 1970s and early 1980s, see H. Wallace (1980, 1983). The Delors-1 package is thoroughly analysed in Shackleton (1990). For a recent overview of the budget and fiscal federalism, see 'Stable Money, Sound Finances', special issue of *European Economy*, no. 53 (1993). For a provocative discussion of the future of EU finances, see Brouwer *et al.* (1995). The most up-to-date volume on the budget is Laffan (1997*b*).

Brouwer, H. J., *et al.* (1995), *Do We Need a New Budget Deal?* (Brussels: Philip Morris Institute).

Laffan, B. (1997*b*), *The Finances of the European Union* (London: Macmillan).

Shackleton, M. (1990), *Financing the European Community* (London: Pinter).

Wallace, H. (1980), *Budgetary Politics: The Finances of the European Community* (London: Allen & Unwin).

—— (1983), 'Distributional Politics: Dividing up the Community Cake', in H. Wallace *et al.* (1983: 81–114).

Chapter 9

Cohesion and the Structural Funds

Transfers and Trade-Offs

David Allen

Contents

Summary

In 1975 the structural funds accounted for less than 5 per cent of European Union (EU) spending. Since the commitment to promote 'economic and social cohesion' was made in 1985, spending has risen to about a third. This might suggest that new opportunities have emerged for a partnership between local or regional authorities and the European Commission, via a form of multi-level governance. However, successive reforms of the funds have shifted much of the control of policy back to national governments. In addition the allocation of the funds between countries and programmes has been a product of high-level bargaining between those governments, making it hard for the Commission to shape policy development. Meanwhile, new preoccupations shape the policy context. Economic and monetary union discourages expansion of public spending and further enlargement will bring new claimants for EU funding. The Agenda 2000 negotiations culminating in Berlin in 1999 suggested that decisions on the structural fund allocations are caught in intense competition between governments to assist their domestic clients and to resist threats to their entrenched advantages from further enlargement.

Introduction

This chapter examines the relationship between the objective of 'economic and social cohesion' and the development of the EU structural funds. Cohesion was written into the Single European Act (SEA) in 1985 to signify the importance of promoting the development of the poorer regions and countries of the EU. It has been articulated as a form of subsidiarity which imposes some obligations on the more affluent regions and countries. The timing of the formal commitment to cohesion was driven by the need to persuade the poorer member states to support the development of the single European market (see Chapter 4). The structural funds have since the mid-1980s provided the main instruments for promoting cohesion. The shorthand term 'structural funds', adopted in 1988, groups together the European Regional Development Fund (ERDF), the European Social Fund (ESF), and the Guidance Section of the European Agricultural Guidance and Guarantee Fund (EAGGF). The Cohesion Fund and the Financial Instrument for Fisheries Guidance (FIFG) were added to this collection in 1992 and 1993 respectively.

In recent years the structural funds have grown to become a significant part of the EU budget (see Table 9.1).[1] From 1975 to 1999 there was a close correlation between the decline in agricultural market expenditure through the Guarantee Section of the EAGGF, and the rise of structural fund expenditure; together they amounted to around 80 per cent of the EU budget. This shift in emphasis partly reflected the growing priority that was given to the goal of 'economic and social cohesion'. In this context the common agricultural policy (CAP) was argued to be both wasteful and

Table 9.1 Growth of the structural funds, 1975–2006

Year	million ecus/€	Percentage of EU budget
1975 (ecus)	257	4.8
1981 (ecus)	1,540	7.3
1987 (ecus)	3,311	9.1
1992 (ecus)	18,557	25.0
1998 (ecus)	33,461	37.0
2002 EU15 (€)	30,865[a]	30.0
2002 EU, enlarged (€)	34,615	35.0
2006 EU15 (€)	29,170[a]	32.0
2006 EU, enlarged (€)	41,250	39.0

Notes:
[a] At 1999 prices.

Sources: Author's compilation from various documents.

counter-productive in so far as it tended to reinforce regional disparities by channelling funds to the wealthier parts of the Union (see Chapter 7). From 1988 to 1999 expenditure on the structural funds rose as expenditure on the CAP fell, but this growth has now been halted. Under the agreements made at the Berlin European Council in March 1999, EU expenditure on the structural funds for the 2000–6 period has been frozen at 0.46 per cent of EU gross domestic product (GDP), an allocation intended to cover both the current EU membership and the enlarged Union.[2]

Regional disparities, both within the Union and within the member states, have always been regarded as barriers to what the original Treaty of Rome termed 'harmonious development', or since the SEA 'cohesion'.[3] The member states are required to conduct and coordinate their economic policies towards this end, and all Union policies, in particular those related to the internal market, are expected to take it into account (Commission 1996c: 6–8). The question, however, is whether the search for economic and social cohesion is simply a rationalization for expenditure on the structural funds, or a real policy goal in its own right. The decision to establish the various funds, and after 1988 to increase significantly the resources at their disposal, can be understood as a series of side-payments designed to facilitate general packages related to the development of the Union as a whole—what John Peterson (1995a) has referred to as 'history-making' decisions. The basic argument of this chapter is that the essence of the structural funds' operations has been determined by a process of high-level inter-state bargaining, primarily resolved by the central governments of the member states, with a kind of collusion by the European Commission and, to a lesser extent, by regional actors. Pollack (1995: 285) has neatly described this process as like a play in which the Commission and the regions are independent actors who are constrained by a script 'written essentially by the member states'. The new arrangements confirmed in Berlin retain a pattern of side-payments and, in effect, compensate the incumbent member states for their acceptance of further enlargement.

Other authors take a different view (Marks 1992; Marks *et al.* 1996; Jeffrey 1997; J. Peterson and Bomberg 1999; Bache 1998); they argue that the way in which the structural funds have been implemented has, either deliberately or inadvertently, challenged the autonomy of governments in the EU. These have been subjected to both the incursions of the Commission's supranational authority and the growing role of sub-national actors, both public and private, at the regional and local level. Many of those interested in the study of regionalism (i.e. a shift of political power to the regions), and in the notion of a 'Europe of the Regions' (Harvie 1994; Keating 1998; Keating and Loughlin 1997), have viewed the EU's structural funds and their attendant institutional arrangements as facilitating regionalization (i.e. a greater role for regional bodies in the administration of public policies). In particular they are impressed by the opportunities for influence apparently afforded to sub-national actors by the implementation of the structural funds. Between 1988 and 1993 the revitalized structural funds gave weight to the arguments of those who perceived the central governments of the member states to be vulnerable to subversion from above and below. The term 'multi-level governance' was developed in the context of the structural funds (Marks 1992), drawing its evidence especially from the implementation of policy in this domain. A critical appraisal of these arguments can be found in Christiansen (1999).

In order to get a handle on this debate, we need to examine the policy implementation process in the light of the 1988, 1992, and 1999 reforms because the state-centric approach is most under challenge from this experience. Our analysis needs to take account of both the institutional arrangements and the philosophy of regional development that the reforms embody. A core contention of this chapter is that the institutional arrangements devised by the European Commission in the 1988 reforms made significant advances in the direction of multi-level governance, but that subsequent developments can be characterized as a reassertion of member state control, revealed as a partial 'renationalization' in the way that the structural funds have been managed.

As far as the philosophy of policy is concerned, the arrangements for structural intervention agreed in Berlin up to the end of 2006 are still tied to the goal of cohesion. However, the way in which economic integration is now being interpreted in the EU seems to suggest that these structural interventions are designed only for the short to medium term, while, in the long run, the operation of the market itself should provide increased welfare for all and reduce regional disparities. There has always been something of a conflict between the competition objectives of the treaties, designed to perfect the working of the market, and the idea of spending programmes to overcome regional disparities as mechanisms that inhibit or 'correct' the working of the market (Frazer 1994). Here we should note that the Commission's evolving approach to the control of state aids (see Chapter 5), in particular vis-à-vis aids from national governments to the regions, could have a significant, even contradictory, impact not just on national regional policies, but on the Union's cohesion policy as well (Wishlade 1998a, b; Thielemann 1998).

An added complication is caused by the prospect of enlargement and its likely impact on cohesion and the evolution of the structural funds (see Chapter 16). In the past there has been a strong connection between enlargement and structural expenditure, as new and poorer member states have been helped to converge economically with the rest of the EU. However, it was argued in the third edition of this volume that the funding arrangements for the EU15 could not easily be extended to encompass the probable new members. It was also argued that the structural funds might no longer be used to facilitate broad Union agreements as they had in the past. As noted above, the European Council concluded another 'historic' agreement at Berlin in March 1999, facilitated in no small way by a deal involving the structural funds. This extended the present arrangements in only slightly reduced and modified form to 2006, not just for the EU15, but also in a form claimed to encompass, if necessary, an EU of twenty-one or so members. However, fundamental reform of the structural funds, as of the CAP (see Chapter 7), both seen as essential for future enlargement, appear to have been postponed until 2005, when the next financial perspective must be negotiated.

The growth of the structural funds to 1999

The establishment of the European Regional Development Fund

The preamble to the Treaty of Rome of 1957 established that the member states were anxious to reduce regional disparities. This, along with the other objectives stated in the preamble, was to be achieved by the 'establishment of a common market and by the progressive approximation of the economic policies of the member states' (Article 2, Treaty of Rome (EEC)). While most of the relevant activity involved the 'negative' process of removing barriers to the free operation of the market, provision was also made for 'positive' intervention. There was to be a common agricultural policy, which would require 'one or more agricultural guidance and guarantee funds' to be set up, a European Social Fund (ESF), and a European Investment Bank (EIB). There was, however, no specific provision for a regional policy or fund, an objective always keenly advocated by the Commission (Bache 1998: 35–8). When, in the early 1970s, the ERDF was established by the member governments, recourse had to be made to the catch-all treaty power in Article 235 (now 308) and to high-level inter-state bargaining at two European summits, both held in Paris in 1972 and 1974.[4] The reasons for establishing the ERDF at that time included the Commission's desire to combine an extension of competence with the beginnings of an attack on regional disparities. However, Helen Wallace (1977) clearly establishes that the ERDF owed its existence mainly to its important part in facilitating a broad deal between the member governments. Wallace argued that 'the first allocations from the ERDF proved little more than an exercise in pork barrel politics' and that it remained to be seen 'whether this will provide a viable basis for a coherent common policy'. The deal sprang from the decisions taken at the 1969 Hague Summit; it was linked both to the enlargement of the EU and to the anticipation of a move towards economic and monetary union (EMU). As we trace the evolution of the structural funds to the present day we shall discover that, as in 1969–75, broad EU deals involving both enlargement and EMU are always explanatory factors.

The 1975 deal established the ERDF, agreed a figure (1.3 billion ecus) for the 1975–8 period, and also set out national quotas for its allocation. The fund was too small to have a significant impact on regional disparities, and thus cannot be seen either as the basis for a real common regional policy or as a significant contribution towards the economic convergence that would have facilitated EMU. Nevertheless, a fund was established and rules had to be devised for its day-to-day management. The Commission devised these rules, which were rationalized in terms of the logic of a regional policy designed to enhance cohesion.

Within the parameters of the basic deal the Commission, in particular Directorate-General (DG) XVI (responsible for regional policy and subsequently cohesion), hoped to influence the selection of projects submitted by the member governments and to prevent them from simply substituting ERDF money for national expenditure. At first the Commission was constrained by the ability of the member governments to limit the total value of their project applications to the size of their agreed quotas, and by their reluctance to provide transparent financial information so that 'additionality' could be ensured. Additionality means spending beyond the levels that would other-wise have resulted from established national programmes. Nevertheless, the imple-menting regulations for the ERDF, which included the creation of a Regional Policy Committee, provided the starting-point for future reforms which would develop the notions of partnership, additionality, and concentration. In parallel, a system for the dispersal of money from the ESF was evolving which from the very beginning sought to involve economic and social 'partners'.

Some minor reforms were introduced in 1979[5] and 1984,[6] but both the Commission and most regional authorities found themselves marginalized in a policy process that rapidly became an instrument of national policy-making (J. Scott 1995). The rules governing the ERDF required unanimity in the Council, which inhibited the Com-mission's ability to engineer more radical reform. The European Parliament's mem-bers, on the other hand, saw an opportunity in that ERDF expenditure qualified as 'non-compulsory expenditure' in the EU budget and was therefore subject to their endorsement. Any increase in the fund, particularly if it were accompanied by greater Commission autonomy *vis-à-vis* the member governments, would also mean add-itional influence for the Parliament.

The Single European Act and Delors-1

However, despite glimpses of the integrative potential of an expanded regional pol-icy, progress was not to be made incrementally. Instead it required the stimulus of major change and pressures for a 'historic' deal to develop structural funds further. This stimulus was provided by the twin impact of 'widening' (to include Greece and later Spain and Portugal), and 'deepening' (the SEA and its centrepiece the single market). Once Greece became an EU member in 1981, its government sought support from the French and Italian governments in winning concessions from the other member states to compensate all of the 'southern' three for the presumed costs of admitting Spain and Portugal. This led to the introduction of the impressively named Integrated Mediterranean Programmes (IMPs), which were justified as measures to address regional backwardness, as well as a kind of solidarity with the existing poorer regions in the EU.[7] None the less, these too can be interpreted as a side-payment designed to ease further enlargement.

The strategy which led to the SEA successfully facilitated a complex bargain in two steps: first, the SEA itself, signed in 1986; and, secondly, the financial consequences, agreed as the Delors-1 package of 1988, which established the first 'financial perspec-tive', or broad framework for multi-annual budgetary allocations. This strategy was successfully repeated in the early 1990s: the Treaty on European Union (TEU) was agreed in December 1991; and the Delors-2 package, in a second financial perspec-tive, which became known as the Maastricht bill, agreed at the Edinburgh European Council of December 1992 (Shackleton 1993*b*; Laffan 1997*b*; and Chapter 8). A similar, although less direct, link can be seen between the Treaty of Amsterdam (ToA), agreed in June 1997, and the Agenda 2000 proposals, launched in June 1997. This was con-solidated in the third financial perspective, agreed at the Berlin European Council in March 1999. This two-stage process links distributive issues to fundamental bargains, but separates the two phases of detailed negotiations (Majone 1994*b*; McAleavey 1994).

The SEA inserted into the Treaty of Rome a new Title V (Articles 130a–e, now 158–62); this, for the first time, linked a concern 'to strengthen economic and social cohesion' with the aim of 'reducing the disparities between the levels of development of the various regions and the backwardness of the least favoured regions, including the rural areas' (Article 130a). Cohesion was to be achieved according to Article 130b, by: EIB loans enhancing the working of the internal market (the 'competitive' approach to eradicating regional disparities); common Community policies (including the structural funds); and the coordination of member states' economic policies. In other words, the structural funds were not designed to bring about cohesion on their own, but rather to supplement the workings of the free market and the economic policies of the member states. Article 130c helped the Commission by providing a direct treaty base for the ERDF, while Article 130d required the Commission to rationalize and to reform the objectives and implementation of the structural funds.

Thus broad changes to the structural funds, including increased expenditure, flowed from the SEA and its surrounding bargains. How far members of the European Council had gone in committing themselves to a particular size for the structural funds at the time of signing of the SEA is not clear from the public record. Some observers of the subsequent behaviour of the member states believe that such a deal was struck, and similarly so at Maastricht and Amsterdam. George Ross, in his study of the Commission under Jacques Delors, argues that in the case of the SEA it was 'a matter of proposing a programme to make good on the social and economic cohesion clauses in the SEA which would combine some serious commitment to preventing the single market from penalizing the EU's less developed members and "paying off" new members Spain and Portugal' (Ross 1994: 40 n. 71).

The Delors-1 package provided for a doubling of the structural funds so that by 1993 they would account for 25 per cent of the Community budget (see Table 9.1). The detailed reforms of the structural funds are covered in the next section, but the point needs to be made here that the basic parameters of this agreement were established by high-level intergovernmental bargaining. Both the French and British governments demonstrated some last-minute reluctance to double the structural funds, but this was overcome by the persistence of the German presidency of the Council, the willingness of Chancellor Kohl to foot the bill, and the negotiating activism of Jacques Delors. There is very little evidence to suggest that the heads of state or government spent very much time debating the advantages and disadvantages of regional policy as they worked to strike a deal.

The Treaty on European Union and Delors-2

The revolution in European affairs that occurred from 1989 onwards stimulated pressures for enlargement and for a further deepening of the EU. This culminated in the signing of the TEU in Maastricht in December 1991 and the promise of a further budgetary bargain to be negotiated in 1992. In the interim it was agreed that the special needs of the five eastern *Länder* now included in a unified Germany would be met by an additional allocation of 3 billion ecus for the 1991–3 period. The money for the eastern *Länder* had to be additional so as not to upset 'the delicate balance in the Funds' allocation of resources and their breakdown by objectives and regions' (Commission 1990d).

The Maastricht agreements were built around a complex intergovernmental bargain, much of which was negotiated at the last moment (Ross 1994: 188–93). It is clear that further changes to the structural funds were central to the bargain. Article B (now 1) of Title 1 (Common Provisions)[8] lists as an objective of the Union the promotion of 'economic and social progress which is balanced and sustainable, in particular through the creation of an area without internal frontiers, *through the strengthening of economic and social cohesion* and through the establishment of economic and monetary union' (my emphasis). Article 3 includes a number of new objectives including 'the strengthening of economic and social cohesion and the encouragement and development of Trans-European Networks' (TENs). Articles 130a to 130e (now 158–62) were similarly amended; special note should be taken of Article 130d, which provides the basis for a further reform of the tasks, objectives, organization, and implementation of the structural funds, as well as for the establishment of a new Cohesion Fund to provide money for the 'poor four' (Greece, Spain, Portugal, and Ireland), in particular to support environmental projects and the TENs. The TEU also established a Committee of the Regions (CoR), and required that it should be consulted on all aspects of ERDF allocation and implementation. Some observers noted the similarity between these limited powers of the CoR and those of the Economic and Social Committee (ESC). Even those sympathetic to its aims have struggled to provide evidence that the CoR has a significant role (Loughlin 1997a).

The member governments approached the TEU much as they had the SEA, detaching agreement on objectives from the exact detail of how these should be financed and implemented. For some member governments the assurance that these details would be resolved in their favour in the future was not enough, and hence a Protocol on Economic and Social Cohesion was annexed to the TEU. This Protocol constituted an interim agreement between the member governments, outlining broadly the changes to be agreed later in Edinburgh and to be incorporated into the enabling rules for the new structural funds which came into force in September 1993.[9]

This Protocol recorded that the doubling of the structural funds between 1988 and 1993 'implies large transfers, especially as a proportion of GDP of the less prosperous member states'. It also noted that the EIB was 'lending large and increasing amounts for the benefit of the poorer regions', and that there was 'a desire for greater flexibility in the arrangements for allocations from the structural funds'. This was the beginning of the rot, as far as the Commission was concerned, because it was a clear reference to the determination of the member governments to free themselves from some of the restraints imposed by the 1988 reforms. Similarly, there was a reference to a 'desire for modulation of the levels of Community participation in programmes and projects in certain countries', as well as a proposal 'to take greater account of the relative prosperity of member states'. Both these suggestions indicated a willingness to devote enhanced structural funds exclusively to the poorer EU states (via the Cohesion Fund), but played down the principle of additionality. Here again we can observe high-level bargaining not just about the basics of the Fund, but also about how governments wanted it to be implemented. Others have suggested that the way the structural funds are implemented impacts on the 'historic' decisions (J. Peterson and Bomberg 1999); yet here we have evidence of the opposite, with the 'historic' deal intruding into the area of future implementation.

The Protocol reveals more of the basic deal that was done at Maastricht in its reference to an agreement that the Cohesion Fund will go to those member states with a GNP per capita of less than 90 per cent of the Community average and which have a programme for fulfilling the economic convergence criteria for EMU. The Cohesion Fund thus represents an incentive to the poor four limited to an EMU rather than a regional development rationale. Both the conditions attached to the Cohesion Fund and those attached to the proposals for a general reform of the structural funds were clearly designed to enhance the power of the member governments at the expense of both the Commission and sub-national actors. None the less, the terms of the TEU left scope for further negotiation in what Marks (1993) refers to as 'post-treaty interpretation and institution-building', although this scope was quite significantly constrained, as can be seen in the Edinburgh Agreement and the 1993 reforms.

At the 1992 Edinburgh European Council the member governments agreed to increase the size of the structural funds from 18.6 billion ecus in 1992 to 30 billion ecus in 1999 (at 1992 prices) (Shackleton 1993*b*) (see Table 9.1). There was also agreement about how the structural funds would be allocated between the various objectives which the Commission had established in its 1988 reforms (see Box 9.1), but only a vague understanding about the shares to be guaranteed to each member state. It was, however, evident that an agreement about how the spoils would be divided up was an essential condition for agreeing the implementing regulations (Allen 1993). At Edinburgh the European Council also allocated an aggregate total of 15 billion ecus to the Cohesion Fund with annual totals rising from 1.5 billion ecus in 1993 to 2.6 billion ecus in 1999. The member governments were primarily interested in the total amount of structural funding that they would each receive. Annexe 3 of the Edinburgh communiqué indicated a rough division of the Cohesion Fund up to 1996 in which Spain would receive between 52 and 58 per cent, Greece and Portugal between 16 and 20 per cent, and Ireland between 7 and 10 per cent. The Irish Prime Minister, for instance, later claimed that he had 'firm pledges of 8 billion Irish punt' from the Edinburgh European Council (*Financial Times*, 2 July 1993), while the Spanish government said it had obtained written assurances that it would receive 6,400 million pesetas (*Financial Times*, 5 July 1993), and the Portuguese government claimed that it was promised 3,500 billion escudos (*Financial Times*, 9 July 1993).

The exact determination of which regions would be eligible for the funds from the various objectives was left until later, although it was clear that outline promises were made in order to facilitate agreement in Edinburgh. It has been suggested, for instance, that the German government, under pressure from the *Länder*, agreed to an extension of the British budget abatement only after it had obtained assurances that the five eastern *Länder* would be eligible for at least 13 billion ecus from Objective One funds. It was only after further negotiation in the Council that each member state's share was established (see Table 9.2) and the enabling legislation passed in late 1993.

Between 1988 and 1999 the structural funds went through a significant expansion. It has been argued by some that this expansion played an important role in facilitating the 'historic' decisions which underpinned the SEA and the TEU, and that much of the haggling over the details was left until later because 'the resolution of both types of decision simultaneously would be practically impossible' (McAleavey 1994). We shall see later that a broadly similar view can be taken of the decisions around the ToA and Agenda 2000 in mid-1997, together with the Berlin Agreement of March

> **Box 9.1** Structural fund objectives, 1988–2006
>
> **1988–99**
>
> ■ *Objective One* was originally meant to cover regions where the GDP per capita was less than 75 per cent of the EU average. Some member states insisted that this criterion be loosened, in order to include particular additional regions, as a condition of their agreement to the overall package. The Council decides eligibility for this objective. Objective One draws on funds from the ERDF, ESF, and EAGGF and represents just under 70 per cent of the total funds.
>
> ■ *Objective Two* covers regions affected by industrial decline, where the unemployment level is above the EU average. Eligibility for this objective is negotiated between the Commission and the Council. Objective Two draws on funds from the ERDF and the ESF and represents around 11 per cent of the total funds.
>
> ■ *Objective Three* is aimed at combating long-term unemployment. In 1993 it was effectively combined with the old Objective Four, which was aimed at facilitating the occupational integration of young people. The post-1993 Objective Four was for facilitating the adaptation of workers to industrial change. The two objectives draw on the ESF and together claim just under 10 per cent of the total funds.
>
> ■ *Objective Five* is subdivided between 5*a*, funded by the EAGGF and earmarked specifically for agricultural and forestry assistance, and 5*b*, which draws on the EAGGF, ERDF, and ESF. Objective 5*b* is aimed at promoting the development of rural areas mainly via diversification away from traditional agricultural activity. Objective 5 receives around 9 per cent of total funds.
>
> ■ *Objective Six* was introduced after the 1995 enlargement for developing sparsely populated Nordic areas. It draws funds from the ERDF, ESF, and EAGGF and accounts for less than 3 per cent of total funds.
>
> **2000–6**
>
> ■ *Objective One* remains as above but with a stricter application of the criterion, but will also include those areas previously eligible for Objective Six.
>
> ■ *Objective Two* is for regions facing major change in the industrial, services, and fisheries sectors, rural areas in serious decline and disadvantaged urban areas.
>
> ■ *Objective Three* covers those regions not covered by the other objectives and is specifically aimed at encouraging the modernization of systems of education, training, and employment.

1999. In the period up to 1999 both the secondary 'distributive' arrangements and the primary 'historic' decisions were dependent on high-level bargaining. It was subsequently, as their implementation began, that other actors began to play a role in the policy process.

The process of implementation does provide some scope for a challenge to the powers of the central governments of the member states, although some care needs to be taken in specifying which central powers are being challenged. Marks (1993) argues that it is necessary to 'go beyond the areas that are transparently dominated by the member states; financial decisions, major pieces of legislation and the Treaties' to understand that 'beyond and beneath the highly visible politics of the member

Table 9.2 Allocation of structural funds to member states, 1988–1999 (per cent)

Member state	1988–92	1993–9
Austria	—	1.04
Belgium	1.18	1.31
Denmark	0.64	0.54
Finland	—	1.09
France	9.38	9.65
Germany	9.56	14.12
Greece	11.96	10.12
Ireland	7.08	4.07
Italy	17.08	14.29
Luxembourg	0.09	0.06
Netherlands	1.15	1.59
Portugal	13.42	10.12
Spain	20.81	22.91
Sweden	—	0.85
United Kingdom	7.05	8.26

Source: Bache (1998: 85), reproduced with kind permission of Sheffield Academic Press.

state bargaining lies a dimly lit process of institutional formation (integration?) and here the Commission plays a vital role'. Others have argued that the implementation of the structural funds involves a mobilization of both public and private sub-national actors which is significant, because it has led to 'an enhancement of the governing capacity of the system as a whole' (Hooghe and Keating 1994). Neither of these arguments necessarily demonstrates that the central governments have lost power. It may be that they have little interest in the implementation stage once they have secured guarantees of a certain level of structural expenditure. It may also be the case that they are either able to control, to manipulate, or even to cooperate with newly enfranchised sub-national actors so as to consolidate, rather than weaken, their central authority. For instance, in the UK in the early 1990s the government, led by John Major, had an interest in encouraging private sub-national actors to partici-pate in EU regional procedures, if this would disturb Labour-controlled local author-ities. Finally, it has also been argued that it is artificial to distinguish between the decision-making and implementation stages of structural fund policy-making (J. Peterson and Bomberg 1999: 155), in that opportunities exist for those involved in implementation, including the Commission and sub-national actors, to have an impact on the big decisions. I will return to these arguments in the conclusions.

The implementation of the structural funds

In the early days of the structural funds the Commission was given little discretion other than over the minuscule ESF. The ERDF was distributed by a system of national quotas, which meant that the member states simply applied for funding up to their quota limit. They usually requested funds for projects that were already planned, or, in some cases, completed. In 1979 the Commission persuaded the Council to agree to a small non-quota section and in 1984 the quotas were relaxed into 'indicative ranges'. This gave the Commission discretion over about 11 per cent of the ERDF budget. The Commission used this new flexibility to develop its own regional priorities, and to introduce its own programmatic approach to regional assistance. In 1984 the Council agreed that 20 per cent of the ERDF would be devoted to programmes, rather than to individual projects. Although most of the programmes would be developed by the member states, some would be initiated and developed by the Commission. Steps were also taken to coordinate better the activities of the three separate funds (ESF, ERDF, and the guidance sectors of the EAGGF). The IMPs and the Integrated Development Programmes (IDPs) were the first that might be said to involve the structural funds as a coordinated group rather than an individual fund, although efforts had been made in this direction since the late 1970s (H. Wallace 1983).

In this early period the Commission took advantage of any opportunity to influence the activities of the funds or to shape their future. The Commission's big opportunity owed much to Delors's success in establishing the concept of cohesion in the SEA and in linking this to increased structural fund expenditure. The SEA (Article 130d, now 161) established that the implementation of the structural funds should be reformed on the initiative of the Commission (another Delors success). Once the financial perspective was agreed in 1988, the Commission duly proposed, and the Council passed, a package of regulations that amounted to a major reform. The TEU subsequently amended Article 130d (now 161), so as to provide the opportunity for further reform in 1993.

In the 1988 reforms the Commission established four principles (see Box 9.2) so as to relate the structural funds to the objective of economic and social cohesion. The Commission was interested in the further development of a common policy and the

---

Box 9.2 The Commission's four principles for implementing the structural funds

- *Concentration* of measures around priority objectives.
- *Partnership*, involving the closest possible cooperation between the Commission and the 'appropriate authorities' at 'national, regional, and local level' in each member state, and at every stage in the policy process from preparation to implementation.
- *Additionality*, such that EU funds complement, rather than replace, national funding.
- *Programming*, whereby multi-annual, multi-task, and occasionally multi-regional programmes, rather than uncoordinated individual national projects, are funded.

creation of a more autonomous role for itself, in part by seeking an alliance with sub-national partners against the stranglehold of the national central governments. The 1993 reforms suggest that this strategy broadly failed in that the member governments took every opportunity to claw back what they conceded in 1988, so much so that some commentators now talk about the partial renationalization of the structural funds (Bache 1998: 127–33). Pollack (1995) argues that the concessions of 1988 were in essence insisted upon by the major donor states. These latter were not destined to receive much from the structural funds and they probably judged that a system that gave an element of control to the Commission was preferable to one that left the major beneficiary states to their own devices.

The ToA made no substantive changes, but it was agreed that the Agenda 2000 package would require yet further reform of the implementation procedures. The main guidelines for these reforms were adopted by the Commission in March 1998 (*Financial Times*, 19 March 1998); the Berlin Agreement of March 1999 paved the way for these to be formally agreed by the Council later in 1999, in order to become operational by the start of 2000 (*Financial Times*, 20 March 1998; Bache 1998: 125–33). Broadly the 1998–9 reforms as proposed are likely to confirm the lines of the 1993 reforms.

Programming

The implementing regulations of 1988 and 1993 provided for the structural funds to be allocated to programmes rather than to individual projects. These programmes could be initiated at the national or Community level, and could be financed by one or more of the funds. In the period between 1988 and 1999 roughly 90 per cent of the funds went towards nationally initiated programmes and 9 per cent towards what became known as Community initiatives (see Table 9.3).

The programmes initiated at the national level were adopted by the Commission under the 1988 rules on the basis of community support frameworks (CSFs); these were separately negotiated between the Commission and each member government, on the basis of either national or regional development plans (RDPs), drawn up by the member government in partnership with its regional authorities. The 1993 reforms streamlined this process, allowing a member state to submit a single programming document (SPD); these are not negotiated with the Commission, in contrast to the CSFs, and contain proposals for programmes from the outset, thus shortening the process. Because of time constraints this can mean the effective exclusion (and confusion!) of 'partners', and the domination of the process by central governments. Once adopted, the programmes are monitored and assessed by monitoring committees at national, regional, and whatever the relevant operating levels are, which may include local authorities or other agencies. The 1999 reform proposals suggest further streamlining, in response to the member governments' demand for 'simplification'; Bache (1998: 127) takes this to mean reducing the role and influence of the Commission. In consequence, the Commission intends to withdraw from much of the day-to-day management of the funds.

Initially, therefore, the Commission was successful at moving away from the uncoordinated funding of nationally selected projects towards the funding of programmes, designed in consultation with the member governments and using

Table 9.3 Community initiatives, 1998–2006

Initiative	Purpose
1988–99	
Interreg	Cross-border, transnational, and inter-regional cooperation
Leader	Rural development
Regis	Support for the most remote regions
Adapt	Adaptation of the workforce to industrial change
SME	Small and medium-size firms in disadvantaged areas
Rechar	Adaptation to industrial change in coal-dependent regions
Konver	Adaptation to industrial change in defence-industry-dependent regions
Resider	Adaptation to industrial change in steel-dependent regions
Retex	Adaptation to industrial change in textile-dependent regions
Urban	Urban policy
Pesca	Restructuring the fisheries sector
Employment	Integration into working life of women, young people, and the disadvantaged
2000–6	
Interreg	Cross-border, transnational, and inter-regional cooperation
Leader	Rural development
Equal	Transnational cooperation to combat all forms of discrimination and inequalities in the labour market

Commission-determined criteria. However, it has been forced over time to concede more and more of the programming to the member governments. As we shall see, the designation of objectives, of the areas that they will cover, and of the programming criteria are increasingly influenced by the bargains struck internally by the member states. The Commission was able to push its programming principle furthest in the one area where it has had considerable autonomy: Community Initiatives (see Box 9.3). Innovative measures added up to 10 per cent of the structural funds budget between 1988 and 1999. Community Initiatives are drawn up on the basis of guidelines established by the Commission alone, although the Regional Policy Committee (a high-level consultative committee with the member governments, established under the ERDF regulations) must be consulted. However, as Hooghe and Keating (1994) have pointed out, the Commission's exercise of this autonomy has caused considerable friction with the national authorities—friction that has often been exacerbated by coordination failures within the Commission itself, resulting in conflicts and contradictions between Commission-initiated programmes and national programmes. In the 1993 reforms a new Council Committee on Community Initiatives was established to tighten member governments' control. For the 1993–9 period the Commission optimistically proposed that the percentage of the structural funds devoted to Community Initiatives be expanded from 9 per cent to 15 per cent. The member governments responded by retaining the 9 per cent limit and in 2000–6 reduced this to just 5 per cent. The Commission has now agreed that there will be just three Community Initiatives in future; some might see this as a retreat, but the Commission is arguing that this is an advance for the principle of concentration.

Concentration

In their six objectives for the funds (see Box 9.1) the Commission sought to impose consistent geographical and functional criteria on their management, and thereby to concentrate spending on the most needy regions and states. To a certain extent this goal has been achieved. The Cohesion Fund furthered this principle of concentration by limiting the recipients to only four member states. There is a constant tension between the Commission's desire for more concentration and the concern of all the member states to obtain and retain as big a share of the structural funds as possible. The 1993 negotiations were replete with examples of individual member states seeking to bend the agreed rules in order to preserve funds for their own favoured regions. The 1999 reforms have sought to extend the principle of concentration even further by reducing the objectives to just three and by reducing the percentage of the EU's population eligible for structural aid from 51 per cent to between 35 and 40 per cent (in the end the Berlin European Council agreed on 42 per cent). Thus in the end the Commission was forced to modify its proposals for further concentration with safety nets and transitional arrangements in order to facilitate an agreement that had 'something in it for everybody' (see Box 9.3).

Additionality

The Commission had repeatedly tried to insist on additionality as a principle for structural fund expenditure. It was successful in the 1988 reforms in making this more respected by the member states, and in constraining them from reducing national expenditure, as they had tended to do in the past. Bache (1998: 77–9, 105–12) documents the battles that the Commission had over this issue, in particular with the UK, but also with the other member states. On this issue the Commission was actively supported by many UK local authorities, a development which provided Marks (1993) with the evidence that he needed to confirm his view that sub-national authorities and the Commission had become significant participants in the EU policy process. However, this overall conclusion is challenged by Pollack (1995), and the actual outcome of the UK dispute is questioned by Bache (1999). Nevertheless, the Commission has pushed the member governments to 'account openly and transparently for the structural funding they receive and for the continuing implementation of national expenditure' (J. Scott 1995). Member governments are now required to demonstrate additionality when they submit their planning documents to the Commission, and the Commission has successfully threatened recalcitrant states with the withholding of funds if they do not comply. But it still has enormous problems in seeking to monitor effectively the devious financial practices of member governments. In the 1999 reforms these problems are acknowledged; as part of its 'simplification' drive the Commission has come up with the notion of 'negotiated additionality'. The intention is that the Commission will negotiate with each member government an agreed level of structural expenditure, one which must at least match what was spent in the previous period.

The Cohesion Fund, on the other hand, appears to strike at the very principle of additionality. This is partly because until 1999 cohesion money was viewed as aid to

---

Box 9.3 Something for everybody! The Berlin agreements and 'particular situations'

- The Berlin European Council of March 1999 agreed structural fund spending for 2000–6 and allocated €11.142 billion for transitional support for all regions and areas which no longer meet the relevant eligibility criteria. In addition, particular situations would be funded as follows:

- €500 million for the development of the Lisbon region

- €500 million for five more years of the Peace Programme, in recognition of the special efforts for the peace process in Northern Ireland, of which 100 million will be allocated to Ireland

- €100 million phasing out treatment under Objective One for the transition region of Ireland resulting from the new classification of regions, and an additional allocation of €550 million under Objective One as a result of the reclassification

- €500 million for the Netherlands to take account of the particular characteristics of labour market participation

- €150 million for Sweden for a special programme of assistance, plus €350 million for Sweden under Protocol Six of its Act of Accession

- €100 million to take account of the special problems of East Berlin in the transformation process

- €96 million for Italy and €64 million for Belgium for the phasing out of allocations for Objective Two

- €15 million for the Hainaut region of Belgium for the phasing out of Objective One

- €300 million for a phasing out programme for the UK Highlands and Islands in view of the particular structural problems resulting from low population density, matched with a high degree of poverty

- €450 million for Greece, €450 million for Portugal, €40 million for Ireland and €200 million for Spain as a special financial allowance to enable these countries to maintain between 2000 and 2006 the overall average level of per capita aid reached in 1999

- €350 million for Austria inside the Community Initiatives

- €550 million for the Netherlands inside the Community Initiatives

Source: European Council (1999).

---

promote convergence for the purposes of EMU. It was thus specifically designed to assist governments from the poorer member states to increase levels of structural assistance (especially for the environment and TENs), without increasing the burden on overall government expenditure. It has become harder to retain this rationale now that three of the four beneficiaries of the Cohesion Fund have joined the single currency. However, the 1999 agreement retains the Cohesion Fund until 2006, with a view to helping those eligible to 'maintain' the convergence that they have managed to date.

Partnership

A great deal of excitement has been generated by the Commission's advocacy of the principle of partnership in the management of the structural funds (Bache 1998: 93–104; 1999). The 1988 reforms called for the close involvement of regional and local bodies with the Commission and the national authorities in the planning, decision-making, and implementation of the structural funds. It is this which is the basis for the interest in sub-national actors (Hooghe 1996) and the notion of multi-level governance (Marks 1993) in this area of policy. The intent was clear: it was not just to improve the efficiency of regional policy, but to give it features specifically designed to penetrate national policy processes (Hooghe 1996). In this sense one core goal was a policy made for the regions and by the regions—in other words, a policy that encouraged not just regionalization, but regionalism. Such an objective was almost certain to encounter resistance from central governments, especially in the more highly centralized member states such as the UK, and especially at a time when they were facing demands for devolution. Some even saw the principle of partnership as an early example of subsidiarity (Bache 1998: 75).

The 1988 partnership proposals included some interesting innovations, which were seized upon by a host of academics searching for a convincing alternative to the intergovernmentalism that had begun to dominate studies of the EU policy process. An advisory Consultative Council of Regional and Local Authorities was established, the forerunner of the Committee of the Regions established later by the TEU. Regional and local authorities became much more active, both individually and collectively, in lobbying in Brussels and in national capitals (McAleavey 1994; Mazey and Richardson 1993b; Hooghe 1996). While some authors have argued that the partnership principle has enhanced regional and local governmental involvement in the policy process (Landáburu 1994; Laffan 1996; Nanetti 1996), others contend that, despite a great deal of mobilization, much of the activity has been symbolic. On this latter view, very little real power has been wrested from national central governments, and very little additional power has flowed to the regions in those member states, such as Germany or Spain, with a decentralized federal structure (Hooghe and Keating 1994; J. Anderson 1996; Bache 1999). McAleavey's (1994) study covers the extensive activity of the lobby which promoted Objective Two and sought to preserve it in the 1994–9 period. He concluded that the impact of the lobbying had been minimal, and that it was not possible to detect sub-national influence on the intergovernmental bargaining in Edinburgh.

Perhaps not surprisingly, the extent of influence of the many regional offices based in Brussels has been questioned by central government officials, in contrast to the claims from regional and local authorities to the political credit for any EU funds that have come their way. Sub-national actors involved in structural fund partnerships have been the subject of a great deal of academic scrutiny (Bache 1998: 93–104; A. Smith 1998) and it is hard to draw firm conclusions across the great variety of EU member states. It does seem that the effectiveness of sub-national access is determined more by the nature of the constitutional arrangements in a particular member state than by the Commission's partnership arrangements. In some cases central governments have been able to strengthen their powers by using Commission procedures to play one set of sub-national actors off against another, or by joining forces with sub-national actors to do battle with the Commission. Examples of the latter case support the liberal intergovernmentalist approach of Andrew Moravcsik (1998), in so far as they show sub-national actors as important in national preference formation, rather than as independent actors at the EU level.

The Commission has been criticized for its choice of partners; in some programmes the Commission prefers regional authorities, in others local authorities, and in yet others partners from the private sector. There is also a tension between the Commission's desire for partnership and its desire for consistent, coherent, and well-coordinated programmes. If the partnership principle really did lead to significant sub-national participation in the design and management of the structural funds, then the enormous variety across the EU, in terms of both organization and influence, would lead to different regions funding many different solutions to similar problems (A. Smith 1998; Bache 1998). We can indeed observe a great deal of regional mobilization; in the Flanders region of Belgium and in the German *Länder* there is extensive involvement in the preparation, financing, monitoring, and assessment of programmes, although J. Anderson (1996) doubts whether the *Länder* have increased their powers *vis-à-vis* the federal government. But this clearly has not been the case in the UK (Bache *et al.* 1996) or in states like Greece, Ireland, and Portugal, which have no elected regional tiers. In these cases the powers of the central government have probably increased, drawing on their ability to influence significantly who participates in the implementation of the structural funds. Devolution in the UK and the recasting of the eligible areas in Ireland may, of course, change the patterns of influence.

It is, however, quite hard to demonstrate that the Commission's advocacy of the partnership principle in itself has significantly challenged the autonomy of the central governments. Where that autonomy is under challenge for different reasons, the management of the structural funds provides an opportunity structure for political positioning, as may well be the case as regards the participation of the UK Highlands and Islands in Objective One funding after 1999. Some EU countries have experimented a good deal with regionalization in recent years, but this is not necessarily to be equated with regionalism as such. As Tsoukalis (1997: 208) concludes, 'European integration may indeed strengthen in the long term the centrifugal tendencies inside some member states. But this will have little to do with the principle of partnership or other such ideas which have often been blown completely out of proportion in the literature.'

Agenda 2000 and the Berlin agreements

The major issue for structural fund policy-makers as a result of the 1993 reforms was how to adapt to EU enlargement. The accession of Austria, Sweden, and Finland in 1995 presented no real problems; it was marked only by the invention of Objective Six (see Box 9.1). The Commission's (1996c) first assessment of cohesion policy was followed shortly by an informative report from the House of Lords Select Committee on the European Communities (1997a). Both reports were inconclusive about the relationship between structural fund expenditure and economic cohesion, although the House of Lords report attributed some significance to the political impact of the funds, in particular to the encouragement which they gave to local participation and thus a sense of 'ownership' of the EU policies. But it was hard to derive a justification for the funds in terms of their impact in diminishing regional disparities.

The prospect of further enlargement would necessarily entail a debate about the future of the structural funds (see Chapter 17). Decisions on this were postponed while the member governments negotiated the ToA, but immediately afterwards the Commission delivered, as requested, its proposals for managing enlargement. The Agenda 2000 documents (Commission 1997i)[10] outlined a third financial perspective and proposed that overall spending on the structural funds, among both the EU15 and the enlarged membership, be frozen at 0.46 per cent of EU GDP (see Table 9.1). The Commission proposed a total expenditure on structural operations within this ceiling of €275 billion, at 1999 prices, between 2000 and 2006. This sum was broken down into €230 billion for the structural funds and the retained Cohesion Fund for the EU15, and €45 billion, to be ring-fenced, for both pre-accession aid for all the applicants (allocated in similar fashion to the Cohesion Fund) and post-accession aid for the six states that were assumed likely to join the EU by 2006. In proposing that the structural funds should remain a high priority, but that their growth should be curtailed, the Commission was constrained in that the member governments were committed to freezing the overall budget at a maximum of 1.27 per cent of EU GDP up to (and probably beyond) 2006, and that they might well not agree to any significant reductions in other areas of expenditure.

The Commission also proposed that the structural funds should be further concentrated and that their implementation should be simplified. To this end it suggested reducing the number of objectives from seven to just three (see Box 9.1) and reducing the coverage of the structural funds from over 50 per cent of the EU population to between 35 and 40 per cent. It was also proposed, in line with the policy concerns about unemployment expressed in the ToA and reinforced by the European Council, that unemployment should become the major criterion for allocating structural funds in the newly created Objective Two regions. This was particularly bad news for the incoming Labour government in the UK, which had inherited a system for measuring unemployment which had been contrived by the previous Conservative government to disguise unemployment as far as possible. The new rules for determining aid in Objective Two regions and the proposed stricter application of the rules for Objective One eligibility would mean that many regions that had received aid between 1988 and 1999 would no longer be eligible.

The potential for sharp negotiations between member governments was high, and this is indeed what occurred between March 1998, when the Commission published its full proposals to implement Agenda 2000, and March 1999, when the European Council concluded a deal (see also Chapter 8). This established that the Commission's overall figure for structural operations expenditure between 2000 and 2006 would be reduced from €275 billion (at 1999 prices) to €258 billion; €45 billion would remain ring-fenced for pre-accession aid and post-accession benefits, and the €213 billion reserved for the current EU15 would include €18 billion for the Cohesion Fund. The Spanish government was particularly vigorous in defending the Cohesion Fund (*Financial Times*, 27–8 March 1999).

The character and results of this lengthy negotiation suggest that intergovernmentalism is not yet dead, and that the Commission may have to accept a further watering down of some of its principles, especially those of partnership and additionality. Even the effort to concentrate further the coverage of the structural funds was modified in the Berlin settlement, although the Commission did gain acceptance for the reduction of the number of objectives. The negotiations themselves were significantly affected by the German national election, which took place in the autumn of 1998. In the period between then and the Berlin European Council, the Commission responded to the pressures from the member governments (themselves often supported by various sub-national actors) and announced a series of safety nets to reassure those who feared that they would lose out under the new rules. Once the Commission had conceded that special transitional arrangements would be tolerated for those regions likely to lose out, that no region would lose no more than one-third of its covered population, and that the Cohesion Fund would continue to be available for the poor four (even though three of them had apparently 'converged' enough to join the single currency), the makings of a deal was there.

The Berlin Agreement was facilitated by acceptance of the principle of providing something for everybody (see Box 9.3), which seemed to leave the member governments in a stronger position than before. This appears to confirm the renationalization of control of structural fund expenditure, and the weakening of the Commission's four principles (Box 9.2), that has been apparent since the 1993 reforms. Formally, the new proposals deal with the immediate problem of enlargement in terms of provisional budgetary allocations, but they are unlikely to have any serious impact on the problem of regional disparities. Furthermore, as Bache points out (1998: 133), the proposals address only the enlargement aspect of the cohesion problem. Politically, the new proposals served the function of facilitating agreement between the member governments, and the Commission may have been wise to respond to the new atmosphere by its proposals to simplify the implementation procedures, and to step back from some of its contacts with sub-national actors. All of these tendencies seem to take the policy process further and further from the concept of multi-level governance and much closer to the modified intergovernmentalism that Bache (1999: 37–42) has described as 'extended gatekeeping'.

Conclusions

The structural funds gained an enormous increase in resources in the period between 1988 and 1999. That increase has now been halted, and consolidation would appear to be the name of the game for the next decade. Nevertheless, structural fund expenditure in pursuit of cohesion has become, and may well remain, one of the EU's core activities. Despite arguments to the contrary (J. Peterson and Bomberg 1999: 155), it is argued here that policy-making as regards the structural funds can best be understood in two distinct stages: the 'historic' decisions emerge as intergovernmental deals, in which the central governments of the member states are the major and determining players. Bargains about the size and allocation of the structural funds have been used to facilitate wider EU developments, particularly in relation to the SEA and the TEU. Some similar elements are visible in the Agenda 2000 outcomes. However, it is not that easy to explain these 'side-payments' in rational economic terms. No real effort has been made to base the cohesion policy on an estimate of the costs for the poorer states of accepting the single market programme, EMU, or the continued enlargement of the EU. Despite a great deal of sub-national activity associated with the structural funds, there is no really convincing evidence that this has weakened the intergovernmental character of policy negotiation. In some member states regional interests must be given serious consideration, and may even be deliberately mobilized by central governments when considering their national negotiating stance and tactics, but this seems to be linked more to the existing political features of individual member states than to the impact of EU programmes.

The Commission has clearly sought, through its establishment and pursuit of the four principles of programming, concentration, partnership, and additionality, to strengthen its own and the EU's position in this area of policy-making. However, these efforts peaked in the 1988 policy reforms; the Commission has been backtracking *vis-à-vis* the member states in the subsequent reforms of 1993 and 1999. Thus Hooghe and Keating (1994) point out that the member governments, armed with the TEU principle of subsidiarity, reasserted their influence over the selection of eligible areas, over a simplified set of implementing procedures, and over the selection of sub-national partners; in addition the Cohesion Fund rules represent a significant 'slackening' of the additionality principle. Similarly Bache (1998: 127–30), in his assessment of the 1998 reforms, argues that the 'while the four principles of 1988 remained intact, and a fifth principle of "efficiency" would be added, the Commission's proposals were relatively modest and in some areas hinted at a further renationalization of the funds'.

It may not be a damaging outcome for European integration that the structural funds have not encouraged further regionalism within the EU. The EU was constructed, and has been sustained by, relatively coherent member states with relatively strong central governments. If structural fund expenditure and the concept of cohesion led to a reinforcement of the power and legitimacy of these governments, then this may be advantageous for European cooperation. A 'Europe of the Regions', encouraged and nurtured by a strong supranational–sub-national alliance over access to the structural funds, might not, in the long term, lead to increased harmony. Already the implementation of the structural funds has given rise to rivalries and conflicts between regional and local authorities and between public and private partners. Not all of this conflict has enhanced the power or authority of the Commission, despite the high profile that has been accorded DG XVI since 1988.

It was argued in the third edition of this volume that the future of the structural funds was challenged by the prospect of continued enlargement to include the states of eastern and central Europe. While enlargement has proved to be a more protracted process than was first anticipated, the EU has reached agreement on a financial perspective for 2000–6 which appears, at least until 2006, to reconcile enlargement and the continuance of the structural funds. This could not have been taken for granted a few years ago. The new 1999 arrangements for the structural funds seem to represent a complex deal between the present member governments, but one which also includes consideration of the claims of likely future members, contrary to the agreement of 1992. This bargain was probably possible because the structural funds have rather less to do with real economic cohesion or the eradication of regional disparities than to do with a modest budgetary redistribution to facilitate the continued development and smooth running of the EU. Even at the levels of funding available to the EU15 until 1999, the structural funds were not large enough to make a significant difference either to regional disparities or to convergence, although we should not forget that for the smaller and poorer states the income was significant (Tsoukalis 1997: 206). Indeed the Commission (1996c) in its first Cohesion Report noted that between 1983 and 1995 regional income and employment disparities widened, despite an overall rise in EU prosperity.

The enlarged EU economy will almost certainly not rely in the future on the redistributive effects of the structural funds. None the less, the EU system of governance may well continue to rely on the structural funds to facilitate and, to a certain extent, to legitimate its complex arrangements. Cohesion will remain important to an enlarged EU, but will probably be sustained more by the operation of the market, by European competition policy, and by the coordinated economic policies of the member governments, than by the structural funds.

Notes

1 In the latest budgetary perspective €215 bn. is planned for all structural operations. This is made up of €198 bn. for the structural funds and €18 bn. for the Cohesion Fund. The figures are for spending amongst the present EU15. The third financial perspective also provides for a small amount of structural assistance (€1 bn.) as part of the pre-accession package, as well as a much larger sum (€40 bn.) for an assumed enlargement to EU21 between the years 2002 and 2006.

2 European Council, *Presidency Conclusions*, Press Release No. SN 100 (Presse) (Brussels, 25 Mar. 1999). See also *Financial Times*, 27–28 Mar. 1999, 2.

3 In the Treaty of Rome (EEC) these were 'differences existing between the various regions and the backwardness of the less favoured regions' (Preamble) and in the Treaty on European Union (TEU) they were 'disparities between the levels of development of the various regions and the backwardness of the least favoured regions, including

the rural areas' (Article 130a (TEU)). The ToA makes one very small change, referring in Article 158 (ex 130a) to 'disparities between the levels of development of the various regions and the backwardness of the least-favoured regions *or islands*, including rural areas' (my emphasis).

4 Article 235 of the Treaty of Rome (EEC) reads: 'if action by the Community should prove necessary to attain, in the course of the operation of the common market, one of the objectives of the Community and this Treaty has not provided the necessary powers, the Council shall, acting unanimously on a proposal from the Commission and after consulting the assembly, take the appropriate measures'.

5 A small non-quota section, under the exclusive control of the Commission, was built into the ERDF allocation process, a predecessor of the Community Initiatives, which were introduced in 1988.

6 Instead of rigid national quotas a

system based on 'indicative ranges' was introduced, giving the Commission a bit more flexibility (about 12% of the ERDF was now effectively at the discretion of the Commission). In 1984 the Commission also made some progress towards replacing the funding of individual projects with the establishment of more wide-ranging 'programmes'. These were designed to give the Commission a greater input into regional expenditure plans.

7 The IMPs were first established in 1985 and involved the transfer of 6.6 bn. ecus over seven years to parts of France and Italy and all of Greece. The Commission advanced its own procedural agenda by only funding integrated programmes rather than individual projects selected by the recipient states.

8 There was no reference to cohesion in the Preamble to the SEA. It has been argued (Frazer 1994) that the fact that there is no reference to the regulation of competition in the TEU Common Provisions suggests that cohesion now has primacy over competition. More recently, see Wishlade (1998a, b).

9 Council Regulations (EEC) Nos. 2080-5/ 1993, all of 20 July 1993 and published in the *OJL*, 193/1.

10 See Avery and Cameron (1998, esp. 101–39) for full details of Agenda 2000.

Further reading

For an excellent overview of the development of EU regional policy and the theoretical debate, see Bache (1998) and Hooghe and Keating (1994). For a good review of the recent literature on 'territorial politics', see the review article by Christiansen (1999). J. Peterson and Bomberg (1999) provide a useful overview of cohesion policy and the debate about the significance of sub-national actors, while Hooghe (1996) provides the most thorough account of research to date on the subject. Marks (1992) remains a clear statement of the multi-level governance concept applied to EU structural policy, and Pollack (1995) stands out as a detailed rebuttal of this view. J. Scott (1995) is useful on the regional development debate, and Le Gales and Lequesne (1998) provide a wide-ranging survey of a number of the themes explored in this chapter.

Bache, I. (1998), *The Politics of European Union Regional Policy: Multi-level Governance or Flexible Gatekeeping?* (Sheffield: Sheffield Academic Press).

Christiansen, T. (1999), 'Territorial Politics in the European Union', *Journal of European Public Policy*, 6/2 June, 349–57.

Hooghe, L. (1996) (ed.), *European Integration, Cohesion Policy and Subnational Mobilisation* (Oxford: Oxford University Press).

—— and Keating, M. (1994), 'The Politics of European Union Regional Policy', *Journal of European Public Policy*, 1/3: 367–93.

Le Gales, P., and Lequesne, C. (1998) (eds.), *Regions in Europe* (London: Routledge).

Marks, G. (1992), 'Structural Policy in the European Community', in Sbragia (1992b: 191–224).

Peterson, J., and Bomberg, E. (1999), *Decision-Making in the European Union* (London and New York: Macmillan and St Martins Press).

Pollack, M. (1995), 'Regional Actors in an Intergovernmental Play: The Making and Implementation of EC Structural Policy', in C. Rhodes and Mazey (1995: 361–90).

Scott, J. (1995), *Development Dilemmas in the European Community* (Buckingham: Open University Press).

Chapter 10

Social Policy

Left to Courts and Markets?

Stephan Leibfried and Paul Pierson

Contents

Summary

Despite the widespread assumption that European Union (EU) involvement in social policy has been minimal, the dynamics of market integration have led to a substantial spill-over on to the Community level. Resistance by national governments to loss of autonomy and conflicts of interests between rich and poor regions, or between employer and employee interests, present formidable obstacles to activist EU policies, though in the 1980s, and especially in the 1990s, the EU has now accumulated substantial regulatory competences in social policy. Nevertheless, member states have lost more control over national welfare policies, in the face of the pressures of integrated markets, than the EU has gained *de facto* in transferred authority. The multi-tiered pattern which has emerged is largely law- and court-driven, marked by policy immobilism at the centre and by negative market integration, which imposes significant constraints on national social policies.

Introduction

Accounts of European social policy generally still present a minimalist interpretation of EU involvement.[1] The sovereign nation state, so the argument goes, leaves little social policy role for the European level. The EU is regarded as focused on market-building, leaving an exclusive, citizen-focused, national welfare state, its sovereignty formally untouched, though perhaps endangered indirectly by growing economic interdependence. 'Welfare states are national states' (Swaan 1992: 33; cf. also Lange 1992). On the face of it, the European welfare state indeed looks national. There is no European welfare law granting individual entitlements against Brussels; there are no direct taxes, or contributions, funding a social budget to back such entitlements; there is no Brussels welfare bureaucracy to speak of. Territorial sovereignty in social policy, so conventional wisdom holds, is alive and well.[2] We disagree. The process of European integration has eroded both the sovereignty (by which we mean legal authority) and autonomy (by which we mean *de facto* regulatory capacity) of member states in the realm of social policy. National welfare states remain the primary institutions of European social policy, but they do so in the context of an increasingly constraining multi-tiered polity (Pierson and Leibfried 1995a,b).

While there have been extensive barriers to any true federalization of European social policy, the economic and institutional dynamics of creating a single market have made it increasingly difficult to exclude social issues from the EU's agenda. The emergence of a multi-tiered structure (Pierson 1995b), however, is less the result of welfare-state-building ambitions of Eurocrats than a result of spill-overs from the single market initiative. By spill-overs we mean the process through which the completion of the internal market has invaded the domain of social policy (see initially E. B. Haas 1958, then Lindberg and Scheingold 1970, and now Falkner 1998: 7–12). Recall that the single market initiative in the 1980s was based on a deregulatory agenda and assumed that initiatives to ensure free movement of goods, persons, services, and capital could be insulated from social policy issues, which would remain the province of member states. This dubious assumption runs directly contrary to the central tenets of political economy, which stress that economic action is embedded within dense networks of social and political institutions (Hall 1986, 1999; North 1990). Already there is significant evidence that the tidy separation between market issues, belonging to the supranational sphere, and social issues, belonging to the national spheres, is unsustainable. Irrespective of the results of 'high politics' struggles over social charters and treaty revisions the movement towards market integration carries with it a gradual erosion of national welfare state autonomy and sovereignty, increasingly situating national regimes in a complex, multi-tiered web of social policy.

This transformation occurs through three processes (see Table 10.1). Positive, or activist, reform results from social policy initiatives taken at the 'centre' by the Commission and the Council, along with the European Court of Justice's (ECJ) often expansive interpretations of what those initiatives mean; in the 1990s the treaty mandate was strengthened, providing a Euro-corporatist anchor, which drew European union and employer organizations towards the activist centre. Negative reform occurs through the ECJ's imposition of market compatibility requirements that

Table 10.1 National welfare states transformed through European integration: processes, key actors, and examples

Processes	Key actors	Examples
Direct pressures of integration → '*positive*' initiatives to develop uniform social standards at EU level	Commission, expert committees, ECJ, and since 1992 institutionally entrusted corporate actors (UNICE, CEEP, ETUC) (background actors: EP, ESC, diverse lobbies)	Gender equality; health and safety; Social Protocol 'corporatism' since 1992, generalized 1997, with expansion of competences and of QMV; 1989 EC Social Charter, 'incorporated' in ToA
Direct pressures of integration → '*negative*' policy reform via market compatibility requirements	ECJ, Commission, Council (national governments), national legal institutions	Labour mobility; since late 1980s freedom to provide services, combined with impact of European 'competition regime'
Indirect pressures of integration → adaptation of national welfare states	Market actors (employers, unions; sensitive sectors: private insurance, provider groups), Council, individual national governments in fields outside social policy	'Social dumping', EMU, harmonization of tax systems, single market for private insurance

restrict and redefine the social policies of member states. Both positive and negative initiatives create direct pressures on national welfare states through new instruments of European social policy. Finally, the process of European integration creates a range of indirect pressures that do not legally require, but none the less encourage, adaptations of national welfare states. These 'ecological' pressures strongly affect national welfare states, but they are not systematically connected to the development of social policy instruments at the European level.

In our first section we briefly review the initially modest direct efforts to develop an activist European social policy. Like others, we stress the formidable obstacles for such policy: institutions that make reform difficult, limited fiscal resources, jealous member state protection of 'state-building' resources, and an unfavourable distribution of power among interest groups. But the 1990s also reveal a growing activity potential and profile. The second section reviews the development of what we call market compatibility requirements—legal challenges to those aspects of national welfare states that conflict with the single market's call for unhindered labour mobility and open competition for services. In the third section we consider the *de facto*, rather than *de jure*, pressures on national regimes. These result from factors such as competitive demands for adaptations of national economies and their institutional environments to a single market and, since 1 January 1999, a single currency area for eleven member states. In the final section we pull together these arguments to highlight some of the distinctive features of this emerging multi-tiered system of social policy.

Positive initiatives from the centre go hand in hand with major and visible social conflicts and have been attempted since the foundation of the European Community

(EC). The 1957 Treaty of Rome, for instance, met stiff resistance in the French National Assembly in part because of concern that weak social clauses endangered the well-developed French welfare state (Marjolin 1989: 284–97). Negative integration efforts were historically less visible, but are just as old. The coordination of rules governing labour mobility was enshrined in one of the earliest EC legislative acts of 1958, although similar action on services dates only from the mid-1980s, reaching a high plateau at the end of the 1990s. Naturally, indirect pressures, the third level distinguished in Table 10.1, are of more recent vintage, since such pressures could only build up as integration intensified.

The limited success of activist social policy

Discussions of social policy generally focus on such prominent actors as the Council, the Commission (most often in tandem with the Directorate-General for Employment, Industrial Relations, and Social Affairs: DG V) and the European Parliament (EP) (with its Committee on Employment and Social Affairs), and the representatives of business and labour interests with their recently matured 'corporatist policy community' (Falkner 1998). The European Commission, in particular, has been a central actor in direct attempts to construct a significant social dimension for its 'European social model' (Commission 1994f)—areas of social policy competence where uniform or at least minimum standards are set at the European level. These attempts have occurred in fits and starts during the past few decades. It has been a saga of high aspirations and modest results, marked by a plenitude of 'cheap talk', produced in the confident knowledge that the requirements of unanimous votes in the Council meant that ambitious blueprints would remain unexecuted. This story has been well told elsewhere (Streeck and Schmitter 1991; Vogel-Polsky and Vogel 1991; Lange 1992). Here we review only the broadest outlines, for our main argument is that the analytical focus on the efforts of Euro-federalists to foist an activist social dimension on a reluctant Council has been somewhat misleading. European integration has indeed altered the making of European social policy, but largely through quite different mechanisms.

The obstacles to an activist role for Brussels in social policy development have always been formidable (Pierson and Leibfried 1995a,b). These include both institutional constraints and the balance of power among relevant social interests. EU institutions make it much easier to block reforms than to enact them. Generally, only narrow, market-related openings for social legislation have been available. Even on this limited terrain reform requires a super-majority, i.e. a qualified majority. The member governments themselves, which serve as gatekeepers for initiatives that require Council approval, jealously protect social policy prerogatives. Economic and geopolitical changes since the second world war have gradually diminished the scope of national sovereignty in a variety of domains. The welfare state remains one of the few key realms of policy competence where national governments still appear to reign supreme. Given the popularity and the electoral significance of most social programmes, national executives have usually resisted losses of social policy authority.

Until the mid-1990s a further barrier was the relative weakness of the social demo-cratic forces most interested in a strong social dimension. Unions and social demo-cratic parties had become weaker since the 1980s in most of Europe, especially among the founding members of the EU. Though social democracy—now less bent on traditional social than on 'new' employment policy—has ascended again among EU member states in the 1990s, union power has not. At the European level organiza-tional difficulties and profound conflicts of interest between high-wage and low-wage areas of the EU limit labour's influence, sometimes leading to new regional inter-class alliances. At the same time, business power has grown considerably, in part because of the increasing capital mobility that European integration—and capital markets throughout the Organization for Economic Cooperation and Development (OECD)—has fostered. This balance of power among social interests has further hindered efforts that institutional blockages, limited fiscal resources, and the tremendous dif-ficulties of harmonizing widely divergent and deeply institutionalized national social policies[3] would have rendered highly problematic in any event.

In this context, substantive policy applications have been rather rare. Expansive visions of Community social policy have had far lower priority than initiatives for an integrated market. Knowing that—surely until 1993—British opposition rendered serious initiatives impossible (see Kleinman and Piachaud 1992*b*), member govern-ments, European officials, and interest groups have made rhetorical commitments to the construction of a social dimension (Lange 1992; Ross 1995; Streeck 1995). Over the last two decades there have been loud public fights over a series of initiatives to increase the social policy competence of the EU. In most cases, the vigour of the rhetorical battle far exceeded the true implications of the proposals at hand. In any case, these initiatives invariably were either defeated outright or radically scaled back. The struggle over the Social Charter in the 1980s was typical (Falkner 1998: 65–9), though the 1989 Community Charter of the Fundamental Social Rights of Workers and the 1961 European Social Charter of the Council of Europe now have both been silently incorporated by simple reference in the Preamble to the 1997 Treaty of Amsterdam (ToA) and its Article 136. Efforts to establish an ambitious programme for European-level legislation were rebuffed by the British, who eventually refused to agree to even the much watered-down version that was signed by the other member states in 1989. The exercise allowed various actors to adopt politically useful public postures, but seemed to give only modest momentum to actual policy initiatives.

Legislative reform until the early 1990s was limited to a few areas where the Treaty of Rome, or the single market project, allowed more significant latitude. A notable example concerns the gender equality provisions of Article 119 of the Treaty of Rome (EEC), now 141 (ToA). Until 1986 this was the only major (then implicit) social policy competence in reach of the then EC. This provision, offered as a face-saving conces-sion to France, lay dormant for almost two decades. In the 1970s, however, the Coun-cil unanimously agreed to a number of directives which gave the equal treatment provision some content. Over the past twenty years the ECJ has played a crucial activist role, turning Article 119 (EEC) and the directives into an extensive set of requirements and prohibitions related to the treatment of female (and occasionally male) workers (Falkner 1994*a*: 77–122; Ostner and Lewis 1995; Hoskyns 1996; Bieback 1997). These rulings have required extensive national reforms—although not always to the benefit of women. To take just one example, ECJ decisions have had a dramatic impact on private and, indirectly, also on public pension schemes. The Court's insistence on equal retirement ages in occupational pension schemes forced Britain to level ages up or down. By choosing to raise the retirement age for women the government saved billions of pounds, while avoiding much of the blame for the cuts. When in the *Barber* case the ECJ in 1990 made a similar ruling for occupational pensions (C-262/1988), fear that the ruling might be applied retroactively to private pensions (at a cost estimated at up to £40 billion in Britain and DM35 billion in Germany) fuelled 'what is probably the most intense lobbying campaign yet seen in Brussels' (Mazey and Richardson 1993a: 15). While this pressure led the negotiators of the Treaty on European Union (TEU) explicitly to limit retroactivity, the impact of the Court's rulings was still dramatic.[4] Thus the EU has come to play a considerable role on gender issues, although the market-oriented nature of the Community and its restricted focus on the paid-labour market has circumscribed such interventions.

A second example is the extension of regulations governing health and safety in the workplace (see Eichener 1993, 1997). The Single European Act (SEA) of 1986 allowed qualified majority voting (QMV) in this area out of fear that national regulations could be used as non-tariff barriers to trade. Surprisingly, policy-making has produced neither stalemate nor lowest-common-denominator regulations. Instead, extensive regulations have generally produced quite a high level of standards. Furthermore, European regulators moved beyond the regulation of products to the regulation of production processes, where the concerns about barriers to trade would seem inapplicable. As Eichener has documented, the Commission's role as 'process manager' appears to have been critical in this low-profile environment. Much of the crucial decision-making took place in committees composed of policy experts (Joerges and Neyer 1998). Some of these experts were linked to business and labour groups, but business interests did not have the option of simply refusing to participate, since regulatory action was likely to proceed without them. Representatives within these committees were often interested in innovation, having gravitated towards Brussels, because in regulatory issues it seemed to be 'where the action is'. In this technocratic context, best practices from many member states (and from then non-member Sweden) were pieced together to form a quite interventionist structure of social regulation. The Commission played a central part by linking together the work of different committees, incorporating concerns of other actors such as the EP, and founding a new specialized 'expertocratic' institution, the European Agency for Safety and Health at Work, active since 1996 in Bilbao, as well as actively promoting particularly innovative proposals.

This development provided one indication that the institutional restrictions on social policy initiatives had loosened somewhat since the mid-1980s. The introduction of QMV in some domains has made social policy the focus of sharp conflict. There have been significant struggles to determine the range of issues that can be decided by QMV, either under Article 100a (SEA, now 94) (covering harmonization of legislation so as to avoid distortions of competition) or under the SEA's exception for proposals governing the health and safety of workers: 'the Treaty-Base game' (Rhodes 1995). Members of the Commission, the EP, and the European Trade Union Confederation (ETUC) have pushed with some success for expansive readings of these clauses. The Union of Industrial and Employers' Confederations of Europe (UNICE), the main employers' organization, has strongly opposed such a move (Lange 1992: 235–56; for a broader view, see Falkner 1998: 84–95). While many proposals connected to the Social Charter and the 1989 Action Programme had been watered down or stalled until the early 1990s, already then the combined impact of what was passed was far from trivial (Addison and Siebert 1993). Early signs of some growing room for social policy initiatives were the enactment of the Atypical Work (health and safety) Directive in 1991 and of the Maternity Directive in 1992, both passed under the 'health and safety' provisions allowing QMV—and both opposed by the UK, the latter also by Italy.[5] This legislation required more generous policies in several EU countries. At the same time, it introduced a policy ratchet, prohibiting other countries from cutting back their existing regimes. But the TEU and its Social Protocol of 1992 achieved a procedural breakthrough and an expansion of competences which led to a series of additional directives (see Table 10.2).

The watershed in the development of social policy competences and their use dates to the mid-1990s. The ToA (1997) reveals a fully developed Social Chapter, a 'one track' Social Europe as a hard constitutional end-point of a soft 1989 Social Charter. The two 'original' mandates (health and safety in the 'working environment'—Article 118a (now 138) (TEU); gender equality 'in pay'—Article 119 (now 141) (EEC)) were kept, but health and safety was broadened to all 'working conditions' and gender equality was extended to all labour force issues (partly following EC practice and the ECJ); all were placed under QMV, an innovation for gender equality. Two additional QMV competences were introduced: worker information and consultation; and integration of persons excluded from the labour market (but not the attendant finances). Unanimous decision-making was explicitly extended to five new topics: social security and protection of workers; protection of workers when the employment contract is terminated; collective interest representation; employment of third-country nationals; and financing measures to integrate the excluded. But also, to tame the scope of treaty clauses with wide powers, three topics were explicitly declared off limits: pay; the right of association; and the right to strike, as well as the right to impose lock-outs. In all these revisions the ToA consolidated and universalized a state of the Union that dated to the 1992 Maastricht Social Protocol for all EU members except the UK, which had opted out of its provisions.[6] The new British government in 1997 reversed its predecessor's opt-out and without exception. Amsterdam thus extended Maastricht progress to the UK. It was also agreed to universalize the new 1992 Euro-corporatist legislative powers of the 'social partners', i.e. the unions and the employers, in what became Articles 138–9 (ex 118a and 118b) in the Consolidated Treaty on European Union (CTEU).

But the ToA also has some original social policy aspects: based on a Swedish initiative, it also included a new Title VIII on employment (Articles 125–30 (CTEU), replacing Articles 109n–s) (see Johansson 1999; Tidow 1998). Although stressing the importance of activist policy, the provisions directly call for largely symbolic actions: the exchange of goals, procedures, guidelines, and reports. In striking contrast to economic and monetary union (EMU), it does not provide any additional fiscal or legal instruments for effective 'positive integration' beyond the small European Social Fund (J. Anderson 1995; Kaluza 1998). The employment competence assigned to the EU level therefore is less about EU employment policy than about co-ordinating national employment initiatives.

Table 10.2 The assignment of explicit[a] social policy competences to the European Union

Competences	EEC 1957	SEA 1986	TEU 1992	Social Protocol 1992	CTEU[b] 1997
Free labour movement	Unan 48–50	QMV	QMV	No impact	QMV 39–40
Gender equality in pay[b]	Unan 119	Unan	Unan +	QMV	QMV 141
Gender equality for labour force[b]	No ref	No ref	No ref	QMV	QMV 137(1) v
Working environment	No ref	QMV 118a	QMV	QMV	QMV 137(1) i
Working conditions (outside former Article 118a)	No ref	No ref	No ref	QMV	QMV 137(1) ii
Worker information and consultation	No ref	No ref	No ref	QMV	QMV 137(1) iii
Integration of persons excluded from labour market	No ref	No ref	No ref	QMV (excl. funding)	QMV 137(2) (excl. funding)
Social security and protection of workers	No ref	No ref	No ref	Unan	Unan 137(3) i
Protection of workers where employment contract is terminated	No ref	No ref	No ref	Unan	Unan 137(3) ii
Collective interest representation, co-determination	No ref	No ref	No ref	Unan	Unan 137(3) iii
Employment of third-country nationals	No ref	No ref	No ref	Unan	Unan 137(3) iv
Funding for employment policy	No ref	No ref	No ref	Unan	Unan 137(3) v
Social security coordination	Unan 51	Unan	Unan	n.a.	Unan 42
Pay	No ref	No ref	Excl 100a.2[c]	Excl	Excl 137(6)
Right of association	No ref	No ref	Excl 100a.2[c]	Excl	Excl 137(6)
Right to strike and to impose lock-outs	No ref	No ref	Excl 100a.2[c]	Excl	Excl 137(6)

Notes: Unan = unanimity required; QMV = qualified majority voting; No ref = no reference to competence; n.a. = not applicable; Excl = competence explicitly excluded.

Heavier shading denotes less competence. Heaviest shading shows explicit denial of competences, anchored in the treaties only since 1992 in these areas.

Numbers refer to articles in each treaty. The CTEU column lists the revised article numbers according to the relevant sections of the 1997 CTEU agreed at Amsterdam.

[a] Explicit mention in the treaties, in contrast to unspecified general powers, as under Articles 100 and 235 (now 95 and 308) (EEC), or non-enabling norms such as Article 129 (now 152) (TEU) on public health.
[b] Between the original Treaty of Rome and the 1992 Social Protocol the ECJ had interpreted gender equality more and more widely.
[c] Article 100a(2) (TEU) exempted provisions on free movement of persons, and on the rights and interests of employees, from QMV, but did not preclude action by unanimity, whereas Article 137(6) (CTEU) specifically withholds competence.

Source: Falkner (1998: 82), supplemented by the authors (with thanks to Josef Falke for his legal advice).

In principle, the revised Social Chapter (Articles 136–45 (CTEU)) facilitates efforts to expand EU social policy, in line with the 1992 Social Protocol. First, any single country's capacity to obstruct legislation has diminished. Already in 1992 the four cohesion states—Greece, Ireland, Portugal, and Spain—no longer commanded enough votes to block reform under the Social Protocol's rules on QMV. This minority status became even more pronounced after the northern expansion to EU15 in 1995. The obstruction that had met the 1989 Social Action Programme (Falkner 1998: 69) had been made impossible. In 1994 a long-delayed European Works Councils Directive was approved under these procedures (Rhodes 1995; Falkner 1998: 96–114), even though in this case the new Euro-corporatist legislative procedure still remained stalled. In 1996 the Parental Leave and in 1997 the Atypical Work (working conditions and distortion of competition) Directives followed suit (Falkner 1998: 114–28, 129–45). These became the first successes for a functioning Euro-corporatism endowed with legislative powers. The social partners were ready to negotiate, now 'in the shadow of the (Council) vote' and based on their own learning experience.

Yet, while most aspects of the Social Charter have moved forward, further initiatives seem likely to be modest and more consolidating in nature, as also indicated by the 1998 Social Action Programme.[7] Through the early 1990s the Commission itself was involved in intensive soul-searching concerning its proper social policy role (Ross 1994: 221–6). Efforts to combat stubbornly high European unemployment have taken centre-stage, as reflected in the ToA in 1997. The Commission seems to have accepted at least some of the British case about the need to promote 'flexibility'. Already the White Paper on Growth, Competitiveness, Employment had revealed a change in emphasis towards reducing labour costs, calling for tax reforms that would generate 'a substantial reduction of non-wage labour costs (between 1 and 2 percentage points of GDP), particularly for the least-skilled workers' (Commission 1993*d*: 116 ff.). The member states seem unlikely to allow the Commission to take the lead on such issues, suggesting that the immediate prospect is for consolidation, with the completion of some current agenda items but few new initiatives.

The dismissals of claims that a significant EU role now exists in social policy are largely based on an examination of 'high politics'—the widely publicized struggles over positive, centre-imposed social policies through devices like the Social Charter in the 1980s and the Social Protocol in the early 1990s. Developments such as the Maternity Directive, the directives under the Social Protocol (1992), and the 'constitutionalized' Social Chapter (1997) suggest that the room for European initiatives is growing. EU legislative activity is now at least as extensive as, for example, federal social policy activity was in the United States on the eve of the New Deal (Robertson 1989; Pierson 1995*a*). Yet, if member states have lost considerable control over social policy in the EU, this is primarily because of processes other than the efforts of Union officials to develop social policy legislation for a new European universe.

European integration and market compatibility requirements

Lost amidst the noisy fights over the Social Charter and the Social Protocol has been the quiet accumulation of EU constraints on social policy connected with market integration. The last four decades, and especially the most recent two, have witnessed a gradual, if incremental, expansion of Community-produced regulations and, especially, court decisions that have seriously eroded national welfare state sovereignties. Until recently (Falkner 1998) political scientists paid scant attention to this area of 'low politics', entranced by the world of 'high politics' and 'high conflicts'. The topic was left to a small set of European (welfare, social security) lawyers who have monitored another centre of policy-making: the Courts.[8]

By now the ECJ has delivered (Table 10.3 gives the figures up to 1995) more than 400 decisions on social security coordination and more than 200 decisions on other 'social policy' matters (within the scope of Articles 117–25 (TEU), now 136–48 (CTEU)). (See also Appendix 10.1.) In addition, the Commission stayed its course by also bringing to court violations of the treaties by member states concerning social policy (*Eureport Social*, 6/1–2 (1998), 13; 6/4–5 (1998), 14–15; 6/8 (1998), 5–6).

Social policy cases account for a growing share (1991–5: 21 per cent) of a rising ECJ caseload (see Tables 1.5 and 1.6, which summarize cases from the Commission's annual *General Reports*). Looking at new cases since the mid-1980s the social policy cases have moved up to permanent and prominent 'major league' status at the ECJ. They are now on par with agriculture and fishery, free movement of workers and services (a category which harbours quite a few social policy decisions in the 1990s, notably *Kohll*), and environment. One special category of social policy cases is excluded from our calculations, namely those brought by staff from EU institutions, for whom

Table 10.3 The distribution of the European Court of Justice caseload, 1961–1995

Period	Social security (Article 51 (EEC) now 42 (CTEU))		Social provisions (Articles 117–22 (EEC), now 136–45 (CTEU))		Free movement of workers (Articles 48–50 (EEC), now 39–42 (CTEU))		Social policy (all)	
	% of cases	No. of cases	% of cases	No. of cases	% of cases	No. of cases	% of cases	No. of cases
1961–70	19.7	20	0.7	1	0.7	1	21.1	22
1971–75	12.5	44	0.3	1	4.3	15	17.1	60
1976–80	10.3	72	1.1	8	2.0	14	13.4	94
1981–85	8.4	63	3.7	28	4.1	31	16.2	122
1986–90	9.1	74	4.2	34	5.0	41	18.3	149
1991–95	10.0	108	8.8	95	2.2	35	21.0	238

Source: Stone Sweet and Brunell (1997: 82–3).

the ECJ serves as a labour and social security court. In 1995 this particular category of cases far exceeded the generic social policy cases. This huge demand on ECJ resources, among others, led to the founding of the Court of First Instance in 1989 (Emmert 1996: 104–6), with the ECJ now serving only as a court of appeals for such cases.

The 600 social policy cases have a distinct pattern of origin. Even after several enlargements, cases emerged mostly from the original EC6 countries and, from the newcomers, mostly and interestingly from the UK, which became quite active in the European legal system. Remarkably, the smaller states, such as Belgium, the Nether-lands, and Denmark, have given rise to a disproportionate share of the social case-load, while France and Italy have consistently produced rather few, with Germany in between and routinely active only in free movement of persons cases (Stone Sweet and Brunell 1997: 81 ff.). Since plaintiffs usually may not appeal to the ECJ directly, the national legal profession plays a critical intermediary role in feeding cases to the ECJ. Indeed, the activist stance of the legal profession as a whole seems crucial. In Ger-many, for instance, lower welfare and labour courts often try to outmanœuvre their national courts, employing the ECJ to overturn firm national precedents from above.

The EU's social dimension is usually discussed as a corrective or counter to market-building, but, in our view, it has instead proceeded largely as part of the market-building process. It is this which has spurred the demand for court decisions, and thus expanded European law in several areas of importance to systems of national social provisions.

Freedom of movement for workers

The nexus between the market and social policy was at least partially acknowledged at the outset, when social policy in the Community was addressed largely in relation to the problem of reducing restrictions on labour mobility. Articles 48–51 (EEC) (now 39–42 (CTEU)) deal with the freedom of movement for workers, with Article 51 (TEU) (now 42 (CTEU)), providing for the direct social policy effects: 'The Council shall, acting unanimously on a proposal from the Commission, adopt such measures in the field of social security as are necessary to provide freedom of movement for workers . . .'.

That a labour mobility regime of 'coordination' restricts welfare state sovereignty was on the minds of treaty-makers in 1957, when Italy, as a labour exporter, and France, with early equal pay legislation, pushed for Community competence (Romero 1993). At the time, however, such impacts were neither very visible nor contentious. An already entrenched intergovernmental consensus existed on which the treaties could build, including: bi- and multilateral social security treaties, the Treaty of Paris establishing in 1951 the European Coal and Steel Community, with its Social Security Treaty for miners and steelworkers, and the standards set by the International Labour Organization (Schulte 1994b: 408, 422). These embedded international legal norms facilitated fast and silent supranationalization. The new regulations, along with the obligations they created for member states, gradually became more deeply institutionalized—mostly in the quiet of the Court's chambers. It was not until the end of the 1980s that member states began to wake up to the full importance of 'coordination' and to struggle with it.

In line with the Community's agenda of market integration, Articles 59–66 (now

49–55, with old 62 repealed) (EEC) also from the outset provided competence to regulate and ensure the freedom to provide services. At first sight this competence does not seem to allow much room for social policy. In contrast to coordination, the EEC Treaty's signatories saw no real connection between the freedom of services and their sovereign welfare state-building. But developments in recent times have shown that this constitutional principle and its implementation entail far-reaching consequences for national social policy regimes. It guarantees both the freedom of movement to consumers of social policy to shop where they want, and the right of service providers to deliver their services 'across the border' into another welfare state. Through the freedom to provide services and through the EU competition regime for private actors the demarcation line between welfare state and market has been redrawn across all member states. This spill-over has become a major terrain for European conflicts over social policy—especially, broadly speaking, over health—reform, as several ECJ decisions in 1998 clearly revealed.[9] In the rest of this section we briefly indicate how creating a free market for labour and services has directly intruded on the sovereignty of national welfare states.

One of the crucial points of tension between national welfare states and the developing common market has arisen over regulations governing the mobility of labour across the jurisdictional boundaries of member states. Intra-European migration—compared with the USA—is small, and member states are quite different in their active migration profiles;[10] there are still only 5 million workers, including their dependants, who actually exercise this freedom (Angenendt 1997). But already these numbers provided more than the critical mass necessary to generate continuous and increasing litigation at the ECJ level. In legal terms, the adaptation of social policy to a developed context of European inter-state commerce does not require a quantum leap in European migration itself. Individuals as litigants and national courts which refer cases to the ECJ are, together with the ECJ itself, the central actors in shaping this multi-tiered EU policy domain. They have instigated a large corpus of national and, especially, supranational adjudication since 1959. Third-country migrants have also prompted important cases,[11] and labour migration generally has been one of the driving forces behind the third pillar and the innovations of the ToA (see Chapter 18).

A detailed review of this case law cannot be attempted here (see Leibfried and Pierson 1995a; Barwig and Schulte 1999; Slaughter *et al.* 1997). Over a period of forty years a complex patchwork of regulations and court decisions has partially suspended the principle of member state sovereignty over social policy in the interest of European labour market mobility. It now spreads to the freedom of service consumers, as well as producers. The net effect is to limit national capacities to contain transfers by territory (Maydell 1991: 231; Eichenhofer 1992; Barwig and Schulte 1999) and to shape welfare state reform trajectories, as we can see from just two examples. First, attempts to create a minimum pension benefit in Germany during the 1980s foundered in part because of concerns that the benefit would be exportable to non-German EC citizens who had worked for some time in Germany (Zuleeg 1993). Secondly, in 1994 German long-term care insurance was strategically targeted to include benefits in kind, straight monetary transfers treated as 'in kind' surrogates, so as to prevent a Europeanization of benefits and thus to preserve territorialization. But in 1998 in *Molenaar* the ECJ did not find this strategy convincing (Case C-160/1996 of 5 March 1998; see Sieveking 1998: 316–70).

To summarize some of the key implications of this section:

- A member state may no longer limit most social benefits to its citizens. As regards 'foreigners' from within the EU, the state no longer has any power to determine whether foreign people have a right to benefits or not. Benefits must be granted to all or withheld from all. This development is remarkable since 'citizen-making' through social benefits—demarcating the outsider—was a watershed in the history of state-building on the continent, especially in France and Germany. This restriction places some weight on attempts to develop innocent-looking, devious mechanisms at the national level.

- A member state may no longer insist that its benefits apply only to its territory and thus may be consumed only there. As a result, today's state can exercise its power to determine the territory of consumption only to a limited extent— basically when providing in-kind or universal means-tested benefits, and still in unemployment insurance (see Husmann 1998: 296).

- A member state is no longer entirely (though still largely) free to prevent other social policy regimes from directly competing on its own territory with the regime it has built. In Germany, for instance, there are many 'posted' construction workers from other EU countries, who work for extended periods at their national wage level, while covered by many of their home country's social regulations. Thus, the state has lost some of its exclusive power to determine how the people living within its borders are protected, though there have been successful attempts in the 1990s to contain these losses through obligatory minimum wages and vacations (cf. Eichhorst 1998; Streeck 1998: 26–30).[12]

- Member states do not have an exclusive right to administer claims to welfare benefits of migrants. Rather, the authorities of other states may also have a decisive say in adjudicating benefit status in individual cases—as quite controversial cases like *Paletta* revealed repeatedly in Germany and other countries (Case C-45/1990 of 3 June 1992).

If complete national *de jure* authority in these respects is what sovereignty in social policy is all about, it has already ceased to exist in the EU. This has been a complex process, in which supranational efforts to broaden access and national efforts to maintain control go hand in hand, and are calibrated from conflict to conflict and court case by court case.

This transformation has not occurred without member state resistance. Individually, member governments have baulked at implementing particular facets of coordination, although they have been effectively taken to task for this by the ECJ. Collectively, the member states have sought to roll back some aspects of coordination in the early 1990s, unanimously agreeing to revisions that will allow member governments to restrict portability in a somewhat broader range of cases following proper 'notification' (Schulte 1994; Fuchs 1998). The impact of this shift is still unclear, though it may partially offset some of the loss of sovereignty. The notification provision must still pass muster with the ECJ.

Coordination, however, has become the entering wedge for an incremental, rights-based 'homogenization' of social policy. Neither 'supranationalization' nor 'harmonization' seems an appropriate label for this dynamic, since each implies more policy control at the centre than currently exists. The process is more like a market-place of 'coordination', with the ECJ acting as market police, a light and visible hand, though enforcing the boundaries of national autonomy. It structures the interfaces of fifteen national social policy systems, with potentially far-reaching consequences for the range of policy options available to national welfare states.

Freedom to provide services and the European competition regime

The treaties, and also secondary European law, focus on economic activity, and entrepreneurial freedoms. Are welfare state measures economic activity? If so, the freedom to provide (financial or social) services (Articles 59–66 (now 49–55) (EEC)) would apply,[13] as would the general European competition regime (see Chapter 5). Wherever the welfare state is involved in economic activity both normative domains usually become relevant at the same time. European integration does acknowledge non-economic, true welfare state activity—but when in doubt economic and not welfare state activity is presumed. There is, as quite a few ECJ cases show, no general exemption for welfare state activity from the treaties' market freedoms (Becker 1998: 360–1.). Rather, drawing—and continually redrawing—this fine line between 'economic' and 'solidaristic' action is what much of the legal conflict is about (see typically *Sodemare*, Case C-70/1995 of 17 June 1997). Schulz-Weidner (1997: 449) has posed the general dilemma well:

There is a permanent tension between the European economic constitution, on the one hand, and the sovereignty of its member states to shape their welfare states, on the other. The European economic constitution and its competition regime have moved out of the national sphere and have become a mostly European competence—and in so far as this is so, the principle of subsidiarity does not protect member states. Consequences for national social security systems have mainly received public attention because of a series of ECJ decisions. As soon as social security institutions are active 'economically'—and the ECJ interprets this quite liberally—they lose their national privileges, and have to conform to the European competition regime and the basic freedoms. Otherwise these institutions would forfeit their (national) 'social security monopoly'.[14] Judged by the present case law of the ECJ the implementation of German pension insurance through public institutions—characterized by an insurance monopoly—is not yet substantially endangered. But this may well change, as pension insurance is now permanently under reform and seems placed on a trajectory where contributions and benefits become ever more 'equivalent', or where even actuarial justice, as in private insurance, is aimed at.

That these stark alternatives (economic versus solidaristic) and (if economic) the freedom to provide services, together with the European 'competition regime', directly and deeply affect national welfare states has become clear. How this constellation shapes the contours of welfare states is still somewhat opaque. To clarify Schulz-Weidner's point some examples may be helpful. A number of reforms to national pension systems are under discussion in member states, such as changing over to a 'capital stock' principle, or staying with the 'pay-as-you-go' system, but weeding out 'foreign' elements (like pensions for East Germans who could not pay contributions before 1989, baby years, survivor insurance). Many of these move social insurance away from redistribution and solidarity. Beyond some, as yet unidentified, threshold such programmes would become just another economic enterprise that must compete with private (pension) insurance and other competitors on a level-playing field. Then a provider monopoly would become unsustainable.

The principles concerning the free movement of workers have been continuously worked out in hundreds of ECJ decisions spanning almost four decades. However, the influence of the 'economic action' doctrine, of the freedom to provide services, and of the competition regime on national welfare states really emerged only after the passage of the SEA in 1986. Such issues have been confronted more systematically only since the late 1990s. Also, the related influence of the freedom of establishment provisions (Articles 52–8 (now 43–8) (EEC)) has been felt only quite recently, although there are already a few leading cases. There are significant prospects for a substantial remoulding of national social policies through this 'market filter', which has been most effective in the large sector of health care, an area exposed to some turmoil in recent ECJ history. Some consequences of these 'regime changes' are detailed by Schulte (1999):

> The struggle is about delimiting a sphere for the welfare state which is intervention-free, be it from the Community or through the market. All in all one might summarise: Member states remain competent to make insurance obligatory, to implement solidarity and to install a redistributive financing system. But wherever there are market traces, national hindrances of any sort are prohibited. It does not matter whether a consumer is buying his own health care (and then is reimbursed) or whether a health care scheme does this for him or her (through 'in kind' provision or 'national health care'). . . . As the health care deliverer steps in for the individual it will have to respect *Kohll* and *Decker* as well: In-kind providers from other member states have a right to a level playing field *vis-à-vis* local providers, so alternatively refund systems will have to be offered for demand and supply from 'out-of-state'. National health systems are affected as well, if they have market or 'quasi-market' elements, as does the UK; the 'vouchers' in use there need to be extended to the EC. Why should consumer demand in an influenza epidemic, as in 1998, stop at the UK border? Shouldn't hospital beds in France or Benelux—just beyond the Tunnel—be just as much on offer as (scarce) UK beds were?

Two cases, *Kohll* (Case C-158/1996) and *Decker* (Case C-120/1995), both of 28 April 1998, have become the prominent ECJ cases testing the 'freedom to provide services' (Maydell 1999; Kötter 1998).[15] Especially *Kohll* is useful to illustrate the continuing struggle over where to draw the line between the market and welfare state privileges. The intensity of the turf fight appears in the spontaneous reactions of one of the many member governments concerned. The German government feared Americanization of the health sector and financial instability for the welfare state in general. But, some sick funds saw new chances to cut costs. And the popular press was drawn to horizons for 'treatment under palm trees' (Becker 1998: 360; Kötter 1998). Both cases—probably initiated by parties interested in the health policy outcomes—were focused on the issue: may a member of a sick fund make use of 'service providers' in other member states? This issue concerns some 90 or more per cent of the population—the insured—in most countries, and also the provider groups.

Both cases are from Luxembourg. *Kohll* is about remunerative orthodontist work done in Germany, outside any hospital infrastructure, by a privately established doctor. *Decker* is about buying a pair of spectacles with corrective lenses on a Luxembourg prescription from a Belgian optician. The sick fund refused to reimburse in each case: In *Kohll* this was because it saw no basis for exceptional treatment abroad. This was not an 'emergency treatment received in the event of illness or accident abroad'; and, since the fund had rejected Kohll's request with reason, the required 'prior authorization of the competent social security institution' was amiss. Decker had not requested prior authorization and presented his bill only.

These cases caught the attention of many member governments, since national interests are highly affected by prying open 'closed shop' health delivery systems. In *Kohll* the governments of Luxembourg, Germany, Greece, France, Austria, the UK, and also the Commission, submitted critical written observations. In *Decker* Luxembourg, Belgium, Germany, Spain, France, the Netherlands, the UK, and the Commission did so.

The Court found such authorizations, or administrative 'necessity testing', not in agreement with EC law. In *Kohll* the Court applied the 'freedom to provide services': 'Article 59 of the EEC Treaty precludes the application of any national rules which have the effect of making the provision of services between Member States more difficult than the provision of services purely within one Member State.' Also, the Court saw no 'objective' justification for such a rule, since it did not see any 'risk of seriously undermining the financial balance of the social security system', which could be an 'overriding reason in the general interest'.

It should be noted . . . that under Articles 56 and 66 of the EC Treaty Member States may limit freedom to provide services on grounds of public health. However, that does not permit them to exclude the public health sector as a sector of economic activity and from the point of view of freedom to provide services, from the application of the fundamental principles of freedom of movement . . .

Since the conditions for taking up and pursuing the profession of doctor and dentist have been taken up in several coordination and harmonization directives, it also 'follows that doctors and dentists established in other Member States must be afforded all guarantees equivalent to those accorded to doctors and dentists established on national territory, for the purpose of freedom of services'. Nor could the Court find that these rules 'were necessary to provide a balanced medical and hospital service accessible to all'. In *Decker*—as would also be the case for all pharmaceuticals—the free movement of goods (Article 30 (now 28)) was in focus, not services. Protection of public health (Article 36 (now 30) (EEC)) was again seen as unaffected, especially since a national ophthalmologist had prescribed the spectacles.

This opening of one major social insurance system to the European market is probably just a beginning, as other cases are coming up which test the limits of welfare state 'closed shops'. The important strategic issue of normal access to hospital treatment in other member states is already waiting for ECJ decision (*van Braekel*, Case C-368/1998). But, in the medium term such 'deregulation' may provoke 'reregulation' in order to provide particular social goods.

The balance between a market and institutionally autonomous national welfare states, two principles embedded in the EU constitution, is not a static but a dynamic one. Here is open terrain for Brussels, with a large potential for restructuring welfare state delivery regimes. This problem is likely to be particularly severe for Sweden and Finland, the two Nordic countries which entered the Union in 1995, since they have built up the most encompassing welfare states and have also systematically pursued a policy of marginalizing competitive pressures in welfare state activity. As Kåre Hagen (1992: 289), already seeing the welfare state *per se* endangered, argued early on:

Political ambitions of providing high- and equal-quality health care to all segments of the population, have required the extensive use of public monopolies that may militate against enterprise freedoms guaranteed by Community legislation. The same applies to state restrictions on private pension insurance and on how their funds are to be managed. In general, any kind of state welfare policy which is deliberately designed to prevent private purchasing power from being reproduced in the consumption of welfare goods supplied by the market, will run counter to the freedoms of the common market. (See also Hagen 1998.)

This position would seem somewhat overdrawn. But, now we can add three further general points to our list of restrictions on member state sovereignty and autonomy:

- The treaty constellation—'economic' versus 'solidaristic' action—now frames the welfare state. It seems to prioritize two polarized trajectories: core welfare state components (redistribution, pay-as-you-go, . . .) remain 'intervention-free', to the extent that they are 'pure' welfare; but the more these functions are provided by market-based services, the more the welfare state (in whole or in parts) tilts towards the sphere of 'economic action', thus becoming subject to market regimes. Thereby the welfare state could gradually be submerged in a single European 'security' market.

- Consumer and provider rights in services have come to the fore since the mid-1990s, also in relation to questioning of welfare state 'closed shops'. Member governments can no longer exclusively decide who may provide social services or benefits. They no longer exclusively organize social service occupations, since mutual recognition of qualifications from other member states intervenes. So they have a radically limited capacity to protect their national service organizations from competition from service organizations in other member states.

- The health area will be a first Europe-wide testing-ground for the turf struggle between national welfare states and the Community plus the market, as represented by private insurance, producers, etc.[16] Health insurance—compared with pensions—has more 'market traces' in most national systems, is more fragmented by provider groups which already operate in markets (medical instruments, pharmaceuticals) or quasi-markets (doctors in sick fund private practice), and has in most countries been traditionally exposed to substantial private provision. National reforms have pointed more and more to 'market cures' and deregulation in recent decades.[17]

To summarize this section, even by looking only at issues of freedom of movement for workers and freedom to provide services, one can see a wide range of market compatibility requirements, through which either EU regulations or ECJ decisions impinge on the design and the reform of national social policies. Examples of other welfare state effects of single market measures could easily be multiplied—for example, restrictions related to subsidies for economic activities in regional policy. In Italy, for instance, the central government used abatements of social insurance taxes as a strategy to attract investment to the Mezzogiorno. While the Commission agreed to permit this until the end of 1993, it then initiated ECJ proceedings against the continuation of the practice on grounds of 'unfair competition' (*Eureport*, 2/5 (1994), 9). In 1993 and 1994 Belgium had lowered contributions for companies especially exposed to European market competition (ECJ *Maribel* Case C-75/1997, still pending). Due to the European Economic Area non-EU member Norway faced just these barriers in 1998 (*Eureport Social* 6/8 (1998), 10). Similarly, improvements in Germany's social insurance for farmers require Brussels' approval, since such changes in a non-universal insurance could be sectoral subsidies if they were part of a package deal with the lowering of prices for agricultural commodities. The broader point is clear: a whole range of social policy designs that would be available to sovereign welfare states—and belong to the traditional policy 'tool kit'—are prohibited, or are made more costly, to member states within the EC's multi-tiered polity.

European integration and *de facto* pressures on national welfare states

The EU now intervenes directly in the social policies of member states in two ways: by enacting significant social policy initiatives of its own; and by striking down features of national systems that are deemed incompatible with the development of the single market. In addition, the process of European integration also has less direct, but none the less significant effects, on member state social policies, as both the economic policies of the EU and the responses of social actors to those policies put pressures on national welfare states. Because these effects are indirect they are difficult to measure, but they none the less add to the general picture of increasing supranational influence over the design of national social policy.

The most frequently cited source of pressure on welfare states within the EU is the possibility that heightened integration may lead to 'social dumping', a debate still going strong though it has partly submerged in the 'globalization' discussion (Rieger and Leibfried 1998). The term refers to the prospect that firms operating where social wages are low may be able to undercut the prices of competitors, forcing higher-cost firms either to go out of business or to relocate to low social wage areas, or to pressure their governments to reduce social wage costs. In extreme scenarios, these actions could fuel a downward spiral in social provision, eventually producing very rudimentary, lowest common denominator, national welfare states. Supporters of social policy in the EU countries with well-developed welfare states—for example, labour confederations like the Deutscher Gewerkschaftsbund—have particularly stressed this concern.

There is some evidence that these kinds of pressures have restricted social expenditures in the USA, where labour (and capital) mobility is far greater than is currently the case in the EU (P. E. Peterson and Rom 1990; for comparative background, see Boltho 1989). Despite widespread attention to this issue, however, the evidence that European integration will fuel a process of social dumping remains limited. As a number of observers have noted, the social wage is only one factor in investment decisions, and firms will not invest in low social wage countries unless worker productivity (relative to wages) justifies such investments (Hauser 1996). This should also hold for east European enlargement, the likely focus of the next major social dumping debate. Also, price and quality competition need to be distinguished. Neo-classical trade theory suggests that high social wage countries should be able to continue their policies as long as overall conditions allow profitable investment. One sign of the ambiguous consequences of integration is the fact that northern Europe's concerns about 'sun belt effects' are mirrored by southern Europe's concerns about 'agglomeration effects' in which investment would flow towards the superior infrastructures and highly skilled workforces of Europe's most developed regions.

Social dumping may generate greater fears than current evidence warrants. The opposite could be the case for some of the other ways that economic integration creates pressures on national social policy systems. The single market is encouraging a gradual movement towards a narrowed band of value added tax (VAT) rates. In theory, governments finding that their VAT revenues have been lowered will be free to increase other taxes, but this may be no simple task. Because it is politically easier to sustain indirect taxes, the new rules may create growing constraints on member state budgets, with clear implications for national social policies (Wilensky 1976; Hibbs and Madsen 1981). This is likely to be a particular problem for Denmark, which relies heavily on indirect taxes, rather than payroll taxes, to finance its generous welfare state (J. H. Petersen 1991: 514–22; 1993; Schulte 1994b: 40). Thus, countries like Denmark and Sweden are resisting 'upper limits' for VAT to make sure that they can finance their welfare states.

The move towards EMU, with its tough ongoing requirements for budgetary discipline, may also encourage downward adjustments in welfare provision (see Chapter 6). For example, to participate in the final stage of monetary union, Italy had to reduce its budget deficit from 10 per cent to about 3 per cent of gross domestic product by the end of the 1990s. This served mainly to legitimate efforts by successive governments to pursue major cuts in old age pensions and other social benefits in 1994 and 1995 (Brunetta and Trenti 1995). EMU seems to have triggered a systematic rebuilding and retrenchment of the Italian welfare state (Ferrera and Gualmini, forthcoming). While most other countries face less radical adjustments, the convergence criteria present formidable problems for almost all of them (Krupp 1995). Here again, the significance of the EU's indirect effects is hard to ascertain. Governments would have faced such pressure for austerity in any event (see Pierson 1998). The convergence criteria do not, of course, require budget reductions—tax increases would also be possible—but they considerably strengthen the hand of those seeking such cuts.

EMU would not only put pressures on national social programmes; it could prod the Community into a more active role in efforts to combat unemployment, a stance the Union has already symbolically enshrined in 1997 in the ToA. Analysis of the prospects for monetary integration in Europe was historically coupled with discussion of the need for accompanying social policies to address the likely emergence of regional imbalances (Ross 1994: 152–3). EMU would strip national governments of significant macroeconomic policy levers, and a Community-wide macroeconomic stance will create significant regional unemployment problems. Somewhat flexible exchange rates allow local adaptations to local economic conditions. Once these instruments are dismantled, combating pockets of regional unemployment at the national level will be more difficult (Eichengreen 1992: 32–7).

Another indirect pressure on national welfare states stems from the rapidly evolving European single private insurance market. As of 1 July 1994 national private insurance has been drawn into the common market of the EU. The furious pace of cross-border mergers and acquisitions is creating a heavily concentrated, or interlocked, insurance sector operating at the European level, though mostly in still very balkanized national markets (due to the 'salesman dependency' and 'label recognition'). Integrated European insurance markets allow for a greater differentiation of policy-holders by risk groups (Stone 1989), and thus for cheaper, more profitable policies with lower operational costs. Also, such an integrated private sector would confront fifteen national, internally segmented, public insurance domains, themselves often caught up in spirals of deregulation and thus already exposed to challenges from private markets (Hagen 1998). Insurance providers with the option of relocating to more lenient member states will gain a growing influence over national social regulation. At the same time, the clash between particular national regulatory styles and the quite different traditions of competing insurers from other member states is likely to be intense.

The results of 'public–private' interplay in the context of a radically altered private sector are difficult to anticipate. There is, however, considerable evidence from studies of national welfare states that the reform of private sector markets can have dramatic effects on public service provision (see e.g. Rein and Rainwater 1986). Public and private insurance compete mainly in areas like occupational pensions, life insurance, and supplemental health insurance. Permanent turf quarrels between public and private seem likely concerning where 'basic' (public) coverage should end and 'additional' (private) insurance may begin. Private (or competing 'out-of-state' public) actors in this turf struggle may arm themselves with the 'economic action' approach. Since the periphery of 'private insurance' is likely to be considered 'economic' action, freedom to provide services and the European competition regime reign freely. This may be seen as part of a broader process in which movement towards the single market challenges existing demarcations between the public and private spheres. The welfare state, which has traditionally been a key area for establishing these demarcation lines, is bound to be affected by such gradual and often indirect redrawing of boundaries (Hagen 1998), often taking place in fields quite beyond the welfare state.

It is difficult to evaluate the consequences for national welfare states of these various indirect pressures. Many of the possible problem areas lie in the future, and some of the others, such as social dumping, are difficult to measure even if they might be occurring now. One has to weigh the pressures for reform against the welfare state's considerable sources of resilience (Pierson 1996a, 1998). Yet the picture that emerges is one where national governments possess diminished control over many of the policies that have traditionally supported national welfare states: macroeconomic policies, public finance, tax policies, and also industrial relations systems. Again, these developments challenge the dominant view that European integration is a 'market-building' process that advances relentlessly while leaving the development of social policy a purely national affair.

Social policy in Europe's emerging multi-tiered system

Scholarly attention has focused largely on Commission efforts to establish a 'social dimension' of Community-wide policies or at least minimum standards. While far from trivial, to date these efforts have modified member state social policies in relatively few areas—most systematically, though, in labour law. But the expansion of EU competences, buttressed by the extended use of QMV, indicates that an 'activist' threshold may have been crossed in the 1990s. Important, though much less visible, have been the social policy effects of the single market's development itself. These have occurred either directly, as the Commission, national courts, and the ECJ have sought to reconcile member state policy autonomy with the effort to create a unified economic space, or indirectly, through pressures on the support structures of national welfare states.

We are living through a period of rapid change in the relations between nation states and an increasingly global market system. '[T]he central question to pose is: has sovereignty remained intact while the autonomy of the state has diminished or has the modern state faced a loss of sovereignty?' (Held 1991a: 213). In the EU member state sovereignty and autonomy have diminished in tandem (Leibfried 1994). The process has been subtle and incremental, but developments within the Community as a whole increasingly constrain national welfare states. Member states now find their revenue bases under assault, their welfare reform options circumscribed, many of their delivery regimes under threat of new competition, and their administrators obliged to share control over policy enforcement.

What is emerging is a unique multi-tiered system of social policy, with three distinctive characteristics: a propensity towards 'joint decision traps' and policy immobilism; a prominent role for courts in policy development; and an unusually tight coupling to market-making processes.

First, policy-makers at the European level are tightly hemmed in by the scepticism of the Council, the density of existing national-level social policy commitments, and the limited fiscal and administrative capacities of the EU. Compared with any other multi-tiered system the EU's social policy-making apparatus is extremely bottom-heavy (Kleinman and Piachaud 1992a; Pierson and Leibfried 1995a). The quite weak 'centre' has limited capacity to formulate positive social policy. As a result, social policy evolution is likely to be more the result of mutual adjustment and incremental accommodation than of central guidance. From the centre come a variety of pressures and constraints on social policy development, but much less by way of clear mandates for positive action.

Yet there has been a considerable weakening of the member states' position as well (Pierson 1995). With the gravitation of authority, even of a largely negative kind, to the European level, the capacity of member governments to design their welfare states as they choose is also diminishing. Significant losses of autonomy and sovereignty occurred without member governments paying a great deal of attention. In some cases—such as Italy's role in pushing for enhanced labour mobility in the Rome Treaty—member governments actively pursued sovereignty-eroding initiatives. While member governments currently resist some of the single market's implications for their own power, their capacity to do so is limited by their fear of jeopardizing the hard-won benefits of European integration. Their resistance is further limited by an institutional ratchet effect. Once you become an EU member you are bound by all ECJ rulings, and can pursue reforms only through the slow and difficult procedures available under Community rules. The combination of diminished member state authority and continued weakness at the EU level is likely to restrict the room for innovative policy. As Fritz Scharpf observes, 'the policy-making capacities of the union have not been strengthened nearly as much as capabilities at the level of member states have declined' (1994a: 219; also 1994b).

Member governments still 'choose', but they do so from an increasingly restricted menu. At a time when control over social policy often means responsibility for announcing unpopular cutbacks, member governments sometimes are happy to accept arrangements that constrain their own options. Given the unpopularity of retrenchment, governments may find that the growing ability to blame the EU allows changes which they would otherwise be afraid to contemplate. The movement towards a multi-tiered political system opens up major new avenues for the politics of 'blame avoidance' (Weaver 1986). It has been suggested that this dynamic strengthens national executives at the expense of domestic opponents, and this may be the case (Milward 1992; Moravcsik 1998: 76 n. 112, 1994; Wolf 1997). Yet in the process of escaping from domestic constraints, national executives have created new ones that profoundly limit their options. Decision-making bodies at both the national and supranational levels face serious restrictions on their capacity for social policy intervention, since they have partly 'locked themselves in' through previous steps towards integration.

The second distinctive characteristic of social policy-making in the EU is that the constraints and requirements which do develop from the centre are unusually law and court-driven.[18] It is as much a series of rulings from the ECJ as the process of Commission and Council initiative that has been the source of new social policy. While the Council and Commission are prone to stasis, the ECJ's institutional design fosters activism. Once confronted with litigation, the ECJ cannot escape making what are essentially policy decisions as a matter of routine. The Court also relies on simple majority votes, taken in secret, sheltering it from the political immobility typical of the EU. Only a unanimous vote of the Council can generally undo ECJ decisions when they relate to primary European law. The structure of EU institutions puts the ECJ on centre-stage. Attempts at corporatist policy-making have generated much of the drama surrounding Europe's social dimension, but until recently (Falkner 1998) businesses and unions have had little direct involvement in the decisions that have actually created legally binding requirements for the social policies of member states. But this seems to be changing.

Legal strategies have had the advantage of leaving taxing, spending, and administrative powers at the national level. It should be emphasized, however, that such a court-led process of social policy development has its own logic. Decisions are likely to reflect demands for doctrinal coherence as much as, or more than, substantive debates about the desirability of various social policy outcomes. The capacity of reforms built around a judicial logic to achieve substantive goals may be limited. Furthermore, courts may have less need to consider political constraints in prescribing solutions. A possible danger is that court initiatives may exceed the tolerance of important political actors within the system. After all, centralized policy-making was made difficult in the EU for a reason, and ECJ activism may generate resentment. This is, of course, one aspect of the current disquiet over the 'democratic deficit'.

Finally, Europe's emerging multi-tiered system of social policy is uniquely connected to a process of market-building. Of course, social policies in mixed economies always intersect in a variety of complex ways with market systems. In the past, however, social policy has generally been seen as part of what Karl Polanyi (1994) described as a spontaneous 'protective reaction' against the expansion of market relations. Social policies have grown up in response to the shortcomings of market arrangements.

At the EU level, however, interventions in the traditional spheres of social policy have generally not taken this Polanyian form. Even in areas such as gender issues where the EU has been activist, policies have been directly connected to labour market participation, while broad issues of family policy have been ignored, although they were thoroughly explored in an Observatory on National Family Policies after 1989. Instead, as the centrality of decisions regarding labour mobility and free service markets reveals, EU social policy interventions have grown up as part of the process of market-building itself. Never before has the construction of markets so visibly and intensively shaped the development of social policy initiatives.

The overall scope of EU interventions has been, we emphasize, extensive. These interventions reveal that national welfare state regimes are now part of a larger, multi-tiered system of social policy. Member governments profoundly influence this structure, but they no longer fully control it. While the governance of social policy occurs at multiple levels, however, the EU's peculiar arrangement is also different in many respects from traditional federal states, distinguished by a weak policy-making centre, court-driven regulation, and strong links with market-making processes. The EU's unique political arrangement is producing a pattern of policy-making quite different from that of any national welfare state (see Streeck 1995, 1998).

Appendix 10.1 The development of cases before the European Court of Justice, 1992–1998

Year	Social Policy (Articles 136–48 (ex 117–25))		Freedom of movement for persons (Articles 39–41 (ex 48–51))		All cases	
	Cases introduced	Cases closed[a]	Cases introduced	Cases closed[a]	Cases introduced	Cases closed
1992	20	23	35	39	442	345
1993	26	36	45	39	490	342
1994	15	24	71	29	354	293
1995	25	—	42	8	415	289
1996	42	—	69	6	423	349
1997	26	—	50	14	445	456
1998	33	—	36	11	485	420

Note. For comparisons with cases in other policy domains, see Tables 1.5 and 1.6.
[a] 1992–4: cases closed by judgment or orders terminating the case (*incl.* removal from the Register, declaration that the case will not proceed to judgment, or referral to the Court of First Instance). 1995– : cases closed by judgments or orders terminating the case by judicial determination (*other* than by removal from the Register, declaration that the case will not proceed to judgment, or referral to the Court of First Instance).

Source: ECJ, Registry, Denise Louterman-Hubeau (communication of 26 Jan. 1999)

Notes

1 This chapter is based on, but substantially revises and updates, Leibfried and Pierson (1996). We are indebted to Michelle Everson for her detailed advice on the private–social insurance interface for the 3rd edition. We also thank Eberhard Eichenhofer, Josef Falke, Petra Kodré, Elmar Rieger, Susanne K. Schmidt, Bernd Schulte, Klaus Sieveking, and Dieter Wolf for their help.

2 For a historical overview on social policy development, cf. Collins (1975) and now Falkner (1998: 55 ff.).

3 Recommendations 92/441 (on Common Criteria Concerning Sufficient Resources and Social Assistance in Social Protection Systems of 24 June 1992) and 92/442 (on Objectives and Policies of Social Security Systems of 27 July 1992) (EEC) (26 Aug. 1992) reflect these difficulties and point to social policy 'convergence' (Maydell 1999: 10). In contrast, in the 1970s 'harmonization' was still the major focus.

4 The retroactivity of *Barber* was weakened by a unanimous amendment to the Treaties in the TEU, which established a somewhat less costly, but not the least costly, version of retroactivity. The ECJ, thus restrained, upheld the TEU solution in *Ten Oever* (Case C-109/1991 of 6 Oct. 1993). Estimated costs of full retroactivity for Germany are from Berenz (1994: 437); for Britain from Mazey and Richardson (1993*a*: 15).

5 Two further directives were passed in 1994: the Young Workers Directive and the Working Time Directive. Italy, Greece, and Spain opposed the former and the UK the latter.

6 The British opt-out from both decision-making and policies *de facto* cautioned the Eleven, later Fourteen, in their use of the Social Protocol as they feared distortions of competition and instinctively preferred to maximize unanimity. Many UK-based firms nevertheless voluntarily implemented the 1995 European Works Council Directive in order to preserve intra-firm uniformity and also to ward off possible consumer conflicts (Falkner 1998: 197). The ECJ never ruled on the legality of the Protocol. Once Britain had opted in, it became bound by the new *acquis* of decisions taken between 1993 and 1997.

7 In 1998 the Commission mainly announced measures to protect people employed in 'tele work', guidelines on subsidies for national training programmes and revisions of some health and safety directives (see *Eureport Social*, 6/4–5 (1998) 3).

8 See Weiler (1991), Burley and Mattli (1993), Stone Sweet and Caporaso (1998); on the general myopia about courts: Shapiro and Stone (1994); and on the state of welfare law, see Barwig and Schulte (1999), Sieveking (1998).

9 In 1998 three major freedom of services cases were decided, of which *Kohll* was the most far-reaching:

■ In *Molenaar* (Case C-160/1996 of 5 Mar. 1998) the Court cleared away hindrances for exporting German care insurance benefits (*Pflegegeld*) out of state. Sieveking (1998) focuses on this decision only.

■ In *Kohll* (Case C-158/1996 of 28 Apr. 1998) the Court cleared away hindrances to obtaining dental care out of state.

■ In *Decker* (Case C-120/1995 of 28 Apr. 1998) the Court cleared away hindrances to obtaining spectacles on a prescription out of state.

One further decision will be central:

- In *van Braekel* (Case C-368/1998) the Court may decide to clear away hindrances to hospital treatment out of state (see *Eureport Social*, 6/11–12 (1998) 8). The decision has not yet been taken.

10 An EU study reported that in 1995 155,000 Germans worked in another EU country, 177,000 French, 197,000 British, and 625,000 Italians; of the 3.5m foreign workers in Germany less than a third were citizens of EU countries, notably 365,400 Italians and 233,000 Greek (*Eureport Social*, 6/3 (1998) 11).

11 For example, on the status of Turkish immigrants in Germany, see *Mehmet Birden* v. *Stadtgemeinde Bremen*: Case C-1/1997 of 26 Nov. 1998 (see Jorens and Schulte 1998).

12 The 1996 Directive on the Posting of Workers was advocated by governments from Austria, France, and Germany, and resisted by the UK and Portugal, both 'donor nations'. The controversy was not about general regime competition, as when capital moves, but about the competition of several social policy regimes on one territory, when workers migrate to benefit from wage differentials, while taking along some of the social and wage policy 'frames' of their country of origin, as when the centre of unified Berlin was rebuilt after 1990.

13 Much welfare state activity falls under 'services' in the terms of the Treaty, not only 'social services'. Private insurance is a matter of financial services. So is the (monetary) 'transfer state', when considered as 'economic' activity rather than 'true welfare state activity', as, for example, when public pensions are shorn of their redistributive elements in welfare state reform.

14 This means 'monopoly' of supply by particular public institutions, i.e. a provider monopoly (see Giesen 1995).

15 An earlier ECJ judgment, in *Höfner and Elsner* v. *Macotron* (C-41/1990 of 23 Apr. 1991), declared illegal the monopoly in employment services of German unemployment insurance as regards senior white-collar employees.

16 Some producers are more likely to take the European route than others, especially private international service organizations involved in hospitals, drug markets, and the provision of medical equipment (Bieback 1993: 171). Such producers are likely to become strong actors at the EU level, be it *vis-à-vis* the Commission or in the Courts.

17 Directive 89/105 set minimum standards for all national systems of drug price control and price-fixing. The Commission has developed proposals for a single drug market, which would strongly, though indirectly, harmonize parts of national health insurance systems, for example by undoing price controls and introducing significant co-payments. In 1994 the European Agency for the Evaluation of Medicinal Products (EMEA) in London started surveillance and licensing work (*Eureport*, 2/2, (1994), 3; 2/5 (1994), 3—and the EMEA *Yearly Reports*). Also, Commission competition policy provides instruments for influencing drug-pricing, with wide potential impact on health policies. Since equivalent pharmaceuticals are much cheaper in most southern European countries, among others German sickness funds have been quite interested in 'importing' such drugs—and the Euro will give another boost to these trends. This ongoing conflict reveals 'the close links between drug prices and health care policy' (Woolcock 1996: 314) and an unresolvable conflict which Michael Noonan, the Irish Secretary of Health, described in 1996: 'Member States cannot give ground on their prerogative to set health policy within their own jurisdiction. Nor is it acceptable that one country can or should impose its choice of health policy on its neighbours by the action

of parallel trade' (Schwarze 1998: 63). One possible resolution, Europe-wide standardization according to Articles 94, 95 (CTEU), to replace diverse national health policies, is strongly resisted by pharmaceutical industry.

18   Gerda Falkner pointed out to us a

budget-driven factor which shapes national thinking on some social problems and policies, in so far as national or local agencies tailor their projects to EU action and research programmes in order to gain funding. Hence even modest EU programmes may leverage significant social impacts.

Further reading

For the main contours of the subject, see Leibfried and Pierson (1995b); the first and last chapters provide a guide to theoretical explanations, while the second chapter details the core social policy contours. More recent analyses are found in Hine and Kassim (1998) and Rhodes and Mény (1998). For a UK 'social policy' view, see Kleinman and Piachaud (1992b); for a 'continental' political science view, Scharpf (1999, ch. 4). On the legal dimensions, see Bieback (1991), Barwig and Schulte (1999: 397–424), and Fuchs (1998: 410–11); and vis-à-vis health policy, see Maydell (1999). Recent ECJ cases may be consulted in all official languages on the web under <http://europa.eu.int/cj/index.htm>. For a comprehensive analysis of the new corporatist perspectives, see Falkner (1998). Both the *Journal of European Social Policy* (1991–) and the *Journal of European Public Policy* (1994–) contain useful articles. Regular policy news is reported monthly in German (since 1993) in *Eureport Social*.

Barwig, K., and Schulte, B. (1999) (eds.), *Freizügigkeit und soziale Sicherheit. Die Durchführung der Verordnung (EWG) Nr. 1408/71 über die soziale Sicherheit der Wanderarbeitnehmer in Deutschland* (Baden-Baden: Nomos).

Bieback, K.-J. (1991), 'Harmonization of Social Policy in the European Community', *Les Cahiers de Droit*, 32/14: 913–35.

Eureport Social is a monthly bulletin, until

vol. 32 (Feb. 1995) titled *Eureport*, produced by the European Representation of German Social Insurance (e-mail: esip.bxl@euronet.be) in Brussels, which is a member of the network European Social Insurance Partners.

Falkner, G. (1998), *EU Social Policy in the 1990s: Towards a Corporatist Policy Community* (London: Routledge).

Fuchs, M. (1998) (ed.), *Nomos Kommentar zum europäischen Sozialrecht* (Baden-Baden: Nomos) (loose leaf).

Hine, D., and Kassim, H. (1998) (eds.), *Beyond the Market: The EU and National Social Policy* (London: Routledge).

Kleinman, M., and Piachaud, D. (1992b), 'European Social Policy: Conceptions and Choices', *Journal of European Social Policy*, 3/1: 1–19.

Leibfried, S., and Pierson, P. (1995b) (eds.), *European Social Policy: Between Fragmentation and Integration* (Washington: Brookings Institution).

Maydell, B., Baron von (1999), 'Auf dem Weg zu einem gemeinsamen Markt für Gesundheitsleistungen in der Europäischen Gemeinschaft', *Vierteljahresschrift für Sozialrecht*, 1: 3–19.

Rhodes, M., and Mény, Y. (1998) (eds.), *The Future of European Welfare. A New Social Contract?* (London: Macmillan).

Scharpf, F. W. (1999), *Governing in Europe: Effective and Democratic?* (Oxford: Oxford University Press).

Chapter 11

Environmental Policy

Economic Constraints and External Pressures

Alberta M. Sbragia

Contents

Summary

Environmental policy was in the 1970s and 1980s a domain of innovation in the European Union (EU). 'Green-minded' governments and advocacy groups were the 'leaders', pulling the 'laggards' towards accepting higher standards of environmental regulation than many could have agreed at the national level. In the 1990s the pattern has changed. A tougher economic climate and recognition of the unanticipated costs of environmentalism have led to a more cautious approach. More prudent governments now frame the discussion, and other economic actors have become more vocal. A less heavy approach to European regulation leaves more scope for individual country variations in the implementation of policy. A parallel set of impulses has come from wider global discussions, for example on the United Nations Framework Convention on Climate Change (UNFCCC). These put the EU under external pressure to define a common approach. Its ability to do so made the EU an influential player in crafting the Kyoto

Protocol in 1997. This set limits to fuel emissions and created the novel system of tradeable quotas.

Introduction

The politics of environmental policy are now being shaped by the fact that so much environmental protection has been legislated so quickly. In Weale's words, 'Completely unanticipated in 1957, environmental policy had moved from silence to salience within thirty years' (Weale 1999: 40). The protection of the environment by the EU has become so extensive and so intrusive that policy-making in this sector is now very much shaped by the impacts of previous legislative achievements. Such achievements have set the stage for the sector's policy-making challenges—in this sector, policy is creating politics (Lowi 1972).

Environmental policy is now one of the major policy areas in which Brussels plays a critical role. No matter whether a member state (such as the UK) has clearly struggled to adapt to EU laws or whether it has traditionally played a leadership role in setting the EU's environmental agenda (Germany, for example), the impact of the EU on that member state's domestic policy is significant (Haigh 1999: 109). Whereas in the 1970s many Commission officials viewed 'the environment as at best voguish and at worst politically irrelevant', it is now seen as an important policy area within the EU's policy portfolio (Jordan 1999a: 5).

The EU's legislative advances in the area owe much to the past political support of environmental protection associated with the 'green' states of Denmark, the Netherlands, and particularly Germany, as well as to an international system in which environmental protection has rapidly gained prominence. Those achievements were obtained as the result of compromises among member governments which varied rather dramatically in their enthusiasm for environmental protection and their capacity to pay for it. The institutional machinery of the EU allowed those governments which adopted comparatively stringent regulatory regimes at home to 'pull' along those member states with national regulatory regimes that were more lax and undeveloped. By 'externalizing' their regulatory regimes, the high-regulation states were able to protect their economic competitiveness (Sbragia 1996).

Environmental policy in the 1990s was characterized by a number of paradoxes. The Single European Act (SEA), the Treaty on European Union (TEU), and the Treaty of Amsterdam (ToA) have cumulatively embedded environmental protection in the EU's policy portfolio through the use of qualified majority voting (QMV) and the increased participation of the European Parliament (EP). The *political salience* of environmental policy—at least as such policy has been traditionally conceptualized—has, however, declined in the 1990s. The impact of German unification, the persistent problem of unemployment, and the very difficult choices implied by stringent environmental restrictions, at a time of increased global competition, all served to lower environmental protection on the EU's political agenda. Institutionally, environmental legislation, now subject to QMV rather than unanimity, is easier to adopt, but the political commitment to impose stringent and intrusive regulations through command and control processes has diminished very significantly.

On the other hand, several landmark pieces of legislation were approved during that decade; a variety of new policy instruments was introduced, and the EU emerged as a key player in international environmental politics. This policy area, although undergoing a period of transition, is characterized by continuous legislative activity, some of which is stimulated by internal dynamics, while some is a response to international agreements in which the EU has played an important negotiating role.

The old cleavage between 'leaders' and 'laggards' has gradually become displaced by new cleavages which have much more to do with how environmental protection should be achieved. What role should traditional 'command and control' instruments play? What role should public administrators play, as opposed to societal actors such as environmental groups? How mandatory should environmental policy be? Can firms be given workable incentives to reduce their polluting activities voluntarily? Should incentives include fiscal instruments such as an 'eco-tax'? Can the marshalling of information and data, by an agency such as the European Environmental Agency, be effective in improving the state of the environment or are tougher enforcement sanctions and penalties required? How far can the EU 'externalize' its own answers to such questions on the global scene?

As new questions have come to the fore, Germany, traditionally the key leader in environmental protection at the European level, has been presented with an unexpected challenge. Its regulatory philosophy is based on traditional command and control regulation, best available technology (BAT) (without consideration of cost), and an exclusion of public interest groups from administrative processes. New approaches to protection, however, challenge those very same concepts. The combination of this new policy agenda and the unexpectedly high costs of unification have eroded Germany's leadership role. The German government is no longer the 'first mover' across the board for environmental issues and proposals. Furthermore, it is often a key opponent of the new policy approaches which are shaping environmental policy-making.

The UK, for its part, traditionally viewed as braking or weakening EU regulations, has emerged as often much better able than Germany to integrate the 'old' and the 'new' approaches. The EU's regulatory regime encouraged the UK to modernize its own domestic system, and this allowed it to incorporate at least some of the new perspectives emerging within the sector. The British government subsequently has been able to play much more of a leadership role in Brussels than it had previously, and it has been able to challenge Germany's hitherto entrenched leadership role.

The politics of environmental policy in the EU therefore now incorporate a contest between regulatory philosophies, as well as the typical bargaining among governments concerned with how environmental protection affects the economic competitiveness of their firms and their public finances. Who shall be forced to adjust the most from environmental legislation adopted in Brussels? To make matters more complicated, the recurring cleavages about issues related to national sovereignty have not disappeared. Therefore, to the extent that environmental policy intersects with issues connected to national sovereignty—as the proposed eco-tax does— political coalitions shift. Finally, the Union as a whole is facing a whole set of challenges from the international arena. The Kyoto Protocol, negotiated within the UNFCCC, introduces an entirely new set of mechanisms alien to the EU. In essence, the Protocol introduces a regulatory philosophy alien to both the EU and its member states.

History

The process by which environmental policy came under EU jurisdiction highlights the role that political salience plays in a policy area which is relatively new on most government policy agendas. The Treaty of Rome (EEC) did not mention environmental protection. However, after the 1972 United Nations (UN) Conference on the Human Environment in Stockholm, the heads of state and government decided in 1973 to move the Community into that policy arena, using Article 235 (now 308) (EEC) which allowed the Community to move into areas that were not explicitly mentioned in the Treaty of Rome. The political importance of environmental protection was increasing, especially in states with important markets like Germany, so that the Community was empowered to move into a new policy area without an explicit treaty provision authorizing such a move. That was an unusual move by the member states' top political leaders, but it illustrates well how sensitive environmental protection can be to prevailing political winds.

Once the heads of state and government had given their approval, the Commission produced the first Environment Action Programme. Although the Commission wanted to move into the environmental arena, because member governments were adopting environmental legislation which could act as trade barriers, it quickly came to embrace environmental protection for its own sake as well. In this period unanimity was the normal decision rule in the Council of Ministers, a requirement under Article 235 (EEC), and the EP played a minor role.

Several key pieces of legislation were adopted. In particular, a directive on bathing-waters and another on drinking-water were passed, which were to withstand the winds of controversy for well over two decades. In this novel policy area many national policy-makers had not fully understood the consequences of their decisions. The British negotiators, for example, did not realize how binding directives actually were on the member states. Directives were passed which were so expensive to implement, and required so much adaptation in some member states, that it is unlikely they would have been passed at a later date, when the implications of environmental restrictions were more fully understood. None the less, adopted they were—and the difficulties of changing legislation once it is adopted in the Community ensured that they remained as key pieces of legislation which the Commission attempted to enforce.

In the early 1980s environmental damage became a major political issue in Germany, as well as in the Netherlands and Denmark. Governments from these three 'green' states pushed for more legislation at the European level. German industrialists in particular were anxious that the costs of environmental protection, which they were being forced to bear under national legislation, would lessen their competitiveness. They therefore supported the 'ratcheting up' of environmental restrictions on industry in other member states. Although opinion in other member states was often reluctant, or at least less enthusiastic, the Community began to adopt environmental legislation more stringent than many member states would have adopted unilaterally. This is why significant pieces of legislation were passed in the area of water- and air-quality policy. An *acquis* accumulated without a specific legal basis in the Treaties, although this made the Commission more cautious in its proposals than it would have been with a sounder legal foundation.

The SEA gave environmental protection a legal basis in the treaties. It gave the Commission more self-confidence, and the pace of environmental legislation picked up noticeably after the SEA came into effect. Environmental legislation linked to the single market mostly came under the provisions of QMV in the Council of Ministers and the procedure for cooperation in the EP. Furthermore, legislation not linked to the single market, but dedicated to the protection of the environment, was also given a treaty basis, although it required unanimity.

The TEU went a stage further and brought those areas of environmental policy not linked to internal market harmonization measures under QMV in the Council of Ministers and the cooperation procedure within the EP. Areas linked to internal market harmonization became subject to the stronger procedure for co-decision within the EP. However, certain areas, including the use of fiscal measures to achieve environmental goals, were still subject to unanimity. Thus, depending on which issue was being decided, one of four procedures would be applicable.

Both the SEA and the TEU explicitly recognized that the Union would have external relations in the field of environmental policy. Over time the Union would begin to play a much more assertive role within the UN framework, culminating in its very visible role in the climate change negotiations which led to the Kyoto Protocol (Sbragia 1998; Sbragia with Damro 1999). The ToA brought more changes than many had expected to the environmental field. The governments from several key member states (France, Germany, and the UK) were reluctant to move in this direction. The German and Dutch governments, for example, in fact wanted the Intergovernmental Conference (IGC) to focus on other issues, such as common and foreign security policy and justice and home affairs. One important factor was the arrival within the EU of Austria, Finland, and Sweden, countries with high environmental standards, and in which this policy area carried high political salience, as had become clear during their accession negotiations (Young and Wallace 2000).

The ToA simplifies decision-making in environmental policy enormously. Most environmental matters are now subject to QMV and the (simplified) co-decision procedure. The EP will play a more significant role in the legislative process for most environmental issues than it did under the TEU. The few exceptions to QMV remain as under the TEU, and are in sectors very important for environmental protection: land use planning, fiscal measures, energy, and water resources (of particular concern to Austria).

During the IGC an effort was made to introduce an 'eco-tax'. The Danes, who already had a domestic eco-tax, proposed a Protocol that would have excluded certain environmental taxes from the general provision that fiscal measures require unanimity in the Council of Ministers. Had it been adopted, this procedure might have made it more likely that some environmental taxes might be adopted. The Danish proposal, however, was not supported, and hence the debate over the use of fiscal instruments in the field of environmental protection has hardly shifted (van Calster and Deketelaere 1998: 19). This is not surprising, given that finance ministers in nearly all countries opposed QMV for fiscal measures (Liefferink and Andersen 1998b).

In addition, a new Protocol to the Treaty makes it clear that 'where possible, Member States should be given the freedom to enforce Community policy and regulation through the means which they prefer, taking into account their traditions and legal systems' (van Calster and Deketelaere 1998: 21). Framework directives, rather than directives with detailed specifications, would therefore seem to be indicated along the lines typically associated with subsidiarity. Finally, the right of citizens to gain access to documents has been strengthened under the new transparency rules. Two changes of perhaps largely symbolic value are: the strengthening of the principle that environmental considerations should be 'integrated' into other sectors; and, as opposed to the TEU's 'sustainable and non-inflationary growth respecting the environment', the inclusion of 'sustainable development' as a formal objective of the EU (Liefferink and Andersen 1998b).

Key actors

In the period between 1973 and 1992 the Commission (aided by the Parliament) and member governments, particularly ministers of the environment, were the primary movers in this policy arena. In the years following 1992 non-governmental organizations (NGOs) increased in importance. Yet the Commission and the member governments are still the primary actors in the policy-making process, with the EP playing an important role in supporting more, rather than less, stringent regulations. The European Court of Justice (ECJ) plays a key strategic role in deciding both which environmental measures are permissible in the context of a single internal market and which potential litigants have the 'standing' to challenge environmental decisions before the ECJ itself.

Institutions

The Commission is a key player within the politics of environmental policy. It is *the* key player at the stage of policy formulation, since the regulatory approach that it adopts can be very difficult to change completely. Commission proposals tend to define the ground on which governments negotiate. For that reason, those member governments interested in externalizing their own domestic regulation try to influence the Commission's initial proposal. The Commission decides what should constitute 'plausible policy responses' and places these on the EU's agenda (Zito 1998: 679).

The Commission is also, however, typically a segmented player. Its structure and culture mitigate against coordinated approaches even more than do most national policy systems. In the field of environmental protection, its segmented nature poses very clear problems. DG XI is the Directorate-General charged with 'environmental protection'. However, many (if not most) environmental problems are products of energy use, transportation policy, agricultural practices, public investment and infra-structure patterns, and economic activity in general. Thus, many 'environmental' problems need the cooperation of the DGs concerned with those sectors, which are generally much less sympathetic to environmental considerations than is DG XI. DG XI is at something of a disadvantage in that it is less powerful within the Commis-sion than are DGs such as DG III (Industry), or DG VI (Agriculture).

The same is true when issues go for resolution in the college of commissioners: the Environment Commissioner needs the partnership of other commissioners in order to win agreements for proposed legislation. In the words of Environment Commissioner Ritt Bjerregaard, 'I am a bit like someone in charge of a car-park where none of the issues which are parked there under the name of the environment are really ones I could call my own. In reality they are in fact issues which really need to be resolved elsewhere by some of my other Commission colleagues' (Wilkinson 1997: 160).

Various attempts have been made to integrate environmental considerations into other policy areas (a goal written into Article 130r.2 (now 174.2) (SEA)) and strength-ened in both the TEU and the ToA). For example, in 1993 DG XI established a new Unit for Political Coordination and Integration, and each DG appointed an 'Integration Correspondent', charged with ensuring that the environmental considerations were incorporated into its policies. However, several of the powerful DGs (Agriculture, Industry) already had their own environmental affairs units, and these continued to operate as they always had. Furthermore, these DGs found that 'integration' gave them the right to influence DG XI and to make it more aware of, for example, the real-world problems of industrial producers. As Wilkinson points out, 'In those DGs with an established environmental role or unit, integration is regarded as a two-way pro-cess in which the sectoral department has as much right to influence DG XI as vice versa' (Wilkinson 1997: 162). The lack of coordination with DG XI was perhaps best manifested by the fact that many Integration Correspondents did not even bother to attend a meeting called by DG XI designed to bring them all together (Wilkinson 1997: 162).

DG XI has, however, been more successful in working with the Budget and Environment Committees of the EP. The election of a former Director-General of DG XI to the EP and his subsequent appointment to the key Budget Committee had an impact here. Some NGOs were able to highlight the environmental damage appar-ently accompanying some programmes funded by the Community structural and cohesion funds. The Parliament's Environment Committee was prompted to raise this issue, and won a commitment from the Regional Affairs Commissioner to strengthen the environmental dimension of the structural and cohesion funds (Wilkinson 1997: 165–8; Lenschow 1999: 53–68).

In general, however, the integration of environmental considerations into other policy sectors has been a very slow process. It is complicated by the types of trade-off which must be made in order to keep European firms competitive in a global econ-omy and the different priority given to environmental considerations in the various member states. Although this notion of integration forms a central part of the debate regarding 'sustainable development' (a term which itself is open to many meanings), the systematic and meaningful incorporation of environmental considerations in, for example, the transport sector's policy-making process is still a very long way off (O'Riordan and Voisey 1997).

The Council of Ministers

The Council of Ministers is the key legislative body for environmental policy, just as it is for the other policy areas discussed in this volume. The Council of Environment Ministers' meetings are attended by the ministers (or their representatives) who exercise responsibility for environmental protection within their national political systems. The ministers from the traditionally 'green' member states—the Nether-lands, Denmark, and Germany—have been able to use the EU's institutional machinery to 'externalize' domestic ideas of environmental protection throughout the Union. This dynamic has, however, gradually been changing as Germany's role as a 'leader' on environmental directives has weakened in the 1990s.

The environment ministers representing the more reluctant member govern-ments, for their part, have drawn on the compartmentalization of the Council, par-ticularly its relative insulation from the influence of ministers of economics, finance, and industry, to raise the profile of environmental protection back home (Collier and Golub 1997: 237). The fact that the environment ministers have usually deliberated amongst themselves in Brussels should not be underestimated. They have acquired an autonomy of action that they often lack at the national level, although how much varies depending on how national policy is coordinated in each member government.

Environment ministers have undoubtedly been able to approve some legislation in Brussels for which they would have been unable to win support in their national cabinets. Even the German Environment Ministry, located in one of the traditionally 'green' countries, has, in the view of other German ministries, gone further than they would have liked in supporting environment controls in the EU. For example, when the negotiations for the Directive requiring an environmental impact assessment were taking place in the Council of Environment Ministers, the negotiator from the German Environment Ministry was accompanied by 'chaperones'—two officials from the Ministry of Transport, one each from the Ministry of Economics, Ministry of Defence, and Ministry of Agriculture, and two representing the *Länder*. These 'chap-erones' had a very specific role: 'they had all been instructed to make sure that the Ministry for the Environment did not go too far in Brussels' (Pehle 1997: 199). The ministerial affiliation of these 'chaperones' illustrates the broad areas of activity upon which environmental regulations can have an impact, as well as the potential influence which an environment ministry might hope to wield in the absence of 'chaperones'.

In a similar vein, the draft Directive on end-of-life vehicles (ELVs) was derailed in June 1999 during the German presidency by the direct intervention of Chancellor Schröder, who was responding to pressure from the Chairman of Volkswagen, the German car manufacturer, who was simultaneously the President of the European Automobile Manufacturers' Association (ACEA). (Schröder had previously sat on Volkswagen's supervisory board and argued that the ELV Directive, because of its cost to manufacturers, would hurt share prices.) The Chancellor overrode the previous position taken by Jurgen Trittin, the Green Party member and Environment Minister, who then faced stinging criticism from within his party (as well as from fellow environment ministers) for having blocked the proposal (*Ends Report*, no. 290 (1999), 51).

The British and Spanish governments, which had been lobbied by Schröder, then supported the new German position. Rover, a major British car manufacturer, and SEAT, a major Spanish one, are both owned by German firms (respectively BMW and Volkswagen). Since the three governments' votes constitute a blocking minority, negotiations had to be restarted over a directive which had previously seemed to be a 'done deal' (*Environment Watch: Western Europe*, 2 July 1999: 6–8).

The implementation of EU legislation is in practice mainly the responsibility of national agencies, rather than the Commission. Governments seem willing sometimes to approve comparatively stringent environmental rules, but then subsequent compliance with them is sometimes patchy, slow, or at worst non-existent. In practice, therefore, legislation does not always have as far-reaching an impact as one might expect. In this sense Council negotiations are at some distance from practice on the ground, one of the factors that helps to explain the persistence of an 'implementation deficit' in the EU policy system.

Thus, environmental regulation proceeded relatively quickly and ambitiously because its real costs and intrusiveness became apparent only slowly. Most member governments did not have a dense regulatory framework already in place, and those governments which did were anxious to externalize it, to avoid placing their domestic industries at a competitive disadvantage. Furthermore, most directives are written with quite long lead-times for implementation, and before expenditure has to be made to meet the new standards. As the Council developed its legislative activity *vis-à-vis* the environment, its members became more cautious, a factor which has begun to undermine the previous advantages of the Commission in pioneering policy.

The accession of three 'green states'—Austria, Finland, and Sweden—in 1995 might have been expected to change the dynamics of environmental policy-making within the Council of Ministers. However, the weakening of Germany's leadership position on environmental issues also weakens the potential of any 'green bloc' within the Council. Liefferink and Andersen concluded that the Nordic countries, for their part, lack the 'critical mass to play a role in the environmental field comparable to that of the French–German cooperation on the integration process at large' (Liefferink and Andersen 1998a: 263). Other commentators (Young and Wallace 2000), however, argue that at least on some issues the new members have tipped the balance towards higher environmental standards.

The European Parliament

The EP stands out among parliamentary institutions in that 'it has had more influence on environmental measures than is typically true for more well-established national Parliaments' (Weale 1999: 37). Its influence has grown as its powers have been enlarged, and its Committee on the Environment, Public Health, and Consumer Protection, under the aggressive chairmanship of Ken Collins, has emerged as among the most important (as well as the most lobbied) parliamentary committees. Collins, a Scottish Labour MEP, succinctly summarized the evolution of the EP's influence on environmental policy: 'In 1979, we were a talking shop, an assembly without teeth. By 1994, we had learnt to do some damage with our gums. Now we have developed some pretty ferocious teeth' (*Environment Watch: Western Europe*, special issue (1999), 7–8). Collins, who retired in 1999, had been the Chair of the Committee for fifteen of the past twenty years, and his long tenure in office undoubtedly helped the Committee to increase its influence over time.

The Parliament has often taken a 'greener' line than either the Commission or the Council. It has forced the passage of more stringent rules than desired by the Council in several important pieces of legislation. Both the cooperation and co-decision procedures have been important institutional instruments in forcing the Commission and the Council to take account of the EP's interventions. MEPs were able to use the cooperation procedure to make the 1989 Directive on Exhaust Emission Standards from small cars more stringent (Tsebelis 1994). In the case of biocide legislation and the 'auto-oil' package (emission limits for cars and vans and fuel quality standards) the 'conciliation' procedure, which is triggered by co-decision, led to more stringent regulations than had been originally agreed to by the Council (*Ends Report*, 280 (1998), 46; *Ends Report*, 281 (1998), 48; Young and Wallace 2000). In 1996 the EP actually killed a draft directive on waste landfill standards. On the other hand, relatively few pieces of environmental legislation have been subject to conciliation, and the Environment Committee has been more successful in using conciliation to make changes to draft directives on consumer affairs and public health dossiers than in the environmental field (*Environment Watch: Western Europe*, special report (1999), 4).

The European Court of Justice

The ECJ historically has supported the intervention of the EU in the field of environmental protection even though it was acting without a treaty base. Since the SEA, its major impact has been to delineate those instances in which the principles of the internal market can be constrained by environmental protection and in restricting the access of environmental groups to the ECJ. In the *Danish Bottle* case of 1988 the Court established that the objective of environmental protection may override the principle of the free movement of goods (Koppen 1993). Secondly, the court is a key instrument for the enforcement of EU legislation in the member states. Many environmental cases brought by the Commission concern the failure of national governments to adopt legislation implementing directives approved in Brussels. Others target the nature of the legislation, arguing that the legislation itself does not fully and adequately translate the Community's directive into national law. At times the threat of such legal action convinces the national government to improve its legislation without further judicial action being needed.

In the field of environmental policy compliance with legislation after its adoption is often a serious problem. However, the Commission does not usually bring cases concerned with post-legislative compliance to the ECJ. Environmental groups, by contrast, are typically concerned with monitoring post-legislative compliance. The judiciary provides a potentially very important access-point for such groups in their efforts to ensure that legislation is actually executed on the ground. In particular, they would like to use the ECJ to force the Commission to pay more attention to such execution. The Court, however, has refused to allow environmental groups the legal 'standing' which would allow them to challenge decisions made by the European Commission. This position was reaffirmed in April 1998 in the case of *Greenpeace International and others v European Commission*. The Treaty of Rome allows the member states and the Council of Ministers, and the Commission, to challenge the legality of decisions made as relevant by the Council or the Commission; the EP can also challenge a decision that affects its own interest or that raises certain systematic issues. However, third parties can gain access to the Court only if the Commission's decision is 'of direct and individual concern to them'. In the view of Richard Macrory (*Ends Report*, 279 (1998), 46–7), the result of the Court's decision in the *Greenpeace International* case is that 'any further progress on standing is now likely to require amendment of the Treaty'. Given that much of the power of American environmental groups comes from their using the courts to force compliance on the ground, the lack of such access by European environmental NGOs to the ECJ limits the pressure felt by the Commission to concern itself with how directives are actually being executed.

The European Environmental Agency

The European Environmental Agency was established to provide 'objective, reliable and comparable information' about the quality of the environment, rather than to enforce environmental regulations. It is essentially an information-gathering institution, rather than one concerned with enforcement or with proposing new environmental legislation. The information it gathers is designed to allow comparisons about environmental issues to be made across the EU member states and to give national and Community policy-makers a common set of empirical indicators from which to work. It is therefore very different from the American Environmental Protection Agency (EPA), which exercises significant powers of enforcement.

The Agency is the successor to the Coordinated Information on the Environment (CORINE) project authorized in 1985. The new Agency was authorized in 1990, but, owing to problems over agreeing its location, it did not become operational until late 1994. Located in Copenhagen, it is independent and has its own Management Board. The Board includes one representative from each member state, plus representatives from Norway and Iceland, a representative from the Commission's DG XI and one from DG XII, and two appointees chosen by the EP. The Chair of the Board is chosen by its members (Wynne and Waterton 1998).

The Agency is very decentralized, with a European Information and Observation Network (EIONET) serving as its core. In practice, it acts to link together national ministries into a network which feeds information into the Agency. While it is largely independent of the Commission, it is closely linked to national environmental bureaucracies. The national ministries of the environment play a more crucial role in the network than they would have if an equivalent entity had been set up within the Commission itself. Critics argue that their key role 'potentially inhibits free access and exchange between the Agency and independent bodies at sub-national or international levels which may be in conflict with member state governments' (Wynne and Waterton 1998: 128). Critics fear that NGOs and local governments, for example, can easily become marginalized given the centrality of national ministerial officials. The issue of whose data is transmitted to Copenhagen has potentially far-reaching impacts on both the type and quality of data gathered by the European Environmental Agency, one reason why the seeming monopoly of national administrations in the network has raised considerable concern.

The Agency's emphasis on providing policy-relevant information echoes an increasing emphasis within the environmental policy culture on the role of public information (Wynne and Waterton 1998: 124). 'Regulation by information' has become associated with a certain regulatory philosophy which questions the appropriateness and effectiveness of 'command and control' activities traditionally carried out by the public administration (Majone 1997). Whereas expertise in the traditional bureaucracy is used to pursue new policy initiatives and to target enforcement activities, the Agency uses expertise to improve the data used in policy formulation and political debate.

Environmental groups

NGOs that support increased environmental protection are a well-developed feature in the 'green' states, but are much less conspicuous or influential elsewhere. The European Environmental Bureau (EEB) was established in 1974 and remained the only major environmental interest group active in Brussels until the mid-1980s. Thereafter, Friends of the Earth Europe, Greenpeace, and the World Wide Fund for Nature (WWF) each established a Brussels office. The EEB, Friends of the Earth, the WWF, and Greenpeace were known as the 'Gang of Four', and they worked closely with DG XI (the first three groups also received Commission funding to help sustain their operations). The group has now expanded to the 'Gang of Seven' with the addition of BirdLife International, Climate Network Europe, and the Transport and Environment Federation. The staff resources of these groups have been very modest, with probably no more than thirty people employed by the groups combined (Long 1998: 107–15).

The European-level NGOs became more important in the 1990s than before, but they remain weaker than the European-level groups representing business or environmental groups in the USA. They have long had access to DG XI, but their access to the other, more powerful, DGs is limited. NGOs have become more visible as the EP has gained powers, and are likely to gain influence as the EP gains further powers under the ToA. It should be noted, however, that there are other vectors than NGOs for feeding environmental considerations into the process.

Policy outcomes, implementation, and compliance

Once an environmental directive is adopted by the Council and Parliament, further work is needed to turn it into practice. 'Implementing measures' may need to be adopted by specialist committees within the comitology procedures. The Council often deliberately leaves technical issues to be resolved and spelled out by these implementing committees. Brendan Flynn concludes that these provide a forum within which 'technical rules are frequently the centre of conflict between contend-

ing interests of the member states, industry and environmentalists . . . EU environmental policy is often contested and negotiated more in the opaque world of comitology . . . than it is at the higher level of policy debate between the Commission,
Council, and the Parliament' (Flynn, 1999).

Member states must transpose directives into their national legal systems, by
whatever their national arrangements are—often a time-consuming and complex
process. The national legislation needs to be applied on the ground, which may
involve new administrative arrangements and enforcement mechanisms being set in
place. Policy implementation depends on what happens inside each member state;
national governments are responsible for compliance, and thus retain a large measure of control in the policy process, although in some member states the operational
responsibilities lie with local or regional authorities, or special agencies.

In practice the quality of implementation varies a great deal between countries and
from case to case. Thus real gaps exist in the implementation of environmental
directives—so much so that it is widely accepted that there is an 'implementation
deficit', and that compliance is a real problem (Sbragia with Hildebrand 1998). Various explanations have been offered for this (Jordan 1999a), but most commentators
agree that problems of implementation keep environmental policy from being as
effective as it should be.

The Commission has the task of monitoring the transposition of EU directives into
national legislation. If a member government either fails to transpose, or does so
inadequately, the Commission can open an infringement proceeding, which, if not
resolved, can lead to a member state being brought to the ECJ. In 1997 the Commission brought infringement proceedings for non-transposition of environmental directives against every member state, with the Netherlands and Denmark being the
only states with a single case brought against them. Furthermore, national legislation
must conform to the provisions of the directives adopted in Brussels. Here, problems
are numerous. The Commission is currently involved in cases charging non-
conformity with all the member states and in all areas of environmental legislation.
Infringement proceedings are especially noteworthy in the area of water pollution:
roughly a quarter of all infringement proceedings under way in 1997 concerned
water pollution legislation.

Transposition and conformity of national legislation with EU directives does not
necessarily ensure that the intent of the legislation is actually executed. Some countries with relatively good transposition records (like Spain) have very poor records
when it comes to actual compliance (Börzel 1999). The Commission does not have its
own inspectorate to gather data about implementation on the ground (Sbragia with
Hildebrand 1998). NGOs and individual citizens, do, however, send complaints to the
Commission about non-compliance, and the Commission can then bring pressure on
the member government to improve its record.

The Commission is faced with the fact that administrative capacity varies widely
within the Union. Some governments implement their national legislation relatively
efficiently while others regularly run into difficulties, Italy being a striking example
of the latter category (Sbragia with Hildebrand 1998). Inspectorates in some member
states are as yet underdeveloped. In several member states environmental protection
is the responsibility of regional governments, and hence implementation involves yet
another layer of the process. Central governments bear the brunt of infringement

proceedings under European law, even when they lack the levers within their own political systems to improve the execution of legislation.

In some cases, implementation problems arise not from the lack of administrative capacity but rather from a 'misfit' between the EU's approach to regulation and the administrative apparatus which exists within a member state. For example, in Germany environmental policy is firmly in the hands of the *Länder*, and hence the federal government, with few exceptions, has limited scope for ensuring that the *Länder* implement measures appropriately. This complication is partly offset by the intermediation of *Bundesländer* working groups, although poor links between the levels of government cause problems.

As long as Germany's regulatory philosophy shaped EU environmental directives, its national regulatory system accommodated them easily, which is hardly surprising. However, once other influences on legislation became more significant, the German system faced enormous challenges, given its dependence on a particularly intricate set of domestic arrangements. German agencies have found it hard to apply EU directives shaped by a different regulatory philosophy (Héritier *et al.* 1996; Börzel 1999; Knill 1998).

As implementation problems have become more prominent, the Commission, under some pressure from the EP, has begun to pay more attention to non-compliance, and since 1983 it has published, at the EP's request, annual reports on the implementation of Community legislation. In 1996 the Commission (1996*h*) proposed that guidelines on minimum criteria for environmental inspections in the member states be explored and that public complaints on national non-compliance with EC legislation be dealt with much more systematically at the national level. In particular, the Communication proposed that national courts should broaden the (currently restricted) access of environmental groups to those same courts when EC environmental law was involved in a case. Since the ECJ has restricted the judicial access of environmental groups at the Community level, the Communication was proposing that environmental groups be given more judicial access at the national level. Such access would at least partially circumvent the restrictiveness of access to the ECJ, since national courts, using the preliminary Article 171 (now 228) procedure, could ask the ECJ for its opinion.

Ministers from the member states have also started to take more interest in implementation and in 1997 asked the Commission to propose minimum criteria for environmental inspections of industrial facilities. Ritt Bjerregaard, the responsible Commissioner, considered proposing mandatory inspection requirements under a new directive, but the political sensitivity of the topic led the Commission as a whole to issue instead, in December 1998, a non-binding recommendation rather than a draft directive. Its criteria suggest that national inspectors should check facilities for their compliance with EU rules, as well as make their reports available to the public. It is expected that the southern member states will have particular difficulty in meeting these criteria, while other countries, such as the UK, will also have to change their current practices (*Ends Report*, 277 (1998), 43; *Ends Report*, 288 (1999), 47–8).

In June 1997 Environment Ministers also decided to strengthen the institutional capacity of the informal EU Network for the Implementation and Enforcement of Environmental Law (IMPEL), created in 1992, by giving it a secretariat within DG XI and allowing it to give formal policy advice. IMPEL is composed of representatives

from the national environmental inspectorates concerned with industrial installations, and is jointly chaired by the Commission and the Council presidency. It drafted
the paper upon which the Recommendation was based (*Ends Report*, 277 (1998), 43;
House of Lords 1997*b*: 56). IMPEL's membership does not include those charged with
enforcing directives concerning habitat, bathing-water, and non-industrial developments (Haigh 1997: 72).

Although the implementation deficit is clearly a problem for environmental
protection, it is harder to judge its significance for the process of integration more
broadly. The EU is a complex and multi-layered system of governance, which cannot
operate like a unitary state. Hence the problems of implementation seem to be mainly
related to the characteristics of its member states (Jordan 1999*a*). Comparison with
the USA sheds a different light on the process: although the federal EPA is a powerful
agency with enforcement powers, it too is dependent on individual American states
to implement and to manage environmental management programmes. In the USA,
too, we find chronic implementation problems, which often come to light only when
environmental groups use the courts to find a remedy. The EPA is far more dependent
on the states than is often assumed. Given the experiences of federal states, including
the relatively centralized US example, what needs to be explained is not why the
Commission has so little power, but rather why it has so much.

Daniel Kelemen argues that the Commission has remarkable power to bring member governments before the ECJ because of non-compliance, a right which it exercises
regularly and persistently. Many federal governments are reluctant to exercise such
powers, because their states or provinces are so resistant to such interference. Kelemen's comparative study of environmental policy in federal systems and the EU
concludes:

Member State control of implementation and enforcement need not be viewed as a sign of
weakness. Delegation of implementation and enforcement to Member States does not distinguish the EU from other federal-type politics. Well-established federal governments, such as
those in the US, Germany, Australia, and Canada also delegate most implementation and
enforcement of regulatory policy to state governments . . . the EU compares favourably with
some federal systems. Community directives and regulations place more detailed requirements
on Member States than do Canadian or Australian laws. The European Commission and the ECJ
do more to enforce EU environmental law than do the central authorities of Australia or Canada
or Germany. (Kelemen 1998: 245–6, 248)

Federal systems find it extraordinarily difficult to centralize the implementation of
environmental legislation. Compliance tends to rely on factors such as: the access of
societal actors to the courts; the technical administrative capacity; and the political
engagement of infranational agencies. This suggests that the EU has more chance of
improving implementation by encouraging the horizontal transmission of 'best practice' among the member states than by efforts to centralize implementation powers
in Brussels.

Policy contestation

Two major debates have characterized the environmental policy arena in the 1990s. One has to do with subsidiarity—that is, the division of competence between different levels of government. The second concerns the choice of which regulatory philosophy should underpin EU policy—command and control or a more flexible, market- and information-based control regime.

Subsidiarity

Subsidiarity, as we have seen, is an issue in all multi-level systems of governance, and the environmental domain particularly illustrates the difficulty of allocating responsibilities between levels of government. Local, as well as national, authorities in most countries have environmental functions. In the EU case, to add yet another level of legislation and policy-making was bound to create some tensions. Indeed, this is why it was in the environmental domain that subsidiarity, as a principle, first crept into the treaties in the SEA (Article 130r, now 174) (Wallace and Wilke 1990). The TEU took the principle further as a more general concept, stressing the importance of public policy being located at the lowest possible level of government.

In the subsequent political debate environmental directives became especially central. Proponents of subsidiarity argued that many directives had gone beyond what could be justified at the European level, and hence that certain elements of environmental policy should be 'renationalized'. In contrast, those in favour of tough standards tended to advocate a strong European legislative framework. This argument has had an impact. Some important proposals were withdrawn by the Commission. Framework (rather than detailed) directives became more widely used, thus giving national governments more latitude. In addition, the pace at which environmental directives were adopted slowed very considerably (Golub 1996). On the other hand, certain key directives—bathing- and drinking-water in particular—remained in place. Jordan (1999a) argues that the subsidiarity issue has been exaggerated, and that no significant 'roll-back' was accomplished.

Contrasting regulatory philosophies

In the 1990s debate has sharpened around the one issue of whether environmental legislation should regulate the sources of potential damage or focus on the environmental quality to be achieved, for example, in relation to water or air. In other words, the argument was between controls over the means and the targeting of ends. An approach favouring controls over emissions was very strongly favoured by Germany, in line with its own domestic regulatory framework and philosophy. The very competitive environmental technology industry in Germany stood to benefit from this approach (Héritier et al. 1996; Knill 1996).

The British, on the other hand, favoured a regulatory approach which would focus on the environmental quality of the medium under discussion, a 'regulatory style derived from the fundamental conception of pollution as the effect of emissions on the receiving medium rather than the presence of emissions themselves' (Golub 1996: 705). Geography also reinforced these differences of philosophy. The UK's pollutants are blown away and its streams run into the ocean, and hence dispersal takes care of much of Britain's pollution. The opposite is the case for Germany.

These two contrasting approaches lead to very different regulatory preferences. The common control approach necessitates very detailed regulations, whereas targeting quality allows much greater latitude to the member states as to the choice of methods. Furthermore, the German approach required BAT, whereas the British approach was based on BAT without excessive economic cost (BAT versus BATNEEC). Implementation under BAT involves sophisticated technology, whereas BATNEEC is much more permissive.

In the field of air quality the Germans set the agenda in the 1980s. For example, the Large Combustion Plant Directive was much influenced by German domestic experience. In that period the British were often regarded as leading the opposition to EU environmental policy. However, in the 1990s Germany started to lose its 'first mover' advantage to the British. After modernizing its own domestic system of environmental protection, the British began to emerge as the leader as regards air quality on the basis of a quite different type of intervention. In the words of Héritier *et al.* (1996: 208), 'It is the British who are now able to call the tune in important areas, and it is in their interest to impose their innovative arrangements on other countries via the EU'. In other areas the record is more mixed. Even though the Commission's position is now much closer to the British than to the German, Héritier *et al.* (1996:276) concluded that 'current developments in European legislation are a mixed "strategic" bag. We find a mixture of intervention philosophies with both typically British and typically German traits.'

Several environmental directives have addressed the procedures through which environmental protection is achieved, an innovation in the Community's legislative framework which has led to many difficulties in nearly all member states. In 1990, for example, a Directive on Public Access to Environmental Information was adopted, but its implementation has been difficult in those member states which do not by tradition allow citizens easy access to information. As Rose-Ackerman (1995: 114) points out, 'the directive runs directly counter to German bureaucratic traditions . . . Access to government files by members of the public with an interest in policy but no personal stake in the outcome is a novel idea in German public law.' Furthermore, the trend of privatizing what were once public services makes it harder to determine which firms have 'public responsibilities' and are therefore covered by the Directive.

We can therefore now observe a reversal of experience between Britain and Germany. As British legislation now shapes a good deal more of EU legislation, the UK's domestic administrative apparatus sits more easily with it. The opposite is the case for Germany: 'the Germans fiercely combat proposals betraying a quality-orientation or serving to improve public rights of access to information, regulatory concepts fundamentally opposed to their own philosophy' (Héritier *et al.* 1996: 276). None the less the debate is not closed in either country. The British government has, for example, been criticized by environmental groups because it has not designated the privatized water authorities as having a 'public responsibility', and therefore argues that they should not be subject to the Directive on public access to environmental information. Although the German government, for its part, opposed the introduction of the (voluntary) eco-audit, German firms have been by far the most receptive to using it.

The history of one of the most important environmental directives to be adopted in the 1990s illustrates the tensions which are now present in most negotiations over environmental legislation. The Integrated Pollution Prevention and Control (IPPC) Directive, a pivotal piece of legislation (coming into force in October 1999), affects numerous industrial installations and sets the stage for future legislation. It was modelled on the British Integrated Pollution Control (IPC) Act introduced in 1990. One of the drafters of the British law played a key role in drafting the Commission's proposal for an integrated pollution approach, eventually adopted as Directive 96/61/ EEC, which would simultaneously regulate pollutants into the water, air, and soil. However, as the Directive was discussed, other governments sought to bend it to suit their own different circumstances.

One of the reasons that the UK government was the 'first mover' in this case was that its new domestic system risked making British industry less competitive if the EU adopted less stringent standards. For example, one version of the draft directive allowed existing plants to defer upgrading to the 'best available techniques' until 2005, whereas the British legislation required such upgrading much earlier. However, the Spanish and Portuguese governments would not agree to an earlier date. The British also supported a centralized system of issuing permits to plants for all processes with environmental impacts, in line with British practice, and proposed an arbitration procedure to handle disputes between regulatory authorities. In contrast, the German public administration has a well-established practice of giving permits for each single medium and found the prospect of having to implement an integrated approach unacceptable. As for rules on disclosure, the British wanted disclosure to use public registers, as its national system required, while the Germans argued that the existing Directive on Public Access to Environmental Information (which it has only partially and very grudgingly implemented) was sufficient. The two approaches, however, were reconciled on the issue of BAT versus BATNEEC, in that the draft directive aimed at BAT, but allowed reference to economic considerations (*Ends Report*, 235 (1994), 37–8; *Environment Watch: Western Europe*, 18 August 1995: 1).

The story, however, changed when the German government took over the Council presidency in mid-1994. Instead of using its role to move the negotiations forward, the German government simply deleted the requirement that regulatory authorities coordinate their issuing of permits, rather than set in train an unwelcome change in domestic practice. 'Germany [had] special problems with the proposal because it would at a minimum require a coordinated input from all the regulatory authorities involved to produce an integrated permitting decision for installations subject to IPPC' (*Ends Report*, 237 (1994), 35). Widely viewed as having abused its presidency, the German government was unable to make progress on the draft directive.

It was not until the subsequent French Council presidency that an acceptable compromise was constructed. The French included costs and benefits in the definition of 'best available techniques'. The new version of BAT now became more similar to BATNEEC, although it was argued in the UK that this extended British practice to the EU (*Ends Report*, 292 (1991), 38–9). Agreement was also found on wording which called for full co-ordination among regulatory authorities. Finally, in June 1995, the Environment Ministers were able to agree unanimously on the Directive. It would indeed require that permits be issued 'whose emissions limit will be set in an "integrated" way that covers emissions to air, water and land simultaneously and prevents the transfer of pollution between them'. Permit applications and the results of emissions monitoring will have to be made public; furthermore, the Commission every three years will publish an inventory of principal emissions and their sources (*Environment Watch: Western Europe*, 7 July 1995: 6–7).

This landmark piece of legislation (which will eventually replace the 1984 Directive on Emissions from Industrial Installations) illustrates the influence of the 'first mover' (in this case Britain), but also indicates that a member government cannot control the agenda enough to get everything it wants. As the 31 October 1999 deadline for transposing the Directive into national legislation approached, it became clear that the IPPC directive, even though relatively compatible with pre-existing British arrangements, would none the less 'introduce far-reaching changes to the UK's existing pollution control regimes' (*Ends Report*, 288 (1999), 35).

New instruments

The Fifth Action Programme (1993–2000) crystallized the Commission's move away from the traditional 'command and control' approach, which had dominated environmental protection since the early 1970s. Reflecting the increased influence of economic concerns in the Commission, the economic effects of the Fifth Action Programme itself were evaluated (Commission 1994g). The traditional approach was viewed as economically inefficient. The pressure for new ways of regulating came from a variety of sources, including firms worried about their competitiveness, and was reinforced by the emphasis on regulatory reform within the EU. Although NGOs were originally sceptical about these new instruments, they gradually became more accepting.

'New instruments are intended to provide the efficiency and positive incentives which command and control lacks' (Golub 1998: 5). Although member governments have experimented with a wide range of such instruments, the Commission has advocated using eco-audits (environmental management systems), eco-labels, and voluntary agreements. Variants of an 'eco-tax' have been frequently discussed, and adopted by some member states, but, as noted earlier, have failed to find general agreement in the EU. Jonathan Golub, however, argues that the EU's record in introducing new instruments is a better one than that of the USA or Japan, and thus, it compares well in international terms, even if some EU members have gone further (Golub 1998: 20–1).

The eco-tax on the use of oil, gas, and coal (all non-renewable energy sources) has been the most fiercely contested policy instrument. Proposed by the Commission in the run-up to the Rio Summit in 1992, it was meant both to help the EU play a leadership role in these global environmental negotiations and to stabilize the carbon dioxide emissions which contribute to climate change (Zito 1995a). The EU's Council of Economic and Finance Ministers (Ecofin) has been the veto point and succeeded in keeping the issue on its agenda rather than that of the Environment Council (Zito 1995a: 444).

The British, Portuguese, Greek, Irish, and Spanish governments have fiercely opposed any such tax. In 1993 the Danish Council presidency came close to a

compromise acceptable to the 'poor four', but the British objections killed the proposal at that stage. The issue did not disappear from the agenda, however. The Spanish presidency in 1996 proposed a different compromise, the Swedish, German, and
Austrian governments judged it too weak, while the British, Greek, Portuguese, and
Irish continued to oppose the idea altogether. The French then suggested an alternative way, and in 1997 the Commission proposed 'energy tax IIIa', but again no consensus could be reached. The new Labour government in the UK began to shift position and Mario Monti, the relevant Commissioner, proposed 'energy tax IIIb', 'an
empty shell which could be filled up much later when the political will was there'
(*European Voice*, 18–24 February 1999, 16). However, the Spanish hostility increased
rather than diminished. In May 1999, under another German presidency, thirteen
members of Ecofin agreed to a compromise which would permit Spain to set low
rates or grant exemptions, but neither the Spanish nor the Irish government would
accept the compromise (*Environment Watch: Western Europe*, 4 June 1999: 6).

Some voluntary policy instruments have, however, been adopted, although even
here progress has been mixed. A Regulation (880/92) to encourage use of the EU
eco-label has not been widely applied, although some national schemes such as
Germany's 'Blue Swan' have been successful. Firms seem reluctant to cooperate in
establishing the criteria for, and then using, eco-labelling for their products unless
there is a threat of binding regulation, except in a few technically homogeneous
sectors. By the end of 1998 only twelve products were covered by European eco-labels,
of which half were indoor paints and varnishes (which contain volatile organic com-
pounds). Even in this case, the negotiation of the criteria for labelling had taken from
May 1991 until January 1996. By contrast, the cosmetics industry refused to participate in negotiations over any products because it opposed the proposed criteria for
hairsprays (Nadai, forthcoming). Firms outside the EU tend to view eco-labelling as a
protectionist measure, a concern similar to those in the biotechnology sector (see
Chapter 12) (Herrup 1999).

The Fifth Action Programme also called for the use of voluntary agreements, of a
kind used in several member states, the Netherlands in particular. In July 1998 the
Commission finalized a key voluntary agreement designed to cut carbon dioxide
emissions from new cars. This was important for the EU's commitment under the
Kyoto Protocol of the UNFCCC (*Ends Report*, 282 (1998), 48). Although the EP at one
stage had supported binding legislation and opposed the use of a voluntary agreement, it finally accepted the agreement (although stressing its scepticism about its
effectiveness). The Commission has insisted that it has the legal right to adopt such
agreements without the approval of either the EP or the Council of Ministers
(*Environment Watch: Western Europe*, 18 September 1998: 8).

The role of the EU in global regimes

At the international level the EU is now widely recognized as a leader, especially in
the crucial climate change negotiations. Although the EU, like many individual countries, often has problems implementing international agreements once ratified, the

impact of the EU as a negotiating bloc within the global system has grown. A crucial threshold was passed once the SEA gave the EU a treaty base for environmental policy. The Commission and the member governments began thereafter to assert collective positions in global regime-building. The Montreal Protocol was the first strong instance of this (Sbragia with Hildebrand 1998). The EU does not have full competence and therefore does not have the status of a 'unitary actor'; none the less, it has made headway in developing coherent agreed positions (Sbragia 1998).

The demands of negotiating UNFCCC, adopted in 1992, led the EU to innovate in its policy-making process. For example, the first joint Council of Energy and Environment Ministers met in October 1990 to draw up a Community position, which proposed the stabilization of CO_2 emissions by the year 2000 at 1990 levels. Furthermore, the member governments committed themselves to a pioneering 'burden-sharing' agreement, whereby those which could only reduce emissions more gradually would be offset by other governments agreeing to reduce theirs disproportionately. The success of the EU in achieving this measure of internal coherence made it much easier to adopt a tough stance at the global level, a result which would not have been expected even a decade ago.

In the run-up to the conference which discussed the Kyoto Protocol (agreed eventually in December 1997) to bind states to implementing the UNFCCC, the EU Environment Council committed the EU to reducing by 15 per cent emissions of three greenhouse gases (CO_2, methane, and NO_x) by 2010. The Commission admitted that such targets would be 'politically challenging ... [as] the only way to reduce CO_2 emissions is through modification of structures, processes, equipment and behaviour which directly or indirectly use fossil fuels' (Commission 1997d: 1–3).

EU policy-makers were pleased with the achievement of embedding legally binding targets into the Protocol which safeguarded EU competitiveness. Their agreed level was an overall 8 per cent reduction of greenhouse gas emissions in the EU, compared to 1990 levels by the year 2012. The US government took much more persuading, even threatening to block the whole process, because of severe difficulties in gaining domestic consent for stringent targets. Eventually the Americans accepted a reduction of 7 per cent in its targets, but only because the Protocol included the so-called 'flexible mechanisms', in particular the unusual (from a European perspective) device of tradeable quotas in emissions reductions. This had not been an EU objective, although the EU (in Article 4 of the Protocol) obtained the permission it sought to fulfil its obligations through intra-EU burden-sharing. This is now legally binding on the EU.

The flexible mechanisms—that is, economic instruments—introduced under the Protocol allow for a system of trading in emissions and transfer of credits earned by those countries which have reduced emissions. These instruments are a new device for the EU and its members, as for other countries. In May 1999 the Commission succinctly outlined the challenge facing the Union:

The Kyoto Mechanisms are fundamentally different from the way the European Community and its Member States have organised their environmental policy over the last decades. Environment policy has been based on technical standards (such as Best Available Technology—BAT), regulatory emission limitations, and more recently on economic instruments such as taxes, charges, and environmental agreements. So far there is hardly any experience in the Community with instruments such as the Kyoto Mechanisms. The policy challenge ahead consists therefore of developing new flexible instruments within European environmental policy, without however undermining the important achievements of the past. (Commission 1999f: 14)

In other words, the EU was unable to export its regulatory regime to the global level, and it will have to develop a new system.

European policy-makers have since Kyoto tried to restrict the use of this system at the global level, and in May 1999, environment ministers approved a 'cap' on this and the other mechanisms approved by the Protocol. The cap is designed to ensure that at least half of the reductions in emissions are obtained through domestic action. The EU submitted this as a proposal to a meeting in June 1999 dealing with the follow-up to Kyoto (*Environment Watch: Western Europe*, 21 May 1999: 10).

In March 1997 the EU government had agreed on an internal allocation of reductions in emissions in order to bolster their leverage during the Kyoto negotiations. These reductions were not, however, binding. In June 1998, under the UK Council presidency, the EU reached a binding agreement to fulfil the 8 per cent agreed at Kyoto (*Ends Report*, 281 (1998), 46). (See Table 11.1.) Climate change policy is the global issue with the highest profile currently being negotiated. Here, as in its internal policies, the EU has a similar challenge of implementation, which depends not only on environment ministers. Their colleagues dealing with energy, transport, and finance hold the levers to the implementation of climate change policy, and can use their EU Council sessions to block agreements. In April 1998 the UK Council presidency convened the first joint Transport and Environment Council to 'take a strategic look at the integration of transport and environment policies'. This does not seem to have been a successful experiment, and it leaves a gap between stated goals and implementation. In part, of course, these differences at the EU level reflect the different streams of policy responsibility within each member state.

Table 11.1 Required change in greenhouse gas emissions, 1990–2010 (per cent)

Member state	March 1997 Proposal	UK Presidency Proposal	Agreed allocation (June 1998)
Austria	−25	−20.5	−13
Belgium	−10	−9	−7.5
Denmark	−25	−22.5	−21
Finland	0	0	0
France	0	0	0
Germany	−25	−22.5	−21
Greece	+30	+23	+25
Ireland	+15	+11	+13
Italy	−7	−7	−6.5
Luxembourg	−30	−30	−28
Netherlands	−10	−8	−6
Portugal	+40	+24	+27
Spain	+17	+15	+15
Sweden	+5	+5	+4
UK	−10	−12	−12.5

Source: *Ends Report*, 281 (1998), 46.

The EU-level process is, however, made more complicated because in some fields relevant to environmental policy the EU has only weak powers: energy policy is a crucial case in point. As Collier argues, 'Member States have managed to retain their sovereignty in all crucial areas of energy policy' (Collier 1997: 49). The commitments made under the Kyoto Protocol make energy policy even more crucial, and it remains to be seen whether the EU members will take the necessary steps in energy conservation at the national level for the EU to meet its Kyoto commitments.

Conclusions

The EU's regulatory framework in the field of environmental protection operated with a combination of two approaches, both the traditional 'command and control' approach, and the new market–information-based elements. The Kyoto Protocol adds new mechanisms to this mix, and will complicate still further the politics of EU environmental policy. The economic character of the Kyoto mechanisms will need to be reconciled with both the single market and competition policy, for example to ensure that trading in emissions does not create state aids in disguise.

Regardless of these complexities, the EU policy process has demonstrated that it is capable of making binding decisions, which most federal systems would find extraordinarily challenging. Although the EU has jibbed at fiscal federalism, the 'burden-sharing' agreement of 1998 stands as an example of 'pollution federalism' with a form of redistribution between member states. To build on this and to develop the EU's bargaining power in global regime-making will need a firmer grasp of the implementation challenge. In all multi-level or federal systems the application of legislation is testing. The EU is now engaged in developing environmental policy at three main levels: global, EU, and national (for some EU members a fourth local or regional level is also important). A key question for the future is how that new global involvement will alter the dynamics of environmental policy-making within the EU.

Further reading

For a good discussion of environmental policy in those European countries which were the most committed to environmental protection, see Andersen and Liefferink (1997). For an analysis of how Britain, France, and Germany have shaped EU environmental policy-making, see Héritier et al. (1996). The House of Lords (1997b) report on the implementation of Community environmental law is excellent. The special issue of Environment and Planning C: Government and Policy (1999) and Zito (2000) both give excellent overviews of EU environmental policy. Golub (1998) reviews the different policy instruments which environmental policy-makers are using at both the Community and national levels.

Andersen, M. S., and Liefferink, D. (1997), *European Environmental Policy: The Pioneers* (Manchester: Manchester University Press).

Golub, J. (1998) (ed.), *New Instruments for Environmental Policy in the EU* (London: Routledge).

Héritier, A., Knill, C., and Mingers, S. (1996), *Ringing the Changes in Europe: Regulatory Competition and Redefinition of the State. Britain, France, Germany* (Berlin: Walter de Gruyter).

House of Lords (1997*b*), Select Committee on the European Communities, *Community Environmental Law: Making it Work*, Report, Session 1996–7 (London: Stationery Office).

Jordan, A. (1999*b*) (ed.), 'Theme Issue: European Union Environmental Policy at 25', *Environment and Planning C: Government and Policy*, 17, Feb., 1–126.

Zito, A. (2000), *Creating Environmental Policy in the European Union* (London: Macmillan).

Chapter 12

Biotechnology Policy

Regulating Risks and
Risking Regulation

Lee Ann Patterson

Contents

Summary

This chapter analyses the development of the European Union's (EU's) biotechnology regulatory framework by exploring: (1) the historical context of the policy debate; (2) the importance of conflicting ideologies in the policy debate; (3) the policy-making process within the Commission; and (4) the role in the policy process of other players, including the other institutions of the EU, the member states, industrial and environmental interest groups, and trade partners. The chapter focuses mainly on the passage and reform of two very important biotechnology regulations: Directive 90/219 on the Contained Use of Genetically Modified Micro-organisms and Directive 90/220 on the Deliberate Release of Genetically Modified Organisms into the Environment. These

Directives serve as framework legislation in the area of biotechnology and are at the centre of a heated regulatory debate in the EU.

Introduction

Few policy debates have been economically as important or politically as explosive as the recent debates on regulating biotechnologies in the EU.[1] Biotechnology regulatory policy will have a critical impact on the technology trajectories of many European industries and on the political economy of the EU as a whole. Sectors which currently utilize biotechnologies account for 9 per cent of the Community's gross value-added and 8 per cent of its employment and the growth rate of industries based on modern biotechnologies is expected to be substantial (Commission 1993*d*). At the same time, the new technology is characterized by uncertainty and a widespread public belief that it could present a risk to human health and the environment. The underlying policy problem is, therefore, how to regulate a critical new technology in a manner which will create a conducive environment for the many Community industries which stand to gain from the new technology, while at the same time protecting consumers and the environment from any risks associated with the new technology.

Many factors have contributed to the complexity of policy-making in this area. First, biotechnology policy is a relatively new policy field which cuts across existing categories of policy management and involves several sectors such as agriculture, medicine, pharmaceuticals, chemicals, and processed foods.[2] This requires a degree of horizontal policy coordination and communication for which there are few precedents.

Secondly, biotechnology policy is being made simultaneously at several different levels of government including the member state level, the EU level, and the international level (at the Organization for Economic Cooperation and Development (OECD) and the United Nations (UN)). The EU stands at the nexus of these multi-level debates. The EU must establish a coordinated EU-wide policy in order to achieve a true internal market, and it must coordinate the positions of its member governments in international policy arenas as well. Both of these tasks have proved to be particularly difficult, because there is no wide-ranging societal consensus in Europe about the appropriate regulatory approach to be taken.

Thirdly, the biotechnology policy debates are influenced by the prevailing ideologies of conflicting social domains. Three domains or 'social spaces' exist in the policy arena: the scientific domain, the environmental domain, and the market domain. Each domain has its own networks of technical experts who help to define risk and, in turn, influence the regulatory process. In the scientific domain a certain risk must be proved to exist before regulations are implemented. In the environmental domain protection of the environment and human health require that regulations should be based on potential risks. In the market domain there is an attempt to balance acceptable risks with economic benefits.

There is little overlap among these various domains. Scientists argue that it is logically impossible to prove that there is no risk, and that any regulations should be based on demonstrated risks not potential risks. However, European public opinion is generally distrustful of scientific risk analysis after the Chernobyl meltdown and the bovine spongiform encephalitis (BSE: mad cow) and thalidomide crises. Consequently, many EU citizens, consumers, and environmental interest groups believe that regulations should be based on potential risks rather than demonstrated risks. Those in the market domain often find themselves trying to square scientific evidence with popular opinion, while making good business decisions about bringing new products to market.[3] The existence of these ideologically driven social domains, in combination with the multiple levels of government, has generated a tremendously complex policy-making environment.

This chapter focuses mainly on how biotechnology policy is made at the EU level. Particular attention is paid to policy-making in the European Commission, since it initiates regulations and its internal debates reflect the various social domains outlined above. Furthermore, by studying the Commission, the interaction between ideas and institutions becomes clearer and we are able to say with greater certainty why some policies were adopted and others were not.

A historical perspective

Biotechnology burst on to the EU policy agenda in the mid-1980s as a result of the many and varied policy discussions which were occurring more or less simultaneously in the international community of biological scientists, the OECD, the member states, and the European Parliament (EP).

The international scientific community

The earliest concerns about recombinant DNA (rDNA) experimentation arose within the community of biological scientists. In 1975 an International Conference on Recombinant DNA Molecules was held in Asilomar, California. Scientists from all over the world attended the meeting to discuss appropriate ways to deal with potential bio-hazards. Two groups of experiments were identified, low risk and high risk. No moratorium was placed on the low-risk procedures. For high-risk procedures, the scientists decided to use biological containment procedures similar to those developed by the Ashby Working Party in the United Kingdom (UK) (Cantley 1995: 516).[4] Already aware that the public was dubious of the new technology, Sydney Brenner of the British Medical Research Council, Laboratory of Molecular Biology, also advocated 'adopting guidelines that would be so evidently tight that no one could reasonably accuse the scientific community of being self serving' (*Science*, 14 March 1975: 932). The guidelines would be revised downward in the future as more knowledge about rDNA techniques and products was gained. The Asilomar Conference raised governmental awareness of both the potential benefits and the potential risks involved in biotechnology.

However, the EU was relatively slow to initiate regulatory action on biotechnology throughout the late 1970s because integration of the common market was proceeding slowly, there was widespread disagreement about whether regulation was needed, and there was no legal basis for European regulation. The first biotechnology policy proposal was developed in the Commission by Directorate-General (DG) XII (Science, Research, and Development) in 1978. DG XII advocated a Community-wide research and development programme in molecular biology, and formulated a proposal for a Council directive which would require notification and authorization by national authorities prior to all research and other work involving rDNA. National authorities were called to develop categorization procedures for rDNA experiments, to keep track of the experiments, and to report annually to the Commission on experiences and problems.

However, in 1980 the Commission withdrew its proposed directive and replaced it with a non-binding Council recommendation requiring notification, not authorization, of rDNA work so that, in the unlikely event of a problem, the origin of the contamination could be traced. This policy change was made in light of the accumulation of experimental evidence in the USA and the UK which indicated that some of the initial fears related to rDNA research had been overblown. In addition, there was a growing belief that legislation was not needed as long as guidelines were in place (Cantley 1995: 518–19). The recommendation was approved by the EP after a lengthy debate and adopted by the Council in June 1982. Key European science organizations, including the European Science Foundation (ESF), the European Molecular Biology Organization (EMBO), and the European Federation of Biotechnology (EFB), agreed with this approach. By July 1983 biotechnology had been incorporated into DG XII's Framework Programme, a multi-year, comprehensive research and development programme. The policy debate on biotechnology was, however, far from over.

In 1983 the Commission itself became concerned that the EU was falling behind Japan and the USA in the development of bio-industries, and therefore, in October 1983, submitted a new Communication to the Council (Commission 1983). This Communication outlined priority objectives for increasing the competitiveness of Europe's bio-industries. It also stated that, because the public and the EP were divided between admiration of the new discoveries and concern for their conjectural risks, it was the role of the Commission to ensure the maintenance of rational standards of public safety, and to monitor the social dimensions of biotechnology and their interfaces with policy. The Communication stated that the application of current Community regulations in the various fields (pharmaceuticals, veterinary medicines, chemical substances, food additives, and bioprotein feedstuffs) appeared to meet regulatory needs provided that there was close cooperation between the Competent Authorities in the member states and the Commission.[5] The 1983 Communication did not call for a horizontal, overarching, regulatory policy which would apply to research in any area using biotechnological processes. Although it recognized the need to take into account the social dimensions of biotechnology policy, the Commission in no way anticipated the degree of social contention which would come to characterize the biotechnology debate over the next fifteen years.

International organizations

The debate about how to regulate biotechnology was taking place not only in international scientific fora, but also among policy-makers in the OECD. In 1983 the OECD's Committee for Scientific and Technological Policy created an *ad hoc* Group of National Experts (GNE) on Safety and Regulation in Biotechnology. This was composed of eighty experts from a wide variety of academic and professional backgrounds, including representatives from the scientific research community and industry, and a wide variety of administrative agencies dealing with science and technology, environment, and public health. In 1986 the GNE reached a consensus on guidelines to be used in biotechnology research, and published them in a report called *Recombinant DNA Safety Considerations* (OECD 1986).

The OECD report found that the vast majority of industrial rDNA applications were of intrinsically low risk and warranted only limited containment consistent with good industrial large-scale practices. The report concluded that 'there was no scientific basis for specific legislation to regulate the use of rDNA organisms' (OECD 1986: 7–8). Instead, the report established a set of guidelines for conducting research. Although the guidelines were not formally binding, the OECD member states stated their commitment to the common scientific framework set out in the report.

National legislation

In the same period some of the member governments of the EU were beginning to develop their own guidelines and regulations. National attitudes about biotechnology varied widely among member states, as their initial attempts to develop biotechnology guidelines and regulations reflected. For instance, in Denmark and Germany the public perceived genetic engineering to be very risky. Consequently, Denmark enacted in June of 1986 one of the first, and most restrictive, gene laws in the EU.

The Danish *Environment and Gene Technology Act* served as a primary model for the EU directives that would be adopted in 1990, in three ways. First, it set a precedent for legislating on the basis of a production technique, genetic modification, rather than on the safety, quality, and efficacy of a specific product. In doing so, the Act totally ignored the findings of the OECD and the ESF, which stated that there was no scientific justification whatsoever for legislation specific for rDNA research. Secondly, the Danish legislation attributed to the Minister of the Environment (rather than a Minister for Research, Technology, or Industry) the primary responsibility for its administration. Finally, the Act required the Minister of the Environment to consult with other ministries, nationwide trade and industrial organizations, consumer organizations, and municipal organizations that would be affected, a prescription for horizontal coordination which would be adopted in a somewhat modified form by the EU. Although fairly restrictive, the Danish Gene Act did establish a review process for the law.

The environment of biotechnology policy in Germany was, and is, extremely contentious. On one hand, the German chemical and pharmaceutical industry, including among others BASF, Bayer, Böhringer Ingelheim, Hoechst, Roussel-Uclaf, and Scherring, is one of the strongest in Europe and the world. On the other hand,

German public opinion shows a deep and abiding concern about the ethical aspects of biotechnology, especially as regards human genetic engineering, including both somatic and germline therapy.[6]

The political success of the Greens in 1983 catalysed a nationwide debate about the risks and ethical considerations of biotechnology research. In 1984 the Bundestag launched an inquiry on the 'Prospects for Gene Technology' which came to be known as the Catenhusen Commission. This Commission was charged with, among other things, investigating possible conflicts between the constitutionally guaranteed freedom of research and other basic rights, exploring criteria for limiting the application of biotechnology on human cells, and producing recommendations for safety standards for industrial applications. After two years of work the Catenhusen Commission recommended that the existing Federal Law on Epidemics should be extended to cover biotechnology and renamed the Law on the Regulation of Biological Safety. In doing so, it rejected a total ban on biotechnology research, although it called for legally binding safety guidelines, much to the dismay of the German chemical manufacturers' association, DECHEMA, which had argued that various sectoral regulations concerning pharmaceuticals, agriculture, food, and chemicals could be modified to accommodate biotechnology research.

The Greens, disagreeing with the Catenhusen Commission and acting in defiance of the unanimously agreed rules of procedure for minority reports, submitted a lengthy document to the Commission one day before the final session and simultaneously released it to the press. They argued that the federal government should: first, stop any application of genetic engineering that was not supported by a broad consensus of society; and, secondly, set up a wide-ranging system of Commissions at local, regional, and national levels to review proposed research plans and to monitor them for adherence to safety regulations and ethical, social, and ecological restrictions. The Greens' document was included in the final Catenhusen Report in order to make it harder for the Greens to present themselves as a persecuted minority (Cantley 1995: 583). The Germans did not, however, enact a gene law until 1990. By that time the EU legislative debate was well under way and the domestic debate in Germany had been transferred to the EP via German members of the EP (MEPs).

The UK and France took a different approach to regulating biotechnology research. The discovery of the double helical structure of DNA occurred in Britain and, since that discovery, the UK has been a major player both in biotechnological research and development and in the definition of appropriate regulatory statutes. In 1977 the UK established the Genetic Manipulation Advisory Group (GMAG) in the Department of Education and Science to maintain surveillance of work involving genetic manipulation. The GMAG's primary contribution was to establish a risk assessment scheme for various types of rDNA research. Categorization of experiments was carried out by local biological safety committees.[7] However, most research fell into the first category, which required only 'good microbiological practice', and this allowed scientists in the UK to continue their work with minimal disruption. The GMAG risk assessment scheme was given statutory force under the existing 1974 *Act on Health and Safety in the Workplace* and focused on getting the right balance between caution and progress. The Act required employers to limit risk and exposure to their employees and to the general public. In essence, the Act required the employer to make a cost–risk analysis and to assess, on the one hand, the risk of the work, and on the other hand, the difficulty and expense involved in avoiding that risk. Thus the emphasis was largely on self-regulation (UK, Laboratory of the Government Chemist, 1991: 19).

France is the home of several well-known research institutes in the biological sciences including the *Institut Pasteur* and the *Institut National pour l'Enseignement et la Recherche Médicale* (INSERM). France pursued a very different regulatory strategy from Denmark and Germany. Until 1989 the French system was, in effect, one of self-control by the scientific community. The applicant for a project would propose a level of risk classification and complete a questionnaire. The application was turned over to a committee composed entirely of scientists. This committee would review the training of the researcher and the existence of a local oversight committee and would decide upon the confinement category required (Cantley 1995: 590).

Several important points are clear from analysing the various regulatory measures being taken in the member states.[8] First, there were conflicting views among the member states about whether guidelines or regulations were required. At one extreme, Denmark and Germany were beginning to institute programmes of government regulations. At the other extreme, the UK and France were employing a system of monitored self-regulation. Secondly, the ability of scientists to influence the policy process varied across member states. Denmark essentially ignored the advice of the ESF. The UK and Germany formed committees which were composed of a combination of bureaucrats, politicians, and scientists. And, until 1989, France utilized an oversight committee composed primarily of scientists. Thirdly, safety issues had become politicized to various extents across these countries, with the Greens in Germany representing the most extreme case of anti-biotechnology campaigning.[9] Fourthly, from a procedural point of view, companies and research labs in these different member states had to follow a wide variety of notification and containment procedures. These varying approaches towards regulation raised the unpleasant possibility of a highly fragmented system of regulations and markets within the EU.

The European Parliament

The EP has been actively involved in the biotechnology policy-making process from the beginning. Its recommendations and amendments often reflect a sort of push–pull tension between expertise and populism. This was evident in the earliest EP reports. In 1986 the Parliament's Committee on Energy, Research, and Technology decided to prepare an 'own initiative' report on biotechnology, known as the Viehoff Report after its *rapporteur*, Mrs Phili Viehoff, a Dutch Socialist MEP. Opinions and formal input into the report came from six parliamentary committees, including: Research and Technology; Agriculture and Food; Environment and Consumer Protection; Economic Affairs and Industrial Policy; Social Affairs and Employment; and Legal Affairs and Citizens' Rights. The final report was adopted by the plenary session in February 1987. The Viehoff Report recognized the vast potential of biotechnology to contribute to socially useful products in medical, agricultural, and environmental areas. It also made frequent mention of the risks involved. Specifically, the report called on the Commission to give priority to studying the problems posed by the potential release into the environment of genetically engineered micro-organisms and demanded that such releases be banned until binding Community safety directives had been drawn up. The report also called for the harmonization of member states' provisions with regard to safety and the environment to provide for common procedures for risk assessment (European Parliament 1987).

As a result of these simultaneous policy developments at different levels of policy-making, the Commission submitted a communication to the Council entitled *A Community Framework for the Regulation of Biotechnology* in November 1986 (Commission 1986). This communication made extensive reference to the OECD Blue Book. It also stated that care should be taken to achieve a measure of harmonization with other countries and that the regulatory framework should provide a clear, rational, and evolving basis for the development of biotechnology. In order to achieve these goals, the Commission stated its intention to draft proposals for legislation on genetically modified organisms (GMOs) by the summer of 1987. The communication did not, however, indicate which DG would draft the guidelines or directives or how the interests of the other DGs would be incorporated into the policy-making process.

Conflict and coordination within the Commission

Biotechnology policy cuts across several sectors. Consequently, it is of considerable interest to a wide variety of DGs including DGs I (External Relations), III (Industrial Affairs), V (Employment, Social Affairs, and Education), VI (Agriculture), XI (Environment, Nuclear Safety, and Civil Protection), XII (Science, Research, and Development), XV (Internal Market), and XXIV (Consumer Policy) (see Table 12.1). Each of these DGs represents a different client base, is embedded in different policy networks, has a different institutional mandate and different standard operating procedures, and is concerned with a slightly different product or problem area related to the use of biotechnology. In addition, these DGs have widely differing beliefs and perceptions about biotechnology and the extent to which biotechnological products and processes require regulation. The process by which these various sub-cultures were merged (or not merged, as the case may be) is critical to understanding the development of EU biotechnology regulations.

Ideological conflict within the Commission

It is not particularly surprising that different DGs have approached the biotechnology regulatory question from different perspectives. A better assessment of these various perspectives can be made by exploring how the four DGs most heavily involved in the policy-making process answered the questions outlined in Box 12.1.

The first question underlies what has come to be known as the product–process debate and is critically important to the regulatory debate. It has two components: the research component and the marketing component. From a research perspective, one must ask if there is anything inherently more dangerous about using genetic modification processes in the laboratory than using traditional biological, chemical, and radiation processes. From a marketing perspective, one must ask if products

---

Table 12.1 The Commission's range of interests in biotechnology

Directorate-General	Areas of competence related to biotechnology
DG I: External Relations	OECD Trade Group; GATT negotiations; international agreements; trade issues
DG III: Industrial Affairs	Industrial affairs in biotech-related sectors: agro-food, chemicals, pharmaceuticals, veterinary medicines, timber and wood products; related regulatory regimes; international–bilateral discussions
DG V: Employment, Social Affairs, and Education	Use of Social Fund; worker safety in biotech industries and agriculture; employment impact of biotech
DG VI: Agriculture	Current or potential impacts on most aspects of plant and animal production; inputs to agriculture; impacts of substitution conversion technologies on competition and trade; agricultural legislation (crop products, animal nutrition, veterinary and zoological legislation, crop regimes, quotas, prices, disease control)
DG XI: Environment, Nuclear Safety, and Civil Protection	Impact of biotechnology on the environment; contained use and deliberate release of GMOs
DG XII: Science, Research, and Development	Research programmes in biotechnology and in many areas of applied life sciences; science and technology for development; rDNA registration; bio-ethics; international scientific relations
DG XV: Internal Market	Intellectual property rights
DG XXIV: Consumer Policy Service	Consumer protection

Source: Derived from Commission DG XII (1985*a*).

Box 12.1 Key questions for the regulation of biotechnology

1. Do genetically modified organisms (GMOs) require special regulations at either the research or marketing stage on the grounds that they are unique by virtue of being produced by a unique process?
2. If regulation is necessary, should it be conducted via a vertical or horizontal regulatory process?
3. Should regulations reflect the precautionary principle or the preventive approach?

---

resulting from genetic modification constitute a distinct class of products requiring a separate regulatory framework for marketing or if these products should be evaluated for safety, quality, and efficacy in the same manner as comparable products produced by different methods.

The second question deals with whether legislation should be vertical or horizontal in nature. If one believes that tomatoes, no matter how they are produced, should meet the same standards of quality and safety, then all tomatoes can be regulated via a vertical framework administered by DG VI. However, if one believes that GMOs are inherently different and constitute a class of products unto themselves, then one would argue for a horizontal directive which cuts across all sectors and applies equally to genetically modified tomatoes, pharmaceuticals, medical devices, pesticides, and vaccines.

The third question revolves around two opposing philosophies of regulation: the precautionary principle and the preventive approach. The precautionary principle is a conservative approach to risk in which regulation anticipates the sort of environmental harm which has not already been documented for a given category of products and which does not take into consideration the relative costs and benefits of regulation to industry and the public. Those advocating a precautionary approach argue that this is necessary to protect the environment from potentially catastrophic events. The possibility of the occurrence of such an event is heightened by both the complexity of eco-systems, which precludes unambiguous identification of cause–effect relations, and by our lack of experience with GMOs, which makes us uncertain about what their impact on eco-systems will actually be (Tait and Levidow 1992: 223). In contrast, a preventive approach seeks to respond to:

scientifically proven adverse impacts that have arisen in earlier generations of products. New products and processes are screened to ensure that they do not give rise to any similar hazards. The regulatory system is built up slowly . . . Decisions about the need for regulation and the level of regulation required are taken in relation to the relevant benefits and costs. (Tait and Levidow 1992: 221)

The fundamental policy problem was that the four DGs most involved in the policy-making process took different positions on these questions (see Table 12.2). For instance, DG XII believed that regulations should be product-based, vertical and preventive, while DG XI thought that regulations should be process-based, horizontal and precautionary.[10]

DG XII's policy frame largely reflected its close contact with the scientific com-

Table 12.2 Conflicting positions on how biotechnology should be regulated

Basis of regulation	Regulation based on safety, quality, and efficacy of product	Regulation based on process by which product is produced
Type of regulation	Vertical regulation—existing sectoral regulations can be modified to ensure human and environmental safety of new biotech products	Horizontal regulation—new cross-cutting regulations need to be adopted to ensure a basic level of human and environmental safety
Philosophy of regulation	Preventive—less conservative regulatory approach which attempts to minimize environmental harm only after existence of harm has been scientifically proven	Precautionary—conservative regulatory approach in which regulation anticipates environmental hazards which have not already been documented but which could conceivably occur

munity composed primarily of biologists and microbiologists who were well versed in the characteristics of specific organisms. The vast majority of these scientists argued that there were no unique bio-hazards associated with rDNA research. Therefore, no specific regulations were required at either the research or marketing stages. Rather researchers should utilize traditional standard operating procedures for dealing with microbes, and large-scale industrial applications should follow the good industrial large-scale practice (GILSP) outlined in the OECD's (1986) *Recombinant DNA Safety Considerations*. If it were deemed necessary to pass some sort of European legislation to assuage public and political concerns, a system of national registration and monitoring with an information exchange at the European level could be passed, as outlined in the 1982 Council recommendation. DG XII also argued that once a product was developed, it should be evaluated on the basis of the qualities of that product, not on the basis of how the product was produced. This could best be accomplished through the application of vertical legislation. Finally, DG XII advocated taking a preventive approach where accumulated knowledge could be used to predict outcomes.

DG XI, on the other hand, took a very different approach. Whereas DG XII is located largely in the network of biologists and microbiologists, DG XI is located in the network of ecologists and environmental interest groups. DG XI tends to view GMOs as unique because they have not occurred via natural mutation. In a widely distributed pamphlet DG XI justifies the need for Community-wide regulatory directives by stating that:

the new techniques of genetic engineering allow the identification of many useful genes and their transfer to other organisms which didn't possess them before. Biological barriers are bypassed and new organisms are created with novel properties not previously existing in nature. Micro-organisms with novel properties could cause adverse effects in the environment if they survive and establish themselves, out-competing existing species or transferring their novel traits to other organisms. (Commission, DG XI/A/2 Biotechnology, n.d.)

Consequently, DG XI advocated the development of horizontal legislation for several reasons. First, because biotechnological products were unique, cross-cutting legislation to deal with them was necessary. Secondly, there was an increasing public phobia about the technology. To allay this, DG XI believed it was necessary to pass a special directive which would assure the public that everything was well regulated, controlled, and contained. Finally, DG XI advocated a horizontal approach as a measure which would fill in the gaps left by the various vertical directives. Using Levidow and Tait's definition of precautionary and preventive, DG XI leaned more towards a precautionary approach than a preventive approach (although the actual word used in the directive is 'preventive') because DG XI argued that the precise nature and scale of risks associated with GMOs were not fully known. They did, however, acknowledge that there were different types of operation and some were more risky than others.

DGs III and VI have a long history of regulating and interacting with producers in specific sectors. To them biotechnology was just a different technology for producing products which would fall under their long-established domains. In general, DGs III and VI tend to believe that a technology is not something which exists on its own, but rather that its relevance is in its use as a new and improved route to the manufacture of products. From a regulatory point of view, it was the product rather than the technology which was important (Commission 1985*b*). Thus they argued that it was not necessary to develop new regulations for the protection of humans and the environment, since existing regulations were quite adequate to cope with biotechnology products and could be easily adapted as necessary. Both services agreed that it was necessary to protect the environment and human health; they argued that they were in the best position to do this, because they could apply the knowledge they had gained through regulating similar products. Thus they advocated a preventive approach, and they were quite clear that industry believed that rash and unnecessary regulation would be a major disincentive to increased investment in biotechnology.

Turf conflict

Superimposed upon these major philosophical differences was an old-fashioned bureaucratic politics fight. No DG wanted to cede autonomy and regulatory authority to another in an area which it believed fell squarely into its own policy domain. Turf claims to biotechnology policy were exacerbated by the passage of the Single European Act (SEA), which allowed each DG to refer to a different treaty base for its involvement in biotechnology. As Anand Menon and Jack Hayward (1996: 273) note, 'Divisions within the Commission engender further confusion and ambiguity when vague Treaty stipulations are operationalized.' DG XII and DG III argued that their participation was justified by Article 130f (now 163) (SEA), which states that:

The Community shall have the objective of strengthening the scientific and technological bases of Community industry and encouraging it to become more competitive at international level, while promoting all the research activities deemed necessary by virtue of other Chapters of this Treaty.

DG XII focused on its role in strengthening the scientific base and DG III focused on improving the competitiveness of European industry. DG XI argued that its participation was justified by Article 130r.1 (now 174.1) (SEA), which states that:

Community policy on the environment shall contribute to pursuit of the following objectives: preserving, protecting and improving the quality of the environment; protecting human health; prudent and rational utilization of resources; promoting measures at international level to deal with regional or worldwide environmental problems.

Furthermore, DG XI noted that Article 100a (SEA) states that:

the Commission in its proposals envisaged in paragraph 1 concerning health, safety, environmental protection and consumer protection, will take as a base a high level of protection.

What distinguished the debate about biotechnology regulatory policy from other examples of bureaucratic politics was that there was little room for compromise, trade-offs, and side-payments because of the existence of very strong and widely divergent world-views about the potential harm that biotechnology posed for humankind and the environment in general.

Early attempts at cooperation

Given these ideological differences and turf conflicts, the problem was how to establish an institutional mechanism which would facilitate intra-DG coordination. The cross-cutting nature of biotechnology called for an institutional paradigm shift from the traditional vertical division of DGs according to sectoral specialisms such as agriculture, industry, and the environment, to a new, horizontal, cross-cutting approach to policy-making. Three institutional attempts to create a cooperative policy environment within the Commission were made. Unfortunately, the first two were dismal failures.

In early 1984 Vice-President Davignon (Research and Development and Industrial Affairs), together with Commissioners Dalsager (Agriculture) and Narjes (Internal Market) put forward a Commission paper calling for internal coordination for biotechnology, and the Biotechnology Steering Committee (BSC) was formed. The BSC was comprised of the heads of DGs III, VI, XII, and XIII (Information Market and Innovation) and was to be open to other DGs when their interests were concerned (see Table 12.3). DG XI was notably absent in the initial organization of the BSC. At that time there was no legal basis for environmental regulation. However, as talk of regulating the contained use and deliberate release of GMOs became more pronounced in 1985, DG XI did start attending the BSC meetings.

The BSC was established to provide a forum for discussion at Director-General level. It was not a decision-making body. Thus the BSC fell into the dialogic tradition in which a public space is created for open deliberation about facts and values. From a governance point of view, the goal of such a body is discursive steering (Linder and Peters 1995). Unfortunately, the BSC failed, primarily because its members were used to making decisions rather than merely discussing policy alternatives. As Cantley (1995: 534) notes, 'the time pressures on senior staff in the Commission made them reluctant to devote time to a mere "debating club". The consequence was the dilution of participation to a more junior level as the years went by and a declining frequency of meetings.'

It became evident that consideration of regulatory options would involve a highly technical discussion which was outside the purview of the Directors-General. Consequently, in July 1985 the BSC agreed to establish the Biotechnology Regulations Inter-service Committee (BRIC), to serve as its technical agent. Although the BSC remained, in theory, the parent of BRIC and was to resolve any disputes within it, in reality BRIC became the centre of biotechnology policy development within the Commission between 1985 and 1990. Although BRIC was intended to serve a coordinating function, each of the individual services was to retain its executive function in the examination, initiation, and management of regulations. The chairmanship of the committee was to alternate between DG III and DG XI. DG XII's Concertation Unit for Biotechnology in Europe (CUBE) was to serve as the Secretariat (Commission, DG XII, 1985b).

As mentioned above, in November 1986 the Commission submitted a Communication to the Council entitled *A Community Framework for the Regulation of Biotechnology* (Commission 1986). This document opened with the statement that there was no *a priori* reason to believe that the use of genetic modification would entail any extra or new risks. Nevertheless, the Commission stated its intention to introduce proposals for Community regulation of biotechnology by summer 1987. These would take account of (1) regulatory action being taken by several of the member states; (2) the belief set out in a report by the agrochemical, pharmaceutical, and food industries that there was a need for Community-wide regulation of biotechnology; and (3) the

Table 12.3 Mechanisms for coordination within the Commission

Date operational	1984–8	1985–1990	1990 onwards
Committee	Biotechnology Steering Committee (BSC)	Biotechnology Regulatory Inter-services Committee (BRIC)	Biotechnology Coordinating Committee (BCC)
Members	DGs III, VI, XII, XIII, and other concerned DGs	DGs III, V, VI, XI, XII, and other concerned DGs and services	DGs I, III, V, VI, XI, XII, XIII, XV, and other concerned DGs and services
Chair	DG XII	To alternate between D III and DG XI	Secretary-General
Secretariat	Concertation Unit for Biotechnology in DG XII	Concertation Unit for Biotechnology in DG XII	Secretariat-General
Mandate	To establish internal communication and concertation network	1. To identify and review existing laws and regulations that may govern commercial applications of biotechnology 2. To review guidelines for rDNA research 3. To clarify the regulatory path that products must follow 4. To determine whether current regulations adequately deal with risk and initiate specific actions where regulatory measures are deemed necessary 5. To ensure the coherence of scientific data which will form the basis of risk assessment and avoid unnecessary duplication of testing between services	1. To discuss new initiatives and prepare policy decisions on all aspects related to biotechnology 2. To verify any biotechnology proposal against policy objectives 3. To develop internal guidelines on broad issues to do with biotechnology such as how to combine the 'horizontal' and the product-by-product approach without creating excessive burdens for industry 4. To solve problems of inter-service overlap 5. To coordinate Commission standpoints to be taken at meetings held with other EU institutions, countries, and organizations 6. To set up a system of round tables between Commission services and industry representatives

fact that micro-organisms do not respect national frontiers. The proposals would deal with levels of physical and biological containment, accident control, and waste management in industrial applications; this eventually became Directive 90/219 on the contained use of genetically modified micro-organisms. They would also deal with authorization of planned release of genetically engineered organisms into the environment; this became Directive 90/220 on the deliberate release of GMOs into the environment.

A key factor in determining policy outcomes is which DG is *chef de file*, a term referring to the service which is given primary responsibility for drafting a directive. DGs III and XI were co-*chef de file* for the directive on the contained use of GMOs, and DG XI was *chef de file* for regulating the deliberate release of GMOs into the environment. The role of *chef de file* is extremely important for two reasons. First, the *chef de file* drafts the directive and, in doing so, sets the terms of the debate. When staff in DG XII saw DG XI's draft proposal for regulating the deliberate release of GMOs into the environment, they were extremely upset and submitted an alternative draft directive to DG XI, focusing on a system of national registration and monitoring with information exchange at the Community level. However, because DG XII was not *chef de file*, its proposal was ignored. Secondly, the service which is *chef de file* defines how the directive is presented to the Council of Ministers. Because DG XI was *chef de file*, the directives went before the Council of Environment Ministers. These ministers, in general, shared the same ideological outlook on the matter as DG XI. Thus, while an individual service is supposed to represent the Commission at large to the Council, in reality there is a functional connection across institutions which may supersede any compromises that may have been made at the inter-service level. Within BRIC DG XII's role was to provide scientific input into the regulatory debates and DG VI was to provide agricultural input. There was no initial controversy over this division of labour.

In reality, DG XI was essentially given free rein to draft the directives with very little input from DG III until very late on. DG III's participation was limited by understaffing and increased responsibilities related to the pending passage of the SEA. Consequently, DG III agreed, under pressure from DG XI, to the terms of the Communication to the Council which said the Commission was going to develop horizontal directives. DG III did insist on co-authoring the legislation on contained use, since that was going to affect industry most immediately. However, DG XI did most of the actual drafting, and the directive went before the Council of Environment Ministers.[11]

Industry, which would be heavily affected by any regulatory framework, was curiously absent in the initial stages of policy formation. Greenwood and Ronit (1995) point to several reasons for this. First, companies were slow to identify themselves as bio-industries on the basis of utilizing a specific technique. Industrialists were accustomed to using a variety of techniques and processes and in the past had formed lobby groups which approached the regulatory process on the basis of categories of products, not techniques. Consequently, there was a significant lag between the formulation of horizontal directives and industry's ability to organize in response to the directives. Secondly, this problem was exacerbated by the existence of many small and medium-sized enterprises (SMEs), all of which were at the initial stages of the product innovation cycle. Because of the many firms involved and the high degree of competition between them, there was a significant collective action problem. Thirdly, even among those who were aware of the likely shift from product-based to process-based regulation, 'there was a view among industrial interests that to coordinate too closely by abandoning sectoral representation and using only dedicated bio-industry associations would be a mistake because it would invite industry to be drawn into accepting horizontal regulation' (Greenwood and Ronit 1995: 36). Fourthly, the existence of both SMEs and large chemical and pharmaceutical companies led to a certain degree of fragmentation of views across companies as regards what would be proper and non-burdensome levels of regulation.

In sum, industrialists were focused on traditional product legislation rather than process-driven legislation. They were slow to make the paradigm shift, and consequently they were slow to coordinate their efforts with other firms across sectors. They had also been lulled into a false sense of security because DGIII and DGVI had succeeded in having their traditional product areas, including pharmaceuticals, animal feedstuffs, plant protection products and novel foods, excluded from the draft horizontal directives. Thus firms within traditional sectors thought their voice was being heard. However, that was not the end of the story.

DGXII, which had very strong reservations about horizontal legislation, was not able to sway the debate against introducing horizontal legislation. The CUBE staff believed that horizontal directives were unnecessary, and, if adopted, would unduly stigmatize biotechnology, a critical research technology for the life sciences. However, the Director General of DGXII, Paolo Fasello, did not enjoy a great deal of support from his Commissioner, Filippo Pandolfi, who believed that the biotech directives would never become operational. Consequently, Fasello preferred to focus his attention on running the EU's research programmes.[12]

Directives 90/219 and 90/220

DGXI was primarily responsible for drafting both Directives 90/219 (Contained Use) and 90/220 (Deliberate Release). The BRIC had little influence on the final form of the proposals. The few compromises that were made in BRIC were essentially eliminated when DGXI took the draft directives before the Council of Environmental Ministers.

For instance, the original proposal for a Council Directive on the contained use of genetically modified micro-organisms had as its legal basis Article 100a (now 95) (SEA). Late in the negotiations the legal basis was changed in the Council from 100a to 130s (now 175), when it became clear that unanimity among the environment ministers was possible. This had two consequences: first, it shifted the primary rationale for the directive from the need to create an internal market to the need to protect the environment and human health. (Of course, the need for an internal market remained as a secondary reason for the directive.) This allowed environment ministers to take a more precautionary approach. Secondly, it allowed individual member governments to exceed the EU directive if they wanted. Thus the emphasis shifted from establishing a common level of protection to establishing a floor for protection. In addition, the notification requirements were substantially lengthened and the final directive agreed in the Council of Ministers contained a new Appendix A, which provided a list of techniques through which genetic modification occurred. This annexe locked in the concept of process-based regulation.

Similar, and in some senses more startling, changes were made in Directive 90/220 on the deliberate release into the environment of GMOs. Part C of this Directive deals with the placing on the market of products containing GMOs. Part C was necessary to justify a legal basis of 100a and it has caused the most problems for DGs III and VI. The original Commission proposal stated that Part C of Directive 90/220:

would *not* apply to medical products; veterinary products; foodstuffs, feedingstuffs and their additives; plants or animals produced or used in agriculture, horticulture, forestry, husbandry and fisheries, the reproductive material thereof and the products containing these organisms, or to any products covered by Community legislation which includes a specific risk assessment. (Commission 1988; my emphasis).

The inclusion of this paragraph was an attempt by the Commission to maintain a distinction between vertical and horizontal legislation. DG III fought bitterly to get this clause placed in the Directive and eventually succeeded in forcing it through the Commission over the protests of DG XI. DGs VI and XII were both aligned with DG III on this. If the products noted above were not included, the Directive could be viewed as a stopgap measure that would keep any product not covered under vertical legislation from falling through the cracks. This approach was acceptable to the members of BRIC.

However, this proposed Directive was also radically changed in the Council meeting. As with 90/219, an Appendix A was added, which defined what techniques constituted genetic modification. However, equally importantly, Part C was changed to read:

Consent may only be given for the placing on the market of products containing or consisting of GMOs provided that . . . the products comply with the relevant Community product legislation and the products comply with this part of the directive, concerning the environmental risk assessment. In the future, Part C would not apply to any products covered by Community legislation which provides for a specific environmental risk assessment *similar to that laid down in the Directive*. (my emphasis)

Consequently, *all products* containing GMOs had to meet not only the Community's relevant product legislation, but also process-based, environmental risk assessment requirements equal to or similar to those laid down in 90/220. Interestingly, this change in the Directive was advocated by the EP Committee on the Environment, Public Health, and Consumer Protection. As John Hodgson (1992) notes: 'There remains a suspicion, therefore, that the exclusion clause in the original document was just a way of getting the proposal out of the Commission and before Parliament and Council: the corollary of that suspicion is that the removal of the exclusion clause later was an act agreed upon by DG XI, the Council, and the Parliament.' In the meantime, both the industrialists and some DG III analysts argued that meeting the requirements of both horizontal and vertical legislation would be extremely burdensome and was largely unnecessary. In practice, however, DG XI had accomplished its goal of extending its influence over all products produced via genetic modification or containing GMOs.

Protest and institutional innovation

The ink had not dried on the paper before the EU fell under heavy criticism from scientists, industry, and the USA for the regulatory approach adopted in Directives

90/219 and 90/220. On 8 February 1990 the European Nobel Laureates in Medicine and Chemistry wrote to the Presidents of the EP, Council, and Commission to say:

Now that the two directives 'contained use' and 'deliberate release' have been carried by the EC Council and reviewed by the Environment Committee of the European Parliament, it appears to us that they contain a number of provisions relating to research which are both based on non-scientific criteria and so unduly burdensome as to be discouraging. (Cantley 1995: 561)

When industrialists became aware of the approach being taken by the Commission, they decided to form a high-level lobby group to address specifically the question of biotechnology regulation. This is consistent with Paul Pierson's observation (1993: 598–9) that 'the activity of interest groups often seems to follow rather than precede the adoption of public policies'. It is the policies that provide incentives that may facilitate the expansion of particular groups; in the case of biotechnology, the directives were viewed as so burdensome that they served as a catalyst for collective action at the EU level by industry.

The Senior Advisory Group for Biotechnology (SAGB) was created in June 1989 specifically to promote a supportive climate for biotechnology in Europe.[13] The founding members were Monsanto Europe, Hoechst AG, ICI PLC, the Ferruzzi Group, Rhône Poulenc, Sandoz, and Unilever. In August 1989 they sent a letter to President Delors and all the other Commissioners stating that they were concerned about: (1) 'the lack of overall coordination and resultant confusion in the proposals for regulation of biotechnology'; (2) the possible use of *ad hoc* solutions, such as moratoria (being recommended in the EP); and (3) the basis of product regulation, which they argued should be efficacy, safety, and quality (not the process by which a product was produced). They also called for the development of a relevant 'science based regulatory framework'.[14] The SAGB was not organized in time to affect the initial passage of the directives, but it did play an important role in the 1991 decision to revise the directives.

A final set of criticisms came from the US government, which had adopted a set of product-based, vertical, and preventive guidelines for biotechnology research and product release. Specifically, the US Food and Drug Administration and the US Ambassador to the European Communities expressed concern that the EU's process-based regulations would hinder research and development, would lead to difficulties in attempts to achieve international harmonization, and could be used to erect non-tariff trade barriers to foreign products (Cantley 1995: 559).

In response to the wide-ranging criticisms of Directives 90/219 and 90/220, President Delors asked his chief of staff, Pascal Lamy, to hold a meeting to discuss internal Commission coordination of biotechnology policy in July 1990. At the meeting agreement was reached that better coordination was needed and could be achieved if there were a single internal coordinating group, and if this group held a series of round tables with industry. (It should be noted that DG XI strenuously objected to the suggestion that inter-agency coordination had failed and that there was a need to institute a new coordinating body.) Thus the Biotechnology Coordinating Committee (BCC) was born and it was given the task of reviewing and elaborating the EU's biotechnology regulatory framework. The establishment of the BCC was an initiative largely driven by President Delors rather than by the Council or the member governments. However, the work of the BCC was generally supported by the Council of

Industry Ministers and many member governments.[15] David Williamson, Secretary General of the Commission, argued that DG III, not DG XI, should be the lead DG for coordination, but, given the history of the subject, he acknowledged that perhaps the Secretary-General should chair the coordinating group, at least in the beginning. The challenge faced by the BCC was somehow to move beyond the inherent conflict between the various DGs in order to create an environment of true policy coordination.

The BCC embodied two critically important structural innovations. First, by bringing all the relevant services together as a team under the leadership of the Secretary-General, the BCC became the technocratic counterpart to the college of Commissioners. Just as the college was concerned with a wide range of political issues, so the BCC was concerned with a wide range of technocratic issues related to biotechnology. This reframing of institutional status facilitated a major change in the way the various DGs thought about coordination. The college of Commissioners is supposed to take an aggregate and horizontal view of policy, while traditionally the DGs have been vertically oriented and policy area specific. The creation of the BCC, a horizontal body at the level of the services, required individual DGs to reframe their views of whom they served. In addition to serving their traditional clients, they would have simultaneously to consider a variety of issues, such as competitiveness, environmental protection, human health, and the ethical implications of some forms of biotechnology research.

Secondly, the appointment of the Secretary-General to the chairmanship of the committee brought a new degree of institutional and political standing to the coordination effort and formalized the coordination process. Although the core role of the Secretariat-General is to coordinate between the services, its staff is extremely busy. It can monitor, but cannot command, coordination between the services. However, the Secretary-General was able simultaneously and iteratively to broker deals in the BCC among the various players at both the technocratic and political levels. His influence was buttressed by his role in chairing the weekly meetings of the *chefs de cabinet* of the Commissioners, where many critical political issues are resolved, and by his direct contact with the President of the Commission.[16]

Elaboration and reform of biotechnology policy

The reform process of the EU's biotechnology regulatory framework illustrates the tension between institutional innovation within the Commission and path-dependency, and the effect of bottlenecks imposed by political debates in the other institutions. The BCC was already limited in its ability to initiate policy reforms by the existence of Directives 90/219 and 90/220. In addition, the BCC was constrained by the wider political context in which it operated. Political debates in the Council, the EP, and on occasion in the college of Commissioners slowed the momentum of reform and on numerous occasions threatened to bring the reform process to an abrupt halt.

In April 1991 the Commission sent a Communication to the EP and the Council entitled *Promoting a Competitive Environment for Industrial Activities Based on Biotechnology within the Community* (Commission 1991a). This had been drafted largely by the BCC, and had three main goals: (1) to ensure a coherent regulatory approach and an efficient and simplified interaction between sectoral and horizontal legislation; (2) to ensure existing legislation is kept under review to reflect rapid developments and technical and scientific progress; and (3) to streamline testing and authorization procedures required for biotech products. The Greens in the EP did not view this Communication favourably. They claimed that the Commission was placing too much emphasis on ensuring the competitiveness of industry, and not enough emphasis on the social, ethical, and environmental considerations related to biotechnology.

The reform effort received added impetus when biotechnology was included in the White Paper on Growth, Competitiveness, and Employment (Commission 1993d), largely due to the efforts of Martin Bangemann, Commissioner responsible for industry. Germany had used Directive 90/219 as a regulatory floor and had instituted even more restrictive policies than it required. In addition, the rules were variously implemented by different *Länder*. This proved to be immensely frustrating for German industry. Because of the extremely negative public perception of biotechnology in Germany, several German industry representatives decided that advocating reform at the EU level would be more expedient than attempting to achieve reform at the German level. In addition, the UK House of Lords Select Committee on Science and Technology published a report entitled *Regulation of the United Kingdom Biotechnology Industry and Global Competitiveness* in July 1993 in which they were highly critical of the EU's biotechnology directives. Martin Bangemann was sympathetic to the complaints of his fellow countrymen and to the House of Lords, and hoped that the White Paper would propel the reform process forward and allow for serious reforms to take place during the German Council presidency at the end of 1994. Box 12.2 lists the main reform objectives outlined in the White Paper.

The White Paper was greeted with varying degrees of enthusiasm. It was supported by the SAGB as a first step forward. However, the British Health and Safety Executive (in juxtaposition to the House of Lords), the Danish Ministry of the Environment, and the EP's Committee on Energy, Research, and Technology varied in their reactions from moderately concerned to highly critical.

Reforming Directive 90/219 became the BCC's top regulatory priority, for which an *ad hoc* drafting group was formed, including representatives from DGs XI and III and three member states.[17] The revisions went through an extensive inter-DG

Box 12.2 Reform objectives outlined in the 1993 White Paper

- Review the regulatory framework to ensure that advances in scientific knowledge are constantly taken into account
- Harmonize the regulatory framework with international practice
- Make full use of the possibilities that already exist under the regulations to simplify procedures
- Increase public investment in biotechnology research and development
- Improve the climate for private investment
- Enhance public understanding of the technology
- Clarify value-laden issues in relation to some applications of biotechnology

consultation process. In addition, consultations were held with industry, environmental groups, scientific organizations, and trade unions. However, the environmental groups eventually boycotted meetings with the Commission, because they were afraid their involvement would imply agreement; they judged that by refusing to meet the Commission they could take their case to the enormously more sympathetic EP.

The final BCC proposal for reforms to Directive 90/219 was ready to go to the college of Commissioners in June 1995. However, a new college of Commissioners had been appointed in January 1995, and the overwhelming support for reform enjoyed by the BCC in 1994 evaporated. The new Commissioner in charge of the environment, Ritt Bjerregaard, was particularly hostile to the proposed reforms. She reportedly broke off all communications with the DG XI officials in the BCC who had been in charge of drafting the reforms and asked her *cabinet* to produce a new draft, which she presented to the Commission. In a most unusual display of divisiveness within the college, an infuriated Bangemann (Commissioner for DG III) and Cresson (Commissioner for DG XII) offered a counter-proposal along the lines of that originally drafted by DG XI and DG III and agreed to by the BCC. The matter came to a vote and the Bangemann–Cresson proposal was passed in December 1995. In order to maintain collegiality, positions taken by the various Commissioners on votes are usually kept confidential. However, in this case, details of this conflict became publicly known, illustrating how politically contentious is the question of how to regulate biotechnology appropriately.

After two readings in the EP, in keeping with the cooperation procedure, the final Directive amending 90/219 was adopted by the end of 1998 (*OJL* 330, 5 December 1998). The revisions were positively received as taking a more scientific approach by applying a risk-based classification of micro-organisms which was closer to international practice. However, the horizontal, process-based approach of the initial directive was left intact.

In June 1994 the Commission also announced its intention to review Directive 90/220. Originally, there was not the same sense of urgency surrounding this as there was surrounding 90/219, since there seemed to be broad agreement on the practical problems presented by 90/219, at a time when there was not much experience with the release of GMOs (except in the area of field trials of genetically modified plants). There were fewer specific complaints about Directive 90/220, and the Commission had already made a number of technical adaptations to the Directive to reflect the wide number of GMO releases in the plant area. Furthermore, DG III was co-*chef de file* with DG XI for Directive 90/219, but not for Directive 90/220. Consequently, it was more difficult for DG III to push for revisions to Directive 90/220.

However, the Commission's approval of the sale of imported genetically modified soya in April 1996 and maize in January 1997 from the USA under Directive 90/220 changed the policy environment. Two issues arose from this decision: first, whether the products should have been approved at all; and, secondly, whether they required labelling. These were addressed under the comitology procedures. Originally, the Commission voted in favour of allowing the imports. The Competent Authorities in Belgium, Finland, France, Ireland, Spain, and Portugal agreed with the Commission, while those in Austria, Sweden, Denmark, and the UK voted against the imports, with other member governments abstaining. The proposal was therefore referred to the

Environment Council, where the French government prevented the Council from reaching the unanimous vote required to amend the Commission proposal, and hence the decision reverted to the Commission. The Commission then consulted three scientific committees, and after receiving their opinions, proceeded to authorize the products. In addition, the US Food and Drug Administration had reviewed summary data provided by both Monsanto and Ciba-Geigy and determined that both products were safe to introduce into the market-place.[18] The Commission's decision was widely deplored by consumer groups, many non-governmental organizations (NGOs), and the EP (Bradley 1998: 207–22). For instance, the European Farmers' Coordination (CPE) urged European farmers and consumers to mobilize against the authorization of genetically engineered maize. They stated that the Commission's decision to allow the import of this product 'fails to take account of numerous warnings of farmers, environmentalists, and scientists, and is a provocation to consumers less than a year after the discovery of the mad cow crisis. The European Union is giving in to very strong pressure by the United States and the chemical, seed and genetic technology multinationals' (*Agence Europe*, 16 January 1997). In addition, Austria, Italy, and Luxembourg invoked the 90/220 safeguard clause and banned the importation of maize into their territory.

The original Commission decision not to require labelling was consistent with the Novel Foods Regulation which was under discussion at the time. This regulation, specifically intended to deal with genetically modified food products, was agreed in January 1997 and entered into force in May 1997. According to the regulation, only products containing live GMOs, or GMO-derived products that were no longer 'equivalent' to a traditional product, required labelling. Other products did not need to be labelled. Since both imported soya and maize were judged to be 'equivalent' to traditional products, neither was required to bear a label indicating that it had been genetically modified. However, there was a huge public outcry about the exemption for maize and soya; consumers demanded labelling, and many food retailers supported them. Some companies, such as Unilever, which uses 7.5 per cent of all EU imports of soya beans, simply refused to buy US soya beans.

The outcry in favour of labelling opened the door for DG XI to make a technical adaptation to Directive 90/220 in June 1997. This adaptation called for mandatory labelling of all genetically modified products approved for placing on the market under the Directive. In the case of products placed on the market with mixtures of non-genetically modified organisms, the label would indicate the possibility that GMOs might be present. Hence, DG XI used Directive 90/220 essentially to overturn the Novel Foods Regulation. Some industries, rather surprisingly, supported this adaptation, because they did not want to be held liable for failing to inform the public about what was in a product.

Directive 90/220 is now undergoing further modifications as a result of the public outcry against genetically modified maize and soya. Current proposals include: introducing mandatory monitoring after the placing on the market of products, linked to a consent granted for a fixed time period (seven to twelve years is currently under discussion) after which the consent must be renewed; introducing a procedure to consult formally a Scientific Committee before placing GMO products on the market; applying a IIIb comitology procedure for the regulatory committee, which would allow the Council to reject a Commission decision by a simple majority rather than a qualified majority (thus increasing the role of the member governments in the decision-making process); further broadening the labelling requirements; and improving the administrative procedures for release.

In general, industrialists have opposed these additional amendments, especially the one which would authorize products for only a fixed time period. Their concern is that these amendments will lead to obfuscation and long regulatory delays which are not scientifically justified. This, in turn, will undermine public confidence and discourage investment. On the other hand, consumers insist that they have a right to know what is in their food supply and what the effects are of releasing GMOs into the environment. The reform of 90/220 was not expected to be completed until the end of 1999.

In addition to power struggles within the Commission, the biotechnology regulatory debate has also been characterized by inter-institutional power struggles. The most blatant example of this can be seen in the EP's refusal to adopt the Commission's first text on intellectual property rights in this domain. This Directive, relating to patenting of genetic products, was not controversial within the Commission. In 1992 it went to the EP for a first reading and the Commission adopted many of the Parliament's amendments. In February 1994 the Council adopted a common position on the Directive. The EP, at its second reading of the Directive in May 1994, proposed three amendments, of which the Commission adopted two, but refused to adopt the third. In November 1994 a conciliation meeting between the Commission, Council, and EP, as directed by the Treaty on European Union (TEU), resolved the issue of the third amendment, after which the Commission expected the Directive to sail through the plenary session of Parliament. However, a new Parliament had been seated in January, many of whose members were unfamiliar with the preceding debates about the Directive. In addition, Greenpeace launched an explosive press campaign to dissuade MEPs from voting for the compromise text, reinforced by pressure from some Catholic organizations.

The EP rejected the compromise text by a vote of 240 to 188, with only 428 of 624 MEPs present. This rejection infuriated the Commission and the Council, because they had made strenuous efforts to reach agreement with the EP, and now they would have to draft a new directive and go though the entire legislative process again. Under the co-decision procedure established in the TEU, an agreement reached by the conciliation committee needs approval from the EP plenary by an absolute majority of the votes cast; otherwise the measure falls. In this case the 240 represented an absolute majority against the Directive. However, the TEU also specified that, when a conciliation committee failed to reach agreement, the EP could veto the common position to which the Council had agreed before the conciliation committee only by an absolute majority of its component members. Thus, had the Council refused to reach a compromise in conciliation with the EP, it would have taken over 312 votes for the EP to veto the Directive. Many officials in the Council and the Commission interpreted the EP's move as a power play meant to exert its new powers under the TEU. They had chosen to do this on a directive which had been extensively discussed with Parliament and was widely viewed as necessary by the Commission, Council, and industry to enhance European competitiveness in the area of biotechnology. A new directive for the protection of biological inventions finally entered into force in July 1998.

Conclusions

The biotechnology policy arena in the EU is tremendously complex. Institutional efforts to bridge the different social domains outlined above have been only partially successful. The Commission realized that new institutional mechanisms were necessary for dealing with cross-cutting policy issues, and hence they established the BCC under the leadership of the Secretary-General. While the BCC made several substantive improvements in the regulatory framework, it was constrained by the path-dependency which grew out of the process-based approach to regulation, which had been previously incorporated into Directives 90/219 and 90/220. The installation in 1995 of a new college of Commissioners, the increased legislative power of the EP after the passage of the TEU, and increasingly effective lobbying efforts by Greenpeace and other environmental NGOs were all factors in the process, as was, most importantly, the sustained public distrust both of scientific facts and of policy-makers who base regulations on scientific findings.

The existence of conflicting ideologies about whether to take a preventive or precautionary approach and the high degree of institutional infighting has also slowed down the reform process. Since agreement was so difficult to achieve initially, all parties have been reluctant to reopen the discussion of whether Directives 90/219 and 90/220 should be completely rewritten. Instead, an incremental approach to reform has been pursued, which does not fundamentally question the horizontal, process-based approach taken in the Directives. Even the incremental changes under discussion are fraught with conflict.

The resulting biotechnology regulatory framework has both social and economic consequences, including for trade. On the one hand, the availability of genetically modified foodstuffs has been limited, and the imposition of restrictive regulations has successfully limited the amount of genetic experimentation within the EU. Both of these achievements seem to meet the social goals of many Europeans. On the other hand, billions of research dollars are flowing out of Europe and into the USA, where there is a preventive, product-based regulatory system. Hence, the USA far exceeds the EU in the number of biotechnology patents. High value-added jobs have been created in the USA rather than the EU, and the USA is generally ahead of the EU in its trajectory of promoting biotechnology. This means that more products are coming to market, which are generating more money for research and encouraging further innovation and discovery. This has given the USA a competitive advantage in perhaps the most important field of technology for the twenty-first century. However, the EU may yet recoup. DG XII and many member governments have developed specific programmes to encourage research and development in biotechnology. Whether these programmes can outweigh the regulatory disincentives for investment and the generally negative public perception of biotechnology in the EU remains to be seen.

Finally, policy-makers on both sides of the Atlantic agree that the differences between the product-based regulatory system in the USA and the process-based regulatory system in the EU will lead to a wide variety of trade conflicts. The issue of labelling genetically modified foods is likely to come before the World Trade

Organisation in the near future. It is unclear whether the USA or the EU system will prevail. Certainly, as Stephen Woolcock points out in Chapter 14, the EU is becoming a powerful player in the international trade arena. However, much of the EU's success in influencing GMO trade issues will depend on its ability to craft cohesive policy positions which take into account the preferences of national governments, civil society, the EP, and the various DGs within the Commission.

Notes

1 Much of the material covered in this chapter was gathered as part of the author's dissertation research. She was located in the Office of the Secretary General in the Biotechnology Unit from August 1994 until July 1995, with access to high-level policy meetings, briefing papers, key policy makers, and archival files. Thanks are due to the Fulbright Foundation, the Social Science Research Council and the European Community Studies Association for funding this research.

2 The Organization for Economic Co-operation and Development (OECD) defines biotechnology as the application of scientific and engineering principles to the processing of materials by biological agents to provide goods and services (A. T. Bull et al. 1982: 21).

3 Some companies, such as Monsanto, have failed to recognize the strength and importance of popular opinion in the EU and consequently have suffered immense opposition to the introduction of their biotechnology products. Other companies, such as Unilever, have been more successful at balancing scientific evidence with popular opinion.

4 Biological containment involves crippling the plasmid vector and its bacterial host so that they will not be able to survive outside the laboratory.

5 Competent Authorities are officials in the member states who are involved in implementing EU legislation and are appointed to represent their countries in EU-wide discussions and clearance processes.

6 Somatic therapy applies to the body cells of a multicellular organism. Mutations in somatic cells do not generally play a significant role in evolution and are unlikely to be passed on to future generations of gametes. Germline cells are those that become differentiated from the somatic cell line and have the potential to undergo meiosis and form gametes. Thus genetic changes in these cells could be passed on to future generations.

7 Local safety committees had previously been established in 1974, when the UK adopted the Health and Safety at Work Act, implemented through the Health and Safety Executive and Factory Inspectorate.

8 Some other EU member governments had also begun to address the regulatory problems associated with biotechnology. The above-noted four have in their countries the headquarters of major multinational companies involved in biotechnology product development and were 'first movers' in the area of setting guidelines or developing regulations to monitor biotechnology research and development.

9 Sheila Jasanoff (1995: 324) has argued that the different approaches taken by the various governments reflect each

country's political culture and regulatory style. Specifically she states that: 'In Britain, regulators appeared initially more prepared to accept the process of genetic modification as the frame for policy making, with concurrent attention to the physical and social dimensions of risk . . . German political debate on biotechnology was unique in taking as its domain the entire programmatic relationship between technology and society, as mediated by the state, a position that led to a full blown discussion of risks.'

10 Shackley *et al.* (1990) make a similar argument about 'contending rationalities' between DGs XI and XII. They identify the main points of contention as the scope of the Deliberate Release Directive, the appropriate regulatory structure (product-based or process-based), and the interactions of political and scientific considerations.

11 Interview with former DG III official, 24 Feb. 1995.

12 Interview with former DG XII official, 8 Nov. 1998.

13 The SAGB is not the only industrial lobby group. National bio-industry associations representing smaller companies were co-ordinated through the European Secretariat of National Bio-industry Associations (ESNBA). Their aims were often in accordance with those of SAGB. On 27 Sep. 1996 SAGB and ESNBA merged into one organization.

14 Letter from the Senior Advisory Group on Biotechnology to Commission President Jacques Delors, 24 Aug. 1989.

15 For instance, several member governments, most notably from the Netherlands, the UK, France and Germany, supported the BCC's attempts at reform. The Danish government, on the other hand, saw little need for reform and, after 1995, was joined by those from Austria, Finland, and Sweden, since their national legislation was already stricter than the EU legislation.

16 Individual services have a route directly to the college of Commissioners via their own Commissioners. But between 1990 and 1995 many inter-service disputes were settled before they reached the level of the *cabinets*.

17 One national official noted that 'the drafting group was a separate, specialist body with particular kinds of Member States' representatives and Commission officials doing all the work . . . It was not the Community working the way you read about it in textbooks on how the Community comes to decisions.'

18 The FDA's policy on foods derived from new plant varieties can be found in the *Federal Register*, 29 May 1992, 57/22984.

Further reading

The following references will help to illuminate various aspects of the biotechnology regulatory debate. Cantley (1995) provides an excellent historical reference on the formulation of EU biotechnology policy between 1974 and 1995. Watson and Tooze (1981) is recommended for those who would like to read a comparative piece on the early development of biotechnology policy in the USA. Wildavsky (1991) outlines rival cultural views with respect to biotechnology. Bradley (1998) provides an excellent analysis of the institutional procedures which resulted in the decision to allow the import of genetically modified maize and soya. For more information on the biotech industry in Europe, see the Ernst and Young *Annual Reports* on the European biotechnology industry. These can be accessed on the internet at: www.eyi.com.

Bradley, K. St Clair (1998), 'The GMO-Committee on Transgenic Maize: Alien Corn, or the Transgenic Procedural Maze', in van Schendelen (1998: 207–22).

Cantley, M. (1995), 'The Regulation of Modern Biotechnology: A Historical and European Perspective. A Case Study in how Societies Cope with New Knowledge in the Last Quarter of the Twentieth Century', in H. J. Rehm and G. Reed (eds.) in co-operation with A. Pühler and P. Stadler (1995), *Biotechnology*, xii D. Brauer (ed.) *Legal, Economic and Ethical Dimensions*, 2nd edn. (Weinheim: VCH), 506–81.

Watson, J. D., and Tooze J. (1981), *The DNA Story: A Documentary History of Gene Cloning* (San Francisco, Calif: W. H. Freeman).

Wildavsky, A. (1991), 'Public Policy', in B. D. Davis, (1991) (ed.), *The Genetic Revolution: Scientific Prospects and Public Perceptions* (Baltimore: Johns Hopkins University Press), 77–104.

Chapter 13
The Common Fisheries Policy
Letting the Little Ones Go?

Christian Lequesne

Contents

Summary

Technological changes, extensions of territorial waters, and successive enlargements of the European Union (EU) have transformed the context since the common fisheries policy (CFP) was first designed in 1970. This is an economically insignificant field, employing some 270,000 throughout the EU15. Nevertheless, its political and social salience is high. There are sharp differences of interest, and of approach, not only among member governments but also within the major fishing countries. In addition to political, social, and economic factors, conservation of fish stocks has become a major preoccupation, articulated by an expert policy community of biologists and economists. The diversity of distinct and geographically concentrated fishing communities has made it difficult for an EU-wide lobby to emerge; instead interests are mobilized locally. A nominally common policy has been implemented in very different ways within different member countries and regions. In recent years challenges to national fisheries regulation have accounted for a rising number of European Court of Justice (ECJ) cases. Negotiations with third countries over access to fishing-grounds have also become a significant aspect of the EU's external relations, and eastern enlargement, bringing in Polish and Baltic fishing fleets, presents a further challenge.

Introduction

A common fisheries policy (CFP) has been on the agenda of the EU since 1970.[1] Although it appears at first sight to be a technical area which affects few European citizens, this policy has not fulfilled the predictions of neofunctionalist theorists, who saw the process of European integration as a matter of experts pooling their problems in order to produce rational compromises. Instead, the CFP shows that the EU has not enabled expertise to supplant politics and politicians. Alongside the Commission officials, who endeavour to preserve fish stocks on the basis of scientific opinion, the CFP illustrates, above all, that the EU is a new arena for the negotiation of compromises between governments and the social actors. These actors comprise not only fishermen, but also manufacturers in the fish-processing industry, consumers, and environmentalists, who occasionally obtain additional resources from the EU for representing their interests. Moreover, the CFP shows that European integration cannot be studied and understood without taking a series of factors into account, such as: the implementation of the CFP in areas where market forces have not erased the idiosyncrasies of the sector; the globalization of trade; the role of borders (both terrestrial and maritime); and the importance of history and of symbols in the process of moulding the interests on the European scene.

The CFP operates not through a transnational process in which experts regulate problems in a rational way; rather it is based on negotiations between diverse political and social actors who defend interests which are anchored in national and local territories. This chapter identifies the conditions and results of this permanent negotiation, using four axes of analysis. First, the historical conditions leading to the inclusion of fisheries on the agenda of the EU are examined. Secondly, the interests at stake are described, and, as we shall see, the European arena supplements, but does not replace, the national and local arenas. Thirdly, the question is asked why the conservation of fish stocks constitutes simultaneously a cornerstone of the CFP and a domain where implementation varies widely between member states. Finally, it will be argued that the EU, as a new arena for reaching social compromise, has developed a redistributive function with regard to the different social actors involved in the fisheries sector, while having to evolve to respond to the forces of globalization.

How fisheries policy came on to the agenda of the EU

Although Article 38 of the Treaty of Rome of 1957 (later Article 32) stated that the rules of the common market would apply to fisheries products, under the same heading as agricultural products, it was not until 1970 that Regulations 2141/70 and 2142/70 introduced the first specific measures for the sector. Three measures were decided: (1) the creation of a common market organization for fisheries products; (2) structural aids for the modernization of the sector; and (3) guarantees of free access for fishing vessels to the waters of all member states, subject to certain conditions.

An additional step was taken in January 1983 with the adoption of Regulation 170/ 83, which established a Community regime for the conservation and management of fisheries resources. This constitutes the cornerstone of the current CFP which, since then, has been amended (in particular to deal with successive enlargements), but not fundamentally altered. Following a report on the CFP, compiled by the Commission in 1991 (Commission 1991*b*), Regulation 3760/92, adopted by the Council in December 1992, established a common regime for fisheries and aquaculture. This applies the rules of access under the previous legislation until 2002, while at the same time setting limits on fishing, for example by the introduction of fishing licences. As is typical of many EU policies, the inclusion of fisheries on the agenda is not a linear process, but an incremental one, marked not only by developments within the evolution of the EU and its member states, but also by the wider international context (see Box 13.1).

The impact of enlargement

Successive enlargements of the EU have been a key factor, first, in promoting the inclusion of the CFP on the agenda of the EU, and, later, in shaping its evolution. At the end of the 1960s the applications of the UK, Ireland, Denmark, and Norway (where the negative referendum on accession in September 1972 was largely due to the opposition of its farmers and fishermen) led to predictions of a quadrupling of fish production within the EU, in comparison with that of the six founding members. In 1970 the government of France, which was the primary producing country, forced the adoption of two important measures. The first created a common market organization for fisheries products, governed by price stabilization mechanisms, even though the German and the Dutch governments were unhappy about the budgetary costs and a structural policy. The second established the principle of free access for member states' vessels to all Community waters. The imminent extension of the exclusive economic zones (EEZ) to 200 nautical miles from the coasts of the applicant countries in the North Sea was perceived as a threat by the French deep-sea fishermen, who in 1970 caught almost 65 per cent of their fish in what would become the British EEZ, and 20 per cent in the Norwegian and Faroese EEZ (Shackleton 1986).

The enlargement to include Spain and Portugal in 1986 was a second step which shaped the evolution of the CFP. It led to a doubling of the number of fishermen, and an increase of 65 per cent in fleet tonnage and of 45 per cent in production. Moreover,

---

Box 13.1 Key dates in the common fisheries policy

- 1970: Adoption of the first regulations establishing the CFP: free access for vessels, common market organization, structural aid

- 1973: Accession of Denmark, Ireland, and the UK to the CFP. Norway does not join, following a negative referendum in which fisheries play an important role

- 1976: The foreign ministers of the EU agree at The Hague to create a 200-mile EEZ from 1 January 1977, to which member states' vessels would have free access. Establishment of the principle of *relative stability*, but failure to introduce an EU regime of TACs and quotas

- 1983: Adoption of a regulation fixing a common regime for fisheries resources: introduction of TACs and quotas, fixing of a system of coastal zones of 12 miles, reserved for the exclusive use of each coastal state; the sole exceptions being 'historical [fishing] rights'

- 1991: Publication of a half-term review on the CFP by the Commission

- 1992: Adoption of a regulation establishing a Community regime for fisheries and aquaculture: continuation up until 2002 of rules of access set in 1983; introduction of a policy to limit catches (licences)

- 1995: Accession of Austria (which has no maritime border), and of Finland and Sweden to the CFP. Following another negative referendum (in which fisheries are less important than in 1972) Norway does not join the EU

- 1998: Exercise in consulting the professionals on reforms to the CFP, to take effect from 31 December 2002

---

the rule of free access to all Community waters had to accommodate the fact that two-thirds of Spanish fishing activity and a quarter of Portuguese were traditionally practised outside their national waters. The governments of these two applicant countries agreed in the Acts of Accession of 1985 to take over the *acquis communautaire* in the domain of the CFP, although with a transitional regime until 2002.[2] Their arrival forced a rethinking of policy. The need to modernize the Spanish and Portuguese fleets—older than the average of the Community—encouraged a stronger emphasis on the structural aspect of the CFP from 1986. Thus enlargement also enhanced the external dimension of the CFP, since the EU had to take over the obligations—including budgetary obligations—of the bilateral fisheries agreements which linked Spain and Portugal with many third countries.

The accession of the three European Free Trade Association (EFTA) countries in 1995 did not, in the event, have a significant impact on the CFP. If the 1994 referendum in Norway had produced a positive result, the situation would have been different, with an increase of 17 per cent in the tonnage of the EU fishing fleet, and of 10 per cent in the number of fishermen, as well as the impact of Norway's strict policy on the conservation of resources.

The issue of conservation

A debate on dwindling stocks has developed at a global level since the 1970s through the impetus of the United Nations (UN) institutions and environmental non-governmental organizations (NGOs). This debate has been propelled by the techno-logical changes to fishing vessels and equipment in most producing countries between 1950 and 1960. The development of vessels with deep-freeze facilities, and of techniques such as deep-sea trawling, significantly increased the volume of catches, as well as making them more indiscriminate (Antoine 1995; Revéret and Weber 1997).

The non-binding recommendations made by scientists in the International Council for the Exploration of the Sea (ICES) and in intergovernmental fisheries commissions, such as the North East Atlantic Fisheries Commission (NEAFC), were not judged strict enough to control overfishing in the eyes of the fisheries departments in EU member states, or of some Commission officials. It became accepted that the EU would need a new regime to manage fishery resources. The expertise of the Commission, which had a 'small' fisheries unit within the Directorate-General for Agriculture, DG VI, and the constraints of Community law provided the discipline which the NEAFC could never achieve, in particular the enforcement of total allowable catches (TACs) (Shackleton 1983).

Extended national territorial waters

Efforts to control overfishing at a global level had another result that influenced EU policy, namely widespread pressure on states to exercise stronger national control over the seas. In 1971 the Icelandic government unilaterally declared that it was henceforth sovereign over the waters up to 50 nautical miles from its coasts. This triggered a 'cod war' with British fishermen, who were excluded, without further ado, from a traditional fishing area. In 1975 Iceland, this time followed by Norway and Canada, extended its national fishing control up to 200 nautical miles, just as the Third Conference of the United Nations on the Law of the Sea, launched in 1973, seemed to legitimate this measure. The impact of this 'nationalization' of the seas on the UK, Ireland, and Denmark, the new members of the EU, was considerable. Accus-tomed to operating in Norwegian and Icelandic waters for generations, British fish-ermen particularly suffered from this exclusion, which was exacerbated by a severe increase in oil prices, and made it more expensive to redeploy vessels to new fishing-grounds.

This pervasive ideology of sovereignty, prompted by the new international law of the sea, encouraged these new member states to press for a collective response which would limit the access of third countries to Community waters. Meeting at The Hague in November 1976, the foreign ministers of the EU decided to create an EEZ of 200 miles for all member states as from 1 January 1977. As part of a larger package, the European Commission was also authorized to conclude fisheries agree-ments with third countries and to negotiate with relevant international organiza-tions, thus signifying a withdrawal of EU members from the NEAFC (Thom 1993). On the other hand, the proposal of the European Commission aimed at introducing a system of TACs in the new EEZs of the member states was not accepted by the governments, and similarly a proposal to establish a common regime of coastal zones under the control of each member state was also shelved. The reservations of the Irish and, above all, of the British governments had a major influence on this failure at The Hague—these two states having already accepted the imposition of the principle of free access as a *fait accompli* during their enlargement negotiations, although the Community fish stocks were concentrated in their EEZs. It was necessary to wait until 25 January 1983, after six long years of negotiation, for an agreement on a common regime, which endorsed the principle of free access for all EU vessels within the 200-mile zone, but reserved a coastal zone of 12-miles for the exclusive use of each coastal state. Only a limited number of vessels from other countries, those which had operated in the 12-mile zone before the establishment of the CFP, could fish in these coastal zones on the basis of what were termed 'historical rights'. No EEZ was established in the Mediterranean and thus the CFP did not originally apply in this area.

The issue of free access heated up with the accession of Spain and Portugal on 1 January 1986. The strong interest of Spanish fishermen in gaining access to the French, Irish, and British EEZs led the governments of these three countries to insist on strict limits on catches and on the number of vessels authorized to operate during the transitional period. While the conditions for access to the Atlantic became more or less the same after 1 January 1996 for Spanish and Portuguese fishermen as those for fishermen from other member states, the North Sea and the Irish Sea remained still closed to them.

Between Brussels and local territories: opposing interests

The fisheries sector is one where political salience seems inversely related to the real economic weight of the sector. In 1999 in no member state of the EU, even Spain, did the value of catches exceed 1 per cent of gross domestic product (GDP). Compared with the total labour force of the EU, fishermen constitute a tiny social group: barely 270,000 people in 1995, as Table 13.1 shows.

This political salience derives from a series of factors which have little to do with the statistical indicators. Fishing remains an occupation that, in most European countries, appeals to images that belong to the maritime past of the nation, to the hardships of fishermen seeking to provide food for the population, and to a harsh occupation which bureaucrats—yesterday national, today European—fail to understand.

The territorial dimension

Another political dimension is the strong regional concentration of the sector. In 1999 in parts of west Galicia 43 per cent of the local population were dependent on fishing and ancillary activities: canning factories, unloading and fish-handling

Table 13.1 Employment in the fishing industry, full- and part-time, 1990–1995

Member state	1990	1991	1992	1993	1994	1995	Percentage change (1990–5)
Belgium	845	818	762	720	652	624	–26.15
Denmark	6,945	6,682	7,277	5,491	5,275	5,055	–27.21
France	32,622	30,953	29,588	28,306	27,598	26,879	–17.60
Germany	4,812	4,291	4,377	4,142	4,979	4,979	3.47
Greece	39,124	40,164	40,164	40,164	40,164	40,164	2.66
Ireland	7,905	7,910	7,805	7,700	7,700	5,500	–30.42
Italy	41,429	39,171	45,620	45,000	45,000	45,000	8.62
Netherlands	3,502	3,932	2,876	2,834	2,796	2,752	–21.42
Portugal	40,610	38,745	36,337	34,454	31,721	30,937	–23.82
Spain	87,351	84,838	82,299	79,369	77,962	75,009	–14.13
UK	24,230	23,820	23,410	23,000	20,766	19,928	–17.75
EU12	288,530	281,324	280,515	271,180	264,613	256,827	–10.99
Finland	3,046	2,884	2,739	2,750	2,372	2,792	–8.34
Sweden	3,823	3,549	3,275	3,000	3,500	3,400	–11.06
EU15	295,399	287,757	286,529	276,930	270,485	263,019	–10.96

Source: European Court of Auditors, compiled from various EU and national sources. Some figures are estimates.

facilities, and shipyards. This is also the case in some Scottish ports such as Lerwick and Scalloway, and in some coastal areas of southern Brittany such as the Pays Bigouden. This concentration helps to forge strong local identities which, if provoked, can mobilize political activity around defence of these occupations. In 1993–4 the fall in the price of fish in France led to the setting-up of a Committee for Survival in southern Brittany, which was supported by the local population, despite violent attacks on public buildings (Couliou 1998). In the UK Save Britain's Fish (SBF) can also be considered as a political movement. Born in the English port of Grimsby, the SBF has since 1990 regularly organized demonstrations including elected representatives of the Conservative Party as well as the Labour Party, and the most radical fishermen have called for the UK to opt out of the CFP. SBF has, however, never resorted to violent action.

Like agriculture, fishing is a heterogeneous sector in the thirteen member states of the EU where it is present. In Spain the fishing techniques, income levels, and professional opportunities of the Basque coastal fishermen have little in common with those of the Galician deep-sea fleet, which fishes for hake off the coast of Ireland. These in turn differ from the concerns of the shipowners of Vigo, who fish for tropical tuna off the African coast. This social diversity, combined with geographical concentration, fragments the interests of fishermen even within their national professional organizations. In France the Union des Armateurs à la Pêche de France (UAPF) traditionally represents industrial fishing, while the Coopération Maritime defends the interests of small-scale fishermen. In Spain the Federación Nacional de Cofradías de

Pescadores primarily represents the inshore fishing sector, while the Confederación Española de Asociaciones Pesqueras and the Federación Española de Armadores de Buques de Pesca defend the interests of the deep-sea fleets. This fragmentation of national representation is sometimes due also to differences which are not functional but territorial. In the UK the National Federation of Fishermen's Organizations (NFFO) represents English and Welsh fishermen, whereas the Scottish Fishermen's Federation (SFF) represents most Scottish fishermen. Although the NFFO and the SFF produced a joint document on the general approach of the 2002 reform of the CFP (NFFO and SFF 1998), their positions are not identical. The Scottish organization has always been more moderate than its Anglo-Welsh counterpart in its criticisms of the CFP and, in particular, has never advocated a renationalization of fisheries policy. The more open position of Scottish deep-sea fishermen can be explained by their privileged access to the stocks protected by the Shetland box, an area off northern Scotland where fishing activity is restricted to a limited number of vessels. Indeed, the EU has often been seen by Scottish fishermen as an additional means for protecting themselves against their main competitors, the Norwegian fishermen.

The fragmentation of interests at the national level has also to be seen in context, since corporatist traditions, which link the state to socio-economic groups, vary between countries. A Comité National des Pêches Maritimes et des Élevages Marins (CNPEM) has existed in France since 1945. This organization is subdivided into regional and local committees, which the various professions linked to fisheries are legally obliged to join (Thom 1993). Similarly, in the Netherlands, a country strongly imbued with the corporatist model, the Produktschap Vis, registered in public law, has represented the interests of all producers and processors of fish since the 1930s. This position is quite different in the UK, where the state has not provided channels for the economic and political engagement of fishermen.

In the EU member states the central authorities responsible for fisheries often continue to consider themselves as sovereign in their domain, even though their administrative and budgetary resources are quite weak, and despite the fact that the bulk of the legislation which they have to enforce is of Community origin. In some countries decentralization of government has added an extra level of local or regional administration. In Spain the Autonomous Communities are responsible for fisheries—including controls—within territorial waters and for aquaculture (Criado Alonso 1996). The officials from the regions most concerned with fishing, such as Galicia (which has its own Ministry for Fisheries at Santiago de Compostela) or the Basque country, therefore tend to be more involved in EU negotiations on the CFP, a situation which the central governments in Madrid have always resisted. The Spanish Autonomous Communities have never hesitated to exploit EU institutions and law at every possible opportunity, in order to involve themselves more in the formulation of the CFP. In July 1996 the autonomous government of Galicia obtained the right to intervene directly on behalf of Galician shipowners in the proceedings which the latter had brought before the Court of First Instance against the Council of the EU. The shipowners wanted to have a Community regulation annulled which, following pressure from Canada, had reduced the European fishing quota for black halibut in international waters off Newfoundland. This was the first time that a regional government of a member state had succeeded in arguing that an economic and social interest justified its recognition in the EU legal process.

In England and Wales all controls over a coastal zone of 6 miles are the responsibility not of the Ministry of Agriculture, Fisheries, and Food (MAFF), but of the twelve Sea Fisheries Committees (SFC), linked to local authorities, for example the Cornwall Sea Fishery Committee. The SFCs issue by-laws which, once vetted by MAFF, establish measures for conservation which are sometimes more severe than national laws. In Scotland the process of devolution directly raises the question of how the future Scottish Minister responsible for fisheries will be involved in negotiations in Brussels, especially given that the Scottish Office had been directly involved before devolution through its Department for Agriculture and Fisheries. Scottish fishermen have already made it known that they find it inappropriate that European negotiations on fisheries (in particular the annual fixing of TACs) should not be prepared in Edinburgh, given that their vessels account for two-thirds of landings in the UK (*Fishing News*, 18 March 1998).

This fragmentation in the way the sector is represented at the national level goes a long way towards explaining the weak organization of fishermen at the European level. The EU-level lobbying group Europêche, created in the 1970s, is a federation of fifteen national associations of producers, but has only limited resources at its disposal in comparison with those of European groups in the agricultural sector. National contributions from national associations provide funds for only a modest secretariat, composed of a part-time secretary-general and an assistant. Certain national fishermen's organizations (such as the Portuguese or the Finnish) have been unable to join Europêche, because they cannot pay the subscription. More fundamentally, Europêche has found it difficult to define common positions with regard to the CFP, and the search for consensus has been made more difficult, as successive enlargements have added to the diversity of its membership. Europêche brings little by way of added value to national fishermen's organizations in terms of information flows in comparison with what the latter obtain directly from their governments or from the Commission. Europêche thus mainly operates as a vehicle through which the national fishermen's organizations agree their official representation *vis-à-vis* the Commission.

The Commission has an official Consultative Committee on Fisheries, established in 1971 on the model of the agricultural committees instituted in the late 1960s for the management of the CAP. These committees reflect the ambitions of the Commission in the 1960s to establish itself as the future government of Europe, and in retrospect they can be seen as milestones in the effort to construct a European corporatist model. Composed of forty-five members nominated for three years by organizations representing producers, trading, processing, and financing, the Consultative Committee for Fisheries has little influence on how the Directorate-General for Fisheries (DG XIV) formulates its proposals. The main reason is that, in contrast to the domain of agriculture, the fishermen have a limited capacity to generate their own expertise. The core *raison d'etre* of the Consultative Committee has been an exercise in mutual legitimization. It allows DG XIV to reply to governments that accuse it of technocratic aloofness that it has regular contact with the grassroots, just as it is a way for the representatives of national organizations to justify their presence in Brussels to their members. As one French representative recollects, 'to come back from meetings of the Consultative Committee and tell my members that their problems have been explained to the Commission helps in the negotiation of each collective position on the CFP'.[3] In July 1999 the Commission proposed a reform of the Consultative Committee, which is less and less considered as a forum for dialogue with the fishermen. The number of members has been reduced—twenty instead of forty-five—and other actors involved in the CFP, like representatives of consumers' organizations or of green NGOs, have been invited to join the Committee.

The Commission as a promoter of expertise

The Commission is the best-placed European institution to gather expertise on fisheries issues. Created in 1976, DG XIV is composed of officials who see themselves as the guardians of expertise in contrast to the face of governments which are under clientelist pressure from fishermen. Their role is to construct a public policy based on a scientific rationale. The cornerstone of this is to work towards a policy of surveillance. In 1999 its staff included a French director and a British head of unit; both came from the circle of marine biologists who direct national oceanographic institutes—such as the Institut Français de Recherche pour l'Exploitation de la Mer (IFREMER) in France or the Centre for Environment, Fisheries, and Aquaculture Science (CEFAS) in the UK—among which ICES is by tradition a sort of 'Vatican'. With their colleagues who remain in the national oceanographic institutes, these officials form a scientific community with a common creed. This has three core beliefs: (1) fish stocks are threatened by the natural tendency of fishermen to overfish; (2) the mission of scientists is to encourage governments to counter this threat with regulatory measures (TACs and quotas); (3) hence it is necessary to devise statistical models to evaluate stocks, so as to be able to demonstrate to politicians the extent of this threat.

This resilient paradigm carries support from meetings of the Scientific, Technical, and Economic Committee for Fisheries (STECF), which has, since 1979, brought together most of the marine biologists who are responsible for submitting advice on fish stocks in the ICES. Since 1993 economists have also been involved in the work of the ICES, as DG XIV has become concerned to increase expertise on questions such as over-investment, competition between fishermen, or rates of return. Fewer in number than the biologists, these economists (drawn from institutes of applied research, but also from universities) have never won a place in the EU decision-making process equal to that of biologists who study fish stocks.

A parallel can be drawn with the environmental policy community. In the fisheries domain the opinions of scientists, even where they are a source of controversy within the scientific community, have provided DG XIV and the successive Commissioners responsible for fisheries (Manuel Marin, Yannis Paleokrassas, Emma Bonino) with very convenient arguments for passing unpopular regulatory measures, such as the establishment of new TACs or reductions in fleet capacity, where it is necessary to convince fishermen and national ministers.

Council negotiations

The Council of Fisheries Ministers is the place where the main decisions over the CFP are discussed, argued over, and finally adopted. Generally meeting in this group three times a year, the Council has powers at its disposal which, in contrast to most other sectors, virtually amount to direct administration. The Council legislates mainly through regulations, directly binding on the member states, and not directives. In contrast to many other policy areas, Article 37 (ex 43), which also covers the CAP, requires no stronger role for the European Parliament (EP) than the right to be consulted. The Council may take its decisions by qualified majority voting (QMV), and this sometimes poses problems for those ministers who have to return to their capitals and explain to fishermen that they found themselves in the minority. This was the case in June 1998, when the Irish and French ministers were overruled by a majority of their colleagues, who favoured the ban of driftnets in the Atlantic and the Mediterranean.

Most of those who comprise the Council of Fisheries are Ministers of Agriculture and Fisheries. However, the Council has its own identity. Its meetings are prepared by a network of high-level national officials who are responsible for fisheries in the capitals, and the fisheries counsellors from the Permanent Representations in Brussels, who attend the fisheries working groups of the Council and accompany Deputy Permanent Representatives to the meetings of Coreper I.

Parliamentary scrutiny

Article 43 (now 37) (EEC) does not allow the EP to exercise much influence on legislation in the area of the CFP, in contrast to most other policy areas. However, the EP looks for ways of intervening through other routes, such as in the annual budgetary process or in debates on the structural funds and their reform.

In 1979 there was only a working group within the EP that covered fisheries; then from 1984 a sub-committee of the Agriculture Committee; and a full Committee since 1994, the first President of which was a Spanish MEP, Miguel Arias Cañete (Steel 1998). The involvement of the British and Spanish MEPs in this Committee has been particularly active. In 1997 and 1999 the presidency of the Committee passed to other Spanish MEPs, Carmen Fraga Estévez (European People's Party: EPP), interestingly the daughter of the President of the autonomous community of Galicia, Manuel Fraga Iribarne, and then Daniel Varela Suanzes-Carpegna (EPP).

The Fisheries Committee holds one or two public meetings a month. It is the sole EU institution which uses its reports and hearings to bring alternative expertise to bear on the proposals of DG XIV. What is striking about the way the Fisheries Committee operates is its deliberate cultivation of expertise as the basis of its efforts to influence the Commission. This approach is quite a contrast to the political rhetoric which tends to excite national parliamentarians on the same subject during debates in their own chambers. The lyrical flights of fancy on fishing or fishermen, observable, for example, in the debates of the House of Commons, are seldom reproduced in the EP, since they appeal to a national symbolism which cannot rally support in a transnational assembly (Lequesne 1998a). The professional organizations in the fisheries sector none the less find some MEPs to act as advocates of specific interests, regions, or occupational groups. One such MEP, from Cuxhaven, is the regular spokesperson for the processing industry in the north of Germany, which favours a liberal import regime for fisheries products. The report on the CFP after 2002, drafted in 1997 by the Committee's President, Carmen Fraga Estévez, reflected the position of Galician shipowners, who favoured complete liberalization of access to community waters by 2002 (Fraga Estévez 1997). In 1999 the Irish MEP Pat 'the Cope' Gallagher wrote a report on the extension of national coastal zones from 12 to 24 miles and on the decentralizing of the management of fisheries to regional units. Its recommendations corresponded quite closely to the views of the Irish Fishermen's Organization.

The EP also provides an arena where environmental NGOs, such as Greenpeace, the WorldWide Fund for Nature (WWF), or the Eurogroup for Animal Welfare can regularly intervene on the CFP. After having long directed their lobbying at the Environment Committee, these NGOs, all with offices in Brussels, understood over the course of the 1990s that it was equally necessary to 'invest' in lobbying other committees of the EP. Indeed they even encouraged the creation of 'intergroups': these are informal bodies for MEPs who share a particular idea or interest on the fringes of the EP's legislative function. Often the secretariats are provided by NGOs, as is the case for the Eurogroup for Animal Welfare. From 1994 the Fisheries Committee became the target of regular approaches from environmental NGOs, not only on the question of the conservation of stocks, but also on the impact of certain fishing techniques on marine flora and fauna (dolphins, turtles, etc.). Its opposition to the use of driftnets is not unconnected to lobbying from environmental NGOs. It has not so much been fishermen themselves, but rather the European fish-processing and distribution industries, that have recognized the implications for their commercial activities of the efforts by NGOs to promulgate environmental standards (precautionary principle or sustainable development). This explains the 1997 initiative taken by Unilever to associate the WWF with the creation of the Marine Stewardship Council (MSC). Based in London, this is an NGO which aims to develop an approach to product-labelling that will promote the marketing of those marine products which take account of the goal of 'sustainable development' (Marine Stewardship Council 1997).

Operating through the courts

Finally, the European Court of Justice (ECJ) and the Court of First Instance have played a crucial role in the evolution of the CFP. Prompted both by cases brought directly by institutions and individuals, and by those referred for preliminary rulings by national courts, the ECJ has since 1970 pronounced regularly on questions concerning quotas, the free movement of capital in the sector, and the external competence of the EU. In his study of which substantive issues came before the ECJ between 1980 and 1989, Christopher Harding (1992) demonstrated that fisheries came in fourth place, after agriculture, competition, and the free movement of goods, with the majority of cases being prompted by complaints originating from one member state: Spain. Some defining points of Community jurisprudence resulted from disputes related to the CFP. Thus the judgment on the 1976 *Kramer* case ([1976] ECR, 1279) reinforced the concept that the definition of an internal EU policy implied parallel external competences for the EU; and the series of *Factortame* cases, notably that in 1991 ([1991] ECR, 3905) established that provisions of national laws which infringed European law could be struck down to prevent discrimination. These were UK cases in relation to the 1988 British Merchant Shipping Act.

Common management of resources and differences in implementation

It is the regime for conserving and managing resources that forms the cornerstone of the CFP. The risk of depleting stocks is real, and the way in which marine biologists have become influential actors in the Commission helped to make conservation a priority issue on the EU agenda.

Setting limits on catches

Conservation policy appeared first as a system of TACs and quotas to regulate the fishing of some 120 stocks in the Atlantic, the North Sea, and the Baltic (Karagiannakos 1997). The system of zones is shown in Figure 13.1. Because the Mediterranean was not covered by an EEZ, the fisheries ministers decided in 1983 that it could be exempted from the system of TACs. However, a recommendation from the International Commission for the Conservation of Atlantic Tuna (ICCAT) showed the extent of the threat to the blue-fin tuna, and the fisheries ministers of the EU then decided, in December 1998, to establish a TAC for this species, including the catches in the Mediterranean.

In December of each year TACs are set for the following year by EU fisheries ministers in a ritual exercise where scientific reasoning confronts political reasoning. The point of departure for the process is scientific advice. A report from the marine biologists on the Advisory Committee on Fishery Management (ACFM) of the ICES is forwarded as early as possible in October–November to DG XIV. This suggests the TACs by species and by geographical division concerning both EU stocks and those shared with third countries, such as Norway or the Faroe Islands (Guegen *et al.* 1990). A majority of these TACs are precautionary, that is to say they aim to protect a resource estimated by scientists to be at risk but for which the specific data allowing for an accurate analysis are missing. The opinion is then transmitted to the EU's STECF, a body which often includes the same biologists who work at ACFM, where it is usually agreed without any significant modifications. This forms the basis from which the conservation unit of DG XIV makes its proposal to member governments.

The officials in the conservation unit of DG XIV regard themselves as 'guardians of stocks'. They see it as their function to ratify the choices made by the scientists, knowing that national officials and ministers will rely quite heavily on the scientific advice and tend to revise downwards their negotiating targets. Ministers also draw on the terms of the proposal of the Commission as a means of adjusting downwards the demands of their own fishermen. Once the Commission issues its proposal to member governments each November, the negotiations move into a political mode, shifting from an emphasis on the protection of stocks to the balance between different geographical areas and the preservation of socio-economic peace.

This double imperative has developed from the principle of *relative stability* established at The Hague in 1976 and later formalized by Regulations 170/83 and 3760/92, and by the jurisprudence of the ECJ.[4] A key is fixed for the allocations of TACs

Figure 13.1 Maritime zones

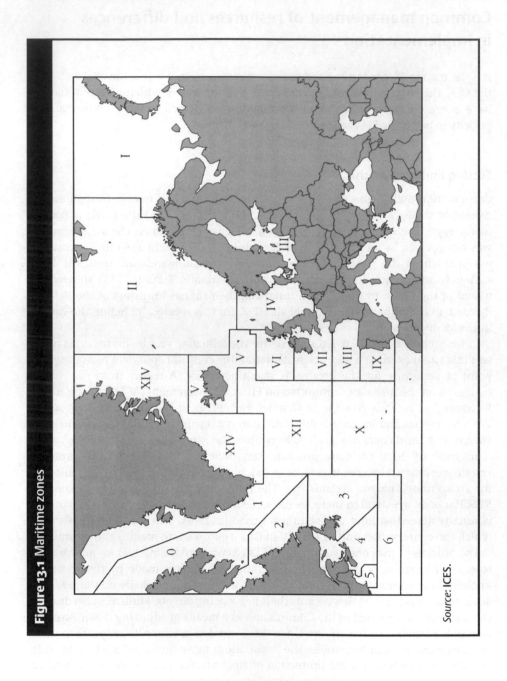

Source: ICES.

between states, based on three criteria which have little to do with biology: the preservation of traditional fishing activities within each member state; the particular needs of those regions most dependent on fisheries; and the loss of catches in the waters of third countries, as they have extended their own fishing zones. The autumn meetings of the Council working groups and the December session of the Fisheries Council provide the arena for defining what relative stability means. At this stage governments engage in intensive bargaining over the levels of the TACs. As in most EU negotiations, the confrontation between many different interests usually ends in a compromise which neither the Commission nor the member governments can totally control. QMV may make arriving at a decision easier, but it sometimes puts ministers who are in the minority in an awkward situation *vis-à-vis* their national fishermen's organizations, which are usually present in Brussels for this event. The Fisheries Council of December 1998, for example, adopted a TAC on blue-fin tuna against the minority opinions of the Italian and Greek delegations.

The system of TACs and quotas has often been criticized for not making a strong impact on the conservation of resources (Oliver 1998). But we should remember that the CFP, like most EU policies, depends on implementation at a national level, which involves different constellations of actors from one state to another. In the UK 95 per cent of TACs are managed directly by nineteen producer organizations. In France quotas are allocated each year by the government according to geographical criteria: the producer organizations, which only represent 35 per cent of vessels but 68 per cent of the total value of catches, then manage TACs for their members (IFREMER 1995). In the Netherlands since 1977 there has been a system of individual transferable quotas (ITQs), which turn TACs into a kind of property right.

Efforts to make controls effective

Whatever the individual merits of different national systems, their effectiveness depends essentially on what controls the national administrations are able to exercise over catches, as well as on how far fishermen are able to regulate themselves through their own producer organizations. The British and Irish administrations have proved stricter than their Spanish and French counterparts in compelling vessels above a certain size to record their catches in their logbooks. The fact that the vast majority of vessels of over 10 metres in length belong to a producer organization makes the work of British and Irish inspectors easier. Strict administration can, however, be counter-productive, encouraging the practice of illegal landings. The problem of 'black fish' is a burning issue in the UK, to the extent that the Anglo-Welsh and Scottish fisheries authorities have required all vessels over 20 metres in length to land their catches solely at thirty-one designated ports and at designated times (*Fishing News*, 20 November 1998).

The historical relationship between a state and its fishermen is a factor which has a deciding influence on the capacity of administrations to control the sector, and which creates distinctive 'policy styles'. In France a trade-off involving 'impunity from fraud in exchange for the preservation of social peace' has historically structured the relationship between fishermen and the state, which makes it hard to root the idea of 'co-management' with the government in operating the TACs. The Dutch system, which obliges the producer organizations themselves to impose fines of a minimum of 5,000 guilders on members who exceed their allocated quota, could not be reproduced in France (Dubbink and van Vliet 1996).[5]

The policy of the conservation of stocks is not limited to the system of TACs and quotas. It also involves a series of other measures established by the EU. A licensing system governs the access of vessels to certain large breeding-grounds of species, which are called 'boxes' (Shetland Box, Irish Box). Numerous measures specify permitted fishing techniques (engine types, size of nets and meshes, and so forth).

There are also plans for fleet reductions, embodied since 1983 in the Multi-annual Guidance Programmes (MAGPs) which lie at the intersection of conservation and structural policy. The MAGPs are adopted by the Fisheries Council on the basis of a proposal by DG XIV, and fix the rate of multi-annual reductions in fleet capacity by country and by sector, with a view to achieving a more appropriate level for managing the resources. They are intended to reduce capacity by decommissioning vessels or exporting to third countries in return for compensatory payments. The fourth MAGP, which calls for a global decrease of approximately 20 per cent (expressed in kilowatts) of the motor power of fleets for the period 1997–2000, was adopted on 15 April 1997, in spite of British and French opposition. These MAGPs are much disliked by fishermen, as they symbolize the regulatory power of the EU over fleets which have been decreasing in size in all EU member states since the late 1980s. Moreover, fishermen find it hard to accept that if they ignore the targets fixed by the MAGPs, the Commission will refuse them permission to put new vessels into service.

At the end of 1996 the majority of states were lagging behind the targets for reducing tonnage and motor power (see Table 13.2). Following the recommendations of the Commission, the French government had in 1998 to make up the reductions of 20,000 kW, to which it was committed under MAGP III (1992–6), before it could discuss with its fishermen the building of new vessels. In their efforts to regulate a reduction of fishing, the MAGPs also represent for fishermen a shift in the responsi-

Table 13.2 Gross tonnage of the Community fleet

Member state	1991	1997	Difference in tonnage (1991–7)	Difference in percentage (1991–7)
Belgium	27,732	22,880	−4,852	−17
Denmark	117,949	98,551	−19,398	−16
France	198,801	196,001	−2,800	−1
Germany	92,775	72,910	−19,865	−21
Greece	129,474	114,587	−14,887	−11
Ireland	56,236	58,502	2,266	4
Italy	274,063	260,603	−13,460	−5
Netherlands	174,274	177,196	2,922	2
Portugal	183,306	123,220	−60,086	−33
Spain	788,232	604,901	−183,331	−23
UK	252,601	253,924	1,323	1
EU 12	2,295,443	1,983,275	−312,168	−14

Source: European Commission, DG XIV

bility for producing a social compromise from the nation state towards the EU. This shift is hard to legitimate given that the implementation of this approach is not identical in each member state. British fishermen feel particularly badly treated because the British Treasury (with its strict approach to expenditure) has always been reluctant to provide generous compensatory payments to supplement the EU subsidy for those fishermen, in contrast to the practice in Spain and France. The legal construction of the single market, with its corpus of rules promoting free movement, moreover, allows shipowners from certain states to counter the restrictions imposed by the MAGPs at the national level by acquiring vessels in other member states and fishing under their quotas. In 1998 there were about fifty-seven Spanish-owned vessels operating in France and approximately eighty in the UK (as well as some Dutch-owned vessels). In France the motor power of Franco-Spanish vessels represented 25,120 kW in 1998, which was more or less equivalent to the reduction in fishing required by MAGP III. The British and French fishermen's organizations never miss an opportunity to highlight the link between MAGPs and the effects of the free movement of capital, captured, since the late 1980s, by the term 'quota-hopping'. The issue became hotly debated in the UK during the negotiation of the Treaty of Amsterdam and the 1997 general election (Lequesne 1998*b*, 1999).

Limits to the common regime

How the policy is implemented, and therefore whether conservation is successful, depends on the system of controls. Although DG XIV has since 1983 had its own corps of fishing inspectors, EU regulations only allow them in their land and sea investigations to accompany national authorities, and not to carry out autonomous controls. In a domain which touches on the sovereignty of their national fleets, the member governments have not been keen to delegate responsibility for these controls to the EU level.

Such controls as these vary greatly in their effectiveness across the member states. As a general rule, the increased cost of controls at sea is never welcomed by national budgetary authorities, in the light of the modest contribution which fishing makes to national GDP. In England and Wales the Treasury regularly expresses its reservations about the cost of inspections undertaken by the Royal Navy on behalf of MAFF, estimated at £20,000 per day in 1998.[6]

None the less, this British system of controls at sea is regarded as 'an example of the way in which the CFP ought to be applied' (Commission 1996*f*: 112). Far less strict controls operate in Belgium, Spain, and Portugal, which are under-equipped in terms of surveillance vessels and aeroplanes. Secondly, the fines which punish infringements of the CFP are much more severe in the UK and Ireland than in Italy or France. Thirdly, governments do not all give the same priority to the exercise of controls. In France the priority of preserving social peace makes the responsible national agency reluctant to appear too coercive in dealing with offenders. For example, in one southern Breton port undersized hake were caught and processed for many years in full view and knowledge of the Administration for Maritime Affairs, which refused to take any action. Finally, the national inspectorates do not form a powerful transnational network, despite regular calls from the Commission (1998*g*) and also from certain governments, such as the Irish, for closer cooperation. The fisheries administrations are, in this sense, very different from the customs authorities, where the mechanisms of control are now largely transnational. This difference is partly explained by the strong historical association of the sea with sovereignty and borders. The development of new inspection technologies, such as satellites, used progressively in the EU to monitor vessels of more than 24 metres in length since July 1998, is likely to improve the exchange of information between national administrations in the future.

How controls are operated within the EEZs also raises the interesting question of how fairly the EU regime is enforced. Actual practice reveals, in effect, a tendency for national administrations to be rather stricter in dealing with non-national fishermen than with their own nationals. This is the case in France as regards Spanish vessels, and in Ireland as regards French vessels and even more so for Franco-Spanish vessels. This situation explains why Spanish deep-sea fishermen, the most active in the EEZs of other member states, generally support giving the Commission its own control powers, judging that they will be less discriminated against than by the current national systems.[7]

The CFP between redistribution and globalization

The EU is often described as a political system deriving its particular features from the fact that its main successes are in the regulatory field, and not in the distribution of resources (Majone 1995). The modest scale of the EU budget seems to support this view, but it is more complex than it appears. Even without pointing out the strong redistributive logic driving the agricultural and regional policies of the EU over many years, we can still observe that the fisheries sector is marked by similar intensive lobbying and claims for financial intervention, albeit from a smaller pot of money.

In practice, a kind of triad of the Commission, governments, and fishermen has established a compromise around a regime of structural aids, conceived as compensation for the social costs of each successive reform. When Emma Bonino, the Commissioner for Fisheries in 1995–9, sought to justify the decision to ban driftnets, she automatically used the argument that reconversion did not pose any problems as 'the structural funds can intervene' (quoted in *Le Figaro*, 7 April 1998). The fishermen's organizations got the message, and continue to press at Brussels, as at national and regional level, for financial aid as a condition of accepting social change.

Financial support for the fishing industry

It was not until the reform of the structural funds in 1993 (see Chapter 9), applicable for the period 1994–9, that the fisheries sector was granted its own Financial Instrument for Fisheries Guidance (FIFG). Granted 2.9 billion ecus (almost 1.9 per cent of the total structural funds), the FIFG was intended to help achieve Objective 5a, which promotes structural adaptation of the cohesion policy in agriculture and fisheries. Some support for the fisheries sector can also be justified under other headings of the European Regional Development Fund and the European Social Fund, as well as through a so-called Community Initiative Programme, Pesca, specifically created to help 'areas dependent on fishing'. (See also Chapter 9.)

Between 1994 and 1999 the main beneficiaries of these structural operations were Spain (40 per cent of the total), Italy, Portugal, and France. In addition to support for the measures imposed under the MAGPs (see above), financial support has been made available for the modernization of vessels, equipment at fishing-ports, the commercial processing of fish products, and some socio-economic help to individual fishermen. In some regions still dependent on fishing—such as Galicia, Brittany, and Scotland—EU aid, added to national and regional aid, formed a substantial injection of public money. For example, the Pesca programme spent 12 million ecus in Brittany between 1994 and 1999, on actions to promote processing, to improve the quality of fish products, or to train or retrain sailors (Thivend 1998).

However, these financial contributions, accumulated from different levels of government (EU, national, and local), have not always favoured the selection of appropriate projects. In southern Brittany many ports have profited from EU aid in order to draw on other funds so as to modernize their auction markets, whereas if less public money had been available, there might have been a more efficient concentration on selected landing-ports (Schirmann-Duclos and Laforge 1998). Also, the rules fixed by the EU for the allocation of funds have sometimes sharpened, rather than reduced, competition between local fishing communities. In Spain the Basque fishermen found it difficult to accept that their equally prosperous Galician counterparts would benefit from a higher level of intervention from the FIFG, over the period 1994–9, because Galicia is classified as a 'region lagging behind in development' while the Basque country is not. Nevertheless, the financial and political incentives generated by the structural funds have led local fishing communities to mobilize themselves differently *vis-à-vis* the EU. Not only do they react against EU regulations which they consider restrictive, but they also mobilize, along with local and national politicians, in order to influence the distribution of funds.

Agenda 2000 provides some relevant examples of local actions designed to prevent the reform of the funds, as proposed by the Commission, from significantly reducing the contribution of the FIFG for the period 2000–6, as compared with the previous period. In southern Brittany the actions of the Pesca Cornouaille association illustrate the mobilization of 'fishermen, companies and local representatives'. One of its objectives is to make the French government, members of the national and European Parliaments, and the EU Committee of Regions aware that the new Objective 2 (see Chapter 9) gives a very wide definition of 'areas dependent on fishing' and does not greatly reduce the rate of financial intervention. More or less identical campaigning is done by Scottish and Spanish fishermen, who work through those of their countries' MEPs who sit on the Fisheries Committee to get their views to Brussels (*Fishing News* 23 March 1998; Arias Cañete 1998).

International trade and Community preference

In contrast to agricultural products, fisheries products have since 1962 been subject to the rules of the General Agreement on Tariffs and Trade–World Trade Organization (GATT–WTO), which have strictly limited the fixing of tariffs in the Common Commercial Tariff (CCT), and have prevented quantitative restrictions and measures having an equivalent effect. Moreover, 60 per cent of EU imports of fish products are governed by preferential agreements with groups of third countries which involve derogations from the CCT: Mediterranean countries; African, Caribbean and Pacific (ACP) countries; those countries benefiting from the generalized system of preferences (GSP); and Norway and Iceland under the European Economic Area (EEA) (see Chapter 15). These various trade arrangements facilitate imports of third-country products to the EU, and have contributed to the deficit in the EU's trade balance for the period 1986–96, as Tables 13.3 and 13.4 indicate. In 1995 only Ireland and the Netherlands had a positive balance of trade: the former due to the modesty of its imports, the latter due to the dynamism of its exports of deep-frozen products.

The marked gap between EU production and consumption has led to a constant pendulum movement within the CFP between, on the one hand, defence of the principle of Community preference and, on the other hand, the need to guarantee imports at low prices for the distribution and processing industries which provide most of the employment in the sector. Managing these two requirements is all the more complicated because the main producing countries (Denmark, Spain, the UK, France, Italy, and the Netherlands) are generally also the main importers of third-

Table 13.3 External trade in fish products

Year	Imports		Exports		Balance	
	Q	V	Q	V	Q	V
1986	3,322	4,593	1,306	1,266	−2,016	−3,327
1987	3,613	5,294	1,237	1,363	−2,376	−3,931
1988	3,548	5,917	1,239	1,372	−2,309	−4,545
1989	3,991	6,390	1,328	1,462	−2,663	−4,928
1990	4,160	6,925	1,220	1,352	−2,940	−5,573
1991	3,998	7,698	1,302	1,471	−2,696	−6,227
1992	4,096	7,655	1,432	1,420	−2,664	−6,235
1993	4,020	7,064	1,478	1,454	−2,542	−5,610
1994	4,723	8,124	1,593	1,682	−3,130	−6,442
1995[a]	4,303	8,271	1,584	1,630	−2,719	−6,641
1996[a]	4,324	8,646	1,509	1,695	−2,815	−6,951

Notes: Q = quantity in 1,000 tonnes; V = value in million ecus. Imports in cif price value; exports in fob price value; inc. all fish products.

[a] EU15

Source: European Commission, DG XIV.

Table 13.4 Total external trade of EU and EEA member states in fish and fish products ('ooo ecus)

Member state	1970			1995		
	Imports	Exports	Balance	Imports	Exports	Balance
Austria	28,087	829	−27,258	144,049	13,310	−130,739
Belgium[a]	84,467	17,724	−66,743	796,770	283,708	−513,062
Denmark	46,045	162,033	115,988	1,215,572	2,050,241	834,670
Finland	20,292	429	−19,862	86,738	17,150	−69,588
France	199,438	36,188	−163,250	2,468,260	766,466	−1,701,794
Germany	259,032	62,490	−196,542	1,928,019	644,604	−1,283,416
Greece	12,235	3,814	−8,421	176,564	135,879	−40,684
Ireland	8,360	11,491	3,130	69,131	264,424	195,293
Italy	156,132	11,875	−144,257	1,894,468	272,556	−1,621,912
Netherlands	91,209	109,328	18,118	942,254	1,179,747	237,492
Portugal	31,662	45,624	13,962	602,775	222,272	−380,503
Spain	45,543	93,414	47,872	2,343,833	936,413	−1,407,419
Sweden	96,633	22,240	−74,393	414,611	195,925	−218,685
UK	287,649	53,875	−233,773	1,496,495	865,600	−630,895
EU15[b]	1,366,783	631,353	−735,430	14,579,539	7,848,296	−6,731,243
Iceland	65	110,454	110,389	30,815	1,026,411	995,595
Norway	18,010	254,302	236,292	374,909	2,387,345	2,012,436
EEA[b]	1,384,858	996,109	−388,749	14,985,052	11,262,052	−3,723,210

Notes: [a] Incl. Luxembourg.   [b] Incl. trade between member states.
Source: Eurostat–FAO.

country products. The only exception is Germany, which produces rather little, but has a processing industry, specializing in deep-frozen products, which is overwhelmingly supplied from outside the EU.

The CFP operates several trade instruments designed to support Community preference. The main one is the common market organization for aquaculture and fisheries products, created in 1970 along the lines of the market organizations used in CAP.[8] Financed from the EU budget, this is a support mechanism for the prices of fresh and frozen products which comes into play when prices reach a threshold level at which they would have to be withdrawn from the market. Aid may be provided for storage and for relaunching products on the market, or indeed for their destruction. One species—tuna—benefits from a specific compensatory payment paid to producers at the moment when a fall in prices significantly affects the Community market. The operation of these market organizations in the member states is not the responsibility of national governments, but of producer organizations, the creation and extension of which has been much encouraged by the EU.

These 150 producer organizations, all located in the member states, are based on the principle of free membership for fishermen, and marketed approximately 80 per cent of the production of those species subjected to price regimes in 1999. Although the figures vary a good deal according to years, countries, and species, less of the production of the fisheries sector is withdrawn from the market than in the agricultural sector (for the contrast, see Chapter 7). Financing from the EU budget nevertheless forms part of the redistributive compromise which was established between fishermen and European governments when the CFP was set up in 1970 (Commission 1997*f*).

The second type of measure which supports Community production involves regularly imposing quotas on imports and, in the case of disturbances to the market, using safeguard clauses. This latter remains rather exceptional, since it requires the Commission to conduct an investigation and to consult the contracting parties of the WTO. It is not surprising that in some of the EU producer countries the fishermen regularly criticize the CFP as ill adapted to international trade and ask for increased protection of external borders. Whatever the real facts of the case, during a crisis in 1993–4 one of the demands of Breton fishermen was that imports from third countries should be blocked. Their opposition to the CFP became all the more violent when the Commission refused the French government's request for the introduction of a safeguard clause, because, so the Commission judged, not all European markets were affected; instead the Commission proposed a system of minimum pricing for imports of seven species which were particularly vulnerable to competition (du Guerny and Bauer 1994). The EU can, in contrast, operate forms of protection welcomed by producers when it moves to prevent unfair practices such as dumping. In April 1998 Scottish and Irish producers thus welcomed the decision of the Council to make definitive the anti-dumping measures taken by the Commission against Norwegian salmon exporters. On these matters of trade it has quite suited national ministers that the Commission had been delegated so many powers to intervene, since the interests of fishermen and those of processors are often at variance inside each member state.

This difficult trade relationship between the EU and the rest of the world as a result of the CFP is mirrored in the arrangements for access to resources. It is estimated nowadays that 35 per cent of the world's seas and oceans are under the jurisdiction of individual states, through the establishment of both EEZs and exclusive fishing zones. Thus EU fleets find themselves excluded from many areas where they operated freely until the 1970s (Del Vecchio 1995).

Negotiating with third countries

In 1976 the governments of the member states entrusted the EU with the power to conclude fishing agreements with third countries concerning access to resources, assuming that their negotiating capacity would be strengthened as a result. The arrival of Spain and Portugal, whose deep-sea shipowners had a specific interest in fishing third-country waters, strengthened this side of the CFP, and there are now some thirty agreements in force. They rest on four main forms of reciprocity (EP 1996):

1. access to resources–access to resources (Norway, the Faroe Islands, Iceland, and the Baltic states);
2. access to resources–financial compensation and access to markets (Morocco);

3. access to resources–financial compensation and access to markets, through the device of joint ventures, the 'second generation' agreements (Argentina); and
4. access to resources–financial compensation and developmental measures, such as the training of local fishermen, landing of a certain quota of captures in local ports, the 'third generation' agreements with ACP countries, such as Senegal, Guinea-Bissau, and the Seychelles.

With the exception of purely reciprocal agreements, which apply to European countries, the other types of agreement thus involve the costs of financial compensation. These are sometimes borne by European shipowners themselves, and sometimes by the EU budget, which contributes—as in the case of agreement with Morocco—to the development of local fisheries networks (for example, port management or canning factories). The budgetary cost is the subject of argument within the EU, because these essentially serve the interests of one category of shipowners from some member states (those who practise deep-sea fishing in the southern seas).

The fleets which benefit from negotiated access to African and Latin American waters are mainly from Spain, Portugal, Italy, Greece, the Netherlands, the UK, and France. Danish and Irish fleets are less concerned and thus have a tendency to consider that these agreements exist to the detriment of the financing of other aspects of the CFP. In its response to the Commission questionnaire on the 2002 reform, the Irish Fishermen's Organization, for example, stressed that 'the cost and consequently the percentage of the EU fisheries budget committed to supporting third-country agreements has risen enormously over the years. It now has to be questioned whether financial support should be continued' (Irish Fishermen's Organization 1998). In contrast, the UAPF, which includes among its members the Breton tuna fleet which fishes off the African coast and in the Indian Ocean, observed in its response to the Commission that the EU should pursue 'an aggressive, dynamic and expansionist policy in the matter of fishing agreements. It no longer suffices to safeguard what already exists, [the EU] should develop what could be!' (Union des Armateurs à la Pêche de France 1998). The difference in interests is so marked that in Spain, the main country which benefits from these agreements, some politicians and representatives of the fishing and processing industries have called for powers to be granted to individual member states to negotiate bilateral agreements with third countries in those cases where the EU does not wish to take on the necessary financial obligations (Fraga Estévez 1997).

The agreement which the EU concluded with Morocco in 1995, for example, affected the regular activities of some 450 Spanish and Portuguese deep-sea fishing vessels. There are 150 vessels employing 1,400 sailors who mainly fish for cephalopods (such as cuttlefish and squid) based in Galicia, and even more in Andalucia. Out of a total of twenty-nine joint ventures which have been approved within the scope of the 'second generation' agreement with Argentina, concluded in 1993, twenty-two are Spanish-owned. The Iberian countries attach all the more importance to these agreements, as their fleets have progressively been excluded from the territorial waters of some coastal states of the north Atlantic. The decision of the Canadian government in 1995 to reduce the TAC for cod came as a severe blow to the Portuguese deep-sea fishing fleet and necessitated its redeployment to other areas and fishing grounds (de Jesus 1998). Similarly, the creation of joint ventures and the transfer of flags to Argentina or to Namibia has provided certain sections of the Spanish fleet (such as the forty deep-freeze trawlers from Vigo, which carry 1,800 sailors) with a way of meeting the requirements of MAGP III. This stratagem has become all the more attractive because aid from the EU budget has covered the costs of transferring the vessels and the production of joint ventures can be exported to the EU market. These agreements can also have a substantial impact on the local economy of the third countries concerned. The government of the Seychelles puts a figure of FF103 million on the net income which it earns from the presence of European tuna fishermen, that is more or less equivalent to its tourism receipts (Parrès 1997).

The durability of such agreements with third countries cannot be taken for granted. There is an imbalance, with some third countries having fish-rich waters, while in general resources in Europe are dwindling and the trade deficit of the EU puts it in a weaker negotiating position. The Moroccan government has therefore been very strict in its application of its fishing agreement concluded with the EU in 1995: it regularly inspects Spanish vessels suspected of violations, and temporarily closes fishing-grounds for biological reasons. In March 1999 it had made no commitments regarding the renewal of the agreement, due to expire on 30 November 1999. The severity of the Moroccan position is reflected in the efforts of the Rabat government to raise the stakes regarding budgetary aid and trade concessions from the EU, the object being eventually to export fish (in particular canned sardines) directly to the Spanish and Portuguese markets. To take another example, in December 1998 the Argentine Senate insisted that in future all officers and 75 per cent of ordinary seamen employed on vessels of joint venture companies should be Argentinian; this is also part of a political strategy aimed at tough negotiation on the terms of trade with the EU (Arocena 1998).

The strong trend towards extending territorial control over fisheries resources shows that EU agreements with third countries over access to fishing resources are not immutable. If they are eroded, there will be severe consequences for the EU; fleets will have to be redeployed and there will be pressures for increased financing for decommissioning. But none of this would rule out in the future new agreements with third countries, focusing on technological or industrial matters relating to the processing of fish products (Chaumette 1998).

Conclusions

This survey of the CFP highlights several distinctive features of the EU policy process in this domain. First, the CFP is one of the few EU policies designed to be implemented by direct administration. The reliance on regulations rather than directives to make legislation is one indication of this, although this formal characteristic should not blind us to the conspicuous variations between member states in their methods of implementation. Secondly, the formulation of the CFP in its early years rested mainly on the political interaction between two institutions: the Commission on the one hand and the Council on the other. This duopoly has been gradually eroded, as the EP has progressively and pragmatically inserted itself into the decision-making process, and by the interventions of the ECJ, in response to cases brought by social actors. Thirdly, the CFP is a policy in which there is very weak representation of interests at the transnational level. Fishermen still prefer to lobby mainly at the level of the state. However, other social groups which are more and more concerned by the CFP, such as the environmental NGOs, have, in contrast, developed lobbying practices, and indeed policies, that are primarily transnational and directed at the Commission and the EP.

The CFP also illustrates a typical feature of European integration, namely the temporal dimension (Abélès 1996). Every major development since 1970 has been accompanied by a timetable, causing those involved in the sector to face up to the next reform. The Regulation of December 1992 establishing a common regime for fisheries and aquaculture defines the terms for its own review: on the basis of a proposal of the Commission, the Council must decide before 31 December 2002 on the adjustments to be made in many areas, of which access is the most important. Inside each institution—the Commission, the EP, the national administrations, and the professional organizations—the daily operation of the CFP has to take into account the 'date of expiry—2002'.

The Commission has held to its primary function as the mobilizer of expertise, a role which it has always known better how to fulfil than that of managing its programmes, as the events leading to the resignation of the Santer Commission in March 1999 revealed. The Commission has been preparing for reform of the CFP since 1998, by initiating a process of consultation with the social groups concerned. This consultation, conducted by DG XIV, took the classic path: a request for an opinion from the Consultative Committee on Fisheries, which delivered an intermediate report in June 1998; and the organization of public meetings with representatives of the sector in member states. It also involved the preparation and dispatching of a questionnaire to a deliberately wide range of 347 recipients (professional fishermen's organizations, but also scientific institutes, environmental NGOs, and suchlike), to which 150 had responded by June 1998.[9] DG XIV asked these organizations also to give their opinions on certain other aspects of the CFP, which were not formally envisaged by the 2002 reform, such as the market organization for fisheries products or the agreements with third countries. This effort to broaden out policy issues is an excellent illustration of the way in which the DGs of the Commission use the work of experts in order to shape the political agenda for future reforms. This tactic did not escape criticisms from some national fishermen's organizations (Union des Armateurs à la Pêche de France 1998).

Forced to position themselves in the debate on reform, the national organizations of shipowners and fishermen have indicated that access to resources remains, as at the beginning of the CFP, the vital issue for all concerned, despite their often opposing interests. The professional organizations from the countries possessing the deep-sea fleets which are most mobile in EU waters (Spain, the Netherlands, and France) argued in favour of maintaining free access to the 200-mile zone after 2002, as well as the 12-mile coastal zone which guarantees the protection of their inshore fishermen. In contrast, the professional organizations of some other member states are in favour of renationalizing some of the current EEZs and, if need be, of suppressing certain historical rights that can still be exercised within the 12-mile coastal zones. A resolution was voted by the Portuguese Parliament in March 1998, and then endorsed by the organization of Portuguese fishermen, which advocated the extension of the coastal zone to 50 nautical miles (de Jesus 1998). The Irish Fishermen's Organization proposes 30 nautical miles (Irish Fishermen's Organization 1998). In a more indirect intervention, the UK NFFO and the SFF have jointly called for the management of the CFP to be decentralized by transferring to the coastal states the responsibility for applying the rules for conserving stock within the 200-mile zone. Such a step could be tantamount to a form of renationalization of fisheries (NFFO and SFF 1998). Sensitive to these arguments, the EP voted in February 1999, by a large majority, in favour of extending the coastal zone from 12 to 24 miles after 2002. All of the national fishermen's organizations declared themselves to be still strongly attached to the principle of *relative stability*, albeit, if necessary, with some modification of the key for allocating stocks. Here lie the beginnings of a debate on the defence of territory, a recurrent theme in the history of the CFP. Of course the outcome could well be to preserve the status quo and leave the essential rules on access to EU waters intact. But 2002 could well introduce some changes, which might include the revising of historical rights within the 12-mile zone, or even the lifting of the ban on access to the North Sea for Spanish vessels.

The deadline of 2002 is fuelling a debate in all member states about the individual responsibility of fishermen regarding fish stocks, even though it is hard to discern concrete suggestions for reform on this subject. With the exception of Dutch fishermen, to whom it already applies, and of some representatives of the deep-sea fishing industry (for example, Galicians or French), most European fishermen remain resistant to the idea of TACs being replaced by individual transferable quotas (ITQs), which would mark the emergence of individual property rights over fisheries resources. The main argument against ITQs is that these favour the concentration of resources around the large ship-owning companies to the detriment of traditional fishermen. It is, however, important to note that the phenomenon of concentration has started to occur without ITQs. Boosted by the free movement of capital, the consolidation of the large European ship-owning groups has been under way since the 1980s (Pescanova in Spain, Jaczon in the Netherlands). These buy up firms in the EU and the rest of the world. The same trend towards concentration can be observed in the deep-sea fishing sector at the national level (Intermarché in France, Stevenson in the UK).

In a sector which needs significant investment competitiveness depends on the search for economies of scale. In the majority of producing countries, however, concentration poses a political problem, namely the image which both the state and society at large have of an occupation which is historically constructed around the figure of the traditional fisherman as an artisan. This question in turn is generating a debate over what the priority objectives of the CFP should be after 2002. Should they be to help certain countries to preserve the historical model of the traditional fisherman by means of redistributive programmes—the traditional option? Or should they, on the contrary, be to accompany the march towards concentration and the demand for competitiveness, despite the price of financing the social costs of transition—the liberal option? Or should they do both at once—the syncretic option (i.e. reconciling different traditions), which would fit with the European social model?

Finally, the CFP cannot escape from the dynamic of the changes which follow further new enlargement of the EU to include many maritime states situated this time in the East: Poland, Latvia, Estonia, and Lithuania. In Poland, which is the main country concerned, the fisheries sector employed 40,000 people in 1995 (Commission 1997g). The Polish fishing fleet is composed of about thirty factory ships operating principally in the Bering Sea and also of many ageing, small, and underpowered boats which fish herring in the Baltic. At the time of accession, the Polish fleet will necessarily find itself confronted with the requirements of the EU to reduce capacity. This would imply subjecting Polish fishing vessels to a restructuring plan, which would presumably have to be financed primarily from the EU budget. Such a change will involve social and political costs for Poland. It would also carry significant costs for the current EU member states and for the Community institutions, by sharpening market competition between fishermen and by modifying the terms of redistribution once more.

Notes

1 This chapter was translated from the French by Orla McBreen. The author would like to thank Jean-René Couliou, Michel Dion, Alain Laurec, and Dominique Levieil for their critical comments.

2 Full integration of Spain and Portugal into the CFP was achieved on 1 Jan. 1996.

3 Interview with Alain Parrès, Union des Armateurs à la Pêche de France, 9 Feb. 1998.

4 See e.g. the judgment of the ECJ C-4/1996 of 19 Feb. 1998.

5 A measure described, in revealing terms, by an official of a French producer organization as 'collabo' (interview, 22 July 1998).

6 Interview with S. J. Ellson, Chief Inspector for Fisheries, MAFF, London, 8 July 1998.

7 Interview with J. Suárez-Llanos Rodriguez, Shipowners' Cooperative of Vigo, Vigo, 30 Oct. 1997.

8 See Ch. 7 for a comparison with agriculture.

9 Interview with Christopher Nordman, Commission official in charge of consultation on the 2002 review, Brussels, 3 June 1998.

Further reading

There is no recent book in English or French on the CFP. The most recent account is Holden (1994), which is a good description of the main CFP mechanisms. The Manual on the CFP, published by the Directorate-General for Research (European Parliament 1994), remains useful for facts on developments. On the governance of fisheries in general, Crean and Symes (1996) and Symes (1999) offer useful analysis and bibliographic information. On the politics of fishing in the UK and northern Europe, see also Gray (1998), with interesting chapters written both by academics and practitioners.

Articles on the CFP are regularly

published in the academic journal *Marine Policy*, published by Elsevier Science Ltd in the UK. The professional press is also a relevant source of information on the national debates: *Fishing News* (UK), *Le Marin* (France), *Industrias Pesqueras* and *Europa Azul* (Spain).

Crean, K., and Symes, D. (1996) (eds.), *Fisheries Management in Crisis: A Social Science Perspective* (Oxford: Fishing News Books).

European Parliament (1994), *Manual on the Common Fisheries Policy* (Brussels: Directorate-General for Research).

Gray, T. S. (1998) (ed.), *The Politics of Fishing* (London: Macmillan).

Holden, M. (1994), *The Common Fisheries Policy* (Oxford: Fishing News Books).

Symes, D. (1999) (ed.), *Alternative Management Systems for Fisheries* (Oxford: Fishing News Books).

Chapter 14

European Trade Policy

Global Pressures and
Domestic Constraints

Stephen Woolcock

Contents

Summary

Common markets require common commercial policies, hence the early decision of the Treaty of Rome in 1957 to provide a framework for this. Over the years the European Commission established itself as the negotiator for the European Union (EU) on trade issues, but always operating under the watchful eyes of the member governments. Much of the impetus for collective EU policy-making has come from successive international trade rounds, most recently the Uruguay Round. Often tense arguments with the USA have injected further pressure on the EU, on trade in general and agricultural trade in particular. The nature of trade regimes is also changing as new issues come on to the agenda. Environmental, labour, and cultural issues are emerging as tricky subjects for the Millennium Round. On the one hand, the agenda is broadening, bringing in new actors, such as non-governmental organizations (NGOs). On the other hand, industries vulnerable to international competition press for protection. EU and national policy-makers are pulled between contradictory pressures, with little opportunity for parliaments (either European or national) to intervene. This leaves open the question of how effective and credible the EU will prove in multilateral trade diplomacy.

Introduction

The establishment of a customs union requires the participating countries to have a common external tariff.[1] The Treaty of Rome therefore granted to the then European Economic Community (EEC) exclusive competence for a common commercial policy.[2] This was necessary because the member states had to speak with 'one voice' in international trade policy negotiations. The early years of collective trade policy-making were not easy, but they were arguably more straightforward than today. In 1957 the international trade agenda had a relatively narrow focus and consisted of tariffs and a few non-tariff issues, such as multilateral rules on anti-dumping and subsidies. Not surprisingly, therefore, the definition of commercial policy, Article 113 (now 133) (EEC) referred to tariffs, anti-dumping, and subsidies as the area of exclusive EEC competence. The EEC was also not yet a major player in international negotiations, which were still shaped by USA leadership and USA policies of multilateral trade liberalization. Article 228 (now 300) (EEC) provided powers for the EEC to conclude trade agreements with third countries.

Things have now changed. Successive General Agreement on Tariffs and Trade (GATT) rounds have reduced tariffs to minimum levels and extended the trade agenda to include first a range of non-tariff barrier (NTB) issues (during the Tokyo Round 1973–79) and then domestic regulatory issues, such as services, environmental policies, food safety, and animal health issues (during the Uruguay Round 1986–94).[3] This extension of the international trade policy agenda has pushed the EU, as it now is, towards extending the scope of its competence in international trade policy. For example, EU trade policy has, in the past, been predominantly technocratic in nature, with decisions taken after discussion between national and Commission officials. The deepening of the World Trade Organisation (WTO)[4] agenda means that WTO rules now touch on the interests of new and more diffuse constituencies, such as those seeking the incorporation of environmental objectives in all policy areas, including international trade. This brings with it a pressure to make EU decision-making more transparent and accountable.

The EU now plays a central role in international trade negotiations, due to its increased economic leverage and the decline in the willingness and ability of the USA to provide leadership in international trade diplomacy. The EU's leverage stems from the fact that it accounts for 20 per cent of international trade flows (or 44 per cent if one includes intra-EU trade) and about 30 per cent of foreign direct investment flows (both outward and inward). The completion of European market integration in the single European market (SEM) gives EU international trade policy very significant leverage, because it can determine conditions of access to the largest unified market in the world. The EU's leverage has also been increased by an enlarged membership and the introduction of the euro as a common currency in 1999. In international trade policy, as in other areas of EU decision-making, enlargement has also made EU membership more heterogeneous and thus made policy-making even more complex.

EU international trade policy also has a potentially more important role to play, because of the declining willingness on the part of the USA to continue to provide a leadership role. The USA still supports multilateralism, but only when this produces the results demanded by a range of domestic constituencies. During the 1980s the USA made progressively more extensive use of unilateral and regional trade policy instruments because these offered quicker results.[5] In short, the EU must now at least share with the USA the 'burden' of sustaining a multilateral trading system. To fulfil this more important role the EU will need to be an effective and credible actor in international trade diplomacy. In other words changes in the nature of trade policy and the more important role of the EU have created a need for EU decision-making to be more transparent, more democratic, and more effective. Two questions arise concerning how the EU uses its greater economic leverage. First, will the EU be able to agree on common positions and thus be a credible actor in international trade diplomacy, or will internal divisions doom it to be reactive and often ineffectual? Secondly, will the EU use its economic potential to promote multilateral (or plurilateral) market-opening agreements, or simply as a means of defending its own market against foreign competition? This chapter mainly addresses the first question. It seeks to provide an overview of the issues concerning the machinery of EU decision-making for trade policy and thus to assist those interested in the substance of EU policy to understand the factors that shape EU policy and thus address the second question.[6]

Issues in EU decision-making

In order better to understand EU decision-making it is helpful first to emphasize the importance of 'competence', namely the assignment of policy powers between the EU and the member states in any given issue area covered in international trade negotiations. For example, trade in goods falls within exclusive EU competence, but investment remains mainly the competence of the member states. Some areas are subject to mixed national and EU competence. Note that it is the EU collectively (i.e. the member states operating through the European institutions) that is competent, not the European Commission on its own. Note also that it is not just a question of which issues fall under EU and which under national competence, but also of the impact on decision-making of a lack of clarity about competence.

It is necessary, then, to break down the EU decision-making process on trade into three different—but interdependent—phases. The first phase involves the *setting of objectives for negotiations*. Decisions here are made by the Council of Ministers, on the basis of a proposal from the European Commission. But there are important questions concerning how this is done, the degree of flexibility given to the Commission, what role, if any, the European Parliament (EP) and the national parliaments play, and what role NGOs play in the agenda-setting phase. The next phase involves the *conduct of negotiations*. In multilateral negotiations the Commission negotiates for the EU. This is so when the policy issues that are the subject of international negotiations come under the exclusive competence of the EU. But the Commission has, at least to date, also been *de facto* the sole negotiator in cases when the policy issues are of mixed national and EU competence. In accordance with Articles 133 (ex 113) and 300 (ex 228) of the Treaty, the Commission negotiates in consultation with the Council, but how much flexibility does the Commission have, and ultimately who decides on negotiating tactics? Phase three of the process is the *adoption of the results*. Here the Council of Ministers (usually the General Affairs Council of foreign ministers) has ultimate authority to adopt agreements by qualified majority voting (QMV) under Article 133, or by unanimity when the EU is adopting the results of an agreement negotiated bilaterally with a third country, such as the Europe Agreements under Article 310 (ex 238). As the chapter will explain, however, practice diverges from the letter of the treaty. Then I look at the question of how the EU operates in the WTO, on issues such as WTO dispute settlement. As arguments involving the EU on trade in bananas, hormones in beef, and others have shown, WTO dispute settlement now plays an important role in interpreting existing trade rules. Finally, the chapter examines how EU decisions are taken to use instruments of commercial defence, such as antidumping.

Competence

As noted above, the progressive extension of the GATT agenda has forced the EU repeatedly to redefine EU competence. In the Tokyo Round the issue was whether subsidies, government procurement, and technical barriers to trade were EU competence or mixed competence. The EU dealt with this pragmatically by mandating the European Commission to negotiate on all issues, but without prejudice to how legal competences were assigned. The rationale for this was that all the issues were linked in this multilateral round, and that it would have been counter-productive for the Commission to respond on some issues and member states to respond individually on others. When it came to ratifying the results, however, it was no longer possible to duck the question of legal competence. In 1980 a political agreement was reached in which both the EU and the member state governments signed the agreement (Bourgeois 1987; Macleod 1997).

Similar questions arose in the Uruguay Round with regard to services, intellectual property, and investment. The member governments claimed that these were national or at least mixed competence. The European Commission, however, argued, as before, that since all the fifteen negotiating groups included in the Round formed part of a global negotiation, it was essential for the EU to 'speak with one voice'. Following the precedent of the Tokyo Round it was decided that the Commission should be sole negotiator, but without prejudice to the question of legal competence, a pragmatic approach which has worked rather well. The EU has not been prevented from participating in negotiations by disputes over legal competence. The Commission has been happy with the arrangement, which has enabled it to provide the single voice and strengthened the Commission's *de facto* authority. Member governments have been particularly vigilant in their oversight of negotiations in the areas where they claim mixed or national competence, but, provided that the Commission has kept them adequately informed, there have not been major tensions. Indeed, it was not in areas of mixed competence that the EU ran into difficulties during the Uruguay

Round, but in agriculture, a sector where exclusive competence has never been in any doubt. Competence might have been more contentious had there been significant policy divergence between member states on the new issues, but during the Uruguay Round this was not really the case.[7] Member governments have also tended to let legal competence issues take a back seat during such negotiations, because they have been more concerned about getting results; legal disputes over competence undermine the credibility of the EU's negotiating position.

As in the Tokyo Round, the real difficulties in the Uruguay Round negotiations emerged when it came to adopting the agreement. The Commission maintained that the Uruguay Round was negotiated as a package, and therefore should also be adopted as a single package by the EU.[8] The member governments argued that agreement on the new issues of services, intellectual property rights, and investment were outside EU competence and therefore had to be ratified by the member states. Efforts were made to find a political solution to this problem, but the Commission, with the support of some member governments, such as Belgium, opted to refer the matter to the European Court of Justice (ECJ). In previous judgments concerning trade competence the ECJ had largely supported the European Commission's expansive interpretation of EU competence, but in its Decision 1/1994 on the 'Competence of the Community to conclude international agreements concerning services and intellectual property' the ECJ leaned towards the view of the governments which had brought the case.[9] The ECJ ruled that services were EU competence only when there was a cross-border supply of services, or when the labour associated with the provision of a service crossed a border. This judgment significantly limits the scope for EU competence in international services, because most services are provided by establishment (investment in a branch or subsidiary in the target market), rather than through cross-border supply.[10]

ECJ Decision 1/1994 poses a number of potential difficulties for the EU (Krenzler and da Fonseca-Wollheim 1998). For example, there is the possibility of contagion in that issues of mixed or national competence may 'infect' areas that have to date been considered to fall under exclusive EU competence. This problem arises because trade in goods and trade in services are hard to disentangle, and must therefore be negotiated together. The absence of exclusive competence for services could thus undermine existing EU competence for trade in goods. This raises the spectre of the EU losing its single voice in negotiations, with member governments challenging the European Commission's authority to negotiate. The ECJ recognized this in its Decision 1/1994 and went out of its way to stress the need for the EU to speak with one voice. In response, the Commission and Council reached agreement on a Code of Conduct for negotiations on services in 1995.[11] This Code of Conduct was agreed without prejudice to the assignment of legal competence, and provided for the Commission to be the sole negotiator, while member governments could attend the negotiations. Informal meetings might take place, at which only the Commission would be present, but in return the Commission would be obliged to inform the member governments immediately of any decisions taken in such meetings (Code 1994).

The ECJ's Decision in 1/1994 may have ripple effects throughout EU decision-making. If services are intrinsically linked to goods, and services remain mixed competence, unanimity will be required to adopt any agreement negotiated. The Council of the EU seldom votes on major trade issues, although the threat of QMV has given the Commission some leverage. The need for unanimity in areas of mixed competence could reduce the credibility that a member government might be outvoted, and this diminishes negotiating flexibility.

A different problem provoked by the ECJ judgment related to the convention of standstill agreements in the period preceding a multilateral negotiation. Standstill agreements oblige all parties to a negotiation not to introduce new measures restricting market access during the course of the negotiation. Without such an agreement any WTO member could introduce new restrictions simply to offer them as concessions during subsequent negotiations, and thus effectively to defend the status quo. The practice in the GATT–WTO has been for standstill provisions to be global, that is to cover all aspects of the negotiations. If member states retain competence over services and intellectual property, unanimity will be required for the EU to offer a general standstill prior to the new Millennium Round. As some member governments, including Britain and France, are unwilling to commit themselves to a standstill in services, the EU may be unable to offer a general standstill and thus undermine its general negotiating credibility. Moreover, if the EU cannot offer a standstill, then other parties may refuse to do so, thus jeopardizing the success of the negotiations.

In the 1996 Intergovernmental Conference (IGC) the Commission argued, as it had in the 1991 IGC, that services and intellectual property should come under exclusive EU competence.[12] This was rejected by the member governments. The compromise solution was the introduction of an enabling clause in the Treaty of Amsterdam (TOA), Article 133(5); this measure, which is sometimes called *Kompetenz Kompetenz*, enables the member states, acting unanimously, to extend exclusive EU competence to include services, without having to change the treaty. This provision could be used to overcome some of the problems mentioned above; thus, for example, the Council could use the provision to grant the EU competence for a limited period, such as for the duration of a new WTO Round.

Setting objectives

In international trade policy, as in any negotiation, agenda-setting plays an important part. In the Uruguay Round the basic structure of the Round and of the eventual trade-offs were determined during the preparatory period in 1985–6. For example, the decision to include agriculture put pressure on the EU to reform the common agricultural policy (CAP). The inclusion of the new issues of services and intellectual property, in the face of opposition from developing countries, and of textiles and clothing, in the face of resistance from developed countries, set the scene for one of the basic trade-offs that underlay the whole negotiation. In effect the developed countries agreed to liberalize the restrictive Multi-Fibre Arrangement (MFA) for quotas on textiles and clothing and in return the developing members of the GATT agreed to open up trade in services and other new issues.

It is the Council, usually meeting as foreign ministers, that formally determines the EU's negotiating 'mandate'. The Council acts on the basis of a Commission proposal, drawn up by Directorate-General I (DGI) in cooperation with other Commission DGs, and, by QMV if necessary, authorizes a mandate from which the Commission

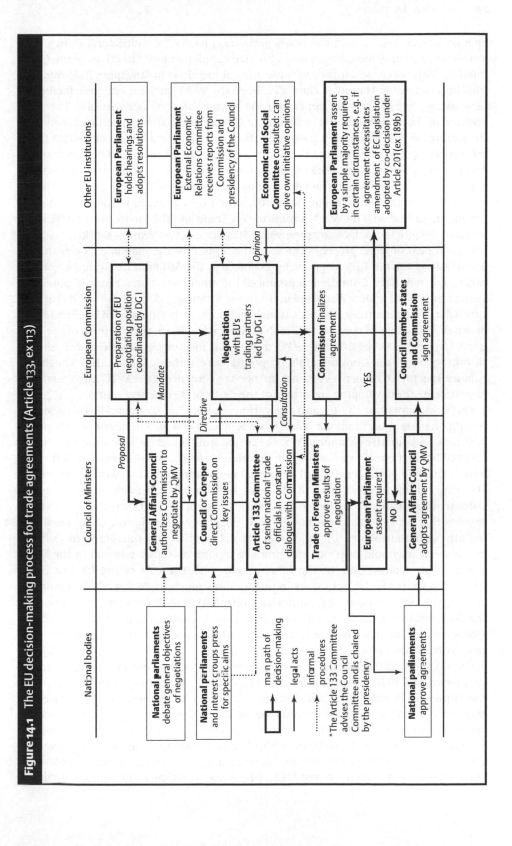

Figure 14.1 The EU decision-making process for trade agreements (Article 133, ex 113)

negotiates (see Fig. 14.1). In the pre-negotiation phase of a multilateral round, and indeed at any time, the Council may also give supplementary directives to the Commission. This was done for the WTO ministerial meetings in Singapore in November 1996 and Geneva in May 1998; these discussed the WTO work programme, including new issues that might later appear on the agenda of WTO negotiations. The EU's position for both meetings was confirmed at Council level, after consultation between the Commission and member governments in the then Article 113 Committee (now the Article 133 Committee), and the Commission spoke for the EU on both occasions. At the Singapore meeting working groups were established to discuss competition and investment. Opposition from developing countries prevented the pursuit of work in the WTO on trade and labour standards, which were referred to the International Labour Organization. The WTO Committee on Trade and the Environment (CTE) was retained despite the lack of any progress in its previous two years of work.

A good deal of work precedes the formal adoption of the mandate. For example, preparations for the EU's negotiating position in the Millennium Round began in early 1999, when the Commission produced informal papers on a range of potential agenda items. These were discussed in the (now) Article 133 Committee and its various specialist sub-committees. The EU's trade position was also influenced by discussions in other formations of the Council, such as, in particular, those on reform of the CAP (see Chapter 7). As regards the WTO ministerial meeting in Seattle at the end of November 1999, the Commission's proposals were rather general. They sought to balance specific EU objectives against the need to convince other WTO members, and in particular the developing countries, of the desirability of a new round.

The involvement of the EP and the various national parliaments in this agenda-setting phase is at best indirect. The EP is not closely involved in developing detailed positions and discusses a summary of the negotiating mandate only after it has been adopted by the Council, rather too late to influence the EU's objectives. The difficulty here is that too public a debate of a detailed negotiating mandate would inform the EU's negotiating partners what the EU's 'bottom line' is; this might undermine the Commission's ability to exchange concessions with other WTO members. For these reasons the formal mandate is not a public document. The EP can, however, shape the atmosphere in which EU objectives are determined and thus have an indirect influence; it may hold hearings and produce reports on topics relevant to the WTO agenda. This indirect role of the EP contrasts with the role of the US Congress, which can shape the US objectives in negotiations much more directly by granting, or by withholding, negotiating authority. Consultation with national parliaments in the EU is left to individual member governments. In most cases national legislatures appear to play no direct part in setting negotiating objectives, and they do not have an opportunity to debate the official EU 'mandate'.

The EU's negotiating objectives are also subject to influence from a range of interest groups and NGOs. The Commission actively encourages input from important constituencies in order to help it shape specific negotiating objectives. In some cases detailed negotiating positions cannot be established without NGO input, such as private sector priorities on market access. Information on impediments to access for European exporters and investors to third-country markets has been improved as a result of systematic efforts by the Commission to collect information centrally. Contrary to the situation in the USA, which has a set of formal Trade Advisory

Committees, there is no formal structure of advisory committees at EU level. Contacts are informal, although reasonably well structured, with bodies such as the Union of Industries of the European Community (UNICE) and other EU-level sectoral associations. The Commission sometimes encourages new channels of communication, when it judges that it does not have adequate input from NGOs, or when it seeks to establish a single point of contact. For example, in late 1998 the Commission promoted the establishment of a European Services Network (ESN) in order to have a single interlocutor for trade in services. In late 1998 the Commission also initiated a new series of consultations on the WTO agenda with 'civil society', i.e. environmental, developmental, and other NGOs. This reflected the heightened awareness of the influence of such groups following the collapse of negotiations on a Multilateral Agreement on Investment (MAI), which was, in part, due to a campaign by NGOs opposed to the agreement.[13]

The conduct of negotiations

A key issue in the negotiating phase is how much flexibility the Commission has to interpret EU objectives. Too much flexibility for the Commission would mean limited control by member governments over the course of negotiations. Too little flexibility would make it impossible for the Commission to negotiate. Critics of EU decision-making in trade policy have accused the EU (meaning the Commission) of being unwilling to negotiate without a mandate from the Council and unable to negotiate once it has a mandate, because mandates tend to be so tightly drafted. In practice the mandates are usually tight only on sensitive issues, such as agriculture. In response to this criticism it has been suggested that the EU adopt a procedure equivalent to the 'fast track' procedure used in the USA. Under the US Constitution, Congress has authority over international commercial policy, and the executive branch can negotiate only when it is granted explicit authority to do so. The granting of negotiating authority has, in recent years, been based on a fast-track procedure, according to which Congress can accept or reject, but not amend, the results of an international agreement negotiated by the US Trade Representative (USTR) on behalf of the President and the executive branch. Consultation between the USTR and Congress is ensured, because the negotiators from the USTR know that whatever they negotiate must be approved by a majority in both the US House of Representatives and the Senate.

Under the Treaty of Rome, as amended by the Maastricht Treaty on European Union (TEU), it is the Council which grants negotiating authority to the European Commission (Articles 133 (ex 113) and 300 (ex 228)), and to which the Commission has to report. The treaty provisions are different from the US arrangement in that they can involve a good deal of discussion back and forth A European fast track would presume that the Commission could negotiate as it wished, subject only to the critical condition that whatever it negotiated would have to be approved by the Council. Such an approach would provide flexibility, while at the same time providing a form of accountability to the Council and thus the European electorate. If American experience can be taken as a model, the likelihood would be that the Commission would maintain regular constant contact with the Council, mindful of the need for its eventual endorsement.

So far, however, the European process differs from that of the USA, in that the member governments are not ready to grant the Commission such discretion over how and when it consults the Council. One reason for this is that issues of mixed competence are being negotiated. Another is the fear that the Commission might strike deals on issues which impinge upon national interests, which member governments would then find it difficult to reverse. In the USA case the USTR must balance different sectoral interests in defining the overall US interest. In the case of the EU the Commission would have to balance different national interests, as well as different sectoral interests, in order to define a Community interest. So far the member governments have wished to retain control over the trade-offs between the various national and sectoral issues.

The member governments therefore favour constant dialogue with the Commission during any negotiation. The main forum for this is the Article 133 (ex 113) Committee, which discusses negotiating positions on individual topics and the links between them. Before all sessions of international negotiations there are preliminary meetings between the Commission and national officials to go over any last-minute modifications to the EU's position. If the negotiations are in Geneva, where the WTO is located, these meetings are normally staffed by members of the member governments' delegations in Geneva, and occasionally include officials from national capitals on very sensitive issues. At important stages of a WTO negotiation the trade ministers from the member states are generally in attendance. This was the case, for example, at the launch of the Uruguay Round in Punta del Este in September 1986, at the mid-term review meeting in Montreal in December 1988, at the Brussels ministerial meeting in 1990, which was supposed to conclude the Round, and, of course, at the final meetings in Geneva in December 1993 and Marrakesh in April 1994.

Constant 'consultation' is needed because of the dynamic nature of international negotiations. Even when the negotiating mandate is tightly drawn, as especially in the case of agriculture, there is always a need to reinterpret it in the course of constantly shifting negotiations. This provides infinite scope for differences of opinion between the Commission and the Council and within the Council and Commission. On the politically less sensitive and technical issues the EU response is decided by the Commission, after consulting the Article 133 Committee. The Article 133 Committee rarely votes formally, but the sense of the meeting is taken informally through the conclusions of the presidency. If the Commission decides to proceed with a policy approach or proposal which does not have the clear backing of the Article 133 Committee, it can expect difficulties in the Council. If the national trade officials on the Article 133 Committee are doing their job properly, they will reflect the preferences of their own ministers (M. Johnson 1998). On more important issues, to interpret the mandate, or to adapt shifts in the negotiating position of other WTO members, the Council may issue formal directives to the Commission as provided for in Article 133. The formal conclusions of Council sessions also give guidance to the Commission.

This consultation process between Commission and Council is at the heart of EU decision-making process in international trade (Woolcock and Hodges 1996). Whether it works well or not depends a great deal on practice. For example, member governments will have confidence that the Commission is reflecting their interests only if it keeps them fully informed of developments. Such consultation is very resource-intensive and the relevant DGI units coordinating policy are small. These limited resources make it, on occasion, difficult to maintain intensive levels of consultation. If, for example, briefing papers arrive late from the Commission, it will be difficult for the members of the Article 133 Committee to consult with their colleagues in other government departments.

The Commission must, on occasion, venture on to the tight-rope of 'exploratory' talks, without the safety net of backing from the Article 133 Committee or Council, for example when the international negotiations reach an impasse and compromises must be made on both sides. The Brussels GATT ministerial meeting in 1990 was a case in point, when an impasse arose over the level of commitments from the EU to reduce agricultural subsidies. The Commission explored a potential deal with the USA government and the Cairns Group of developed and developing country agricultural exporters, without the backing of the Council. The EU member governments with a hard line on agriculture at that time (France, Ireland, and Germany) had ensured that the Commission had a negotiating mandate with little flexibility. The national trade and agricultural ministers present in Brussels got wind of the Commission's exploratory talks from the EU's negotiating partners and called the Commission to heel, thus effectively undermining the negotiating credibility of the Commission and the EU as a whole. What had been planned as the final phase of the Uruguay Round collapsed in part as a result of this, as Woolcock and Hodges (1996) explain in detail.

Neither the Commission nor the Council is a homogeneous actor. Proposals from the Commission are coordinated by DGI, but virtually every area of policy has an external dimension, whether this is agriculture, the environment, or industry. Coordination within the Commission can be very tricky, especially on some of the new trade policy issues, such as those which touch upon 'domestic' (i.e. EU) regulatory competence. A good example is the importation of meat produced by countries allowing the use of hormones or antibiotics banned in the EU. In this case EU policy requires a common position to be reached between the different DGs responsible for agricultural, environmental, and consumer policies. Each of these DGs will have different concerns. In the past these concerns have generally been pursued independently of international trade policy considerations. This makes the task of reconciling EU regulation with international trade rules especially challenging. Chapters 7, 12, and 15 provide further illustrations.

Similarly, the positions and preferences of the member governments may also be less than homogeneous. Member governments have different ministries leading, or coordinating, national inputs into EU international trade policy. For example, in Germany it is the Ministry of Economics which leads; and in Britain it is the Department of Trade and Industry. But often coordination is not easily achieved, and governments, like the Commission, have to reconcile trade considerations with domestic concerns.

A complex machinery has developed to coordinate trade issues: the Article 133 Committee; Coreper (permanent representatives of the member governments in Brussels) and the General Affairs Council (consisting usually of foreign ministers); but other specialist councils (agriculture, industry, finance, environment, etc.), each with its own preparatory committees, develop sectoral policies. There is no systematic forum for trade ministers, although they do sometimes meet informally or under the aegis of the General Affairs Council. These different representatives of the member governments have their own institutional interests and may espouse different policies. For example, the Article 133 Committee tends to try to keep international trade policy away from Coreper (M. Johnson 1998). Trade ministers may take a broader view than ministers for agriculture, but the latter may still be able to hold wider interests hostage to their own sectoral aims (Hayes 1993). The General Affairs Council, usually composed of foreign ministers, mostly takes ultimate responsibility, but is often preoccupied with 'high politics' issues, the wider EU agenda, or common foreign and security policy (CFSP) issues; and they may also temper decisions on trade with wider foreign policy interests. Occasionally decisions rise to the level of heads of state or government in the European Council.

At the agenda-setting stage it is hard for other bodies to exert influence. The EP is consulted on negotiations as they proceed, and in recent years the Commission has gone out of its way to keep its External Economic Relations (REX) Committee informed. The EP now also has the opportunity to send an observer (usually the Chair of the REX Committee) in the EU's delegation to some major events, such as the launch of a new round, but with no speaking rights. The EP is, however, excluded from the key consultations (between the Commission and the Council) that determine EU negotiating positions, and hence its representatives tend to be passive observers rather than active participants.

The issue of control over negotiations has created more tensions in EU trade policy than that of competence. A number of proposals have been made to help remedy these tensions. It has been suggested that the Council, in the shape of the presidency, should be present in all negotiations 'alongside' the Commission. This was suggested by several member governments during the 1996 IGC, but opposed by the Commission on the grounds that it would undermine the principle of a single (Commission) voice for the EU. There have also been proposals for a general code of conduct to govern consultations between the Commission and Council, but efforts to draft one have failed to find a compromise acceptable to both Commission and Council. The consensus among practitioners in both the Commission and the Article 133 Committee has so far been that the costs in terms of reduced flexibility would outweigh any benefit in terms of tighter control by member governments. The process therefore continues to rest on the ability of the Commission and national officials to maintain effective communication.

The adoption of results

The Council of Ministers is responsible for adopting the results of international trade agreements. When the EU has exclusive competence, decisions are taken by QMV; in the case of bilateral association agreements the Council decides by unanimity (see Fig. 14.2). Even where the Treaty provides for QMV, however, the practice has been to seek consensus on important trade agreements, such as for the conclusion of GATT rounds, in order to avoid direct clashes on issues that are sensitive for individual governments. This is much the same as happens in many other policy domains where QMV is the decision rule, but consensus decisions are the practice. On trade issues, as on decision-making on the SEM, the possibility of a vote provides an incentive for member governments likely to be outvoted to work for compromises (see Chapter 4). In trade policy the threat of a vote is perhaps less potent, partly because in bilateral

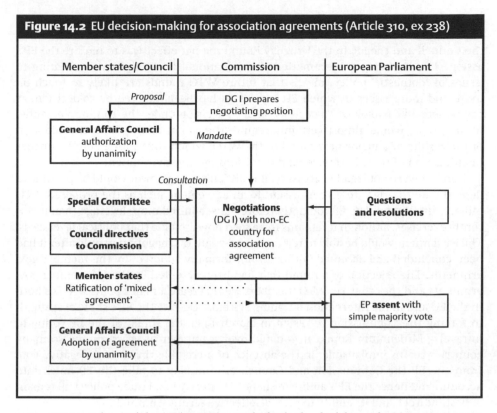

Figure 14.2 EU decision-making for association agreements (Article 310, ex 238)

agreements under Article 310 (ex 238) unanimity is the decision rule. Moreover, as we saw earlier, tensions over the assignment of competence have tended to reduce the feasibility of calling votes.

The lack of recourse to voting at the stage of the adoption of agreements has an impact on the prior negotiating process. If consensus is the norm, the Commission has limited room for manœuvre, because it cannot appeal to a qualified majority of member governments to outvote minority interests. Member governments which oppose elements in a proposed package, such as further liberalization of agriculture, may effectively be able to exercise a veto on the outcome. It should be stressed that this tends to happen only when a member state sees its 'vital national interests' affected. On issues of less importance, informal or implicit voting does occur in the Article 133 Committee. In other words, when there is a clear qualified majority in favour of a policy within the Committee, member governments in the minority will not generally hold out for very long. This may help to explain why the EU manages to reach common negotiating positions most of the time, but runs into difficulties if member governments dig in their heels.

The EP has no power under the treaty provisions concerning trade policy; indeed, in the 1991 IGC member governments went out of their way to exclude the EP from any role in adopting the results of multilateral trade agreements. This contrasts with the situation as regards bilateral association agreements under Article 310 (ex 238), to which the EP must give its assent by a simple majority vote. However, Article 300 (ex 228), dealing with other kinds of bilateral trade agreement, does require the assent of the EP for any agreement which has institutional or budgetary implications, or when a trade agreement requires changes to EU legislation adopted by co-decision between the Council and the EP. In the Uruguay Round the net effect was to require the EP's assent. The changing subject-matter of international trade diplomacy, relating to issues of 'domestic' policy, means that future WTO rounds are likely to touch on more and more issues in which EU legislation has been adopted by co-decision, as can be seen in Chapter 12. The extension of co-decision under the ToA, implemented in May 1999, would almost certainly require the assent of the EP to the adoption of the results of a major new round of the WTO, which cover, for example, further liberalization of trade in services and provisions on the environment.

Even if it were not legally necessary, it is difficult to see how it would be possible to deny the EP the right to give its assent to an agreement such as the proposed WTO Millennium Round. The EP could, therefore, have aquired more leverage than it currently exercises, although it remains to be seen how credible that political leverage is. The Parliament would be able to reject the end-result of a negotiation only after it had been concluded and accepted (although not formally adopted) by the member governments. The rejection of a round that had been accepted by the EU member governments and the other 112 WTO members would create a major political crisis both in the EU and in the international trading system.[14] Despite the EP's show of strength in forcing the Commission to resign in March 1999, the threat of the EP voting to unravel a Millennium Round negotiated over a number of years among so many countries seems implausible. In the absence of a credible threat of a negative vote from the EP the Commission and Council are unlikely to take the EP much into account, and hence the EP's ability to shape EU international trade policy will remain at best indirect, and its ability to provide effective scrutiny limited.

National parliaments could perhaps help to fill this democratic deficit in EU trade policy, but scrutiny at the national level is not systematic and largely superficial. National parliaments have an opportunity to exercise a scrutiny role by their influence over their own governments, but the remoteness of international trade negotiations limits this possibility, making it hard for national parliamentarians to follow the events, or to have any effective impact. The negotiations are hard to follow, because in the multiple layers of bargaining national positions are modified first within the EU and then in the exchange with the other WTO partners. Most national parliamentarians therefore feel that they have no effective voice in the process, and hence the formal adoption of the results of international trade negotiations by national parliaments becomes a rubber-stamping exercise. However, on a few issues with a more populist dimension, national and European parliamentarians may become more engaged. For example, the case of the European ban on fur imported from countries permitting the use of metal leg-hold traps comes to mind. In this case the EP pressed for a ban, and national parliamentarians pressed ministers to support a policy that was in direct conflict with the EU's international obligations under the GATT. Animal rights groups argued that international trade rules should not limit national policy preferences on animal rights. But national parliaments, which do not systemically scrutinize European or international trade policy, do not generally balance animal rights concerns against the wider trade interests, which might include maintaining a rules-based international trading system. This need to balance special interests against wider public interests in trade policy is not, of course, new. What has changed is that increasingly the special interests are no longer specific industries, such as textiles or footwear, seeking protection, but wider constituencies responding to the more intrusive nature of international trade diplomacy.

To sum up, policy-making in trade is located in the interchange between the Commission and member governments, in the Council and the Article 133 Committee. This delivers outcomes, but the process is not especially transparent or accountable. Political control of EU trade policy by the EP or national parliaments (or both) might improve democratic accountability, but such a 'politicization' of EU trade policy would certainly add inertia to the EU decision-making process, and considerably constrain the EU's room for manœuvre.

The EU and WTO trade disputes

In 1994 a new Dispute Settlement Understanding (DSU) was adopted as part of the Uruguay Round; it has considerably strengthened the dispute settlement procedures of the WTO. In the past it was possible for any Contracting Party (CP) to the GATT to frustrate dispute settlement by blocking either the establishment of a panel or the adoption of a panel report. The new DSU made the establishment of a panel more or less automatic in the event of a dispute, and made adoption of panel reports much more likely; decisions can now be blocked only if all members of the Dispute Settlement Body (DSB), effectively the whole WTO membership, agree that the panel report should *not* be adopted. As a result of these changes, there has been increasing response to dispute settlement procedures within the WTO, a development which is becoming an important aspect of EU trade policy.[15]

This new development poses a number of important questions for the EU. First, who should decide whether and when the EU initiates a procedure against a trading partner? The initiation of a dispute settlement procedure is an important trade policy decision. One case in point was the decision, taken in February 1999, to initiate a procedure against the USA on the grounds that US 'fair trade' laws, such as the infamous Section 301, are inconsistent with GATT rules. The EU has repeatedly complained about Section 301, and claimed that it is in violation of the GATT, but to challenge it directly in the WTO could be interpreted as an aggressive act with important implications for EU–USA relations. The practice to date has been for the Commission to initiate WTO cases, after taking soundings from the Article 133 Committee. Only when the issue is very sensitive have such decisions been taken in the Council or Coreper. In 1998 and 1999 the Council Secretariat argued that this practice was illegal, because WTO dispute settlement cases may affect the EU's international obligations and only Coreper and the Council had a sufficiently wide perspective on the EU's broad international interests. These proposals from the Council Secretariat were resisted by trade policy practitioners, including the national officials on the Article 133 Committee, with the riposte that formal voting in the Council on dispute settlement cases would produce decisions more slowly and less effectively than under the current arrangements.[16] Response time in WTO disputes can have important consequences; using its current practices the EU tends to react more quickly than the

USA government, where it is necessary to go through a series of inter-departmental committees.

Issues of competence and control arise in relation to WTO disputes, as they do in EU trade policy in general. Thus if a dispute arises in an area of mixed national and EU competence, it could result in both the Commission and member governments speaking at the WTO dispute settlement panels. This danger was recognized by the ECJ in its Decision 1/1994, but the discussions since 1994 between the Commission and the Council on a Code of Conduct have failed to resolve this issue. For the time being, the practice is that the Commission speaks for the EU on matters concerning the interpretation of WTO rules, even when disputes touch on issues of mixed competence. It remains to be seen what would happen if an individual EU member state were found to be in violation of its obligations under the General Agreement on Trade in Services (GATS), where there is mixed competence. Under the DSU an aggrieved country which wins its case may ultimately be able to take cross-sector retaliation against the EU; thus the failure of one member state to comply fully with its WTO obligations in an area of mixed or national competence could result in trade 'sanctions' ('compensation' in WTO terminology) against the EU as a whole in trade in goods. This hypothetical case is presented only as a means of illustrating the kind of tensions that may arise, although, to date, there have been no such cases. On dispute settlement issues, as in other areas of EU trade policy, a choice has to be made between continued use of informal arrangements and a codification of procedures. The former may be more effective, but is not conducive to transparency, while the latter facilitates greater transparency and might encourage more democratic control, but could well result in a less effective decision-making.

Instruments of commercial defence

There is another pillar of EU trade policy which is based on the application of instruments of commercial defence. These are mainly deployed to defend EU industries against the 'unfair' trade practices of the EU's trading partners. These instruments include: anti-dumping duties, applied when exporters into the SEM sell at below the costs of their domestic production; countervailing duties imposed when exporters into the EU receive subsidies; and remedies under the 1994 Trade Barriers Regulation against 'unfair trade practices' of the EU's trading partners that impede market access for EU exporters.[17] The EU, like other WTO members, may also take safeguard actions under Article XIX of the GATT (as revised 1994), when an industry suffers from—or is threatened with—serious injury as a result of a surge in imports into the SEM, even though this is not the result of 'unfair' trade practices. The EU can also, subject to some limits, build reciprocity provisions into single market directives, such as the Second Banking Coordination Directive, or the Utilities Directive on public procurement in utilities (energy, water, and telecommunications). Finally, it has been argued that certain regulatory instruments, such as definitions of rules of origin, have been used as protectionist instruments.

Anti-dumping measures are by far the most commonly used instrument of commercial defence in the EU. Countervailing duties have been little used by the EU, in part because EU member governments have maintained that national subsidies are legitimate policy instruments and should not be penalized under the GATT rules. Safeguard actions have not been favoured, because GATT rules require that these cannot be applied selectively, and that any GATT member that applies them must compensate all the exporting countries affected.

Anti-dumping procedures

Anti-dumping actions are the most frequently used instrument for 'commercial defence'. Article VI of the GATT provides considerable scope for WTO members to apply anti-dumping duties selectively on particular products exported to them, when it is found that these have been dumped. There is no obligation to provide compensation.

The EU introduced its own regulation for imposing collective anti-dumping measures in 1968, to replace the previously disparate national regimes. These provisions have been repeatedly revised, either to conform with changes in GATT rules or as a result of EU initiatives. The current EU provisions require three main tests before anti-dumping duties can be applied: evidence of dumping; injury or the threat of injury to a European industry; and a demonstration that the imposition of anti-dumping duties would be in the 'Community interest'. The EU rules follow GATT law and are more liberal than GATT rules, in that they provide for a 'Community interest' test. But GATT rules have been shaped by the EU and other major users of anti-dumping measures, such as the USA and Australia, in such a fashion that it is not difficult to use them as a protectionist instrument, while remaining technically within the letter of GATT law.

Figure 14.3 sets out the basic elements of the EU policy process in the application of anti-dumping provisions. Broadly speaking the Commission has more power in the application of anti-dumping measures than in international trade policy in general. Whereas the Commission has right of initiative in general trade policy, it has decision-making powers in applying anti-dumping measures. For example, it is the Commission that decides whether the EU initiates an investigation in response to complaints from European industry (which must represent 50 per cent of the sector concerned)[18] or from a member government. It is also the Commission which determines whether there is a case for imposing anti-dumping duties, by applying the dumping, injury, and Community interest tests. In other countries these tests are carried out by different bodies; for example, in the USA the Department of Commerce determines dumping margins, but the more independent International Trade Commission determines whether there is injury.[19] The GATT sets out the methods to be used when measuring dumping margins and determining injury, but the wording of Article VI provides for considerable discretion on the part of the agency implementing the measures.

With regard to the third test of 'Community Interest', Article 21 of the Basic Regulation on Anti-Dumping sets out the principles to be applied.[20] In 1997 the Commission, in response to criticism of its application of the Community interest provision, produced new guidelines after consulting European industry, consumers, and other interested parties. The code provides for analysis of: the relevant market and

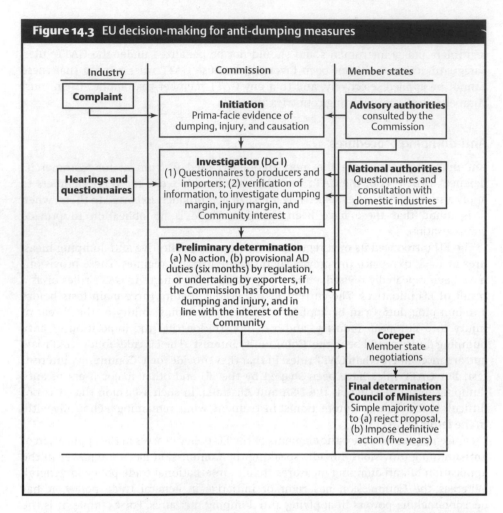

Figure 14.3 EU decision-making for anti-dumping measures

competition within it; the interests of producers, traders, upstream and downstream users of the products; and the impact on consumers. The Commission's guidelines state that hearings will be organized to comment on the definition of Community interest at the request of the interested parties. These reforms were designed by the Commission to make it harder for narrow and protectionist interests to drive anti-dumping actions. None the less the Commission retains considerable discretion in applying the Community interest test and remains subject to continued criticism for the way it applies this.

The Commission also decides whether the EU should impose provisional (anti-dumping) duties. Such duties are allowed under GATT rules on the grounds that dumped imports can inflict considerable damage on an industry in the period before definitive duties can be procedurally authorized. A provisional duty stands for six months (with a possible extension to nine months), unless the Council decides, by QMV, to reverse the Commission decision. The Commission must propose, and Council adopt, a definitive duty before the provisional duty expires. But when it comes to adopting the definitive duty, the Council needs only a simple majority of member governments. Until the end of the Uruguay Round decisions on anti-dumping were subject to QMV. As part of the internal settlement on the adoption of the Uruguay Round, France, with support from some other member governments, insisted on the lower hurdle of simple majority for agreeing definitive duties. This was opposed by the Netherlands, Britain, and initially Germany, but the German government shifted its position to create a majority in favour of the change. The aim appears to have been to encourage effective and speedy implementation of EU remedies against 'unfair trade' as a *quid pro quo* for agreeing to the liberalization resulting from the Uruguay Round.

One further element of the process gives the Commission yet more power, namely the scope to negotiate (price) 'undertakings' with exporters found to be responsible for dumping products, as an alternative to the imposition of duties. These undertakings are provided for under GATT and have certain attractions to exporters, because part of the economic rent from an anti-dumping action then goes to the exporter in the shape of higher revenue, at the expense of the EU consumer. As in the case of provisional dumping duties, the undertaking negotiated stands unless there is a qualified majority in the Council opposed. The Commission has opted to make extensive use of undertakings, with the result that the EU settles far more dumping cases through price undertakings than any other WTO member.

The Commission is largely responsible for implementing EU anti-dumping measures, but subject to a number of checks. The member governments are consulted throughout via an Advisory Committee, chaired by a Commission official, and can therefore influence Commission thinking at every stage. The Commission has the advantage, however, of generally having more information at its disposal than national officials. The Council is ultimately responsible for the imposition of anti-dumping duties, although the shift to a simple majority vote for the approval of definitive duties enhances the power of the Commission. However, we should note that the enlargement of 1995 to include 'liberal traders' such as Sweden strengthened the more liberal coalition in the Council.

Some of this debate is reflected within the Commission as well. Different DGs have different interests which may have a bearing on a specific case. DG IV (Competition) tends to be more wary of anti-dumping actions than DG III (Industry), although the latter may sometimes champion the downstream users of a product in the definition of Community interest. In 1997 Sir Leon Brittan, then the responsible Commissioner, argued against imposing anti-dumping duties on D-RAM integrated circuits from South Korea, even though the anti-dumping unit in DG I had proposed them. Even within DG I there may be differences between the individual units responsible for determining dumping and dumping margins and injury and Community interest.[21]

The Trade Barriers Regulation

Remedies against unfair trade can be applied in response to measures which violate GATT–WTO rules, as well as to certain practices of other WTO members which do not violate GATT rules, the so-called non-violation cases. For example, restrictive business practices in another WTO member, which represent a barrier to market access or distort trade, might be seen as 'unfair' practices and are not covered by any explicit GATT or GATS rule. The EU introduced a general 'unfair trade' provision in 1984, the

New Commercial Policy Instrument (NCPI),[22] modelled on the US Section 301, which has been the main instrument with which the USA has pursued aggressive unilateralism (Bhagwatti 1991). Under Article XXIII of the GATT it is possible to bring an action against a WTO member if it is believed that the benefits of membership are nullified, even if there is no violation of the GATT. But the NCPI required QMV in the Council, and there has not been a mobilizable majority in favour of an aggressively unilateralist policy (Bhagwatti 1991).[23] The EU may have used unilateralist rhetoric in trade relations, for example, in its criticism of domestic regulation in Japan, which limits market access for EU exporters; yet it has not been able plausibly to threaten unilateral measures in the same way as the USA. At the conclusion of the Uruguay Round a number of member governments, led by France, called for the introduction of an EU 'fair trade' instrument with more teeth. The result was the Trade Barriers Regulation (TBR), adopted in December 1994. This provides the opportunity to act against 'unfair' measures in other countries which inhibit, or prevent, access to third-country markets as well as against 'unfair trade' practices which result in, or threaten, material injury to an EU industry. In other words the TBR is not confined to the EU domestic market and not primarily intended to result in measures imposed at the frontiers of the EU, but to put pressure on third countries to eliminate barriers to trade. The TBR covers measures that are illegal under GATT rules, as well as non-violation issues. In other words, it was intended as an instrument of aggressive unilateralism that could be used more readily than the NCPI.

The procedures used for the TBR are set out in Figure 14.4. A new element in this Regulation is that individual firms can initiate investigations by the Commission, as can member governments. The Commission makes its appraisal of the complaint by gathering information from member governments and consulting with the third country concerned. It has five months to consider the case, after which it must decide whether to initiate a WTO dispute settlement action against the third party concerned, a decision which requires prior consultation with the Article 133 (ex 113) Committee. In contrast to the procedure for Section 301 in the USA, the TBR requires the EU first to exhaust all available multilateral dispute settlement procedures. If the third party concerned fails to comply with the WTO dispute settlement panel decision, the TBR provides a basis for imposing sanctions against the country concerned, although the EU must seek authorization from the WTO DSB before taking retaliatory measures. Use of the TBR requires a qualified majority of member governments in favour of taking trade sanctions. So far, the balance of opinion within the Council of Ministers is against the pursuit of aggressive unilateralism, and hence the TBR seems more likely to be used mainly as a means of identifying potential WTO dispute settlement cases.

The European trade policy process

EU international trade policy has become more multilateral and more liberal over the past fifteen years. In recent years it has also become more proactive, compared to a previously reactive and defensive approach to trade diplomacy; how liberal or

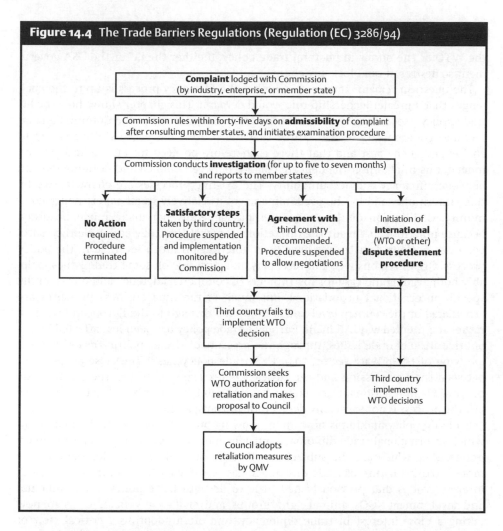

Figure 14.4 The Trade Barriers Regulations (Regulation (EC) 3286/94)

Complaint lodged with Commission (by industry, enterprise, or member state)

Commission rules within forty-five days on **admissibility** of complaint after consulting member states, and initiates examination procedure

Commission conducts **investigation** (for up to five to seven months) and reports to member states

No Action required. Procedure terminated

Satisfactory steps taken by third country. Procedure suspended and implementation monitored by Commission

Agreement with third country recommended. Procedure suspended to allow negotiations

Initiation of **international** (WTO or other) **dispute settlement procedure**

Third country fails to implement WTO decision

Commission seeks WTO authorization for retaliation and makes proposal to Council

Third country implements WTO decisions

Council adopts retaliation measures by QMV

protectionist is widely debated. Trade economists tend to see the EU as protectionist (M. Wolf 1994). Nevertheless, the consensus of quasi-impartial reports (GATT 1991–5) on EU trade policy in recent years suggests there has been a trend towards a more liberal position, even if this falls short of the expectations of liberal economists. Indeed, the much trumpeted 'fortress Europe' was never constructed (Hanson 1998).

The EU has also made a determined effort to be more proactive in international trade policy. This is reflected in the vigour with which in 1998–9 the EU took the initiative in pressing for an ambitious new round of the WTO, to be known as the Millennium Round. This contrasts with the mid-1980s, when the EU resisted US and Japanese calls for what became the Uruguay Round. These changes, together with the continued economic strength of the EU and the establishment of a single currency, mean that it is now in a better position to play a leading role in the international trading system. The EU also has more of an opportunity to exert its influence at the multilateral level because the USA appears to have lost its way in international trade diplomacy, at least for the time being. In practice neither the EU nor the USA can shape the international trading system alone. Broad agreement between the EU and USA will be needed if future trade negotiations are to change the nature and scope of the WTO or the norms in bilateral trade policy. If either the EU or the USA government so desires, it can block any change.

The question remains, however, whether the EU policy process is up to the challenges that a greater leadership role would demand. This chapter shows how the EU trade policy process has evolved over the years. Practitioners in the Commission and member governments tend to argue that the process has successfully adapted to challenges in the past and that there is therefore no need for any radical reform. Indeed, this might upset the delicate balance between Council and Commission and between efficiency and accountability. The existing processes are characterized by their informality and by the predominance of a relatively small expert policy community. Codification of the procedures has generally not made much headway, because practitioners favour the discretionary power that they enjoy. Neither European nor national legislatures have been able to gain much leverage in the policy process. Organized business interests play an active role on some trade issues, palpably both arguing the case for instruments of commercial defence and on sectorally specific international negotiations. But much of the time business pressures are articulated at the country level and are only fed through to the European level in a rather fragmented way. All in all, European trade policy has been less affected by the politicization of trade issues, through the pressure of elected politicians or by direct lobbying of the private sector, than USA trade policy has.[24] The close cooperation between the Commission and the Article 133 (ex 113) Committee, the technocratic heart of EU international trade policy, has undoubtedly contributed to its efficiency. But the process is not especially democratic or transparent.

EU trade policy-making is now under growing pressure because of the manner in which international trade diplomacy intrudes more and more into domestic policy preferences, which are the subject of either EU or member state legislation. This more intrusive nature of trade diplomacy has provoked a reaction from a range of interest groups that previously had little to do with trade policy. Environmental and development NGOs, animal rights groups, and 'civil society' in all forms are now taking a close interest in trade diplomacy, and often adopting a critical view of existing or proposed multilateral rules. Such 'civil society' groups often criticize the rules-based system of the WTO, which has been hailed as an important advance by international trade experts, for putting the priorities of international liberalization and the interests of multinational business above those of the environment, consumers, or balanced economic development.

In addition, the issue of competence remains on the table. The issues raise by ECJ Decision 1/1994 still need to be resolved, in order to prevent tensions about competence eroding the effectiveness of EU decision-making. Further enlargement of the EU will be an added complication that may overload the inherited and largely informal structures.

Evolutionary change

What might be done to remove or reduce some of these tensions? If they are not mitigated, they could undermine the ability of the EU to pursue credible strategies in international trade. It has been argued that all phases in the process are linked: agenda-setting, negotiation, adoption of results, and dispute settlement. Thus decisions about competence, including the 'contagion' of areas of exclusive competence by others with mixed competence, have important implications for decision-making. The extension of mixed competence may well reduce the credibility of QMV in the adoption of the results of a negotiation and thus reduce the EU's margins of manœuvre. Yet it is difficult to see how the competence issue can be resolved. None the less, although much is made of the need for a single voice in negotiations, these difficulties over competence have not created insurmountable difficulties for the EU. The EU has adopted the pragmatic approach of allowing the Commission to negotiate on all issues without prejudice to legal competence, and of operating by a kind of common-sense consensus-building. The enabling clause in the ToA also provides an additional means of responding to problems over competence.

A more difficult problem is one of how negotiating mandates for the Commission are decided. Proposals for a code of conduct to structure consultations between the Council and Commission were, in 1999, a dead letter, leaving everything to depend on open and effective communication. One simple palliative would be to increase the staffing of DGI so that it might be more responsive to the needs of the member governments. Until recently, such a suggestion would have little chance of running, but the efforts being made to reform the Commission, including by internal restructuring, may offer an opportunity for the Commission to regain some lost ground.

One major feature of the decision-making process is the weak, and arguably further weakening, importance of QMV. This not only makes the adoption of agreements harder, but reduces the EU's flexibility in so far as individual member governments exercise a kind of veto power. Simply to insert QMV in more places in the treaties would in itself not be enough; member governments have to be willing to take votes in the Council. With regard to the use of instruments of commercial defence, such as anti-dumping duties, there might be a case for harmonizing voting procedures and reverting to QMV for adopting definitive anti-dumping duties, although such a policy change would be strongly resisted by France and some other member governments.

The EU trade policy process is not particularly transparent or accountable. There is scope for both the EP and national parliaments to exercise more oversight. The EP probably has sufficient powers to play a more active role in scrutiny, but, on the evidence so far, seems unlikely to use these powers to veto complex international trade agreements in the assent procedure. A different approach for the EP would be to try to engage with the process at the negotiation phase—not so odd a suggestion if we make a comparison with the American trade policy process. It would be difficult for the EP to have much influence unless it could credibly threaten to block a major trade deal negotiated by the Commission on behalf of the EU. There is not much sign that MEPs are keen to pay more attention to this policy domain. A more probable development may turn out to be more active attention from national parliaments, given the degree to which trade impacts on other issues: food safety, the environment, human rights, animal rights, and so forth. Here we can see the tension between efficiency and democracy in sharp form, not least since domestic political preferences are beginning to have far-reaching repercussions on EU trade policy. On trade matters, as in other areas of public policy, parliamentarians often take partial views of the process and may not be particularly interested in the wider (European) Community interest.

European trade policy is also under rather more pressure from NGOs to be more transparent, more open, and accommodating of other policy considerations.[25] Broadly speaking, the policy-makers have gone a good way in this direction within the WTO, as was reflected, for example, in the positions adopted by the major WTO members at the Geneva WTO Ministerial in May 1998. But this leaves to be resolved which NGOs should be consulted and when. So far in the EU what has happened is that a variety of forms of informal consultation take place with a range of NGOs—the mechanism planned for the WTO Millennium Round in particular. The alternative option of formal structures has, probably wisely, been avoided. Experience from the USA with formal Trade Advisory Committees suggests that these do not prevent NGOs from lobbying through alternative channels. On the other hand, the US system favours more transparency, helped by the assignment of responsibility for evaluating injury to an independent agency, a device from which the EU could learn a valuable lesson in defining 'Community interest'.

The picture is one of incremental and piecemeal adjustments in the trade policy process in response to both internal and external developments, and to changing political claims and constraints. By and large incrementalism over the years has edged the EU in a more, rather than less, liberal direction. Yet this is to understate some of the new forces bearing down on trade policy. On one side, we can see pressures of fragmentation and contestation, as societal interests and preferences impinge on the policy process. These constrain the EU positions on the new sensitive trade issues, these days as likely to be society-driven as producer-driven, especially in the EU and the USA, where 'civil society' groups are well organized and increasingly alert on trade and investment issues. On the other hand, there are pressures for a more coherent and integrated approach to policy. The EU now has a single currency and hence potentially a quite different weight in international economic diplomacy. The EU is on the verge of developing a collective defence identity as well, in turn perhaps a spur to a more vigorous common foreign policy. The common trade policy used to be the mainstay of the EU's collective external economic relations. It now occupies more crowded territory.

Notes

1 This chapter is dedicated to Dr Michael Hodges, my friend, colleague, and co-author of an equivalent chapter in the 1996 edition of this volume, who died suddenly in June 1998. I would like to thank Joakim Rieter for his very competent research assistance.

2 This chapter refers to the European Union's international trade policy. It uses 'EU', in preference to 'EC', and includes issues included in EC exclusive competence, as well as issues on which competence is mixed (i.e. partly EC and partly national competence). It uses 'international trade policy' rather than 'commercial policy', because 'trade policy' is the term in common English usage. It must be stressed that trade policy in this chapter is defined as including both border measures, such as tariffs and quantitative restrictions, and those regulatory issues that were previously seen as 'domestic' policy, but which now constitute the core of 'trade' policy.

3 For information on the substance of the Uruguay Round, see Croome (1995).

4 The GATT Secretariat was replaced by the WTO in Jan. 1995. The WTO provides a single institutional framework, including dispute settlement for GATT 1994, the system of trade rules developed since 1948, and the General Agreement on Trade in Services (GATS).

5 On trends in USA trade policy see, e.g. Low (1993) or Destler (1995).

6 For a balanced but descriptive view of EU trade policy, see GATT (1991–5).

7 See Paemen and Bensch (1995) and Woolcock and Hodges (1996) for an extensive treatment of the EU in the Uruguay Round.

8 The European Commission had initialled the agreement struck in Dec.

1993, but this was subject to ratification by the Council of Ministers.

9 Opinion 1/94, *European Court Reports I* 5267 (15 Nov. 1994).

10 The General Agreement on Trade in Services (GATS) identifies four modes of supply: cross-border supply (international phone services); the consumer of services moving to the provider (tourism); the supplier moving to the customer (professional services); and establishment within the host country.

11 This was necessary despite the fact that the Uruguay Round had been completed, because the sector negotiations in financial services, telecommunications, and transport implementing the GATS framework agreement continued throughout the 1995–7 period.

12 For a debate on the 1991 IGC as it relates to commercial policy, see Maresceau (1993).

13 The failure of the MAI was probably due to other factors, such as the EU and Canada seeking the exclusion of 'cultural' (i.e. film and audio-visual) industries from the obligation to provide right of establishment, and the USA seeking a broad 'national security' exemption. The intensity of non-business NGO lobbying on the MAI issue nevertheless illustrated the growing influence of such interests and led the Commission to seek a closer dialogue with them.

14 The EP would prefer to have a positive power to shape EU trade policy, see De Clercq (1995).

15 The case could be made that WTO panels are being asked to rule on issues, such as a number of trade and environment cases, that should really be the subject of intergovernmental

agreement rather than a quasi-legalistic WTO panel.

16 Interviews with Council and Commission officials.

17 Council Regulation 3286/94, adopted by the Council on 22 Dec. 1994.

18 In the case of an industry complaint the complainant must represent 50% of EU production in the sector concerned.

19 Before 1995 a single unit with just 120 staff within DG I decided on dumping and injury. There are now two units, one determining the dumping margin and the other dealing with injury and Community interest, and the number of staff has been more than doubled.

20 Council Regulation (EC) 384/96 of 22 Dec. 1995.

21 Another case in point was Sir Leon Brittan's resistance to the use of anti-dumping actions in the steel sector in 1998–9, despite claims from the industry that steel was being diverted from Asian markets as a result of the Asian economic recession and dumped on the SEM. Steel industries in the USA and the EU were under intense pressure, and action by either the USA or the EU would have resulted in a downward spiral of protective actions with damaging effects on the prospect of economic recovery in Asia.

22 Regulation 2641/84, *OJL* 252, 20 Sept. 1984.

23 US policy was aggressively unilateralist because, in contrast to the use of countervailing or anti-dumping duties (which protect domestic industries from unfair import competition), the US policy of the 1990s sought to force third-country governments to change national policies in order to facilitate improved (i.e. 'fair') market access opportunities for US exporters of goods and services.

24 This refers to the work of the Article 133 Committee in international trade diplomacy. With regard to the application of trade instruments, such as anti-dumping duties (where the European Commission determines the dumping margin and degree of injury, and the Commercial Questions Group decides on whether the EU takes action) there is not the same counter-balance to vested interests as in the Article 133 Committee.

25 Business-based NGOs have been active in trade policy for a longer period and have to a greater or lesser degree been able to represent business and sector views in trade policy.

Further reading

On the issues of competence and the institutional framework of EU international trade policy-making, see van den Bossche (1997) and for a wider view including all aspects of EU trade and external economic relations, Maresceau (1993), and Macleod *et al.* (1996). On the more political aspects of decision-making, see Johnson (1998), and for a summary of some of the substantive policy issues, see Hanson (1998) and Paemen and Bensch (1996).

Hanson, B. T. (1998), 'What Happened to Fortress Europe? External Trade Policy Liberalization in the European Union', *International Organization*, 52/1: 55–86.

Johnson, M. (1998), *European Community Trade Policy and the Article 113 Committee* (London: Royal Institute of International Affairs).

Macleod, I., Hendry, I. D., and Hyett, S. (1996), *The External Relations of the European Communities* (Oxford: Clarendon Press).

Maresceau, M. (1993) (ed.), *The European*

Commercial Policy after 1992: The Legal Dimension (Dordrecht: Nijhoff).

Paemen, H., and Bensch, A. (1995), *From the GATT to the WTO: The European Community in the Uruguay Round* (Leuven: Leuven University Press).

van den Bossche, P. (1997), 'The European Community and the Uruguay Round Agreements', in J. Jackson and A. Sykes, *Implementing the Uruguay Round* (New York: Clarendon Press, 1997), 23–103.

Chapter 15

Trade with Developing Countries

Banana Skins and Turf Wars

Christopher Stevens

Contents

Summary

European Union (EU) policies towards developing countries have evolved from their post-colonial origins under changing internal and external pressures. World Trade Organization (WTO) rules on preferential agreements are tighter than those of the General Agreement on Tariffs and Trade (GATT). Mediterranean enlargement of the EU has increased resistance to concessions on agriculture and textiles. Economic development in the more successful former colonies has improved their competitiveness in sensitive goods. EU policies towards central and eastern Europe, and towards the southern Mediterranean countries, have created alternative priorities and aid programmes. Turf wars within the Commission, and divergent interests among member governments, have inhibited the adjustment of EU policies. The story of the banana regime vividly illustrates the tensions and the constraints, including the impact of new WTO procedures and intense US pressure. Another example is the trade negotiations with post-apartheid South Africa, which presented the EU with awkward choices. The established pattern of EU trade policy towards developing countries is giving way under these multiple pressures.

Introduction

Policy-making in EU trade and aid towards developing countries used to be a relatively simple affair. It was focused on one major instrument and one Directorate-General (DG) of the Commission. While the member governments remained the ultimate decision-makers, they were not heavily involved except at five-year intervals. During the 1980s, and especially the 1990s, things became a lot more complex. By 1999 four DGs, five Commissioners, and the European Parliament (EP) were all closely and directly involved in the formulation and implementation of policy (if transition economies are included), and the member governments were also deeply enmeshed in the process. Moreover, decisions had to be framed in response to pressures in Geneva (from GATT and later the WTO) as well as Brussels and the national capitals. The reasons for this are varied, and include the need to find portfolios for an increasing number of Commissioners.

One striking feature of the recent period has been for trade policy to evolve away from non-reciprocal trade preferences for developing countries within a multilateral framework towards a hub-and-spoke system of reciprocal trade accords. While portrayed by its supporters as a move towards liberal trade and WTO compatibility, critics can point to evidence in the opposite direction. If the latter are to be believed, the tenor of EU trade policy towards developing countries is rather different from that described by Woolcock (Chapter 14) on trade policy towards other developed states.

The change is illustrated in this chapter by the decisions in 1995 to deny post-apartheid South Africa trade membership of the Lomé Convention, and in 1998 to propose the replacement of Lomé by a set of regional economic partnership agreements (REPAs). Both decisions were influenced by the challenge within the GATT–WTO to the legitimacy of EU policy, prompted by a dispute over bananas and by jostling between DGs I, IB, and VIII.

Pressures for change

The Lomé Convention, administered by the Commission's Directorate-General for Development (DG VIII), used to sit at the centre of the EU's development policy as a unique agreement, combining a liberal trade regime with substantial aid within a framework of jointly agreed principles and institutions. It is unique no longer: the EU now has a host of other preferential trade agreements; its aid to non-African, Caribbean, and Pacific (ACP) states has been growing much faster; and the Treaty on European Union (TEU) provides a broad statement of the aims of development cooperation.

By the same token, DG VIII is pre-eminent no longer (see Fig. 15.1). It shares trade policy towards developing countries with DG IB, and aid policy with DG IA (for the

Figure 15.1 Commission responsibilities for development

(*a*) as at July 1999

Commissioner **Sir Leon Brittan** **DG I**	Commissioner **Hans van den Broek** **DG IA**	Commissioner **Manuel Marin** **DG IB**	Commissioner **João de Deus Pinheiro** **DG VIII**
• Multilateral trade policy–WTO • GSP • Trade with East Asia and APEC • Sectoral trade policy (textiles, clothing, footwear) • Anti-dumping	Aid to FSU (the former Soviet Union)	Aid to: • South and South-East Asia • Latin America • Mediterranean	Trade with and aid to: • ACP • South Africa

Commissioner **Emma Bonino** **ECHO** Humanitarian aid world-wide	**Joint Service for Management of Community Aid to non-Member Countries (SCR)** Administration of development aid world-wide

(*b*) as (proposed) at September 1999

Commissioner for **Development and Humanitarian Aid** **Poul Nielsen** **Development DG**	**Commissioner for External Relations** **Chris Patten** **External Relations DG**	Commissioner for Trade **Pascal Lamy** **Trade DG**
• Development policy and development-related issues • Incorporating much of ex-DG VIII but not trade policy, CFSP elements on human rights, but incorporating parts of ex-DG IB	• Inherits most of ex-DG IA • *Inter alia* takes over human rights and CFSP units of ex-DGVIII • Coordinates all external relations activities of Commission • Relations with Western industrialized countries and Far East	• Bilateral and multilateral trade policy and instruments including GSP and trade role of ex-DG VIII

ECHO Humanitarian aid world-wide	**SCR** Common Service for External Relations (role to be revised)

states of eastern Europe and the former Soviet Union) and DG IB (for Asia and Latin America). A new common service now administers all development aid. Emergency aid policy and administration are handled by the European Community Humanitarian Office (ECHO), with its own Commissioner. To the extent that EU accords must be made WTO-compatible, DG I became pre-eminent.

The current importance of the WTO results partly from a chance set of events (the banana dispute). This has had a disproportionate impact by shattering the shell of a relationship that already had been fundamentally weakened by decades of gradual underlying change. It has given impetus to the search for a new model which has also involved competition between DG I and DG VIII, between the member governments and the EP, and between different conceptions of the relationship between the EU's bilateral and multilateral trade policies.

The rest of this section sketches some of the fundamental pressures for change, as well as the impact of more personal turf wars. It is followed by an extensive analysis of the principal catalyst for change: the dispute in the WTO over EU trade policy on bananas. The next two sections deal with the manifestation of this change: the first negotiation from scratch of a free trade agreement (FTA) with a non-candidate, non-neighbour (South Africa), and the subsequent attempt to apply the same approach to the recasting of the Lomé relationship.

Tensions between formal policy and effective interests

At the heart of this shift has been an evolution of Europe's economic and political priorities. A change in the structure of Europe's economy led to a growing disparity between the focus of the EU's formal development policies and its economic and political interests in the South. At the same time, the collapse of communism to the east and concern with political and demographic patterns in its southern neighbours refocused political attention closer to home.

Over the past decades there has been a change in the relative importance of various sources for European growth, with non-traded services and trade between developed countries increasing in relative significance. The distortions caused by the common agricultural policy (CAP) (see Chapter 7) have simply accentuated a trend away from the traditional colonial trade pattern of importing raw materials from the South and exporting manufactures to it. In its place, a trade has developed with parts of the South that emphasizes a two-way flow of manufactures and services.

But the countries at the centre of the EU's formal policies are not well represented in this new trade pattern. The ACP's share of EU trade has fallen dramatically over the period of the Lomé Convention. Whereas imports from other developing countries have increased substantially, those from the ACP have stagnated in current terms (see Fig. 15.2).

Over time a tension developed between the focus of formal policy towards the South and the focus of the EU's immediate economic interests. The tension was initially defused because each EU member state retained control over many of the most potent commercial policy instruments. But as powers have been transferred increasingly from national to Union level, this capacity to run an independent shadow policy has withered; the emphasis of Union-level policy has acquired a direct importance for national interests. This was the broader significance for Euro–South

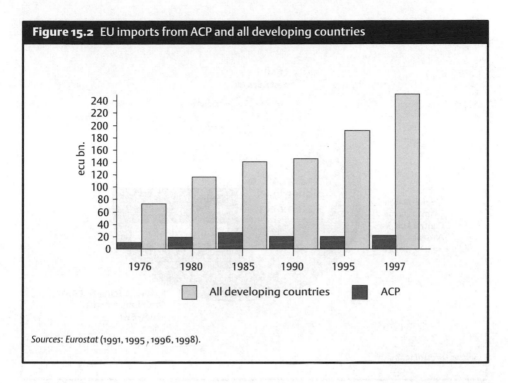

Figure 15.2 EU imports from ACP and all developing countries

Sources: Eurostat (1991, 1995 , 1996, 1998).

relations of the single European market (SEM), which led directly to the WTO dispute over the EU banana regime.

The EU has managed over the years to fashion with some skill a quasi-foreign policy based on a limited range of Union-level instruments. Trade preferences have bulked large in the relationship with the South. The system that has grown up is particularly complex. It provides different degrees of preference to various groups of developing countries. The depth and breadth of these preferences are not necessarily related to the level of development of the recipient country and, indeed, access better than most-favoured nation (MFN) is not limited to developing countries.

The EU's current trade policy defines three broad bands of states, each of which accounted for approximately one-third of EU imports in 1995 (Fig. 15.3). The first and most favourable access is made available to the 121 developed, developing, and transition states that fall in turn under three types of trade regime (all with different and, as will be seen, questionable justification within the WTO). They are: the Lomé Convention (seventy trade members); the bilateral agreements that the EU has with thirty-one of its southern and eastern neighbours plus the remaining members of the European Free Trade Association (EFTA); and a superior tranche of the Generalized System of Preferences (GSP) available to twenty states. The second group comprises the newly industrialized, middle-income, and poor countries that receive only the standard GSP, numbering some forty-seven. Last, and at the base, with the least favourable access, is a group of ten states that receive the misnamed *most*-favoured-nation treatment: these include the advanced industrialized states that do so by virtue of their WTO membership, together with states that are not in the WTO (such as North Korea), but to which the EU offers autonomously MFN access.

Figure 15.3 The EU's tariff system

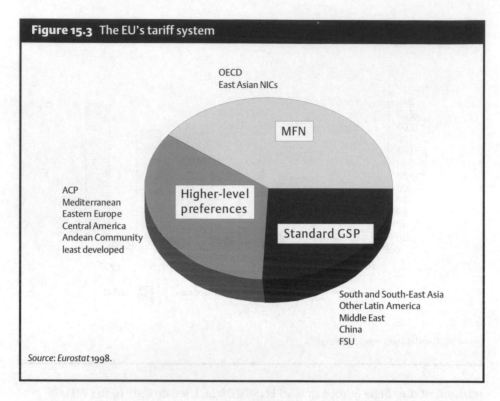

OECD
East Asian NICs

MFN

ACP
Mediterranean
Eastern Europe
Central America
Andean Community
least developed

Higher-level preferences

Standard GSP

South and South-East Asia
Other Latin America
Middle East
China
FSU

Source: Eurostat 1998.

The value of trade preferences to the beneficiary is related inversely to the level of protectionism (at least if the matter is viewed only in a short-term, static perspective). The 1990s have been a decade of liberalization, reducing the vitality of any preferences. Hence, the whole edifice built up over the years by the EU is subsiding gently as its foundations are weakened by liberalization. The trade preferences of the ACP, the Mediterranean, and some Latin American states will tend to lose their vitality over the next decade as liberalization reaches important products. The two most important Lomé preferences on the EU market are privileged access for some CAP products and exemption from the Multi-Fibre Arrangement (MFA). Under the Uruguay Round agreement the MFA will be phased out by the end of 2004.

This will leave just one really important preference in agricultural trade via guaranteed prices for some ACP states under the Lomé Convention for certain temperate agricultural products, and through tariff cuts for the ACP, Mediterranean, eastern European, Andean, and Central American states and many others. These are valuable to their beneficiaries only as long as the CAP maintains artificially high prices in Europe. The CAP has withstood many attempts at fundamental reform, as is clear from Chapter 7, but it will come under pressure in the next WTO Agricultural Round scheduled to commence in 2000, which some are arguing should be broadened to cover the concerns of the developing countries.

Institutional competition

Despite the declining economic importance of the EU's favoured partners, and the dwindling value of its preferences, the force of institutional inertia might well have left policies intact had change not been forced. The principal catalyst was the banana dispute, but change was also mediated by turf wars between Commissioners. In particular, the combination of dismal economic performance by the ACP and growing interest in 'emerging markets' elsewhere contributed to a competition between DGs VIII and I over portfolio responsibility for South Africa. Prior to the South African elections of April 1994, which brought the African National Congress (ANC) to power, Sir Leon Brittan (then also responsible for the Europe agreements) had visited South Africa and flown the kite of an FTA between Europe and South Africa. This struck a chord both in the white establishment (which had sponsored South Africa's classification in the GATT as an industrialized country, partly to distance itself from other African states) and among elements in the ANC that associated the Lomé Convention with much poorer countries.

In the event, DG VIII managed to assert its portfolio responsibility for the post-apartheid negotiations with South Africa, but the proposal that these be in the form of an FTA stuck. This, in turn, provided DG VIII with an entrée into the world of reciprocal agreements, similar in most respects to trade accords that had traditionally been the responsibility of DG I. As recognition grew of the importance of the WTO as an arbiter of the multilateral legitimacy of all these agreements, this new approach provided DG VIII also with a basis for involvement in the Union's deliberations on multilateral trade policy.

At the same time there were institutional forces operating in the opposite direction to keep the Lomé Convention distinct from other Union actions. These pressures were evident primarily in the field of aid, because of the differing legal basis of the Union-level assistance channelled through the Lomé Convention and that channelled through the annual budget. The Lomé activities are financed through the European Development Fund (EDF), which is not part of the Union's budget but is funded by direct contributions from the national budgets of the member states. The legal basis for the EDF is an Internal Financing Agreement drawn up between the governments of the member states. This reflected member state ambivalence in the 1950s and 1960s to funding what was then the largest Community-level aid programme from the normal budget.

Apart from aid channelled under the Lomé Convention, the Union now funds a wide range of aid programmes directly from the EU budget. These include programmes for aid to countries in the Mediterranean, eastern and central Europe and the former Soviet Union, Asia and Latin America, as well as food aid and emergency aid. Before the TEU, most broad policy decisions on Community aid policy outside of the Lomé framework were taken at the Development Council, on the basis of the original Article 235 of the Treaty of Rome (EEC). This allowed the Council, acting unanimously, to pursue a Community objective for which the EEC Treaty had not provided appropriate powers.

The arrangements for budgetary aid, based to a significant extent on broad interpretation of these treaty clauses and administrative regulations, was superseded in the TEU by a clearly defined set of objectives. Title XVII of the TEC establishes the legal basis for Union-level activities. Article 130 u (now 177) includes the provision that 'Community policy in the sphere of development cooperation . . . shall be complementary to the policies pursued by the Member States'. The phrase 'shall be complementary' has been taken to imply that development cooperation is not an area in which the principle of subsidiarity is dominant, i.e. aid is not an instrument that must be exercised at either a Union or a national level. On the contrary, the phrase provides legal justification to the view that there are sixteen aid programmes, one each for the member states plus one for the Commission. Union-level aid policy is neither superior nor inferior to national policy.

Another consequence of the TEU for development cooperation concerns decision-making. Along with other areas of Union decision-making, action on development cooperation can now be approved by qualified majority voting in place of the unanimity previously required. One very important exception to this rule, however, is the EDF. As an extra-budgetary arrangement, unanimity remains the rule. The retention of unanimous voting in the Council is not the only consequence of this anomalous status of the EDF. It also means that the EP has no direct powers to influence either the level or the distribution of the aid. Both features have endeared the EDF (and hence Lomé) to successive UK governments. The budgetary fate of a post-Lomé aid regime has still to be decided.

The banana problem

Origins

The WTO banana dispute has cast a shadow not only on the Lomé Convention, but also on most elements in the EU's complex set of trade policies with developing countries. These have all evolved over the years and in an international environment that differs markedly from today's. The dispute arose because of tension between parallel changes in the EU (the completion of the SEM) and in the GATT (the Uruguay Round). To a certain extent the rules administered by the WTO are more stringent than the old regime under the GATT, but this is not the main source of change. Rather, it is a change of attitudes which evolved during the Uruguay Round: exceptions from MFN treatment are now viewed in a more sceptical light than in times past.

In the opinion of the Union, the preferential access provided to ACP exports was justified under Article XXIV of the GATT, read in the light of Part IV, and, in particular, Article XXXVI, para. 8, under which developed countries 'do not expect reciprocity' for preferences given in trade negotiations to less developed countries. This position was challenged in 1993 by the GATT panel established to investigate Latin American complaints concerning the European banana regime.

The SEM Link

The banana problem had its origin in the EU's difficulty in balancing three sets of demands:

- those arising from the changes required for the completion of the SEM;
- the Union's treaty obligations under the Lomé Convention; and
- its obligations under the GATT.

While often portrayed in terms of a simple clash between 'liberal traders versus protectionists', the range of interests underlying the conflicting positions was more complex. The completion of the SEM involved changes to the market for bananas, because they were one of the few agricultural products not yet covered by common rules. Not only were bananas not subject to the CAP, they were also not subject, in effect, to the common commercial policy. As a result there were three tariff regimes operating within Europe:

- duty-free imports, by virtue of preferences for specific exporters under the Lomé Convention's Banana Protocol (in France, the UK, and Italy);
- duty-free imports, by virtue of a special derogation for the importer (Germany); and
- 20 per cent duty-paid imports in the Benelux countries, Ireland, and Denmark.

Relatively high-priced Caribbean and African bananas found a market in the first group of states. Lower-priced 'dollar' fruit from Latin America dominated in the other two.

This differentiated regime survived because member states could use licensing to control direct imports of 'non-preferred' fruit and Article 115 to control indirect imports. Both mechanisms fell victim to the SEM. They had either to be replaced by something else or the preferred suppliers would lose market share to the lower-cost dollar fruit.

Interest groups

This complex mixture of long-established national regimes spawned close links between importing governments, exporting governments, and commercial interests. It is not surprising, therefore, that it spawned an intricate set of interest groups. In consequence, the number of parties active in the negotiation of a successor regime was substantial. (See Table 15.1.)

The European Commission played a central role but did not have an entirely consistent position. DG VI (Agriculture) was primarily responsible for the formulation of a new regime but, because the pre-SEM competences were largely national, its leadership role was not as marked as is normally the case for agricultural products. DG VIII, as custodian of the Lomé Convention, had responsibility for ensuring effective implementation of the Banana Protocol under any new regime. In addition, DG I (External Relations) had an interest in the banana debate, both because its North–South Directorate was responsible for relations with Latin America and, more importantly, because of its responsibilities for the GATT and the concurrent Uruguay Round negotiations. Figure 15.1 lists the distribution of Commission responsibilities. For conversion and comparison the recent reorganization of the European Commission is also shown.

The EP played a role in the banana story, even though it had no formal right of initiative. Both the Development Committee and the External Relations Committee prepared reports on the subject that were generally favourable towards ACP interests.

Table 15.1 Banana interest groups

Main types	Sub-divisions	Interests
European Commission	DG VI DG VIII DG I	Support for EU producers Support for ACP Support for GATT negotiations
European Parliament	Development and External Affairs Committees	Support for ACP
Member states	UK, France, Italy Belgium, Germany Netherlands	Continuation of preferential links Unrestricted imports (most via Antwerp) As Belgium and Germany, but balanced with development concerns for Caribbean and Surinam
Companies	Geest, Fyffes[a] United Fruit, Standard Fruit, EU importers and ripeners	Protection for high-cost trade (plus access to other markets) Unrestricted imports; maintenance of dominant position in 'dollar' trade
Supplying states	Caribbean Africa Latin America	Strong protection in traditional markets Protection in traditional markets Unrestricted imports

Note: [a] The Caribbean suppliers were Fyffes and Geest, which then sold its interests to WIDBECO, a joint venture of the Windward Islands producers and Fyffes.

The member states were divided into two groups (see Box 15.1). The companies involved in transporting, marketing, and, in some cases, producing the fruit fell into two similar categories, but once again with some cross-cutting interests. The two European companies most closely involved with the import of fruit from the Caribbean, Geest and Fyffes, were active in pushing for a new regime that would defend their traditional markets. Geest, in particular, is believed to have worked in close alliance with Caribbean producers lobbying in support of the Banana Protocol (Pedler 1994: 70). On the other side, the US companies involved in plantation production in Central America and in transporting dollar fruit—United Fruit (Dole) and Standard Fruit (Chiquita)—together with importers and ripeners based in Belgium, the Netherlands, and Germany, wanted a removal of restrictions on the banana trade. As will be seen from the riposte to the new banana regime, described below, such 'protectionist' and 'free trade' stances were not quite as clear as they might seem. What both sets of companies really wanted was to fend off competition in their traditional markets, while opening up possibilities elsewhere in the EU.

The supplying states can be roughly categorized into the same two groups— protectionist suppliers of EU and Lomé bananas and liberal suppliers of dollar

Box 15.1 The member governments' line-up on bananas

Those member governments with strong interests in the matter tended to act in two main groups, but with some movement between them, which turned out to be of critical importance in obtaining a final agreement.

The UK, France, and Italy all consistently supported a regime that would give clear guarantees to their preferential sources of supply.

Germany was equally clearly in the opposite camp, demanding a continuation of its duty-free access to bananas from any source. Bananas had acquired a symbolic importance in Germany, linked to the recovery of prosperity after the Second World War, and probably accentuated by their association in the eastern part of the country with the change of regime in 1989–90.

Germany was supported strongly by Belgium, which, in addition to supplying its domestic market with dollar fruit, had an interest in the role of Antwerp as a port of entry for much of Germany's consumption. The Netherlands was in a somewhat ambivalent position: its consumption of dollar bananas, as well as support for liberal trade and successful completion of the Uruguay Round, counselled support for the German position; on the other hand, the Netherlands' traditional interest in development matters, together with its close ties to Surinam, tended in the other direction.

fruit—but here again these broad distinctions hide subtle variations. Among the ACP centres there was a latent tension between the Caribbean and African banana exporters. The former are the highest-cost external producers; they need absolute guarantees in their traditional market and would not benefit from improved access to other European markets. African producers, by contrast, are medium cost and might be able to offset losses in their traditional market against gains in the other European markets. The Latin American states favoured a liberal trade regime, although each had its own interests (depending in part on whether production was indigenously controlled or undertaken by a US company, or both), resulting in policy differences.

The new regime

The square of mutually incompatible positions was circled to produce a common decision by the usual combination of chance and design (see Box 15.2). The solution adopted by the EU was to implement a two-tier import regime. A temporary regime was introduced to cover the first half of 1993, and a permanent system established thereafter. In both cases Caribbean and African bananas continued to enter the Union duty free, but dollar fruit were subject to a two-tier tariff. A tariff quota (set initially at 2 million tonnes) of imports from Latin America paid a specific duty of 100 ecus per tonne (equivalent to an *ad valorem* tariff of 24 per cent at 1992 unit values); for imports above this threshold, the duty increased to 850 ecus per tonne (206 per cent *ad valorem* equivalent). The object of the two-tier tariff was to allow the Latin American countries to continue to supply their traditional share of the market while imposing a serious barrier to attempts to increase their market share at the expense of preferred suppliers. Caribbean and African suppliers no longer had an absolute advantage in the UK and French markets, but they had a substantial tariff advantage, *provided that* the Latin American tariff quota had been set at a level that would leave space for them.

An additional feature of the new regime, which fuelled much of the subsequent

Box 15.2 How the banana decision was reached

The Commission proposed to introduce a CAP regime for bananas under Article 43 (EEC). This meant that the matter would be decided in the Agricultural Council and any decision would be taken by qualified majority vote (Pedler 1994: 78). The draft proposal issued on 1 August 1992 was broadly favourable to the cause of EU–ACP bananas. A quick review of the voting strengths of the main protagonists would have suggested that the 'free traders' would have sufficient votes to form a blocking minority. Germany, Benelux, Denmark, and Ireland had twenty-eight votes between them, with only twenty-three required to block the proposal. Yet the final decision, reached after votes in December 1992 and February 1993, was broadly in line with the Commission's initial proposal (the main trade-related difference being that the latter proposed an absolute quota of 2 million tonnes from all sources).

This came about because countries did not vote entirely in accordance with their assumed position within the 'protectionist' and 'free trade' camps. That they did not do so was a result partly of persuasion, partly of accident, and partly of broader considerations. The fact that the UK was President of the Council during the second half of 1992 and lobbied hard in favour of the ACP is likely to have enhanced the persuasion element of the equation. Ironically, the assumption of the presidency by Denmark (a 'free-trader') also benefited the 'protectionist' cause, but for different reasons.

A first vote was taken at the Agricultural Council on 17 December 1992 which dealt only with the trade aspects of the new Banana Trade Regime, leaving the internal implementation to be dealt with at the February 1993 meeting. Although the details were significantly changed from the Commission's original proposal, it remained fundamentally geared to the preservation of protected markets for EU and ACP fruit. The Belgian government voted for the regime (although it would have been expected to support freer trade). Later, the Belgian government claimed that it had been misled over the exact effects of voting for the package (Pedler 1994: 85).

When the matter came back to the next Agricultural Council, in February 1993, for the internal details to be agreed, there was again a qualified majority, although the Belgians changed sides. Denmark, in the presidency, had the casting vote and decided in the interests of Community decision-making to vote for the proposal.

controversy, was the introduction of three types of licence for importers of the 2 million tonne quota for dollar fruit. The reason for this innovation was that the new regime was expected to lead to a fall in prices in the protected markets and to an increase in price in the free markets. The companies engaged in supplying the former argued, successfully, that their profit margins would be eroded. The licences were designed to allow them to make profits in the free market in order to achieve a rate of return overall that would enable them to continue to ship Caribbean and African fruit. One consequence, of course, was that the traditional suppliers of dollar fruit found themselves with unwelcome new competitors in their traditional back yard.

Defending the new regime

As is the fate of compromises, this one was attacked by many of the interests it was supposed to balance. In general, it found favour with the preferred suppliers, but it was opposed vociferously by German importer interests and Latin American exporters. As a result of these complaints, two third parties—the GATT and the USA—became involved, together with the European Court of Justice (ECJ).

Intra-EU complaints

The complaint of the German importers, which was taken up by the German government and backed by those of Benelux, centred on the imposition for the first time of a tariff, albeit a relatively low one. The German government sought a ruling from the ECJ that it was guaranteed unimpeded access to the fruit, and that the measure amounted to an expropriation and redistribution of market share. The Court ruled against the two petitions (in respect of the interim and the longer-term regulation), on the grounds that the new regime did not cause 'serious and irreparable damage' to Germany, since the regulation allows the Commission to raise the tariff quota in line with demand. This provided a reiteration of the power of the ECJ in providing legal solutions to problems that are essentially commercial and political.

The GATT complaint

The dollar fruit exporters were concerned by the imposition for the first time of a tariff on exports to Germany and, more particularly, by the size of the quota to which the low tariff applied and the punitive nature of the high tariff. They claimed that the tariff quota of 2 million tonnes was insufficient. Five of the aggrieved Latin American exporters lodged two complaints in the GATT (one in relation to each of the EU's regulations). They were supported in their action by the USA which was concerned, at a critical time in the final negotiations of the Uruguay Round of trade liberalization, not to permit the EU to move in the opposite direction by increasing tariffs and introducing new quotas at a time of 'tariffication'.

The GATT panel on both complaints ruled in the Latin American states' favour. Since the EU had justified its actions on the basis of the Banana Protocol of the Lomé Convention, the panel in these rulings moved beyond the specific case of bananas to comment unfavourably on the GATT compatibility of the entire Lomé Convention. This view was not put immediately to the test, because a compromise was hatched between the EU and the main Latin American banana exporters. Under a Framework Agreement on Bananas reached in mid-1994 with four of the GATT complainants (Costa Rica, Colombia, Nicaragua, and Venezuela), the EU agreed to raise the tariff quota and to grant the four Latin American countries specific quotas based on their past share of the market. In return, the four dropped their GATT complaint.

Another feature of the deal was that the four Latin American states were authorized to issue export licences, i.e. to determine which suppliers could take advantage of the EU's import licences. This was seen by them as enhancing their negotiating position *vis-à-vis* the US companies that have dominated the trade in dollar fruit to Europe.

The WTO complaint

This agreement stirred up, in turn, its own controversy. It was rejected by other Latin American suppliers (including Guatemala, which had been party to the GATT complaint, plus Ecuador, Honduras, Panama, Mexico, and the Dominican Republic).

The agreement was also opposed by two US banana companies that felt discriminated against by the overall tariff quota, by the country quotas for the four Latin American signatories, and by increased competition with other companies. The decision to allocate part of the 'free market' in Europe to the two traditional suppliers of Caribbean fruit, together with the Latin American agreement that linked the allocation of licences to the possession of an export certificate issued by the Latin American state concerned, restricted the traditional activities of Dole and Chiquita. The companies sought action from the US government, which responded by launching an investigation under Section 301 of the US Trade Act and then lodging a complaint in the WTO.　The WTO panel issued a report in May 1997, which upheld the complaint. Importantly, the report did not take issue with the duty-free preferences for the ACP, but found fault with aspects of the licensing system. The EU appealed, but the appellate body upheld the panel's decision.

This did not bring matters to a close: indeed, they became a lot more messy in autumn 1998 and spring 1999, when the inadequacies of the WTO's follow-up mechanisms became apparent. The US government charged that the changes introduced by the EU in response to the appeal ruling were inadequate to deal with the complaint. It threatened to take the ultimate sanction permitted by the WTO—the imposition of punitive tariffs on imports from the EU. The EU, for its part, argued that such sanctions were *ultra vires*, until the WTO had ruled that its compliance measures were, indeed, inadequate. The situation became especially heated in March 1999, when a deadline for compliance imposed unilaterally by the USA expired before the WTO had adjudicated on the adequacy of the EU's measures. The USA imposed sanctions equivalent to 100 per cent tariffs on fourteen European products. These were subsequently scaled down when the WTO finally ruled that the EU's compliance had been inadequate but that the USA had overstated the level of damage caused to it by this failure. On 15 July 1999 the *Financial Times* carried the story that the Caribbean and Ecuadorian producers were entering discussions to see if they, as producers, could find a solution. The story recalls a similar transnational producer coalition between competing beet and cane sugar producers identified in the first edition of this volume (Stevens and Webb 1983). In the sugar case, frustration at the inadequacies of the EU policy process led the producers, in spite of their differences, to negotiate an extra-institutional solution. In October 1999 the European Commission proposed as a solution a two-stage plan with first a five-year period of adaptation for ACP producers and then a single tariff for both ACP and dollar bananas. The Commission, however, insisted that any such solution would be conditional upon the US and Latin American governments undertaking not to challenge the new regime in the WTO (*European Voice*, 21–7 October 1999).

The implications for other agreements

It is important not to exaggerate the tightness of the boundaries that the banana dispute places on EU members' freedom of action. The dispute has been particularly difficult for the EU precisely because opinion within the Union is so divided. The new banana regime was not the only possible solution: it was the solution for which majority support could be marshalled. Internal pressures give the Union greater scope in other trade policy areas to design changes that are acceptable both to EU stakeholders and to WTO members.

None the less, while it did not result in a fundamental challenge to the Lomé Convention's multilateral legitimacy, the banana dispute has had two major effects on EU thinking:

- it established that the EU's trade agreements could no longer be passed 'on the nod', and would need to be justified in the multilateral fora; and

- it demonstrated that the WTO's new, more muscular dispute settlement procedures could throw unwanted light into murky corners of EU policy and bring into question arrangements and understandings not directly related to the point at issue.

This second point may turn out to be the more important, since the ruling appears to have established an order of precedence between the different parts of the WTO accords, with potentially wider implications. The Uruguay Round texts are in two main groups: a set of principles to which all members have agreed, and extensive lists of the detailed policies that each member will implement to give effect to these principles. The latter include tens of thousands of lines of tariff schedules, many of which pass unscrutinized, unless and until a challenge arises. The banana dispute was one such challenge; there could be others.

An argument made by the EU in its defence against the WTO complaint was that the quotas were justified in its Uruguay Round tariff schedules. But the panel ruled that provisions in the schedules could not be sustained if they contravened fundamental WTO principles. This judgement could open the way to further challenges in other areas of EU trade policy currently given effect by the detailed provisions of its tariff schedules. One such is the Sugar Protocol, under which the EU imports at the domestic price a fixed quantity of cane sugar from selected ACP states.   The initial response to the challenge presented to the Lomé Convention was for the Union to seek and obtain in 1994 a waiver from the MFN rule under GATT Article XXV. This removed the immediate questions about the validity of the Lomé Convention. But while the waiver, since renewed by the WTO, has provided some respite, the problem has not gone away. The banana disputes provided a stimulus to find a new formulation that would remove the danger.

The options for WTO conformity

The basic problem is that a fundamental GATT–WTO principle is non-discrimination, but the EU's preferential accords are by definition discriminatory. The task is to transform Lomé (and the EU's other accords) so that they can hang on one of the pegs under which members may seek justification for discriminatory treatment of one group of trading countries *vis-à-vis* others. It can be noted in passing not only that the 'WTO problem' is not limited to Lomé, but also that it is not limited to the EU. Both the USA and Canada, for example, provide discriminatory preferences to favoured states that could be challenged if another WTO member was so minded.

The pegs on which to hang discrimination are:

- if the countries concerned are creating an FTA or customs union (covered by Article XXIV);

- if the trade partners are developing countries subject to 'special and differential treatment' (covered by the 1979 Enabling Clause); or

■ if a waiver has been obtained under WTO Article IX (formerly GATT Article XXV).

Article XXIV

The formal procedure for obtaining WTO approval for an FTA is fairly straight-forward, but in practice there is ample scope for doubt. This is because Article XXIV is vague—by design rather than by accident, because members have been unwilling to restrict themselves through a more precise formulation. Two salient requirements of Article XXIV are that the FTA must be completed 'within a reasonable length of time' (newly defined in the WTO as a period that 'should exceed ten years only in exceptional cases') and that 'duties and other restrictive regulations of commerce . . . are eliminated on substantially all the trade between the constituent territories' (GATT 1947: Part 3, Article XXIV, paras 5(c) and 8(b); WTO 1995: 32). The formal requirements for legitimization of an FTA are high, since it requires universal approval (because of the practice of achieving consensus). But in the past a failure to achieve consensus has not proved to be a barrier to those countries wishing to create an FTA (see Box 15.3).

The current procedure following the successful completion of an FTA is for it to be referred for consideration to the WTO Committee on Regional Agreements. This committee has a large backlog of agreements to consider: it is still assessing accords notified before the completion of the Uruguay Round (and hence subject to GATT rules), and so has not yet begun to establish any guidance for the interpretation of the regulations under the WTO. On past form, it is unlikely to give a straightforward approval or disapproval of any agreement. In the absence of clear guidance from the Committee, it would still be open to any aggrieved WTO member to file a complaint under the dispute settlement mechanism. This could pass to a quasi-judicial body the task of defining such terms as 'substantially all' trade. As will be seen, the EU in its negotiations with South Africa stated clearly its understanding of the term.

Special and differential treatment

There is provision in the WTO for developing countries to be treated differently from developed states in various regards. These include the provision by developed

---

Box 15.3 How FTAs were approved under GATT

Because WTO procedures have not yet been tried and tested (given the backlog of work arising under GATT), the old procedures are still a relevant guide. The parties to the agreement had to notify the GATT following signature of an FTA. Such notification was generally followed by the establishment of a working group (membership of which was open to any country that felt it to be in their interests to belong) which produced a report that had then to be adopted by consensus by the GATT membership.

Practice has been a lot less clear-cut than is suggested by this procedure. The majority of the cases notified to the GATT were interim agreements, some of the provisions of which came into effect before the relevant working group had completed its deliberations. As of January 1995 a total of ninety-eight agreements had been notified under Article XXIV, but only six (of which only two are still operative) had been explicitly acknowledged as being in conformity with Article XXIV.

countries of trade preferences in favour of developing states. In other words, developed states may discriminate against other developed countries in their trade policy provided that it benefits developing countries. This is permitted under the inelegantly named 1979 Enabling Clause.

The main problem for an EU attempt to justify any of its preferential accords other than the Standard GSP in this way is that they do not cover all developing countries. In this respect, therefore, Lomé is no different from the Mediterranean and central European bilateral accords that have not yet been transformed into FTAs and, arguably, the superior tranche GSP, given that it is not limited to a recognized group of especially poor countries. It would seem impossible to overcome this limitation, unless either the liberality of the Lomé preferences were extended to all countries or they were reduced to the level currently available under the GSP, or something in between. While the first would make EU trade policy more liberal by extending deep preferences to the more competitive, larger developing countries, the second would effectively increase the EU's absolute level of protection. The arguments for and against have come to the fore in the negotiation of a successor to the Lomé Convention (see below).

A waiver

The third option is the one adopted by the EU in 1994 to seek a waiver from the MFN rule under Article XXV of GATT–Article IX of WTO. The WTO members can waive any of the rules if they wish so to do. A majority of the twenty-eight waivers granted since the inception of GATT have involved preferences granted by developed to developing countries on a non-reciprocal basis. The Marrakesh Agreement establishing the WTO has made more onerous the rules for approving a waiver than was the case under GATT (when the Lomé waiver was agreed). The level of support required for approval of a waiver has been increased from a two-thirds majority under the GATT to a 75 per cent majority under the WTO. But, given the practice of seeking consensus for all decisions, the change has limited operational significance.

The provision is well used. Both the USA and Canada, for example, justify their preference agreements with the Caribbean in this way. So long as they continue to do so, an EU waiver for Lomé would appear to be safe from attack from this quarter—but not necessarily from others. However, the proposed Free Trade Agreement of the Americas (FTAA) would remove the necessity for the US and Canadian waivers. The target date for the FTAA is 2005—a year that, through no coincidence, figures prominently in the EU's proposals for a post-Lomé relationship (see below).

The South African FTA

Origins

To a significant extent the trade agreement reached between the EU and South Africa in 1999 provides a model for the Commission's vision of future Euro–South accords. It has proposed similar agreements with Mercosur and Mexico, and that the whole Mediterranean should be a zone of free trade. And it underpins the negotiating mandate for a post-Lomé accord with the ACP.

Unlike the ACP and Mediterranean states, South Africa started the negotiations from a low position in the EU's hierarchy of preferences. And unlike the central and east European states (which also began from a low base), there is no suggestion that the trade accord is a precursor to full membership (see Chapter 16). Partly for this reason, the negotiations (and especially those internal to the EU and to the Commission) revealed in a stark fashion the tension in trade policy formation. At the outset South Africa was accorded only MFN access to the EU market, and then only qualified GSP treatment. Only in the final phase of the negotiations did it obtain full Standard GSP access, placing it in the middle of the three broad bands of the EU's trade hierarchy (see Figure 15.3).

This was because the legacies that the new South African government inherited in 1994 from the country's apartheid past included its isolation in global trade policy. The ending of sanctions did not remove the international constraints under which South Africa's exporters operated. During the three decades preceding majority rule, when South Africa was internationally isolated, a complex network of trade agreements evolved, giving many countries advantages in their export markets compared with some of their competitors. South Africa was absent from this process.

In the case of South African exports to the EU, the effects of this exclusion from preferences were mitigated during the apartheid era by the commodity composition of trade. Partly to evade sanctions and partly because of the pattern of South African competitiveness, exports were concentrated on relatively insensitive mineral products. Sensitive manufactures were largely absent from South African exports because of the country's lack of international competitiveness. The one segment of exports that did cause problems was South Africa's fruit, vegetable, and wine products. It exported these to Europe at a disadvantage compared with its competitors from Israel, Turkey, North Africa, and Latin America.

For the new ANC government the effects of South Africa's unfavourable treatment were more serious. The lifting of the more severe restrictions of sanctions increased the relative importance of trade policy discrimination. Moreover, the government wished to foster the expanded exports of labour-intensive manufactures and to build upon the agricultural exports. Improved access to its main market in Europe would facilitate achievement of this goal.

The negotiating process

Initially the new South African government dithered, absorbed as it was by other matters and the conflicting signals coming from Brussels over the advantages of Lomé versus a tailor-made bilateral deal with the EU. Arguably this delay cost it dear, as portfolio responsibility in Europe passed from the desk of premiers and foreign ministers, who might have taken a broad view, to those of agriculture and industry ministers, whose approach was much narrower and more short-term.

It was not until November 1994 that the then South African Minister of Trade and Industry, Trevor Manuel, proposed a joint council with the Lomé Convention signatories to investigate South Africa's eligibility for membership of the Convention. This followed its conclusions that Lomé was more advantageous because:

- it would facilitate intra-regional trade (since all of South Africa's neighbours in Southern Africa are also members);
- it would ease diplomatic problems (because these neighbours and the other Convention members would be involved as of right in the negotiating process);
- it offered reduced tariffs on many of South Africa's current exports; and
- it was particularly appropriate for the fluid nature of the South African economy under a new set of policy stimuli.

Lomé's suitability for South Africa's fluid economy stems from two of its features: it offers a *carte blanche* approach in the form of duty-free access for *all* industrial goods; and the existing Convention lasted only until the end of the decade. Since South Africa's economy was expected to change radically during this period, the in-built termination of Lomé provided an automatic date for renegotiating the terms of any agreement once the nature and direction of the changes in South Africa's economy were better understood.

However, these two key features of Lomé's flexibility were exactly what made it unacceptable to European political opinion. EU policy-makers were concerned that South Africa would become internationally competitive in a wide range of sensitive manufactures which would have unrestricted access to the European market. Having initially granted Lomé terms, it would be difficult politically to scale these back, once South Africa's competitiveness became clear.

By a deft political manœuvre, the EU managed to accede to the South African government's eventual request for Lomé membership, while covering itself against these potential pitfalls. It offered South Africa membership of the Lomé Convention, but exclusion from the trade chapters.[1] The negotiations during 1995 to 1999 concentrated on the form that South Africa's bespoke trade agreement should take.

These negotiations were often fraught because of South Africa's poor initial access and the highly competitive exports of items covered by the CAP. The negotiations were led by DG VIII, but with very heavy involvement by DG VI. Given the commodity composition of South Africa's exports, DG VI effectively held a veto on a successful conclusion to the negotiations, unless and until it was overruled by the Council. Little scope existed to offer improved access in the 90 per cent of South Africa's exports to the EU which were non-sensitive goods facing zero or low tariffs. Only if it won significant concessions on the remaining 10 per cent of products could the South African government hope to sell the deal to its own producers, which would face increased competition from EU goods. But four-fifths of these sensitive products were agricultural. Faced with the concurrent negotiation of the Agenda 2000 reforms of the CAP, the continuing renegotiation of the Mediterranean accords, and the prospect of FTA negotiations with Mercosur and the WTO Agricultural Round due in 2000, DG VI's position was to give very little ground.

The very restricted nature of its initial position is illustrated by the fact that at one point the EU's offer for the 'free' trade area was less liberal than that already accorded under the GSP. In other words, had South Africa concluded an agreement on that basis, exports of some products would have received better access under the GSP than under the FTA! The EU also attempted to pin on to the market access negotiations ancillary demands on fishing rights in South African waters for European fishermen and on trademarks (in relation to South African wine and spirit names).

DG VI's strength was enhanced because the initial negotiating mandate handed down by the EU Council of Ministers in 1995 was very restrictive. The reason for this was that the southern European states that could have been expected to oppose liberal access on fruit, wine, and vegetables were joined by Germany, which also took a very restrictive line. This was partly because the German agriculture ministry was given an important role in federal decision-making on the issue. It was also rumoured that the well-established German investors in South Africa's protected industrial sector were unenthusiastic about the prospect of an FTA and the increased competition it would produce for their affiliates. The UK supported a generous offer to South Africa but, in the dying years of the Conservative administration, when the Eurosceptics were in the ascendant, its voice in the Council was relatively weak.

For its part, the South African government had to move cautiously on liberalization. It inherited a highly protected economy with an import regime even more complex than that of the EU. Manufacturers feared competition from more efficient European production, and farmers feared losing their market to dumped EU beef and cereals. South Africa's partners in the Southern African Customs Union (Botswana, Lesotho, Namibia, and Swaziland) feared both, and also the loss of tariff revenue that formed a major part of their tax income.

Over the four years of negotiation the two sides moved closer together, partly by enhancing their offers of liberalization and partly by scaling down the scope of the enterprise. As such they have effectively established a benchmark for the extent of liberalization within a *free* trade area. It remains to be seen whether or not this benchmark will be scrutinized in the WTO—and if it is, whether it will be upheld.

Even so, a final agreement was in the balance until the very end. Deadlines for the 'end of the negotiations' were trumpeted several times, and passed unheeded. It was hoped first to unveil the accord at the June 1998 Council summit in Cardiff, addressed by President Mandela. Tony Blair, the British Prime Minister, went to great efforts to try and complete a deal so as to bring the UK presidency to an auspicious conclusion. The UK had made this one of the priorities of its presidency during the first half of 1998. But the attempt failed: the two sides could not agree because the EU offer still excluded large parts of South Africa's fruit and wine exports. An autumn deadline was then set, but this too passed.

The breakthrough at Commission level came in February 1999, when Commissioner Pinheiro and South Africa's trade minister, Alec Erwin, met at Davos to reach agreement in principle on the outstanding issues. But obtaining member state approval proved to be an additional obstacle. EU foreign ministers could not reach agreement on the deal at their 22 March 1999 Council meeting, and deferred a decision. It was left to European heads of government to approve the deal on 25 March at the Berlin Summit (concerned more with Kosovo than with South Africa), following intense negotiation led by Gerhard Schröder and Tony Blair with Spain, Portugal, France, Italy, and Greece to overcome their concerns.

The WTO dimension

The characteristics of the agreement

The South African negotiations thus illustrate the EU's understanding of the various WTO requirements, and its treatment at Geneva may provide guidance for the acceptability or otherwise of the EU's other proposed changes, such as the post-Lomé REPAs. The EU–South Africa accord includes effective definitions of the two salient WTO requirements that an FTA should cover 'substantially all' trade, and that it should be completed within a 'reasonable length of time'. The EU has interpreted 'substantially all' as meaning an *average* of 90 *per cent* of the *items currently traded* between the two partners. All three italicized elements could be challenged: the figure of 90 per cent, its relationship to the items currently traded, and the averaging between partners. The 90 per cent figure is, perhaps, the least controversial. Evidently, the phrase 'substantially all' implies that less than 100 per cent of trade is liberalized. The EU claims to have canvassed in Geneva the 90 per cent figure, and to have received assurances from trade partners on its acceptability.

But this raises the question: 90 per cent of what? Should the calculation be made in relation to the goods actually traded between the two partners, or should it be in relation to all possible traded goods? The difference is important. The effect of heavy protectionism (such as is provided by the CAP) is either to eliminate trade or to keep it at very low levels. If trade does not occur, or is slight, a calculation based upon current flows will show the excluded items to be a very small proportion of the total. Ironically, therefore, the more polarized a country's trading regime (between unsensitive goods and exceptionally sensitive ones), the easier it will be to meet the 90 per cent target, since the latter group can easily be excluded without upsetting the arithmetic. The alternative would be to make the calculation in relation to every item in the tariff nomenclature (which describes all possible traded goods and allocates them a unique numeric code). This in turn would have its problems. The trade nomenclature is particularly detailed on products which are sensitive, in order to allow import regimes to target precisely the goods that are to be kept out. Hence, the exclusion from an agreement of a small number of very sensitive products would have a disproportionate effect on the arithmetic compared with the inclusion of non-sensitive items. This would make the 90 per cent threshold more difficult to achieve.

As part of its commitment to an asymmetrical agreement (under which the requirements on South Africa are less onerous than those on the EU) the parties have agreed that a larger proportion of EU imports must be made duty-free than is necessary for South African imports. Hence, while 96 per cent of the goods imported into the EU will be covered by the FTA, only 86 per cent of those imported into South Africa will be covered.

The agreement also includes a definition of the term 'a reasonable length of time'. The new WTO agreement indicates that this should 'normally' be not more than ten years, which implies that abnormally it could be longer. But how much longer? Most products referred to in the EU–South Africa FTA will be liberalized over a period of twelve years. The EU will liberalize over ten years, but South Africa has an additional two. This might not, of itself, cause problems, but in addition South Africa has put into a series of protocols a range of goods on which it is not willing, at the moment, to agree liberalization but which could come on to the agenda at a later stage (particularly if the EU is willing to extend its offers). Such products are therefore covered by the FTA, but will not be liberalized within twelve years or, indeed, any specified finite period.

Obtaining WTO approval

As explained above, the formal procedure for WTO scrutiny of the new accord (and its interpretation of Article XXIV) via the Committee on Regional Agreements may not result in the speedy application of the seal of approval or disapproval. Appeal to the WTO's dispute settlement provisions might fulfil this task instead.

For example, if the US considered that an EU–South Africa FTA disadvantaged its exporters, it might post a complaint. But this would be risky. There is very little guidance available on how the weasel words of Article XXIV are to be interpreted. As the banana dispute has shown, the WTO has given birth to a strong dispute settlement mechanism. Any country launching a complaint would have to weigh up the possible consequences of multilateral trade policy being established in a quasi-judicial framework rather than through intergovernmental negotiation. There could be far-reaching implications from this 'case law', and some of these might rebound on the complainant in unexpected ways. On the other hand, the USA is not the only country that could lodge a complaint: any WTO member might do so. And not all countries facing trade diversion in either the South African or the EU market will necessarily attach much weight to the danger of a precedent being established. So the accord could be vulnerable to challenge.

Applying the new approach to Lomé

Faced with the difficulties presented by the banana panel ruling, the Commission entered into a two-year period of public consultation on the future of Lomé in 1996–7. Following the commissioning of consultancy reports on various aspects of a post-Lomé relationship during 1996, it produced a Green Paper identifying challenges and possible options for a new partnership (Commission 1997h). Four principal options were put forward: maintenance of the status quo; integration of Lomé into the GSP; and two variations of regimes in which the ACP would offer trade reciprocity in return for their privileged access to the EU market.

In its proposal to the Council for a negotiating mandate submitted in autumn 1997, the Commission opted for a two-stage approach. Initial negotiations would be for a Framework Agreement, setting out the principles for trade and aid cooperation following the expiry of Lomé IV (and its WTO waiver) in February 2000. It would also seek a further WTO waiver (under Article IX) for the continuation of Lomé preferences to 2005. During this second stage ACP states would be invited to negotiate REPAs. Least developed states that failed to agree REPAs would continue their current access to the EU market, but under an improved GSP provision open to all least developed states. Other ACP members not in REPAs would be downgraded to the Standard GSP. The choice of the year 2005 for the end of the waiver was not unrelated to the fact that it was the target date for the inauguration of the FTAA. If this occurs it will leave the EU as the only developed state requiring an Article IX waiver for trade agreements with developing countries.

Although its status as leader of the post-Lomé negotiations was unchallenged, DG VIII found that, in formulating its proposals, it had to accept limitations imposed by DGs I and VI. In a formulation in mid-1997 DG VIII had sought to dissipate some of the tension that its 'REPA or GSP' choice would provoke by offering a third way—a vague Regional Economic Cooperation Agreement that would not require ACP reciprocity. But this was shot down by DG I as being WTO-incompatible.

DG VIII's attempts to produce an offer that would appeal to the ACP were also restricted by limits to what could be said in relation to CAP products. Since Lomé preferences already provide virtually unrestricted access on manufactures, agriculture is the only product area in which the EU could offer improvements for the exports of REPA members. But this was ruled out, at least until the final negotiating rounds, by DG VI's insistence that improvements on CAP products could not be contemplated. DG VIII was left, therefore, with the less than easy task of selling to the ACP an offer in which they could be required to open up their markets to EU exports simply in order to retain the status quo for their exports.

In practice, the task of selling the new approach was even more difficult because considerations of the CAP and WTO required DG VIII to underplay the costs of being downgraded to the GSP and, hence, the relative attractiveness of the REPA alternative. DGs I and VI insisted that nothing be said that would undermine the EU's claim that its Sugar and Beef protocols were WTO-compliant (by virtue of their inclusion in the EU's Uruguay Round tariff schedules—see above). To do so would weaken the EU's credibility in the WTO, not only in respect of the Protocols, but also in relation to other elements of trade policy that are justified by the specifics of the Uruguay Round schedules. The implication was that these Protocols (which for their beneficiaries are the most valuable part of their preferences) could continue after Lomé, even if countries failed to enter a REPA.

During the first half of 1998 there was intensive negotiation between the member states on the mandate proposal. Two clear viewpoints emerged. One, with Germany as a prominent exponent, was to support the Commission's proposals as a way of fostering a liberal trade policy in ACP states and integrating the Lomé Convention into the 'mainline' provisions of the WTO. The other, with the UK (then in the presidency) in the driving seat, was to reduce the contrast between the post-2005 options by improving the Standard GSP. This was seen as a method both of reducing friction in the negotiations with the ACP and of promoting a wider liberalism in EU trade policy (since enhancements to the GSP would tend to benefit all developing countries).

The result was a mandate agreed in the dying hours of the UK presidency at the end of June 1998 that combined both approaches. On the one hand, it committed the EU to 'offer a process to establish free trade areas . . . [to] be negotiated during the five years following the expiry of the current convention (2000–2005)'. On the other hand, a footnote provides that:

Notwithstanding the primary objective set out in the mandate with regard to FTAs, the Council and the Commission agree to assess, in 2004, the situation of the non-LDC ACPs who are *for objective reasons* not in a position to join such FTAs with the EU.

They will examine all alternative possibilities ... to provide ... a new framework for trade between them and the European Union which is equivalent to their existing situation under the Lomé Convention and in conformity with WTO rules. In particular the Council and the Commission will take into account their interests in the review of the GSP in 2004, making use of the differentiation permitted by WTO rules. (Council of the European Union 1998: 18, footnote 1.) (my emphasis)

No agreement had been reached at the time of writing.

Conclusions

Context and history

Union-level trade policy towards developing countries grew out of the pre-existing interests of the member states and has evolved as the balance between national and Union competences has altered. The single most important internal event has been the completion of the SEM. This provided the catalyst for changes that were increasingly required by the shifting geographical orientation of European economic interests and the demands of the international community.

The Lomé Convention was very much the descendant of the colonial policies of the member states. It grew out of the Yaoundé Conventions that had linked the original six to the former colonies of France, Belgium, and Italy in sub-Saharan Africa. This group was joined by some of the ex-British colonies (mainly the smaller and poorer ones) in 1975 to negotiate the first Lomé Convention.   In both its trade and aid provisions the Lomé Convention reflected these origins. Whilst there has never been a time when some products were not 'sensitive' in the EU, in the mid-1970s such sensitivities were less marked in relation to the ACP than they are today. On the one hand, the CAP was still focused primarily on northern grains and livestock products; on the other, the ACP were either exporting non-competitive items, such as cocoa and coffee, or, if they were competitive (as with sugar), the trade was of long standing and well integrated into European commercial culture. On the aid side, the transfers to the ACP were very large by comparison with the Community's other development assistance programmes and quite large in relation to other aspects of Community expenditure. They were protected, however, by the provision of the Treaty of Rome, which had channelled aid through the EDF as a separate financial mechanism, which remained outside the EU budget.

By the end of the 1990s all of this had changed. Some ACP states had proved themselves to be adept at exporting sensitive clothing (Mauritius) or horticulture (Kenya and Zimbabwe) or rice (Surinam). It was no longer an advantage that the EDF was outside the EU budget, because the effect was to restrain its volume, thereby limiting the volume of aid available to the poorest countries in the ACP, as compared with those in Latin America, the Mediterranean, and former Soviet Union. On the other hand, the special decision-making arrangements for the EDF provided a last-ditch defence against the transfer of responsibility for aid from national to Union level.

Policy initiation

The catalyst for change was the need to create a new banana regime following the completion of the SEM. This proved to be a tough nut to crack, precisely because Europe was so divided on the issue. Opinion was split almost equally between those wishing to preserve traditional ACP interests and those who wanted to end them. Within the Commission three Directorates-General (I, VI, and VIII) were involved, and the member states fell into two main camps. This differentiation has continued into the WTO dispute and is one reason why it has been so difficult to resolve. The EU regime that has been struck down by the WTO panel was a delicate compromise between competing interests; finding an alternative that is acceptable within the EU, as well as being compatible with the WTO ruling, will be difficult.

This chapter has assessed the effects of the changed stance following the WTO dispute on two areas of policy: the negotiation of an FTA with South Africa; and the preparations for a post-Lomé agreement with the ACP. In both cases policy initiation has lain with DG VIII, but it has had to work closely with DGs I and VI. This has proved not to be an easy relationship. For chance reasons of history, South Africa illustrated in a stark way a more general problem that continues to bedevil EU efforts to negotiate trade accords with developing countries. This is that the most attractive part of any package for the trade partner is precisely that which the EU finds most difficult to concede: improved access on CAP products. As Chapter 7 argues, one of the effects of the CAP is to maintain prices in the European market at an artificially high level. If foreign suppliers can capture part of this market they have the possibility of achieving much higher profits than they would on sales to other countries. But DG VI sees its duty as defending the interests of the group for which the artificially high prices have been created: European farmers.

Policy decision

Because the trade negotiations have come to be seen as a zero-sum game, in which gains for developing countries mean losses for European farmers, it has become increasingly difficult to bring them to a successful conclusion at official level. It would be interesting to know whether events would have been different had Nelson Mandela obtained from Europe's leaders, in advance of the 1994 South African elections, a commitment to offer Lomé-style access following the creation of a multiracial government. He did not do so because the ANC had many other priorities, and the result was four years of grinding negotiations between trade and agricultural officials. Deadlock was finally broken by the intervention of the heads of government in March 1999—on terms that were not necessarily greatly different from those that could have been offered in 1994 had the political commitment been made earlier.

The prospects for policy change

Unless there is a sharp reversal in the trend towards liberalization of merchandise trade, the current pattern of the EU's trade policy towards developing countries will fade rapidly over the next decade. Hence, even if the post-Lomé regime turns out to have strong similarities to the current policy *vis-à-vis* the ACP, the practical value of the agreement will decline.

To a certain extent, this will facilitate a change in the direction of European policy. Old agreements will not need to be torn up and the costs of abandoning them in the face of external pressure from the WTO will decline. The 'new' trade hierarchy will be created in the 'new areas' of trade policy: agreements on services, intellectual property, standards harmonization, investment measures, etc. These are all in their infancy. It remains to be seen whether or not it is either desirable or politically feasible to negotiate agreements in these areas at a sub-multilateral level. If it does prove to be desirable and feasible, it remains to be seen with which countries the EU forges such accords. But it is reasonable to surmise that the most likely candidates for such pacts will be the states (developed or developing) which have the greatest economic or political importance for the EU. And it is also reasonable to speculate that these countries will not be identical to those that were at the pinnacle of the EU's old trade policy regime, based as it was on preferences for merchandise trade.

Notes

1 It also, by mutual consent, excluded South Africa from the aid provisions of Lomé. Because of the arcane split in the sources of European aid between the EDF and the budget, South Africa is likely to receive substantially more aid by being outside the Lomé framework than it would do if it were inside.

Further reading

For general background on EU policy towards the developing countries, see Lister (1988), Grilli (1993), and the House of Lords (1993, especially pp. 5–32). Pedler (1994) tells part of the banana story. Mendoza et al. (1999) sets the recent debate on revisions to the Lomé Convention in its broader context. McMahon (1999) supplies further details on the negotiations.

Grilli, E. (1993), *The European Community and the Developing Countries* (Cambridge: Cambridge University Press).

House of Lords (1993), *EC Aid and Trade Policy*, Select Committee on the European Communities (London: HMSO).

Lister, M. (1988), *The European Community and the Developing World* (Aldershot: Avebury).

McMahon, J. A. (1999), 'Negotiating in a time of turbulent transition: the future of Lomé', *Common Market Law Review*, 3: 599–624.

Mendoza, M. R., et al. (1999), *Trade Rules in the Making: Challenges in Regional and Multilateral Negotiations* (Washington: Brookings Institution Press for the Organization of American States).

Pedler, R. (1994), 'The Fruit Companies and the Banana Trade Regime (BTR)', in R. Pedler and M. P. C. M. van Schendelen (eds.), *Lobbying the European Union: Companies, Trade Associations and Issue Groups* (Aldershot: Dartmouth).

Chapter 16

Eastern Enlargement

Strategy or Second Thoughts?

Ulrich Sedelmeier and Helen Wallace

Contents

Summary

The end of the cold war necessitated a radical reorientation of European Union (EU) policy towards its eastern neighbours. The immediate response was technical and financial assistance for reforms. The search for a long-term policy began with the initial design of the Europe Agreements. EU policy-makers were caught between the high expectations of their new partners and internal resistance to change. From 1994 onwards the debate shifted to eastern enlargement. Ten candidates from central and eastern Europe were addressed by a 'pre-accession' strategy. In 1997 the EU's Agenda 2000 began to lay a basis for enlargement, and negotiations opened with five candidates in 1998, and in 2000 with all ten. It became evident that successful enlargement required radical rethinking of core EU policies and its institutional design. The issues relating to both Europe Association and enlargement require of the EU the capability to develop a 'composite policy', both at the 'macro' level and in more specific 'meso' policy domains.

Introduction

The need to devise a policy towards the countries of central and eastern Europe (CEECs) shot on to the EU's agenda in the late 1980s. It was prompted by dramatic political changes, against the backdrop of *perestroika* and *glasnost* in the Soviet Union, and its subsequent break-up. This sudden insertion in the agenda of a new policy with potentially far-reaching effects is a reminder for the student of European integration of the dangers of assuming the relative stability of integration patterns at any given moment, and of neglecting the outside world.

These events generated new policy for the EU agenda (rather than being dealt with bilaterally by the member states) in part because it was quickly agreed among EU governments and the Commission that the EU would be the most appropriate forum for a response, and in part because politicians from the CEECs directed their expectations directly at the EU. Devising an appropriate policy presented a major challenge for EU policy-makers, compared with the previously extremely limited relationship with the CEECs. New options, including the prospect of eastern enlargement, had potentially far-reaching implications for the EU. First sketching and then managing the new relationship required a significant degree of innovation, creativity, and strategic policy-making. As thinking has evolved towards an enlargement policy, the EU has had to confront the complex and difficult task of identifiying and agreeing options for the internal reforms necessary to accommodate the accession of the CEECs. In this sense eastern enlargement has become a dimension which permeates almost every other domain in EU policy, as other chapters in this volume demonstrate.

The challenge of devising strategy in a composite policy domain

On the surface, EU policy towards the CEECs sits somewhat uneasily among the other chapters in this volume: it is not a policy area in its own right; it is not a single-issue policy; and it does not have a single location in the policy process. Nor is it simply a case of cross-sectoral policy impacts in which certain measures within one policy domain also have an effect on another (such as the link between transport and environmental policy). It is rather that policy towards the CEECs is a broad policy framework, which draws its substance from a range of distinctive policy areas.

This overarching characteristic leads us to use the term 'composite policy' to describe this domain (Sedelmeier 1998a). This requires an analytical distinction between two dimensions of policy: (1) decisions about the macro level of policy, to determine the overall objectives and parameters of policy; and (2) decisions about the specific detail and substance of policy, generally dealt with by the various policy-makers that have the relevant technical expertise and decision-making competences.

Decisions at the macro level of policy have to specify the overall objectives of policy and set the broad framework and parameters of policy. For EU policy towards the CEECs, this includes, for example, an agreement on the direction in which the relationship should evolve (for example, 'standard' external relations; 'special relationship'; or eventual membership) and on which policy instruments to use to develop the relationship. The latter consists of decisions on both the general framework of policy (for example, sectoral trade agreements, association agreements, regulatory regime) and which policy areas to include (for example, in which specific sectors to liberalize trade; whether to include political cooperation; regulatory alignment; free movement of workers; and so on). In principle, decisions at the macro level could also involve the setting of parameters for cooperation in the policy areas that are included, such as: gradual or immediate removal of trade barriers; which trade barriers are removed; substantial liberalization or only limited reciprocal concessions; and what form and level of financial assistance to provide.

Yet to translate these objectives into substantive policy outputs requires a decision not only on what instruments to use, but also on how to use them. These involve highly detailed, specific decisions across a wide range of EU policy areas. Such decisions concern, for example, the precise extent and speed of tariff reductions within a particular sector; the specific mechanisms through which the EU might consult the CEECs on foreign policy issues; and the identification of the specific measures within a specific regulatory policy with which the CEEC should align. 'Policy towards eastern Europe' thus does not exist independently of those decisions which make up these separate sub-policies. In other words, the macro policy is composed of a range of distinctive meso policies, and it is these which define the substance of policy, and feed back into the overall policy (see Table 16.1).

The meso policies that constitute EU policy towards the CEECs are simultaneously parts of other policy areas. Instruments that this policy uses to achieve its objectives are at the same time instruments that are employed in other policy areas and for quite different purposes. In general, the more the objectives of policy towards the

Table 16.1 EU policy towards the CEECs: a composite policy

Policy dimension	Type of decision	Examples	Principal policy-makers
Macro policy	Overall objectives, broad framework, and parameters of policy, including:		In the Commission: Commissioners, their *cabinets*, and DGs responsible for external relations
	■ direction for the evolving relationship	■ 'standard' external relations ■ 'special relationship' ■ eventual membership	In the member states: Foreign Ministry officials; Foreign Ministers; heads of state or government
	■ policy instruments: —framework of policy	■ sectoral trade agreement ■ association agreements ■ regulatory regime	
	—range of policy areas such as:	■ assistance–investment ■ trade liberalization ■ regulatory alignment ■ free movement of persons ■ political cooperation	
Meso policies	detailed decisions across range of EU policies relevant to links with CEECs	■ programmes of technical and financial support ■ tariffs, quotas, etc. by product ■ specific regulatory measures ■ issues and mechanisms for foreign policy consultation	Sectoral policy-makers in both Commission and member states

CEECs represent a shift from previous policy, the more this is likely to challenge the status quo in other policy areas. To translate broad objectives into concrete measures in the meso policies therefore requires horizontal coordination. This has two main implications:

■ policy-making is less characterized by inter-state bargaining than by bargaining between distinctive groups of policy-makers and by transgovernmental alliances; and

■ it generates obstacles to strategic policy-making.[1]

Some clues about the factors that affect the likelihood of strategic policy-making can thus be found in the literature on national intra- and inter-ministerial coordination (see, e.g. Scharpf 1993), as well as in the principal–agent literature. A specific characteristic of EU policy towards the CEECs is that the macro-policy-makers occupy positions at the top of the decision-making hierarchy within the relevant political systems (national and EU). The likelihood of strategic policy-making depends on:

- the congruence of the macro-policy-makers' preferences, since the greater their diversity, the more difficult is strategic policy-making; and

- the structure of the *policy coordination process* between macro- and meso-policy-makers.

The more diverse the preferences, the more fragmented the policy process, and thus the greater is the autonomy of the meso-policy-makers, the harder it is to achieve strategic policy-making. The more hierarchical the coordination and the more centralized the decision-making, the more likely it is that the collective preferences of the macro-policy-makers will prevail.

Yet the flip-side is that, while centralized policy-making might lead to more strategic policies within the context of policy towards the CEECs, the impact on the meso policy areas might lead to dysfunctionalities and incoherence within the context of these specific policy areas.

The starting-points of policy towards the CEECs

The relationship with the CEECs until the late 1980s

Before Gorbachev took office in the Soviet Union, relations between the EU and the CEECs were virtually non-existent (Pinder and Pinder 1975; Pinder 1991: 8–23). Cold war antagonism precluded formal relations with the Council for Mutual Economic Assistance (CMEA), or its individual members, and the centrally planned economies did not engage much in foreign trade. EU activities were limited to sectoral agreements designed to protect the 'sensitive' sectors of agriculture, coal, steel, and textiles (Marescau 1989*b*), and the frequent use of anti-dumping procedures (Jacobs 1989). EU governments also used trade policy to encourage individual CEECs to take more independent positions from the Soviet Union, which rewarded Yugoslavia in the early 1970s with substantial trade concessions, and Romania in 1980 with a (more limited) trade agreement.

More political overtures depended largely on initiatives from individual member governments, notably the German *Ostpolitik*. Coordination within the framework of European Political Cooperation (EPC) for the Conference on Security and Cooperation in Europe (CSCE) was a rare and positive experience of collective diplomacy by the member states (W. Wallace 1983*b*); it began to generate other forms of light cooperation and communication. The new *détente* under Gorbachev led to the tentative attempts to establish 'more normal' relations, particularly a joint EC–CMEA declaration in June 1988 (Lippert 1990).

Immediate responses to the political upheavals of the late 1980s

Ten years after the event it might be difficult for some readers to imagine just how unexpected these changes were for publics, analysts, and policy-makers alike. The cold war context in which the EU had been conceived and developed had not laid down a 'European policy', but rather set a clear geographical boundary to the EU, and provided it with a 'counter-image' of itself. New relations had to be built virtually from scratch, and with no mental map to define the new relationship.

The EU's immediate response had the following features:

- enthusiastic pledges of support for the changes;
- consensus that the EU should be the main channel for policy;
- the leadership role played by the Commission;
- hyperactivity and a proliferation of initiatives;
- a focus on 'normalization' and technical relations; and
- short-termism.

Pledges of support

At the level of discourse the European integration project always sought to end the division of the continent, as well as to defend the liberal democracies and market economies. Scripts for public speeches and statements were readily available for politicians and policy-makers at both the national and EU levels. The Rhodes European Council in December 1988 reaffirmed the EU's 'determination to act with renewed hope to overcome the division of the continent' (*Bulletin of the European Communities* (December 1988)). In Strasbourg in December 1989, when the extent of change became more apparent, the European Council pledged full support for transformation in the CEECs.

The Community and its Member States are fully conscious of the common responsibility which devolves on them in this decisive phase in the history of Europe.... They are prepared to develop ... closer and more substantive relations ... in all areas.... The Community is at the present time the European identity which serves as the point of reference for the countries of Central and Eastern Europe.... The Community has taken and will take the decisions necessary to strengthen its cooperation with peoples desiring liberty, democracy and progress, and with states which demonstrate their commitment to the principles of democracy, pluralism, and the rule of law. The Community will encourage, by all the means at its disposal, the necessary economic reforms. (*Bulletin of the European Communities*, December 1989)

Agreement on an EU response

It was not self-evident that the key role in delivering a response should be assigned to the EU. The collective rhetoric of the macro-policy-makers helped by alluding to the special role of the EU in supporting the transformations. However, although the member governments shared an interest in geopolitical stabilization of the region and the long-term economic opportunities, the intensity of these interests varied considerably, particularly among the bigger member states (Niblett 1995). The West German government was keen to re-establish historical ties in the region, particularly with the German Democratic Republic (GDR). However, German influence in the CEECs, and particularly German unification, became key concerns of the French and British governments. In the smaller member states there was some anxiety lest unilateral activities of the bigger member states create tensions within the EU. EU coordination was a reassuring way forward. The German government favoured a collective response, seeing the advantages of burden-sharing and greater efficiency. The French and British governments, albeit reluctant to see their capacity for unilateral action constrained, saw this as preferable to unilateral German initiatives.

The scope for a strong EU role was brought into sharper focus by external demands and expectations. The new CEEC governments framed their goals of reforms with explicit references to the core values of European integration. It seemed therefore natural that their principal foreign policy objective was to 'join Europe' by entering the EU (Kolankiewicz 1994; Saryusz-Wolski 1994; Inotai 1998). The US Administration repeatedly encouraged this aspiration, although it was becoming a less present actor in European affairs (Baker 1989). Once German unification was under way it also appeared that the Soviet Union could live with an EU enlarged eastwards.

The leadership role of the Commission

The activism and leadership provided by the Commission were crucial elements in establishing that the EU would play a central role in promoting systemic transformation in the CEECs and in coordinating Western policy more generally. The first move from the Commission was to develop bilateral Trade and Cooperation Agreements (TCAs) with individual countries, as they embarked on political and economic reform (Lequesne 1991; Sedelmeier and Wallace 1996: 357–8). Following a suggestion by the then US President, George Bush, at the G7 summit in July 1989, Jacques Delors accepted on behalf of the Commission the task of coordinating aid from the so-called G24 (the Western industrialized countries), with which other international organizations and agencies (the Organization for Economic Cooperation and Development (OECD), World Bank, International Monetary Fund, and the Paris Club) were associated.

Although this initiative took by surprise the few staff in the Commission dealing with the CEECs, the Commission was able to exploit its first such political mandate. It submitted its own Action Plan, intended as a 'framework for action by the Community and as an incentive for the other members of the G24 to take similar and coordinated initiatives' (*Bulletin of the European Communities* (October 1989): 8). The Action Plan included measures ranging from emergency humanitarian aid to the improvement of market access, and from the provision of macroeconomic assistance to the setting up of the Community's own programme for technical assistance, the Phare programme (Pologne–Hongrie: Assistance à la Restructuration des Économies; the acronym borrows the French word for 'lighthouse'). Phare was operated by a new service in the Directorate-General for External Relations (DG I). Its primary instrument of direct grants turned the Commission into the role of the patron *vis-à-vis* the CEECs. It became locked into direct bilateral and contractual relationships with individual recipient countries and had to invent a philosophy to sustain the programme. The result was a curious mix of ambition and caution.

The Commission became the channel of wide-ranging advice about economic transformation and imposed demanding conditions on the clients of its policy, though deliberately confining its conditionality to market-developing measures. It was only later that the European Parliament (EP) insisted on building a 'democracy' line into the general budget for 1992, in order to focus more attention on politics and civil society. The Phare 'democracy programme' was very different in character from other Phare programmes (Blackman 1994). Lacking the resources of staff and expertise within the house, the Commission turned to outside bodies and groups as its advisers and intermediaries. Early on Phare came to depend on an army of consultants from western Europe under contract to the Commission, which led to a disturbing bias in actual expenditure away from the intended CEEC beneficiaries. Efficiency of aid was also hampered by the relative lack of resources allocated to the management of the programme, and by the considerable pressure that the coordination of programmes put on the overstretched staff in DG I, subsequently assisted by the Commission delegations in the CEECs (for more detail on Phare, see Sedelmeier and Wallace 1996: 357–62; Mayhew 1998: 138–50). Notwithstanding these problems, the Commission's activism was key to establishing the EU as the anchor of the Western response to the changes in eastern Europe, as well as in fostering a leadership role for itself (Pelkmans and Murphy 1991).

Normalization and assistance

Despite the activism and some more innovative elements, the overall thrust of policy was still rather conventional. This was reflected in the two principal characteristics of policy: a focus on the normalization of relations; and the provision of technical assistance.

First, normalization meant ironing out distortions stemming from the communist period and then fitting the CEECs into the EU's hierarchy of external relations. The TCAs were the convenient starting-point and became the standard framework for cooperation. They dated back to steps to develop tentative relations between the EU and the CMEA, the first TCA with Hungary having been concluded in 1988. The TCAs removed those forms of trade discrimination which related to those previously imposed against the CEECs as state trading countries; after 1989 their primary importance was symbolic in normalizing trade relations. They did not give the CEECs a preferential position, since the concrete concessions remained limited (Lequesne 1991: 364).[2]

The second focus of policy was on technical economic assistance. This approach ran through the work of the Phare programme and of the European Bank for Reconstruction and Development (EBRD). This latter was set up by the EU and its Western partners to provide public loans for investment until private capital became available (for more details on the EBRD, see Dunnet 1991; S. Weber 1994; Sedelmeier and Wallace 1996: 362–64). On the one hand, this provided a means to advocate that the CEECs imitate west European policy models and rules. To support economic and political transformation was to help the CEECs to 'become like us' (which was, of course, also a declared goal of the new CEEC governments). From early on this approach established an asymmetrical relationship, in which the EC set the conditionality for assistance, and ultimately for accession. On the other hand, the focus on assistance revealed a perception of transition as a predominantly technical problem, solvable through a transfer of expertise and financial resources. Therefore, although EU rhetoric put a strong emphasis on the *finalité politique* of economic cooperation and assistance, this political dimension proved hard to insert and the policy had somewhat mixed results (La Serre 1994: 24).

Short-termism

The easy part was to state the shared aim of helping to root the principles and practices of both political democracy and market economy; it became clear that to achieve this was much more demanding. Despite the initial consensus it became apparent that the EU found it easier to devise *ad hoc* policy than to design a more rounded approach. In practice the individual elements of policy were not always coherent. The efficiency and appropriateness of the substance of policy were not always evident, especially as regards some of the more innovative elements. The pace of change meant that policy was often outdated by events and had constantly to adapt. Some glimpses of more strategic elements appeared in the political and economic conditionality that determined eligibility of individual CEECs for assistance through Phare and the EBRD and in the differentiation which determined which of the CEECs were offered trade agreements and when (Pinder 1991: 32–4). The inclusion of an explicit suspension clause hardened the political conditionality, an approach which also resulted from efforts to coordinate more closely with the EPC framework in policy towards the CEECs (Nuttall 1992).

It is perhaps not surprising that policy responses were *ad hoc*. The EU had been unprepared for these unexpected changes, and was operating under time pressure and uncertainty about their speed, depth, and durability. This inexperience led to a lack of clear-cut prescriptions or policy blueprints for appropriate responses at the technical level. Shortages of staff and of expertise were another complication. Both EU and national agencies had to construct policy machinery, as staff were rapidly redeployed from other tasks, often from teams experienced in development assistance programmes for the Third World (Pinder 1991: 91). Policy was invented with little clarity about the matching of short-term action to crafted future goals. The resulting mix of tradition and innovation reflected a sense that 'something had to be done', but not a policy. Not surprisingly, therefore, difficulties emerged once the focus of the debate shifted from the symbolic dimension of the relationship to the substance and the need to deliver economic results.[3]

Towards a longer-term policy framework: the Europe Agreements

Attempts to move towards a more long-term framework for relations with the CEECs were supported notably by the UK government, the German government, and parts of the Commission. The difficulty of devising a more coherent and strategic policy was evident not from any explicit controversy, but rather from the striking absence of thorough debate. Policy-makers were busy with other issues, but they were also nervous about opening up a potentially divisive debate about the future of the EU integration model. To the extent that a discussion took place it was mainly framed by the conventional antithesis of 'widening versus deepening' and the new geopolitical balance in Europe (Sedelmeier 1994: 7–20). Two more innovative ideas were floated: the French President Mitterrand's suggestion of a European Confederation (Vernet

1992); and the proposal for a European Political Area put forward by Frans Andriessen (1991), then the Commissioner for External Relations. Neither idea gathered much support.

Instead EU policy-makers invented the formula of association agreements, first suggested by the UK government in November 1989, although this drew on previous precedents (Kramer 1993). The Strasbourg European Council in December 1989 agreed to devise 'an appropriate form of association' and the Commission, in particular DG I and Andriessen, moved quickly to sketch a broad framework (Commission 1990*d*). The special meeting of the European Council in April 1990, summoned for other reasons, agreed without much discussion to 'create a new type of association agreement as a part of the new pattern of relationships in Europe'. These Europe agreements (EAs) were to be offered to Hungary, Poland, and Czechoslovakia, which were identified as the most advanced among the CEECs.

This decision reflected the balance of opinion emerging in the 1991 Intergovernmental Conference (IGC) in favour of giving priority to deepening rather than widening. EU policy-makers found it convenient to address the CEECs as an 'external' problem, separate from their internal agenda (Rollo and Wallace 1991; Sedelmeier and Wallace 1996: 366–7; Niblett 1995). The Commission presented further proposals on the contents of the EAs in August (Commission 1990*a*), and these were to frame the subsequent negotiations. The formula was locked to the established paradigm of a classical trade agreement, supplemented by a 'political dialogue', intended to underline the CEECs' special character, and backed by technical and financial assistance and economic cooperation. The main features are set out in Box 16.1.

Box 16.1 The Europe Agreements

General character—based on Article 238 (EEC)

Unlimited duration; preferential agreements; mixed competences; for an example of full text see *OJL 348* (31 Dec. 1993) (Poland–EU).

Modified by:

- added clause on respect for democratic principles, human rights, and principles of market economy for all new agreements (Council statement, 11 May 1992)
- conditional acceptance of eventual membership (Copenhagen European Council, see Box 16.3).

Political dialogue

Regular bilateral meetings and consultations on all topics of 'common interest', at highest level, including ministerial (Association Council); to promote convergence on foreign policy matters.

Modified by:

- the Copenhagen European Council on 'reinforced and extended multilateral dialogue' (see Box 16.3)
- Council conclusion on reinforcing political dialogue of 7 March 1994
- the Essen European Council on a 'structured relationship' (see Box 16.4).

Free movement of goods

- Progressive establishment of *free trade in industrial goods* (transition period for EU five years, for CEECs ten years):

1. tariffs: immediate elimination for some products, one to five years for most others
2. quantitative restrictions: immediate elimination, with *exceptions* for sensitive sectors: (a) ECSC products (*coal*: quotas after one year and tariffs after four years, with special derogations for Germany and Spain; *steel*: quotas immediately and tariffs gradually within five years); (*b*) *textile products*: quotas within not less than five years and tariffs gradually within six years)

- *agricultural products*: consolidation of previous concessions and some reciprocal concessions
- special provisions for *rules of origin* (at least 60 per cent 'local content' required)
- *safeguards*: anti-dumping provisions; special and general safeguard clauses; unilateral measures possible
- *consolidation of GSP benefits* (and withdrawal from list of GSP beneficiaries, normally reserved for developing countries)
- *acceptance as market economies*, hence removal from the scope of Regulation 1765/82 and 3420/83.

Modified by:
the Copenhagen European Council to accelerate market access (see Box 16.3).

Other freedoms of movement

- *movement of workers*: equal treatment for workers legally established in the EU
- *right of establishment*: full application of national treatment for establishment and operation of new economic and professional activities; transitional periods for application by the associates; restriction on freedom of movement through limitation to 'key personnel'
- *supply of services*: progressive allowance of cross-border supply of services; special rules for transport
- *payments and movement of capital*: freedom of financial transfers for commercial transactions, provision of services, and investment operations; repatriation of capital or investment benefits.

Approximation of legislation

- Associates make legislation compatible with EU laws with EU technical assistance
- *competition policy*: associates adapt their legislation to EU rules within three years
- non-discriminatory public procurement
- protection of intellectual, industrial, and commercial property similar to that in EU within five years.

Modified by:
decisions to prepare the CEECs for integration into the single market.

Dimensions of cooperation

- *economic cooperation*: covering all sectors of mutual interest
- *cultural cooperation*: extending EU cultural cooperation programmes to associates
- *financial cooperation*: grants under Phare and loans from EIB; possibility of macroeconomic assistance through G24; no financial protocol.

Institutions

- *Association Council*: ministerial level at least once a year; supervises the agreement's implementation; possibility of binding decisions and dispute settlement
- *Association Committee*: assists the Association Council
- *Parliamentary Committee*: advisory role.

Acceptance of the EA formula as the mainstay of policy still left open the question of their concrete substance. This required delegation to, or negotiations with, sectoral policy-makers within both the Commission and the member governments. The macro-policy-makers had to confront disputes over how to balance policy towards the CEECs with the vested interests of particular domestic groups in the incumbent member states. These intra-EU dimensions shaped the drafting of the negotiation mandates on the basis of which the Commission conducted the negotiations on behalf of the member states with the governments from the CEECs.

The initial framework presented by DG-IE built on intensive consultations with the three CEECs and was fairly ambitious. Some of this ambition was lost as the Commission's specialist services filled in the detail and as sectoral experts in the member states' Permanent Representations became more involved, often functioning as channels for domestic interest groups. The final mandates agreed by the Council were even more limited. The asymmetry of bargaining power between the EU and the CEECs put the EU very much in the driving seat.

The EA negotiations opened in December 1990 with Poland, Hungary, and Czechoslovakia, and brought into sharp focus the gap between CEEC expectations and concrete proposals from the EU. The dissatisfaction of the three governments from the CEECs (at the time often referred to as the Visegrád group) led to two periods of deadlock, first in late March 1991 and again from July 1991, when notably the Polish delegation refused to send a high-level delegation to the negotiations. On each occasion the Commission successfully persuaded the Council to amend the negotiation directives in order to take better account of CEEC demands.[4] Despite some improvements on the original offer, the CEECs were still far from enthusiastic about the final outcome of the negotiations.

One key criticism was that the EAs did not establish a clear link to future membership of the EU. The Commission had attempted to pre-empt argument by stating that there was 'no link either explicit or implicit' between association and accession, and while 'membership is not excluded when the time comes', it was 'a totally separate question' (Commission 1990a). In its negotiation mandate the Council advised the Commission simply to refer to Article 237 (EEC): any European state may apply for membership. In the revised mandate the EU took a somewhat more flexible position, under pressure from the Commission negotiators and the British and German governments. A formula in the preamble to the EAs noted that the EU recognized eventual membership as the associates' 'final objective', and that 'this association, in the view of the parties, will help to achieve this objective'. This fell short of a firm commitment and was interpreted quite widely as antipathy to enlargement.

The other main area of CEEC discontent was over the economic substance of the EAs, primarily with regard to trade liberalization and financial assistance. The EU had committed itself in principle to free trade in industrial products over five years. However, the special protocols and annexes covering 'sensitive' sectors, notably agriculture, textiles, coal, and steel, offered slower and limited liberalization. Yet these sectors accounted for the bulk of CEEC exports and reflected their medium-term comparative advantages. Even though extensive liberalization was envisaged eventually, the provisions for contingent protection provided an instrument for EU producers to hamper CEEC exports (Hindley 1992), a deterrent to potential foreign investors.

Thus, in their general design the EAs were undoubtedly the most wide-ranging agreements ever concluded by the EU with third countries. Yet their effectiveness was reduced by the EU's inability to deliver comprehensive, predictable, and unconditional market access. However generous their economic content relative to other trade agreements, they were seen by the CEECs as grudging.

Although the discussion about the EAs had excited some bargaining between EU member governments, the debate over policy substance was not really a clear-cut confrontation between different national positions (Sedelmeier 1994; Niblett 1995; Torreblanca 1997). Rather the debate within both individual governments and the Commission was polarized between macro-policy-makers, emphasizing longer-term political objectives, and various groups of meso-policy-makers, under pressure from short-term economic problems. Within the Commission this manifested itself in the rivalry between DG I and DGs III (Industry) and VI (Agriculture), as well as inside DG I, between the units dealing respectively with the CEECs and those responsible for trade defence instruments. Within most member governments the foreign ministry was competing with ministries of industry and agriculture that were subjected to pressures from sectoral producer lobbies. The ability of the sectoral logic to constrain a more politically motivated agreement was greatly facilitated by the fragmentation of the policy process and lack of close oversight by the macro-policy-makers in the member governments.

Defensive sectoral interests were able to insulate specific aspects of the EAs from political pressures for a more generous approach to the CEECs and to set the baseline of what would be on offer. As some of those involved on the CEEC side were able to observe, as fast as they identified issues on which they wanted to press for more open market access, they found that an EU-based lobby had beaten them to the EU negotiators.

The distinctiveness of the EAs compared with conventional trade agreements led the Council to set up a different group from the Article 113 Committee (see Chapter 14); the Working Group on Eastern Europe monitored the negotiations, its national delegates often coming from capitals with narrow briefs to defend particular domestic producers in specific sectors. Fragmentation was facilitated, and its effects exacerbated, by the lack of clear oversight by foreign ministries. Once they had agreed on the principle of association agreements, the macro-policy-makers in the member governments mostly disengaged from the policy process. In Germany, for example, the Foreign Office turned its attention to the CSCE, and unification absorbed political attention.

The ability to accommodate the demands and expectations of the CEECs thus rested essentially on how far the Commission negotiators could persuade the member governments to grant more substantive concessions. At times the context of the negotiations allowed them to manipulate the policy process in such a way as to force greater involvement of foreign ministers in the General Affairs Council to adjudicate in disputes over national negotiation positions. On occasion, such as on the question of voluntary restraints on steel trade (see Sedelmeier 1998a, ch. 4; Torreblanca 1998), this device facilitated more generosity towards the CEECs. The overstretched team in DG I, however, had to rely on the individual national policy-makers to withstand the pressure from their sectoral lobbies.

From association to pre-accession

The Copenhagen European Council and the prospect of membership

The European Council had already agreed at Maastricht, in December 1991, to examine the general implications of enlargement at Lisbon, in June 1992. The Lisbon Report (Commission 1992*b*) distinguished between the countries of the European Free Trade Association (EFTA) as immediately eligible for membership, and both the southern applicants (Cyprus, Malta, and Turkey) and the CEECs (Michalski and Wallace 1992). This had left hanging the question of what kind of 'partnership' to develop for the CEECs beyond Europe Association.

The Commission therefore proposed a new formula of 'reinforced association' in a communication (Commission 1992*e*) for discussion at the extraordinary European Council in Birmingham in October 1992. In the event the debate was sketchy; and the Edinburgh session in December was too preoccupied with other issues to discuss the Commisssion's report in detail. It deferred to its next meeting 'decisions on the various components of the Commission's report in order to prepare the associate countries for accession to the Union' (*Bulletin of the European Communities*, December, 1992), the first official indication that the CEECs might be considered as candidates for membership of the EU. The Commission (1993*f*) set out more concrete measures for the deepening of association, mostly endorsed by the General Affairs Council on 8 June 1993.

The declarations at the Copenhagen European Council in June 1993 marked an important qualitative change in the evolution of policy; they both endorsed eventual membership as a goal and agreed to improve market access (see Box 16.2). This fragile compromise had been forged by a mix of internal political engineering, external pressure, and a certain 'learning process'. It left much to be determined about how the new policy would be achieved.

Policy advocacy and political leadership from the Commission again played a key part in the reformulation of policy at Copenhagen. The services of DGI and the Andriessen *cabinet* had reopened the debate within the Commission. This gathered momentum with the arrival in 1993 of two new External Relations Commissioners, Hans van den Broek and, particularly, Sir Leon Brittan. The challenge was to build a sustainable coalition against the erosion of this new approach. The Commission team worked closely with the British and Danish Council presidencies and with the German government. The careful formulation of the qualitative criteria for membership minimized the ground for opposition from the macro-policy-makers in the more hesitant member governments.

We can observe a kind of staccato learning process over this period, a kind of acknowledgement that the EU was in uncharted waters and that the CEECs could not be treated on a 'take it or leave it' basis. This learning process was induced partly by criticism from the CEECs, partly by some inescapable evidence of shortcomings in the implementation of the EAs, and partly by the strictures of the outside 'expert community'. There had been an unusually intense involvement of newly expert groups of outside analysts in advising the Commission and the member governments

---

Box 16.2 The Copenhagen European Council

EU accepts conditionally eventual membership of the CEECs

provided that CEECs have:

- stable institutions (guarantee of democracy, rule of law, human rights, minority rights)
- functioning market economy and capacity to cope with competitive pressures inside the EC
- ability to adopt the *acquis*; accepted aims of political, economic, and monetary union; and provided that *EU* has:
- capacity to absorb new members without endangering the momentum of European integration.

Accelerated market access to the EU

More rapid (than EAs) opening of EU markets across products, including (although to a more limited degree) the sensitive sectors (Additional Protocols, *OJL* 25 (29 January 94)).

Structured Relationship with the Institutions of the EU

- *political dialogue* (second pillar): shift from bilateral towards multilateral framework; reinforced through additional meetings at expert level and greater frequency
- extension to *other EU policy areas* (multilateral meetings at ministerial level and heads of state–government); particularly energy, environment, transport, science–technology, and JHA.

Reorientation of Phare assistance

Up to 15 per cent of Phare budget available for infrastructure projects.

---

on policy. Many of the same experts had given advice to CEEC governments and may well have heightened the latter's awareness of the limitations to the EAs. Although probably too heterogeneous to be called an 'epistemic community', these various experts were largely unanimous in denouncing the shortcomings of EU policy (see, e.g. Langhammer 1992; Winters 1992; Messerlin 1993; Rollo and M. A. M. Smith 1993; Baldwin 1994; M. A. M. Smith and Wallace 1994; Faini and Portes 1995). Academic criticism provided the advocates of a more open policy with important arguments to reopen the debate.

A further part of this 'learning process' had to do with developments in the CEECs. The scale and difficulties of the transformation process became more evident, and the first indications emerged of decreasing public support in the CEECs for vigorous reforms. Meanwhile, the EU seemed unable to resist all of the calls to use instruments of commercial protection,[5] and it was running a trade surplus with the CEECs.[6] These matters were politically highly sensitive within the CEECs and contributed to some cooling of support for integration with the EU. Meanwhile, the conflict in the former Yugoslavia was a salutary reminder of the costs of failed transition from communism to liberal democracy (see Chapter 17). Thus it became harder to set aside criticisms from CEEC governments, especially on the gap between EU rhetoric and substance. The two Visegrád memoranda (of September 1992 and June 1993) were important signals and showed the glimmerings of a collective response from several of the associates.

This policy shift owed a great deal to the re-engagement of the macro-policy-makers in the member states. Chancellor Kohl backed the Commission's proposals within the German government's deliberations; interestingly, similar active support came from Felipe Gonzales, the Spanish Prime Minister, and Beniamino Andreatta, the Italian Foreign Minister. The involvement of the European Council focused the attention of the macro-policy-makers. Centralization of policy coordination was important for the agreement on the substance of accelerated trade liberalization. A high-level group of senior officials took on the task of obtaining comprehensive con-cessions horizontally across the range of sectors, thus sidelining the technical experts at the working-group level.

The Essen European Council and the Pre-accession strategy

To maintain momentum on the agreement to the principle of CEEC membership of the EU, the policy advocates in DG I and the Brittan *cabinet* set out to put it on to a concrete working footing. Their main idea was to build a strategy to prepare for accession which centred on helping the CEECs to align with EU legislation—the *acquis communautaire*. Significant progress would make it more difficult for the EU to justify stalling on accession. Alignment would, in any case, be beneficial in its own right by underpinning economic restructuring and facilitating the internationalization of the CEEC economies, as long as the process remained sufficiently flexible for the CEECs to set their own priorities. Especially in the areas of competition and state aids it could deliver immediate benefits by undermining calls from within the EU for the use of instruments of commercial defence.

In March 1994 an internal review of policy by the Commission revealed that among many Commissioners there was a mood for 'consolidation' of existing policy rather than new initiatives. However, Brittan and van den Broek seized the opportunity to lay out more comprehensive proposals to prepare the CEECs for accession. In addition to regulatory alignment, these included: improved trade opportunities through liberalization in agriculture; limiting the use of commercial defence instruments; a cumulation of rules of origin; more effective use of the Phare programme (following the structural funds model); and making the structured dialogue more operational.

The debate was echoed in the discussion among national policy-makers. A British–Italian initiative, launched by Douglas Hurd and Beniamino Andreatta as foreign ministers, proposed to deepen the political dialogue by allowing for more direct participation by the governments of the CEECs in the second and third pillars (common foreign and security policy (CFSP) and justice and home affairs (JHA)) (*Agence Europe*, 22 December 1993: 6).

Some other governments were more hesitant. The French and Spanish govern-ments wanted a comparable investment in an active Mediterranean policy, with pol-itical and security dimensions as well as economic. Some tensions emerged during the closing phases of the accession negotiations with the EFTA applicants.[7] A kind of strategic bargain was struck in which the French and Spanish accepted eastern enlargement as a goal, as well as immediate EFTA enlargement, in return for German support for what became the Barcelona process to develop a new Mediterranean policy.

Informal cooperation between the Commission team and the German government resulted in the call at the Corfu European Council in June 1994 for the Commission to report on 'the strategy to be followed with a view to preparing for accession' (*Bulletin of the EU* (June 1994)). This mandate gave those inside the Commission who favoured a more engaged policy towards the CEECs a crucial advantage. The Commission report of 13 July 1994 outlined a 'pre-accession' strategy (Commission 1994*u*). Agreement on the complementary substantive paper (Commission 1994*c*) was more difficult, given the range of internal disagreement within the Commission. Especially on commercial defence, agricultural subsidies, rules of origin, and financial transfers, the college as a whole took a cautious view and watered down the original proposals. The two surviving cornerstones were the 'structured dialogue' with EU institutions and the progressive integration of the CEECs into the single European market through regulatory alignment. The Commission promised a White Paper on those parts of the *acquis* essential for the CEECs to adopt in their own legislation, as well as the legal and institutional framework required.

In July 1994, as the German presidency opened, the Council largely endorsed the Commission's approach, though it did not command universal enthusiasm. Informal meetings followed in September, including a bilateral Franco-German discussion in Paris on 20 September 1994, which agreed to agree on the merits of a White Paper, in spite of persistent differences of emphasis. In October 1994 the Council agreed in principle to the 'structured dialogue' and to press ahead with the White Paper. Final agreement on the structured dialogue proved difficult, because some governments felt that the Germans were trying to give the associates backdoor membership. These difficulties were reflected in an embarrassing row over the reluctant endorsement of the planned invitation to the CEECs' heads of government to attend part of the European Council meeting in Essen.

Arguments also continued over the concrete accompanying measures on trade and financial aid, albeit already watered down inside the Commission. Most EU governments were internally divided, including the German. The German Council presidency averted further weakening of the proposals by keeping negotiations at the level of Coreper, the final text being adopted in a Coreper *restreint*. The Germans also won agreement to negotiate EAs with the Baltic states, knowing that the new Nordic EU members would support this. The results from Essen (see Box 16.3) may seem undramatic compared with some expectations, but none the less produced a more multilateral approach and were geared to making accession seem feasible.

The Commission White Paper on regulatory alignment

The White Paper was published in May 1995 and agreed at the Cannes European Council in June 1995 (Commission 1995*b*). It used the methodology of the 1985 Commission White Paper on the single European market (see Chapter 4) to identify how the CEECs might adopt EU market regulations in terms of core legislation and phased convergence. It stressed the importance of the legal and administrative infrastructure, not just the 'transposition' of legislation. By making so many of the issues technical and horizontal it reduced the opportunities for veto groups on the EU

Box 16.3 The 'pre-accession' strategy (Essen European Council)

Structured relationship
Making the agreement in principle of Copenhagen more operational
- reaffirmation of multilateral framework to complement bilateral dialogue of the EAs
- schedule for joint meetings at the beginning of each year in agreement between the two presidencies (more systematic framework than previous *ad hoc* meetings)
- concrete decisions on issue areas and frequency of meetings connected to corresponding Council (General Affairs: semi-annual; Internal Market, Ecofin, Agriculture: annual; Transport, Telecommunications, Research, Environment: annual; JHA: semi-annual; Culture, Education: annual); annual meetings on the margins of European Council (stronger emphasis on meetings of the Fifteen with CEEC counterparts, rather than Troika–Commission format).

Preparation of the CEECs for integration into the single market
Creation of conditions to allow the single market to function after eastern enlargement.
EU action:
- identification of key *acquis* essential for the creation and maintenance of the internal market in each sector
- suggested sequencing for legal approximation; priority measures to be tackled first (but not priorities between sectors)
- specification of administrative and organizational structures for effective implementation and enforcement (formal transposition of legislation insufficient)
- suggested adaptation of Phare assistance for pre-accession strategy
- Technical Assistance Information Exchange Office (database on alignment with internal market; clearing-house to match requests for assistance with expertise available in Commission, member states, and private bodies)
- monitoring of implementation of recommendations.

CEEC action:
- phased adoption of legislation, regulatory systems, standards, and certification methods compatible with EU
- establishment of national work programmes to identify sectoral priorities and timetables for alignment.

Supporting policies to promote integration
Development of infrastructure; cooperation in TENs; intra-regional cooperation; environmental cooperation; CFSP; cooperation in JHA, culture, education, and training; supported through Phare.

---

side to intervene and block progress. There were both practical and tactical reasons for using this approach to policy development.[8]

The drafting of the White Paper marked a shift in the centre of gravity of policy and in how it was coordinated: DG XV, responsible for the single market, was in the lead, working with DG IA. DG II and DG IV seem to have supported this, with the acquiescence of DG XI and criticism from DG V. As a result, the document also breached an important taboo in two senses. Implicitly it suggested that some parts of the *acquis* were more important than others. It also distinguished those areas of legislative alignment needed to enable *products* to be traded from those that defined the *processes* for making products and generating services. The latter were excluded from the White Paper's menu, with the exception of social policy.

This is a persistently important issue, given that high process standards are costly, and more easily achieved by advanced than by under-developed economies, for example as regards standards of social and environmental protection. Yet to make such an argument runs counter to the dominant policy paradigm underpinning the single European market (Sedelmeier 1998b). Some of this would feed into the debate about what level of convergence would be required for full accession, what could be left for post-accession transition, and what scope there would be for the CEEC governments to express regulatory preferences of their own (Rouam 1994; McGowan and Wallace 1996; M. A. M. Smith *et al.* 1996; Young and Wallace 2000).

There followed an extensive effort to provide technical support for regulatory convergence, including through the creation of a new agency attached to the Commission, the Technical Assistance Information Exchange Office (TAIEX), working closely with the relevant agencies in the member states.

Towards an enlargement policy

The Madrid European Council

Over the next few months attention shifted to the new Mediterranean policy favoured by the French and Spanish governments during their Council presidencies. In addition some momentum was lost within the new Commission college presided over by Jacques Santer. His reorganization of the responsibilities for external relations by geographical portfolios replaced the somewhat dysfunctional separation of external economic relations (DG I) from external political relations (DG IA). In the ensuing contest Hans van den Broek 'won' DG IA, now responsible for the CEECs and former Soviet Union, from Leon Brittan, who took the DG I portfolio. This broke up the team that Brittan had built up over the previous years in his *cabinet* and DG I.

The Madrid European Council in December 1995 none the less shifted the discussion towards an enlargement policy. It agreed:

- to ask the Commission to prepare its opinions (*avis*) on the candidates 'as soon as possible' after the conclusion of the IGC due to start in 1996;

- to ask the Commission to prepare a 'composite paper' on enlargement, both to evaluate the effects of enlargement on the EU's policies, particularly agriculture and the structural policies, and to make proposals for the 'financial perspective' from 2000 for the EU budget; and

- to set an indicative date to open accession negotiations with the CEECs, alongside Cyprus and Malta, six months after the end of the IGC. (Council of the European Union 1995b: 23)

The prompt for these developments came mainly from member governments. The German government in particular lobbied discreetly, but actively, among its partners for some key decisions to be taken at Madrid, after a strategic review of policy by an

Enlargement Task Force, established in the Foreign Office in 1994, had advocated moves from a 'pre-accession' to an accession strategy. In particular the Germans sought to separate the IGC from the enlargement agenda, a committed date for opening negotiations, as well as a target date of 2000 for completing them, the speedy preparation of the *avis*, and an open mind about which of the CEECs would be ready to meet the accession criteria of Copenhagen.

None the less, Chancellor Kohl was widely reported as favouring the opening of accession negotiations initially with only Poland, the Czech Republic, and Hungary. This started a debate, which has rumbled on ever since, about whether or not to 'differentiate' between the applicants, and, if so, at what stage in the accession process. One concern has been not to weaken the incentives for reform. Another was that too many candidates at once would make the negotiation process unmanageable. In addition individual EU members had their own favourites among the applicants, because of geographic and historical ties. The Spanish presidency brokered a solution whereby the European Council made no priorities among applicants and underlined that the EU would treat them all on an equal basis. The timetable was agreed rather easily because in April 1995 the Greek government had insisted on a date for negotiations with Cyprus in return for allowing the customs union with Turkey to go ahead.[9]

Thus, by the end of 1995 the focus of policy debate had shifted from association and pre-accession towards an eastern enlargement policy, though the follow-through would have to await the end of the IGC. The parameters were set for substantive negotiations about the adjustment measures needed on the side of the EU and about candidate selection. A new feature of the policy process was that the member governments had assumed the central role that the Commission had previously occupied.

Institutional reform: the IGC and the Amsterdam treaty

Enlargement has always generated institutional and constitutional debates in the EU; an increased membership generates both management problems and greater heterogeneity of interests. The initial reason for convening an IGC in 1996 was mainly to review the workings of the pillar structure, but the link was made early with enlargement, even to the extent that some participants thought that this should be the central focus of the IGC. Both the Reflection Group of representatives of heads of government, charged with preparing for the IGC, and the Commission presented enlargement as a main rationale for the IGC (Reflection Group 1995a: 1; 1995b: 6–8; Commission 1996g: 3–4).

De facto institutional reform became a kind of precondition for the accession process, although in the event the reforms most relevant to enlargement were not agreed. MEPs and others had long argued that more extensive reforms were needed to accommodate the EFTA enlargement, let alone an eastern enlargement. Successive European Councils had noted that the EU needed the institutional capacity to handle enlargement (see, for example, the Essen conclusions in Council 1994: 7). For some member governments the institutional issues were also a convenient excuse for not going ahead too quickly with enlargement.

The relevant institutional agenda came to be defined as ensuring:

- the efficiency of EU decision-making;
- 'fair' representation for each member state; and
- greater accountability, transparency and legitimacy.

The capacity of the EU's decision-making structures to reach collective agreements was widely argued to be under pressure, as more and smaller countries joined the EU. Calls became commonplace for an extension of qualified majority voting (QMV), to be balanced by a reinforced weight for the larger member states (Kerremans 1998; Edwards 1998). These were generally accompanied by a proposed trade-off that the larger member states would nominate only one Commissioner each (Dinan 1998). The inherited formula for QMV had been deliberately generous to the smaller member states, an arrangement that increasingly irritated politicians from the larger countries. Hence the issue crystallized around proposals for a reweighting of votes, on which numerous models were put forward (for example, Raunio and Wiberg 1998; Hosli 1996; Schmitter and Torreblanca 1997). This emerging conventional wisdom is, it should be noted, at variance with the empirical evidence. The Council votes rather little, operating mostly by consensus, and smaller member governments do not gang up on the larger member states. Coalitions depend more on the topics under discussion (Hayes-Renshaw and Wallace 1997).

Another issue in the IGC purported to be about enlargement, namely whether or not a formula could be found to facilitate a more flexible model of integration, that would allow smaller groups of member states to cooperate more closely on some issues. The assumption was that there would be an increasing number of issues on which not all member states would be engaged (Deubner 1995; H. Wallace and Wallace 1995; Stubb 1997; La Serre and Wallace 1997; Ehlermann 1997).

Table 16.2 The main changes in the Treaty of Amsterdam with regard to enlargement

Issue	Result
Extension of QMV	Only very limited
Number of commissioners	Only one commissioner per member state from the next enlargement if the weighting of votes has been modified
Weighting of votes	No decision, but indication of an eventual reweighting of votes, or introduction of a 'dual majority' (i.e. of votes in the Council as well as share of population)
Insertion of 'flexibility clauses'	Circumscribed as a 'last resort' (must involve a majority of members; must respect rights and obligations of non-participants; can be vetoed if 'important national interests' at stake)
Number of MEPs	Limit agreed
Review of institutional arrangements	Comprehensive review at least one year before EU membership exceeds twenty
'Schengen'	Schengen *acquis* to be applied *in full* by new members

All these pressures notwithstanding, the IGC reached only limited decisions on these issues, and enlargement did not provide the lever for reform (Sedelmeier 2000). Essentially decisions were deferred on 'the institutional problem', although the conclusion of the 1996–7 IGC did indeed pave the way for accession negotiations to open. One other new clause insisted that new members would have to apply the Schengen *acquis* in full (see Chapter 18). Table 16.2 summarizes the changes incorporated in the Treaty of Amsterdam. The Belgian, French, and Italian governments immediately recorded their insistence that enlargement could not go ahead without first a settlement on the institutional issues. Perhaps the feeble results of the IGC imply a weakening of commitment to enlargement. On the other hand, experience suggests that the EU is prone to defer politically difficult issues unless and until the pressures are overwhelming. The convening of another IGC is now scheduled in 2000, with these remaining institutional issues at the apparent core of its agenda.

Internal policy reforms and Agenda 2000

In July 1997 the Commission published the reports requested by the Madrid European Council in three volumes, ambitiously entitled *Agenda 2000* (Commission 1997i). These covered four main areas:

1. *The Commission's opinions on the candidates*: none was judged to meet fully all the Copenhagen criteria, but the Commission recommended a differentiated approach, with accession negotiations to open first with the Czech Republic, Estonia, Hungary, Poland, and Slovenia, as those considered to be in a position to meet the conditions in the medium term.

2. *A framework enlargement strategy*: this assumed that the *acquis* would be applied fully upon accession (although some transitional arrangements might be agreed in accession negotiations), with a reinforced pre-accession strategy for all applicant countries, based on both pre-accession aid (through a revamped Phare programme), and new Accession Partnerships (APs), to pursue regulatory alignment, to be annually reviewed.

3. *An impact study*: the effects of enlargement on the Union's internal policies were examined, as well as options for reform, especially agriculture (see Chapter 7) and the structural funds (see Chapter 9), the two areas of EU expenditure most relevant to most of the candidates given that their economic structures and their levels of gross domestic product (GDP) per capita were well below the EU average.

4. *A proposed new financial perspective (2000–2006)*: the budgetary impact of enlargement would need to be accommodated without exceeding the available sources of revenue and in a form that was acceptable to incumbent member states, according to a formula for pluri-annual budgeting (see Chapter 8).

Agenda 2000 took the enlargement discussion on to new ground, in which many of the policy and political issues started to come into much sharper focus. The policy debate shifted from questions of trade liberalization towards issues of policy adjustment, thus opening up some of the hardest and most sensitive questions about enlargement. If acceptable solutions could be found, one of the greatest obstacles to enlargement might be removed. New actors and interests now moved to the centre of the debate, and different alliances started to emerge. On questions of overall budgetary balances and reform of the structural funds, the negotiations would be between the beneficiaries of EU funding and those who paid the costs, typically through inter-state bargaining. On agricultural issues, the argument lay between the status quo beneficiaries and the advocates of reform, including particularly the finance ministries, but within the context of awkward debates about the social welfare functions of the common agricultural policy (CAP).

The EU now also began to be much more specific about the timetable for eastern enlargement. The Commission's opinions about individual candidates injected some realism into the speculations about what was feasible. Previously both Chancellor Kohl and President Chirac had voiced the year 2000 as a possible date, but this looked increasingly implausible. The Commission's assessments suggested a medium-term perspective of about five years, implying 2002 as the earliest possible date. This began to gain acceptance within the EU as a realistic, even optimistic, reference-point.

Agenda 2000 gave the Commission a chance to reinsert itself at the centre of the enlargement debate, by setting important parameters and by making enlargement look a credible and not over-costly process for incumbents. It sketched an incremental pathway for a sequencing of enlargement-related decisions, including candidate selection, the opening of accession negotiations, and institutional and policy reform—especially the CAP and structural funds. The underlying view also assumed the full adoption of the *acquis* by the CEECs. While this incremental approach had the advantage of pragmatism, it lacked a more strategic or visionary view of the character of an EU of twenty-six plus members, let alone of how to develop relations with countries that might not join in the medium term.

The sequencing of both intra-EU decisions and accession negotiations started to take a much clearer shape. The Luxembourg European Council of December 1997 would have to decide on the Commission's recommendation about which candidates should negotiate in the first group. The detailed discussion of Agenda 2000 would have to address the nitty-gritty of policy reform to the CAP and the structural funds, as well as the budgetary envelope. March 1999 was set as the deadline for agreement. Finally, the EU had to take a decision on how to deal with the outstanding questions of institutional reform; the Cologne European Council of June 1999 announced that the next IGC would be convened in early 2000 and completed at the end of 2000.

Towards accession

Selecting the candidates: the Luxembourg European Council

The queue for EU membership included ten candidates from central and eastern Europe, two from southern Europe (Cyprus and Malta), and Turkey, also waiting in the wings as a declared candidate for EU membership. Choosing which to engage in negotiation was necessarily a tough challenge. Until the Commission's opinions were published the debate on selection was muted (Commission 1998*h*). Some member governments hoped that the Commission would grasp the nettle, an irony given that the Commission had cautioned against Greek accession in the late 1970s, only to be overruled by the Council.

The opinions were organized in sections examining the ability of the applicants to meet the several Copenhagen criteria (Avery and Cameron 1998; Grabbe and Hughes 1998: 41–54), on the basis of responses by the applicants to a long questionnaire about their progress in adopting the *acquis*. In addition, the Commission drew on data compiled by its delegations in the candidate countries, and from the international economic organizations (the Organization for Economic Cooperation and Development (OECD), World Bank, EBRD), the Council of Europe, the Organization for Security and Cooperation in Europe (OSCE), academic sources (for example, Kaldor and Vejvoda 1998), and NGOs. On this apparently objective basis the opinions assessed their ability to meet the conditions in the medium term (see Table 16.3). The Commission recommended early accession negotiations with the Czech Republic, Estonia, Hungary, Poland, and Slovenia (in addition to Cyprus).[10]

Yet the process was profoundly political. It had involved some arguments within the Commission, and among member governments: the Nordic EU countries supported Estonia, and Slovenia was favoured by the Austrians. There was open pressure from the US government for the EU to 'compensate' the Baltic states for being ruled out of early North Atlantic Treaty Organization (Nato) membership. Some policy-makers argued against differentiation and for the 'regatta' option; all of the candidates should start the accession race, but row at different speeds towards the finishing-line, depending on the pace of their convergence with the EU and the success of their domestic reforms. Part of the case for this was to keep up the encouragement for reform and stabilization. The point of decision was the Luxembourg European Council in December 1997, where the Commission's selection was essentially endorsed. However, the distinction between the two groups was somewhat blurred, as, in particular, the Swedish, Danish, and Italian governments argued successfully for an inclusive process so as not to create new divisive boundaries (Friis 1998).

Specifically, the Luxembourg European Council decided that:

- formal accession negotiations would open simultaneously with *all* ten CEEC candidates (plus Cyprus);

- the screening process would cover all candidates, for the first five CEECs and Cyprus in individual discussions with the Commission, and the remainder in a less detailed and multilateral group;

- financial aid would be independent of accession, with equal treatment for all candidates and priority to the countries with the greatest need;

- the Commission would provide regular progress reports on the candidates, and might recommend that a country be promoted to the faster group (thus creating a language of 'ins' and 'pre-ins', rather than 'ins' and 'outs'); and

- a European Conference would be established, as the new multilateral framework for political consultations following up on the structured dialogue, and partly to try to involve Turkey.

Accession negotiations

Accession negotiations opened formally on 31 March 1998 under the British presidency, and substantively under the following Austrian presidency; the General Affairs Council of 5 October 1998 decided to proceed with substantive negotiations

Table 16.3 The Commission's opinions on the candidate countries, 1997

Country	Political[a]	Economic criteria[b]	Adoption of *acquis*[c]
Bulgaria	+	–	–
Czech Republic	+	Fairly close to meeting the criteria	+ Provided more progress in specific sectors
Estonia	+	Functioning market economy, but not yet adapted to competitive pressures	Substantial efforts necessary
Hungary	+	Very close to meeting the criteria	+ Provided more progress in specific sectors
Latvia	+	–	Very substantial efforts necessary
Lithuania	+	–	Very substantial efforts necessary
Poland	+	Very close to meeting the criteria	+ Provided more progress in specific sectors
Romania	+	–	–
Slovakia	–	Adapted to competitive pressures, but not fully functioning market economy	+ Provided efforts are much strengthened and more progress made in specific sectors
Slovenia	+	Fairly close to meeting the criteria	Considerable efforts necessary

Notes: + = positive; – = negative.
[a] (1) democracy and the rule of law; (2) human rights; (3) respect for minorities.
[b] In the medium term: (1) existence of a functioning market economy; (2) capacity to withstand competitive pressure and market forces within the Union.
[c] Ability to adopt the main parts of the *acquis* in the medium term, including: (1) obligations set out in the EAs; (2) transposition and effective implementation of the measures in the White Paper; (3) transposition and implementation of other parts of the *acquis*. In addition, a broader category, the ability to meet 'other obligations of membership', includes (*a*) the aims of political, economic, and monetary union; and (*b*) the administrative and judicial capacity to apply the *acquis*.

with the five CEECs and Cyprus, and these opened on 10 November.[11] The first stage is a process of 'screening', conducted by the Commission, to examine the ability of the candidates to apply the *acquis* and to identify potentially controversial issues for negotiations. For the five+one, screening was conducted on a bilateral basis by the Commission's Task Force on Enlargement; and for the remainder it was carried out by staff of DG IA in a multilateral format and in less detail. The next stage is for the Commission to recommend to the EU member governments the opening of accession conferences (in intergovernmental format) for substantive negotiations. Then the discussion covers issues such as transition periods and their duration, either to meet a candidate's needs, or because of a preoccupation of the incumbent members, for example on free movement of workers (as when Spain and Portugal joined).

The Commission published its first progress report on 4 November 1998 (Commission 1998*h*). It noted some economic stagnation in the Czech Republic and Slovenia, and highlighted the progress in Latvia and, to a lesser extent, in Lithuania and Slovakia. The latter was confirmed by the political developments after Prime Minister Meciar lost office. The Commission can make recommendations to promote individual CEECs to a faster track, a possibility that gained plausibility during 1999. External events also bear on this process. One result of the Kosovo war in 1999 was the beginning of a rethink about how to deal with other countries in eastern and especially south-eastern Europe.

The Commission announced in October 1999 a review of policy in its Composite Paper (Commission 1999*h*). This recommended that full accession negotiations start with the other five CEECs, though some conditions were further specified in relation to individual countries. The Helsinki European Council endorsed this in December 1999. The Commission also indicated that negotiations with some of the candidates might be completed by as soon as 2000.

The Accession Partnerships

The APs were proposed by the Commission to develop regulatory alignment through a 'reinforced pre-accession strategy'. They are more directly focused on helping the CEECs to adopt the *acquis* than the previous Phare assistance, which supported economic restructuring more generally. The APs are a more rigid approach than the original pre-accession strategy; member governments are more involved; and there is less chance that the Commission can use them to pre-empt accession negotiations. In addition there is rather little scope for the candidates themselves to shape their pace and content, causing considerable criticism that the language of partnership disguises rather thinly the imposition of EU priorities. One sign of this is the EU member governments' insistence on incorporating the APs into a Council Regulation (Grabbe 1999).

The European Conference

The French government first floated the idea of a European Conference in 1996, as a framework to make the accession process more inclusive and to reinforce multi-lateralism in pre-accession relations with the CEECs.[12] The idea was strongly reminiscent of the proposal for a 'European confederation' made in early 1990 by the late President Mitterrand. The Commission included this proposal in Agenda 2000, to replace the unsatisfactory 'structured dialogue' as the forum for consultations between the EU and all the applicants in the areas of CFSP and JHA.[13] The Luxembourg European Council had also been attracted to the idea as a way of involving Turkey, in a period when accession negotiations had been ruled out. However, the Turkish government declined the invitation to participate, feeling slighted by its exclusion from the accession process and after an ill-tempered exchange with the German government. The Turkish complication continues to cast a shadow over the enlargement process in general, as well as in relation to the Cypriot candidacy.

The formula for the European Conference involves annual meetings at heads of government and foreign minister levels, starting respectively on 12 March and 6 October 1998. Switzerland was invited as a 'member-elect' after the Vienna European Council of December 1998, and Malta, after the Commission's positive re-evaluation of the Maltese application in February 1999. The Helsinki European Council in December 1999 was set to review the membership, a question now changed in character by the efforts to find ways of developing dialogue with the other countries of south-eastern Europe.

Policy reform and funding: the Berlin European Council

The CAP and the structural funds were early identified as problem areas in relation to eastern enlargement (see Mayhew 1998: 236–311; Grabbe and Hughes 1998: 90–103; W. Grant 1998; Josling 1998; Begg 1997; Baldwin et al. 1997). On paper the CEECs would be eligible for significant budgetary transfers on both counts, a difficulty both for existing beneficiaries in the EU15 and for the overall impact on the EU budget. The details of each set of issues are to be found in Chapters 7, 8, and 9 of this volume. The agreement reached at the Berlin European Council of March 1999 on paper made provision for what the Commission judged to be adequate amounts for both pre-accession aid to the CEEC candidates and post-accession receipts for some new members within the financial perspective for 2000–6. The ring-fenced figures run from €6.45 billion in 2002 to €16.78 billion in 2006. These presume that new CEEC members might have allocations at relatively modest levels compared with current member states. Pre-accession aid would meld with EU budget flows after accession.

The Commission had used its agenda-setting power to present enlargement as feasible without an increase in the budget, and without demanding too many sacrifices from the incumbent member states. This implied some optimistic assumptions, notably real growth of the budget through annual growth in EU GDP of 2.5 per cent, but politically the important message was that the reforms needed for enlargement were 'yesable'. The Commission made efforts to develop the outlines of a package deal, although in the final stages of negotiation in early 1999 its influence waned after the forced resignation of the college. This contrasted with the way the Delors-1 package was crafted just after the accession of Portugal and Spain.

The enlargement dimension set a considerable discipline on the positions of member governments, as they faced the uncomfortable issues raised by Agenda 2000. As on previous macro negotiations over budgetary issues, the eventual decisions were prepared by a mix of horizontal and vertical coordinating mechanisms. Given the sharpness of the argument about net national contributions, one might have expected the package-dealing to be controlled by finance ministers and their officials. Yet this was not the case. Instead it was foreign ministers in the General Affairs Council who shaped much of the final agreement put to heads of state or government for resolution in Berlin.

Moreover, the deadline for agreement held, as set by the Cardiff European Council in June 1998. What is not quite clear is what conditioned this outcome, given the unusual circumstances of both the forced resignation of the Commissioners and the war in Kosovo. Both sets of factors served to remind the member governments how much was at stake in Berlin in terms of the overall credibility of the EU. The coincidence of a German presidency of the Council helped to maintain the linkage between budget, policy reform, and the enlargement process.

Relationships with other Europeans

Three other big issues hung over the way the EU addressed the question of eastwards enlargement: how to deal with candidates not yet admitted to accession negotiations, notably Turkey; how to deal with the eastern neighbours of the candidates; and what kind of relationships to develop with those other south-east European countries that did not even have Europe Association agreements. Each of these issues had its own complications, but together they raised a broader set of questions about 'pan-Europe', and they took on sharper focus in the light of the continuing war across the former Yugoslavia.

Turkey continues to present the EU with difficult dilemmas. A strong defence partner in Nato (see Chapter 17), but a contested EU partner, and with delicate domestic politics, Turkey provokes a mix of ambiguous and ambivalent responses from the EU and its member governments. In 1998 the Commission (1998*i*) attempted in a paper to set out its views on how the relationship might develop, but much depends on bilateral relationships with individual EU governments, on developments within Turkish politics, and how the defence and security relationship plays into the politics of the EU. On the one hand, the development of a more stable and rounded relationship with Turkey would be a major achievement in its own right. On the other hand, there is a persistent risk of complications for the EU's enlargement policy because of the unresolved division of Cyprus. The Cologne European Council of June 1999 failed to find a way of taking policy forward. In October the Commission (1999*h*) recommended that Turkey be given 'candidate status' and an Accession Partnership, so that a firmer path towards EU membership could be envisaged, even though the conditionality attached would be strict.

Whatever decisions the EU takes about enlargement, it will certainly not switch to a policy of open-ended inclusiveness for all those other European countries that have aspirations to join the EU family. Ukraine and Russia in particular keep pressing for enhancements of their relationships with the EU, and both are contiguous with current or likely future members. These two countries raise sharply the issue of how to manage the future boundary between the EU and the non-EU parts of Europe. In principle the EU is developing 'strategies' towards both countries. Yet, as this chapter reveals, to be strategic in a composite policy is one of the biggest of challenges for the EU policy process.

An acute version of this challenge has beset the EU since the Federal Republic of Yugoslavia collapsed. Those parts of the federation that 'escaped' have looked to the

EU for support. The Croatian government has made it clear that it would like to follow the Slovenes on a trajectory towards EU membership. Macedonia is in search of a closer and supportive relationship. Albania similarly has aspirations to move closer to the EU. Both Bosnia and Kosovo are fragile protectorates, in the aftermaths of war. Montenegro is seeking a pathway out of the federation and towards the EU. A huge question hangs over the evolution of Serbia. Meanwhile, the EU's associates and candidate members in the region, Bulgaria and Romania, have had their already vulnerable economies further damaged by the Yugoslav wars. In summer 1999 the EU was endeavouring to develop a stabilization package for the whole of the region, as well as to craft appropriate relationships with each of the countries and territories in the region—another huge test for composite policy-making.

One possible way forwards to alleviating some of the trade and economic discussion being canvassed was the creation of some form or other of a 'pan-European free trade arrangement' (Sapir 2000). Whatever precise form it might take it would offer only a partial solution, but might at least provide a helpful basis for addressing some of the practicalities of economic cooperation.

Conclusions

The unexpected political changes of 1989 suddenly confronted the EU with the need to invent from scratch a framework for relations with the CEECs and indeed a 'European policy'. Policy has been driven by the perception that the EU has a special role in reintegrating the continent and supporting the political and economic transformations, as well as by a notion, not always well defined, about the opportunities arising from successful transformation and the risks entailed by failure.

The challenge was not only to devise a policy towards a very different set of partners and to do so in a context that had changed considerably—internally and externally. A rounded and long-term policy also meant confronting many of the paradoxes and idiosyncrasies of the west European integration process. Nor was the challenge just about what policy to adopt; it was also about how to deliver whatever policy was agreed. In short, policy towards the CEECs tests the policy process and political capacities of the EU to the limits.

Ten years on eastern enlargement seems firmly on the agenda and appears an almost deceptively conventional process, although many issues are still outstanding. The IGC to be convened in 2000 has to return to the question of institutional reform, and the jury is still out on the Agenda 2000 agreement. Policy-makers also still have to get to grips with the question of how to manage the impact of the accession of some CEECs on those for whom this is not an immediate prospect, as well as how to square it with relations with the more extended neighbourhood. Finally, only the result of accession negotiations will tell to what extent the incumbents can resist the temptation to make the candidates bear the brunt of the adjustment burden.

The main pattern of policy has been the incremental nature of its overall development and the difficulties found in matching declared broader goals with substantive policy practice. The chapter has suggested that these difficulties relate to the specific characteristics of the policy process, namely that EU policy towards the CEECs is what we have called a 'composite policy'. We have emphasized two key factors that hamper or facilitate strategic policy-making for a composite policy:

1. how divergent or convergent the preferences of the macro policy-makers are; and
2. how centralized or fragmented the policy coordination process between macro- and meso-policy-makers is on questions of policy substance.

Fragmentation of the policy process at the level of detail made it easier for the meso-policy-makers to insulate some of the substantive policy issues from broader political objectives and to prevent more far-reaching moves to accommodate the concerns of the CEECs. Some specific features of policy towards the CEECs have encouraged strategic policy-making, in particular that the macro-policy-makers occupy high places in the decision-making hierarchy of their respective political systems. This hierarchy has facilitated centralized policy-making some of the time and induced a more coherent policy.

For example, the EA negotiations and those over Agenda 2000 were conducted in a more tightly coordinated way. It proved possible to wrest decisions on concrete substance from the veto power of the meso-policy-makers and to disentangle them from their narrower sectoral logic. European Councils have played a very important part in this process. So have foreign ministers in national governments and their interlocutors in the Commission in DG I, and later DG IA.

However, the forces of divergence and fragmentation have also been present, especially when grand policy had to be turned into detailed implementation and on more technical issues. Hence, for example, the use of commercial defence instruments has persisted, and periodically the EU has taken inflexible positions on the adjustments that the CEECs needed to make to be allowed to develop their relationships with the EU. Thus we can also find plenty of evidence of incoherence and dysfunctionalities at the level of detailed policy delivery.

The lack of a clear consensus about the longer-term perspective meant that the macro policy could be constructed only in fits and starts. Yet there was sufficient collective sense of purpose for policy to evolve, albeit incrementally and interspersed with more defensive reactions at the meso level, especially because the relationship with the CEECs raises so many awkward questions for the incumbent members of the EU. However, the process that we observe does not fit a neat template in which 'history-making decisions' are made through inter-state bargaining, while the middle-range decisions are left to the technicians. It is rather that some policy-makers from both governments and the Commission have been engaged in the development of macro policy, while different policy-makers—from both member governments and the Commission, and at all levels of the decision-making hierarchy—have dealt with the sectoral and more day-to-day questions. Thus the tensions between macro and meso are distributed across the European and national levels of governance.

Part of the tension between the two that makes this policy domain so interesting is the way in which it raises such challenging issues of self-definition for the EU itself. On the one hand, policy was perceived and presented as a case of enlightened self-interest in a stable neighbourhood and economic opportunities. This left open the question of how far this would require taking into account the specific preferences of CEEC policy-makers. On the other hand, the political credibility of the EU's self-proclaimed role has been at stake, since it would have been an enormous failure if policy towards the CEECs had dissolved into fragments of defensiveness. Yet to move from rhetoric to substance, and from association to membership, requires quite radical rethinking of the status quo. We can see moments where the former has prevailed over the latter, and moments where the reverse has been true, a pattern of inconsistency that seems unlikely to be easily broken. Are the CEECs to be seen as external objects, or are they part of the EU 'family', and of the 'future us' (Avery 1995: 1)?

The fragility of the consensus between the macro-policy-makers on this core question, compounded by their difficulties in getting some of their own colleagues to buy the argument, made the role of policy advocates, and advocacy alliances, crucially important. A team of policy advocates formed inside the Commission, and ensured that policy moved from the EAs to Copenhagen and the pre-accession strategy. They used the consensus among the macro-policy-makers about the inappropriateness of defensive opposition to enlargement to move policy forward incrementally. They made effective use of agenda-setting power and successfully forged alliances. Allies were to varying degrees found in certain member governments, notably the German government, and especially during their Council presidencies. But we have put it this way round. Some national macro-policy-makers have played a part in this process and occasionally taken important initiatives. But none, not even those in the German government, has sustained a role of leadership over this policy domain. There have been too many other preoccupations, both internal and external, for powerful and sustained policy leadership from the side of the member governments. And as yet no stable transgovernmental coalition has emerged.

We should therefore expect these tensions and constraints which emanate from the composite character of this policy domain to continue to characterize the policy process. Indeed they seem more, not less, likely to characterize the development of policy as the exigencies of preparing for enlargement take over from the association policy. The framework of accession negotiations might facilitate centralized oversight and direct influence from the macro-policy-makers. However, enlargement requires many more substantive and detailed decisions, and allows less creative scope for initiative to sidestep the vested interests. The scope for accommodating the preferences of the CEECs is largely predetermined by existing arrangements among and for the incumbent members. In this sense enlargement is a more path-dependent process than association.

Our account of the policy process has focused on the Commission, the Council, and relevant national policy-makers. In the story so far other policy actors have had quite muted voices. The European Parliament has not been very prominent, although by and large supportive of both association and enlargement. Organized socio-economic interests have intruded episodically, especially at the meso level and especially on issues of commercial defence. But their role so far should not be exaggerated. Indeed it is one of the features of the policy domain so far that much of the policy has been set horizontally rather than vertically, leaving limited scope for organized interests to impinge. But we should also note that the advocacy alliance that has helped to keep the macro policy moving has had little by way of outside support on which to draw, either from socio-economic groups that might stand to gain, or from broader political circles, or from public opinion. This may be a handicap in taking the enlargement process forward.

Appendix 16.1 Overview of relations between the CEECs and the EU and Nato

Country	Europe Agreements			EU Accession		Nato		
	Signed	Interim agreement	Into force	Application to EU	Start of negotiations	North Atlantic Cooperation Council[a]	Partnership for Peace	Membership
Hungary	16.12.91	01.03.92	01.02.94	31.03.94	31.03.98	20.12.91	08.02.94	12.03.99
Poland	16.12.91	01.03.92	01.02.94	05.04.94	31.03.98	20.12.91	02.02.94	12.03.99
CSFR	16.12.91	01.03.92				20.12.91		
Czech Republic	04.10.93	(as CSFR)	01.02.95	17.01.96	31.03.98	01.01.93	10.03.94	12.03.99
Slovakia	04.10.93	(as CSFR)	01.02.95	27.06.95	pending	01.01.93	09.02.94	
Romania	01.02.93	01.05.93	01.02.95	22.06.95	pending	20.12.91	26.01.94	
Bulgaria	08.03.93	31.12.93	01.02.95	14.12.95	pending	20.12.91	14.02.94	
Estonia	12.06.95	(01.01.95[b])	01.02.98	24.11.95	31.03.98	20.12.91	03.02.94	
Latvia	12.06.95	(01.01.95[b])	01.02.98	13.10.95	pending	20.12.91	14.02.94	
Lithuania	12.06.95	(01.01.95[b])	01.02.98	08.12.95	pending	20.12.91	27.01.94	
Slovenia	10.06.96	01.01.97	01.02.99	10.06.96	31.03.98	29.01.97	30.03.94	
Albania	Eligible for SAA[c]					05.06.92	23.02.94	
Macedonia	Eligible for SAA[c]					11.03.96	15.11.95	
Croatia	In principle eligible for SAA[d]							
Bosnia-Herzegovina	In principle eligible for SAA[d]							
Yugoslavia	Not yet considered for SAA[e]							

Notes:
[a] Replaced on 30 May 1997 by the Euro-Atlantic Partnership Council (EAPC), as the overarching framework for consultations and cooperation under PfP.
[b] Free Trade Agreement.
[c] Proposed Stabilization and Association Agreement (SAA); the Commission to report on feasibility of opening negotiations, with Macedonia likely to be the first (Commission 1999g)
[d] The Commission (1999g) does not regard it appropriate to consider opening negotiations until the relevant conditions are fulfilled.
[e] In principle and in the longer term eligible for an SAA, but the Commission (1999g) considers the most fundamental of the relevant conditions are currently flouted.

Notes

1 'Strategic policy' is usually understood as one which maximizes the collective long-term interests of the EU member states. In our more limited use of the term strategic policy requires: (*a*) clearly articulated goals; and (*b*) coherence between declared goals and policy practice. This does not presuppose a specific view as to the nature of the interests or the policy chosen to pursue them. For a longer account of the relevance for composite policy, see Sedelmeier (1998*a*).

2 Under the Action Plan the EU offered as trade concessions to remove some forms of non-specific discrimination, which amounted to positive discrimination. Although intended as temporary, these were renewed.

3 This contrasts starkly with the treatment of the east German *Länder*, not covered here. Spence (1991) describes the unusual and highly adaptive EU policy of accepting their transformation as an intra-EU task.

4 See *Agence Europe*, 28 Mar. 1991: 9; *Financial Times*, 19 Apr. 1991: 6; *Guardian*, 15 July 1991: 7; *Bulletin of the European Communities*, Sept. 1991: 45.

5 Since the entry into force of the Interim Agreements the EU has used safeguards or anti-dumping measures for: pig-iron and ferro-silicum imports from Poland; seamless steel and iron tubes from Poland, Czechoslovakia, and Hungary; urea ammonium nitrate from Bulgaria, Poland, and so on. Among the most publicized restrictions was the temporary ban on live animal and dairy imports of Apr. 1993 (*Euro-east*, Apr. 1993: 26).

6 Much depends on the structure of the deficit; an imbalance which reflected a valuable influx of investment goods would be encouraging.

7 A diplomatic row broke out over remarks attributed to François Scher, former French Ambassador to Germany, on the increasingly assertive tone of German European policy (*Frankfurter Allgemeine Zeitung*, 16 Mar. 1994: 1; and 18 Mar. 1994: 2; and *Le Monde*, 19 Mar. 1994: 6).

8 We regard this as a constructive approach, although Rouam (1994) took a more critical view.

9 Malta was included on the list until the incoming Labour government suspended the membership application. The Nationalist Party, back in office, revived the application in Sept. 1998. In Cologne in June 1999 the European Council delayed until its Helsinki meeting in December 1999 the decision on whether to include Malta in accession negotiations, subject to a Commission Opinion on Maltese preparations for accession.

10 The Commission did not explicitly rank the candidates, but the detailed assessments implied a comparison, with Hungary slightly ahead of Poland and the Czech Republic, followed by Slovenia and then Estonia, Latvia, Lithuania, and Slovakia not far behind, but Bulgaria and Romania much further behind.

11 Negotiations started on the seven chapters (out of thirty-one) judged to cause least problems, since the candidates expected to be able to apply the *acquis* in full on accession: science and research; telecoms and IT; education and training; culture and audiovisual; industrial policy; small and medium-sized enterprises; and CFSP.

12 The bilateral Association Councils continue to meet in parallel.

13 Especially on relations with Russia, Ukraine, and other CIS countries, and

European security, organized crime, terrorism, corruption, drug-trafficking, illegal arms' sales, money-laundering, and illegal immigration.

Further reading

For an overview of the issues relating to association and eastern enlargement, see Mayhew (1998). Preston (1997) and Michalski and Wallace (1992) set these issues in the context of earlier enlargements. On the earlier period of responses to the 1989 changes, see Sedelmeier and Wallace (1996) and Friis (1998). K. E. Smith (1998) and Torreblanca (1997) situate the subject in the context of EU foreign policy. For recent accounts of the economic issues, see Baldwin *et al.* (1997) and Estrin and Holmes (1998).

For overviews and updates on ongoing developments, see the websites of DG IA, <http://europa.eu.int/comm/dg1a/enlarge/index.htm> and the European Parliament, <http://www.europarl.eu.int/enlargement/briefings/en/index3.htm>.

Baldwin, R., François, J. F., and Portes, R. (1997), 'The Costs and Benefits of Eastern Enlargement: The Impact on the EU and Central Europe', *Economic Policy*, 24: 125–76.

Estrin, S., and Holmes, P. (1998) (eds.), *Competition and Economic Integration in Europe* (Cheltenham: Edward Elgar).

Friis, L. (1998), *The End of the Beginning of Eastern Enlargement—Luxembourg Summit and Agenda-Setting*, European Integration Online Papers, 27, <http://eiop.or.at/eiop/texte/1998-007a.htm>.

Mayhew, A. (1998), *Recreating Europe: The European Union's Policy towards Central and Eastern Europe* (Cambridge: Cambridge University Press).

Michalski, A., and Wallace, H. (1992), *The European Community: The Challenge of Enlargement* (London: Royal Institute of International Affairs).

Preston, C. (1997), *Enlargement and Integration in the European Union* (London: Routledge).

Sedelmeier and Wallace (1996), 'Policies towards Central and Eastern Europe', in H. Wallace and Wallace (1996: 353–87).

Smith, K. E. (1998), *The Making of EU Foreign Policy: The Case of Eastern Europe* (London: Macmillan).

Torreblanca, J. I. (1997), *The European Community and Central Europe (1989–1993): Foreign Policy and Decision-Making*, Ph.D. thesis, Instituto Juan March de Estudios e Investigaciones (Madrid: Ediciones Peninsula; Aldershot: Ashgate, forthcoming).

Chapter 17

Common Foreign and Security Policy

From Shadow to Substance?

Anthony Forster and William Wallace

Contents

Summary

The member governments of the European Union (EU) committed themselves to a common foreign and security policy (CFSP) in the wake of German unification and the end of the cold war. This built on twenty years' experience of cooperation among national foreign ministries, coordinated by each government in turn through the Council presidency. The break-up of Yugoslavia demonstrated, however, that rhetorical commitments and intergovernmental exchanges provided only a flimsy basis for common action; the USA continued to dominate politico-military cooperation among European North Atlantic Treaty Organization (Nato) members. The 1996–7 Intergovernmental Conference (IGC) made a number of institutional changes, in spite of diverse national inhibitions. Convergence of attitudes between Britain and France, historically antagonists on how to approach foreign policy and defence, however, led to the launch of a bilateral European defence initiative in 1998, intended to lead to a 'European Pillar' within the Atlantic Alliance, with the merger of the Western European Union (WEU) into the EU. There remain, however, many obstacles to the development of effective common policies.

Introduction

Defence and diplomacy, like border controls, policing, and citizenship—and money—are part of the core of state sovereignty, around which practitioners of functional integration tiptoed throughout the formative years of the EU. Transfer of effective authority (and budgetary allocation) over foreign policy and defence would create—or require—a European federation. Policy cooperation in this field has therefore operated under contradictory pressures, in which the rationality of common action and of sharing scarce resources has been balanced by concern for the preservation of national sovereignty and of diverse national traditions and taboos. Thirty years after the establishment of European Political Cooperation (EPC), preoccupation with procedure, status, and constitutional authority remains at the heart of this policy domain, and is reflected in its weak institutionalization and marginal policy output. Stronger institutions and obligations for common foreign and security policy (CFSP) have preoccupied negotiators through three IGCs, in 1986, 1991, and 1996–7, with so far limited results.

Yet in the course of 1999 significant steps towards an effective CFSP appeared to be under way. Successive European Councils were registering progress towards European defence cooperation, with defence ministers joining foreign ministers in the General Affairs Council, with plans to incorporate WEU into the EU. The movement of Javier Solana, Nato Secretary-General, to the position of Secretary-General of the Council of Ministers signalled a change in the relationship between the EU and Nato which may mark a turning-point in the development of a CFSP.

Foreign policy and defence have been coordinated among west European states since 1949 within the broader framework of the North Atlantic Treaty, under American leadership. For as long as the cold war lasted, maintenance of the American commitment seemed to most west European governments vital to their security. Behind concerns about the Soviet threat lay parallel concerns about Europe's 'alternative hegemon', Germany, with a truncated West German state re-emerging as the dynamo of the west European economy under firm American tutelage. Proposals to develop an autonomous capability to coordinate foreign and defence policies among European Community members thus opened up fundamental questions about the transatlantic relationship, and about the balance of influence and power within Europe itself: about 'the Atlantic idea and its European rivals' and the Gaullist challenge to American security leadership (van Cleveland 1966; Grosser 1980).

None of the three founding treaties touched on foreign policy, let alone defence. The European Economic Community (EEC) was given only limited competences to conduct external relations, under Articles 113–16 (common commercial policy), 228–31 (relations with third states and international organizations), and 238 ('agreements establishing an association involving reciprocal rights and obligations, common action and special procedures' with 'a third State, a union of States or an international organization'). In the distinction which Gaullists made between 'high' and 'low' politics the EEC was clearly limited to the low politics of commercial diplomacy, leaving the high politics of foreign policy and defence to sovereign states. Walter Hallstein, as the EEC Commission's first President, sought to enhance its status through formalizing diplomatic relations with missions from third states in Brussels, provoking President de Gaulle to accuse him of using 'all his skill' to create an 'artificial country springing from the brow of a technocrat' (Loth *et al.* 1998: 134). The French government nevertheless allowed the EEC to develop some aspects of a politically driven external policy, using the provisions of Article 238 (now 310) to negotiate association agreements, first with Greece, then with Turkey, then with a succession of other states around the Mediterranean and beyond.

Yet issues of national security and foreign policy were fundamental to the development of west European integration. The Schuman Plan for a European Coal and Steel Community was launched in 1950 by the French government in response to intense American pressure to accept the full reconstruction of German heavy industry, in a divided Germany facing apparent internal and external communist threats. American pressure to accept West German rearmament, after the outbreak of the Korean War, led a reluctant French government to advance the Pleven Plan for a European Defence Community (EDC), into which German units might be integrated. The European Defence Treaty, signed in Paris in May 1952, committed its signatories (under Article 38) to examine the form of the political superstructure needed to give the EDC direction and legitimacy. The resulting de Gasperi Plan for a European political community would have transformed the Six into an effective federation, with a European executive accountable to a directly elected European Parliament.

After the death of Stalin and the Korean armistice in 1954, however, this direct attack on the core of national sovereignty was rejected by the French National Assembly. An intergovernmental compromise, promoted by the British, transformed the 1948 Treaty of Western Union (signed by Britain, France, the Netherlands, Belgium, and Luxembourg, as a preliminary commitment in the negotiations which led to the Atlantic Alliance) into the seven-member WEU, bringing in Germany and Italy. The WEU had a ministerial council, a small secretariat, a consultative assembly, and an armaments agency (primarily to control German arms production). Its military functions, however, were explicitly integrated into Nato. The package deal also abolished the Allied High Commission in Germany, ended the occupation statute, and admitted Federal Germany to Nato. The collapse of these ambitious proposals for defence and political communities was a defeat for European federalists, who concluded that future developments could only be gradual and indirect, through economic and social integration. It was also a defeat for American policy-makers, who looked to the development of an integrated Europe as a future partner with the USA, which would shoulder a larger share of the burden of Western international order which the United States had carried since 1947. John Foster Dulles, President Eisenhower's Secretary of State, had gone so far as to threaten 'an agonizing reappraisal of basic United States policy' towards western Europe if the EDC were to fail (Fursdon 1980; Lundestad 1998).

Five years later President de Gaulle chose foreign policy cooperation as the ground on which to make his twin challenge to American hegemony and to the supranational ambitions of the infant EEC. A conference of heads of state and government and foreign ministers of the Six met, at French invitation, in Paris in February 1961 'to discover suitable means of organizing closer political cooperation' as a basis for 'a progressively developing union'. This Fouchet Plan was vigorously opposed by the Dutch, and found little support even within the German government. With Britain applying to join the EEC, and the Kennedy Administration calling for a new 'Atlantic partnership', this was an evident challenge to American leadership and to Nato as such. After the collapse of the Fouchet Plan, de Gaulle pursued a more direct means of harnessing German economic strength to French international ambitions, rapidly negotiating and signing the Franco-German Élysée Treaty in March 1963. The treaty included extensive provisions for bilateral defence collaboration. But during the ratification debate the Bundestag, against Chancellor Adenauer's wishes, added a firmly Atlanticist preamble. De Gaulle subsequently withdrew French forces from Nato's integrated structure—leaving foreign policy and defence consultations among other EEC members firmly within the Nato framework.

European political cooperation, 1970–1990

The 'relaunch' of European integration at the summit meeting in The Hague in December 1969, which followed de Gaulle's departure, was a carefully crafted package deal. French acceptance of 'widening' the negotiations for British accession was balanced by insistence on 'completion' of the system of agricultural finance within the Community budget and by commitments to 'deepen' economic and monetary union (EMU), and to a renewed effort at 'political cooperation'. Yet EPC in its early years more clearly served German international interests than French. It provided Western multilateral support for *Ostpolitik*, through the Conference on Security and Cooperation in Europe (CSCE), in a period when American policy-makers were preoccupied with Vietnam; and it provided a caucus within which to operate when Federal Germany was admitted into the United Nations (UN) in 1973.

The initial scepticism of other governments lessened as foreign ministers discovered the utility of informal consultations, and as their diplomats learned to appreciate this private framework for multilateral diplomacy. EPC was an entirely intergovernmental process, outside the treaties, agreed among governments and managed by diplomats. Foreign ministers' meetings were prepared by the Political Committee, consisting of political directors from foreign ministries, under which developed a network of working groups. The Commission was rigorously excluded in the early years, though the overlap between foreign policy and economic relations in the CSCE soon gave European Commission officials a limited role. In sharp contrast to the leaky policy-making processes of the EEC, EPC was managed confidentially, with little reporting to national parliaments and little coverage in the press. Coreu, a secure telex link managed by the Dutch foreign ministry, provided direct communications; working groups, joint reporting from EPC embassies in third countries, and later exchanges of personnel, slowly transformed working practices within national diplomatic services.

The evolution of EPC during the first twenty years of its operation can be seen as a cycle of hesitant steps to strengthen the framework, followed by periods of increasing frustration at the meagre results achieved, culminating in further reluctant reinforcement of the rules and procedures. Relations with the USA were a significant factor in this cycle. Secretary of State Kissinger provoked a debate on the links between European and Atlantic political cooperation in his 'Year of Europe' speech of April 1973. Divergent reactions to the Arab–Israeli War of October 1973 escalated the debate into a bitter Franco-American confrontation, with other west European governments caught in between. The dispute was resolved in the Ottawa Declaration of June 1974, in the context of a Nato Summit; this set up an additional consultative mechanism between the rotating presidency of EPC and the US State Department before and after each EPC ministerial meeting (W. Wallace 1983b). The French, who had attempted to reshape WEU as the vehicle for a more autonomous European defence, remained formally outside Nato's integrated structure, though in the years which followed they attached informal 'liaison missions' to Nato headquarters. Extensive military cooperation among other EU members developed during the 1970s and 1980s within the Nato framework, largely without French participation; the lightly armed Franco-German Brigade, which was formed in 1983, was little more than a symbolic alternative.

European dismay at the drift of US policy towards confrontation with the USSR, in 1979–81, and at the failure to manage a concerted response to the Soviet invasion of Afghanistan, led to renewed efforts to promote cooperation, with the 1981 London Report, and the much more ambitious Genscher–Colombo Plan of 1982. But other governments, in particular the Danish, the neutral Irish, and the Greeks (who joined the EC and the EPC procedures in 1981), retained strong reservations over sharing sovereignty in such a sensitive area, in which the views of the larger member governments were likely to prevail. The 1986 Single European Act (SEA) formally brought EPC together with the EC under the 'single' framework of the European Council and thus provided for only limited reinforcement of foreign policy consultations among member governments (Schoutheete 1986; Nuttall 1992).

Western Europe's self-image as a 'civilian power' in the 1970s and 1980s partly reflected the exclusion of security and defence issues which followed from the unresolved Gaullist challenge to American security leadership (H. Bull 1982). It took accumulated dissatisfaction with the quality of American leadership at the end of the 1970s to weaken the taboo. A Franco-German defence dialogue was relaunched in 1982, and then extended through a trilateral meeting with the British into a revival of six-monthly WEU ministerial meetings (of foreign and defence ministers) in 1983 (W. Wallace 1984). WEU membership expanded to nine with the accession of Spain and Portugal in 1987, following their accession to the EC, although not without a sharp debate on the merits of expansion. But warnings from Washington continued to accompany every gesture towards closer European cooperation, with the German, Dutch, and British governments in particular anxious to reassure the Atlantic hegemon of their prior loyalty to the Atlantic alliance (Menon *et al.* 1992).

By the end of the 1980s the procedures of EPC had evolved into an extensive network, drawing in some thousands of diplomats in the foreign ministries of the member states, in their embassies outside the EU, and in missions to international organizations. The rotating Council presidency acted as convenor and coordinator; French determination to keep EPC out of the hands of the Brussels institutions meant that meetings also rotated with each presidency around national capitals. The development of the Council presidency into a key EU institution, indeed, was partly due to the development of EPC. But the discontinuities created by the six-monthly rotation led first to the development of the 'rolling troika' and then to the slow emergence of a secretariat, a mixed group of seconded officials who moved with each presidency from capital to capital. The SEA settled the EPC Secretariat in Brussels, though the French government maintained the Gaullist heritage and limited its effectiveness by insisting that it remain separate from the Council of Ministers' Secretariat.

Looking back over twenty years, the transformation of diplomatic working practices was evident. Traffic around the Coreu telex network had grown from an initial 2,000–3,000 telegrams a year to some 9,000 in 1989. Desk officers in foreign ministries now dealt directly with their opposite numbers, meeting them regularly in their appropriate working group, in touch by telephone and Coreu whenever necessary. Cooperation and joint reporting among embassies in third countries was of particular value to smaller member governments. The habits and assumptions of a generation of national diplomats were thus reshaped, reinforced by joint training courses, exchanges of personnel, even sharing of embassy facilities in some third countries (Nuttall 1994). Commission officials, who had at first been rigorously excluded on French insistence from participation, had been accepted as observers into working group after working group. The small EPC office within the Commission Secretariat-General grew after the SEA into a Directorate (Nuttall 1994). See Table 17.1.

For its defenders, in London and Paris, EPC in 1989 represented a working model of intergovernmental cooperation without formal integration. The model had indeed been extended to justice and home affairs (JHA), a similarly sensitive area in terms of sovereignty, as Chapter 18 notes. Foreign ministers, and foreign ministries, now spent much of their working life within this multilateral context, moving from EC Councils of Ministers to EPC ministerial meetings to WEU, each with their subordinate committee structures, meeting with each other more often than they met with their colleagues in national cabinets. But it was entirely self-contained within this circle of foreign ministries. Defence ministries remained entirely outside EPC; nine EU defence ministries and armed forces (all except those of France, Spain, and Ireland) worked together instead in Nato's integrated military structure. Outside critics, in economic ministries for instance, contrasted the extensive scale of activity with the modesty of output. The structure resembled a diplomatic game, providing work for officials without engaging or informing parliaments, or press, let alone public opinion. It thus failed to promote any substantial convergence of national attitudes. There was little evidence that EPC had exerted any direct influence on Arab–Israeli relations, for example, or on events in sub-Saharan Africa or in the Persian–Arabian Gulf (Redmond 1992). American arms and American diplomacy still determined the course of Western interests throughout the regions to Europe's immediate south.

European transformation and political union, 1990–1992

The IGC planned for 1990–1 was initially intended to focus on monetary union and its institutional consequences, not directly on political union defined in terms of foreign and defence policy. It was the revolutions in central and eastern Europe in the course of 1989, and the rapid moves towards German unification which followed in 1990, that forced foreign and security policy up the IGC agenda. One of the underlying purposes of west European integration since the Schuman Plan had after all been to constrain the sovereignty of a reconstructed Germany (Soetendorp 1990: 103).

Washington was the first to respond, offering a reformulation of the idea of Atlantic political community. Secretary of State James Baker, in his Brussels speech of 12 December 1989, proposed a redefined transatlantic bargain to reflect the end of western Europe's security dependence, to be based on both North American and European pillars and with an agenda extended across the full range of politico-military, economic, and environmental issues. West European governments resisted the idea of incorporating this redefined relationship into a formal new treaty. The Transatlantic Declaration, which was signed in the autumn of 1990, more modestly formalized and extended the network of contacts between the EC, the EPC presidency, and the US Administration (J. Peterson 1994), and it did not touch the defence relationship.

The USA thus responded to geopolitical transformation by reasserting the strategy it had pursued in 1961–2 and in 1973–4. The path which its west European allies took in these radically changing circumstances was also shaped by attitudes and institutions developed over the previous thirty to forty years. In March 1990, as political developments across central Europe continued to move faster than most west European governments wished, the Belgian government proposed a second IGC on 'political union' to consider strengthening the EC and to run in parallel with the IGC on EMU already agreed. Putting aside differences between Paris and Bonn, Mitterrand and Kohl issued a joint letter the following month in which they endorsed the Belgian initiative and demanded that the IGC formulate a joint CFSP as a central feature of the European Union (Laursen and Vanhoonacker 1992). This proposal gained support as the pace of German unification quickened, with other governments recognizing the logic of strengthening the EC to contain the potential regional hegemony of a united Germany. Thus, against London's preference, the majority view at the Dublin European Council in June 1990 acknowledged a formal link between German unification, political union, and EMU.

It soon became clear, however, that there were significant differences over the character of that link, and much reluctance to recognize that rhetorical commitments implied real resources and practical obligations. Chancellor Kohl and the German political élite saw their acceptance of monetary union as part of a package which must include substantial strengthening of the political institutions of the Community. Political union, for them, should include the development of common foreign policy within an integrated (and democratically accountable) Community framework, and thus end the legacy of Gaullism, the separation of EPC from EC. The Benelux states shared this perspective. The French and British governments, however, resisted the transfer of authority over foreign policy from a confidential

Table 17.1 From EPC to CFSP: a history of major developments

Event/date	Aims	Procedures	Instruments
The Hague Summit December 1969	Launch of political cooperation	Preparation of a report on political cooperation	
Luxembourg Report October 1970	■ to give shape and will to the Union ■ to exercise Europe's growing responsibilities ■ to match the political with economic policies ■ gradual action in areas of common agreement	■ regular exchange of information ■ coordination of positions ■ foreign ministers' meetings (two per year) ■ political directors' meetings (four per year) ■ meetings in national capitals	Common positions
Copenhagen Report July 1973	■ to act in the world as a distinct entity ■ to seek common solutions ■ the aim of consultation is now common policies	■ increased meetings of foreign ministers ■ presidency role elaborated ■ correspondents' group confirmed ■ working groups formalized ■ Coreu established	Political dialogue
London Report October 1981	■ goal of EPC is now joint action ■ coordination of political aspects of security	■ strengthened presidency role ■ troika secretariat confirmed ■ national secondment to presidency ■ stronger commitment to consult ■ full association of Commission	Sanctions, trade, aid
Solemn Declaration on European Union June 1983	■ greater coherence and even closer coordination between EC and EPC ■ to consider economic aspects of security	■ European Council issues general guidelines for EC and EPC ■ each presidency of the European Council presents a report to the EP	

Single European Act February 1986	• to transform relations as a whole into a European Union • to be achieved by consistency and solidarity • to reduce further the differences between the instruments of EPC and EC • treaty review by 1993	• legal treaty basis for EPC • common actions by information and consultation • establishment of EPC secretariat • decisions by consensus but governments must refrain from blocking consensus	• economic and political instruments
Treaty on European Union February 1992	• a common foreign and security policy is established • CFSP is a Union and not a Community responsibility • instruments of EC and CFSP fully combined but institutional distinction maintained through 'pillared' structure • treaty review by 1996 • sub-contracts defence to WEU	• merging of General Affairs Council and EPC • merging of EPC secretariat into Council Secretariat • DGIA and Commissioner created for External Political Affairs • Coreper directly involved • majority voting is permissible • all meetings held in Brussels • synchronization of procedures with WEU	• common action not just common positions • joint actions on all issues except defence • request WEU action on defence issues
Treaty of Amsterdam October 1997	• EU can examine all aspects of foreign and security policy • closer links with WEU • held out the possibility of an EU–WEU merger	• strengthened CFSP planning • creation of High Representative • decision-making on the basis of 'constructive abstention' • secured the basis of financing CFSP	• EU can 'avail itself' of WEU on defence issues
Helsinki European Council December 1999	• develop common European security and defence policy	• General Affairs Council to include defence ministers • Political and Security Committee • Military Committee • Military staff attached to EU Council • combine Secretary-General of EU Council with that of WEU	• create joint military force of 50,000–60,000 persons • prepare for rapid responses within 60 days • sustainable force for up to 1 year

Source: Amended version of Wallace and Wallace (1996, table 16.1).

intergovernmental framework to the Community proper, since this implied an accretion of power to the Commission (and indirectly to the European Parliament), and would generate pressures to move from consensual decisions towards majority voting and joint action. On security policy and defence there was a different dividing line between Atlanticists (in Britain, the Netherlands, and Portugal), resisting any substantial weakening of the Nato framework, and Europeanists (in France, Belgium, and Italy), with the German government in the middle (Gnesotto 1990). Negotiations over preferred policy outputs were thus entangled with ideological and constitutional questions throughout the IGC.

As important a dividing line, less willingly recognized by many delegations, lay between those states with the capacity and the domestic support for active foreign policies and those for which an engaged foreign policy (let alone defence) was surrounded by political inhibitions. Here France and Britain lay at one end of the spectrum, with Germany, the government most determinedly pushing for a CFSP, at the other. When Iraq invaded Kuwait in August 1990, Britain responded to American calls for military support by sending an armoured division; France (to the embarrassment of its military and political leaders, who wished to demonstrate a comparable commitment) could assemble and dispatch from its depleted conventional forces only an under-strength and lightly armed division, which the Americans considered of marginal utility. Germany contributed (substantially) to the financial costs of the military operation, without any military involvement. This reflected historical and constitutional inhibitions about the projection of military power beyond German borders, a reticence to which public opinion and the opposition parties within the Bundestag remained firmly committed. Belgium turned down a British request for ammunition to supply its forces in the Gulf, mainly, it was rumoured, because the ammunition was unreliable.

It was impossible to contemplate options for European defence integration without first establishing how these might affect the relationship between the Atlantic Alliance and the EU (Forster 1994: 58). The USA was thus an active external player throughout the IGC, across the whole CFSP dossier. Successful agreement on the conclusions of the Alliance Strategic Review, launched in April 1990 and running in parallel with the EU deliberations, was a precondition for successful agreement among the Twelve (Menon *et al.* 1992). Negotiations thus proceeded in 1990–1 in three parallel fora, Nato, WEU, and EU–IGC, with overlapping but non-identical memberships. Since these were politico-military negotiations, focusing on security and defence policy rather than on the question of defence *per se*, the political sections of foreign ministries led in all three negotiating fora, with defence ministries in second place in the Nato and WEU discussions and absent from the EU–IGC. There was thus a symbolic quality to the negotiations, with the military and financial consequences of the initiatives proposed left unexplored. The Benelux and German governments saw commitment to a CFSP as part of their broader commitment to 'ever-closer union': France clung to the rhetoric of common foreign policy, while still reserving French freedom to act unimpaired by Community institutions.

The 1991 IGC

If the negotiators had been rational actors, able to focus on the issues at stake undistracted by extraneous developments, the Maastricht package on CFSP might conceivably have been tied up more neatly. But external developments intruded from beginning to end, to preoccupy ministers with more immediate crises and with their longer-term implications. As the Iraq–Kuwait crisis evolved, several of the former socialist states of central and eastern Europe volunteered non-combat forces, to demonstrate their commitment to early membership of the EU, WEU, and Nato. This raised the unwelcome prospect of rapid enlargement of western Europe's institutions and security commitments. US forces transferred from Germany to the Gulf returned direct to the USA in 1991, accelerating a rundown of American troops in Europe from 350,000 in 1989 to a target of 100,000 by 1994. Within west European states, as in the USA, the promise of a 'peace dividend' pushed governments towards uncoordinated cuts in defence spending, with defence ministries warming to regional integration as a means both of reducing costs and of saving commitments from finance ministry attack.

Foreign ministers were also preoccupied by the fraught atmosphere of US–EC negotiations (and intra-EC differences) in the final stages of the Uruguay Round. Tensions in the Baltic states in January 1991 between Soviet forces and nationalists loomed over the initial stages of IGC negotiations on the CFSP dossier. When the Yugoslav crisis broke in June 1991, many of the most sensitive issues remained unresolved. Ministers assembled to discuss the principles of future common policy, but found themselves disagreeing over immediate actions. Some governments had illusory expectations of what western Europe could achieve. The Luxembourg foreign minister, as President of the Council for the first six months of 1991, unwisely declared that 'This is the hour of Europe, not of the United States.' The attempt to establish a ceasefire in Croatia quickly moved beyond the traditional instruments of EPC to the deployment of EC peace monitors, and then, reluctantly, to the dispatch of peacekeeping forces under the auspices of the UN. The attempted *putsch* of 19 August in Moscow, and the progressive disintegration of the Soviet Union from then until the declarations of independence in its constituent states in December 1991, accompanied the final stages of the IGC negotiations.

Foreign ministers and their representatives were caught up in negotiating the terms under which they might act together, while under acute external pressures to take common action in a rapidly changing international environment. Yet to a remarkable degree the two dimensions were handled separately. A common foreign policy towards the former socialist states of central and eastern Europe would have required an integrated economic and security strategy, and a political response to the insistent demand for a 'return to Europe' through membership of the EU (see Chapter 16). But governments and the Commission had agreed to leave the question of Community enlargement off the IGC agenda. American dominance of western policy towards the Middle East was brought home brutally by the Gulf conflict. And on Yugoslavia, where the American Administration had clearly signalled that it expected its European allies to take the lead, west European governments showed themselves unprepared and disunited. As the IGC reached its endgame, the German government, which had been pressing for a binding commitment to a CFSP, was threatening to recognize Croatia unilaterally, in defiance of the consensus among its partners not to do so.

Negotiations within the IGC focused instead on institutional issues. The German and Benelux governments were in favour of bringing foreign policy—and in time defence—within the integrated framework of the EC. The French and British argued, against this, that it was illusory to imagine that an effective foreign policy, which included the 'hard' issues of security and defence, could be built upon the weak legitimacy of the Community; it could rest only on the commitment of governments representing states. The Luxembourg presidency's first 'non-paper', circulated in April, sketched out a 'pillar' model, with CFSP and JHA remaining outside the EC proper. This recognized the strength of French and British (and Danish, Irish, Greek, and Portuguese) opposition to full integration. It attracted strong criticism from the Commission, as guardian both of the treaties and of its own institutional interests, though the presidency paper which followed, after extensive consultations, in June was similar. The succeeding Dutch presidency was more determinedly *communautaire*. Piet Dankert, its ministerial negotiator, produced a new paper in September 1991, proposing a structure which would fully integrate foreign and security policy within the EC. The radical nature of these proposals prompted general dismay; only the Belgian delegation gave them active support. It was quickly agreed, to the presidency's embarrassment, to return to the Luxembourg 'pillared' text (Cloos *et al.* 1994; Buchan 1993).

Three other issues were caught up in these institutional negotiations: decision rules, consensus versus majority voting; the determination of some delegations to facilitate decisions leading to 'joint actions'; and the role and status of the EPC Secretariat and the Commission in this field. As in the parallel negotiations on JHA, delegations also differed over whether the pillar structure might serve as a long-term alternative to the 'Community method' or as a temporary expedient, from which *passerelles* (pathways) should be provided for the progressive transfer of functions and power to the Community proper.

Negotiations on the appropriate link between the EU and WEU proceeded in parallel, focusing on similar issues of institutional coherence, decision rules, and authority over implementation. On this the French and Dutch governments exchanged positions, with the Dutch (and the British) visualizing WEU as a permanent 'bridge', linking the EU and Nato, and the French (supported by the Belgian, Italian, and Spanish delegations) preferring the image of a 'ferry' which would gradually transfer defence functions from Nato to the Union. The French, supported ambivalently by the Germans, wanted WEU to acquire an operational capability with the right to operate within as well as outside the Nato area. The British, supported by the Dutch, wanted it to remain primarily an institutional forum for discussion among European defence and foreign ministers. The underlying division, echoing earlier disputes, was over whether a WEU integrated into the EU would develop into an alternative defence organization to Nato, or whether the object was to construct a more effective European pillar of the Atlantic alliance (Delors 1991). See Table 17.2.

A WEU ministerial meeting preceded the Luxembourg European Council in late June 1991 (where the British Prime Minister, with Greek support, attempted unsuccessfully to raise the issue of a potential conflict in Yugoslavia with heads of government). One day before an informal Gymnich foreign ministers' meeting on 4 October, the British and Italians launched a joint proposal. This defined WEU as the European pillar of Nato, with a WEU Rapid Reaction Force based on 'double-hatted' Nato and national contributions.[1] Determined not to lose the initiative, the French (to Dutch presidential fury) issued an invitation to other governments to meet in Paris to discuss—outside the framework of the IGC—the further integration of European defence. This was followed by a Franco-German proposal (rapidly prepared by their foreign ministries without consultation with their defence colleagues) for an 'organic link' between WEU and EU, which also proposed to transform the Franco-German Brigade into a 'Eurocorps' as the basis for an integrated European military structure (Menon 1992; Forster 1994).[2] But it was the Nato Rome Summit of 7–8 November which built the basis for a compromise, after some sharp exchanges between French and American leaders, from presidents down. The new Nato 'Strategic Concept', which heads of government agreed, approved the development of European multinational forces, but also reaffirmed the primacy of Nato as the forum for defence cooperation.

The Maastricht Treaty

The confident opening statement of Article J of the Treaty on European Union (TEU)— 'A common foreign and security policy is hereby established'—was thus qualified by carefully crafted subsequent clauses, which registered unresolved differences. Heads of government arrived in Maastricht to find square brackets and alternative drafts scattered throughout the CFSP text. They devoted much of their time to other politically sensitive chapters, leaving to foreign ministers and political directors the task of negotiating mutually acceptable language.

The outcome represented a modification of existing institutional arrangements rather than a major change (see Fig. 17.1.). Policy initiative, representation, and implementation were explicitly reserved to the Council presidency, 'assisted if need be by the previous and next member states to hold the Presidency' (an arrangement dubbed the troika, after the Russian three-horse sleigh). The Commission was to be 'fully associated' with discussions in this intergovernmental pillar, and 'the views of the European Parliament . . . duly taken into consideration' (Articles J.5, J.9, J.7). The WEU was designated 'an integral part of the development of the Union', with its Secretariat strengthened and moved from London and Paris to Brussels (Article J.4.2; Declaration on Western European Union). Ambiguous language allowed for 'joint actions' in pursuit of agreed common aims, and referred to 'the eventual framing of a common defence policy, which might in time lead to a common defence' (Articles J.3, J.4.1). An unresolved dispute between the British and the French over further enlargement of WEU was overtaken by the Greek government's last-minute declaration that it would veto the entire Treaty unless it was allowed to join. This forced negotiators to offer associated status to Turkey and to other European Nato members as well.

The most remarkable aspect of the CFSP negotiations in 1990–1 was how successfully they were contained within the network of foreign ministries established through EPC, and how little attention was paid to them by the press, by politicians

Table 17.2 Key dates in European foreign policy and defence cooperation

Date	Event	Signatories/participants	Substance
1948	Brussels Treaty on Western Union	Belgium, France, Luxembourg, Netherlands, UK	Defence treaty with a guarantee to mutual defence (Article V)
1949	North Atlantic Alliance (Washington Treaty)	USA, Canada, and Western Union Signatories	Defence treaty with soft commitment to mutual defence (Article V)
1950	Creation of Nato	All Washington Treaty Signatories	Military structure created in response to Korean War. US Supreme Allied Commander and integrated military command
1951	Negotiation of the European Defence Community and European Political Community treaties	Belgium, France, FRG, Italy, Luxembourg, Netherlands	Eventually rejected in 1954 by the French National Assembly
1954–5	Revision of the Brussels Treaty to form Western European Union (WEU)	Western Union signatories and FRG and Italy	Supranational approach to defence and security in response to US demands for FRG to be allowed to join the North Atlantic Alliance and Nato and to rearm
1961	Fouchet Plan	EEC members. Plan rejected by France's partners in 1962	French plan to incorporate defence and foreign policy into the EEC on intergovernmental lines. Secretariat to be based in Paris
1963	Élysée Treaty	France and FRG	Bilateral defence cooperation as a substitute to the Fouchet Plan. Bundestag effectively made the Treaty stillborn
1966	French withdrawal from Nato		French declaration of withdrawal from Nato (but not the Washington Treaty) and expulsion of Nato HQ from France
1969	Hague Summit	EEC heads of state and government	Agreement to enlarge the EEC, commit to EMU and political cooperation

Year	Document	Participants	Description
1974	Nato's Ottawa Declaration	Nato members	Stronger links between US State Department and rotating presidency of EPC
1981	London Report	EEC members	Coordination of political aspects of security
1983	Relaunch of Franco-German dialogue	France and FRG	Discuss defence issues of mutual concern and creation of the Franco-German Brigade
1983	Solemn Declaration on European Union	EEC members	To consider economic aspects of security
1986	Single European Act	EEC members	SEA reaffirms that nothing should be done which undermines Nato and WEU
1987	Hague Platform	WEU members	Link between the EC and the WEU was made explicit. Need for continued American military presence reaffirmed
1991	Rome Declaration	Nato members	Acceptance of European defence identity through Europeanization of Nato; reorientation of Nato towards more political tasks, e.g. North Atlantic Cooperation Council
1992	Treaty on European Union	EU members	A common foreign and security policy established. Sub-contracts defence to WEU. Creation of Eurocorps at the disposal of the European Union
1992	WEU Petersberg Declaration	WEU members	WEU commits itself to peacekeeping and peacemaking tasks
1997	Amsterdam Treaty	EU members	Strengthens ability of the European Council to 'instruct' WEU to carry out missions
1998	St Malo Agreement	Franco-British initiative	Agreement to enhance defence cooperation inside the EU
1999	Helsinki European Council	EU members	Agreement to develop common European security and defence policy

Figure 17.1 Common foreign and security policy: the tangled web of policy-making in early 1999

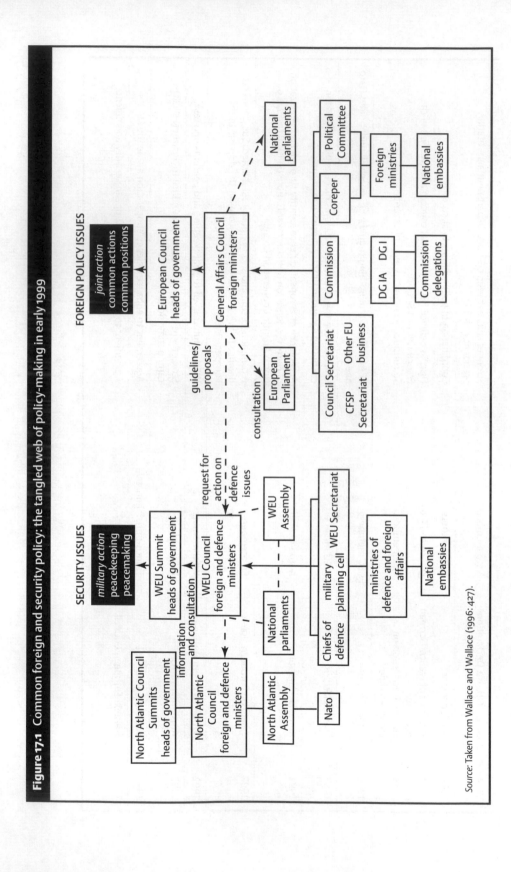

Source: Taken from Wallace and Wallace (1996: 427).

outside government, by national parliaments, or by the wider public. Even defence ministries in Paris and Bonn were excluded from consultation on Franco-German policy initiatives, a factor which explained the absence of detail in successive French proposals. If negotiators had addressed the resources and capabilities required to fulfil the expectations raised by their ambitious rhetoric, then finance ministries and parliaments would have had to be drawn in, with press and public following (Hill 1998). But much of the CFSP negotiations at Maastricht amounted to shadow-boxing behind the security cover which the USA provided, while monetary union and social policy preoccupied heads of government. Article J.4 committed the signatories to report on the operation of CFSP to a further IGC, to be convened (under Article N) in 1996, linking this to the fifty-year review of the WEU Treaty due in 1998. 'We now have four years to demonstrate that the intergovernmental model can work', the British Foreign Secretary declared (Hurd 1992). 'The structure was never intended to work,' a senior Commission official remarked more sceptically two years later.

Learning by doing, 1992–1996

Subsequent developments, however, resolved some of Maastricht's unfinished business, without waiting for ratification. Partly under the pressure of events in eastern and south-eastern Europe, partly thanks to the excellent personal relations between Nato's German Secretary-General and his Dutch counterpart at WEU, the WEU ministerial meeting in Bonn in June 1992 was able in the Petersberg Declaration to outline a distinctive role for WEU in undertaking peacekeeping and peacemaking operations (WEU 1992). Franco-British rivalry over European joint forces abated; the Franco-German Brigade, which was now to be joined by double-hatted Spanish and Belgian contingents to become a Eurocorps, was in future to be 'assigned' to WEU alongside other double-hatted 'European' forces in Nato (most importantly the British-led Rapid Reaction Corps) and 'made available' for possible WEU use (Forster 1994). A West European Armaments Agency brought the Eurogroup together with the French-inspired Independent European Programme Group, though this made only a limited contribution to the problems of common procurement and of integrating Europe's national arms industries in a rapidly shrinking market.

The evolution of the Yugoslav crisis was a painful learning process for governments on both sides of the Atlantic (see Table 17.3). West Europeans had instinctively looked to the USA to provide leadership, while the US Administration had firmly signalled that the west Europeans should take responsibility. WEU lacked the command and control structures required to mount the complex intervention needed in Croatia and Bosnia. The French commander of the UN Protection Force in Bosnia (Unprofor), the initial peacekeeping force, based his headquarters on a Nato structure, with American and German officers taken out and French brought in. Franco-American institutional rivalry led to the initial dispatch of two naval forces to the Adriatic, one under Nato and one under WEU, each commanded by Italian admirals. Aerial surveillance was provided by Nato's multinational aircraft crews, provoking an agonized

Table 17.3 The EU and the conflict in Bosnia

June 1991	EU's decision to lend 730 million ecus to the Yugoslav Federal Government, aimed at avoiding the civil war
June 1991	Slovenia and Croatia declare independence from the Federal Republic of Yugoslavia. EU sends troika to Yugoslavia; they declare 'the hour of Europe'
July 1991	EU arms embargo imposed and diplomatic isolation as Yugoslav army attacks Slovenia
July 1991	Brioni Agreement creates a truce in Slovenia and deployment of EU peace monitors. War spreads as Yugoslav army attacks Croatia
Sept. 1991	Appointment of EU special envoy Lord Carrington, who is asked to formulate a peace plan within two months
Oct. 1991	UN appoints Cyrus Vance as mediator in the Balkans
Dec. 1991	EU agrees to recognize Croatia and Slovenia under pressure from the German government, which threatens unilateral recognition despite Maastricht Treaty commitment to common policies and joint action
Jan. 1992	UN enforces ceasefire in Croatia; Unprofor deployed with a peacekeeping mandate
Apr. 1992	War breaks out in Bosnia-Herzegovina, after a majority in a referendum opt for independence. EU collectively recognizes Bosnia
June 1992	EU and UN oil sanctions embargo. Lisbon Agreement of EU governments not to recognize the former Yugoslav Republic of Macedonia under pressure from the Greek government. Nato approves the use of military force if necessary. Appointment of Lord Owen as EU special envoy
July–Aug. 1992	Sponsored EU–UN peace talks in Geneva and London Conference. Reports of genocide and human rights violations in Bosnia
Oct. 1992	No-fly zone over Bosnia declared by UN and EU and enforced by Nato. Serb leadership rejects Carrington Plan for a peaceful settlement. 6,000 Unprofor troops sent to Bosnia
Jan. 1993	UN–EU Vance–Owen Plan announced and then rejected in May
Dec. 1993	Appointment of former Swedish Prime Minister Carl Bildt as EU envoy to replace Lord Carrington
Aug. 1993	Nato policy of air strikes in support of UN 'safe areas' set up by Unprofor in Bosnia
Oct. 1993	Recognition of FYROM by Belgium and four months later by Denmark, France, Germany, Italy, Netherlands, UK
Mar. 1994	Owen–Stoltenberg Plan announced. Washington Accords establish a Muslim-Croat Federation in Bosnia-Herzegovina
July 1994	Creation of British, French, and German 'Contact Group', with the USA and Russia leading to a new peace plan eventually rejected by Milosevic in Feb. 1995
July 1995	UN safe area at Srebrenica attacked by Yugoslav army leading to death of 6,000 Muslims and subsequent Nato air attacks on Yugoslav forces
Nov. 1995	Peace deal negotiated in Dayton, Ohio and signed in Dec. leading to the deployment of Nato-led Implementation Force (Ifor) with 60,000 troops. Nato takes over from Unprofor
Dec. 1996	Nato-led Ifor replaced by a Stabilization Force to remain in Bosnia for eighteen months

Note: This chronology was compiled with the assistance of Robert Dover.

debate within Germany over whether the German air force personnel among their crews could be permitted to overfly Bosnia.

The Americans were sharply critical of the hesitant and incoherent west European policies in former Yugoslavia; but it was not evident that any clearer approach could have been hammered out within Nato. Manœuvring between three (sometimes four) local protagonists, with American and Russian sensitivities, Islamic pressures, and UN politics in the background, made it hard to achieve consistent policy. The French and the British provided the largest single forces on the ground; the Spanish and Dutch also contributed substantial contingents. Five of the other eleven EU member states had troops in Bosnia or Croatia in early 1995, Danes and Swedes with Norwegians and Finns in a joint Nordic battalion. Ten out of fifteen had ships maintaining the naval blockade in the Adriatic.[3] French attitudes both to Nato and to Britain shifted further under the experience of cooperation with British forces in the field, and with greater appreciation of the utility of Nato military assets, now partly under French command. An active, though confidential, Franco-British defence dialogue was under way by the end of 1993; the two foreign ministers publicly announced its existence in November 1994, setting up a joint air wing (van Eekelen 1993; Gnesotto 1994).

Despite the permissive conclusions of the Rome Nato Summit, both the US State Department and the Pentagon assumed that Nato would continue to define European security. They regarded WEU's creation of a consultative forum with the foreign and defence ministers of eight central and east European states as a competitor to Nato's recently created North Atlantic Cooperation Council (NACC).[4] While west European governments collectively and individually provided by far the largest proportion of economic assistance to the former socialist states, including Russia, the USA defined east–west political strategy. The Organization for Security and Cooperation in Europe (OSCE), of which Russia was a full member, was sidelined in favour of the NACC and Nato's 'Partnership for Peace'. The Clinton Administration again proposed a reformulation of the Atlantic politico-military partnership at the Brussels Nato Summit of January 1994, now to include enlargement of Nato to Poland, Hungary, and the Czech Republic.

The EU's approach to eastern enlargement, in contrast, was hesitant, as Chapter 16 makes clear. It was handled neither as a strategic foreign policy objective nor as a transformation of Europe's international order, but as a process managed by the Commission in which the applicants were expected to accommodate to the EU's existing *acquis*. The piecemeal approach to enlargement was most starkly evident in the late-night agreement at the Corfu European Council in June 1994, under the Greek presidency, to position Cyprus and Malta in the queue for early entry. This exposed the EU to the continuing Greek–Turkish conflict over divided Cyprus, and risked further antagonizing Turkey, a Nato member and key Western ally in relations with Central Asia and the Middle East (K. E. Smith 1998; Zielonka 1998). Similarly, the EU and its members were providing the largest share of economic assistance to the Palestinians, but without any significant influence over Israeli–Palestinian relations. Successive foreign ministers holding the EU Council presidency visited Jerusalem, to be humiliated by Israeli governments, which looked to Washington for advice and support. The EU's southern members pressed for Mediterranean programmes, oriented particularly at the Maghreb, to parallel the eastern-oriented Pologne-

Hongrie: Assistance à la Restructuration des Économies (Phare) and Technical Assistance for the CIS Countries (TACIS), and with a comparable share of the EC budget; the Spanish presidency convened a Euro-Mediterranean Conference in Barcelona in November 1995, which committed the EU in principle to a generous long-term programme (Barbé 1998).

The machinery, activity, and personnel involved in CFSP nevertheless expanded, in Brussels and elsewhere. The EPC Secretariat now became an autonomous unit within the Council Secretariat, with twenty staff. It had, however, little contact with the WEU Secretariat and almost none with the Nato Secretariat, both less than 7 kilometres away. For the European Commission, external relations were fast becoming one of its most thickly staffed fields. The rapid expansion of Community activities in central and eastern Europe and in the former Soviet Union led to the creation of Commission representations in those states. With over 100 trade missions, it had a denser network than many member states, with significant funds to distribute in developing countries and in the former socialist states. In the allocation of portfolios for the new Commission in January 1992, Jacques Delors as Commission President expanded the EPC Directorate into a full Directorate-General: DG IA (External Political Relations), alongside (and partly duplicating the work of) DG I (External Economic Relations). This tactical move provided prestigious posts for two rival Commissioners, Sir Leon Brittan and Hans van den Broek, at the cost of institutionalizing competition among Commissioners and officials. Relations with Mediterranean states were the responsibility of Manuel Marin, the senior Spanish Commissioner; the African, Caribbean, and Pacific states, associated through the Lomé Convention, were the preserve of DG VIII and Commissioner Pinheiro. This scarcely made for an integrated approach to economic and political issues, or for a global approach to the EU's external relations. (See Figure 15.1)

There were also institutional obstacles within national governments to integrating the political, security, and economic strands of foreign policy. Most foreign ministries had separate political and economic directorates, the former relating to CFSP and Nato, the latter to the EU, with separate national missions in Brussels to Nato and to the EU. Some Atlanticist governments designated their Nato Ambassadors to be their representatives to the WEU, other more *communautaire* governments chose their bilateral ambassadors to Belgium, while the French nominated their EU Ambassador. Coordination of this unwieldy machinery depended heavily on foreign ministers, most of whom attended Nato Councils and WEU ministerial meetings, as well as General Affairs Councils and formal and informal CFSP meetings. But foreign ministers were often distracted by immediate issues or domestic politics, and had limited time or inclination either to ensure that different organizations dovetailed neatly or to think strategically.

The Bosnian conflict was not the only issue on which EU member governments found it difficult to agree on a common approach. French engagement in the linked conflicts in Zaire and Rwanda embarrassed other member states. The Greek government's sustained veto over recognition of the former Yugoslav Republic of Macedonia infuriated its partners. The diversity of approaches within the EU increased further in 1995. The addition of three more non-aligned states (Austria, Finland, and Sweden) further complicated attempts to add defence to EU responsibilities. The emergence of a northern perspective among a strengthened Nordic group also shifted the focus of concerns towards the Baltic and Barents Seas and to problems of stability and nuclear safety in north-western Russia, and generated vigorous support for the Baltic states in their approach to EU membership.

Geographical diversity created unavoidable differences of priorities in national capitals. The German government was most directly concerned about its eastern neighbours, about Ukraine and Russia, and about its delicate relations with Turkey, the country of origin of its largest ethnic minority. Relations with Algeria were acutely sensitive for France, not to be subordinated to consultations with its partners. The Greek government focused on immediate problems in Albania and Macedonia, and sought to use its influence over EU–Turkey relations to provide support for Cyprus and for Greek security concerns in the eastern Aegean. Finland's concern was with its long land frontier with Russia and with broader EU–Russian relations. Spain was preoccupied with Morocco, and with the stability of North Africa as a whole.

Issues of national identity and statehood shaped attitudes to common defence. Belgian and Italian political leaders were open to the idea of a common European army; 'there is no longer any justification for a Belgian army', one senior Belgian remarked in explaining his government's proposal to contribute troops both to the Nato Rapid Reaction Force and to the Eurocorps, 'unless it forms part of a larger entity'. In Britain and France, on the contrary, pride in national military tradition both provided support for military deployment abroad and made the idea of sinking those traditions into a European army unthinkable.

France, Germany, and Britain were the key players in moves towards a more effective CFSP. Painful reassessment of post-cold war German responsibilities was leading to a gradual 'normalization' of German foreign policy, with German aircrew deployed in multinational AWACs aircraft over Bosnia in 1992. Nevertheless, continuing support for the principle of a citizen army, based on conscription, left its armed forces poorly structured or equipped for the different demands of peacekeeping and peacemaking. Attitudes in the French and British governments, antagonists in the debate about European versus Atlantic frameworks for foreign policy and defence over the previous forty years, were converging. The French government had explicitly modelled its post-Gulf War defence review on the British, ending conscription to focus on a smaller, better-equipped, and more deployable military force. Cooperation on the ground in Bosnia was building mutual respect between the French and British military. At the political level the British and French shared similar frustrations over the reassertion of American leadership in the Balkans, with its assumption that the European allies would support the imposition of the Dayton Agreement in December 1995—a settlement less generous to the Bosnians than earlier EU proposals which the USA had refused to support. All this contributed to a convergence of attitudes between London and Paris, though the strength of Euro-scepticism within the Conservative Party and within the British press meant that its implications did not become evident until well after the election of a Labour government in May 1997 (Neville-Jones 1997).

Amsterdam and after

There was little enthusiasm among member governments for the major review of progress towards CFSP which they were committed by the TEU to conduct in 1996. With ratification of the TEU completed only in 1993, there was little useful experience to draw on; nor was there any consensus about whether to strengthen, transform, or abolish WEU when the Treaty reached its fiftieth anniversary in 1998 (Deighton 1997). The pre-negotiation stage started with the appointment of a Reflection Group, chaired by Carlos Westendorp, in early 1995. Proposals from member governments revived the debate of five years before, with some added refinements.

The French government pressed for the appointment of a High Representative of the Union (usually labelled M/Mme PESC, from the French acronym for CFSP), to provide for the continuity and leadership which—French ministers claimed—the rotating presidency and the troika were unable to ensure. Governments from the smaller states saw this as an attempt to consolidate large-state dominance of CFSP, already evident in the Bosnian Contact Group, within which the British, French, Germans, and Italians worked with Russia and the USA. Those with long memories saw similarities with the Fouchet Plan, for which the French had unilaterally designated a site outside Paris to house its proposed Political Secretariat, on the assumption that others would accept French leadership. French insistence that the CFSP post required a high-profile figure with political authority was accompanied by rumours that Paris was designing this post for former President Valéry Giscard d'Estaing. There was broader agreement on the appointment of a policy planning unit within the Council Secretariat, to strengthen central support for the intergovernmental structure of CFSP; though French (and British) preference for a small unit was seen by governments of the smaller states as another move by their larger partners to dominate policy-making in this field. Several preliminary papers reopened the question of qualified majority voting (QMV); the French, in mid-IGC, proposed to move on from joint actions to 'common strategies' (B. Smith 1999). The British Conservative government, determinedly focusing on 'practical' measures, saw the High Representative post as a useful contribution to greater continuity, but most sensibly to be integrated into the Council Secretariat and reporting to the Council and presidency; the German government, like the British, saw this as a post for a senior official, who would not compete with national foreign ministers.

As in 1990–1, intra-European negotiations on security policy and defence moved in parallel with developments within Nato. The French and American governments had been attempting to find a compromise between their formerly entrenched positions since their agreement on the new Nato Strategic Concept in November 1991. At the Brussels Nato Summit in January 1994 the American delegation launched the concept of Combined Joint Task Forces (CJTF). This was intended to enable European governments to form 'coalitions of the willing' for operations without direct American commitment, but also with the right to request the use of Nato's headquarters, command facilities, communications systems, and logistical support—Nato assets disproportionately provided by the Americans. France in its turn had been edging back towards participation in the Nato integrated military structure, impressed in particular by the value of Nato training, structures, and assets in Bosnia. The concept of a

European Security and Defence Identity (ESDI), to which the alliance was now committed, expressed American willingness to accommodate French sensitivities, as well as American insistence that the European allies should play a larger role in maintaining the security of their own region.

In December 1995 the French government announced a formal return to some parts of the Nato structure; though President Chirac made clear, in a speech to the US Congress the following February, that France expected a genuine 'Europeanization' of the alliance in return. The June 1996 Berlin Nato Summit agreed that the role of European governments within Nato would be enhanced through a reform of Nato's regional commands, thus moving towards meeting the French government's conditions for full French reintegration. But President Chirac (to the dismay of his defence ministry) then publicly demanded that a French officer take over Nato's southern command, in Naples, to which the US Sixth Fleet and US aircraft made the predominant contribution. This directly challenged American strategic priorities in the eastern Mediterranean, and was refused—dashing hopes in several capitals that this *rapprochement* might lead to full French re-entry into Nato, thus permitting the emergence of a stronger European pillar within the alliance, closely integrated with the EU.

Paradoxically, therefore, Franco-British convergence on defence was not reflected in the formal outcome of the 1996–7 IGC. Both governments were inhibited by opposition within their own parliaments from publicly admitting how far they had moved; both therefore stressed practical cooperation, an approach with much more content but much less symbolism than that which characterized Franco-German defence cooperation. The French government continued to press for the integration of WEU into the EU, supported by the Belgian, Luxembourg, Spanish, and Italian delegations in a joint paper, as well as by the German foreign ministry. The German defence minister, and civilian and military staff within his ministry, were, however, much more cautious about making commitments of this sort. The Finnish and Swedish governments, new members and neutrals, had submitted a joint paper in April 1996 proposing closer association between the WEU and EU in crisis management, conflict prevention, and peacekeeping—the Petersberg tasks. The Irish presidency in the second semester of 1996, a neutral with less enthusiasm for the active peacekeeping envisaged by the Petersberg tasks, had little interest in pressing this dossier forward. The Dutch government, which took over the presidency in January 1997, was internally divided between different coalition parties and different ministries over how far Atlantic defence integration should be modified by Europeanization. Confusion in Paris, after the blocking of moves towards full re-entry into Nato's military structure, left the Italians, Luxembourgers, Belgians, and Spanish as the strongest protagonists of a full merger of WEU and EU in the IGC endgame.

Hardly surprisingly, the language of Article 17 of the Treaty of Amsterdam (ToA) was thus opaque: much longer than Article J.4 of the TEU, but littered with qualifying clauses and conditional verbs. The European Council could now 'avail itself' of WEU action, rather than the slightly weaker 'request' contained in the TEU. Links between the two organizations could be developed further, with the possibility of a merger 'should the European Council so decide'. Article 11 (replacing Article J.1) now defines CFSP as 'covering all aspects of foreign and security policy'; Article 13 (ex J.3) declares that the European Council 'shall define the principles and general guidelines' for

CFSP, 'including for matters with defence implications', leaving for future negotiation what matters might be agreed.

Progress on foreign policy procedures was also limited. The exaggerated declaration which opened Title V of the TEU had, diplomats admitted, opened up 'a capabilities–expectations gap' between what observers thought the EU could do and what it was actually capable of doing (Hill 1993). The new instruments established by Title V—common positions (statements of the EU on foreign policy issues), which required unanimity, and joint actions (implementation of agreements), which allowed for QMV—had been used sparingly, and to little effect. Fewer than forty joint actions had been adopted between the ratification of the TEU and the end of 1996, mostly reactions to developments in the Balkans, the Middle East, and Africa (Stavridis 1997; Regelsberger *et al.* 1997). The concept of common strategies, introduced by the French to the IGC as late as March 1997, appears in Article 13: 'to be implemented by the Union in areas where the Member States have important interests in common . . . in particular by adopting joint actions and common positions'. But there was no common understanding as to what this implied.

Irritation at the way in which the Greeks had blocked common policies on Macedonia and Turkey had, however, led to some movement away from insistence on unanimity, registered in Article 23. Decisions could be taken on the basis of 'constructive abstention', where abstentions by member states representing up to a third of the weighted votes would not prevent the Union adopting a position. A member state when abstaining 'may qualify its abstention by making a formal declaration', in which case 'it shall not be obliged to apply the decision, but shall accept that the decision commits the Union'; 'in a spirit of mutual solidarity, the Member State concerned shall refrain from any action likely to conflict with or impede Union action based on that decision'—language clearly intended to inhibit future Greek behaviour (Article 23.1). Majority voting would apply when the Union adopted joint actions or common positions, or took a decision on the basis of a common strategy (Article 23.2). Member governments were by now well aware that changes in voting procedures were a secondary issue in the pursuit of effective common policies; convergence of interests and understandings was the primary requirement.

Treaty commitment (in Articles 18 and 26) to a High Representative marked potentially a larger step forward: empowered to 'assist the Council . . . in particular through contributing to the formulation, preparation and implementation of policy decisions and, when appropriate and acting on behalf of the Council at the request of the Presidency, through conducting political dialogue with third parties'. The post of High Representative was to be combined with that of Secretary-General of the Council, with a new Deputy Secretary-General post to manage the Council Secretariat. This neatly postponed the question of whether the person to be appointed should be—like previous Council Secretaries-General—an official, or a political figure. The emerging consensus that the rotating presidency was no longer an adequate foundation for concerted diplomacy was further reflected in clause 5 of Article 18. This empowered the Council to appoint 'a special representative' with a mandate in relation to particular policy issues, thus generalizing the experiment adopted (with Lord Carrington, David Owen, and Carl Bildt) in the Bosnian conflict. Acceptance that a new policy planning unit would be created to advise the Secretary-General/High Representative, alongside the existing CFSP Secretariat, registered the continuing increase in the size and influence of the Council Secretariat. Insistence from the smaller member states that they should be represented in this unit, together with staff seconded from the Commission and from the WEU Secretariat, foreshadowed a directorate of twenty or more, rather than the half-dozen the French and British had envisaged.

Distracted heads of government, among them new prime ministers from both Britain and France, did not wish to move further on this difficult dossier when they met at Amsterdam to settle the final terms of the Treaty. Official agreement as the IGC progressed had produced texts which registered marginal strengthening of the positions of the Commission and the European Parliament (EP) in the second pillar. The Commission was now to be 'fully associated' (Article 18.4), but the Council and presidency retained the initiative; the presidency 'shall consult the European Parliament on the main aspects and basic choices' of the CFSP (Article 21). Expenditure on CFSP had been a contentious issue in the Maastricht IGC, because of French and British resistance to the EP acquiring an oversight of spending which might give it future leverage over CFSP. Article 28 charges administrative expenditure and non-military operational expenditure to the EC budget, leaving 'operations having military or defence implications' to be funded by those states which have not exercised their right of constructive abstention. This was a clause which could have considerable implications for the Community budget in the long term, if moves towards common foreign policy continued to advance.

Modest improvements in machinery thus left for post-IGC negotiation many of the most contentious issues which governments had been reluctant to address at Amsterdam. Key factors in the unblocking of the defence dimension in the eighteen months after the end of the IGC, and in acceptance of the French case for a senior figure as High Representative, were the continuing learning experience provided by conflict in south-eastern Europe, and further convergence of views between the British and French governments. European–American differences were evident as conflict developed in Kosovo in late 1998, in the Rambouillet Conference in February 1999 and in the military response which followed. The US Administration favoured the use of air power alone, in which its contribution was also dominant; the French and British were more willing to use ground forces.

The new British government had conducted its own strategic defence review in the course of 1997–8, with the European dimension only a background factor. Tony Blair, the British Prime Minister, was now shocked to discover how limited a force the European allies were able to mobilize in an emergency, and how dependent they were on American transport and communications; the mantra that European governments spent two-thirds as much as the Americans on defence, but could deploy only 10 per cent as many troops, was thereafter repeated in prime ministerial speeches and government statements. Contingency planning for a ground invasion of Kosovo, too late to prevent Serbian expulsion of a substantial proportion of its ethnic Albanian population, depended heavily on the professional forces provided by the British and French. The unilateral style of American policy towards Serbia, as refugees poured into Macedonia and Albania and from there into Italy, Germany, and other EU member states, shifted opinion in London, The Hague, and Bonn further towards accepting the principle of a European pillar within the Atlantic alliance. German willingness to deploy ground troops, with over 1,000 posted to Macedonia in 1998, met another necessary precondition for an autonomous European defence capability.

In parallel with developments in Kosovo, the British were now moving from laggard to leader in promoting European defence integration. At the Pörtschach informal European Council in October 1998 Tony Blair introduced a number of proposals on closer defence cooperation. This was followed by the Franco-British St Malo Declaration of December 1998, which robustly stated that 'the Union must have the capacity for autonomous action, backed up by credible military forces', with member governments operating 'within the institutional framework of the European Union', including 'meetings of defence ministers' (see Box 17.1).[5] With British acceptance that the EU should provide the framework for a European pillar, and French acceptance that this should complement but not attempt to duplicate existing Nato structures, the two governments now set out to persuade their European and American partners. Intensive Franco-British consultations between political directors and senior defence officials expanded bilaterally to other key EU governments, and then to the Americans, Norwegians, and Turks. Within the EU the Germans and Dutch were most closely drawn in, although the new coalition government in Bonn, with a social democrat defence minister and a green foreign minister, found it hard to formulate a coherent response. The Vienna European Council later in December 1998 marked the first stage in gaining agreement from the rest of the fifteen member states.

American acquiescence was vital. Initial reactions in Washington were mixed; like so many of its predecessors, the Clinton Administration publicly supported the greater Europeanization of Nato, but warned of the danger of such an initiative being misconceived or mishandled. The North Atlantic Council which met in Washington

---

Box 17.1 The Franco–British St Malo defence initiative

Aims
- The Europeans must be able to act without US participation
- The aim is to create an operational European defence capability
- To focus on political will and effective military forces

Institutional issues
- The governments have no reservations concerning institutional issues
- The Transatlantic Alliance remains the primary institution for territorial defence, US engagement in Europe, and pan-European defence and security
- Nato is the organization to be Europeanized
- The EU should have a defence competence
- The EU should absorb WEU's security functions and some defence functions

Procedures
- Intergovernmentalism must be the decision-making method for defence
- Governments must retain their national veto
- No involvement of supranational institutions in defence decisions
- The Europeans must have free access to national assets committed to Nato when the US does not want to participate in missions

Practical measures
- Creation of a European strategic air transport, satellite, and reconnaissance capability
- Enhanced policy planning and military early warning unit
- European-led intelligence-gathering and capacity to analyse information

in April 1999 to celebrate the fiftieth anniversary of the Atlantic alliance and to welcome three new members—Poland, the Czech Republic, and Hungary—declared in its carefully balanced communiqué that 'we reaffirm our commitment to preserve the transatlantic link', but also 'welcome the new impetus given to the strengthening of a common European policy in security and defence'. Discussions then moved forward, under the German presidency of both the EU and WEU, through a meeting of the WEU Council of foreign and defence ministers in Bremen, and through EU foreign ministers in the General Affairs Council of Ministers, to the Cologne European Council in early June. Its communiqué stated that 'we are now determined to launch a new step in the construction of the European Union. . . . our aim is to take the necessary decisions by the end of the year 2000. In that event, the WEU as an organization would have completed its purpose.'

There were other indications of a transformed consensus on CFSP in the first half of 1999, based on Franco-British partnership and the support of the German presidency. At the informal meeting of foreign affairs ministers in March, the presidency proposal to establish an EU military committee met with some resistance, most strongly from the neutral Irish. But the British proposal to create a permanent committee of deputy political directors in Brussels (in parallel with Coreper) to improve coordination of CFSP was generally welcomed. After the meeting the Spanish Foreign Minister told the press that he had the impression he was 'seeing the beginning of a process similar to that which marked the beginning of reflection leading to the single currency' (*Agence Europe*, 15 March 1999). In June the German government proposed a broader EU stability pact for south-eastern Europe. At the Cologne European Council member governments adopted their first 'Common Strategy', a lengthy statement of principles for future relations between the EU and Russia.

Perhaps most significantly, there was now general agreement that the new Secretary-General should be a senior political figure, rather than an official who would assist the presidency. The nomination of Javier Solana, former Spanish Foreign Minister and current Nato Secretary-General, was both appropriate and symbolic. The Secretary-General of Nato had always been a European, accepted by the Americans as an *interlocuteur* on behalf of its allies; Solana was already well known, and well trusted, in Washington. Twenty-five years earlier Henry Kissinger had supposedly complained of European pretensions to foreign policy cooperation that he did not know who to phone when he wanted to talk to 'Europe'. The transfer of Javier Solana from Nato to the EU Council Secretariat might begin to provide an answer. George Robertson, the British Defence Minister, who had played a leading role in promoting the Franco-British initiative, succeeded Solana as Nato Secretary-General.

From rhetoric to substance, at last?

Fifty-one years after the signature of the Treaty on Western Union (the original WEU Treaty), thirty years after the launch of EPC, west European cooperation in foreign policy and defence may at last be moving from rhetoric to substance. Previous initiatives for closer cooperation, sparked by disillusion with American leadership, have run into the sand when US foreign policy-makers have regained the confidence of their European allies. The impact of the Kosovo conflict was a crucial element in the post-Amsterdam surge towards more effective foreign and defence cooperation.

Whether this momentum will be maintained once memories of Kosovo fade remains to be seen. Already in the summer of 1999 there were signs of backtracking on commitments made to south-eastern Europe, as EU governments considered the costs to the EU, and to national budgets, of implementing the stability pact and of preparing all states in the region for the long-term prospect of EU membership.

The Franco-British strategy has been to focus first on capabilities, and only later on institutional reform. They have challenged their European partners to reshape their armed forces, and in some cases to increase their defence spending, in order to enable European states to manage conflicts in their own region, and perhaps even to contribute to peacekeeping operations outside their region, without depending on the US for crucial equipment and reinforcement. Their intention, outlined in the Cologne communiqué, was to gain commitments from their partners to greater common efforts to build deployable European forces, and then to merge WEU into the EU, most probably within the framework of the IGC planned to conclude in December 2000.

Many problems, however, remain. WEU has a complex pattern of membership, which has never coincided with that of the EU. American policy-makers have always resisted any suggestion that states might join WEU without also joining Nato. Yet there was little public enthusiasm within any of the four EU neutrals for parallel accession to Nato. Norway, Iceland, and Turkey were associated with the WEU as European Nato members; the delicate question of Turkey's role in the evolving structure of European institutions would be impossible to avoid as the majority of America's European allies shifted the framework for defence cooperation into a framework from which Turkish political leaders felt themselves excluded. WEU as an institution had provided, from the early 1990s, a forum within which the central and east European EU candidates—a third group of associate members—could discuss security and defence with their West European neighbours. Integration of WEU into the EU thus unavoidably raises wider questions about European defence and security, about the enlargement of both the EU and Nato, even about the future pattern of US–European politico-military relations.

Conclusions

Most EU member governments had answers to none of these questions in the summer of 1999. After several years during which EU governments had been forced to squeeze national budgets to meet the convergence criteria for the single currency, the prospect of spending more on defence, to satisfy a new set of 'convergence criteria', was daunting. To increase defence spending while also finding additional sums to support the reconstruction of south-east Europe, to speed eastern enlargement, and to underwrite a more active foreign policy towards the EU's Mediterranean neighbours was more than most political leaders wished to contemplate. As throughout the whole history of European foreign policy cooperation, the developments of 1998–9 had been agreed among ministers and officials, with little involvement of parties or parliaments, and only limited coverage in national media. Governmental commitments had moved far ahead of public awareness, on issues close to the heart of national sovereignty and identity which it was easy for opposition populists to exploit. CFSP thus depended on élite commitments and understandings, without the firmer foundations of public acceptance and support.

Looking back over thirty years, the framework within which west European governments make foreign policy has been transformed, through the development of an intensive transgovernmental network. It has become normal practice within EU foreign ministries to work with diplomats seconded from other states, even in planning staffs and defence policy departments. Information and intelligence are widely shared, dispatches drafted in common; foreign ministers meet several times a month, formally and informally. Defence ministries and military officers from European Nato members have interacted as intensively, but through a separate network, with which until the mid-1990s the French were only loosely associated, while the four neutral member states remained outside. The St Malo process, if carried through by the British and French to its intended conclusion in December 2000, would bring these two networks together.

Institutional innovation and reform has been important, from the creation of EPC in 1970 to the transformation of the role of the Council Secretary-General in the 1997 ToA. Yet responses to crises, incremental changes in working practices, initiatives from presidencies or individual governments, have shaped CFSP as much as package deals at IGCs. Indeed it is striking how little the package deals struck in The Hague, at Maastricht, and at Amsterdam either satisfied the protagonists or achieved the results intended. Developments between IGCs have in many ways been more significant, formalized later through incorporation into the treaties, as in the SEA in 1986 and, potentially, the IGC planned for 2000.

Policy-making in CFSP has been characterized by a very different approach to integration from that of the first pillar, the European Community. Governments have retained the initiative, with the Commission at best playing an auxiliary role, and with the Council Secretariat emerging in the 1990s behind the presidency as the framework for administrative support and coordination. The European Parliament has had little influence, and has devoted little attention; national parliaments have been informed partially and intermittently. The Court of Justice has no authority in this field. Nor have interest groups, active in external relations and north–south relations, played any visible role. Questions of sovereignty and of distinctive national interests have remained important; cooperation has edged forward on the basis of consensus. The major players have most often been from the larger states. It is, however, arguable that governments from the smaller states have gained disproportionately from participation in CFSP, in terms of international and domestic prestige from their turns in the presidency, as well as of information flows and multilateral influence outside the EU. Their foreign ministers and diplomats now form part of a transgovernmental policy community, which operates within international organizations and in third countries throughout the world as well as across the EU.

Some of the classic characteristics of European integration have, nevertheless, been evident in this field: the importance of socialization through working together, the proliferation of working groups as a basis for policy-making and policy implementation, the hierarchy of committees through which ministers and prime ministers set general objectives and officials struggle to translate these into detailed policies. Yet the weakness of central institutions, the marginal common budget, the dependence on mutual trust and consensus more than on rules, mark the second pillar out from all other areas of European integration—except JHA. Federalists and neofunctionalists long ago agreed that integration of foreign policy and defence was comparable to adoption of a single currency, or the development of common policies and institutions on domestic order. Effective integration in any of these fields, it was argued, would mark the crucial transition from political community to federation. Under the impact of German unification, at the Strasbourg European Council in July 1990, EU governments briefly recognized the link between EMU, CFSP, and political union. Ten years later they were, however, attempting to move towards effective integration in each of these fields without accepting any such logical link.

Declaratory diplomacy, without direct budgetary or military implications, was, however, an easy basis on which to build the appearance of common policy for a civilian power, while the United States continued to provide leadership in crises and in hard decisions. The challenge posed by the 1998 Franco-British initiative, to governments which had declared their greater willingness to support common foreign policies through successive IGCs, was to translate declarations into actions and expenditure.

Postscript

The conclusions of the Helsinki European Council, in December 1999, registered substantial further progress towards what was now described as 'the common European security and defence policy (CESDP)'. 'Recalling the guiding principles agreed at Cologne', heads of government committed themselves to the specific target of creating by 2003 a 'a militarily self-sustaining' force of 15 brigades (50,000–60,000 persons), capable of deployment in full within 60 days, with its 'rapid response' elements available and deployable far more quickly, sustainable for 'at least one year' and with appropriate air and naval support. The task of elaborating this objective was entrusted to 'the General Affairs Council, with the participation of Defence Ministers'.

The Helsinki conclusions also set out a list of consequential institutional reforms: 'a standing Political and Security Committee (PSC) in Brussels . . . composed of national representatives of senior/ambassadorial level'; 'the Military Committee (MC) . . . composed of the Chiefs of Defence, represented [for regular meetings] by their military delegates . . . [to] give military advice and make recommendations to the PSC'; and 'the Military Staff (MS) within the Council structures . . . [to] provide military expertise and support to the CESDP', including 'early warning, situation assessment and strategic planning for Petersberg tasks, including identification of European national and multinational forces.' These were to start operation as of March 2000, as 'interim' bodies, without waiting for the lengthy process of treaty amendment and ratification. Javier Solana, who took up his post as EU Council Secretary-General in October 1999, was also appointed Secretary-General of WEU the following month, signalling a consensus among WEU members in favour of integration with the EU. These new commitments were all the more remarkable for their achievement under the presidency of one the EU's four non-aligned member states.

Notes

1 This practice of informal meetings of foreign ministers, usually over a weekend in a pleasant country house, without a detailed agenda and without officials sitting in, was initiated by Hans Dietrich Genscher during the German presidency of 1974, with an invitation to his colleagues to join him at the former archbishop's palace of Gymnich. Regularized under successive presidencies, it brought foreign ministers together for extensive discussions in pleasant surroundings every six months, acting to socialize new foreign ministers into the EPC 'club', with its many long-serving members. In 1991 Genscher himself was (by some distance) its longest-serving member.

2 Only the Spanish and German governments accepted the French invitation; it was to other governments a serious breach of the procedural conventions of the IGC.

3 Since neither Luxembourg nor Austria have navies, and neither Ireland nor Finland have appropriate ships for this task, this means that every capable EU member except Sweden contributed to the naval force.

4 This left some confusion as to the configuration in which the WEU Council should meet, in effect leaving it as neither the defence arm of the Union nor a European pillar of Nato. WEU could meet at ten (the full WEU members); at fifteen (the ten plus the two EU observers and the three European Nato associates); at twenty-three (plus the eight central and east European associates). Numbers of associates and observers grew further with the division of Czechoslovakia, the addition of Slovenia to the group of central and east European associates, and the EU accession of Sweden, Finland, and Austria, to a total of twenty-eight for full meetings.

5 In fact the St Malo Declaration comprises two documents: a statement from the heads of state and government, and a secondary statement between defence ministers.

Further reading

There is now a substantial literature on EPC and CFSP. Nuttall (1992) provides an overall history; a revised edition is due in 2000–1. Regelsberger *et al.* (1997) cover the disappointments and frustrations of the post-TEU years. J. Peterson and Sjursen (1998) and Zielonka (1998) also offer useful surveys.

Nuttall, S. (1992), *European Political Cooperation* (Oxford: Clarendon Press).

Peterson, J., and Sjursen, H. (1998) (eds.), *A Common Foreign Policy for Europe? Competing Visions of the CFSP* (London: Routledge).

Regelsberger, E., Schoutheete de Tervarent, P. de, and Wessels, W. (1997), *Foreign Policy of the European Union: From EPC to CFSP and Beyond* (Boulder Colo.: Lynne Rienner).

Zielonka, J. (1998) (ed.), *Paradoxes of European Foreign Policy* (The Hague: Kluwer Law International).

Chapter 18
Justice and Home Affairs
Integration through Incrementalism?

Monica den Boer and William Wallace

Contents

Summary

Cooperation among national agencies concerned with combating crime, managing borders, immigration, and asylum, and with the judicial and legal implications of rising cross-border movement, became in the late 1990s the most active field for meetings convened under the Council of Ministers. A policy network among national enforcement agencies had developed from the mid-1970s, and was incorporated (as the 'third pillar') into the Maastricht Treaty on European Union (TEU). TEU negotiations on justice and home affairs (JHA), however, were marked by frequent disputes about the role of the European Union (EU) institutions, resulting in an *acquis* which was riddled with soft law, delicate compromises, and reservations by member governments. Nevertheless, the Amsterdam Treaty incorporated the Schengen agreements on the abolition of internal border controls into the EU treaty framework, and transferred migration and asylum policy from the third pillar to the first. Since then cooperation has gathered momentum. Europol became operational in 1999, and an ambitious work programme was presented to a special European Council on JHA questions in Finland in October 1999. But many legal and institutional issues remain to be settled before this policy domain becomes firmly rooted.

Origins of justice and home affairs cooperation

The Maastricht Treaty formalized the network of intergovernmental cooperation among national ministries of justice and the interior, and among related national agencies, into a 'third pillar'. Title VI of the TEU, consisting of Articles K.1 to K.9, covers 'cooperation in the fields of justice and home affairs. . . . for the purposes of achieving the objectives of the Union, in particular the free movement of persons'. Its subject-matter was heterogeneous, defined in K.1 as including asylum policy, rules on external border controls, immigration policy, and rules for third-country nationals within the EU, combating drug addiction and international fraud, judicial cooperation in civil and in criminal matters, customs cooperation, and police cooperation 'for the purposes of preventing and combating terrorism, unlawful drug trafficking and other forms of serious international crime'. A Declaration on Police Cooperation attached to the treaty noted the much more ambitious proposals put forward by the German government during the IGC, and agreed 'to consider on the basis of a report, during 1994 at the latest, whether the scope of such cooperation should be extended'.

The free movement of persons is one of the four basic freedoms set out in the 1957 EEC Treaty. Article 3c listed among the Community's intended 'activities . . . the abolition, as between Member States, of obstacles to the free movement of goods, persons, services and capital'. Nearly thirty years later, however, controls on most internal borders were still in place, in spite of a radical increase in cross-border movement by both citizens of member states and third-country nationals. A parallel increase in cross-border crime, and an upsurge of cross-border terrorism, had, however, pushed member governments into informal cooperation among security services and law enforcement agencies: first through the Pompidou Group on drugs, set up in 1972 within the wider Council of Europe, and then within the framework of European Political Cooperation (EPC) (Edwards and Nuttall 1994: 84; Anderson et al. 1995: 113). The Trevi Group was created in December 1975 by the Rome European Council, in order to coordinate anti-terrorist efforts among European governments faced with Irish, Italian, German, and Palestinian groups operating across their borders, with some evidence that these were receiving support from radical governments in the Middle East and from eastern Europe. A resolution of member governments of 29 June 1976 stated Trevi's objectives as: cooperation in the fight against terrorism; exchange of information about terrorist organizations; and the equipment and training of police organizations, in particular in anti-terrorist tactics.

Trevi was a network of national officials from ministries of justice and the interior, cryptically named after its first chairman, A. R. Fonteijn, and the Trevi Fountain in Rome, where the first meeting was convened. It developed a structure of working groups, reporting to occasional ministerial meetings. The first Working Group (WG I), created in 1977, carried responsibility for anti-terrorism, exchanges of information and intelligence, and the security aspects of air traffic, nuclear installations, and cross-border transport. WG II focused on police tactics, organization, and equipment. Its mandate was widened in 1985, when it also became responsible for technical and tactical cooperation issues in relation to other issues of cross-border public order, such as football vandalism (van der Wel and Bruggeman 1993: 43–49). In the mid-1980s a new WG III was created to enhance cooperation in the area of serious international crime, such as drug-trafficking, bank robbery, and arms-trafficking. Trevi 1992, the Mutual Assistance Group '92 (MAG '92—customs), an Ad hoc Group on Organized Crime and another Ad hoc Group on Immigration, and a Judicial Cooperation Group were later added, reflecting the rise in activities which accompanied the single market programme. The European Council in Rhodes in 1988 established a Group of Coordinators to hold together this proliferation of consultations and proposals. This group then presented the Palma Document to the Madrid European Council in June 1989, setting out a programme of 'compensatory measures' to maintain internal security within the completed single market. A European Drugs Intelligence Unit, the forerunner of Europol, was agreed between the Trevi ministers in June 1990 in Dublin, when Trevi issued a Programme of Action.

Despite the lack of a permanent secretariat, an extensive network had thus developed by 1991, which operated under the overall authority of the European Council on several political and executive levels, ranging from the responsible ministers through directors-general of the relevant ministries to middle-ranking civil servants and representatives of police forces and other agencies. The Maastricht TEU thus incorporated and adapted an already established structure into the third pillar.

The growth of cooperation among member governments in this broad field over the two decades before Maastricht had been largely responsive in character, reacting to perceived threats and to public anxieties through limited initiatives. The underlying rationale for building intergovernmental cooperation follows from the cross-border character of crime, the international mobility of criminals, the permeability of national boundaries among open economies and democratic societies, and the fragmentation of jurisdictions. The difficulties law enforcement agencies face in prosecuting criminals beyond the national frontier becomes a more serious obstacle as border-crossing increases, and as improvements in transport and communications make both legal and illegal activities more mobile.

Changing patterns of migration provided a second set of pressures for closer cooperation, as the flows from southern Europe into northern Europe which characterized the 1950s and early 1960s gave way to increasing flows from outside Europe in the late 1960s and 1970s, while slower growth and rising unemployment within the EU sharpened resistance to immigrant labour. Tightened controls on immigration in the 1980s coincided with a global rise in the number of refugees, leading to a surge of asylum-seekers arriving in western Europe. United Nations High Commission for Refugees (UNHCR) figures estimate that the number of asylum-seekers arriving in Europe had averaged 100,000 a year from the early 1970s, with some 70 per cent of these originating from eastern Europe. Larger numbers from other continents began to arrive in the early 1980s. In 1986, 200,000 sought asylum; in 1989, 300,000, and in 1992 almost 700,000, including Kurds from Turkey and Iraq, Tamils from Sri Lanka, Somalis, Sudanese, and Sierra Leoneans fleeing domestic disorder.

Other aspects of increasing interdependence, such as cross-border marriage, second homes in second countries, cross-border work and retirement, raise jurisdictional problems for civil law. The idea of a European Judicial Space had first been floated by French President Giscard d'Estaing and Spanish Prime Minister Felipe Gonzalez in the 1970s within the framework of the Council of Europe, both as a new initiative in European integration and as a means of resolving jurisdictional problems in criminal and civil justice. Many of the issues at stake, however, touch on sensitive issues of social order and national tradition. It took, for example, five years to negotiate the Convention on Jurisdiction and the Recognition and Enforcement of Judgements in Matrimonial Matters (the Brussels II Convention, signed in May 1998), which deals with issues such as custody of children and the division of property on the break-up of cross-border marriages; it may well take another five years for all national parliaments to ratify it. The pursuit of common rules for extradition was complicated by French and Belgian reluctance to end political asylum for Basque terrorists, who had been welcomed during General Franco's authoritarian regime, even after democratic Spain had joined the EU.

The preservation of domestic order from the threat of external order, the distinction between national territory and foreign lands and between the citizen and the alien, are fundamental aspects of national statehood, sovereignty, and identity. The loosening of border controls, let alone their complete removal, thus raises acute problems for national governments. Integration implies the transfer both of legal sovereignty and of citizenship to a European federation; limited cooperation among governments compromises sovereignty without providing effective results. Foreign threats, real, exaggerated, or imagined, provide powerful imagery in the rhetoric of domestic politics; influxes of outsiders conjure up fears not only of competition for jobs and welfare benefits but also of challenges to national solidarity and culture.

German concerns and anxieties have been a key factor in the development of common policies. Federal Germany had a particularly sensitive history and geographical position, a citizenship law based on ethnic descent rather than birth within the national territory, a liberal asylum law drafted in the aftermath of the Third Reich as the cold war divided Europe, a large *gastarbeiter* population attracted by its strong economy, and a structural ambivalence about sovereignty and nationhood. Experience of terrorism on German soil, from the Baader-Meinhof gang and from radical Middle Eastern groups, combined with the threat of subversion from across the eastern border to create a climate of insecurity. Chancellor Kohl's call for a 'European FBI', in 1988, was reportedly triggered by police reports that the Italian Mafia had infiltrated the restaurant trade in German cities. Demolition of the Berlin Wall in November 1989 increased anxieties that millions of migrants and asylum-seekers, some of them linked to criminal networks, would pour into Germany. In the early 1990s nearly two and a half million people from the former socialist countries arrived in Germany as *Aussiedler*, claiming German citizenship by virtue of distant descent. With them came a steady trickle of disadvantaged minorities from the region (most significantly gypsies from east-central Europe and Jews from Russia), and a modest flow of economic migrants: far fewer than alarmists had predicted. Organized criminals began to smuggle people—and drugs, and even nuclear materials—from East to West, and executive cars from West to East. External security and internal security concerns thus merged into a 'security continuum', in which migration and crime across Europe's eastern and southern borders increasingly preoccupied politicians, press, and public opinion (den Boer 1994b; Bigo and Leveau 1992).

The emergence of the third pillar added an extra dimension to an already crowded policy space. Interpol, a largely European organization until the 1960s, grew out of a conference convened by Prince Albert of Monaco in 1914, to consult about the threat of anarchist and revolutionary groups. Formally it was an association of police forces, not an intergovernmental organization. Re-established in Lyons after the second world war, it had grown by the 1980s into a global organization, with 150 members. Critics of its utility for intensified cooperation among European governments pointed to the slowness of its information exchanges, the absence of screening of its personnel or of a uniform data protection regime, and its lack of a treaty basis (Anderson *et al.* 1995: 52; den Boer 1996). The Council of Europe had provided a framework for negotiating conventions among West European governments on cross-border civil and criminal legal issues since 1949; the Organization for Economic Cooperation and Development (OECD) and a number of United Nations (UN) agencies were concerned with financial fraud, migration, refugees, and asylum policy. Council of Europe and UN conventions, including the European Convention on Human Rights and the 1951 Geneva Convention on the Status of Refugees, provided a framework of international law. The Hague Conference on Private International Law brought together legal experts to discuss differences in domestic civil law, and to propose the approximation of domestic laws (through international conventions) where incompatibilities created acute problems.

There were several overlapping rationales for developing common policies within the EU: the rhetoric of European integration, which declares in the Preamble to the EEC Treaty that its signatories are 'determined to lay the foundations of an ever closer union among the *peoples* of Europe' (our emphasis); the requirements of the single market, including 'free movement of persons'; the intensification of cross-border movement among geographically compact, densely populated countries as prosperity rose and communication links improved; the magnetic attraction of this prosperous, secure, and integrated area to migrants; and the parallel development of illegal cross-border activities alongside legal economic integration. The success of the 1992 internal market programme in removing controls on goods crossing internal frontiers focused attention on the remaining controls on people at the EU's internal frontiers; the further surge in border-crossing which the internal market programme encouraged also alerted law enforcement agencies to the need to agree on 'compensatory measures' to maintain public order across the EU.

The concept coined during the 1996–7 IGC of a Europe of 'freedom, security, and justice' neatly pulls together these different motivating factors. But it also encapsulates the inbuilt tensions in this field. Freedom of movement for those within the EU is balanced by rigorous external frontier controls, justified as providing security for EU citizens. Justice is defined primarily in terms of improving links between prosecuting authorities in pursuing cross-border criminals, together with judicial cooperation in civil law and improving access to justice across borders for EU citizens; justice as a limiting principle, as protecting the rights of citizens against the state, and the human rights of outsiders against arbitrary exclusion receives much less attention. Non-governmental organizations (NGOs) concerned with refugees and immigrants have contended that the underlying purpose of EU integration in JHA has been to create a 'Fortress Europe', with a well-defended border to divide insiders from outsiders, the privileged and rich from the excluded and poor. Member governments have dismissed such charges as a crude caricature of the complex and balanced package of measures they are struggling to introduce. The Austrian presidency's draft Strategy Paper on Asylum and Migration, circulated in September 1998, however, came close to fitting the caricature.

Until the mid-1980s member governments had resisted moves towards the removal of internal frontier controls, even though the steady rise in cross-border traffic had led both to lengthy queues at frontiers and to lighter controls. Three common travel areas, within which frontiers were open, overlapped with the expanded EC: Benelux, UK–Ireland, and the Nordic Area, which linked Denmark to four non-member states. Strict French enforcement of administrative controls on trucks carrying imported goods, in the context of a rising imbalance of French trade in the early 1980s, led first to protests from the German government and then to a strike of French lorry-drivers which blocked French frontiers for ten days in the winter of 1983–4. There followed Franco-German negotiations on bilateral frontier opening, extended at the request of the Benelux governments into the five-country Schengen Agreement, signed at a small village in Luxembourg in June 1985. From then until the ratification of the Treaty of Amsterdam, negotiations among the Schengen states and developments within Trevi and the third pillar overlapped, with a gradually expanding core group setting the pace for other EU governments to follow.

The slowness with which negotiations moved forward even among these five governments, sharing permeable land frontiers across the Rhine valley and delta, exemplifies the intense tensions between sovereignty and integration in this field. It took over four years to negotiate the Schengen Implementing Convention (SIC), signed in June 1990, setting out 'compensatory measures' for the removal of frontier controls covering asylum, a common visa regime, illegal immigration, cross-border police competences, and a common computerized system for the exchange of personal data (the Schengen Information System, SIS). 'Technical' problems then delayed the full implementation of what had been agreed until 1995, with French attacks on the liberal Dutch regime on drugs and questioning the effectiveness of other states' immigration controls, and Dutch concerns over data protection in cross-border information exchanges. In the intervening years Italy, Spain, Portugal, and Greece acceded, with Austria, Finland, and Sweden following, alongside Denmark, after they joined the EU in 1995. French doubts about the effectiveness of Italian frontier controls, however, delayed Italy's full participation until 1997, while Greece—with an extended maritime border and great difficulties in policing its Albanian frontier—did not meet the conditions for lifting internal frontier controls until 2000. Mutual trust in this sensitive area was reinforced by an intergovernmental system of inspection, in which teams of officials from member governments checked on the adequacy of controls on the external borders. The UK claimed that its island status justified maintaining controls on the 'internal frontier', thus enabling it to avoid such domestic controls as identity cards and checks on hotels as were practised elsewhere; Ireland therefore also remained outside in order to maintain its existing common travel area with the UK. When, in 1996, Denmark opted to lift its controls at the internal frontier, alongside Finland and Sweden, additional negotiations were necessary to maintain the Nordic Union travel area with Norway and Iceland.

By the time that the IGC which the Maastricht negotiators had agreed to convene to review the effectiveness of the intergovernmental pillars began in 1996, the pattern of cooperation in JHA was thus both extensive and untidy. A number of intergovernmental conventions had been agreed; others were awaiting ratification or under negotiation. The SIS was now in operation, with over 20,000 terminals holding millions of items of information on undesirable immigrants, criminals, and stolen goods.

As in the second pillar, habits of consultation and information exchange had become well established among national officials, but most member governments still hesitated to move beyond that to common policies and effective institutions.

The third pillar after Maastricht

The German government had been committed in principle to full integration of JHA into the EU during the 1991 IGC. The British government had been firmly opposed. The French government was ambivalent, declaring its support for common action while protective of state sovereignty. The Luxembourg presidency's April draft treaty accepted that foreign policy and internal security would remain primarily intergovernmental, in separate 'pillars'. Rapid dismissal in September of the Dutch presidency draft, which proposed instead to bring both CFSP and JHA into a single integrated structure, demonstrated the general reluctance to transfer authority over such sensitive issues of domestic citizenship and law and order (Laursen *et al.* 1992: 15). The TEU thus formalized the existing network of committees, without transforming the framework of authority and accountability.

The greatest procedural innovation was to transfer the preparation and management of meetings to a new Directorate-General of the Council Secretariat, under the direction of the rotating presidency. The Commission, with limited rights of initiative in this field, maintained a small 'task force' within the Secretariat-General to represent its interests and to manage the overlap between Community competences and third-pillar issues; DG XV, responsible for the internal market, also monitored the development of policy. A handful of staff, reporting to a Commissioner with prior interests—Padraig Flynn, whose main responsibility was for social policy (DG V), though on the changeover in 1995 JHA was defined as one of Anita Gradin's main responsibilities—had little opportunity to shape the flow of policy. The EP made less effort to monitor the flow of proposals than in the second pillar, though its Civil Liberties Committee came to develop an interest in the years which followed. Whether or not the jurisdiction of the ECJ might extend to the interpretation of JHA Conventions became a topic for tedious debate.

Nevertheless, there was in this highly heterogeneous field a considerable overlap between the competences of the revised Treaty of Rome (TEC) and those of the TEU's Title VI, reflecting the unresolved tensions embedded in the Maastricht compromise. The new Article 100c (TEC) and Article K.1 (3a) both addressed visa policy, with the former explicitly giving the right of initiative to the Commission. Article 129 (TEC), on public health protection, referred to 'Community action . . . directed towards . . . drug dependence', while Article K.4 relates to 'combating drug addiction'; Article 209a (TEC) referred to fraud 'affecting the financial interests of the Community', while Article K1.5 referred to 'combating fraud on an international scale'.

A determined Commission, with a senior Commissioner and a well-staffed Directorate-General, might have made much of these ambiguities, and sought to exploit the permissive language of Articles 100c(6) and K.9, which allowed for the transfer of policy-making from the third to the first pillar by unanimous agreement (the

> **Box 18.1** Justice and home affairs in the Treaty on European Union
>
> New Title VI, Articles K.1–9
>
> ■ K.1: '. . . Member States shall regard the following areas as matters of common interest:' asylum policy, rules and controls on external border-crossing, immigration policy (including conditions of entry and residence within the EU for third-country nationals), 'combating unauthorized immigration', combating drug addiction, 'combating fraud on an international scale', judicial cooperation both in civil and in criminal matters, customs cooperation, police cooperation 'for the purposes of preventing and combating terrorism, unlawful drug trafficking and other serious forms of international crime', reference to 'the organization of . . . a European Police Office (Europol)'.
>
> ■ K.2: cooperation to be in compliance with the European Convention on Human Rights and the 1951 Geneva Convention on the Status of Refugees.
>
> ■ K.3: collaboration to take the form of joint positions and joint actions, promotion of cooperation, and negotiation of conventions to be ratified by the member states 'in accordance with their respective constitutional requirements'.
>
> ■ K.4–6: establish Coordinating Committee of senior national officials; voting rules by unanimity except (by prior agreement) when implementing joint actions; Commission to be 'fully associated', Parliament to be regularly informed.
>
> ■ K.7: permits closer cooperation in this field among smaller groups (reference to Schengen).
>
> ■ K.8–9: refer to parallel clauses in EC Treaty; assign administrative expenditure to the EU budget and operational expenditure (unless unanimous decision to draw on EU budget) to member states; also permit transfer of dossiers from Title VI to procedures under (new) Article 100(c) (TEC), by unanimous vote (the *passerelle*).

so-called *passerelle*). For the second (common foreign and security policy) pillar after Maastricht, in contrast, the directorate within the Secretariat-General was expanded into a full Directorate-General (DG IA), reporting to Commissioner van den Broek, a former Dutch Foreign Minister (see Chapter 17). But the Commission found neither the determination nor the staff to attempt a comparable effort in the third pillar.

The second pillar brought together officials from national foreign ministries, with a shared professional approach and the common experience (and personal links) of diplomatic postings in third countries. Participants in the extended network of Council committees which constituted the third pillar, in contrast, were drawn from diverse national ministries, forces, and agencies, rooted in distinctive state traditions. The division of functions between ministries of the interior and of justice differed from state to state; Germany's federal structure, and the UK's separate system of Scottish law, made for particular complexities in national representation and policy preparation. The policing of internal order was organized along national lines in France and Italy, with both paramilitary (Gendarmerie and Carabinieri) and civil forces. The philosophy of policing in the UK, on the contrary, was of single forces locally recruited and accountable, with the London Metropolitan Police providing a loose coordinating role. The increasing cross-border character of crime and of cooperation were motivating factors in the creation in 1992 of the National Criminal

Intelligence Service, through which UK forces channelled their contacts with third-pillar committees and the European Drugs Unit (EDU).

Different national traditions (and geographical circumstances) were also evident in the non-congruence of national agencies combating financial fraud, smuggling, and border control—Germany's Bundesgrenzschütze, for example, Italy's Guardia di Finanza, the UK's Customs and Excise. Legal traditions, judicial training, court procedures, even concepts of crime and of the appropriate hierarchy of penalties, were also deeply and distinctively embedded in each state structure and society. Each national professional community tended to assume that their tried and tested rules were best, and that foreign laws and foreign practices were deficient. Each professional grouping nevertheless shared a certain mutual respect and a certain style, which set police apart from lawyers and judges, and both from the *fonctionnaires* who attempted to coordinate their activities (Anderson *et al.* 1995).

The evolution of the third pillar in the 1990s may thus be compared to an archipelago, with islands of cooperation loosely linked through the coordinating K.4 Committee and through JHA Councils (Frissen 1996: 293). A lengthy process of reciprocal learning was needed in order to establish the foundations for common policies, and to build sufficient mutual trust to support their implementation. Intelligence services and anti-terrorist units had exchanged information since the upsurge of cross-border terrorism in the early 1970s. Customs authorities had developed limited patterns of cooperation as the common market had taken shape, which were intensified as the 1992 Programme had moved forward; the Mutual Assistance Group, 1992 (MAG '92), set up by heads of national customs services in 1989 to agree an External Frontiers Strategy, set the parameters for third-pillar customs cooperation for most of the 1990s (House of Lords 1998a: 48). Judges and prosecuting authorities, on the contrary, were still discovering each other's particular styles and assumptions, and discovering also how diverse were definitions of crime, of civil wrongs, and of legal remedies in each other's countries. Police cooperation, a matter only for specialists ten years before, was now developing rapidly, as rising cross-border traffic presented day-to-day problems for which international contacts were self-evidently useful. Ministry of interior officials had remained among the least internationally minded within national governments throughout the first forty years of west European integration, working within an ideological framework which clearly separated domestic law and order from events beyond national boundaries. To learn the habit of transgovernmental cooperation therefore required a substantial reorientation of working assumptions.

Law and order were matters of executive control in all states. It was therefore understandable for the third pillar to develop as a network of executive agencies reporting to ministers, with national parliaments scarcely informed. Ministers and officials saw themselves as responding to public anxieties about crime and immigration, but did not think it necessary to inform the public of the practical steps they were taking together for their better protection. Nor did the media in any country pay much attention to this esoteric process of negotiating intergovernmental conventions and of exchanging information, except when a proposed new institution like Europol, or an ambitious concept like the European Judicial Area, made copy for a headline or material for a scare story. The Schengen process was far more visible, because frontier controls were ceasing to operate and compensatory measures such

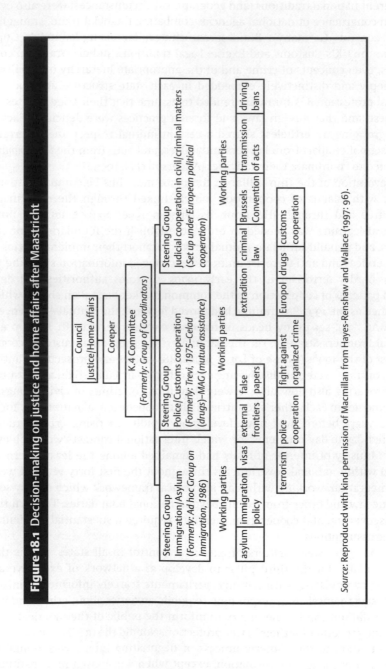

Figure 18.1 Decision-making on justice and home affairs after Maastricht

Source: Reproduced with kind permission of Macmillan from Hayes-Renshaw and Wallace (1997: 96).

as extended patrols and checks on travellers in border areas directly affected the travelling public. Schengen's visibility also linked directly to anxieties about statehood; part of the sensitivities of implementing Schengen, particularly in France, flowed from the fears articulated by politicians and journalists that France without frontiers would have lost control of the national territory.

Nor was this an area thickly populated with organized bodies outside government, even within national politics. Civil liberties organizations and legal bodies extended their activities to some extent to the European level in parallel with the development of the third pillar; networks concerned with migrants, racial and gender discrimination, and refugees had operated internationally long before. Small and poorly funded NGOs and networks with a particular European orientation—Statewatch, for example, and Fair Trials Abroad—now emerged alongside such established groups as Amnesty International, Justice, and the Fédération Internationale des Ligues des Droits de l'Homme, and better-funded networks of immigration and civil liberty lawyers. With neither parliaments nor press actively engaged, such groups had to rely primarily on their expertise, their contacts with insiders, and their persuasiveness for what influence they gained.

The scale of activity within the third pillar steadily increased during the first half of the 1990s. After the 1992 Programme was completed, with the working groups concerned disbanded or less active, this became the largest single field for which the Council Secretariat serviced meetings, amounting in 1997 to a third of the meetings convened and over 40 per cent of the papers circulated. During the Luxembourg presidency in the second semester of 1997, ministers of interior and justice met twice as the JHA Council, with one additional informal gathering; the K4 Committee met six times. Seventy working group meetings were held over the six months, with a further eight meetings of the Horizontal Drugs Group. The busiest of the three broad areas of JHA was police cooperation and organized crime: the British National Criminal Intelligence Unit sent staff to forty-four meetings, most of them lasting two days, including groups on Europol, the Europol computer system, drugs, and organized crime. Legal officials took part in six working group meetings on civil law. Customs officials attended six two-day meetings of the Customs Cooperation Working Group, as well as participating in most discussions on drugs-trafficking, people-smuggling, and organized crime (House of Lords 1998a). Immigration and asylum issues, and the development of a common visa regime, were discussed as actively within the Schengen network (then still without the UK and Irish governments) as in the third pillar; other governments were thus committed to a further calendar of supplementary or separate committee meetings. Intelligence and security service personnel also took part in many meetings, most importantly those on terrorism.

This represented a transformation of the working practices of interior ministries and of police forces, with the emergence of an intense transgovernmental network: supplemented by the posting of a rapidly rising number of police liaison officers to each other's capitals. The British Home Office, which had maintained scarcely any direct international contacts ten years earlier, reported that 'some 68 Home Office officials currently spend all or most of their time on EU-related business' (House of Lords 1998a: minutes of evidence 1, 34). Ministries of justice were drawn in more slowly; the administration of law, the gathering of evidence, and the preparation of prosecutions remained firmly matters of domestic sovereignty. There was a structural tension between increasingly cross-border crime and civil litigation and stubbornly domestic jurisdictions, evident in the slow processes of extradition and in the rising number of citizens of one EU member state in prison in other member states, not only after conviction but also while awaiting trial. But judges and lawyers inherit strong traditions about the inherent superiority of their national system of law. It was not until the revival of the concept of a European Judicial Area, after the Treaty of Amsterdam, that justice ministries began to be drawn into a similar European network on a similar scale.

The flow of policy

As in the second pillar, the initiation and management of policy depended primarily on the presidency, with the assistance of the Council Secretariat. Every six months, therefore, priorities might shift, with particular national concerns—or external events—hijacking the agenda. The Irish presidency in the second semester of 1996, for example, particularly emphasized the control of drugs and cooperation against drugs-trafficking, pushing through a number of resolutions and joint actions in this area: issues of immediate domestic concern after a rise in drug-related crime in Dublin, including the killing by drugs-traffickers of one of Ireland's best-known journalists. During the same presidency the eruption of a major paedophile scandal in Belgium triggered new proposals for joint actions to combat people-smuggling for sexual purposes and child pornography. Multi-annual programmes agreed by the JHA Council served to provide greater continuity; work programmes and action plans proliferated in the aftermath of the 1996–7 IGC. Presidencies which introduced such programmes drafted their preferences into the text, in the same way as Commissioners did under the first pillar. The Austrian presidency's projection of its domestic preoccupations with popular resistance to immigrants into its draft Strategy Paper on Asylum and Immigration, in September 1998, provoked vigorous attacks from non-governmental organizations; the (British) Immigration Law Practitioners Association attacked it as xenophobic, intended to exclude immigrants and asylum-seekers from 'Fortress Europe'. The action plan text agreed at the Vienna European Council in December, after extended negotiations in the K4 Committee, Coreper, and the JHA Council, was much milder in tone.

The discreet staff of the Council Secretariat, both DG H (Justice and Home Affairs) and the Legal Service, played a significant role in managing the flow of policy, as provider of agendas and drafts. DG H was more generously staffed than the Commission task force on JHA throughout the early 1990s, with additional staff recruited in 1998–9. The Treaty of Amsterdam provided for the separate Schengen Secretariat, which had been co-located with the Benelux Secretariat in Brussels, to be integrated into DG H (provoking strong protests from staff unions in the Council Secretariat). Permanent representations of the member states in Brussels were also drawn in, adding legal advisers and officials seconded from interior ministries to their staff. These new additions assisted national officials as they came in and out of Brussels, and managed the overlap between first- and third-pillar business through Coreper I and Coreper II.

Once an initiative had been launched, negotiation of the framework for policy—an intergovernmental convention, or a joint action—has been devolved to about twenty JHA working groups of middle-level or junior national officials. As in other areas of EU policy-making, these disaggregated strategic policies into functional–technical sectors, within which professional and personal relationships helped to build a sense of common purpose. Experts and representatives from relevant EU agencies (such as the EDU, later Europol, and the European Monitoring Centre for Drugs and Drugs Addiction, established in Lisbon in 1993) were invited to take part in meetings. But unlike first-pillar committees and working groups, the involvement of other outsiders, let alone experts from the private sector, has been minimal—except when bids for the architecture of an electronic information system were at stake (Kroon 1997: 167–8). The membership of some working groups was rather fluid, limiting the development of mutual confidence through mutual learning. In this sense, JHA working groups resembled 'issue networks' (J. Peterson 1995a: 77; Richardson 1996a: 9). However, at the same time third-pillar working groups usually enjoyed a core leading group of long-serving members, within which should be included participants from the Council Secretariat and the Commission Task Force (Beyers and Dierickx 1998: 313).

The number of working groups has fluctuated. New groups have been created when new issues are placed on the political agenda; others have been dissolved when the draft they have been asked to prepare is completed (Beyers and Dierickx 1998: 290). Even outside the intergovernmental working sphere it is sometimes difficult to know how many working groups are active at one time (Hayes-Renshaw and Wallace 1997: 15; van Schendelen 1998). During the 1997 Luxembourg presidency, for example, two groups were created to prepare for the incorporation of Schengen into the EU treaties and to prepare for the conclusion of the association agreements with Norway and Iceland (den Boer 1998b: 11). Closure or reconstitution of issue-specific working groups could also serve to prioritize issues or redefine their scope; thus in 1997 two working groups, on international organized crime and on drugs and organized crime, were replaced by the Multidisciplinary Working Group on Organized Crime. Working groups have usually been most active during the first three months of an EU presidency term. It is widely accepted among officials in the JHA field that if a dossier is not ready by the end of the first three months of a presidency, the chance of achieving political agreement during that presidency becomes minimal.

With few exceptions, it has been civil servants, rather than representatives of executive agencies, who have negotiated in working groups. Professional input into the drafting of conventions and other instruments, from the customs or immigration officials or police officers who would have to implement them, has often been marginal—to their discontent. The extent to which senior personnel from such agencies were successful in representing their views on the practicability or enforceability of the measures proposed has varied considerably from one country to another, with professional pride and professional rivalry coming into play. International networking among customs officers and police, however, provided an alternative source of mutual support and influence. The growth of international conferences, training courses, and informal contacts among domestic police organizations was one of the striking developments of the early 1990s, as the police responded to greater cross-border challenges. Bodies such as the International Police Working Group on Undercover Policing provided opportunities to learn about each other's working practices and so to learn how to operate together, outside the restrictions of formal accountability. Judges and magistrates, on the other hand, felt far less need for such informal exchanges.

Several training programmes administered by the Commission under Title VI (TEU) were intended to promote greater mutual learning and to create or strengthen professional networks: Odysseus, covering those involved in managing immigration, asylum, and external borders; Grotius, for legal practitioners; STOP, bringing together those concerned with people-smuggling and sexual exploitation of children; Oisin, for law enforcement agencies; and Falcone, for those in police, customs, and other agencies concerned with combating organized crime. Member governments, drawing on the EC budget and the support of the Commission, were thus contributing to the gradual establishment of policy communities, issue networks among professionals, as a necessary underpinning to the formal processes of JHA policy-making (Stehr 1994: 174).

The third pillar inherited from Trevi a heavily hierarchical structure of policy-making. Three steering groups of senior officials monitored the progress of working groups, in immigration, asylum, and external borders (SG I), police and customs cooperation, drugs, and organized crime (SG II), and judicial cooperation (SG III). The steering groups in turn were responsible for proposing an annual work programme to the coordinating K4 Committee, which had to be reviewed six months later; they then reported back to the K4 Committee at the end of the year. Many delegations saw the steering groups as an extra layer in an already overburdened hierarchy. They met less frequently as one presidency succeeded another, and their abolition was proposed during the early stages of the 1996–7 IGC—though in the end the Treaty of Amsterdam said nothing, leaving them to fade away. The unavoidable overlap between agencies and issues in dealing with border control, organized crime, legal and illegal immigration, drugs-trafficking, financial fraud, terrorism, and prosecution and conviction of people accused of cross-border crime, has led instead to the development of a succession of 'horizontal', or 'high level', groups: to link together the detailed and technical negotiations within the different working groups, and to manage and push forward multi-annual programmes and action plans. The Horizontal Group on Drugs, the High-Level Group on Organized Crime, the High-Level Group on Asylum and Migration, and other cross-agency and cross-pillar groups concerned with data protection issues and judicial cooperation thus in effect replaced the steering groups as strategic groups within the third pillar.

The next layer in the hierarchy has been the Coordinating Committee—the formal title of the K4 Committee, renamed the Article 36 Committee after the Treaty of Amsterdam—which brings together in Brussels senior officials from national ministries normally once a month. A certain rivalry was apparent at the outset between K4 and the fortnightly Coreper II. Coreper members are Brussels-based, working closely with the Council Secretariat, and (where needed) the Commission, to monitor week by week the cycle of working group meetings and to prepare agendas for JHA Councils. This allows them in effect to act as a gateway between the collective gathering of senior officials and the collective Council which brings together the ministers to whom they report. The K4 Committee was slower to clear dossiers through its less frequent meetings, tempting officials within the permanent representations to seize control and assemble agreed 'A-points' for the JHA Council agenda. Attachment of staff from interior and justice ministries to permanent representations has mitigated this rivalry, while moving the permanent representations further towards becoming offices of national administrations in Brussels rather than the predominantly diplomatic representations they were in the early years of the EEC. Every permanent representation except Luxembourg's contained officials from these ministries by 1995 (Hayes-Renshaw and Wallace 1997: 221).

Coreper's strong position also derives from its embodiment of the 'institutional memory of the Council', in keeping track of the vetoes and concessions across the range of EU policies traded by member states (Héritier 1996: 157). Developments in entirely different areas of EU negotiation might, after all, impinge on policy-making within the third pillar. The stalemate over the bovine spongiform encephalitis (BSE) crisis in 1996, during which the UK government blocked agreement on proposals across all three pillars in response to the Commission's ban on British beef exports, affected JHA proposals as much as those within the EC itself.

The formal pinnacle of the policy-making hierarchy, since cooperation first emerged in the 1970s, has been the European Council. Strategic commitments have been registered—and thus legitimated—in European Council communiqués. Until the special European Council convened in Tampere in October 1999, however, there was little space on their crowded agendas for more than expressions of concern—about refugee flows, or threats of cross-border crime—and of support for further cooperation; the JHA Council has effectively provided the final point for political decision. The emergence of the JHA Council as one of the regular formations of the Council of Ministers has marked a further stage in displacing the 'general' role of the General Affairs Council of foreign ministers. Four formal meetings a year from 1991, plus one or two informal meetings, lasting up to two days, brought ministers of interior and justice together as a group every other month. Bilateral conversations between meetings, necessary to explain national positions and to build coalitions, gave to ministerial diaries the transgovernmental dimension that finance ministers had acquired twenty years earlier. Interior ministers were becoming accustomed to addressing each other on first-name terms, as colleagues within an established EU institution.

The rhythm of policy-making within the third pillar has in some ways been regular, and in other ways highly erratic. Agendas have been shaped partly by the progress of working groups and the six-monthly pattern of successive presidencies, but also by the pressure of outside events or the shifting preferences of presidency ministers or of other leading governments (Barrett 1997: 11). Unlike in the first pillar, where the disciplines of Commission proposals and parliamentary co-decision imposed a timetable, dossiers in the third pillar might move forward rapidly from initial draft to adoption, or change shape radically between first and final draft, as presidency officials or *ad hoc* working groups sought consensual agreement. On sensitive issues, however, such as the External Frontiers Convention or the Eurodac Convention (which provided for the creation of an EU-wide computerized fingerprint database to check against multiple applications for asylum), progress might be stalled through successive presidencies. One issue that has been alternately pushed forward and held back is that of 'burden-sharing', or 'solidarity', over asylum-seekers: code for redistributing surges of refugees across the EU's eastern border from the immediate recipient countries to other member states. For obvious reasons each German presidency—with hundreds of thousands of refugees from former Yugoslavia on its territory—vigorously pressed the issue, as did the Dutch and, after their 1995 accession, the Austrians.[1] For equally obvious reasons, however, other governments preferred to set it aside.

The weaknesses of the third pillar

Title VI (Article K) of the TEU was a compromise between a whole range of incompatible objectives. The British and French governments had explicitly resisted yielding sovereignty to new EU institutions in this field, as in the second pillar; most other governments had implicit reservations, or had adopted integrationist positions without thinking through the implications for their domestic courts, their law enforcement agencies, or their freedom to define their own social choices (on, for example, family law or drug control) through national law. The protocols and declarations attached to the TEU, reserving Danish laws to restrict sales of second homes to non-residents, protecting Article 40.3.3 of the Constitution of Ireland (a deliberately obscure reference to the Irish ban on abortion), and protecting the right of each member state to define 'who are to be considered their nationals for Community purposes', demonstrate how close to fundamental national choices about land, social order, and citizenship this field was already seen to be. The policy-making framework negotiated was, however, intricate and slow-moving, too weak to support the expectations of common action which the German and Dutch governments above all held. Three weaknesses in particular stand out: ambiguity about the legal and constitutional framework, evident in the frequency with which institutional issues were entangled with policy proposals; the low political visibility and accountability of this essentially bureaucratic framework for policy, which allowed the practice of cooperation to develop far beyond what was reported to parliaments or to national publics; and the absence of mechanisms for ensuring national ratification or implementation of what had been agreed.

Ambiguity about the legal and constitutional framework for common actions in JHA was embedded in the TEU. Article K.2 declares that actions in this field shall be conducted 'in compliance with the European Convention on Human Rights . . . and the Convention relating to the Status of Refugees', but provides no new mechanism for challenging actions that fall short of the principles these set. The only reference to the ECJ is in Article K.3.2(c), which notes that conventions drawn up by member states under this Title 'may stipulate that the Court of Justice shall have jurisdiction to interpret their provisions and to rule on any disputes regarding their application'. This implicitly excluded the ECJ from judicial review of joint positions and joint actions—the looser instruments of consensual decisions developed through European Political Cooperation—and opened the door to negotiations about this issue in every proposed convention. The British government systematically refused to extend the jurisdiction of the European Court of Justice (ECJ) in this way, while the Dutch insisted that judicial review was needed to protect civil liberties and fundamental freedoms within the EU, as national law enforcement was extended to EU level. For the Europol Convention, the Fraud Convention, and the Customs Information System Convention, all signed by member governments in July 1995, a general 'opt-in' provision was thus agreed, by which willing member states could declare that they would recognize ECJ jurisdiction over the measures agreed. By the beginning of 1999 six states had made the required declaration: Belgium, the Netherlands, Luxembourg, Germany, Austria, and Greece.

Attempts by Commission officials to play a more active role might well have provoked further disagreement among member governments about the interpretation of Article K.4.2, which declared that 'the Commission shall be fully associated with the work . . . referred to in this Title'. The reluctance in particular of justice ministries to permit the Commission to establish a role in their field suggests it was wise for Commission officials to adopt a participant observer role in most working groups, concentrating their efforts on the development of a common visa regime as outlined in new Article 100c (TEC). Even here progress was agonizingly slow. The Commission proposed a common list of 129 third states to the Council in December 1993. There followed extended negotiations, before the Council adopted a revised list of 101 in September 1995. The EP then successfully challenged this decision before the ECJ, arguing that the original proposals had been so substantially modified as to require reconsultation. The Council finally approved the Regulation, with two minor amendments from the list of countries agreed four years earlier, in March 1999.

Article K.6 was similarly ambiguous about the position of the EP, calling on the Council presidency to 'regularly inform the European Parliament of discussions in the areas covered by this Title' and to 'consult . . . on the principal aspects of activities in the areas referred to', while also permitting it to address questions on JHA to the Council. No presidency-in-office, however, consulted the EP on the Europol Convention until after the Council had agreed it; while at the end of the Belgian presidency in December 1993 M. Dehaene refused to answer a direct question from an MEP on whether the Council would undertake to inform and consult the Parliament before taking decisions on issues of internal security (den Boer 1998a: 97). The Civil Liberties Committee was not, however, one of the strongest committees in the Parliament; resolutions were passed protesting at the Council's behaviour, but MEPs were more concerned to push forward their influence in areas within the first and second pillars.

In formal terms political accountability in this intergovernmental pillar was the responsibility of national parliaments, to which the ministers who formed the JHA Council should report. The secrecy with which JHA business was conducted, however, limited parliamentary access. Information on the status of proposals before working groups was hard to come by; scrutiny of documents available only in one or two working languages, which might be changed by consensus and rushed through by the presidency in a matter of weeks, was almost impossible. Those national parliamentary committees which attempted to follow JHA thus found it extremely difficult to influence the flow of policy. After a critical report from the House of Lords in 1993, the British government undertook to provide Parliament with documents at an appropriate stage in the formulation of policy. A further report in 1997 noted the difficulties that all national parliaments had faced in obtaining documents in time to comment before governments were collectively committed, and called for the six-week national scrutiny reserve which had just been won in the Treaty of Amsterdam to be applied immediately, without waiting for ratification (House of Lords 1997c). There have been occasional efforts to compare national practices in the six-monthly meetings of COSAC (Conférence des Organes Spécialisées aux Affaires Communautaires; the Conference of the Parliaments established by a declaration attached to the TEU, attended by members of national scrutiny committees); but a number of national parliaments were largely inactive in this field, and little progress had been made by 1999.

British and Swedish journalists, and the British-based NGO Statewatch, had some success in using EU procedures to gain access to JHA documents on public interest grounds. John Carvel, of the *Guardian*, challenged the Council's refusal to supply him with the minutes of meetings on youth employment, police, and immigration matters before the ECJ in May 1994; the ECJ ruled in his favour the following year. Tony Bunyan, of Statewatch, lodged five complaints of maladministration regarding access to Council JHA documents with the European Ombudsman, in November 1996. The Council first challenged the competence of the Ombudsman over third-pillar matters, but then in June 1997 accepted part of his case and released a number of documents. Pressure from these and from another pending ECJ case brought by a Swedish journalist contributed to member governments' acceptance in the Treaty of Amsterdam of a more open and ordered approach to the circulation of documents (den Boer 1998a: 100–3). In the years between Maastricht and Amsterdam, however, the difficulties of discovering what proposals were under discussion had discouraged the media from attempting to cover this expanding field of intergovernmental activity. The thinness both of parliamentary attention and of press reporting made for a widening gap between what governments were now undertaking in common and what their publics understood.

The 'double lock' on agreement and implementation provided by the need for unanimity among member governments and for ratification of binding agreements—conventions—by each member state constituted one of the most severe weaknesses within the third pillar (O'Keeffe 1995). The Dublin Convention 'determining the state responsible for examining applications for asylum lodged in one of the member states of the European Communities' was signed in June 1990, before Trevi had transmuted into the third pillar. National hesitations over the measures which it proposed to prevent 'asylum shopping' in successive states, and over the unbalanced burdens it might impose if the first state in which a refugee sought asylum was responsible for deciding and, if necessary, granting asylum, delayed ratification for over seven years; the Convention entered into force on 1 September 1997. The proposed European Police Office (Europol) was specifically mentioned in Article K.1.9 of the TEU; but it needed a further three years to agree on the Europol Convention, and another two more from signature to completion of national ratification in July 1997. The Convention thus entered into force in October 1998, and Europol finally became fully operational in July 1999. The Fraud Convention, which overlapped the first pillar competences of the European Commission and the responsibilities of national finance ministries and bank regulators as well as ministries and agencies more familiar to the third pillar, took two years to negotiate, with the French presidency of 1995 splitting off a separate protocol on corruption in the hope of attracting agreement and ratification on a more limited agenda. The External Frontiers Convention became snagged in the Spanish–British dispute over the status of Gibraltar, a British dependency claimed by Spain (with a history of smuggling between Spain and Morocco).

There has in consequence been a 'spiralling-down' effect on the kind of legal instruments produced, in order to circumvent the slow and heavy ratification process. A list of the JHA *acquis* which was drafted in May 1998 to provide an overview for the candidate countries showed that 130 legal instruments had been adopted, of which only nine were conventions, while a further six were protocols. The vast majority of instruments can best be characterized as 'soft law': rules of a non-binding legal nature, such as recommendations, resolutions, and conclusions, none of which have a formal legal basis in Title VI of the TEU (Monar 1997: 329). The degree to which third-pillar decisions bind member states has often been unclear to national parliaments and civil services (Müller-Graff 1996). Resolutions in the field of immigration and asylum, for instance, have had little effect on national policies. Changes in German asylum and immigration law in 1993, for example, considerably reduced the inflow to that country; statistics, however, indicated a consequent diversion of the flow to the Netherlands and to other member states. The French and British governments altered domestic laws on immigration during the 1990s with scarcely any reference to the European context. Citizenship questions, which touch on the acceptance and assimilation of refugees, remain sufficiently close to the core of national sovereignty to build in implicit resistance to acceptance of this developing European framework (Monar 1997: 326).

Even more strongly than in the first pillar, implementation of third-pillar decisions depends upon the administrations of member states. The third pillar thus suffers from an 'implementation deficit' (From and Stava 1993: 58), with delays and shortcomings in transposing intergovernmental decisions into national practice. Beyond the most technical aspects of police or customs cooperation, this requires coordination among ministries and executive agencies within national capitals and across the national territory. It also requires efficient executive agencies, willing to adapt national styles to fit within EU rules, without the sanctions the first pillar provides for the Commission or others to challenge its practices before the ECJ.

Progress within the Schengen group, without the constant institutional hesitations of the British and—until 1996—the Danes, ought in principle to have been easier. Schengen certainly suffered from comparable problems of secrecy and non-accountability. It operated through a network of working groups, with no government reporting in full to its national parliament, accumulating an intergovernmental *acquis* of conventions, decisions, and declarations. French mistrust of Benelux standards on pursuing criminals and controlling drugs, and French hesitations over the concessions of sovereignty involved, delayed the full implementation of the SIC for five years. The problem of mutual trust and mutual confidence in other states' implementation of controls at the external border, and of compensatory measures within the national territory, was, however, addressed, through the development of a system of inspection by multinational teams. This invasion of domestic sovereignty seems to have been accepted by the Italians because it was a condition of their acceptance into the frontier-free regime, and by the French and Germans because it resolved their doubts about the quality of controls at Italy's extensive maritime border.

There was no provision in Title VI for monitoring implementation. An innovative mechanism of transgovernmental monitoring is, however, emerging, modelled on previous practice among customs agencies and on the system of mutual inspection already developed within Schengen. A joint action adopted in December 1997 established 'a mechanism for peer evaluation of the application and implementation at national level of Union and other international acts . . . in the fight against organized crime' (97/827/JHA: Article 1.1). It proposed teams of three 'experts', selected from member states other than that being inspected, to conduct at least five inspections a year. A further joint action in June 1998 (98/427/JHA) extended this mechanism to judicial cooperation, with mutual evaluation of 'good practice in mutual legal assistance in criminal matters'. Teams were operating in both of these areas by 1999. Officials involved in this system of peer review claimed it as an important part of the evolving culture and style of JHA.

Nevertheless, after five years of operation, the third pillar by the time of the 1996–7 intergovernmental review had developed an extensive network not only of meetings but also of instruments and institutions. Europol was taking shape, even though the Europol Convention had not yet been ratified by all member states. The Customs Information System was being computerized, to be managed by the Commission with respect to both its first-pillar and third-pillar usage. Two other databases, for Europol and for Eurodac (this latter similarly to be managed by the Commission), were under development. The SIS was already up and running, with 14 million entries relating to banned entrants to the 'Schengen Area', and a parallel database on stolen property and related cross-border crime.

External relations had also become a major preoccupation. EU governments responded to American requests for closer cooperation in anti-terrorism and in managing refugee flows through development of a parallel network under the umbrella of G7–8. Relations with the EU applicants from east-central Europe included substantial negotiations on border controls, and assistance with police and judicial training. Here too the Americans were an active external partner (and competitor), establishing a police training academy in Budapest and paying particular attention to the overlap between organized crime, drug-trafficking, money-laundering, and people-smuggling. Neither on transatlantic relations nor on eastern Europe, however, was cross-pillar coordination strong (see Chapter 16). It was to be expected that the 1996–7 IGC would wish to reconsider the compromises struck at Maastricht, covering this increasingly important field.

From Amsterdam to Tampere

Title VI had contained no reference to a further review of the framework of the third pillar within a limited timescale, unlike the explicit commitment to review the second pillar in 1996 contained in Article J.4.6. Delays in ratifying the TEU, in the wake of the Danish and French referenda, a constitutional challenge in Germany, and parliamentary resistance in the UK, meant that the Maastricht Treaty had formally been in operation for less than two years when the Westendorp Reflection Group convened to discuss priorities for the next IGC agenda. One of the eight areas the Spanish presidency had identified for the group to consider was development of cooperation in JHA. This emerged in the group's report to the Madrid European Council in December 1995 as one aspect of the broader theme of 'making Europe more relevant for its citizens' (McDonagh 1998; Monar 1997). The link the Reflection Group (1995a) made (in paras. 24–9) between 'serving the citizens' interests' and the claimed 'demand on the part of the public for greater security', extending to 'the citizens calling for better handling of the challenge posed to the Union by the growing migratory pressures' set out the rationale for the warm phraseology written into the Treaty, of 'establishing an area of freedom, security and justice'. The Council of Ministers' report (Council of the European Union 1995a) to Madrid on 'the functioning of the Treaty on European Union' noted, however, that 'extremely limited use has been made of the instruments provided for in Title VI'; it also noted that 'the juxtaposition of a large number of procedures sometimes makes it difficult for the Union to be understood by the outside world'.

It says much about the indirection and drift of EU policy-making, including at the strategic and constitutional level, that few governments anticipated that the 1996–7 IGC might lead to significant changes in the framework of the third pillar. Only the Dutch and German governments were actively canvassing such changes. Constitutional and rhetorical preferences rehearsed during the 1991 IGC were nevertheless repeated in the preparatory papers circulated by member governments. The Dutch, Belgian, Luxembourg, German, French, Italian, Portuguese, and Austrian governments called for external frontier issues to be transferred from the third pillar into the regular Community structure: 'communitarization', in the jargon of Brussels negotiators. This implied moving away from the three-pillar structure agreed at Maastricht towards the integrated Community envisaged in the 1991 Dutch presidency draft treaty. The Austrian government, preparing for its first IGC, adopted the German position, proposing that matters relating to crime, terrorism, and drug-trafficking 'should be dealt with on the basis of supranational coordination of legal and police authorities'. The UK government, on the contrary, opposed any such transfer; while the French government was in favour of partial communitarization, but considered that police cooperation should remain intergovernmental. Six member governments suggested that the incorporation of the Schengen system into the EU proper should be on the agenda: the three Benelux countries, Italy, Spain, and Austria (B. Smith 1999).

The Treaty which emerged at Amsterdam eighteen months later nevertheless contained substantial changes to the framework for JHA, more substantial than for CFSP. A new Title IV of the TEC transferred migration and other related policies to the first pillar. Police cooperation and judicial cooperation in criminal matters are detailed in a revised and lengthened Title VI (see Box 18.2). The greatest surprise was the incorporation of the Schengen conventions and *acquis* into the Treaty. It had not been actively under negotiation during the Italian and Irish presidencies in 1996; Ireland was not a member of Schengen, and the Irish delegation had failed, in spite of several requests, to obtain a copy of the *acquis*. The Dutch presidency in the first semester of 1997, however, drove this, together with the other changes to the framework of JHA, through the final stages of the IGC, succeeding in part because of internal divisions in both the French and German positions, and in particular because of French

Box 18.2 Changes to justice and home affairs in the Treaty of Amsterdam

New Title IV, Articles 61–9 of the revised and renumbered TEC

■ registers the transfer of 'visas, asylum, immigration and other policies related to free movement of persons' from the third to the first pillar (Article 61)

■ 'flanking measures' (Articles 62–3) to compensate for free movement within EU, including common procedures for controls on persons at the EU's external borders, common rules on visas for third-country nationals, common measures on the reception and treatment of asylum-seekers and on the 'temporary protection' of refugees, and similar common rules on immigration policy. The target for adoption of these common policies is set for five years after the entry into force of the ToA

■ 'judicial cooperation in civil matters having cross-border implications' also transferred to the Community proper (but not judicial cooperation in criminal matters)

■ a series of reservations, largely at French insistence, limiting the Commission's powers of initiative, offering the European Parliament only 'consultation' during the five-year transitional period, and setting strict limits to rights of reference to the ECJ (Articles 64, 67–8)

■ different opt-outs for Denmark (wishing to be inside the free movement area, but formally under an intergovernmental regime), the UK, and Ireland (maintaining their opt-out from the lifting of internal frontier controls) (Article 69)

Revised Title VI (TEU), renumbered as Articles 29–42

■ Articles 29–34 provide more detail on 'common action' in police cooperation and judicial cooperation in criminal matters, including references to 'operational cooperation' among law enforcement agencies, and collection and storage of data. Convoluted language on Europol reflects unresolved dispute between German government, seeking an operational agency, and British and French, resisting

■ Articles 35–9 reflect parallel unresolved dispute on the involvement of the EU institutions (Commission, Parliament, ECJ) in this field; lengthy section on ECJ reflects sensitivity of extending cooperation in legal administration and law enforcement without providing for judicial review

■ Article 40 extends provision for 'closer cooperation' among smaller groups of member states, and registers the integration of the Schengen *acquis* 'into the framework of the European Union' (set out in more detail in an attached protocol)

distractions during their election campaign and unexpected change of government (B. Smith 1999: 173–213). The influence of the presidency, when other governments were undecided about their national preferences, was striking. When the Council Secretariat, as guardian of continuity between presidencies, refused to incorporate the full Dutch proposals on Schengen into the negotiating text, the Dutch delegation broke with the normal drafting procedures and inserted its own paper as the presidency draft (B. Smith 1999: 268).

Distracted heads of government—two of them, from France and the UK, newly in office—emerged from the Amsterdam endgame without a clear understanding of what they had signed. There was indeed no definitive or agreed text of the Schengen *acquis*, as gradually emerged from lengthy official negotiations over the next eighteen months; what there was consisted, in addition to the conventions and accession agreements, of an uncatalogued miscellany of decisions and agreed working practices—disjointed incrementalism *par excellence*. The member states had thus

Figure 18.2 Decision-making on justice and home affairs after Amsterdam

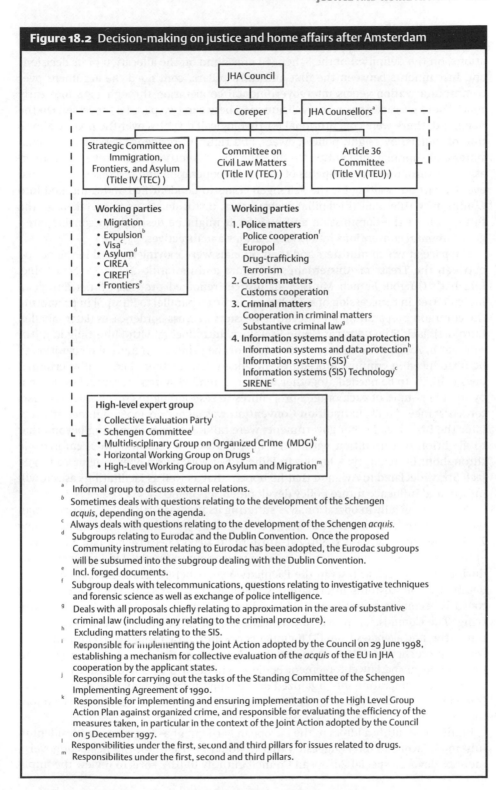

a   Informal group to discuss external relations.
b   Sometimes deals with questions relating to the development of the Schengen *acquis*, depending on the agenda.
c   Always deals with questions relating to the development of the Schengen *acquis*.
d   Subgroups relating to Eurodac and the Dublin Convention. Once the proposed Community instrument relating to Eurodac has been adopted, the Eurodac subgroups will be subsumed into the subgroup dealing with the Dublin Convention.
e   Incl. forged documents.
f   Subgroup deals with telecommunications, questions relating to investigative techniques and forensic science as well as exchange of police intelligence.
g   Deals with all proposals chiefly relating to approximation in the area of substantive criminal law (including any relating to the criminal procedure).
h   Excluding matters relating to the SIS.
i   Responsible for implementing the Joint Action adopted by the Council on 29 June 1998, establishing a mechanism for collective evaluation of the *acquis* of the EU in JHA cooperation by the applicant states.
j   Responsible for carrying out the tasks of the Standing Committee of the Schengen Implementing Agreement of 1990.
k   Responsible for implementing and ensuring implementation of the High Level Group Action Plan against organized crime, and responsible for evaluating the efficiency of the measures taken, in particular in the context of the Joint Action adopted by the Council on 5 December 1997.
l   Responsibilities under the first, second and third pillars for issues related to drugs.
m   Responsibilites under the first, second and third pillars.

signed, and ratified, a treaty without having agreed the text of one of its most
sovereignty-sensitive subordinate documents (House of Lords 1998b). Post-IGC negotiations, on the definition of the Schengen *acquis* and on the allocation of its decisions
and instruments between the first and third pillars, continued the argument over
communitarization versus intergovernmental cooperation through 1998 into early
1999. There was an extraordinary disjunction between two parallel processes. On the
one hand, there were constitutional (or theological) disputes over the precise allocation of judicial oversight, police powers, and rights of residence between sovereign
states and supranational entity. On the other hand, inertial forces drove JHA cooperation forward, under the impetus of practical cooperation and responses to external
events, without waiting for the Schengen *acquis* to be identified and translated into
Community rules and third-pillar instruments, or for decisions to be taken on the
future role of the Commission and how far it might be desirable to convert intergovernmental conventions into EC regulations and directives.

The pace at which ministers and their officials were moving forward in the period
between the Treaty of Amsterdam's signature and its ratification was remarkable.
Élizabeth Guigou, French Minister of Justice, refloated proposals for a European
Judicial Area in a succession of speeches, including a parallel to Europol in promoting
the common preparation of prosecuting dossiers in cross-border cases (later labelled
Eurojust). Jack Straw, British Home Secretary, introducing with Mme Guigou a JHA
seminar in Avignon in October 1998, called for the principle of mutual recognition to
be introduced in criminal procedures; he added that 'further alignment of criminal
laws is likely to be needed', together with an extended system of mutual evaluation
by member states of each other's procedures in responding to cross-border requests
for assistance. An EU Extradition Convention was signed in 1996; eighteen months
later the British and other governments were talking openly of moving beyond that
to abolition of extradition within the EU in favour of 'Eurowarrants' enforceable
throughout EU territory. A European Judicial Network began operating in mid-1998;
Jack Straw declared in Avignon that he hoped 'that as well as facilitating cases it will
inform and influence future policy development in the EU'.

The SIS, now fully in operation, was suffering its first scandals: a Belgian policeman
with access to its terminals was accused of selling information to criminals; a New
Zealand woman was denied entry at Amsterdam airport because her name had been
entered in the Schengen system as a Greenpeace activist involved in demonstrations
during French nuclear tests in the Pacific two years before. Three further computer
databases (the Customs Information System, Europol, and Eurodac) were moving
towards becoming operational. Activities in central and eastern Europe were intensifying. The Commission provided financial support for 'twinning' between national
ministries and agencies from EU member states and those in applicant countries, and
sent a succession of intrusive missions and questionnaires to monitor progress in
bringing legal and law enforcement bodies up to defined EU standards. Action plans
on European migration, on organized crime, and on implementation of the area of
freedom, security, and justice were coming up to ministers and heads of government
for approval.

In his six-monthly address to the European Parliament as Commission President in
July 1998, Jacques Santer suggested that it would be useful for the heads of government to devote a special European Council entirely to JHA, so as to review the impli-

> **Box 18.3** People-smuggling
>
> 'People-smuggling' became one of the major preoccupations of EU law enforcement agencies in the late 1990s. The tightening of border controls and rules on asylum-seekers in the early 1990s, together with the stabilization of the immediate post-cold war flow of dissidents and disaffected minorities, had contributed to a fall in the number of asylum-seekers in 1993–5. Worsening conditions within Bosnia, and the collapse of law and order in Albania, then led to a further surge of European refugees into Austria, Italy, Greece, and Germany. Continuing civil wars in Africa, and the desperate drive of aspirant poor people (from North Africa, South Asia, even China) to gain access to the rich world, fed the extra-European flow. Deepening resistance to further immigration from within the EU, and consequent tightening of border controls and of conditions for entry, created an illegal market to supply this pent-up demand, smuggling desperate people across the EU's eastern border in containers and trucks, and across its Mediterranean border in fast boats: illegal immigration, out of which organized groups were making substantial profits.
>
> Part of the rationale for the Barcelona Plan for an integrated Mediterranean strategy, agreed under the Spanish presidency in 1995, was that substantial financial assistance and technical advice would be needed to create the conditions under which young people around the Mediterranean's southern coasts would prosper at home rather than seek to move into the EU. Recognition of the immense difficulties of stemming such pressures has contributed to some of the most ambitious items on the agenda for the 1999 Tampere European Council, committing EU members to an active foreign and development policy in order to prevent forced migration following from state collapse, or economic or ecological crisis.

cations of the Treaty of Amsterdam and other developments now under way. The Spanish Prime Minister took up the idea at the informal European Council in Pörtschach in October 1998; formal acceptance of this was registered in the communiqué of the December Vienna European Council.[2] The Finnish government, just beginning to prepare for its first presidency in the second half of 1999, seized on the proposal. It sent round a joint prime-ministerial letter (with its German predecessor) in April 1999, and followed this up with a ministerial tour of capitals in May. This active approach generated a flow of preparatory speeches and papers, for an agenda broadly divided into immigration and asylum questions, cooperation against organized crime, and measures connected to the proposed European judicial area, for a meeting in Tampere in mid-October 1999. Even British ministers were talking ambitiously, in the approach to this European Council, of a work programme for JHA comparable to the '1992' single market programme which had driven the pace of European integration throughout the late 1980s. One Finnish diplomat, asked what the underlying purpose of the Tampere Summit was, more cynically replied that it was intended 'to make sure that our heads of government at last understand what they signed up to at Amsterdam'.

The Tampere Communiqué listed a series of 'milestones' on the road towards 'a Union of Freedom, Security and Justice', including measures on the 'management of migration flows', mutual recognition of judicial decisions, better access to justice across the EU, and closer cooperation against crime, and also directives against racism, xenophobia and other forms of discrimination, to implement Article 13 of the

ToA. Over 200 measures were implied by the commitments agreed, a work programme comparable in scale to the single market programme. The Tampere Council also set up a group drawn from governments, national parliaments, the EP and the Commission, to draft an EU Charter of Fundamental Rights.

Conclusions

JHA has thus gradually moved from the outer fringes of European integration towards the centre, more than two decades since the start of Trevi. Movement in this field has come from intergovernmental integration, but with far-reaching scope: against all the conventional wisdom of neofunctionalist theories, yet driven by functionalist imperatives. This is a policy sector in which the Commission has never taken the lead, nor ever played a very active role. Member governments have rarely held coherent positions across different ministries and agencies. Successive presidencies have provided leadership, with the Council Secretariat providing continuity. National governments have responded to the consequences of regional integration for internal order and domestic law not as rational and strategic actors and as defenders of national sovereignty, but as incremental policy-makers. Interior ministries, judicial authorities, and law enforcement agencies have begun to combine efforts and share expertise in what had previously been regarded as a core area of national sovereignty, in a way that has insulated their collective decisions from parliamentary and judicial review at both national and EU levels. The outcome, as of 1999, in some ways resembles the encapsulated world of agricultural policy of thirty years before. Central coordination by prime ministers' offices of developments in this sector appear to be weak. Agencies operate with a good deal of autonomy, within the overall framework set by the transgovernmental network of interior and justice ministries.

The Treaty of Amsterdam, with all its inbuilt reservations and five-year delays, takes JHA further towards full integration with Community institutions. It gives the Commission, the EP, and the ECJ some access, with the expectation of increased access in the future. Some of the items agreed at Tampere would take the EU's judicial system and mechanisms for law enforcement some way towards an effectively federal structure. Political leaders in London, Paris, Copenhagen, and other national capitals, and also within such subordinate levels of government as the German *Länder*, resist that conclusion. The underlying tensions which have marked this field since the beginning of European cooperation thus remain. But so do the dynamics of increasing cross-border interaction which have driven closer cooperation so far.

Notes

1 The Netherlands, of course, does not have a direct frontier with the ex-socialist countries; but refugees from there (as also Kurds from Turkey and Iraq) spilled over its open frontier from Germany in larger numbers than into France or Belgium.

2 José Maria Aznar, the Spanish Prime Minister, had been asked to introduce the discussion of JHA at this informal European Council; Spanish officials reportedly picked up Jacques Santer's proposal and put it into his briefing notes while searching for innovative suggestions to make. The comment of a British official on this is worth recording, as illustrative of the disjointed, half-accidental character of European decision-making: 'this demonstrates the dangers of informal European Councils. Blair was asked to introduce the discussion on CFSP, and launches a defence initiative; Aznar was asked to introduce on JHA, and lands us all with Tampere.'

Further reading

On the development of the third pillar, see Monar and Morgan (1994), and Bieber and Monar (1995). Anderson *et al.* (1995) describes the development of police cooperation; Barrett *et al.* (1997) also covers judicial cooperation; Guild (1999) focuses on migration. Several chapters in Monar and Wessels (forthcoming) discuss the changes to JHA in the Treaty of Amsterdam. Monar (forthcoming) provides an overview of the field. Successive reports from the House of Lords European Communities Committee, from 1997 to 1999, provide further detail on recent developments.

Anderson, M., den Boer, M., Cullen, P., Gilmore, W. C., Raab, C. D., and Walker, N. (1995), *Policing the European Union. Theory, Law and Practice* (Oxford: Clarendon Press).

Barrett, G. (1997) (ed.), *Justice Cooperation in the European Union* (Dublin: Institute of European Affairs).

Bieber, R., and Monar, J. (1995) (eds.), *Justice and Home Affairs in the European Union: The Development of the Third Pillar* (Brussels: European University Press).

Guild, E. (1999) (ed.), *The Legal Framework and Social Consequences of Free Movement in the EU* (The Hague: Kluwer).

Monar, J. (forthcoming), *Justice and Home Affairs in the European Union* (London: Macmillan).

—— and Morgan, R. (1994) (eds.), *The Third Pillar of the European Union: Cooperation in the Field of Justice and Home Affairs* (Brussels: European University Press).

—— and Wessels, W. (forthcoming) (eds.), *The Treaty of Amsterdam: Challenges and Opportunities for the European Union* (London: Pinter).

Part III

Conclusions

Chapter 19
Collective Governance
The EU political process

William Wallace

Contents

Summary

Policy-making within the European Union (EU) is shaped by rules and procedures which have evolved with successive modifications and extensions over more than forty years. There is no single pattern of policy-making; the different demands of distinctive issue areas, the different actors and institutions drawn in, make for diversity. The flow of policy, from initial proposals through more precise definition, consultation, and negotiation, to final agreement, ratification, and implementation, cannot easily be divided into technical preparations and strategic decisions. Commitments in principle alter as negotiators discover their implications, or as working groups produce detailed plans. Outcomes are rarely entirely anticipated by those who strike strategic bargains; EU policy-making is a process of mutual learning, resting on mutual trust, in which ideas as well as interests shape the search for consensus. Policy-making in the 1990s has been marked by governmental entrepreneurship more than by Commission leadership and the demands of transnational economic interests. But it is too soon to identify this as a long-term trend, rather than a reflection of the emphasis in EU policy development on foreign policy, defence, and public order. European policy-making should be situated within the broader context of global multilateralism. The development of common

European policies partly responds to external challenges, and the perception of European élites that common approaches to global negotiations maximize their ability to promote their interests and protect their values.

The established pattern

The EU now has a well-established political process. Its core institutions, designed over forty years ago, have developed extensive procedural rules and standard operating procedures, embedded in successive revisions of the treaties—the EU's proto-constitution. An extended network of committees links the Brussels institutions to those of the member states. The rules and rituals which form all stable patterns of policy-making are firmly entrenched within the EU, shaping the behaviour of ministers and officials, judges and parliamentarians, lobbyists and journalists. The familiar annual cycle of European Councils, Councils of Ministers, and subordinate committees interacts with the six-monthly cycle of changing presidencies and the longer, five-year terms of office of European parliamentarians and the college of Commissioners. Even the 'history-making' Intergovernmental Conferences (IGCs) are becoming institutionalized. The EU in 2000 is moving towards the fourth IGC in fifteen years, following procedures which have grown out of negotiating the Single European Act (SEA), the Maastricht Treaty on European Union (TEU), and the Treaty of Amsterdam (ToA). As successive chapters in this volume have emphasized, the density and intensity of interactions among many thousands of actors marks the EU out from any other intergovernmental policy-making system or international regime. The EU dimension of policy has become part of the daily work of national officials, lobbyists, ministers, even heads of government.

The case-studies above have illustrated the diversity of policy-making patterns in different domains. The European Court of Justice (ECJ), for example, is a key actor in competition policy, exerts significant influence in social policy and the single market, and has decided a large number of cases in fisheries policy; but it has played no significant role in economic and monetary union (EMU) so far, and is so far virtually excluded from common foreign and security policy (CFSP) and justice and home affairs (JHA). The European Parliament (EP) exerts considerable authority over the allocation and implementation of the EU budget, and has intervened actively in the process of formulating many legislative decisions, including the controversial directives on biotechnology; but it has far less influence—and has been far less active—in the shaping of other policies, especially those dealing with external relations, such as policy towards the central and east European countries (CEECs) or towards developing countries. Expert committees are central to the policy process in some fields, organized interests in others.

There is thus no single pattern of policy-making in the EU. Different modes of policy-making, as Chapter 1 argues, have emerged in different policy domains. Negotiation and implementation of the structural funds, for example, bring the Commission into direct relations with sub-national authorities in ways that lend credence to a multi-level governance approach—though David Allen argues in Chapter 9 that member governments retain control of the political bargains which set the framework for the distribution of funds. Budgetary packages and IGCs, characterized by more explicitly political negotiations among member governments, give comfort to those who see the EU as an international regime within which rational state actors bargain on the basis of long-term state preferences. The evolution of JHA demonstrates an intensity of interaction among agencies of member states, with Community institutions only marginally involved, which strongly supports an emphasis on transgovernmentalism.

Many years ago Donald Puchala compared contending theories of European integration to the rationalizations of blind men who had felt their way around different parts of an elephant (Puchala 1972). Today's observers, provided with studies of a wide range of EU negotiations and policy domains, need not be so blind. There is no case for insisting that only one interpretation of EU policy-making can be correct, any more than one can squeeze the diverse patterns of American politics—or German, or Italian—into the iron framework of a single model.

The flow of policy

A number of commentators—including the editors of this volume—have attempted to categorize EU policy-making according to levels of politicization, from constituent (or history-making) decisions to redistributive bargains, distributive politics, and regulatory adjudication (W. Wallace 1983*b*, 1996; J. Peterson 1995*a*). Each of these levels, we argued, were characterized by distinctive actors and distinctive patterns of policy-making. As the chapters in this edition have, however, shown, these categories overlap and spill into each other. Both the Maastricht and Amsterdam grand bargains postponed a number of the most contentious issues on the table. One aspect of IGC treaty revision has become the incorporation into the constitutional framework of practices which have developed out of the flow of policy and of responses to exogenous events in the preceding years. This has been particularly evident in the second and third pillars, but has also been evident in social policy and in other areas of court-led integration.

The extension of EU regulation over areas in which state ownership (and state patronage) had been the norm—airlines, telecommunications, electricity supply—has upset long-standing corporatist networks, provoking strong resistance from national governments and necessitating delicate political manœuvring by the Commission. Narrow sectors of regulatory and distributive politics, where limited economic interests are at stake—the classic examples in this volume are fisheries and bananas—blow up into political confrontations which preoccupy ministers at successive Council meetings, and heads of government in European Councils. Bovine spongiform encephalitis (BSE) almost brought EU business to a halt. Environmental issues, food safety, animal welfare, hunting, issues where public passions may disrupt rational policy-making, can erupt from regulatory committees to preoccupy heads of government at European Councils—even threatening to push discussion of more strategic issues off the agenda.

The flow of policy is shaped by established procedures and institutional frameworks. The difficult processes of building consensus and reaching agreement on frameworks for policy among multiple governments, agencies, and outside interests has built in a high degree of inertia, evident in frequently repeated commitment to the *acquis*. The inertia of EU policy-making is classically illustrated by the difficulties which actors outside the established framework of agricultural policy-making and policy management have experienced in attempting to limit expenditure and intro-duce reform. The ability of successive British governments to defend the budget rebate against attempts to reopen the Fontainebleau package, over fifteen years, also illustrates how resistant entrenched agreements are to renegotiation. The German and Dutch governments found it easier to imitate the British by asking for the rebate principle to be extended, as Chapter 8 shows, than to call into question the broader budget *acquis*.

More than this, the case-studies in this volume provide support for those who argue that institutions matter, and that governing ideas matter, in shaping agendas and formulating preferences (Pierson 1996*b*; Bulmer 1994*a*). Governments hesitate to reopen agreed policies or to question the established *acquis*, where it does not suit their immediate interests, because they have embedded interests in other policy fields, and because they are pursuing other interests through parallel negotiations which they hesitate to put at risk. But they also *define* their preferences within the context of the continuous multilateral processes which constitute the EU collective governance system: they learn from each other, they develop a common discourse, and they explore the potential outlines of consensus. Given their commitment to the continuation of the system, actors internalize its constraints. The calendar of meet-ings does not allow for dispassionate calculation of state preferences in the intervals between major multilateral negotiations. Member governments are engaged in a continuous multilateral and bilateral dialogue, at all levels from heads of government to junior officials, punctuated by formal negotiations and mediated through the Commission and other EU institutions. Proposals are floated, criticized by interested organizations and parliamentarians, modified, examined in detail, before final adop-tion. Concepts—Community preference, solidarity, subsidiarity, flexibility, con-vergence, stabilization, sustainability—interact with perceived interests in shaping acceptable options for agreement.[1]

Thus we agree with Laura Cram that 'day-to-day events in the policy-making pro-cess must be understood as a fundamental aspect of the process of European integra-tion, altering the environment in which major decisions are taken and even the very perceptions which actors, such as national governments, hold of their own interests' (Cram 1997: 6). There *are*, on occasion, major turning-points at which heads of gov-ernment set out new priorities in the context of transformed external circumstances or reconsidered state preferences. But even here, as Chapter 6 makes clear, the flow of policy development alters the parameters of decision. Within the framework of assumptions provided by successful operation of the European Monetary System (EMS) and of substantial progress with the single market programme, the Hanover European Council in 1988 took the contingent decision to establish a committee to consider what detailed proposals for EMU might form the basis for agreement. Achievement of a unanimous report by the Delors Committee, including the signa-tures of the heads of the UK and German central banks, redefined the agenda for decision.

It was, nevertheless, possible for the British Prime Minister to resist the developing consensus, as Mrs Thatcher did. But the costs of resistance had been raised substantially, and her ability to carry her own ministers with her gravely weakened. Heads of government can maintain the coherence of their governments' position only if they are able to carry with them the support of the many others who also participate in this intensive transgovernmental process. National policies are themselves formulated partly through consultation with other governments and with EU institutions, as well as through discussions with domestic interests similarly exploring the boundaries of possible EU policy changes through transnational networks. The feedback through this continuous dialogue modifies the framework for national policy debate, introducing or redefining concepts which shape the discourse. Those who resist an emerging group consensus, as British government representatives did on a range of issues in the 1980s and early 1990s, exclude themselves from the group. Beyond a certain point, it became easier to allow the British to opt out than to attempt to accommodate their divergent views, as other EU member governments responded on EMU and on social policy in the TEU.

The significance of the extensive substructure of Council and Commission committees and working groups which characterizes the EU system lies largely in the role they play in transmitting detailed information and ideas, and transforming disparate working assumptions into a framework for common policy (van Schendelen 1998). The Commission uses consultative groups to learn about the diversity of national working practices and the areas of potential common ground, as well as to coopt national officials into a collective endeavour. Heads of government depend upon the network of committees and working groups which sustains the flow of policy from one European Council to another to convert agreements in principle into detailed and practicable proposals.

Identifying the policy entrepreneur in this process of mutual learning is not as easy as neofunctionalists (who saw the Commission as defining the agenda, socializing other participants into recognizing that their interests might better be served through common action on the basis of what the Commission proposed) or as inter-governmentalists (who see heads of governments as agenda-setters, EU institutions as agents for these principal actors) have suggested (E. B. Haas 1958; Lindberg 1963; Moravcsik 1998). The chapters in this volume have shown that policy initiatives emerge from many different sources, often from more than one. Commission initiatives may be taken up by particular member governments, just as presidency proposals may be modified and developed by the Commission through extensive consultation with affected interests and national agencies. Scholars have long argued (as Chapter 4 notes) over whether the single market initiative was launched by the Commission, by key national governments, or by organized business interests. The successful launch of the initiative, however, reflected the convergent ideas of these different policy entrepreneurs, coming together to agree in principle, to define and then to support an ambitious programme.

It follows from this that policy outcomes are not necessarily—and never entirely—the product of deliberate bargains among strategically oriented rational actors. Deliberations move through too many fora, with too many players involved, for coherence to be maintained by any single political leader throughout the policy process. Heads of government must turn their attention to other issues as negotiations proceed, while those around them follow the flow of papers and the succession of proposals and counter-proposals. The outcome of multilateral negotiation is difficult to predict at the outset, partly because the definition of the issue changes as negotiations proceed, as unexpected aspects emerge, and as external actors intervene. No EU government had a clear and settled preference as to the detailed outcome of negotiations with the former socialist states after the Berlin Wall came down, as Chapter 16 shows; most were uncertain as to whether they should be strategically committed to enlargement. Similarly, negotiations with post-apartheid South Africa were a process of learning, in which the intended objective altered as the negotiations moved forward. Heads of government may hope to strike strategic bargains within the confines of a single conference; but the devil is in the detail, and the bargains struck subtly alter as post-negotiations clarify what has been broadly agreed. Margaret Thatcher discovered that the bargain she thought she had struck in the SEA carried implications of commitment to further integration that she had not intended; the French government's response in the Schengen Agreement to immediate problems on the Franco-German border committed it far more to the integration of domestic policing and migration policy than it had appreciated at the time. Policies flow, through European Councils and through day-to-day discussions; political leaders may succeed in diverting or redirecting the flow, but rarely manage entirely to control the process.

A macropolitical perspective on EU policy-making offers a broad landscape of strategic decisions, agreed among political leaders. A micropolitical perspective, in contrast, offers a crowded and confused picture of multiple activities: a Breughel, rather than a Monet. In North-South relations and in biotechnology, as Chapters 15 and 12 show, fragmented networks, which link the Commission's Directorates-General to functional agencies within national governments and to interested groups, make for a struggle even to define a coherent agenda. Functionalists *prefer* fragmented networks, developing common interests within limited fields; intergovernmentalists have faith that heads of government nevertheless manage to impose order and priority on the mass of activity below. The EU political process is particularly fragmented. The weakness of its central institutions, its dependence on Councils and committees constituted largely by actors whose primary focus and commitments lie outside the EU process, compound the complexity which follows from the wide range of its policy domains. European Councils can get through their agendas only by leaving decisions on most issues to others, in technical committees or specialist Councils of Ministers. Again, however, one should not exaggerate the uniqueness of the EU. Modern government is highly complex, and highly technical; national governments also struggle to distinguish between strategic issues for political decision and meso- or micropolitical questions which can safely be left to individual ministers or to officials to decide. Nor do national political leaders and their advisers always succeed in identifying potentially explosive political issues within the daily flow of papers with which they deal, nor to anticipate the long-term implications of agreements in principle or declarations of intent. Politics is politics, at whatever level.

Ideas and identities

The role of ideas in influencing the evolution of policy comes across in almost every chapter in this volume. Governing ideas—the conventional wisdom, the implicit ideologies of practical policy-makers—set limits to conceivable or acceptable policy

COLLECTIVE GOVERNANCE **529**

options. As governing ideas change, so new ways of formulating policy open up. The shift from a dominant Keynesian economic consensus towards monetarism in the late 1970s and 1980s, as Tsoukalis makes clear in Chapter 6, narrowed the debate on EMU, enabling policy-makers to focus on monetary policy without taking broader macroeconomic and fiscal implications into consideration. Divergent national assumptions about social policy and the future of the welfare state inhibited the formulation of EU-level rules in this field, leaving to the ECJ the task of adjudicating on difficult cases, stepping in where member governments had feared to tread. When new issue areas emerge, as with the environment or biotechnology, the pre-negotiation phase focuses on how best to define the issue: whether in terms of pre-dominantly economic interests, or of social concerns, or of scientific expertise.

European policies are constructed and reconstructed through the moving consensus which limits acceptable intellectual approaches to political problems. This, we note, differs from the way in which national policies are constructed and reconstructed only in the unfocused character of the broader political debate at the political level. Scharpf's lament of 'the lack of Europe-wide policy discourses', however, overstates the weakness of political intellectual exchanges at European level (Scharpf 1999: 187). Compared to the focus which national parliaments, parties, and media provide for domestic political debate, the Europe-wide discourse is weak. But exchanges among élites, conducted through the many élite networks which link expert groups and influentials within European societies, do shape and reshape policy assumptions. McGowan in Chapter 5 notes the importance of the epistemic community of economists and lawyers which links the separate national discourses on competition policy. Meetings between political leaders from the same political families before European Council meetings, and other exchanges among political leaders and parties, search—often with limited success—for shared attitudes and campaigning themes (Hix and Lord 1997). There were elements of an EU-wide debate over reshaping social democracy at the end of the 1990s, with the British 'Third Way' and the German 'Neue Mitte' meeting with mixed responses from social democrats in France and the Nordic countries. So transnational policy discourses on such underlying issues as the relationship between the state and the market, and the appropriate boundaries between the public and the private sector, are emerging.

Almost all actors in the EU policy process have multiple identities, and may play multiple roles (J. Peterson and Bomberg 1999: 234–5). Neither Commissioners nor Commission officials entirely abandon their national links and loyalties in making policy, as our discussions of agriculture, of fisheries, and of trade in particular make clear. Most Commissioners are recruited from national governments, and many return after their term of office to national political life. National political leaders take their turns in the Council presidency, and play their EU-wide representative and policy roles in most respects conscientiously; they value the national prestige which they gain from being seen to act successfully on a wider stage. Ambitious national officials work for periods in Brussels, in Commissioners' *cabinets*, in Commission services, or in their governments' permanent representations, learning to balance national perspectives with institutional roles. Outside experts and interest groups leaders see themselves as players on both national and European stages—and sometimes on a wider transatlantic or global stage as well.[2] It would be a caricature of this intricate policy process to counterpose national actors and supranational entrepreneurs as separate élites, promoting opposed interests. The EU system, through the intensive interactions of transnational and transgovernmental networks which now characterize it, has become a collective government, resting on over-lapping élites.

Government without statehood

The EU is a collective political system, not an intergovernmental regime. Almost all European scholars start from this assumption (Majone 1996*b*; Taylor 1996; Rometsch and Wessels 1996; Cram 1997; Scharpf 1999; J. Peterson and Bomberg 1999). Some international relations scholars, however, remain 'trapped in the supranational–intergovernmental dichotomy', insisting that the EU must conform to one overall conceptual model or another of transactions among states (Branch and Øhrgaard 1999). Moravcsik (1999: 494–501) and Mattli (1999) both place the EU in the same category as the North American Free Trade Area (NAFTA) and the Asia–Pacific Economic Council (APEC) as examples of complex international regimes. Comparison of NAFTA and the EU, however, demonstrates how far the dispute settlement procedures of NAFTA are from the federal jurisdiction of European law, the complex balance of multilateral negotiation and coalition-building within the fifteen-member EU from the US-dominated procedures of NAFTA. The density of transnational and transgovernmental networks, the parallel emergence of an extensive network of organized economic and political interests at the EU level, the mutual penetration of law, regulation, even political campaigning deep into what political scientists had long characterized as the core of domestic politics, define a level of politics and of governance which is most straightforwardly described as a political system.

Policy-making within a stable system of governance, outside the framework of the state, challenges the classical dichotomy between domestic politics within sovereign states, and international relations among states. These were, however, two exclusive ideal types, which never entirely corresponded to the intermediate examples of untidy reality (W. Wallace 1994*b*). The monolithic centralization of republican France, 100 years ago, differed from the Prussian-dominated, but semi-federal, German Reich; both of these differed from the loosely integrated Italian state. Austria–Hungary, with its dual structure and its sixteen official languages, offered a still looser model. The United States, until the New Deal and the second world war still a loose federation within which political power and financial clout in crucial domains rested with the component states, takes us still further away from the ideal type of the monolithic sovereign state. Contemporary Canada and Australia offer examples of relatively loose federations, within which the component states strike inter-governmental bargains and haggle over redistributive package deals. Within the EU, as the case-studies in this volume have made clear, authority, political accountability, budgetary capacity, and administrative capability all remain primarily with the component states. But these component states *share* authority and administrative capability over a significant range of policy domains.

Both the federalist enthusiasts for a United States of Europe, fifty years ago, and the neofunctionalists who predicted a progressive transfer first of interests and then of loyalties from the national to the supranational frame, believed that interests, loyalty, and power must lie at one level or another: to be *retained* by states, or *transferred* to a new entity. The experience of the EU over the past two decades has, however, demonstrated how far all these three elements of politics can be shared and dispersed. Multiple identities, multiple tiers of policy-making and policy implementation, interlocking processes of ratification and scrutiny, make for a far less tidy process than that which characterized the centralized French or British states of a century ago. Some observers have seen it also as unavoidably slow-moving and resistant to change, 'interblocking' as well as interlocking (Scharpf 1988). But all modern government is slow-moving, held back by the diversity of interests at stake and the inflexibility of administrative structures. The loosely structured government of the EU has a far more diverse group of interests to persuade or to override than any of its component state systems, and must rely for implementation on the varied quality and entrenched traditions of the different national administrations. Nevertheless, it moves: not as fast or as smoothly as some would like, but so far without seeing the majority of politicians or public from any of its members jump off the juggernaut.

One demonstration of the resilience of the EU as a system of government is that it does *not* simply serve—as Moravcsik suggests—as a forum for intergovernmental bargaining among its largest states (Moravcsik 1998). German and French political leaders, certainly, have most often attempted to define the terms for negotiation, and to strike strategic bargains bilaterally. The personal commitment of Helmut Kohl was crucial to the achievement of the single currency, as Tsoukalis notes in Chapter 6. British leaders, similarly, have attempted to impose their priorities on EU negotiations rather than to converge on the multilateral consensus—successfully, after years of hard bargaining, on the budget, though less successfully in fisheries, in social policy, and elsewhere. But it is impossible to explain policy outcomes within the EU without taking into account the interests, and the initiatives, of other governments as players.

The Dutch, for example, have played an active part in shaping policy and in crafting compromises across the whole range of EU policy domains, since the Treaties of Paris and Rome were negotiated; Dutch presidencies in the last stages of the 1991 and 1996–7 IGCs left their distinctive imprint on the Treaties of Maastricht and Amsterdam. The Danes have been significant players in the development of environmental policy, as Chapter 11 indicates. The Spanish have successfully promoted their own interests in fisheries and in North–South relations, as well as in cohesion funds. Greek political leaders have stood out against majorities in defence of national interests as determinedly, and as successfully, as the British. Small states benefit disproportionately from the added voice and standing which strong institutions give them in negotiating with their larger neighbours. The EU remains a firmly supported system of collective government because it is seen to serve the interests of *all* its members, large and small.

Twenty years ago it was plausible to picture the Community system as a provisional political structure, halfway between sovereignty and integration. After over forty years of operation, the observer must remark on the persistence and adaptability of the provisional. Member governments and national publics appear more comfortable with the deliberate ambiguity of this semi-confederation, this *Staatenverbund*—as the German constitutional court has described it—than with the logical alternative of a full federation (Ress 1994). Ambiguity of objectives, agreement to disagree, the postponement of difficult but non-urgent decisions until later, are characteristic features of this relatively stable *provisorum*; but they are not unique to the EU. Canadian federal politics, American federal politics, German and Italian national politics, the processes of constitutional reform within the United Kingdom and France, display similar elements of deliberate imprecision.

Students of comparative and international politics should be careful not to exaggerate the coherence of national policy-making, nor the rationality of multilateral intergovernmental negotiation. One of the oddest aspects of American international relations scholarship about the European Union is that it imagines a political system so much more rational than what one may observe in Washington. American trade policy emerges out of a messy process of lobbying, log-rolling, side-payments, and inter-institutional conflicts. It should not be surprising that European trade policy, for example, emerges from a similarly political process, in which the rational calculations of different actors are bounded by the conflicting assumptions and expectations of the many other players, as well as by the institutional conventions and constraints within which they operate. US environmental diplomacy in the late 1990s has been marked by internal contradictions, inconsistent objectives, and consequent incoherence; the twists and turns of European environmental diplomacy look relatively rational by comparison. Multi-level and multi-issue policy-making is an inherently complex activity. States and federations, as well as this non-state system of government, do not always manage to pursue strategic objectives as they balance among conflicting pressures and priorities.

Post-sovereign politics

Policy-making within the EU may thus be described as post-sovereign. It spills across state boundaries, penetrating deep into previously domestic aspects of national politics and administration. It embodies the principle of mutual interference in each other's internal affairs, now extending (as Chapter 18 notes) even to mutual inspection of each other's judicial procedures. It depends upon mutual trust, on collective consent, to implement European law and regulation through national administrations (W. Wallace 1999). States, as represented by national governments, remain central to the EU policy process, but they are no longer the *only* significant actors—and are not always the predominant actors. Their actions are constrained by institutional frameworks, and moderated by the intervention of institutionally autonomous actors such as the Commission, the ECJ, even at the margins the EP. More importantly, as previous chapters have shown, they are constrained by their diminished control of their own governments, administrations, and national political processes, as information on their own negotiating objectives is traded in transnational and transgovernmental interactions in return for information on the intentions of others, feeding backwards and forwards assumptions and expectations which shape possible outcomes.

We do not go as far as Wolfgang Wessels, who concludes that the density of networks and intensity of activities within them amounts to an effective 'fusion' of national administrations into the collective EU framework (Wessels 1997). We do, however, insist that no government in Europe is sovereign in the sense understood by diplomats or constitutional lawyers of fifty years ago. The concept of collective government implies a degree of shared commitment to the common enterprise, of ongoing cooperation within a framework of shared experience and assumptions. The relative robustness of the EU political system—the impetus of activities, the expansion of policy development in response to the emergence of new demands, in spite of frequent failures to agree on desired common policies—depends in large part on the intensive calendar of meetings at all levels, and the expectation from most of those caught up in such meetings that more is to be gained through pursuing common policies than from blocking them, or from seeking alternative frameworks for negotiation.

The EU remains, however, a partial polity, without many of the features which one might expect to find within a fully developed democratic political system. Fritz Scharpf characterizes it as resting on 'output-oriented legitimacy', while lacking 'input-oriented legitimacy'. He argues that it provides government for the people, but does not represent government by the people. 'In the absence of political accountability' and of a strong sense of collective political identity, 'the legitimacy of politically salient European decisions depends on their effectiveness in achieving consensual goals' (Scharpf 1999: 6, 22). Passive popular consent, from his perspective, rests upon the ability of this slow-moving consensual policy-making system to provide outcomes sufficiently satisfactory to avoid provoking active dissent. This partial polity is particularly dependent on regulatory instruments as policy outcomes—as Chapters 4, 10, and 11 in particular illustrate. That makes, however, for an opaque policy process and a technical and non-transparent series of policy outcomes, drafted in terms accessible to expert élites but beyond the interest or understanding of the broader public. National governments rebuilt and maintained collective identity, after the second world war, through large-scale spending programmes for economic development and welfare. The small size of the EU budget forecloses this option.

European policy-making is an élite process, into which non-governmental organizations, the EP, and national parliaments and opposition parties intrude, without succeeding on most policy issues in attracting much wider public attention. Those issues on which wider opinion is aroused, as we have seen, are most frequently questions of taste or values—food safety, biotechnology, environmental protection. Paul Taylor (following Ralf Dahrendorf) has labelled the EU political system a 'cartel of elites', through which—as in the 'consociational' representative democracy characteristic of the post-war Netherlands and of contemporary Switzerland—popular opinion is indirectly represented, each group relying on its own participating élites to take care of its interests and to deliver satisfactory outcomes (Taylor 1996). Collective government, from this perspective, moves slowly, co-opting as broad a coalition of interested groups as possible into the consultative committees and hierarchy of working groups through which it operates, in order to legitimate the policy outcome. Environmental organizations, and non-governmental organizations (NGOs) concerned with social policy and food safety, are invited into the Brussels process in order to engage their leaders in the common enterprise, and so inhibit them from attacking the eventual compromise that may emerge. This is a costly process, involving lengthy consultations over successive draft proposals, sometimes extending over several years (van Schendelen 1998). But it is a necessary part of a policy-making process that rests on such a weak foundation for legitimacy: a post-sovereign political system in which the outcomes agreed justify the continuing collective input.

Policy-making in the 1990s: a shifting pattern?

The completion of the single market programme, and the shift in the course of the 1990s first to the achievement of the single currency and then to the development of policies in the second and third pillars, have altered the balance of EU policy-making. The negotiation and management of the common agricultural policy, and the Commission's attempts to develop parallel common policies, made for an EEC policy-making process in the 1960s characterized—as Chapter 1 has noted—by a distinctive Community method. Strict limits on distributive policies involving budgetary expenditure, together with a shift in approaches to economic management, made for a predominantly regulatory style of policy-making in the 1980s, evident in the single market programme, the rising importance of the ECJ, and the rule-making and rule-enforcing roles of a number of Commission Directorates-General. A further shift of focus, to foreign policy and defence, to migration, border control, and action against organized crime, has brought with it a parallel shift in the predominant pattern of policy-making.

Monetary integration in the 1990s has been influenced at the margins by the demands of transnational economic interests, exerted both through national governments and through direct lobbying in Brussels. But, as Tsoukalis underlines in Chapter 6, it has been the political commitment by key member governments and national political leaders which has been decisive. Transnational economic interests have been far less engaged in promoting common foreign policy, and almost entirely absent from EU initiatives on defence, or on JHA.[3] Nor has the Commission played the role of policy initiator and entrepreneur in either of these two developing fields. Jacques Delors's speech to the International Institute of Strategic Studies in March 1991, in which he called for a Europeanization of national defence policies, was widely seen as a speech too far; the Commission had no standing, and no expertise, to comment on defence issues. As Chapter 18 notes, the Commission held back from building up staff, or exploiting its limited competences, on JHA matters.

So it has been governments which have initiated policy in the key fields of EU activity in the 1990s: not the Commission, nor the Court, nor organized interests, the motors and entrepreneurs for policy development in other domains. German and French political leaders defined the parameters for EMU, with additional intellectual input—as Chapter 6 notes—from officials of central banks, in particular from the Italian central bank. The British and French governments led on CFSP in 1998–9. The Dutch had led on the incorporation of Schengen into the TEU, and the German government, and German law enforcement agencies, have led since then in pushing co-operation further.

The locus and timing of the history-making decision to move ahead to EMU is clear. The decision was taken among heads of government, in the context of the Maastricht IGC. Observers may argue about how far preparatory policy-making from 1988 to 1991 prefigured that decision, and about how crucial the many post-decision reaffirmations of what had been agreed were to the achievement of the single currency eight years later; the strategic bargain is nevertheless easy to identify. It is, however, more difficult to pin down the crucial turning-points in CFSP or in JHA, or to locate them within the strategic framework of history-making European Council package deals and IGCs. Incremental policy-making, learning by doing rather than strategic choice, marks both these major policy domains. Commitments have grown up through intensive transgovernmental interactions as much as through deliberate inter-governmental intervention.

The 1996–7 IGC was convened specifically to address the effectiveness and poten-tial reform of CFSP, as provided for in Articles J.4.6 and N.2 of the TEU. Yet the Amsterdam ToA emerged with little progress under this Title. It was a bilateral initia-tive by two member governments, drawing on their shared learning experience in Bosnia, which relaunched this dossier late in 1998. That dossier was prepared and progressed through intensive consultations between officials from the French and British foreign and defence ministries, a transgovernmental process extended bilaterally to other governments. The aim was to construct a multilateral consensus through multiple dialogues, to be ratified through the EU framework once sufficient agreement had been reached, and to arrive at any necessary changes in the treaties through an IGC only when clear commitments on policy and spending had been given.

It is still harder to locate the crucial turning-points in the development of JHA. The TEU had incorporated, and modified, an extensive pre-existing network of cooper-ation among national ministries and law enforcement agencies into the formal struc-ture. In the early months of 1997 the Deputy Foreign Minister in the Dutch presidency drove through the incorporation of Schengen into the ToA, and the transfer of some dossiers from the third to the first pillar, without this becoming a major issue in the endgame among heads of government in Amsterdam. One justification for convening the special European Council at Tampere in October 1999, an official of the Finnish presidency remarked to a visiting group of British parliamentarians some months before, was to explain to heads of government the implications of the commitments they had accepted at Amsterdam two years earlier. Ministers of justice had been drawn into an increasingly intensive network; but until Tampere heads of govern-ment had been involved only intermittently.

The evolution of enlargement on the other hand, as Chapter 16 shows, offers a pattern of policy which is more familiar to established patterns of EU policy-making. Strategic decisions have been taken by heads of government, at successive European Councils, and by the General Affairs Council of Ministers, responding to proposals from an active—though not always united—Commission. Mesopolicy has been shaped by a wide variety of actors, dealing with detailed sectoral issues. The Com-mission has acted throughout the process so far as a source of information and expertise, and a progress-chaser: circulating detailed questionnaires to applicant governments, assembling opinions on individual countries into the multi-volume *Agenda 2000*, thus setting the agenda to which national governments responded. The macropolicy-makers in both the Commission and member governments have strug-gled to maintain coherence of approach, against the fragmenting pressures of agricultural, steel, and textile interests, recipients of cohesion funds, and lobbies representing the claims of those forced westward from the applicant states after the second world war, in constant tension between overall direction and detailed obs-tacles to progress. Political commitment to enlargement carries complex economic implications, with diverse interests at stake. Far more than CFSP or JHA, it therefore involves extensive interaction between private economic actors and public policy-makers.

Cycles and trends

Extrapolation of long-term trends from current developments is always a difficult task. Proposals to shift significant expenditure under CFSP or JHA from national budgets to the EU budget, or attempts to integrate national diplomatic services or law enforcement agencies into Europe-wide structures, would alter the pattern of policy in these domains; these would lead to a sharp increase in the size of the common EU budget, providing a much sharper public focus for EU-level politics and policy-making. They remain distinctive from other fields of EU policy partly because they have succeeded so far in limiting common policy to cooperation among national agencies, at national expense. The development of Europe-wide computer networks, managed by the Commission on behalf of national governments, indicates a poten-tial shift of emphasis in the management of JHA. So does the commitment by incom-ing Commission President Prodi to a substantial increase in Commission staffing and attention in this field. The continuing expansion of the Council Secretariat's services in CFSP may possibly foreshadow the development of a common administration, alongside the collective efforts of national administrations which have managed CFSP so far. The inclusion of defence for the first time on the EU agenda might lead in the long-run to a major shift in the location of decision-making, administration, and funding.

The EU in 1999 presents an image of collective government in which national governments provide a great deal of the system's dynamism and initiation of policy. The college of Commissioners, forced to resign in March 1999, had lost prestige and credibility. Exposure of maladministration and (petty) corruption within the Com-mission services had damaged the institution as a whole. European Councils, for-mally convened every six months, met three times in 1998 and four times in 1999, offering a powerful image of multilateral political leadership. The IGC as a locus for strategic rule-making among member governments appeared to be becoming a regular dimension of the EU cycle, as noted above, with the fourth such conference in fifteen years taking place in 2000.

Yet the Commission's authority and credibility has fallen and risen before, in the swings of the pendulum which Chapter 2 outlines. After Walter Hallstein's departure there followed a period of weak Commission Presidents and colleges. The search for new initiatives in the long recession of the 1970s, however, encouraged heads of government to agree on Roy Jenkins, chosen as President for a stronger college. A similar cycle is observable in the subsequent nomination of a weaker Commission, presided over by the former Luxembourg Prime Minister Gaston Thorn, and the swing back to Commission dynamism with the choice of Jacques Delors as Thorn's successor. A further swing is observable from the activist Delors Commission to the consolidating Santer college (led by another Luxembourg Prime Minister) and back to the carefully vetted Prodi team.

The increasing frequency of IGCs may yet prove to reflect accidental, more than systemic, factors. It was, more than any other factor, the resistance of the British government at Maastricht to closer commitments on CFSP which led to the postponement of further negotiations to a second IGC, to be convened five years later. The disintegrating British Conservative government in 1996–7 presented an obstacle to progress which both prolonged the Amsterdam IGC and postponed detailed negotiation on institutional reform from then until a later conference. Yet a larger EU, caught in a continuing process of enlargement negotiations and absorption of new member states over the next decade and beyond, might find itself forced to adjust decision rules more frequently. Certainly, it is likely to prove more difficult to strike multilateral bargains among a larger group of governments. Those who see the macropolitics of European integration as driven by strategic bargains among major states should note that Polish governments are likely to prove as important players as Spanish, with as determined a commitment to the promotion of their perceived interests: making for six major players, without allowing for the negotiating skills and initiatives often exhibited by representatives of smaller states.

The persistence of the provisional

The EU has demonstrated considerable flexibility in adapting its institutional practices to the demands of a shifting agenda over the past fifteen years. The frequency of heads of government meetings and sectoral Councils has fallen and risen as circumstances have changed. Committees and working groups have been convened to formulate proposals, following well-recognized standard procedures, and in most cases dissolved when their tasks are complete. The flexibility of this cumbersome, stateless political system appears more remarkable if one considers the counter-factual: the number of alternative outcomes which EU actors have avoided in keeping this provisional system of collective government in place. There were, for example, many within France, Germany, and the Benelux who argued in the early 1990s that neither progress towards EMU nor further enlargement would be practicable without the creation of an inner core of member states. Yet eleven of the fifteen member states participated in the launch of the single currency, in January 1999, with opinion within the remaining four wavering over how soon to follow. Finland and Austria, new members from 1995, have already become among the more active and effective players on the EU stage.

The conventional wisdom from many consultative groups and academic studies, from 1970 to 1990, was that monetary union was not achievable without political union, and that further movement to integrate foreign policy and defence, or internal policing and justice, would necessitate the transformation of the EU into a federation. By 1999, however, the first of these was under way, and member governments and EU institutions were moving towards closer integration of the second and third, without addressing the hard choices of transferring sovereignty to federal institutions. Political logic, clarity of decision-making and accountability, administrative efficiency, external representation, all argue for stronger central institutions. Member governments, and most of their publics, prefer to live with ambiguity, accepting the costs in terms of slow-moving mechanisms for policy-making in return for the benefits of national representation and accountability this consociational cartel of élites continues to provide. Further moves towards common policies in public order and defence, the development of more active macroeconomic and fiscal policies to accompany monetary union, would make it more difficult to maintain this ambiguous system of collective government. Further enlargement, with a more geo-graphically and economically diverse Union of twenty or more states, would make it harder still. The perceived benefits of this post-sovereign system of multilateral policy-making to most member governments are, however, sufficient for political leaders to seek to maintain this provisional but stable balance through successive interim package deals, rather than address the awkward choices involved in any more fundamental transformation.

European government between national policy-making and global negotiation

Policy-making within the EU, as earlier chapters have illustrated, responds both to internal and to external demands. Changes in the EU external environment force changes in embedded bargains. It has, for example, been sustained pressures from successive General Agreement on Tariffs and Trade (GATT) rounds, reinforced by surpluses on world agricultural markets and the uncertainties of Russian demand for EU exports, which have (as Rieger notes in Chapter 7) pushed through the McSharry reforms to the CAP, and provided impetus for Commissioner Fischler's continuing efforts. Fisheries policy has developed within the context of changing international rules on national fishery limits and on sustainable levels of fish catches. Environmental policy has been shaped within a broader world-wide debate, drawing on scientific evidence from outside the European continent as well as within. Migration policy is intrinsically a response to pressures from outside, including the disappearance of the EU's secure eastern frontier after 1989, and the impact of ethnic conflict and state collapse to the EU's east and south.

Technological change, with global competition in emerging technologies, has also driven EU policy. The exploitation of biotechnology, both within the EU and within the USA, set the framework within which European policies had to be defined and developed. US and European companies were competing to capture new patents and potential markets, as European and American scientists compared research findings and environmental NGOs exchanged their concerns. The transformation of tele-communications through the information revolution altered the acceptable framework for policy, as state telephone monopolies faced the challenges of rising traffic, new equipment, falling unit costs, and a rapidly developing international market. One of the many reasons why EU policies and policy-making in the late 1990s differ in character from the patterns which prevailed some twenty years before is that the problems which they face have been transformed, and the instruments available to manage those problems are often of a different order. The information which flows through global television, radio, and now also the internet, has increased the surges of asylum-seekers which cross the external borders of the EU after successive external conflicts. But the availability of computer networks makes it possible in turn for EU governments to monitor each surge more effectively, to record each arrival, and to inhibit 'asylum shopping' from immigrants, making multiple applications to different member governments.

The USA is an active presence, sometimes almost a participant, in many of the policy domains we have described. US and European interests overlap across a wide range of EU concerns. These include management of the linked processes of EU and North Atlantic Treaty Organization (Nato) enlargement, for example, and maintenance of stability in the Mediterranean and the Middle East. The US Mission to the European Communities, in Brussels, is more generously staffed than the permanent representations of most member governments. It intervenes to protect and to promote American interests as early as possible in the long process of formulating and negotiating EU policies. The American Chamber of Commerce in Brussels (Amcham) is one of the most active of economic lobbies. It promotes the interests of American multinationals within the EU, and of American industrial and service standards as the basis for global regulation and the model which European negotiators should follow. Negotiation and consultation within the EU interact with consultation within the Organization for Economic Cooperation and Development (OECD); over half the OECD's members are EU member states. G7 and G8, again with half of their participants drawn from EU member governments, address agendas which overlap substantially with EU concerns, based on preparatory papers from groups of experts who also serve on EU committees. The Uruguay Round, like earlier trade rounds formally global, operated on several dossiers primarily as a bilateral US–EU negotiation, with other advanced industrial countries doing their best to intervene. The Montreal and Kyoto Conferences on international environmental regulation also saw the EU and its member governments acting as major players within a wider multilateral forum, in which the USA was the most significant other player. Attempts to reconcile US and European proposals again preoccupied negotiators as a key element in constructing a global package deal.

The flow of EU policy, the introduction of new concepts and information into the policy debate, thus takes place within a wider context: not fully global, since most developing countries (and Russia and China) remain marginal players, but consisting of the widening group of advanced industrial democracies, working through the formal mechanisms of multilateral conferences and organizations, as well as the informal and semi-formal networks of expert communities and advisory groups. Much of what we have described as characterizing the transformation of intra-European policy-making—intensifying transgovernmental and transnational interactions, exchanges of information and ideas among agencies within governments, multi-level lobbying by economic interests and NGOs—has also modified patterns of national policy-making within other OECD member states. Business leaders and management experts exchange ideas with politicians and officials in Davos and Denver; Greenpeace campaigns in North America, Australia, and New Zealand as well as in western Europe. The specificity of western Europe's experience lies partly in its geographical concentration. Collective government, through Councils and committees constituted from responsible ministers and officials regularly travelling out from their national capitals, is far easier within a region in which it is possible to arrive from one's home base by train or plane in good time for a late morning meeting, and return home after an extended session the same night.[4]

In Chapter 5 McGowan reformulates the concept of multi-level governance with reference to competition policy, as operating at the global–OECD–transatlantic level, the European, and the national. This, we suggest, may usefully be applied more widely to EU policy-making, which takes place in constant interaction not only with national policy-making but also with wider international regimes, within a global context. European integration is not an autonomous phenomenon; it is nested within the liberal world economy, under American leadership. Its rules and regulations are moderated by the constraints imposed by international regimes.

Two questions follow from this. First, how far should we think of European policy-making in the 1990s as driven by pressures to respond to American-led global regimes? Secondly, how useful is it to compare European integration with other regional policy frameworks within the global economy? The way in which several member governments have approached European social and competition policies has certainly been influenced by their concern to maintain some distinctive aspects of the European social market model against the growing predominance of Anglo-American market assumptions (Scharpf 1999). The pressure of American (and East Asian) competition has been a constant external reference-point for European policy-makers over the past two decades. Modernizing élites in Russia, Japan, and Turkey a century or more ago attempted to select from the culture, political, and economic structures of their European models those aspects they regarded as most useful, while resisting other aspects they saw as harmful to their own values. Similarly, the aim of social democratic and Christian democratic élites, in Germany, France, the Low Countries, and the Nordic countries since the second world war has been to learn from and copy some parts of the American model, while resisting others. Part of the underlying rationale for EU common policies is that a common European negotiating position enables European governments to bargain with the USA on much more equal terms over global rules, regimes, and standards. In environmental negotiations, on genetically modified foods, on common rules affecting multinational companies and foreign investment, on domestic content rules in television and cinema transmissions, many European politicians and NGOs argue that political values—not simply economic interests—are at stake. Regional integration, through the EU, thus acts to moderate the pressures of global integration, enabling governments which can aspire on their own only to minor influence over global regimes to gain greater influence through combining with their like-minded neighbours.

Regional integration schemes are also under way in other continents. As in the 1960s, when, in the first flush of enthusiasm for regional integration, common markets were set up in East Africa, the Caribbean, and Latin America, the renewed dynamism which European institutions have displayed since the mid-1980s prompts questions about comparison between European processes and preconditions and those in other regions (W. Wallace 1994a; Mattli 1999). The three-member NAFTA, the four-member Mercosur (Brazil, Argentina, Uruguay, and Paraguay), and the sixteen-member APEC might be seen, at the end of the 1990s, as possible comparators to the EU.[5] We question the closeness of the comparison.

One underlying theme throughout this volume has been the dependence of EU policy-making on extensive networks of officials, experts, influentials, and activists, operating across national boundaries on the basis of a relatively high degree of mutual trust and mutual understanding. That rests upon common expectations that each other member state and society are equipped not only with fully democratic government but also with a relatively non-corrupt and efficient national administration, an independent system of justice and administrative redress, an autonomous media, and a vigorous civil society of competing political movements and organized groups. Post-war American hegemony, through the Marshall Plan and other agencies, together with the social democratic compromise of corporatist consultation and welfare provision, helped to root these standards, social institutions, and habits of behaviour firmly across most of western Europe. In Spain, Portugal, and Greece (and in some respects in Ireland) the transition towards an open society was slower and later. In all of these countries, it should be noted, it is widely believed that participation within the EU has played a significant part in entrenching (and monitoring) the full development of civil institutions and democratic standards. The lengthy process of transition to EU membership within the former socialist states, as Chapter 16 notes, is partly about assisting and monitoring the development of democratic standards and civil institutions, now specifically included in the accession negotiations as a precondition for membership.

Outside western Europe similar conditions of mutual trust, based upon extensive interaction among official and non-official élites, obtain between the USA and Canada, but only marginally extend across Mexico. Within APEC they clearly obtain between Australia and New Zealand, between these two and the USA, and to some extent between these three and Japan. But it would be premature to argue that such conditions extend between this core group and Chile, or Korea, or Indonesia, while China remains a half-closed society deeply mistrustful of many of its APEC partners. The broader interaction between governments and societies which we have described as intensive transgovernmentalism and extensive transnationalism holds the advanced industrial democracies together, and provides a foundation of mutual understanding and trust. Scholars who focus primarily on state actors, or concentrate on economic interests to the exclusion of political values and mutual trust, ignore the significance of the substructure of shared ideas and overlapping networks in providing a framework within which political leaders negotiate. Regional integration in other continents of any comparable depth and complexity to the EU political system we have described will require a comparable substructure, extending beyond governments into societies and across borders into other national societies and their domestic élites. The relationship between the USA, Canada, and Mexico through NAFTA is more directly comparable to that between the EU and the rump members of the European Economic Area (Switzerland, Norway, and Iceland), and between the EU and its Mediterranean partners. Both are highly asymmetrical; formal institutions allow for consultation, but in practice the associated states have little alternative, except where clear national economic interests are threatened, but to follow the legislative lead of their dominant partner.

We have not offered any single theoretical model for the EU policy process in this volume. We have preferred to allow the case-studies to illustrate the complexity and diversity of EU policy-making, pointing out common features and offering a range of models which best illuminate different aspects of the political process. Single models are unavoidably reductionist, shutting out significant aspects of political interaction in order to achieve the clean lines of parsimonious simplicity. But politics is not a simple business, and political actors rarely devote their undivided attention to the pursuit of singular and well-defined strategic objectives. The EU is a partial polity, with a profoundly political process of policy-making: a stable structure of collective governance, which serves the mixed purposes of its constituent member states relatively well.

Notes

1 This point has been widely accepted by many scholars. See e.g. Sandholtz (1993b: 3):'the national interests of EC states do not have independent existence; they are not formed in a vacuum and then brought to Brussels. Those interests are defined and redefined in an international and institutional context that includes the EC.'

2 One small illustration of how national networks of non-governmental organizations (NGOs) now operate as part of a broader European network is provided by the frequency with which British NGOs giving evidence to parliamentary inquiries on EU issues include experts from other member states in their presentations. One sub-committee of the Lords European Communities Committee in 1998 met German and Dutch professors and a Danish lawyer, joining in giving evidence from British NGOs.

3 The involvement of the European Round Table and the Union of Industries of the European Community (UNICE) in the establishment of the Transatlantic Policy Network in the early 1990s (as well as the Transatlantic Business Dialogue, which grew out of it) reflected concern by business leaders and their representatives that the weakening of the security link would make governments on both sides of the Atlantic more resistant to compromise in economic issues. The willingness of these business leaders to discuss the relationship between Nato and the EU, western strategy towards Russia, and eastern enlargement with American

business and political leaders reflected their determination to remind their American counterparts that the underlying rationale for the transatlantic relationship remained political, and that differences over trade and international regulation should be contained within that framework.

4 The distance from San Francisco to Washington is further than the distance between any of the capitals of the EU and Brussels. The difficulties of maintaining a regular dialogue among ministers and officials at greater distances was exemplified after the Iranian and Afghan revolutions, when the Japanese foreign ministry attempted to build links to European Political Cooperation through sending responsible officials from Tokyo to consult their European counterparts. I remember the head of a Japanese diplomat sinking onto the table as he attempted to brief me about these exchanges, having flown into London from Tokyo for the second time in two weeks, with a stopover in Washington to exchange views with the Americans as well.

5 Identification of the Association of South East Asian Nations (ASEAN) with this grouping of regionally integrating institutions has suffered from the divergent impact of the Asian financial crisis on its members, from revelations of systemic domestic corruption within several states, and above all from prolonged disorder within its largest member, Indonesia.

References

Most institutions can be researched on the world wide web:

- the Council: http://ue.eu.int/en/summ.htm
- the Commission under http://europa.eu.int/comm/index-en.htm
- the Commission's DG V: http://europa.eu.int/comm/dg05/index-en.htm (and similarly for other DGs) but subject to alteration as DG titles change.
- the European Court of Justice's decisions: http://europa.eu.int/cj/index.htm
- the European Parliament: http://www.europarl.eu.int/
- the European Parliament's Committee on Employment and Social Affairs (ESOC): http://www.europarl.eu.int/committees/en/default.htm#ESOC (and similarly for other committees)
- other actors, such the European Trade Union Confederation (ETUC): http://www.etuc.org; the Union of Industrial and Employers' Confederations of Europe (UNICE), only via e-mail: main@unice.be

Abélès, M. (1996), *En attente d'Europe* (Hachette: Paris).

Adams, W. J. (1992) (ed.), *Singular Europe* (Ann Arbor: University of Michigan Press).

Addison, J. T., and Siebert, W. S. (1993), 'The EC Social Charter: The Nature of the Beast', *National Westminster Bank Quarterly Review*, Feb., 13–28.

Agence Europe, various issues.

Aguilar, S. (1993), 'Corporatist and Statist Designs in Environmental Policy: The Contrasting Roles of Germany and Spain in the European Community Scenario', *Environmental Politics*, 2/2: 223–47.

Allen, D. (1993), 'Dividing the Spoils for 1994', *European Brief*, 1/2: 38–9.

Allsopp, C., and Vines, D. (1998), 'The Assessment: Macroeconomic Policy after EMU', *Oxford Review of Economic Policy*, 14/3: 1–23.

Altenstetter, C. (1992), 'Health Policy Regimes and the Single European Market', *Journal of Health Politics, Policy and Law*, 17/4: 813–46.

Alter, K. J., and Meunier-Aitsahalia, S. (1994), 'Judicial Politics in the European Community: European Integration and the Pathbreaking *Cassis de Dijon* Decision', *Comparative Political Studies*, 26/4: 535– 61.

Anania, G., Carter, C. A., and McCalla, A. F. (1994*a*), 'Agricultural Policy Changes, GATT Negotiations, and the US–EC Agricultural Trade Conflicts', in Anania *et al.* (1994*b*: 1–39).

———— ——— ——— (1994*b*) (eds.), *Agricultural Trade Conflicts and GATT: New Dimensions in US–European Agricultural Trade Relations* (Boulder, Colo.: Westview Press).

Andersen, M. S., and Liefferink, D. (1997), *European Environmental Policy: The Pioneers* (Manchester: Manchester University Press).

Andersen, S. S., and Eliassen, K. A. (1993) (eds.), *Making Policy in Europe: The Europeification of National Policy-Making* (London: Sage).

Anderson, J. (1995), 'The Structural Funds and the Social Dimension of EC Policy', in Leibfried and Pierson (1995*b*: 123–58).

—— (1996), 'Germany and the Structural Funds: Unification Leads to Bifurcation', in Hooghe (1996: 163–94).

Anderson, K., and Hayami, Y. (1986), *The Political Economy of Agricultural Protection: East Asia in International Perspective* (Sidney: Allen & Unwin).

Anderson, M. (1993), *Control of Organized Crime in the European Community*, Working Paper No. IX (Edinburgh: University of Edinburgh, Department of Politics).

—— (1994), 'The Agenda for Police Cooperation', in Anderson and den Boer (1994: 3–21).

—— and den Boer, M. (1992) (eds.), *European Police Cooperation: Proceedings* (Edinburgh: University of Edinburgh, Department of Politics).

—— —— (1994) (eds.), *Policing across National Boundaries* (London: Pinter).

—— —— and Miller, G. (1994), 'European Citizenship and Cooperation in Justice and Home Affairs', in Duff *et al.* (1994: 104–22).

—— —— Cullen, P., Gilmore, W. C., Raab, C., and Walker, N. (1995), *Policing the European Union: Theory, Law and Practice* (Oxford: Clarendon Press).

Andriessen, F. (1991), 'Towards a Community of Twenty-Four?', speech to the 69th Assembly of Eurochambers, Brussels, 19 Apr.

Angenendt, S. (1997) (ed.), *Migration und Flucht. Aufgaben und Strategien für Deutschland, Europa und die internationale Gemeinschaft* (Bonn and Munich: Bundeszentrale für politische Bildung and R. Oldenbourg).

Antoine, L. (1995), 'Quand la controverse tourne à l'impasse: la guerre du thon', *Natures, Sciences, Société*, 3/1: 6–15.

Argyris, N. (1989), 'The EEC Rules of Competition and the Air Transport Sector', *Common Market Law Review*, 26/1: 5–32.

—— (1993), 'Regulatory Reform in the Electricity Sector', *Oxford Review of Economic Policy*, 19/1: 31–44.

Arias Cañete, M. (1998), *Report on the Proposal for a Council Regulation Relating to Structural Actions in the Fisheries' Sector* (Brussels: European Parliament, Fisheries Committee).

Arkleton Trust (1992), *Farm Household Adjustment in Western Europe, 1987–1991: Final Report on the Research Programme on Farm Structures and Pluriactivity* (Luxembourg: Office for Official Publications of the European Communities).

Armstrong, K., and Bulmer, S. (1998), *The Governance of the Single European Market* (Manchester: Manchester University Press).

Arocena, J. (1998), 'Argentine: inquiétude des Espagnols', *Le Marin*, 27 Feb.

Asbeek Brusse, W., and Griffiths, R. (1997), 'Early Cartel Legislation and Cartel Policy in the Netherlands. In Memoriam: The Economic Competition Act (1956–97)', *Acta Politica*, 32/4: 375–405.

Atkinson, M. M., and Coleman, W. D. (1989), *The State, Business and Industrial Change in Canada* (Toronto: University of Toronto Press).

Attwood, E. A. (1963), *The Origins of State Support for British Agriculture*, Manchester School of Economics and Social Studies No. 31 (Manchester).

Avery, G. (1995), *The Commission's Perspective on the EFTA Accession Negotiations*, Sussex European Institute Working Paper No. 12, June (Falmer).

—— and Cameron, F. (1998), *The Enlargement of the European Union* (Sheffield: Sheffield Academic Press for UACES).

Averyt, W. F., Jr. (1977), *Agropolitics in the European Community: Interest Groups and the Common Agricultural Policy* (London: Praeger).

Axelrod, R., and Keohane, R. O. (1988), 'Achieving Cooperation under Anarchy: Strategies and Institutions', *World Politics*, 38/1: 226–54.

Bache, I. (1998), *The Politics of European Union Regional Policy: Multi-level Governance or Flexible Gatekeeping?* (Sheffield: Sheffield Academic Press).

—— (1999), 'The Extended Gatekeeper: Central Government and the Implementation of the EC Regional Policy in the UK', *Journal of European Public Policy*, 6/1: 28–45.

—— George, S., and Rhodes, R. (1996), 'The European Union, Cohesion Policy and Sub-national Authorities in the United Kingdom', in Hooghe (1996: 294–319).

Baker, J. (1989), *A New Europe, a New Atlanticism: Architecture for a New Era*, speech to the Berlin Press Club, 12 Dec., Europe Documents, No. 1588, 15 Dec.

Baker, S., Milton, K., and Yearly, S. (1994) (eds.), *Protecting the Periphery: Environmental Policy in Peripheral Regions of the European Union* (Essex: Frank Cass).

Balassa, B. (1962), *The Theory of Economic Integration* (London: Allen & Unwin).

—— (1975), *European Economic Integration* (Amsterdam: North-Holland).

Baldwin, P. (1996), 'Can we Define a European Welfare State Model?', in Greve (1996: 29–44).

Baldwin, R. (1994), *Towards an Integrated Europe* (London: CEPR).

—— et al. (1992), *Monitoring European Integration, iii: Is Bigger Better? The Economics of EC Enlargement* (London: CEPR).

—— François, J. F., and Portes, R. (1997), 'The Costs and Benefits of Eastern Enlargement: The Impact on the EU and Central Europe', *Economic Policy*, 24: 125–76.

Banting, K. G. (1995), 'The Welfare State as Statecraft: Territorial Politics and Canadian Social Policy', in Leibfried and Pierson (1995b: 269–300).

Barbé, E. (1998), 'Balancing Europe's Eastern and Southern Dimensions', in Zielonka (1998: 117–30).

Barrett, G. (1997) (ed.), *Justice Cooperation in the European Union* (Dublin: Institute of European Affairs).

Bartolini, S. (1998), *Exit Options, Boundary Building and Political Structuring*, European University Institute Working Papers No. SPS 98/1 (Florence: European University Institute).

Barwig, K., and Schulte, B. (1999) (eds.), *Freizügigkeit und soziale Sicherheit. Die Durchführung der Verordnung (EWG) Nr. 1408/71 über die soziale Sicherheit der Wanderarbeitnehmer in Deutschland* (Baden-Baden: Nomos).

Bauer, M. (1995) (ed.), *Resistance to New Technology* (Cambridge: Cambridge University Press).

Bayliss, B. T., *et al.*, (1994): *Road Freight Transport in the Single European Market*, (Committee of Enquiry, Brussels: European Commission, Directorate-General for Transport).

Becker, U. (1998), 'Brillen aus Luxemburg und Zahnbehandlung in Brüssel. Die Gesetzliche Krankenversicherung im Europäischen Binnenmarkt', *Neue Zeitschrift für Sozialrecht*, 7/8: 359–64.

Begg, I. (1997), *Reform of the Structural Funds after 1999*, European Policy Paper Series, (Pittsburgh: University of Pittsburgh, Center for West European Studies, Aug.).

Bellamy, C., and Child, G. (1996), *Common Market Law on Competition* (London: Sweet & Maxwell).

Benelux (1990), *Future EC Regulation on the Import of Bananas*, Memorandum of the governments of the Benelux countries, BEB (90) 5, 27 Sept.

Bennett, C., and Howlett, M. (1992), 'The Lessons of Learning: Reconciling Theories of Policy Learning and Policy Change', *Policy Sciences*, 25/3: 275–94.

Bennett, G. (1992), *Dilemmas: Coping with Environmental Problems* (London: Earthscan).

Benyon, F. (1992), 'Les "Accords européens" avec la Hongrie, la Pologne et la Tchécoslovaquie', *Revue du Marché Unique Européen*, 2: 25–50.

Benyon, J., Turnbull, L., Willis, A., Woodward, R., and Beck, A. (1993), *Police Cooperation in Europe: An Investigation* (Leicester: University of Leicester Press).

Berenz, C. (1994), 'Hat die betriebliche Altersversorgung zukünftig noch eine Chance?', *Neue Zeitschrift für Arbeitsrecht*, 11/9: 385–90, 11/10: 433–8.

Berghahn, V. (1986), *The Americanisation of West German Industry* (Leamington Spa: Berg).

Bergsten, C. F. (1999), 'America and Europe: Clash of the Titans?', *Foreign Affairs*, 78/2: 20–34.

Besley, T., and Seabright, P. (1999), 'State Aids: Making EU Policy Properly Reflect Geography and Subsidiarity', *Economic Policy*, 28: 13–42.

Beyers, J., and G. Dierickx (1998), 'The Working Groups of the Council of the European Union: Supranational or Intergovernmental Negotiations?, *Journal of Common Market Studies*, 36/3: 289–317.

Beyme, K. von, and Schmidt, M. G. (1985) (eds.), *Policy and Politics in the Federal Republic of Germany* (New York: St Martin's Press).

Bhagwatti, J., and Patrick, H. T. (1991) (eds.), *Aggressive Unilateralism: America's 301 Trade Policy and the World Trading System* (London: Harvester Wheatsheaf).

Bieback, K. -J. (1991), 'Harmonization of Social Policy in the European Community', *Les Cahiers de Droit*, 32/4: 913–35.

—— (1993), 'Marktfreiheit in der EG und nationale Sozialpolitik vor und nach Maastricht', *Europarecht*, 28/2: 150–72.

—— (1997), *Die mittelbare Diskriminierung wegen des Geschlechts. Ihre Grundlagen im Recht der EU und ihre Auswirkungen auf das Sozialrecht der Mitgliedstaaten* (Baden-Baden: Nomos).

Bieber, R., and Monar, J. (1995) (eds.), *Justice and Home Affairs in the European Union: The Development of the Third Pillar* (Brussels: European University Press).

Bigo, D. (1994), 'The European Internal Security Field: Stakes and Rivalries in a Newly Developing Area of Police Intervention', in Anderson and Boer (1994: 161–73).

—— and Leveau, R. (1992), 'L'Europe de la sécurité intérieure', end of study report for the Institut des Hautes Études de la Sécurité Intérieure, Paris.

—— (1996), *Polices en réseaux: l'expérience européenne* (Paris: Presses de la Fondation Nationale des Sciences Politiques).

Birk, R. (1997), 'Die Europäisierung des Arbeitsrechts', in K. Kreuzer *et al.* (eds.), *Die Europäisierung der mitgliedstaatlichen Rechtsordnungen der Europäischen Union* (Baden-Baden: Nomos), 55–9.

Blackman, D. (1994), 'Aid to the Democratically Elected Parliaments of Central and Eastern Europe: The European Parliament's Programme', paper presented at the Workshop of Parliamentary Scholars and Parliamentarians, Berlin, 19–20 Aug.

Blanchard, O. J. and Muet, P. A. (1993), 'Competitiveness through Disinflation: An Assessment of the French Macroeconomic Strategy', *Economic Policy*, Apr., 11–56.

Boehmer-Christiansen, S., and Skea, J. (1992), *Acid Politics: Environmental and Energy Policies in Britain and Germany* (London: Belhaven).

—— and Weidner, H. (1992), *Catalyst versus Lean Burn: A Comparative Analysis of Environmental Policy in the Federal Republic of Germany and Great Britain with Reference to Exhaust Emission Policy for Passenger Cars, 1970–1990*, FS II 92–304 (Berlin: Wissenschaftszentrum Berlin für Sozialforschung).

Börzel, T. A. (1999), *The Domestic Impact of Europe: Institutional Adaptation in Germany and Spain* (Florence: European University Institute).

Boltho, A. (1989), 'European and United States Regional Differentials: A Note', *Oxford Review of Economic Policy*, 5/2: 105–15.

Bonvicini, G., *et al.* (1991), *The Community and the Emerging European Democracies* (London: Royal Institute of International Affairs).

Boons, F. (1992), 'Product-Oriented Environmental Policy and Networks: Ecological Aspects of Economic Internationalization', *Environmental Politics*, 1/4: 84–105.

Bourgeois, J. (1987), 'The Common Commercial Policy: Scope and Nature of the Powers', in E. L. M. Volker (ed.), *Protectionism in the European Community* (Deventer: Kluwer Law and Taxation).

—— Berrod, F., and Gippini Fourier, E. (1995) (eds.), *The Uruguay Round Results: A European Lawyer's Perspective* (Brussels: EIP).

Bowler, I. R. (1985), *Agriculture under the Common Agricultural Policy: A Geography* (Manchester: Manchester University Press).

Bradley, K. St Clair (1994), 'Better Rusty than Missin': Institutional Reforms of the Maastricht Treaty and the European Parliament', in O'Keeffe and Twomey (1994: 193–212).

—— (1998), 'The GMO-Committee on Transgenic Maize: Alien Corn, or the Transgenic Procedural Maze', in van Schendelen (1998: 207–22).

Branch, A. P., and Øhrgaard, J. (1999), 'Trapped in the Supranational–Intergovernmental Dichotomy: A Response to Stone Sweet and Sandholtz', *Journal of European Public Policy*, 6/1: 123–143.

Bresserts, H., Huitema, D., and Kuks, S. M. M. (1994), 'Policy Networks in Dutch Water Policy', *Environmental Politics*, 3/4: 24–51.

Brinkhorst, L. J. (1991), 'Subsidiarity and European Environmental Policy', in *Subsidiarity: The Challenge of Change* (Maastricht: European Institute of Public Administration).

Brittan, L. (1992), *European Competition Policy: Keeping the Playing Field Level* (London: Brassey).

—— (1999), 'The EU Needs a New Framework Agreement on Competition', Paper presented at the OECD Conference on Trade and Competition, Paris, 29 June.

Brouwer, H. J., *et al.* (1995), *Do We Need a New Budget Deal?* (Brussels: Philip Morris Institute).

Brunetta, R., and Trenti, L. (1995), 'Italy: The Social Consequences of Economic and Monetary Union', *Labour*, 149–201.

Buchan, D. (1993), *Europe: The Strange Superpower* (Aldershot: Dartmouth).

Bueno de Mesquita, B., and Stokman, F. N. (1994), *European Community Decision-Making* (New Haven: Yale University Press).

Buigues, P., and Sheehy, J. (1994), 'European Integration and the Internal Market Programme', paper presented at the ESRC/COST A7 Conference, University of Exeter, 8–11 Sept.

—— Ilzkovitz, F., and Lebrun, J.-F. (1990), 'The Impact of the Internal Market by Industrial Sector: The Challenge for the Member States', *European Economy: Social Europe*, special edition, 3–7.

Buksti, J. A. (1983), 'Bread-and-Butter Agreement and High Politics Disagreement: Some Reflections on the Contextual Impact on Agricultural Interests in EC Policy-Making', *Scandinavian Political Studies*, 6/4: 261–80.

Bull, A. T., Holt, G., and Lilly, M. (1982), *Biotechnology International Trends and Perspectives* (Paris: OECD).

Bull, H. (1982), 'Civilian Power Europe: A Contradiction in Terms?', *Journal of Common Market Studies*, 21/1 2: 149 65.

Bulletin of the European Communities, various issues.

Bulmer, S. (1984), 'Domestic Politics and EC Policy-Making', *Journal of Common Market Studies*, 21/4: 349–63.

—— (1994a), 'The Governance of the European Union: A New Institutionalist Approach', *Journal of Public Policy*, 13/4: 351–80.

—— (1994b), 'Institutions and Policy Change in the European Communities: The Case of Merger Control', *Public Administration*, 72/3: 423–44.

—— (1997), *New Institutionalism, The Single Market and EU Governance*, ARENA Working Paper No. 25 (Oslo: ARENA, Oct.).

Bulmer, S., and Scott, A. (1994) (eds.), *Economic and Political Integration in Europe: International Dynamics and Global Context* (Oxford: Blackwell).

Bundesverfassungsgericht (1994), 'The Maastricht Decision', in Winckelmann (1994: 751–99).

Burley, A.-M., and Mattli, W. (1993), 'Europe before the Court: A Political Theory of Legal Integration', *International Organization*, 47/1: 41–76.

Cafruny, A. W., and Rosenthal, G. G. (1993) (eds.), *The State of the European Community*, ii: *The Maastricht Debates and Beyond* (Boulder, Colo: Lynne Rienner).

Cameron, D. R. (1992), 'The 1992 Initiative: Causes and Consequences', in Sbragia (1992*b*: 23–74).

Cantley, M. (1995), 'The Regulation of Modern Biotechnology: A Historical and European Perspective. A Case Study in how Societies Cope with New Knowledge in the Last Quarter of the Twentieth Century', in H. J. Rehm and G. Reed (eds.) in cooperation with A. Pühler and P. Stadler (1995), *Biotechnology* xii: D. Brauer (ed.), *Legal, Economic and Ethical Dimensions*, 2nd edn. (Weinheim: VCH), 506–81.

Caporaso, J. A., and Keeler, J. T. S. (1993), 'The European Community and Regional Integration Theory', paper presented at the Third Biennial International Conference of the European Community Studies Association, Washington, 27–9 May.

Cappelletti, M., Secombe, M., and Weiler, J. H. H. (1986) (eds.), *Integration through Law: Europe and the American Federal Experience* (Berlin: Walter de Gruyter).

Carlsnaes, W., and Smith, S. (1990) (eds.), *European Foreign Policy* (London: Sage).

Cawson, A. (1992), 'Interests, Groups and Public Policy-Making: The Case of the European Consumer Electronics Industry', in Greenwood *et al.* (1992: 99–118).

Cayseele, P. van, Sabbatini, P. and van Meerbeeck, W. (forthcoming), 'National Competition Policies', in J. Pelkmans (ed.), *Regulation in the EU* (Brussels: CEPS).

CDU/CSU–Fraktion des Deutschen Bundestages (1994) (Christian Democratic Union/Christian Social Union), 'Reflections on European Policy', Bonn, 1 Sept.

Cecchini, P., with Catinat, M., and Jacquemin, A. (1988), *The European Challenge 1992: The Benefits of a Single Market* (Aldershot: Wildwood House).

CEPR (1992) (Centre for Economic Policy Research) *The Association Process: Making it Work: Central Europe and the EC*, CEPR Occasional Paper No. 11 (London: CEPR).

—— (1995), *Flexible Integration* (London: CEPR).

CEPS (1998) (Centre for European Policy Studies), *Network Industries in Europe: Preparing for Competition*, CEPS/CRI (London: CIPFA).

Chaumette, P. (1998), 'La Politique commune de pêches', in *Droits maritimes: exploitation et protection de l'Océan* (Lyon: Juris-Service).

Christiansen, T. (1999), 'Territorial Politics in the European Union', *Journal of European Public Policy*, 6/2: 349–57.

Cini, M. (1994), 'Policing the Internal Market: The Regulation of Competition in the European Commission', University of Bristol Ph.D. thesis.

—— and McGowan, L. (1998), *Competition Policy in the European Union* (London: Macmillan).

Cloos, J., Reinesch, G., Vignes, D., and Weyland, J. (1994), *Le Traité de Maastricht: genèse, analyse, commentaires* (Brussels: Bruylant).

Cochrane, W. W. (1965), *The City Man's Guide to the Farm Problem* (Minneapolis: University of Minnesota Press).

Cockfield, Lord (1994), *The European Union: Creating the Single Market* (London: Wiley Chancery Law).

Collier, U. (1997), 'The EU and Climate Change Policy: The Struggle over Policy Competences', in

U. Collier and R. E. Lofstedt (1997) (eds.), *Cases in Climate Change Policy: Political Reality in the European Union* (London: Earthscan), 226–42.

—— and Golub, J. (1997), 'Environmental Policy and Politics', in M. Rhodes, P. Heywood, and V. Wright (1997) (eds.), *Developments in West European Politics* (New York: St Martin's Press), 226–42.

Collins, D. (1975), *The European Communities: The Social Policy of the First Phase*, 2 vols., (London: Martin Robertson).

Comanor, W., *et al.* (1990) (eds.), *Competition Policy in Europe and North America: Economic Issues and Institutions* (London: Harwood).

Commission (1969–), *The Agricultural Situation in the European Communities* (Luxembourg: Office for Official Publications of the European Communities).

—— (1972– , 1992–), *General Report of the European Communities* (from 1992: *Union*) (Luxembourg: Office for Official Publications of the European Communities).

—— (1981–), *Annual Reports on Competition Policy* (Luxembourg: Office for Official Publications of the European Communities).

—— (1983), *Biotechnology in the Community*, Communication from the Commission to the Council, COM (83) 672 final/2.

—— (1985*a*), *Completing the Internal Market: White Paper from the Commission to the European Council*, COM (85) 310 final.

—— (1985*b*), internal memo from DG III to DG XI, photocopy.

—— (1986), *A Community Framework for the Regulation of Biotechnology*, Communication from the Commission to the Council, COM (86) 573 final.

—— (1987*a*), *Making a Success of the Single Act*, EC Bulletin, suppl., 1/87.

—— (1987*b*), *Report by the Commission to the Parliament on the Financing of the Community Budget*, COM (87) 101 final.

—— (1988*a*), *Research on the 'Cost of Non-Europe': Basic Findings*, 16 vols., (Luxembourg: Office for Official Publications of the European Communities).

—— (1988*b*), *Seventeenth Report on Competition Policy* (Luxembourg: Office for Official Publications of the European Communities).

—— (1988*c*), *Proposal for a Council Directive on the Contained Use of Genetically Modified Micro-organisms*, COM (88) 160 final.

—— (1989*a*), *Community Public Finance: The European Budget after the 1988 Reform* (Luxembourg: Office for Official Publications of the European Communities).

—— (1989*b*–), *Surveys of State Aids in the European Community* (Luxembourg: Office for Official Publications of the European Communities).

—— (1990*a*), *Association Agreements with the Countries of Central and Eastern Europe: A General Outline*, COM (90) 398 final, 27 Aug.

—— (1990*b*), *Commission Communication to the Council on the Uruguay Round Negotiations: Progress and Prospects*, Feb.

—— (1990*c*), *Commission Opinion of 21 October 1990 on the Proposal for Amendment of the Treaty Establishing the EEC with a View to Political Union*, COM (90) 600 final, 23 Oct.

—— (1990*d*), *The Development of the Community's Relations with the Countries of Central and Eastern Europe*, SEC (90) 194 final, 1 Feb.

—— (1990*e*), 'One Market, One Money', *European Economy*, 44, Oct.

—— (1990*f*), *Twenty-Fifth General Report on the Activities of the European Communities, 1990* (Luxembourg: Office for Official Publications of the European Communities).

—— (1990*g*), *Industrial Policy in an Open and Competitive Environment*, COM (90) 556.

Commission (1991a), *Promoting a Competitive Environment for Industrial Activities Based on Biotechnology within the Community*, Commission Communication to the Parliament and the Council, SEC (91) 629 final.

—— (1991b), *Report 1991 from the Commission to the Council and the European Parliament on the Common Fisheries Policy*, SEC (91) 2288 final.

—— (1992a), *From the Single Act to Maastricht and Beyond: The Means to Match our Ambitions*, Feb.

—— (1992b), 'Europe and the Challenge of Enlargement', *Bulletin of the EC*, suppl., 3/92.

—— (1992c), *The European Community and the Uruguay Round*, Nov.

—— (1992d), *The Operation of the Community's Internal Market after 1992: Follow-Up to the Sutherland Report*, SEC (92) 2277 final, 2 Dec.

—— (1992e), *Towards a Closer Association with the Countries of Central and Eastern Europe*, SEC (92) 2301 final, 2 Dec.

—— (1993a), *Commission Report to the European Council on the Adaptation of Community Legislation to the Subsidiarity Principle*, COM (93) 545 final.

—— (1993b), *The Community Budget: The Facts and Figures* (Luxembourg: Office for Official Publications of the European Communities).

—— (1993c), *Conducting the Uruguay Round*, Dec.

—— (1993d), *Growth, Competitiveness, Employment: The Challenges and Ways Forward into the 21st Century*, COM (93) 700 final.

—— (1993e), 'Stable Money—Sound Finances', *European Economy*, 53.

—— (1993f), *Towards a Closer Association with the Countries of Central and Eastern Europe*, SEC (93) 648 final, 18 May.

—— (1993g), *Twenty-Second Report on Competition Policy* (Luxembourg: Office for Official Publications of the European Communities).

—— (1994a), *The Europe Agreements and Beyond: A Strategy to Prepare the Countries of Central and Eastern Europe for Accession*, COM (94) 320 final, 13 July.

—— (1994b), *The European Union's Cohesion Fund* (Luxembourg: Office for Official Publications of the European Communities).

—— (1994c), *Follow-Up to Commission Communication on 'The Europe Agreements and Beyond: A Strategy to Prepare the Countries of Central and Eastern Europe for Accession'*, COM (94) 361 final, 27 July.

—— (1994d), *Twenty-Third Report on Competition Policy* (Luxembourg: Office for Official Publications of the European Communities).

—— (1994e), *The Uruguay Round Background Brief*, updated, May.

—— (1994f), *European Social Policy: A Way Forward for the Union. A White Paper*.

—— (1994g), *Potential Benefits of Integration of Environmental and Economic Policies: An Incentive-Based Approach to Policy Integration* (London: Graham & Trotman).

—— (1995a), *Commission's Work Programme for 1995*, COM (95) 26 final.

—— (1995b), *Preparation of the Associated Countries of Central and Eastern Europe for Integration into the Internal Market of the Union*, COM (95) 163 final, 3 May.

—— (1995c), *Report on the Operation of the Treaty on European Union*, Brussels, 10 May.

—— (1995d), 'Transposition du Livre Blanc: le sueil de 90% est atteint', *DG XV News*, 1, Mar.

—— (1995e), *2000—Sound Financial Management*, Information Note from Commissioners Liikanen and Gradin, SEC 95/477, 20 Mar.

—— (1996a), 'Economic Evaluation of the Internal Market', *European Economy*, 4.

—— (1996b), *The Impact and Effectiveness of the Single Market*, COM (96) 520 final, 30 Oct.

—— (1996c), *First Report on Economic and Social Cohesion* (Luxembourg: Office for Official Publications of the European Communities).

—— (1996*d*), *Green Paper on the Review of the Merger Regulation*, COM (96) 19.

—— (1996*e*), *Competition Policy in the New Trade Order*, COM (96) 284.

—— (1996*f*), *Monitoring the Common Fisheries Policy*, COM (96) 100 final.

—— (1996*g*), *Reinforcing Political Union and Preparing for Enlargement*, 28 Feb.

—— (1996*h*), *Communication on the Implementation and Enforcement of the Environmental Law*, COM (96) 500, 22 Oct.

—— (1996*i*), 'Notice on Services of General Economic Interest', *OJ* C281, 26 Oct.

—— (1997*a*), *The Community Budget: The Facts in Figures*, SEC (97) 1200 final.

—— (1997*b*), *The Impact of Structural Policies on Economic and Social Cohesion in the Union 1989–99* (Luxembourg: Official Publications).

—— (1997*c*), 'External Access to European Markets', *Single Market Review*, subser. IV/4 (London: Kogan Page Earthscan).

—— (1997*d*), *Communication from the Commission to the Council, the European Parliament, the Economic and Social Committee and the Committee of the Regions: Climate Change—The EU Approach to Kyoto*, COM (97) 481.

—— (1997*e*), *Green Paper on Vertical Restraints in European Community Competition Policy*, COM (97) 721.

—— (1997*f*), *The Future for the Market in Fisheries Products in the European Union: Responsibility, Partnership, and Competitiveness*, Communication from the Commission to the Council and the European Parliament, COM (97) 719.

—— (1997*g*), *Commission Opinion on Poland's Application for Membership of the European Union*, COM (97) 2002.

—— (1997*h*), *Green Paper on Relations between the European Union and the ACP Countries on the Eve of the 21st Century: Challenges and Options for a New Partnership*.

—— (1997*i*), *Agenda 2000: For a Stronger and Wider Union*, COM (97) 2000 final, 15 July.

—— (1997*j*), *An Action Plan for the Single Market* (Brussels).

—— (1998*a*), *Agenda 2000: Financing the European Union*, DG XIX, Mar.

—— (1998*b*), *Commission Report on the Operation of the Own Resources System*, 8 Oct.

—— (1998*c*), *Social Action Programme 1998–2000*, COM (98) 259 final.

—— (1998*d*), *Single Market Scoreboard*, no. 3, Oct.

—— (1998*e*), *Climate Change: Towards an EU post-Kyoto Strategy*, Communication from the Commission to the Council and the European Parliament, COM (98) 353.

—— (1998*f*) *Commission Strengthens the Fight against Cartels*, Press Release IP/98/1060.

—— (1998*g*), *Fisheries Monitoring under the Common Fisheries Policy*, Communication from the Commission to the Council and the European Parliament, COM (98) 92.

—— (1998*h*), *Report on the Progress towards Accession by each of the Candidate Countries*, Composite Paper, COM (98) 712 final, 4 Nov.

—— (1998*i*), *European Strategy for Turkey: The Commission's Initial Operational Approach*, COM (98) 124, 4 Mar.

—— (1999*a*), *Assessment of the Single Market Action Plan, June 1997 – December 1998*, COM (99) 74 final, 18 Feb.

—— (1999*b*), *Mutual Recognition in the Context of the Follow-Up to the Action Plan for the Single Market*, 16 June.

—— (1999*c*), *Single Market Scoreboard*, no. 4, June.

—— (1999*d*), *White Paper on Modernisation of the Rules Implementing Articles 85 and 86 of the EC Treaty*.

—— (1999*e*), *Report on the Application of EC State Aid Law by the Member State Courts*.

Commission (1999f) *Preparing for Implementation of the Kyoto Protocol*, Communication from the Commission to the Council and the European Parliament, COM (99) 230, 19 May.

—— (1999g), *The Stabilisation and Association Process for the Countries of South-Eastern Europe*, COM (99) 235, 26 May.

—— (1999h), *Composite Paper: Reports on Progress towards Accession by each of the Candidate countries*, Oct.

——, DG VI (1998), *Agricultural Situation and Perspectives in the Central and East European Countries* (Brussels).

—— (1999), 'Agricultural Council: Political Agreement on CAP Reform', *Newsletter*, special edition, 11 Mar.

——, DG XI A/2 Biotechnology (n.d.), *The European Community and the Contained Use of Genetically Modified Micro-organisms*.

——, DG XII (1985a), *Biotechnology at the Community Level: Concertation*, Concertation Unit for Biotechnology in Europe (Brussels).

——, DG XII (1985b), , *The Commission's Approach to the Regulation of Biotechnology*, Biotechnology Regulatory Interservices Committee.

——, DG XII (1994), *The Views of the Research Community on the Regulatory Framework: DG XII Survey, Executive Summary*.

——, Office of the Secretariat General (1994), Fiche No. 4: *Biotechnology*, 27 Sept.

Committee of Independent Experts (1999), *First Report on Allegations regarding Fraud, Mismanagement, and Nepotism in the European Commission*, Mar. (Brussels).

Conference de la Charte Européenne de l'Énergie (1994), *Traité de la charte de l'énergie*, 14 Dec.

Corbett, R., Jacobs, F., and Shackleton, M. (1995), *The European Parliament*, 3rd edn. (London: Cartermill; new edn. forthcoming).

Corden, W. M. (1997), *Trade Policy and Economic Welfare*, 2nd edn. (Oxford: Clarendon Press).

Cot, J.-P. (1989), 'The Fine Art of Community Budgeting Procedure', *Contemporary European Affairs*, 1: 227–39.

Couliou, J.-R. (1998), *La Pêche bretonne: les ports de Bretagne sud face à leur avenir* (Rennes: Presses Universitaires de Rennes).

Council of the European Union (1994), *Conclusions of the Presidency*, Essen European Council, SN 300/94, 10 Dec., 9–10.

—— (1995a), *Report on the Functioning of the Treaty on European Union*, SN 1821/95, 14 Mar., (Brussels).

—— (1995b), *Conclusions of the Presidency*, Madrid European Council, 15–16 Dec., SN 400/95.

—— (1998), *Negotiating Directives for the Negotiation of a Development Partnership Agreement with the ACP Countries*, Information Note 10017/98, 30 June.

Coutu, D., Hladik, K., Meen, D., and Turcq, D. (1993), 'Views of the Business Community on post-1992 Integration in Europe', in Jacquemin and Wright (1993b: 47–80).

Cowles, M. G. (1994), 'The Politics of Big Business in the European Community: Setting the Agenda for a New Europe', University of Washington Ph.D. thesis.

—— (1997), 'Organizing Industrial Coalitions: A Challenge for the Future?', in H. Wallace and Young (1997: 116–40).

Cox, A. (1992), 'Implementing 1992 Public Procurement Policy: Public and Private Obstacles to the Creation of the Single Market', *Public Procurement Law Review*, 2: 139–54.

Cram, L. (1996), 'Integration Theory and the Study of the EU Policy Process', in Richardson (1996b: 40–58).

—— (1997), *Policy-Making in the European Union: Conceptual Lenses and the Integration Process* (London: Macmillan).

Crean, K., and Symes, D. (1996) (eds.), *Fisheries Management in Crisis: A Social Science Perspective* (Oxford: Fishing News Books).

Criado Alonso, F. (1996), 'Regional Participation in Governance in the EU: The Cases of Galicia, the Basque Country, Scotland in the Fisheries Policy Field', College of Europe, Bruges, thesis for the Master of European Studies.

Croome, J. (1995), *Reshaping the World Trading System: A History of the Uruguay Round* (Geneva: WTO).

Curtin, D. (1993), 'The Constitutional Structure of the Union: A Europe of Bits and Pieces', *Common Market Law Review*, 30/1: 17–69.

—— (1998), 'Democracy, Transparency and Political Participation: Some Progress post-Amsterdam', in V. Deckmyn and I. Thomson (eds.), *Openness and Transparency in the European Union* (Maastricht: European Institute of Public Administration), 107–20.

—— and H. Meijers (1997), 'The Principle of Open Government in Schengen and the European Union: Democratic Regression?', in H. Meijers *et al.*, *Democracy, Migrants and the Police in the European Union: The 1996 IGC and Beyond*, Standing Committee of Experts in International Immigration, Refugee and Criminal Law (Utrecht: Forum), 13–44.

Daedalus (1995), 'What Future for the State?', Proceedings of the American Academy of Arts and Sciences, 124/2.

Dahrendorf, R. (1973), *Plädoyer für die Europäische Union* (Munich: Piper).

Dam, K. W. (1967), 'The European Common Market in Agriculture', *Columbia Law Review*, 67/2: 209–65.

—— (1970), *The GATT: Law and International Economic Organization* (London: University of Chicago Press).

Dashwood, A. (1977), 'Hastening Slowly: The Communities' Path towards Harmonization', in H. Wallace *et al.* (1977: 273–99).

—— (1983), 'Hastening Slowly: The Communities' Path towards Harmonization', in H. Wallace *et al.* (1983: 177–208).

Davidow, J. (1977), 'EEC Fact-Finding Procedures in Competition Cases: An American Critique', *Common Market Law Review*, 14/2: 175–89.

Davis, B. (1991) (ed.), *The Genetic Revolution: Scientific Prospects and Public Perceptions* (Baltimore: Johns Hopkins University Press).

De Clercq, W. (1995), 'Closing Address', in Bourgeois *et al.* (1995: 511–17).

De Grauwe, P. (1992), *The Economics of Monetary Integration* (Oxford: Oxford University Press).

—— (1994), 'Towards European Monetary Union without the EMS', *Economic Policy*, 18: 147–85.

—— and Papademos, L. (1990) (eds.), *The European Monetary System in the 1990s* (London: Longman).

Dehaene, J.-L., Simon, D., and von Weizäcker, R. (1999), *The Institutional Implications of Enlargement*, Report to the Commission (Brussels: mimeo, Oct.).

Dehousse, R. (1994) (ed.), *Europe after Maastricht: An Ever Closer Union?* (Munich: C. H. Beck).

—— (1998a), *The European Court of Justice* (London: Macmillan).

—— (1998b), 'General Conclusions', in M. den Boer, A. Guggenbühl, and S. Vanhoonacker (eds.), *Coping with Flexibility and Legitimacy after Amsterdam*, Current European Issues (Maastricht: European Institute of Public Administration), 231–42.

—— (1999), *Amsterdam: The Making of a Treaty* (London: Kogan Page).

Deighton, A. (1997) (ed.), *Western European Union 1954–1997: Defence, Security, Integration* (Oxford: St Antony's College).

de Jesus, J. A. R. (1998), 'The Portugese Fisheries Policy in the Context of European Integration: Challenges and perspectives', College of Europe, Bruges, Thesis for the Master of European Studies.

Delors, J. (1991), 'European Integration and Security', *Survival*, 23/2: 99–109.

—— *et al.* (1989), *Report on Economic and Monetary Union in the European Community*, Committee for the Study of Economic and Monetary Union, (Luxembourg: Office for Official Publications of the European Communities).

Del Vecchio, A. (1995), 'La Politique de la pêche: axe de développement', *Revue du Marché Unique Européen* 2: 27–36.

den Boer, M. (1991), *Schengen: Intergovernmental Scenario for European Police Cooperation*, Working Paper No. V (Edinburgh: University of Edinburgh, Department of Politics).

—— (1994a), 'Europe and the Art of International Police Cooperation: Free Fall or Measured Scenario?', in O'Keeffe and Twomey (1994: 279–94).

—— (1994b), 'The Quest for European Policing: Rhetoric and Justification in a Disorderly Debate', in M. Anderson and den Boer (1994: 174–96).

—— (1996), 'The Evolution of Cross-border Policing in Europe', *Current Politics and Economics of Europe*, 5/2–3: 107–27.

—— (1998a), 'Steamy Windows: Transparency and Opennness in Justice and Home Affairs', in V. Deckmyn and I. Thomson (eds.), *Openness and Transparency in the European Union* (Maastricht: European Institute of Public Administration), 91–105.

—— (1998b), *Taming the Third Pillar: Improving the Management of Justice and Home Affairs Cooperation in the EU*, Current European Issues Paper (Maastricht: European Institute of Public Administration).

—— (forthcoming), 'The Incorporation of Schengen into the TEU: A Bridge too Far?', in Monar and Wessels (forthcoming).

—— and Walker, N. (1993), 'European Policing after 1992', *Journal of Common Market Studies*, 31/1: 3–28.

Denmark (1986), Environment and Gene Technology Act No. 288, June 4.

Denza, E. (1996), 'The Community as a Member of International Organizations', in N. Emiliou and D. O'Keeffe (eds.), *The European Union and World Trade Law: After the Uruguay Round* (Chichester: Wiley), 3–18.

Deringer, A. (1964), 'The Interpretation of Article 90(2) of the EEC Treaty', *Common Market Law Review*, 2/2: 129–38.

Destler, I. M. (1995), *American Trade Politics*, 3rd edn. (Washington: Institute for International Economics and Twentieth Century Fund).

Deubner, C. (1995), *Von Maastricht nach Kerneuropa* (Baden-Baden: Nomos).

Deudney, D. H. (1995), 'The Philadelphian System: Sovereignty, Arms Control, and the Balance of Power in the American States-Union, 1787–1861', *International Organization*, 49/2: 191–228.

Devos, S., Woolcock, S., Bressant, A., and Raby, G. (1993), 'Study on Regional Integration', paper presented to the OECD Trade Directorate's Trade Committee, TD/TC (93) 15.

Devuyst, Y. (1995), 'The European Community and the Conclusion of the Uruguay Round', in C. Rhodes and Mazey (1995: 449–468).

Diebold,W. (1959), *The Schuman Plan: A Study in Economic Cooperation 1950–9* (New York: Praeger).

Dinan, D. (1998), 'The Commission and Enlargement', in J. Redmond and G. Rosenthal (eds.), *The Expanding European Union, Past, Present, Future* (Boulder, Colo.: Lynne Rienner), 17–40.

—— (1999), *Ever-Closer Union: An Introduction to the European Union*, 2nd edn. (London: Macmillan).

Dorbey, C. (1995), 'Dialectical Functionalism: Stagnation as a Booster of European Integration', *International Organization*, 49/2: 253–84.

DTI (1991) (Department of Trade and Industry), *Competition Policy: How it Works* (London: HMSO).

Dubbink, W., and van Vliet, M. (1996), 'Market Regulation versus Co-management', *Marine Policy*, 20/6: 499–516.

Duchêne, F. (1994), *Jean Monnet: First Statesman of Interdependence* (New York: Norton).

—— Szczepanik, E., and Legg, W. (1985), *New Limits on European Agriculture: Politics and the Common Agricultural Policy* (London: Croom Helm).

Duff, A., Pinder, J., and Price, R. (1994) (eds.), *Maastricht and Beyond: Building the European Union* (London: Routledge).

du Guerny, S., and Bauern, A. (1994), 'Bruxelles n'accordera pas de clause de sauvegarde à la pêche', *Les Échos*, 14 Feb. (Paris).

Dumez, H., and Jeunemaître, A. (1996), 'The Convergence of Competition Policies in Europe: Internal Dynamics and External Imposition', in S. Berger and R. Dore (eds.), *National Diversity and Global Capitalism* (Ithaca, NY: Cornell University Press).

Dunn, J. (1994) (ed.), 'Contemporary Crisis of the Nation State?', *Political Studies*, 42, special issue.

Dunnet, D. (1991), 'The European Bank for Reconstruction and Development: A Legal Survey', *Common Market Law Review*, 28/3: 571–97.

Dyson, K. H. F. (1992) (ed.), *The Politics of German Regulation* (Aldershot: Dartmouth).

—— (1994), *Elusive Union: The Process of Economic and Monetary Union in Europe* (London: Longman).

The Economist, various issues.

Edwards, G. (1998), 'The Council of Ministers and Enlargement: A Search for Efficiency, Effectiveness, and Accountability', in J. Redmond and G. Rosenthal (eds.), *The Expanding European Union, Past, Present, Future* (Boulder, Colo.: Lynne Rienner), 41–64.

—— and Nuttall, S. (1994), 'Common Foreign and Security Policy', in Duff *et al.* (1994: 84–103).

—— and Spence, D. (1994) (eds.), *The European Commission* (London: Longman).

Ehlermann, C. D. (1997), *Differentiation, Flexibility, Closer Cooperation: The New Provisions of the Amsterdam Treaty* (Florence: Robert Schuman Centre, European University Institute).

Eichenberg, R. C., and Dalton, R. J. (1993), 'Europeans and the European Community: The Dynamics of Public Support for European Integration', *International Organization*, 47/4: 507–34.

Eichener, V. (1993), *Social Dumping or Innovative Regulation? Processes and Outcomes of European Decision-Making in the Sector of Health and Safety at Work Harmonization*, EUI Working Papers in Political and Social Sciences (SPS) No. 92/28 (Florence: European University Institute).

—— (1997), 'Effective European Problem Solving: Lessons from the Regulation of Occupational Safety and Environmental Protection', *Journal of European Public Policy*, 4/4: 591–608.

—— and Voelzkow, H. (1994) (eds.), *Europäische Integration und verbandliche Interessenvermittlung* (Marburg: Metropolis Verlag).

Eichengreen, B. (1992), 'Should the Maastricht Treaty be Saved?', Princeton Studies in International Finance, 74 (Princeton: Princeton University Economics Department).

—— (1998), 'European Monetary Unification: A *Tour d'Horizon*', *Oxford Review of Economic Policy*, 14/3: 24–40.

—— and Frieden, J. (1994) (eds.), *The Political Economy of European Monetary Unification* (Boulder, Colo.: Westview Press).

—— and Wyplosz, C. (1993), *The Unstable EMS*, Brookings Papers on Economic Activity, 1 (Washington: Brookings Institution).

Eichenhofer, E. (1992) (ed.), *Die Zukunft des koordinierenden Europäischen Sozialrechts* (Cologne: Carl Heymanns).

Eichhorst, W. (1998), 'European Social Policy between National and Supranational Regulation:

Posted Workers in the Framework of Liberalized Services Provision', DP 98/6 (Cologne: Max Planck Institute for Social Research).

Emerson, M., Aujean, M., Catinat, M., Goybet, P., and Jacquemin, A. (1988), *The Economics of 1992: The EC Commission's Assessment of the Economic Effects of Completing the Internal Market* (Oxford: Oxford University Press).

Emmert, F. (1996), *Europarecht* (Munich: C. H. Beck).

Ends Reports, various issues.

Environment Watch: Western Europe, various issues.

Esping-Andersen, G. (1990), *The Three Worlds of Welfare Capitalism* (Cambridge: Polity Press).

Estrin, S., and Holmes, P. (1998) (eds.), *Competition and Economic Integration in Europe* (Cheltenham: Edward Elgar).

Eurobarometer, various issues.

Euro-East, 23 Apr. 1993.

Europe, various issues.

European Council (1984), *Conclusions of the Presidency*, Fontainebleau European Council, June.

—— (1999), *Presidency Conclusions: Berlin European Council*, 24–5 Mar.

—— (1999a), *Presidency Conclusions: Tampere European Council*, 15–16 Oct.

European Court of Auditors (1998), Information Note on the *Annual Report of the ECA Concerning the Financial Year 1997* (www.eca.eu.int/english/noteinfora97.htm).

—— (1978–), *Annual Reports* (Luxembourg: Office of Official Publications of the European Communities).

European Parliament (1984), *Draft Treaty Establishing the European Union* (Luxembourg: European Parliament).

—— (1987), *Resolution on Biotechnology in Europe and the Need for an Integrated Policy*, doc. A2–134/86, 23 Mar.

—— (1993), *The Powers of the European Parliament in the European Union*, Directorate-General for Research, Working Paper Series E-1 (Luxembourg: European Parliament).

—— (1994), *Manual on the Common Fisheries Policy* (Luxembourg: European Parliament, Directorate-General for Research).

—— (1995), *The World Trade Organisation and the European Community*, Working Paper Series PE165.187, E-1 8 (Luxembourg: European Parliament, Directorate-General for Research).

—— (1996), *Bilateral Agreements and International Fishing Conventions* (Luxembourg: European Parliament, Directorate-General for Research).

European Union (1999), *The European Union Selected Instruments Taken from the Treaties*, bk. 1, vol. 1 (Luxembourg: Office for Official Publications of the European Communities).

European Report, various issues.

European Voice, various issues.

Eureport, Eureport Social, various issues.

Eurostat, various editions.

Evans, P. B., Jacobson, H. K., and Putnam, R. D. (1993) (eds.), *Double-Edged Diplomacy: International Bargaining and Domestic Politics* (Berkeley: University of California Press).

Faini, R., and Portes, R. (1995) (eds.), *European Union Trade with Eastern Europe: Adjustment and Opportunities* (London: CEPR).

Fairburn, J., Kay, J., and Sharpe, T. (1986), 'The Economics of Article 86', in G. Hall (ed.), *European Industrial Policy* (London: Croom Helm), 21–43.

Falkner, G. (1993), 'Die Sozialpolitik im Maastrichter Vertragsgebäude der Europäischen Gemeinschaft', *SWS-Rundschau*, 33/1: 23–43.

—— (1994a), 'Die Sozialpolitik der EG. Rechtsgrundlagen und Entwicklung von Rom bis Maastricht', in Haller and Schachner-Blazizek (1994: 221–46).

—— (1994b), *Supranationalität trotz Einstimmigkeit. Entscheidungsmuster der EU am Beispiel Sozialpolitik* (Bonn: Europa Union Verlag).

—— (1998), *EU Social Policy in the 1990s: Towards a Corporatist Policy Community* (London: Routledge).

Feld, W. (1980), 'Two-Tier Policy Making in the EC: The Common Agricultural Policy', in Hurwitz, L. (ed.), *Contemporary Perspectives on European Integration* (Westport, Conn.: Greenwood), 123–49.

Feldstein, M. (1997), 'EMU and International Conflict', *Foreign Affairs*, 76/6: 60–73.

Fennell, R. (1997), *The Common Agricultural Policy: Continuity and Change* (Oxford: Clarendon Press).

Ferge, Z., and Kolberg, J. E. (1992) (eds.), *Social Policy in a Changing Europe* (Boulder, Colo.: Westview Press).

Ferrera, M., and Gualmini, E. (forthcoming), 'Italy: Rescue from Without?', in F. W. Scharpf and V. A. Schmidt (eds.), *From Vulnerability to Competitiveness: Welfare and Work in the Open Economy* (Oxford: Oxford University Press).

Financial Times, various issues.

Fischler, F. (1999), Speech to the 6th East-West Agricultural Forum, Berlin, 23 Jan.

Fisher, R., and Ury, W. (1981), *Getting to Yes: Negotiating Agreement without Giving In* (London: Hutchinson).

Fitoussi, J.-P. (1995), *Le Débat interdit: Monnaie, Europe, Pauvreté* (Paris: Arlea).

Flemming, J., and Rollo, J. M. C. (1992) (eds.), *Trade, Payments, and Adjustment in Central and Eastern Europe* (London: Royal Institute of International Affairs and European Bank for Reconstruction and Development).

Flora, P. (1993), 'The National Welfare States and European Integration', in Moreno (1993: 11–22).

—— (1999) (ed.), *State Formation, Nation-Building and Mass Politics in Europe: The Theory of Stein Rokkan* (Oxford: Oxford University Press).

Flynn, B. (1999), 'Postcards from the Edge of Integration? The Role of Committees in EU Environment Policy Making' in *Administering the New Europe: The Role of Committees in the European Union* (Manchester: Manchester University Press).

Forrester, I., and Norrall, C. (1996), 'Competition Law', in *Yearbook of European Law 1995*, xv, (Oxford: Oxford University Press), 321–407.

Forster, A. (1994), 'The EC and the WEU', in Moens and Anstis (1994: 135–158).

—— (1995), 'Empowerment and Constraint: Britain and the Negotiation of the Treaty on European Union', University of Oxford D.Phil. thesis.

Forsyth, M. (1981), *Unions of States* (Leicester: Leicester University Press).

Foster, E. (1992), 'The Franco-German Corps: A "Theological" Debate?', *RUSI Journal*, 137/4: 63–7.

Fraga Estévez, C. (1997), *Report on the Common Fisheries Policy after the Year 2002*, EP 220.887 (Luxembourg: European Parliament).

Frankfurter Allgemeine Zeitung, various issues.

Franklin, M., Marsh, M., and McLaren, L. (1994), 'Uncorking the Bottle: Popular Opposition to European Unification in the Wake of Maastricht', *Journal of Common Market Studies*, 32/4: 455–73.

Frazer, T. (1992), *Monopoly Competition and the Law: The Regulation of Business Activity in Britain, Europe and America* (London: Harvester Wheatsheaf).

—— (1994), 'The New Structural Funds, State Aids and Interventions in the Single Market', *European Law Review*, 20/1: 3–19.

Freeman, C., Sharp, M., and Walker, W. (1991) (eds.), *Technology and the Future of Europe* (London: Pinter).

Friis, L. (1998), *The End of the Beginning of Eastern Enlargement: Luxembourg Summit and Agenda-Setting*, European Integration Online Papers, 2/7, <http://eiop.or.at/eiop/texte/1998-007a.htm>.

—— and Murphy, A. (1999), 'The European Union and Central and Eastern Europe: Governance and Boundaries', *Journal of Common Market Studies*, 37/2: 211–32.

Frissen, P. (1996), *De virtuele staat* (Schoonhoven: Academic Service).

From, J., and Stava, P. (1993), 'Implementation of Community Law: The Last Stronghold of National Control?', in Andersen and Eliassen, (1993: 55–67).

Fuchs, M. (1994–8) (ed.), *Nomos Kommentar zum europäischen Sozialrecht* (Baden-Baden: Nomos) (loose leaf).

Fursdon, E. (1980), *The European Defence Community: A History* (London: Macmillan).

Garcia, S. (1993) (ed.), *European Identity and the Search for Legitimacy* (London: Pinter).

Gardner, B. D. (1995), *Plowing Ground in Washington: The Political Economy of US Agriculture* (San Francisco: Pacific Research Institute for Public Policy).

Garrett, G. (1992), 'International Cooperation and Institutional Choice: The European Community's Internal Market', *International Organization*, 46/2: 533–60.

—— (1994), 'The Politics of Maastricht', in Eichengreen and Frieden (1994: 47–65).

—— (1995), 'The Politics of Legal Integration in the European Union', *International Organization*, 49/1: 171–81.

Gatsios, K., and Seabright, P. (1989), 'Regulation in the European Community', *Oxford Review of Economic Policy*, 5/2: 37–60.

GATT (1947), *The General Agreement on Tariffs and Trade*, in WTO, *The Results of the Uruguay Round of Multilateral Trade Negotiation: The Legal Texts* (Geneva: WTO, 1995).

—— (1986), *General Agreement on Tariffs and Trade: International Trade, 85–86* (Geneva: GATT).

—— (1991–5), *Trade Policy Review: The European Community* (Geneva: GATT).

—— (1993): *General Agreement of Tariffs and Trade: The European Communities, 1993*, 2 vols. (Geneva: GATT).

—— (1994*a*), *The Results of the Uruguay Round of Multilateral Trade Negotiations: The Legal Texts* (Geneva: GATT).

—— (1994*b*), *Code of Conduct Established between the Council of the Member States and the Commission Concerning the post Uruguay Round Negotiations on Services*, decided in procés-verbal at the 1756th session of Council, May 1994, annexed to Document 6948/94 GATT 85 (Geneva: GATT).

Gautron, J.-C. (1991) (ed.), *Les Relations Extérieures de la Communauté Européenne: Europe de l'Est* (Paris: Economica).

Genscher, H. D. (1982), 'Redefining the European Idea', *Europäische Zeitung*, Mar. (London: German Embassy Press Office).

George, K., and Jacquemin, A. (1990), 'Competition Policy in the European Community', in Comanor *et al.* (1990: 206–45).

George, S. (1991), *Politics and Policy in the EC* (Oxford: Oxford University Press).

—— (1997), 'Britain and the IGC', in G. Edwards and A. Pijpers (eds.), *The Politics of European Treaty Reform: The 1996 Intergovernmental Conference and Beyond* (London: Pinter), 100–18.

Gerber, D. (1994), 'The Transformation of European Community Competition Law?', *Harvard International Law Review*, 35/1: 97–147.

Geroski, P., and Jacquemin, A. (1985), 'Industrial Change, Barriers to Mobility, and European Industrial Policy', in Jacquemin and Sapir (1991: 298–333).

Giavazzi, F., and Pagano, M. (1988), 'The Advantage of Tying One's Hand: EMS Discipline and Central Bank Credibility', *European Economic Review*, 32: 1055–82.

Giesen, R. (1995), *Sozialversicherungsmonopol und EG-Vertrag* (Baden-Baden: Nomos).

Gilchrist, J., and Deacon, D. (1990), 'Curbing Subsidies', in P. Montagnon (ed.), *European Competition Policy* (London: Royal Institute of International Affairs), 31–51.

Gillingham, J. (1991), *Coal, Steel and the Rebirth of Europe, 1945–1955: The Germans and the French from Ruhr Conflict to Economic Community* (Cambridge: Cambridge University Press).

Giscard d'Estaing, V. (1995), 'Europe: les raisons de l'échec', *Le Figaro*, 10 Jan.

Gnesotto, N. (1990), 'Défense européenne: pourquoi pas les Douze?', *Politique Etrangère*, 55/4: 881–3.

—— (1994), *Lessons of Yugoslavia*, Chaillot Paper No. 14 (Paris: WEU Institute on Security Studies).

Godard, O. (1997) (ed.), *Le Principe de précaution dans la conduite des affaires humaines* (Paris: Éditions de l'EHESS).

Goldstein, J. (1993), *Ideas, Interests, and American Trade Policy* (Ithaca, NY: Cornell University Press).

—— and Keohane, R. O. (1993) (eds.), *Ideas and Foreign Policy: Beliefs, Institutions and Political Change* (Ithaca, NY: Cornell University Press).

Golub, J. (1994), 'British Integration into the EEC: A Case Study in European Environmental Policy', University of Oxford D.Phil. thesis.

—— (1996), 'British Sovereignty and the Development of EC Environmental Policy', *Environmental Policies*, 5/4: 700–28.

—— (1998) (ed.), *New Instruments for Environmental Policy in the EU* (London: Routledge).

Goodin, R. E., and Klingemann, H.-D. (1996) (eds.), *New Handbook of Political Science* (Oxford: Oxford University Press).

Goodman, J. (1992), *Monetary Sovereignty: The Politics of Central Banking in Western Europe* (Ithaca, NY: Cornell University Press).

Grabbe, H. (1999), *A Partnership for Accession?*, EUI Working Paper (Florence: European University Institute).

—— and Hughes, K. (1998), *Enlarging the EU Eastwards* (London: Pinter for the Royal Institute of International Affairs).

Grant, C. (1994), *Delors: Inside the House that Jacques Built* (London: Nicholas Brealey).

Grant, W. (1993), 'Transnational Companies and Environmental Policymaking: The Trend of Globalization', in Liefferink *et al.* (1993b).

—— (1998), 'Agenda 2000 and the CAP Reform Process', paper presented at the UACES Research Conference, Lincoln, Sept.

Gray, T. S. (1998) (ed.), *The Politics of Fishing* (London: Macmillan).

Greenwood J., and Ronit, K. (1995), 'The Organization of Biotechnology Interests in the European Union', Report to the European Commission from study contract B102-CT93-0603 (Aberdeen: Robert Gordon University).

—— Grote, J. R., and Ronit, K. (1992) (eds.), *Organized Interests and the European Community* (London: Sage).

Greve, B. (1996) (ed.), *Comparative Welfare Systems: The Scandinavian Model in a Period of Change* (London: Macmillan).

Grieco, J. M. (1995), 'The Maastricht Treaty, Economic and Monetary Union and the Neo-realist Research Programme', *Review of International Studies*, 21/1: 21–40.

Griffiths, R. (1997) (ed.), *Explorations in OEEC History* (Paris: OECD).

Gros, D., and Thygesen, N. (1998), *European Monetary Integration: From the European Monetary System towards Monetary Union*, 2nd edn. (London: Longman).

Grosser, A. (1980), *The Western Alliance: European–American Relations since 1945* (London: Macmillan).

Guegen, J., Laurec, A., Maucorps, A. (1990), 'La gestion des pêcheries communautaires et les mécanismes de décision', in Lebullenger and Le Morvan (1990: 145–61).

Guild, E. (1999) (ed.), *The Legal Framework and Social Consequences of Free Movement in the EU* (The Hague: Kluwer).

Haas, E. B. (1958), *The Uniting of Europe: Political, Social, and Economic Forces, 1950–1957* (Stanford, Calif.: Stanford University Press).

Haas, P. M. (1992), 'Introduction: Epistemic Communities and International Policy Coordination', *International Organization*, 46/1: 1–35.

—— (1993), 'Protecting the Baltic and North Seas', in P. M. Haas *et al.* (1993: 133–82).

—— Keohane, R. O., and Levy, M. A. (1993) (eds.), *Institutions for the Earth: Sources of Effective International Environmental Protection* (Cambridge, Mass.: MIT Press).

Hagen, K. (1992), 'The Social Dimension: A Quest for a European Welfare State', in Ferge and Kolberg (1992: 281–303).

—— (1998), 'Towards a Europeanisation of Social Policies? A Scandinavian Perspective', in MIRE, *Comparing Social Welfare Systems in Nordic Countries and France* (Paris: MIRE), 405–22.

Haigh, N. (1992a), 'The European Community and International Environmental Policy', in Hurrell and Kingsbury (1992: 228–49).

—— (1992b), *Manual of Environmental Policy: The EC and Britain* (Harlow: Longman).

—— (1997), *Community Environmental Law: Making it Work*, Background paper for invited experts and participants, House of Lords Select Committee on the European Communities. (London: Stationery Office), app. 5.

—— (1999), 'European Union Environmental Policy at 25: Retrospect and Prospect', *Environment and Planning C: Government and Policy*, 17, Feb., 109–12.

Hailbronner, K. (1994), 'Visa Regulations and Third-Country Nationals in EC Law', *Common Market Law Review*, 31/5: 969–95.

Hall, P. (1986), *Governing the Economy: The Politics of State Intervention in Britain and France* (New York: Oxford University Press).

—— (1999), 'The Political Economy of Europe in an Era of Interdependence', in H. Kitschelt, P. Lange, G. Marks, and J. D. Stephens (eds.), *Continuity and Change in Contemporary Capitalism* (Cambridge: Cambridge University Press), 135–63.

—— and Taylor, R. C. R. (1996), 'Political Science and the Three New Institutionalisms', *Political Studies*, 44/5: 936–57.

Haller, M., and Schachner-Blazizek, P. (1994) (eds.), *Europa—Wohin? Wirtschaftliche Integration, soziale Gerechtigkeit und Demokratie* (Graz: Leykam).

Hallstein, W. (1962), *United Europe: Challenge and Opportunity* (Cambridge, Mass.: Harvard University Press).

—— (1969), *Der unvollendete Bundestaat* (Dusseldorf: Econ Verlag).

Hancher, L., and Moran, M. (1989), 'Introduction: Regulation and Deregulation', *European Journal of Political Research*, 17/2: 129–36.

Hanny, B., and Wessels, W. (1998), 'The Monetary Committee: A Significant though not Typical Case', in van Schendelen (1998: 109–26).

Hanson, B. T. (1998), 'What Happened to Fortress Europe? External Trade Policy Liberalization in the European Union', *International Organization*, 52/1: 55–86.

Hardach, K. (1980), *The Political Economy of Germany in the Twentieth Century* (Berkeley: University of California Press).

Harding, C. (1992), 'Who Goes to Court in Europe? An Analysis of Litigation against the European Community?', *European Law Review*, 17/2: 105–25.

Hardy-Bass, L. (1994), 'The US–EC Confrontation in the GATT from a US Perspective: What did we Learn?', in Anania *et al.* (1994*b*: 236–45).

Harvie, C. (1994), *The Rise of Regional Europe* (London: Routledge).

Hauser, R. (1996), 'Sozialpolitische Optionen in der Europäischen Union', in W. Fricke (ed.), *Jahrbuch für Arbeit und Technik 1995* (Bonn: Dietz), 232–44.

Hawkes, L. (1992), 'The EC Merger Control Regulation. Not an Industrial Policy Instrument: The De Havilland Decision', *European Competition Law Review*, 13/1: 34–48.

Hayes, J. P. (1993), *Making Trade Policy in the European Community* (London: St Martin's Press).

Hayes-Renshaw, F., and Wallace, H. (1997), *The Council of Ministers of the European Union* (London: Macmillan).

Heidhues, T., Josling, T. E., Ritson, C., and Tangermann, S. (1979), *Common Prices and Europe's Farm Policy*, Thames Essay No. 14 (London: Trade Policy Research Centre).

Held, D. (1991*a*), 'Democracy, the Nation-State and the Global System', in Held (1991*b*: 197–235).

—— (1991*b*) (ed.), *Political Theory Today* (Stanford, Calif.: Stanford University Press).

Henderson, D. (1999), *The Changing Fortunes of Economic Liberalism* (London: Institute of Economic Affairs).

Herbst, L., Bührer, W., and Sowade, H. (1990), *Vom Marshallplan zur EWG. Die Eingliederung der Bundesrepublik Deutschland in die westliche Welt* (Munich: Oldenbourg).

Héritier, A. (1993) (ed.), *Policy-Analyse: Kritik und Neuorientierung* (Opladen: Westdeutscher Verlag).

—— (1994), ' "Leaders" and "Laggards" in European Policy-Making: Clean-Air Policy Changes in Britain and Germany', in Waarden and Unger (1994: 278–305).

—— (1996), 'The Accommodation of Diversity in European Policy Making and its Outcomes: Regulatory Policy as a Patchwork', *Journal of European Public Policy*, 3/2: 149–67.

—— Knill, C., and Mingers, S. (1995), *The Changing State in Europe: Changes in Regulatory Policy* (Berlin: Walter de Gruyter).

—— —— —— (1996), *Ringing the Changes in Europe: Regulatory Competition and Redefinition of the State. Britain, France, Germany* (Berlin: Walter de Gruyter).

Herrup, A. (1999), 'Eco-labels: Benefits Uncertain, Impacts Unclear?', *European Environmental Law Review*, 8/5: 144–52.

Hesse, J. (1994) (ed.), *European Yearbook of Public Administration and Comparative Government, 1994* (Oxford: Oxford University Press).

Hibbs, D. A., and Madsen, H. J. (1981), 'Public Reactions to the Growth of Taxation and Government Expenditure', *World Politics*, 33/3: 413–35.

Hildebrand, P. M. (1992), 'The European Community's Environmental Policy, 1957 to "1992": From Incidental Measures to an International Regime?', *Environmental Politics*, 1/4: 13–44.

Hill, C. (1993), 'The Capability–Expectations Gap, or Conceptualising Europe's International Role', *Journal of Common Market Studies*, 31/3: 305–28.

—— (1998), 'Closing the Capability–Expectations Gap', in Peterson and Sjursen (1998: 18–38).

Hindley, B. (1992), 'Exports from Eastern and Central Europe and Contingent Protection', in Flemming and Rollo (1992: 144–53).

Hine, D., and Kassim, H. (1998) (eds.), *Beyond the Market: The EU and National Social Policy* (London: Routledge).

Hirschman, A. O. (1981), *Essays in Trespassing: Economics to Politics and Beyond* (Cambridge: Cambridge University Press).

Hix, S. (1994), 'The Study of the European Community: The Challenge to Comparative Politics', *West European Politics*, 19/4: 1–30.

—— (1999), *The Political System of the European Union* (London: Macmillan).

—— and Lord, C. (1997), *Political Parties in the European Union* (London: Macmillan).

Hodgson, J. (1992), 'Europe, Maastricht, and Biotechnology', *Bio/Technology*, 10/11: 1421–6.

Hoekman, B. (1997), 'Competition Policy and the Global Trading System', *World Economy*, 4/4: 383–406.

Hoffman, S. (1966), 'Obstinate or Obsolete: The Fate of the Nation-State in Europe', *Daedalus*, 95/3: 862–915.

—— (1990), 'A New World and its Troubles, *Foreign Affairs*, 69/4: 115–22.

Hogan, M. J. (1987), *The Marshall Plan: America, Britain, and the Reconstruction of Western Europe, 1947–52* (Cambridge: Cambridge University Press).

Holden, M. (1994), *The Common Fisheries Policy* (Oxford: Fishing News Book).

Holmes, P., Kempton, J., and McGowan, F. (1996), 'International Competition Policy and Telecommunications: Lessons from the EU and Prospects for the WTO', *Telecommunications Policy*, 20/10: 755–67.

Hooghe, L. (1996) (ed.), *Cohesion Policy and European Integration: Building Multi-level Governance* (Oxford: Oxford University Press).

—— and Keating, M. (1994), 'The Politics of European Union Regional Policy', *Journal of European Public Policy*, 1/3: 367–93.

Hoskyns, C. (1996), *Integrating Gender: Women, Law and Politics in the European Union* (London: Verso).

Hosli, M. O. (1996), 'Coalitions and Voting Power: Effects of Qualified Majority Voting in the Council of the European Union', *Journal of Common Market Studies*, 34/2: 255–73.

House of Commons (1990), *Practical Police Cooperation in the European Community*, Home Affairs Committee, 7th Report, vol. 1 (London: HMSO).

House of Lords (1985), Select Committee on the European Communities, *External Competence of the European Communities*, 16th Report (London: HMSO).

—— (1993), Select Committee on the European Communities, *Enforcement of Community Competition Rules*, Session 1993–4, HL Paper 7 (London: HMSO).

—— (1997a), Select Committee on the European Communities, *Reducing Disparities within the European Union: The Effectiveness of the Structural and Cohesion Funds*, Report, Session 1996–7, 11th Report (London: Stationery Office).

—— (1997b), Select Committee on the European Communities, *Community Environmental Law: Making it Work* (London: Stationery Office).

—— (1997c), Select Committee on the European Communities, *Enhancing Parliamentary Scrutiny of the Third Pillar*, Session 1997–8, 6th Report (London: Stationery Office).

—— (1998a), Select Committee on the European Communities, *Dealing with the Third Pillar: The Government's Perspective*, Session 1997–8, 15th Report (London: Stationery Office).

—— (1998b), Select Committee on the European Communities, *Incorporating the Schengen Acquis into the European Union*, Session 1997–8, 31st Report (London: Stationery Office).

Howorth, J. (1990), 'France since the Fall of the Berlin Wall Defence and Diplomacy', *World Today*, 46/7: 126–30.

Howson, S., and Moggridge, D. (1990) (eds.), *The Wartime Diaries of Lionel Robbins and James Meade, 1943–45* (London: Macmillan).

Hucke, J. (1985), 'Environmental Policy: The Development of a New Policy Area', in Beyme and Schmidt (1985: 156–75).

Hurd, D. (1992), speech to the Cambridge University Conservative Association, 7 Feb. (London: Foreign and Commonwealth Office Verbatim Service).

—— (1997), 'CFSP, WEU and NATO: Bringing Order to European Security's Jumbled Alphabet', *Oxford International Review* (Winter), 25–31.

Hurrell, A., and Kingsbury, B. (1992) (eds.), *The International Politics of the Environment: Actors, Interests, and Institutions* (Oxford: Clarendon Press).

—— and Menon, A. (1996), 'Politics Like any Other? Comparative Politics, International Relations, and the Study of the EU', *West European Politics*, 21/4: 802–4.

Hurwitz, L., and Lequesne, C. (1991) (eds.), *The State of the European Community: Politics, Institutions and Debates in the Transition Years* (Boulder, Colo.: Lynne Rienner).

Husmann, M. (1998), 'Koordinierung der Leistungen bei Arbeitslosigkeit durch EG-Recht', *Die Sozialgerichtsbarkeit*, 45/6: 245–52 (pt. 1), 7: 291–8 (pt. 2).

ICC (1958) (International Chamber of Commerce), *Les Pratiques commerciales restrictives et le Traité de Rome*, Resolution of the Council of the ICC, Document 225, 12 May (Paris).

—— (1973), *EEC Competition*, ICC Information, 39/7: 2.

IFREMER (1995), 'Les Organisations de producteurs des pêches maritimes françaises:—situation et typologie', Direction des ressources vivantes.

Ikenberry, G. J. (1989), 'Rethinking the Origins of American Hegemony', *Political Science Quarterly*, 104/3: 375–400.

IMF (1993) (International Monetary Fund), *International Capital Markets: Exchange Rate Management and International Capital Flows* (Washington: IMF).

Inotai, A. (1994), 'Die Beziehungen zwischen der EU und den assoziierten Staaten Mittel- und Osteuropas', *Europäische Rundschau*, 22/3: 19–35.

—— (1998), 'The CEECs: From the Association Agreements to Full Membership', in J. Redmond and G. Rosenthal (eds.), *The Expanding European Union, Past, Present, Future* (Boulder, Colo.: Lynne Rienner), 157–76.

Institute of European Affairs (1999), *Agenda 2000: Implications for Ireland* (Dublin: IEA).

Ireland, P. (1995), 'Fragmented Social Policy: Migration', in Leibfried and Pierson (1995*b*: 231–66).

Irish Fishermen's Organization (1998), 'Response to CFP questionnaire', (Dublin).

Jachtenfuchs, M. (1993), *Ideen und Interessen. Weltbilder als Kategorien der politischen Analyse* (Mannheim: Mannheim Centre for Social Research).

—— (1995), 'Theoretical Perspectives on European Governance', *European Law Journal*, 1/2 115–33.

—— and Kohler-Koch, B. (1995) (eds.), *Europäische Integration* (Leverkusen: Leske & Budrich).

Jacobs, F. (1989), 'Anti-Dumping Procedures with Regard to Imports from Eastern Europe', in Maresceau (1989*b*: 291–308).

Jacquemin, A., and Sapir, A. (1991) (eds.) *The European Internal Market: Trade and Competition* (Oxford: Oxford University Press).

—— Lloyd, P., Tharakan, P., and Waelbroeck, M. (1998), 'Competition Policy in an International Setting: The Way Ahead', *World Economy*, 21/8: 1179–83.

—— and Wright, D. (1993*a*), 'Corporate Strategies and European Challenges post-1992', *Journal of Common Market Studies*, 31/4: 525–37.

—— —— (1993*b*) (eds.), *The European Challenges post-1992: Shaping Factors, Shaping Actors* (Aldershot: Edward Elgar).

Jasanoff, S. (1995), 'Product, Process, or Programme: Three Cultures and the Regulation of Biotechnology', in Bauer (1995: 311–31).

Jeffrey, C. (1997) (ed.), *The Regional Dimension of the European Union: Towards a Third Level in Europe?* (London: Frank Cass).

Jobert, B. (1994) (ed.), *Le Tournant néolibéral en Europe* (Paris: L'Harmattan).

Joerges, C. (1994), 'European Economic Law: The Nation-State and the Maastricht Treaty', in Dehousse (1994: 29–62).

—— and Neyer, J. (1998), 'Vom intergouvernementalen Verhandeln zur deliberativen Politik. Gründe und Chancen für eine Konstitutionalisierung der europäischen Komitologie', in B. Kohler-Koch (ed.), *Regieren in entgrenzten Räumen* (Opladen: Westdeutscher Verlag), 207–33, *Politische Vierteljahresschrift*, special issue, 29.

Johansson, K. M. (1999), 'Tracing the Employment Title in the Amsterdam Treaty: Uncovering Transnational Coalitions', *Journal of European Public Policy*, 6/1: 85–101.

Johnson, C., and Colignon, S. (1994) (eds.), *The Monetary Economics of Europe* (London: Pinter).

Johnson, D. G. (1991), *World Agriculture in Disarray* (London: Macmillan, for the Trade Policy Research Centre).

Johnson, M. (1998), *European Community Trade Policy and the Article 113 Committee* (London: Royal Institute of International Affairs).

Joilet, R. (1981), 'Cartelization, Dirigism and Crisis in the European Community', *World Economy*, 3, pt. 1.

Jong, H. de (1975), 'EEC Competition Policy towards Restrictive Practices', in K. George and C. Joll (eds.), *Competition Policy in the UK and the EEC* (Cambridge: Cambridge University Press), 33–61.

Jordan, A. (1999a), 'Editorial Introduction: The Construction of a Multilevel Environmental Governance System', *Environment and Planning C: Government and Policy*, 17, Feb., 1–17.

—— (1999b) (ed.), 'Theme Issue: European Union Environmental Policy at 25', *Environment and Planning C: Government and Policy*, 17, Feb., 1–126.

Jordan, F. (1990), 'Policy Communities Realism versus "New" Institutionalist Ambiguity', *Political Studies*, 38/3: 470–84.

Jorens, Y., and Schulte, B. (1998) (eds.), *European Social Security Law and Third Country Nationals* (Brussels: die keure-la charte).

Josling, T. (1998), 'Can the CAP Survive Enlargement to the East?', in J. Redmond and G. Rosenthal (eds.), *The Expanding European Union, Past, Present, Future* (Boulder, Colo.: Lynne Rienner), 89–106.

Judge, D. (1992), ' "Predestined to Save the Earth": The Environment Committee of the European Parliament', *Environmental Politics*, 1/4: 186–212.

—— and Earnshaw, D. (1994), 'Weak European Parliament Influence? A Study of the Environment Committee of the European Parliament', *Government and Opposition*, 29/2: 262–76.

Kaelble, H. (1990), *A Social History of Western Europe, 1880–1980* (Dublin: Gill & Macmillan).

Kaldor, M., and Vejvoda, I. (1998) (eds.), *Democratization in Central and Eastern Europe* (London: Cassell).

Kaluza, H. (1998), *Der europäische Sozialfonds. Seine Entwicklung und Funktion in der europäischen Integration mit einem Exkurs zu seiner Bedeutung für die bundesdeutsche Arbeitsförderung* (Baden-Baden: Nomos).

Kamieniecki, S. (1993) (ed.), *Environmental Politics and Policy: Some Recent Controversies and Developments* (Albany, NY: SUNY Press).

Kapteyn, P. (1991), ' "Civilization under Negotiation": National Civilizations and European Integration. The Treaty of Schengen', *Archives Européenes de Sociologie*, 32/2: 363–80.

—— (1995), *The Stateless Market: The European Dilemma of Integration and Civilization* (London: Routledge).

Karagiannakos, A. (1997), 'Total Allowable Catch and the Quota Management System in the European Union', *Marine Policy*, 20/3: 235–48.

Kassim, H., and Menon, A. (1996), *The European Union and National Industrial Policy*, (London: Routledge).

Katzenstein, P. J. (1987), *Policy and Politics in West Germany: The Growth of a Semi-sovereign State* (Philadelphia: Temple University Press).

Keating, M. (1998), 'Is there a Regional Level of Government in Europe?', in Le Gales and Lequesne (1998: 11–30).

—— and Loughlin, J. (1997) (eds.), *The Political Economy of Regionalism* (London: Frank Cass).

Kelemen, D. R. (1998), 'Regulatory Federalism: The European Union in Comparative Perspective', Stanford University Ph.D. thesis.

Kenis, P. (1991), 'Social Europe in the 1990s: Beyond an Adjunct to Achieving a Common Market?', *Futures*, 23/7: 724–38.

Kennan, J., and Stevens, C. (1997), *From Lomé to the GSP: Implications for the ACP of Losing Lomé Trade Preferences*, Report prepared for Oxfam, UK (Brighton: Institute of Development Studies, Nov.).

Keohane, R. O. (1986), 'Reciprocity in International Relations', *International Organization*, 40/1: 1–28.

—— and Hoffmann, S. (1990), 'Conclusions: Community Politics and Institutional Change', in W. Wallace (1990: 276–300).

Kerremans, B. (1998), 'The Political and Institutional Consequences of Widening: Capacity and Control in an Enlarged Council', in P.-H. Laurent and M. Maresceau (eds.), *The State of the European Union, iv: Deepening and Widening* (Boulder, Colo.: Lynne Rienner), 87–109.

Kersbergen, K. van (1998), *Nationale politieke stelsels* (Amsterdam: KUN).

Keynes, J. M. (1933), 'National Self-Sufficiency', in *The Collected Writings of John Maynard Keynes*, xxi, (Cambridge: Cambridge University Press, 1982), 233–46.

Kim, C. (1992), 'Cats and Mice: The Politics of Setting EC Car Emission Standards', CEPS Working Document No. 64 (Brussels: Centre for European Policy Studies).

—— (n.d.), 'The Making of Maastricht: EC Environmental Policy'.

Kleinman, M., and Piachaud, D. (1992*a*), 'Britain and European Social Policy', *Policy Studies*, 13/3: 13–25.

—— —— (1992*b*), 'European Social Policy: Conceptions and Choices', *Journal of European Social Policy*, 3/1: 1–19.

Klip, A. (1997), 'Europol: Who is Watching You?', in H. Meijers *et al.* (eds.), *Democracy, Migrants and the Police in the European Union: The 1996 IGC and Beyond*, Standing Committee of Experts in International Immigration, Refugee and Criminal Law (Utrecht: Forum), 61–73.

Knill, C. (1998), 'European Policies: The Impact of National Administrative Traditions', *Journal of Public Policy*, 18: 1–28.

Kötter, U. (1998), 'Die Urteile des Gerichtshofs der europäischen Gemeinschaften in den Rechtssachen Decker und Kohll. Der Vorhang zu und alle Fragen offen?', *Vierteljahresschrift für Sozialrecht*, 4: 233–52.

Kohler-Koch, B., and Eising, R. (1999) (eds.), *The Transformation of Governance in the European Union* (London: Routledge).

—— and Woyke, W. (1995) (eds.), *Europäische Union* (Munich: C. H. Beck).

Kolankiewicz, G. (1994), 'Consensus and Competition in the Eastern Enlargement of the European Union', *International Affairs*, 70/3: 477–95.

Kolinsky, E. (1994), 'The German Greens: Neither Left nor Right but Backwards?', *Environmental Politics*, 3/1: 164–8.

Koppen, I. (1993), 'The Role of the European Court of Justice', in Liefferink *et al.* (1993*b*: 126–49).

Korah, V. (1997), *An Introductory Guide to EC Competition Law and Practice* (Oxford: Hart).

Kramer, H. (1993), 'The European Community's Response to the "New Eastern Europe"', *Journal of Common Market Studies*, 31/2: 213–44.

Kramer, L. (1992), *Focus on European Environmental Law* (London: Sweet & Maxwell).

Krenzler, H., and da Fonseca-Wollheim, H. (1998), 'Die Reichweite der gemeinsamen Handlespolitik nach dem Vertrag von Amsterdam. Eine Debatte ohne Ende?', *Europarecht*, 3, May–June.

Kroon, N. (1997), *Europese informatiesystemen. Grensverleggend? Een verkenning naar barrières in de bouwfase van het Schengen Informatie Systeem en het Social Security Network* (Delft: Eburon).

Krugman, P. (1990), 'Policy Problems of a Monetary Union', in De Grauwe and Papademos (1990: 48–64).

—— (1995), *Growing World Trade: Causes and Consequences*, Brookings Papers on Economic Activity, 1 (Washington: Brookings Institution), 327–77.

—— (1997), 'What should Trade Negotiators Negotiate About?', *Journal of Economic Literature*, 35: 113–20.

Krupp, H.-J. (1995), 'Die Rahmenbedingungen für die Sozialpolitik auf dem Weg zur europäischen Wirtschafts- und Währungsunion', in Riesche and Schmähl (1995: 173–88).

Küsters, H. J. (1982), *Die Gründung der europäischen Wirtschaftsgemeinschaft* (Baden-Baden: Nomos).

Ladrech, R. (1994), 'Europeanization of Domestic Politics and Institutions: The Case of France', *Journal of Common Market Studies*, 32/1: 69–88.

Laffan, B. (1996), 'The Politics of Identity and Political Order in Europe', *Journal of Common Market Studies*, 34/1: 81–102.

—— (1997a), 'From Policy Entrepreneur to Policy Manager: The Challenge Facing the Commission', *European Journal of Public Policy*, 4/3: 422–38.

—— (1997b), *The Finances of the European Union* (London: Macmillan).

—— O'Donnell, R., and Smith, M. (1999), *Europe's Experimental Union: Rethinking Integration* (London: Routledge).

Lamassoure, A. (1995), *Press Conference Given by M. Alain Lamassoure, Minister Delegate for European Affairs*, Statements, SAC/95/48 (London: French Embassy).

Landáburu, E. (1994), 'How to Make Ill-Placed Regions Fit to Compete', *European Affairs*, 4/2: 97–9.

Lange, P. (1992), 'The Politics of the Social Dimension', in Sbragia (1992b: 225–56).

—— (1993), 'The Maastricht Social Protocol: Why Did They Do It?', *Politics and Society*, 21/1: 5–36.

Langhammer, R. (1992), *Die Assozierungsabkommen mit der CSFR, Polen und Ungarn. Wegweisend oder abweisend?*, Discussion Paper No. 182 (Kiel: Kiel Institute for World Economics).

La Serre, F. de (1994), 'A la recherche d'une Ostpolitik', in La Serre *et al.* (1994: 11–41).

—— and Wallace, H. (1997), *Flexibility and Enhanced Cooperation in the European Union: An Illusionary Bright Idea* (Paris: Groupement d'Études et de Recherches 'Notre Europe').

—— Lequesne, C., and Rupnik, J. (1994) (eds.), *L'Union Européenne: ouverture à l'Est?* (Paris: Presses Universitaires de France).

La Spina, A., and Sciortino, G. (1993), 'Common Agenda, Southern Rules: European Integration and Environmental Change in the Mediterranean States', in Liefferink *et al.* (1993b: 217–36).

Laursen, F. (1992), 'The Maastricht Treaty: A Critical Evaluation', in Laursen and Vanhoonacker (1992: 249–65).

—— and Vanhoonacker, S. (1992) (eds.), *The Intergovernmental Conference on Political Union* (Maastricht: European Institute of Public Administration).

—— and Wester, R. (1992), 'Overview of the Negotiations', in Laursen and Vanhoonacker (1992: 3–24).

Lebullenger, J., and Le Morvan, D. (1990) (eds.), *La Communauté Européenne et la mer* (Paris: Economica).

Legg, W. (1993/4), 'Direct Payments for Farmers?', *OECD Observer*, 185, Dec./Jan., 26–8.

Le Gales, P., and Lequesne, C. (1998) (eds.), *Regions in Europe* (London: Routledge).

Leibfried, S. (1994), 'The Social Dimension of the European Union: *En Route* to Positively Joint Sovereignty?', *Journal of European Social Policy*, 4/4: 239–62.

—— and Pierson, P. (1992), 'Prospects for Social Europe', *Politics and Society*, 20/3: 333–66.

—— —— (1995a), 'Semi-sovereign Welfare States: Social Policy in a Multi-tiered Europe', in Leibfried and Pierson (1995b: 43–77).

—— —— (1995b) (eds.), *European Social Policy: Between Fragmentation and Integration* (Washington: Brookings Institution).

—— —— (1996), 'Social Policy', in H. Wallace and W. Wallace (1996: 185–208).

Lenschow, A. (1999), 'The Greening of the EU: The Common Agricultural Policy and the Structural Funds', *Environment and Planning C: Government and Policy*, 17: 91–108.

Lepsius, M. R. (1991), 'Nationalstaat oder Nationalitätenstaat als Modell für die Weiterentwicklung der europäischen Gemeinschaft', in Wildenmann (1991: 19–40).

Lequesne, C. (1991), 'Les Accords de commerce et de coopération de la Communauté Européenne: pays d'Europe de l'Est', in Gautron (1991: 357–71).

—— (1998a), 'Comment penser l'Union Européenne?', in Smouts (1998: 103–34).

—— (1998b), 'Market vs. Local Communities? Quota Hopping and the EU Fisheries Policy', paper presented at the ECPR-ISA Joint Conference, Vienna, 16–19 Sept. 1998.

—— (1999), 'Capteurs de quotas: la pêche européenne entre territoires et marché', *Critique Internationale*, 2: 121–31.

Leslie, P. M. (1991), *The European Community: A Political Model for Canada?* (Ottawa: Minister of Supply and Services).

Levidow, L., and Tait, J. (1992), 'Release of Genetically Modified Organisms: Precautionary Legislation', *Project Appraisal*, 7/2: 93–105.

Lewis, J. (1998a), 'Is the "Hard Bargaining" Image of the Council Misleading? The Committee of Permanent Representatives and the Local Elections Directive', *Journal of Common Market Studies*, 36/4: 179–504.

—— (1998b), *Constructing Interests: The Committee of Permanent Representatives and Decision-Making in the European Union*, University of Wisconsin at Madison Ph.D dissertation.

Liefferink, D., and Andersen, M. S. (1998a), 'Strategies of the "Green" Member States in EU Environmental Policy-Making', *Journal of European Public Policy*, 5/2: 254–70.

—— —— (1998b), 'Greening the EU: National Positions in the Run-Up to the Amsterdam Treaty', *Environmental Politics*, 7, Autumn, 66–93.

—— Lowe, P. D., and Mol, A. J. P. (1993a), 'The Environment and the European Community', in Liefferink *et al.* (1993b: 1–13).

—— —— —— (1993b) (eds.), *European Integration and Environmental Policy* (London: Belhaven).

Lindberg, L. N. (1963), *The Political Dynamics of European Economic Integration* (Stanford, Calif.: Stanford University Press).

—— and Scheingold, S. A. (1970), *Europe's Would-Be Polity* (Englewood Cliffs, NJ: Prentice-Hall).

—— —— (1971) (eds.), *Regional Integration: Theory and Research* (Cambridge, Mass.: Harvard University Press).

Linder, S., and Peters, B. G. (1995), 'The Two Traditions of Institutional Designing: Dialogue vs. Decision?', in Weimer (1995: 133–59).

Lippert, B. (1990), 'EC–CMEA Relations: Normalisation and Beyond', in G. Edwards and E. Regelsberger (eds.), *Europe's Global Links: The European Community and Inter-regional Cooperation* (London: Pinter), 119–40.

Lodge, J. (1993) (ed.), *The European Community and the Challenge of the Future*, 2nd edn. (London: Pinter).

Long, T. (1998), 'The Environmental Lobby', in P. Lowe and S. Ward (eds.), *British Environmental Policy and Europe: Politics and Policy in Transition* (London: Routledge), 105–18.

Loth, W., Wallace, W., and Wessels, W. (1998) (eds.), *Walter Hallstein: The Forgotten European?* (London: Macmillan), trans. from the German (Bonn: Europa Union Verlag, 1995).

Loughlin, J. (1997*a*), 'Representing Regions in Europe: The Committee of the Regions', in Jeffrey (1997: 147–65).

—— (1997*b*), 'Regional Policy in the European Union', in Stavridis *et al.* (1997: 439–66).

Lovett, A. W. (1996), 'The United States and the Schuman Plan: A Study in French Diplomacy 1950–2', *Historical Journal*, 39/2: 425–51.

Low, P. (1993), *Trading Free: The GATT and US Trade Policy* (New York: Twentieth Century Fund Press).

Lowi, T. (1972), 'Four Systems of Policy, Politics and Choice', *Public Administration Review*, 32/4: 298–310.

Ludlow, P. (1982), *The Making of the European Monetary System* (London: Butterworth).

—— (1989), *Beyond 1992: Europe and its Western Partners*, CEPS Working Paper No. 38 (Brussels: Centre for European Policy Studies).

Lundestad, G. (1998), *Empire by Integration: The United States and European Integration, 1945–1997* (Oxford: Oxford University Press).

Maasacher, M. H. J. M. van, and Arentsen, M. J. (1990), 'Environmental Policy', in Wolters and Coffey (1990: 70–8).

McAleavey, P. (1994), 'The Political Logic of the European Community Structural Funds Budget: Lobbying Efforts by Declining Industrial Regions', EUI Working Paper RSC No. 942 (Florence: European University Institute).

McDonagh, Bobby (1998), *Original Sin in a Brave New World* (Dublin: Institute of European Affairs).

MacDougall, D., *et al.* (1977), *Report of the Study Group on the Role of Public Finance in European Integration*, Economic and Financial Series, A13, Apr. (Brussels).

McGowan, F. (1993), 'The European Community and Privatisation', in T. Clarke and C. Pitelis (1993) (eds.), *The Political Economy of Privatisation* (London: Routledge), 70–90.

—— and Seabright, P. (1995), 'Regulation in the European Community and its Impact on the UK', in M. Bishop, J. Kay, and C. Mayer. (1995) (eds.), *The Regulatory Challenge* (Oxford: Oxford University Press), 227–53.

—— and Wallace, H. (1996), 'Towards a European Regulatory State', *Journal of European Public Policy*, 3/4: 560–76.

MacLachan, D., and Swann, D. (1967), *Competition Policy in the European Community* (Oxford: Oxford University Press).

McLaughlin, A., Jordan, G., and Maloney, W. A. (1993), 'Corporate Lobbying in the European Community', *Journal of Common Market Studies*, 31/2: 191–212.

Macleod, I., Hendry, I. D., and Hyett, S. (1996), *The External Relations of the European Communities* (Oxford: Clarendon Press).

Maher, I. (1997), 'Alignment of Competition Laws in the European Community', *Yearbook of European Law 1996*, 16: 223–42.

Majone, G. (1989), *Evidence, Argument and Persuasion in the Policy Process* (New Haven: Yale University Press).

—— (1991), 'Cross-National Sources of Regulatory Policymaking in Europe and the United States', *Journal of Public Policy*, 2/1: 79–106.

—— (1992), 'Regulatory Federalism in the European Community', *Environment and Planning C: Government and Policy*, 10/3: 299–316.

—— (1993), 'The European Community between Social Policy and Social Regulation', *Journal of Common Market Studies*, 31/2: 153–70.

—— (1994a), 'Independence vs. Accountability? Non-majoritarian Institutions and Democratic Government in Europe', in Hesse (1994: 117–40).

—— (1994b), 'The Rise of the Regulatory State in Europe', *West European Politics*, 17/3: 77–101.

—— (1995), *La Communauté Européenne: un État régulateur*, (Paris: Montchestien).

—— (1996a), 'Public Policy: Ideas, Interests and Institutions', in Goodin and Klingemann (1996: 610–27).

—— (1996b), *Regulating Europe* (London: Routledge).

—— (1997), 'The New European Agencies: Regulation by Information', *Journal of European Public Policy*, 2, June, 262–75.

March, J. G., and Olsen, J. P. (1989), *Rediscovering Institutions* (New York: Free Press).

—— —— (1998), *The Institutional Dynamics of International Political Orders*, ARENA Working Paper (Oslo: ARENA).

Marenco, G. (1983), 'Public Sector and Community Law', *Common Market Law Review*, 20/3: 495–527.

Maresceau, M. (1989a), 'A General Survey of the Current Legal Framework of Trade Relations between the European Community and Eastern Europe', in Maresceau (1989b: 3–20).

—— (1989b) (ed.), *The Political and Legal Framework of Trade Relations between the European Community and Eastern Europe* (Dordrecht: Nijhoff).

—— (1994) (ed.), *The European Commercial Policy after 1992: The Legal Dimension* (Dordrecht: Nijhoff).

Marine Stewardship Council (1997), *Principles and Criteria for Sustainable Fishing* (London: Marine Stewardship Council).

Marjolin, R. (1989), *Architect of European Unity: Memoirs 1911–1986* (London: Weidenfeld & Nicolson).

Marks, G. (1992), 'Structural Policy in the European Community', in Sbragia (1992b: 191–224).

—— (1993), 'Structural Policy and Multilevel Governance in the EC', in Cafruny and Rosenthal (1993: 390–410).

—— Hooghe, L., and Blank, K. (1996), 'European Integration from the 1980s: State-Centric v. Multi-level Governance', *Journal of Common Market Studies*, 34/3: 341–78.

Marshall, T. H. (1963), 'Citizenship and Social Classes', in Marshall (ed.), *Sociology at the Crossroads, and Other Essays* (London: Heinemann), 67–127.

—— (1985), *Social Policy in the Twentieth Century*, 5th edn., ed. A. M. Rees (London: Hutchinson).

Marston, G. (1973), 'The Continental Can Case', *Journal of World Trade Law*, 7/4: 476–82.

Martin, S. (1998) (ed.), *Competition Policies in Europe* (Amsterdam: Elsevier).

—— (forthcoming), 'State Aids', in J. Pelkmans (ed.), *Regulation in the EU* (Brussels: CEPS).

Mason, E. (1946), *Controlling World Trade: Cartels and Commodity Agreements* (London: McGraw-Hill).

Matthews, D., and Mayes, D. G. (1995), 'The Role of Soft Law in the Evolution of Rules for a Single European Market: The Case of Retailing', paper presented at the Fourth Biennial International Conference of the European Community Studies Association, Charleston, SC, 11–14 May.

Mattli, W. (1999), *The Logic of Regional Integration: Europe and Beyond* (Cambridge: Cambridge University Press).

—— and Slaughter, A.-M. (1995), 'Law and Politics in the European Union: A Reply to Garrett', *International Organization*, 49/1: 183–90.

—— —— (1998), 'The ECJ, Governments, and Legal Integration in the EU', *International Organization*, 52/1: 177–210.

Maydell, B., Baron von (1991), 'Einführung in die Schlussdiskussion', in Schulte and Zacher (1991: 229–36).

—— (1999), 'Auf dem Weg zu einem gemeinsamen Markt für Gesundheitsleistungen in der Europäischen Gemeinschaft', *Vierteljahresschrift für Sozialrecht*, 1: 3–19.

Mayhew, A. (1998), *Recreating Europe: The European Union's Policy towards Central and Eastern Europe* (Cambridge: Cambridge University Press).

Mazey, S., and Richardson, J. (1992), 'Environmental Groups and the EC: Challenges and Opportunities', *Environmental Politics*, 1/4: 109–28.

—— —— (1993a), 'Introduction: Transference of Power, Decision Rules, and Rules of the Game', in Mazey and Richardson (1993b: 3–26).

—— —— (1993b) (eds.), *Lobbying in the European Community* (Oxford: Oxford University Press).

—— —— (1994), 'Policy Coordination in Brussels: Environmental and Regional Policy', in S. Baker *et al.* (1994: 22–44).

Mazower, M. (1998), *Dark Continent* (London: Penguin).

Menon, A., and Hayward, J. (1996) (eds.), 'States, Industrial Policies and the European Union', in Kassim and Menon (1996: 267–288).

—— Forster, A., and Wallace, W. (1992), 'A Common European Defence?', *Survival*, 34/3: 98–118.

Mény, Y., Muller, P., and Quermonne, J.-L. (1996) (eds.), *Adjusting to Europe: The Impact of the European Union on National Institutions and Policies* (London: Routledge).

Mercer, H. (1995), *Constructing a Competitive Order: The Hidden History of British Antitrust Policies* (Cambridge: Cambridge University Press).

Messerlin, P. (1993), 'The EC and Central Europe: The Missed Rendez-Vous of 1992?', *Economics of Transition*, 1/1: 89–109.

Mestmäcker, E.-J. (1972), 'Concentration and Competition in the EEC', *Journal of World Trade Law*, 6/6: 615–47, 7/1: 36–63.

Metcalfe, L. (1992), 'After 1992: Can the Commission Manage Europe?', *Australian Journal of Public Administration*, 51/1: 117–30.

Miall, H. (1994) (ed.), *Redefining Europe: New Patterns of Conflict and Cooperation* (London: Pinter).

Michalski, A., and Wallace, H. (1992), *The European Community: The Challenge of Enlargement* (London: Royal Institute of International Affairs).

Miert, K. van (1996), 'The Proposal for a European Competition Agency', *Competition Policy Newsletter*, 2/2: 1–4.

—— (1997), 'La Conférence Intergouvernementale et la politique communautaire de concurrence', *Competition Policy Newsletter*, 3/2: 1–5.

Millstone, E. (1991), 'Consumer Protection Policies in the EC: The Quality of Food', in Freeman *et al.* (1991: 330–43).

Milward, A. S. (1981), 'Tariffs as Constitutions', in Strange and Tooze (1981: 57–66).

—— (1984), *The Reconstruction of Western Europe, 1945–51* (London: Methuen).

—— (1992), *The European Rescue of the Nation-State* (Berkeley: University of California Press).

—— Lynch, F. M. B., Romero, F., and Sørensen, V. (1993) (eds.), *The Frontier of National Sovereignty: History and Theory, 1945–1992* (London: Routledge).

Mint, J., and Simeon, R. (1982), *Conflict of Taste and Conflict of Claim in Federal Countries* (Toronto: Institute of International Relations).

Moens, A., and Anstis, C. (1994) (eds.), *Disconcerted Europe: The Search for a New Security Architecture* (Oxford: Westview).

Monar, J. (1997), 'European Union—Justice and Home Affairs: A Balance Sheet and an Agenda for Reform', in G. Edwards and A. Pijpers (eds.), *The Politics of European Treaty Reform: The 1996 Intergovernmental Conference and Beyond* (London: Pinter/Cassell), 326–39.

—— (forthcoming), *Justice and Home Affairs in the European Union* (London: Macmillan).

—— and Morgan, R. (1994) (eds.), *The Third Pillar of the European Union: Cooperation in the Field of Justice and Home Affairs* (Brussels: European University Press).

—— and Wessels, W. (forthcoming) (eds.), *The Treaty of Amsterdam: Challenges and Opportunities for the European Union* (London: Pinter).

Monnet, J. (1976), *Memoirs* (London: Collins).

Montagnon, P. (1990), *European Competition Policy* (London: Pinter for RIIA).

Moravcsik, A. (1991), 'Negotiating the Single European Act: National Interests and Conventional Statecraft in the European Community', *International Organization*, 45/1: 19–56.

—— (1993), 'Preferences and Power in the European Community: A Liberal Intergovernmentalist Approach', *Journal of Common Market Studies*, 31/4: 473–524.

—— (1994), 'Why the European Community Strengthens the State: Domestic Politics and International Cooperation'.

—— (1998), *The Choice for Europe: Social Purpose and State Power from Messina to Maastricht* (London and Ithaca, NY: UCL Press and Cornell University Press).

Moreno, L. (1993) (ed.), *Social Exchange and Welfare Development* (Madrid: Consejo Superior de Investigationes Cientificas).

Morgan, R., and Bray, C. (1984) (eds.), *Partners and Rivals in Western Europe: Britain, France and Germany* (Aldershot: Gower).

Mortensen, J. (1990), 'Federalism vs. Coordination: Macroeconomic Policy in the European Community', CEPS Paper No. 47 (Brussels: Centre for European Policy Studies).

Mosley, H. G. (1990), 'The Social Dimension of European Integration', *International Labour Review*, 129/2: 147–64.

Müller, W. C., and Wright, V. (1994) (eds.), *The State in Western Europe: Retreat or Redefinition?* (Ilford: Frank Cass).

Müller-Graff, P.-C. (1994), 'The Legal Bases of the Third Pillar and its Position in the Framework of the Union Treaty', *Common Market Law Review*, 31/3: 493–510.

—— (1996), 'Europäische Zusammenarbeit in den Bereichen Justiz und Inneres. Funktion, Ausgestaltung und Entwicklungsoptionen des dritten Pfeilers der Europäischen Union', in P.-C. Müller-Graff (Hrsg.), *Europäische Zusammenarbeit in den Bereichen Justiz und Inneres* (Baden-Baden, Nomos), 11–39.

Murphy, A. (1990), *The European Community and the International Trading System*, 2 vols., (Brussels: Centre for European Policy Studies).

Myrdal, G. (1957), 'Economic Nationalism and Internationalism', *Australian Outlook*, 11/4: 3–50.

Nachbaur, A. (1998), 'Europol-Beamte und Immunität. Ein Sünderfall des Rechtsstaats', *Kritische Justiz*, 31/2: 231–38.

Nadai, A. (1999), 'Industry Cooperation to the Development of Product Ecolabel: The Case of Paints and Varnishes European Ecolabelling Criteria', manuscript.

—— (forthcoming), 'Conditions of a Development of a Product Ecolabel', *European Environment*.

Nanetti, R. (1996), 'EU Cohesion and Territorial Restructuring in the Member States', in Hooghe (1996: 59–88).

Neven, D., Nuttall, R., and Seabright, P. (1993), *Merger in Daylight: The Economics and Politics of European Merger Control* (London: Centre for Economic Policy Research).

—— Papandropoulos, P., and Seabright, P. (1998), *Trawling for Minnows: European Competition Policy and Agreements between Firms* (London: Centre for Economic Policy Research).

Neville-Brown, L. (1981), 'Agricultural Byzantinism and Prospective Overruling', *Common Market Law Review*, 18/4: 509–19.

Neville-Jones, P. (1997), 'Dayton, IFOR and Alliance Relations', *Survival*, 38/4: 45–65.

NFFO and SFF (1998), National Federation of Fishermen's Organizations and Scottish Fishermen's Federation, 'European Fisheries after 2002: Decentralization of the Common Fisheries Policy'.

Niblett, R. C. H. (1995), 'The European Community and the Central European Three, 1989–92: A Study of the Community as an International Actor', Oxford University Ph.D. thesis.

Noetzold, J. (1995), 'European Union and Eastern Central Europe: Expectations and Uncertainties', *Aussenpolitik*, 46/1: 14–23.

North, D. C. (1990), *Institutions, Institutional Change and Economic Performance* (Cambridge: Cambridge University Press).

Nugent, N. (1999), *The Government and Politics of the European Union*, 4th edn. (London: Macmillan).

Nuttall, S. J. (1992), *European Political Cooperation* (Oxford: Clarendon Press).

—— (1994), 'The Commission and Foreign Policy-Making', in Edwards and Spence (1994: 287–303).

OECD (1986), (Organization for Economic Co-operation and Development), *Recombinant DNA Safety Considerations* (Paris: OECD).

—— (1993a), *Assessing the Effects of the Uruguay Round* (Paris: OECD).

—— (1993b), *OECD Environmental Performance Reviews: Germany* (Paris: OECD).

—— (1994), *Economic Outlook*, 56, Dec.

O'Keeffe, D. (1995), 'Recasting the Third Pillar', *Common Market Law Review*, 32/4: 893–920.

—— and Twomey, P. M. (1994) (eds.), *Legal Issues of the Maastricht Treaty* (London: Chancery Law).

Oliver, T. (1998), 'Can Quotas Save Stocks?', in Gray (1998: 68–80).

Olsen, J. P. (1995), 'Europeanization and Nation-State Dynamics', ARENA Working Paper No. 9 (Oslo: ARENA).

O'Riordan, T., and Voisey, H. (1997), 'The Political Economy of Sustainable Development', *Environmental Politics*, 6, Spring, 1–23.

Ostner, I., and Lewis, J. (1995), 'Gender and the Evolution of European Social Policy', in Leibfried and Pierson (1995b: 159–93).

Outrive, L. van (1992a), *The Entry into Force of the Schengen Agreements* (Brussels: European Parliament Committee on Civil Liberties and Internal Affairs).

—— (1992b), *Police Cooperation* (Brussels: European Parliament Committee on Civil Liberties and Internal Affairs).

Paarlberg, R. L. (1992), 'How Agriculture Blocked the Uruguay Round', *SAIS Review*, 12: 27–42.

—— (1995), *Leadership Begins at Home: The United States in a More Deeply Integrated World Economy* (Washington: Brookings Institution).

Padoa-Schioppa, T. (1987), *Efficiency, Stability and Equity* (Oxford: Oxford University Press).

—— (1994), *The Road to Monetary Union in Europe* (Oxford: Clarendon Press).

Paemen, H., and Bensch, A. (1995), *From the GATT to the WTO: The European Community in the Uruguay Round* (Leuven: Leuven University Press).

Page, E. (1997), *People who Run Europe* (Oxford: Clarendon Press).

Papaconstantinou, H. (1988), *Free Trade and Competition in the EEC: Law Policy and Practice* (London: Routledge).

Parekh, B. (1994), 'Discourses on National Identity', *Political Studies*, 42/3: 492–504.

Parrès, A. (1997) *Affirmer la place des pêches maritimes françaises face aux défis mondiaux*, Rapport au Conseil Économique et Social (Paris).

Paterson, W. E. (1991), 'Regulatory Change and Environmental Protection in the British and German Chemical Industries', *European Journal of Political Research*, issue 19: 307–26.

Pearce, J. (1983), 'The Common Agricultural Policy: The Accumulation of Special Interests', in H. Wallace *et al.* (1983: 143–76).

—— and Sutton, J. (1985), *Protection and Industrial Policy in Europe* (London: Routledge).

Pedler, R. H. (1994), 'The Fruit Companies and the Banana Trade Regime (BTR)', in Pedler and van Schendelen (1994: 67–91).

—— and van Schendelen, M. P. C. M. (1994) (eds.), *Lobbying the European Union: Companies, Trade Associations and Issue Groups* (Aldershot: Dartmouth).

Peffekoven, R. (1994), *Die Finanzen der Europäischen Union* (Mannheim: BI Taschenbuch Verlag).

Pehle, H. (1997), 'Germany: Domestic Obstacles to an International Forerunner', in Andersen and Liefferink (1997: 161–99).

Pelkmans, J. (1984), *Market Integration in the European Community* (The Hague: Martinus Nijhoff).

—— (1990), 'Regulation and the Single Market: An Economic Perspective', in Siebert (1990b: 91–125).

—— and Murphy, A. (1991), 'Catapulted into Leadership: The Community's Trade and Aid Policies *vis-à-vis* Eastern Europe', *Journal of European Integration*, 14/2–3: 125–51.

—— and Winters, L. A., with Wallace, H. (1988), *Europe's Domestic Market* (London: Royal Institute of International Affairs).

Pentland, C. (1973), *International Theory and the European Community* (London: Faber).

Peters, B. G. (1992), 'Bureaucratic Politics and the Institutions of the European Community', in Sbragia (1992b: 75–122).

—— (1994), 'Agenda-Setting in the European Community', *Journal of European Public Policy*, 1/1: 9–26.

Petersen, J. H. (1991), 'Harmonization of Social Security in the EC Revisited', *Journal of Common Market Studies*, 29/5: 505–26.

—— (1993), 'Europäischer Binnenmarkt, Wirtschafts- und Währungsunion und die Harmonisierung der Sozialpolitik', *Deutsche Rentenversicherung*, 1/2: 15–49.

Petersen, N. (1993), 'Game, Set and Match: Denmark and the European Union from Maastricht to Edinburgh,' in Tiilikainen and Damgaard Petersen (1993: 79–106).

Peterson, J. (1994), 'Europe and America in the Clinton Era', *Journal of Common Market Studies*, 32/3: 411–26.

—— (1995a), 'Decision-Making in the European Union: Towards a Framework for Analysis', *Journal of European Public Policy*, 2/1: 69–93.

—— (1995b), 'European Union R&D Policy: The Politics of Expertise', in C. Rhodes and Mazey (1995: 391–412).

—— and Bomberg, E. (1999), *Decision-Making in the European Union* (London and New York: Macmillan and St Martin's Press).

—— and Sjursen, H. (1998) (eds.), *A Common Foreign Policy for Europe? Competing Visions of the CFSP* (London: Routledge).

Peterson, P. E., and Rom, M. C. (1990), *Welfare Magnets: A New Case for a National Standard* (Washington: Brookings Institution).

Petersmann, E.-U. (1996), 'The GATT Dispute Settlement System as an Instrument of the Foreign Trade Policy of the EU', in N. Emiliou, and D. O'Keeffe (eds.), *The European Union and World Trade Law: After the Uruguay Round* (Chichester: Wiley), 253–77.

Pierson, P. (1993), 'When Effect Becomes Cause: Policy Feedback and Political Change', *World Politics*, 45/4: 595–628.

—— (1995a), 'The Creeping Nationalization of Income Transfers in the United States', in Leibfried and Pierson (1995b: 301–28).

—— (1995b), 'Federal Institutions and the Development of Social Policy', *Governance*, 8/4: 449–78.

—— (1996a), 'The New Politics of the Welfare State', *World Politics*, 48/2: 147–79.

—— (1996b), 'The Path to European Integration: A Historical Institutionalist Analysis', *Comparative Political Studies*, 29/2: 123–63.

—— and Leibfried, S. (1995a), 'Multi-tiered Institutions and the Making of Social Policy', in Leibfried and Pierson (1995b: 1–40).

—— —— (1995b), 'The Dynamics of Social Policy Integration', in Leibfried and Pierson (1995b: 432–65).

—— (1998), 'Irresistible Forces, Immovable Objects: Post-industrial Welfare States Confront Permanent Austerity', *Journal of European Public Policy*, 5/4: 539–60.

Pinder, J. (1968), 'Positive Integration and Negative Integration: Some Problems of Economic Union in the EEC', *World Today*, 24/3: 88–110.

—— (1991), *The European Community and Eastern Europe* (London: Pinter).

—— and Pinder, P. (1975), 'The European Community's Policy towards Eastern Europe', Chatham House European Series No. 25 (London: Royal Institute of International Affairs).

Polanyi, K. (1994), *The Great Transformation* (New York: Rinehart).

Pollack, M. (1995), 'Regional Actors in an Intergovernmental Play: The Making and Implementation of EC Structural Policy', in C. Rhodes and Mazey (1995: 361–90).

Poole, K. T., and Rosenthal, H. (1993), 'Spatial Realignment and the Mapping of Issues in American History: Evidence from Roll Call Voting', in Riker (1993: 13–39).

Portes, R., and Rey, H. (1998), 'The Emergence of the Euro as an International Currency', *Economic Policy*, 26: 307–43.

Preeg, E. H. (1995), *Traders in a Brave New World: The Uruguay Round and the Future of the International Trading System* (Chicago: University of Chicago Press).

Preston, C. (1997), *Enlargement and Integration in the European Union* (London: Routledge).

Previdi, E. (1997), 'Making and Enforcing Regulatory Policy in the Single Market', in H. Wallace and Young (1997: 69–90).

Pridham, G. (1994), 'National Environmental Policy-Making in the European Framework: Spain, Greece and Italy in Comparison', in S. Baker *et al.* (1994: 80–101).

Prodi, R. (1999), 'Speech Given by Mr Prodi to the European Parliament', 13 Apr., <http://www.europa.eu.int/comm/commissioners/prodi/speeches/130499_en.htm>

Pryce, R. (1994), 'The Treaty Negotiations', in Duff *et al.* (1994: 36–52).

Puchala, D. (1971), 'International Transaction and Regional Integration', in Lindberg and Scheingold (1971: 128–59).

—— (1972), 'Of Blind Men, Elephants, and International Integration', *Journal of Common Market Studies*, 10/3: 267–84.

Putnam, R. D. (1988), 'Diplomacy and Domestic Politics: The Logic of Two-Level Games', *International Organization*, 43/2: 427–60.

Quermonne, J.-L. (1994), *Le Système politique européenne* (Paris: Montchristiensen).

Raunio, T., and Wiberg, M. (1998), 'Winners and Losers in the Council: Voting Power Consequences of EU Enlargement', *Journal of Common Market Studies*, 36/4: 549–62.

Rausser, G. C., and Irwin, D. A. (1988), 'The Political Economy of Agricultural Policy Reform', *European Review of Agricultural Economics*, 15: 349–66.

Redmond, J. (1992) (ed.), *The External Relations of the European Community* (London: Macmillan/St Martin's Press).

Reflection Group (1995a), *Reform of the European Union (Interim Report)*, Madrid, 10 Nov., SN 517/95 (REFLEX 18).

—— (1995b), *Reflection Group's Report to the Intergovernmental Conference*, Brussels, 5 Dec., SN 520/95 (REFLEX 21).

Regelsberger, E., Schoutheete de Tervarent, P. de, and Wessels, W. (1997) (eds.), *Foreign Policy of the European Union: From EPC to CFSP and Beyond* (Boulder, Colo.: Lynne Rienner).

Rehbinder, E., and Steward, R. (1985), *Environmental Protection Policy: Integration through Law* (Berlin: Walter de Gruyter).

Rehm, H. J., and Reed, G. (1995) (ed.), *Biotechnology*, 12 (Weinheim: VCH).

Reif, K. (1994), 'Less Legitimation through Lazy Parties? Lessons from the 1994 European Elections', paper presented at the XVIth World Congress of the International Political Science Association, Berlin, 21–5 Aug.

Rein, M., and Rainwater, L. (1986) (eds.), *Public–Private Interplay in Social Protection: A Comparative Study* (Armonk, NY: M. E. Sharpe).

Reiner, R., and Spencer, S. (1993) (eds.), *Accountable Policing: Effectiveness, Empowerment and Equity* (London: Institute for Public Policy Research).

Reinicke, W. (1992), *Building a New Europe: The Challenge of System Transformation and Systemic Reform* (Washington: Brookings Institution).

Reinke, S. (1992), 'The EC Commission's Anti-fraud Activity', in M. Anderson and den Boer (1992: 13–30).

Ress, G. (1994), 'The Constitution and the Maastricht Treaty: Between Cooperation and Conflict', *German Politics*, 3/3: 47–74.

Revéret, J.-P., and Weber, J. (1997), 'L'Évolution des régimes internationaux de gestion des pêches', in Godard (1997: 245–58).

Rhodes, C., and Mazey, S. (1995) (eds.), *The State of the European Community*, iii: *Building a European Polity?* (Boulder, Colo. and Harlow: Lynne Reinner and Longman).

Rhodes, M. (1995), 'A Regulatory Conundrum: Industrial Relations and the "Social Dimension"', in Leibfried and Pierson (1995b: 78–122).

—— and Mény, Y. (1998) (eds.), *The Future of European Welfare: A New Social Contract?* (New York and Basingstoke: St Martin's Press and Macmillan).

Richardson, J. (1994), 'EU Water Policy: Uncertain Agendas, Shifting Networks and Complex Coalitions', *Environmental Politics*, 3/4, Winter, 139–67.

—— (1996a), 'Policy-Making in the EU: Interests, Ideas and Garbage Cans of Primeval Soup', in Richardson (1996b: 2–23).

—— (1996b) (ed.), *European Union: Power and Policy-Making* (London: Routledge).

Richter, J. H. (1964), *Agricultural Protection and Trade: Proposals for an International Policy* (New York: Praeger).

Rieger, E. (1995a), *Politik supranationaler Integration. Die Europäische Gemeinschaft in institutionentheoretischer Perspektive*, Arbeitspapiere Arbeitsbereich I/9 (Mannheim: Mannheim Centre for Social Research).

Rieger, E. (1995b), 'Protective Shelter or Strait-Jacket? An Institutional Analysis of the Common Agricultural Policy', in Leibfried and Pierson (1995b: 194–230).

—— (1995c), 'Der Wandel der Landwirtschaft in der Europäischen Union. Ein Beitrag zur soziologischen Analyse transnationaler Integrationsprozesse', Kölner Zeitschrift für Soziologie und Sozialpsychologie, 47/1: 65–94.

—— and Leibfried, S. (1995), Globalization and the Western Welfare State: An Annotated Bibliography (Bremen: Centre for Social Policy Research).

—— —— (1998), 'Welfare State Limits to Globalization', Politics and Society, 26/4: 363–90.

Riesche, H., and Schmähl, W. (1995) (eds.), Handlungsspielräume nationaler Sozialpolitik (Baden-Baden: Nomos).

Riker, W. (1993) (ed.), Agenda Formation (Ann Arbor: University of Michigan Press).

Riley, A. (1997), 'The European Cartel Office: A Guardian without Weapons', European Competition Law Review, 18/1: 3–16.

Riley, L. (1993), Counterterrorism in Western Europe: Mechanisms for International Cooperation, Working Paper No. X (Edinburgh: University of Edinburgh, Department of Politics).

Risse-Kappen, T. (1996), 'Exploring the Nature of the Beast: International Relations Theory Meets the European Union', Journal of Common Market Studies, 34/1: 53–80.

Robertson, D. B. (1989), 'The Bias of American Federalism: The Limits of Welfare State Development in the Progressive Era', Journal of Policy History, 1/3: 261–91.

Rodger, B., and Wylie, S. (1997), 'Taking the Community Interest Line: Decentralisation and Subsidiarity in Competition Law Enforcement', European Competition Law Review, 18/8: 485–91.

Rollo, J. M. C., and Smith, M. A. M. (1993), 'The Political Economy of Eastern European Trade with the European Community: Why so Sensitive?', Economic Policy, 16: 139–81.

—— and Wallace, H. (1991), 'New Patterns of Parnership', in Bonvicini et al. (1991: 53–64).

Romero, F. (1993), 'Migration as an Issue in European Interdependence and Integration: The Case of Italy', in Milward et al. (1993: 33–58, 205–8).

Rometsch, D., and Wessels, W. (1996) (eds.), The European Union and the Member States: Towards Institutional Fusion? (Manchester: Manchester University Press).

Rosamond, B. (2000), Theories of Integration (London: Macmillan).

Rose-Ackerman, S. (1995), Controlling Environmental Policy: The Limits of Public Law in Germany and the United States (New Haven: Yale University Press).

Rosenblatt, J., Mayer, T., Bartholdy, K., Demekas, D., Gupta, S., and Lipschitz, L. (1988), The Common Agricultural Policy: Principles and Consequences (Washington: International Monetary Fund).

Ross, G. (1994), Jacques Delors and European Integration (Oxford: Polity Press).

—— (1995), 'Assessing the Delors Era in Social Policy', in Leibfried and Pierson (1995b: 357–88).

Rouam, C. (1994), 'L'Union Européenne face aux pays d'Europe centrale et orientale: délocalisations industrielles ou harmonisation des conditions de concurrence?', Revue du Marché Commun et de l'Union Européenne, 383: 643–8.

Rudig, W., and Kraemer, R. A. (1994), 'Networks of Cooperation: Water Policy in Germany', Environmental Politics, 3/4: 52–79.

Ruggie, J. G. (1982), 'International Regimes, Transactions and Change: Embedded Liberalism in the Post-war Economic Order', International Organisation, 36/2: 379–415.

—— (1993) (ed.), Multilateralism Matters: The Theory and Praxis of an International Form (New York: Columbia University Press).

Ruggiero, R. (1991), 'The Place of the GATT Trading System in the European Community's External Relations', remarks to the Royal Institute of International Affairs, London, 6 Mar.

Ruimschotel, D. (1993), *The EC Budget: Ten Per Cent Fraud? A Policy Analysis*, EUI Working Paper No. 93/8 (Florence: European University Institute).

Sabatier, P. A. (1988), 'An Advocacy Coalition Framework of Policy Change and the Role of Policy-Oriented Learning Therein', *Policy Sciences*, 21: 129–68.

—— (1998), 'The Advocacy Coalition Framework: Revisions and Relevance for Europe', *Journal of European Public Policy*, 5/1: 98–130.

Sandholtz, W. (1993*a*), 'Institutions and Collective Action: The New Telecommunications in Western Europe', *World Politics*, 45/2: 242–70.

—— (1993*b*), 'Choosing Union: Monetary Politics and Maastricht', *International Organization*, 47/1: 1–39.

—— (1998), 'The Emergence of a Supranational Telecommunications Regime', in Sandholtz and Stone Sweet (1998: 134–63).

—— and Stone Sweet, A.(1998) (eds.), *European Integration and Supranational Governance* (Oxford: Oxford University Press).

—— and Zysman, J. (1989), '1992: Recasting the European Bargain', *World Politics*, 42/1: 95–128.

Santer, J. (1995), 'Speech to the European Parliament', 17 Jan.

Sapir, A. (2000), 'Trade Regionalism in Europe: Towards an Integrated Approach', *Journal of Common Market Studies*, 38/1.

Sarris, A. H. (1993), 'Implications of EC Economic Integration for Agriculture, Agricultural Trade, and Trade Policy', *Journal of Economic Integration*, 8/2: 175–200.

Saryusz-Wolski, J. (1994), 'The Reintegration of the "Old Continent": Avoiding the Costs of "Half-Europe" ', in Bulmer and Scott (1994: 19–28).

Sbragia, A. M. (1992*a*), 'Thinking about the European Future: The Uses of Comparison', in Sbragia (1992*b*: 257–91).

—— (1992*b*) (ed.), *Euro-Politics: Institutions and Policymaking in the 'New' European Community* (Washington: Brookings Institution).

—— (1996), 'Environmental Policy: The "Push–Pull" of Policy-Making', in H. Wallace and W. Wallace (1996: 235–57).

—— (1998), 'Institution-Building from Below and Above: The European Community in Global Environmental Politics', in Sandholtz and Stone Sweet (1998: 283–303).

—— with Damro, C. (1999), 'The Changing Role of the European Union in International Environmental Politics: Institution Building and the Politics of Climate Change', *Environment and Planning C: Government and Policy*, 17, Feb. 53–68.

—— with Hildebrand, P. M. (1998), 'The European Union and Compliance: A Story in the Making', in E. Brown Weiss and H. K. Jacobson (eds.), *Engaging Countries: Strengthening Compliance with International Environmental Accords* (Cambridge, Mass.: MIT Press), 215–52.

Schäuble, W., and Lamers, C. (1994), *Reflections on European Policy* (Bonn: CDU/CSU Fraktion).

Scharpf, F. W. (1988), 'The Joint-Decision Trap: Lessons from German Federalism and European Integration', *Public Administration*, 66/3: 239–78.

—— (1991), Die Handlungsfähigkeit des Staates am Ende des 20. Jahrhunderts', *Politische Vierteljahresschrift*, 32/4: 475–502.

—— (1993), 'Positive und negative Koordination in Verhandlungssystemen', in Héritier (1993: 57–83).

—— (1994*a*), 'Community and Autonomy: Multi-level Policy-Making in the European Union', *Journal of European Public Policy*, 1/2: 219–42.

—— (1994*b*), 'Mehrebenenpolitik im vollendeten Binnenmarkt', *Staatswissenschaft und Staatspraxis*, 5/4: 475–502.

Scharpf, F. W. (1994c), *Optionen des Föderalismus in Deutschland* (Frankurt-on-Main: Campus).

—— (1997), *Games Real Actors Play: Actor-Centred Institutionalism in Policy Research* (Boulder, Colo.: Westview Press).

—— (1999), *Governing in Europe: Effective and Democratic?* (Oxford: Oxford University Press).

Schaub, A. (1998a), 'International cooperation in Antitrust Matters: Making the Point in the Wake of the Boeing MDD Proceedings', *Competition Policy Newsletter*, 4/1: 2–5.

—— (1998b), 'EC Competition System: Proposals for Reform', Paper presented at the Fordham Law Institute, Conference on International Antitrust Law and Policy, New York.

Schiller, K. (1939), *Marktregulierung und Marktordnung in der Weltagrarwirtschaft* (Jena: Fischer).

Schimmelfennig, F. (1999), *The Double Puzzle of EU Enlargement: Liberal Norms, Rhetorical Action, and the Decision to Expand to the East*, ARENA Working Papers No. 99/15 (Oslo: ARENA).

Schindler, P. (1970), 'Public Enterprises and the EEC Treaty', *Common Market Law Review*, 7/1: 57–71.

Schirmann-Duclos, D., and Laforge, F. (1998), *La France et la mer* (Paris: Presses Universitaires de France).

Schmidt, S. K. (1998), 'Commission Activism: Subsuming Telecommunications and Electricity under European Competition Law', *Journal of European Public Policy*, 5/1: 169–84.

Schmitter, P. C. (1992), 'Interests, Powers, and Functions: Emergent Properties and Unintended Consequences in the European Polity'.

—— and Torreblanca, J. I. (1997), *Old 'Foundations' and New 'Rules' for an Enlarged European Union*, European Integration Online Papers, 1/1, <http://eiop.or.at/eiop/texte/1997-001a.htm>.

Schnapper, D. (1992), 'L'Europe, marché ou volonté politique?', *Commentaire*, 60, Winter.

Schnutenhaus, J. (1994), 'Integrated Pollution Prevention and Control: New German Initiatives in the European Environment Council', *European Environmental Law Review*, 3/11: 323–8.

Schott, J. (1994), *The Uruguay Round: An Assessment* (Washington: Institute for International Economics).

Schoutheete, P. de (1986), *La Cooperation politique européenne*, 2nd edn. (Brussels: Labor).

Schreiber, K. (1991), 'The New Approach to Technical Harmonization and Standards', in Hurwitz and Lequesne (1991: 97–112).

Schulte, B. (1991), 'Einführung in die Schlussdiskussion', in Schulte and Zacher (1991: 237–252).

—— (1994a), 'Comments on Articles 4, 10a, and 5 of Reg. 1408/71', in Fuchs (1994).

—— (1994b), 'Sozialrecht', in Lenz (1994: 407–78).

—— and Zacher, H. F. (1991) (eds.), *Wechselwirkungen zwischen dem europäischen Sozialrecht und dem Sozialrecht der Bundesrepublik Deutschland* (Berlin: Duncker & Humblot).

—— (1999), Communication to the authors of Ch. 10.

Schultz, T. W. (1943), *Redirecting Farm Policy* (New York: Macmillan).

Schulze, H. (1994), *Staat und Nation in der europäischen Geschichte* (Munich: C. H. Beck).

Schulz-Weidner, W. (1997), 'Die Konsequenzen des europäischen Binnenmarktes für die deutsche Rentenversicherung', *Deutsche Rentenversicherung*, 8: 445–73.

Schuppert, G. F. (1994), 'Zur Staatswerdung Europas. Überlegungen zu Bedingungsfaktoren und Perspektiven der europäischen Verfassungsentwicklung', *Staatswissenschaft und Staatspraxis*, 5/1: 35–76.

Schutte, J. J. E. (1990), 'Strafrecht in Europees Verband', *Justitiële Verkenningen*, 16/9: 8–17.

Schweitzer, C.-C., and Detef, K. (1990) (eds.), *The Federal Republic of Germany and EC Membership Evaluated* (New York: St Martin's Press).

Scott, A. (1993), 'Financing the Community: The Delors II Package', in Lodge (1993: 69–88).

Scott, J. (1995), *Development Dilemmas in the European Community* (Buckingham: Open University Press).

—— (1996), 'Tragic Triumph: Agricultural Trade, the Common Agricultural Policy and the Uruguay Round', in N. Emiliou and D. O'Keeffe (eds.), *The European Union and World Trade Law: After the Uruguay Round* (Chichester: Wiley), 165–80.

Sedelmeier, U. (1994), *The European Union's Association Policy towards Central and Eastern Europe: Political and Economic Rationales in Conflict*, SEI Working Paper No. 7 (Falmer: Sussex European Institute).

—— (1998*a*), 'The European Union's Association Policy towards the Countries of Central and Eastern Europe: Collective EU Identity and Policy Paradigms in a Composite Policy', University of Sussex Ph.D. thesis, Apr.

—— (1998*b*), 'Regulatory Governance in the EU and Regulatory Alignment of the CEECs: Competing Policy Paradigms for the Internal Market', paper presented at the British Council Ionian Conference 'Making Enlargement Work', Athens and Corfu, 14–17 May.

—— (2000), 'East of Amsterdam: The Implications of the Amsterdam Treaty for Eastern Enlargement', in K. Neunreither and A. Wiener (eds.), *European Integration: Institutional Dynamics and Prospects after Amsterdam* (Oxford: Oxford University Press).

—— and Wallace, H. (1996), 'Policies towards Central and Eastern Europe', in H. Wallace and W. Wallace (1996: 353–87).

Shackleton, M. (1983), 'Fishing for a Policy? The Common Fisheries Policy of the Community', in H. Wallace *et al.* (1983: 349–72).

—— (1986), *The Politics of Fishing in Britain and France* (Aldershot: Gower).

—— (1990), *Financing the European Community* (London: Pinter).

—— (1993*a*), 'The Community Budget after Maastricht', in Cafruny and Rosenthal (1993: 373–90).

—— (1993*b*), 'Keynote Article: The Delors II Budget Package', *Journal of Common Market Studies*, 31, Annual Review of Activities, 11–26.

Shackley, S., Levidow, L., and Tait, J. (1990), 'Contending Rationalities and Regulatory Politics', manuscript.

Shapiro, M., and Stone, A. (1994), 'The New Constitutional Politics of Europe', *Comparative Political Studies*, 26/4: 397–420.

Shaw, J. (1997), 'The European Dimension of Socio-legal Studies', in P. Thomas (ed.), *Socio legal Studies* (Aldershot: Dartmouth), 310–41.

Siebert, H. (1990*a*), 'The Harmonization Issue in Europe: Prior Agreement or a Competitive Process', in Siebert (1990*b*: 53–90).

—— (1990*b*) (ed.), *The Completion of the Internal Market* (Tübingen: J. C. B. Mohr).

Sieveking, K. (1998) (ed.), *Soziale Sicherung bei Pflegebedürftigkeit in der Europäischen Union* (Baden-Baden: Nomos).

Sinn, H.-W. (1994), 'Wieviel Brussel braucht Europa? Subsidiarität, Zentralisierung und Fiskalwettbewerb im Lichte der ökonomischen Theorie', *Staatswissenschaft und Staatspraxis*, 5/2: 155–86.

Skjærseth, J. B. (1994), 'The Climate Policy of the EC: Too Hot to Handle?', *Journal of Common Market Studies*, 32/1: 25–45.

Slaughter, A.-M., Stone Sweet, A., and J. H. H. Weiler (1998), *The European Court and National Courts* (Oxford: Hart).

Smith, A. (1995), 'L'Intégration communautaire face au territoire: les fonds structurels et les zones rurales en France, en Espagne et au Royaume Uni', Université Pierre Mendès (Grenoble) Ph.D. thesis.

Smith, A. (1998), 'The Sub-regional Level: Key Battleground for the Structural Funds', in Le Gales and Lesquesne (1998: 50–66).

Smith, A. D. (1992), 'National Identity and the Idea of European Identity', *International Affairs*, 68/1: 55–76.

Smith, B. (1999), 'Politics and Policy-Making at the 1996–1997 European Union Intergovernmental Conference', London School of Economics Ph.D. thesis.

Smith, J. (1999), *Europe's Elected Parliament* (Sheffield: Sheffield Academic Press for UACES).

Smith, K. E. (1998), *The Making of EU Foreign Policy: The Case of Eastern Europe* (London: Macmillan).

Smith, M. (1994), 'The Commission and External Relations', in Edwards and Spence (1994: 50–66).

Smith, M. A. M., and Wallace, H. (1994), 'The European Union: Towards a Policy for Europe', *International Affairs*, 70/3: 429–44.

—— Holmes, P. M., Sedelmeier, U., Smith, E., Wallace, H., and Young, A. R. (1996), *The European Union and Central and Eastern Europe*, SEI Working Paper No. 15 (Falmer: Sussex European Institute).

Smouts, M.-C. (1998), *Les nouvelles relations internationales: pratiques et théories* (Paris: Presses de Science Po), Eng. trans. (London: Hurst, forthcoming).

Snyder, F. G. (1985), *Law of the Common Agricultural Policy* (London: Sweet & Maxwell).

Soetendorp, B. (1990), 'The Evolution of the EC/EU as a Single Foreign Policy Actor', in Carlsnaes and Smith (1990: 103–19).

Spence, D. (1991), 'Enlargement without Accession: The EC's Response to German Unification', RIIA Discussion Paper No. 36 (London: Royal Institute of International Affairs).

Spencer, M. (1990), *1992 and All That: Civil Liberties in the Balance* (London: Civil Liberties Trust).

Spierenburg, D., and Poidevin, R. (1994), *The history of the High Authority of the European Coal and Steel* (London: Weidenfeld & Nicolson).

Spinelli, A., *et al.* (1983), *Report on the Substance of the Preliminary Draft Treaty Establishing the European Union*, Committee on Institutional Affairs, PE 83.326/final, European Parliament Working Document 1–575/83 (Brussels).

Stavridis, S. (1997), 'The Common Foreign and Security Policy of the European Union: Why Institutional Arrangements are not Enough', in Stavridis *et al.*, (1997: 87–122).

—— Mossialos, E., Morgan, R., and Machin, H (1997) (eds.), *New Challenges to the European Union: Policies and Policy-Making* (Aldershot: Dartmouth).

Steel, D. (1998), 'The Role of the European Parliament in the CFP', in Gray (1998: 33–51).

Stehr, N. (1994), *Knowledge Societies* (London: Sage).

Stein, J. G. (1993), 'Political Economy and Security', in Evans *et al.* (1993: 77–103).

Stern, J. (1990), *European Gas Markets: Challenge and Opportunity in the 1990s* (London: Royal Institute of International Affairs).

Stevens, C., and Webb, C. (1983), 'The Political Economy of Sugar: A Window on the CAP', in H. Wallace *et al.* (1983: 321–48).

Stoffaes, C. (1995) (ed.), *Europe à l'épreuve de l'intérêt général* (Paris: ASPE).

Stone, D. A. (1989), 'At Risk in the Welfare State', *Social Research*, 56/3: 591–633.

Stone Sweet, A., and Brunell, T. L. (1997), 'The European Court and the National Courts: A Statistical Analysis of Preliminary References, 1961–95', *Journal of European Public Policy*, 5/1: 66–97.

—— and Caporaso, T. (1998): 'From Free Trade to Supranational Policy', in Sandholtz and Stone Sweet (1998: 92–133).

Story, J. (1993) (ed.), *The New Europe: Politics, Government, and Economy since 1945* (Oxford: Blackwell).

Strange, M. (1988), *Family Farming: A New Economic Vision* (London: University of Nebraska Press).

Strange, S., and Tooze, R. (1981) (eds.), *The International Politics of Surplus Capacity: Competition for Market Shares in the World Recession* (London: George Allen & Unwin).

Strasser, D. (1992), *The Finances of Europe*, 7th edn. (Luxembourg: Office for Official Publications of the European Communities).

Streeck, W. (1992), *Social Institutions and Economic Performance: Studies of Industrial Relations in Advanced Capitalist Economies* (London: Sage).

—— (1995), 'From Market Making to State Building?', in Leibfried and Pierson (1995b: 389–431).

—— (1998), *The Internationalization of Industrial Relations in Europe: Prospects and Problems*, DP 98/2 (Cologne: Max Planck Institute for Social Research).

—— and Schmitter, P. C. (1991), 'From National Corporatism to Transnational Pluralism: Organized Interests in the Single European Market', *Politics and Society*, 19/2: 133–64.

Stubb, A. (1997), 'The 1996 Intergovernmental Conference and the Management of Flexible Integration', *Journal of European Public Policy*, 4/1: 37–55.

Sun, J.-M., and Pelkmans, J. (1995), 'Regulatory Competition and the Single Market', *Journal of Common Market Studies*, 33/1: 67–89.

Sutherland, P., Albrecht, E., Babusiaux, C., Corby, B., Green, P., and Tramontana (1992), High-Level Group on the Operation of the Internal Market, *The Internal Market after 1992: Meeting the Challenge* (Luxembourg: Office for Official Publications of the European Communities).

Swaan, A. de (1992), 'Perspectives for Transnational Social Policy', *Government and Opposition*, 27/1: 33–52.

Swann, D. (1983), *Competition and Industrial Policy in the European Community* (London: Methuen).

—— (1992) (ed.), *The Single European Market and Beyond* (London: Routledge).

Swinbank, A. (1989), 'The Common Agricultural Policy and the Politics of European Decision-Making', *Journal of Common Market Studies*, 27/4: 303–22.

Symes, D. (1999) (ed.), *Alternative Management Systems for Fisheries* (Oxford: Fishing News Books).

Tait, J., and Levidow, L. (1992), 'Proactive and Reactive Approaches to Risk Regulation: The Case of Biotechnology', *Futures*, 24/3, Apr., 219–31.

Taschner, H. C. (1990), *Schengen oder die Abschaffung der Personenkontrollen an den Binnengrenzen der EG*, Vorträge, Reden und Berichte aus dem Europa-Institut No. 227 (Saarbrücken: Universität des Saarlandes).

Taylor, P. (1996), *The European Union in the 1990s* (Oxford: Oxford University Press).

Thatcher, M. (1984), 'Europe—the Future', paper presented to the European Council, Fontainebleau, 25–6 June.

Thielemann, E. (1998), 'EC State Aid Control: Driving a Wedge between Europe and the Regions', paper presented at the Third UACES Research Conference, University of Lincolnshire and Humberside, Lincoln, 9–11 Sept.

Thivend, P. (1998), *Les Fonds structurels en Bretagne dans une Union élargie*, Rapport au Conseil Économique et Social de la région Bretagne (Rennes).

Thom, M. (1993), 'The Governance of a Common in the European Community: The Common Fisheries Policy', University of Strathclyde Ph.D. thesis.

Tidow, S. (1998), *Europäische Beschäftigungspolitik. Die Entstehung eines neuen Politikfeldes. Ursachen, Hintergründe und Verlauf des politischen Prozesses*, Marburg University, Research Group on the European Communities, Working Paper 18 (Marburg: Marburg University).

Tiersky, R. (1992), 'France in the New Europe', *Foreign Affairs*, 71/2: 131–46.

Tiilikainen, T., and Damgaard Petersen, I. (1993) (eds.), *The Nordic Countries and the EC* (Copenhagen: Copenhagen Political Studies Press).

Tiratsoo, N., and Tomlinson, J. (1997), 'Exporting the "Gospel of Productivity": United States Technical Assistance and British Industry 1945–1960', *Business History Review*, 71/1: 41–81.

Topfer, K. (1992), 'The ECO-nomic Revolution: Challenge and Opportunity for the Twenty-First Century', *International Environmental Affairs*, 4/3: 273–80.

Torreblanca, J. I. (1997), *The European Community and Central Europe (1989–1993): Foreign Policy and Decision-Making*, Instituto Juan March de Estudios e Investigaciones Ph.D. thesis (Madrid: Ediciones Península; and Aldershot: Ashgate, forthcoming).

—— (1998), Overlapping Games and Cross-Cutting Coalitions in the European Union', *West European Politics*, 21/2: 134–53.

Tracy, M. (1989), *Government and Agriculture in Western Europe* (New York: Harvester Wheatsheaf).

Transpol (1994) (ed.), *Internationalisering door grenzeloze samenwerking* (Lelystad: Koninklijke Vermande bv).

Tsakaloyannis, P. (1991), 'The Acceleration of History and the Reopening of the Political Debate in the European Community', *Journal of European Integration*, 14/2: 87–9.

Tsebelis, G. (1990), *Nested Games* (Berkeley: University of California Press).

—— (1994), 'The Power of the European Parliament as a Conditional Agenda-Setter', *American Political Science Review*, 88/1: 128–42.

Tsoukalis, L. (1977), *The Politics and Economics of European Monetary Integration* (London: Allen & Unwin).

—— (1993), *The New European Economy: The Politics and Economics of Integration*, 2nd edn. (Oxford: Oxford University Press).

—— (1997), *The New European Economy Revisited* (Oxford: Oxford University Press).

—— (1998), *The European Agenda: Issues of Globalization, Equity and Legitimacy*, Jean Monnet Chair Papers (Florence: European University Institute).

—— (forthcoming), *European Political Economy*, 2nd edn. (Oxford: Oxford University Press).

—— and Silva Ferreira, A. da (1980), 'Management of Industrial Surplus Capacity in the European Community', *International Organization*, 34/3: 355–75.

—— Smith, A., and Hall, R. (eds.) (forthcoming), *Competitiveness and Cohesion: An Evaluation of EU Policies* (Oxford: Oxford University Press).

Tugendhat, C. (1985), 'How to Get Europe Moving Again', *International Affairs*, 61/3: 421–9.

UK (United Kingdom), Laboratory of the Government Chemist (1991), *Biotechnology: A Plain Man's Guide to the Support and Regulations in the UK* (London: Department of Trade and Industry).

Union des Armateurs à la Pêche de France (1998), 'Réponse de l'UAPF au questionnaire de la Commission sur la politique commune de la pêche après 2002', *La Pêche Maritime*, May–July, 322–34.

Usher, J. A. (1988), *Legal Aspects of Agriculture in the European Community* (Oxford: Clarendon Press).

Valence, G. (1990), 'L'Engrenage européen', *L'Express*, 19 Oct.

van Calster, G. van, and Deketelaere, K. (1998), 'Amsterdam, the Intergovernmental Conference and Greening the EU Treaty', *European Environmental Law Review*, 7, Jan., 12–25.

van Cleveland, H. B. (1966) (ed.), *The Atlantic Idea and its European Rivals* (New York: McGraw-Hill).

van den Bossche, P. (1997), 'The European Community and the Uruguay Round Agreements', in J. Jackson and A. Sykes, *Implementing the Uruguay Round* (New York: Clarendon Press), 23–103.

van der Wel, J., and Bruggeman, W. (1993), *Europese Politieke Samenwerking: Internationale Gremia* (Brussels: Politeia).

van Eekelen, W. (1993), 'WEU Prepares the Way for New Missions', *Nato Review*, 5 (Oct.), 19–23.

van Schendelen, M. P. C. M. (1998) (ed.), *EU Committees as Influential Policy-Makers* (Aldershot: Ashgate).

Vasey, M. (1988), 'Decision-Making in the Agricultural Council and the "Luxembourg Compromise"', *Common Market Law Review*, 25/4: 725–32.

Vaubel, R. (1994), 'The Political Economy of Centralization and the European Community', *Public Choice*, 59/1: 151–85.

Verhoeve, B., Bennett, G., and Wilkinson, D. (1992), *Maastricht and the Environment* (London: Institute for European Environmental Policy).

Vernet, D. (1992), 'The Dilemma of French Foreign Policy', *International Affairs*, 68/4: 655–64.

Vesterdorf, B. (1994), 'Complaints Concerning Infringements of Competition Law within the Context of European Community Law', *Common Market Law Review*, 32/1: 77–104.

Villain, C., and Arnold, R. (1990), 'New Directions for European Agricultural Policy', Report of the CEPS CAP Expert Group (Brussels: Centre for European Policy Studies).

Visegrád (1992), *Memorandum of the Governments of the Czech and Slovak Federal Republic, the Republic of Hungary, and the Republic of Poland on Strengthening their Integration with the European Community and on the Perspective of Accession*, 11 Sept.

—— (1993), Aide-Memoire, 2 June.

Vogel, D. (1993a), 'Environmental Policy in the European Community', in Kamieniecki (1993: 181–97).

—— (1993b), 'The Making of EC Environmental Policy', in S. S. Andersen and Eliassen (1993: 115–32).

Vogel-Polsky, E., and Vogel, J. (1991), *L'Europe sociale 1993: illusion, alibi ou réalité?* (Brussels: Éditions de l'Université Libre de Bruxelles).

Volcansek, M. (1992), 'The European Court of Justice: Supranational Policy Making', *West European Politics*, 15/3: 109–21.

Waarden, F. van, and Unger, B. (1994) (eds.), *Convergence or Diversity? The Pressure of Internationalization on Economic Governance Institutions and Policy Outcomes* (Aldershot: Avebury).

Waever, O., Buzan, B., Kelstrup, M., and Lemaître, L. (1993), *Identity, Migration and the New Security Agenda in Europe* (London: Pinter).

Walker, N. (1993a), 'The Accountability of European Police Institutions', *European Journal on Criminal Policy and Research*, 1/4: 34–52.

—— (1993b), 'The International Dimension', in Reiner and Spencer (1993: 113–71).

—— (1994), 'European Integration and European Policing: A Complex Relationship', in M. Anderson and den Boer (1994: 22–45).

—— (1998), 'European Policing and the Politics of Regulation', in P. J. Cullen and W. C. Gilmore (eds.), *Crime sans frontières: International and European Legal Approaches*, Hume Papers on Public Policy, 6/1–2: 141–60 (Edinburgh: Edinburgh University Press).

Wallace, H. (1973), *National Governments in the European Communities* (London: PEP/RIIA).

—— (1977), 'The Establishment of the Regional Development Fund: Common Policy or Pork Barrel?', in H. Wallace *et al.* (1977: 137–64).

—— (1980), *Budgetary Politics: The Finances of the European Community* (London: Allen & Unwin).

—— (1983), 'Distributional Politics: Dividing up the Community Cake', in H. Wallace *et al.* (1983: 81–114).

—— (1984), 'Bilateral, Trilateral and Multilateral Negotiations in the European Community', in Morgan and Bray (1984: 156–74).

—— (1991), 'The Europe that Came in from the Cold', *International Affairs*, 67/4: 647–63.

Wallace, H. (1993), 'European Governance in Turbulent Times', *Journal of Common Market Studies*, 31/3: 293–303.

—— (1994), 'The EC and Europe after Maastricht', in Miall (1994: 19–24).

—— (1995), 'Die Dynamik des EU Institutionsgefüges', in Jachtenfuchs and Kohler-Koch (1995: 141–64).

—— (1999*a*), *The Domestication of Europe: Contrasting Experiences of EU Membership and Non-Membership*, 6th Daalder Lecture (Leiden: Leiden University), 13 Mar.

—— (1999*b*), 'Whose Europe is it Anyway?', *European Journal of Political Research*, 35/3: 287–306.

—— and Wallace, W. (1995), *Flying Together in a More Diverse European Union* (The Hague: Netherlands Scientific Council for Government Policy).

—— —— (1996) (eds.), *Policy-Making in the European Union*, 3rd edn. (Oxford: Oxford University Press).

—— and Young, A. R. (1997) (eds.), *Participation and Policy-making in the European Union*, (Oxford: Oxford University Press).

—— Wallace, W., and Webb, C. (1977) (eds.), *Policy-Making in the European Community* (Chichester: Wiley).

—— —— —— (1983) (eds.), *Policy-Making in the European Community*, 2nd edn. (Chichester: Wiley).

Wallace, W. (1983*a*), 'Less than a Federation, More than a Regime: The Community as a Political System', in H. Wallace *et al.* (1983: 403–36).

—— (1983*b*), 'Political Cooperation: Integration through Intergovernmentalism', in H. Wallace, *et al.* (1983: 337–402).

—— (1984), 'European Defence Cooperation: The Reopening Debate', *Survival*, 26/6: 251–61.

—— (1990*a*), 'Introduction: The Dynamics of European Integration', in W. Wallace (1990*b*: 1–24).

—— (1990*b*) (ed.), *The Dynamics of European Integration* (London: Pinter).

—— (1990*c*), *The Transformation of Western Europe* (London: Pinter).

—— (1994*a*), *Regional Integration: The West European Experience* (Washington: Brookings Institution).

—— (1994*b*), 'Rescue or Retreat? The Nation State in Western Europe, 1945–93', *Political Studies*, 42, special issue, 52–76.

—— (1996), 'Government without Statehood: The Unstable Equilibrium', in H. Wallace and W. Wallace (1996: 439–60).

—— (1999), 'The Sharing of Sovereignty: The European Paradox', *Political Studies*, 47/3: 502–21.

—— and Allen, D. (1977), 'Political Cooperation: Procedure as Substitute for Policy', in H. Wallace *et al.* (1977: 227–42).

—— and Smith, J. (1995), 'Democracy or Technocracy? European Integration and the Problem of Popular Consent', *West European Politics*, 18/3: 137–57.

Watson, J. D., and Tooze, J. (1981), *The DNA Story: A Documentary History of Gene Cloning* (San Francisco, Calif.: W. H. Freeman).

Weale, A. (1992*a*), *The New Politics of Pollution* (Manchester: Manchester University Press).

—— (1992*b*), 'Vorsprung durch Technik? The Politics of German Environmental Regulation', in Dyson (1992: 159–84).

—— (1997), 'The Single Market, European Integration and Political Legitimacy', in D. G. Mayes (ed.), *The Evolution of the Single European Market* (Aldershot: Edward Elgar), 199–225.

—— (1999), 'European Environmental Policy by Stealth: The Dysfunctionality of Functionalism?', *Environment and Planning C: Government and Policy*, 17, Feb., 37–52.

—— and Williams, A. (1992), 'Between Economy and Ecology? The Single Market and the Integration of Environmental Policy', *Environmental Politics*, 1/4: 45–64.

—— —— (1994), 'The Single Market and Environmental Policy', paper presented at the ESRC/COST A7 Conference, University of Exeter, 8–11 Sept.

Weatherhill, S., and Beaumont, P. (1993), *EC Law* (London: Penguin).

Weaver, R. K. (1986), 'The Politics of Blame Avoidance', *Journal of Public Policy*, 6: 371–98.

Webb, C. (1983), 'Theoretical Perspectives and Problems', in H. Wallace *et al.* (1983: 197–226).

Weber, M. (1978), *Economy and Society*, ed. G. Roth and C. Wittich (Berkeley: University of California Press).

Weber, S. (1994), 'Origins of the European Bank for Reconstruction and Development', *International Organization*, 48/1: 1–38.

Weiler, J. H. H. (1991), 'The Transformation of Europe', *Yale Law Journal*, 100/8: 2403–83.

—— (1992) 'After Maastricht: Community Legitimacy in post-1992 Europe', in Adams (1992: 11–41).

—— (1993), 'Journey to an Unknown Destination: A Retrospective and Prospective of the European Court of Justice in the Arena of Political Integration', *Journal of Common Market Studies*, 31/4: 417–46.

—— (1994), 'A Quiet Revolution: The European Court of Justice and its Interlocutors', *Comparative Political Studies*, 26/4: 510–34.

—— (1997), 'The Reformation of European Constitutionalism', *Journal of Common Market Studies*, 35/1: 417–46.

—— (1999), *The Constitution of Europe: 'Do the New Clothes Have an Emperor?' and Other Essays on European Integration* (Cambridge: Cambridge University Press).

Weimer, D. (1995) (ed.), *Institutional Design* (Norwell, Mass.:).

Wellens, K., and Borchardt, G. (1989), 'Soft Law in European Community Law', *European Law Review*, 14/5: 267–321.

Werner, P., *et al.* (1970), 'Report to the Council and the Commission on the Realization by Stages of Economic and Monetary Union in the Community', *Bulletin of the EC* suppl., 11.

Wessels, W. (1990), 'Administrative Interaction', in W. Wallace (1990*b*: 229–41).

—— (1992), 'Staat und (westeuropäische) Integration. Die Fusionthese', *Politische Vierteljahresschrift*, special issue, 23/92, 36–61.

—— (1997), 'An Ever Closer Fusion? A Dynamic Macropolitical View on Integration Processes', *Journal of Common Market Studies*, 35/2: 267–99.

Wester, R. (1992), 'The Netherlands and European Political Union', in Laursen and Vanhoonacker (1992: 205–14).

Westlake, M. (1994), *A Modern Guide to the European Parliament* (London: Pinter).

—— (1995), *The Council of the European Union* (London: Cartermill).

WEU (1992), *Petersberg Declaration*, WEU Council of Ministers, Bonn, 19 June (London: WEU Press and Information Service).

Widgrén, M. (1994), *The Relation between Voting Power and Policy Impact in the European Union*, CEPR Discussion Paper No. 1033 (London: CEPR).

Wiener, A.(1998), 'The Embedded *Acquis Communautaire*: Transmission Belt and Prism of New Governance', *European Law Journal*, 4/3, Sept., 294–315.

Wildavsky, A. (1991), 'Public Policy', in B. D. Davis (ed.), *The Genetic Revolution: Scientific Prospects and Public Perceptions* (Baltimore: Johns Hopkins University Press), 77–104.

Wildenmann, R. (1991) (ed.), *Staatswerdung Europas? Optionen für eine europäische Union* (Baden-Baden: Nomos).

Wilensky, H. J. (1976), *The 'New Corporatism': Centralization and the Welfare State* (London: Sage).

Wilkinson, D. (1997), 'Towards Sustainability in the European Union? Steps within the European Commission towards Integrating the Environment into Other European Policy Sectors', *Environmental Politics*, 6, Spring, 153–73.

Wilks, S., and McGowan, L. (1995*a*), 'Discretion in European Merger Control: The German Regime in Context', *Journal of European Public Policy*, 2/1: 41–68.

—— —— (1995*b*), 'Disarming the Commission: The Debate over a European Cartel Office', *Journal of Common Market Studies*, 33/2: 259–73.

Willgerodt, H. (1983), *Die Agrarpolitik der europäischen Gemeinschaft in der Krise*, Ordo, 34 (Stuttgart: Fischer).

Winand, P. (1993), 'Lobbying, Democracy, the Action Committee for the United States of Europe and its Successor: A Case Study', paper presented at the international seminar 'Démocratie et construction européenne face aux défis de l'Union politique et de la Grande Europe', European Parliament, 11–12 Nov.

Winckelmann, I. (1994) (ed.), *Das Maastricht Urteil des Bundesverfassungsgerichts vom 12. Oktober 1993*, Dokumentation des Verfahrens (Berlin: Duncker & Humbolt).

Winters, L. A. (1992), 'The Europe Agreements: With a Little Help from our Friends', in CEPR (1992: 17–33).

Wishlade, F. (1998*a*), 'EC Competition Policy and Regional Aid: The Trojan Horse Approach to Regional Policy-Making', paper presented at the Third UACES Research Conference, University of Lincolnshire and Humberside, Lincoln, 9–11 Sept.

—— (1998*b*), 'Competition Policy or Cohesion Policy by the Back Door? The Commission Guidelines on National Regional Aid', *European Competition Law Review*, 6: 343–57.

Wolf, K. D. (1997), 'Entdemokratisierung durch Selbstbindung in der Europäischen Union', in Wolf (ed.), *Projekt Europa im Übergang? Probleme, Modelle und Strategien des Regierens in der Europäischen Union* (Baden-Baden: Nomos), 271–94.

Wolf, M. (1994), *The Resistible Appeal of Fortress Europe* (Washington: American Enterprise Institute for Public Policy Research).

Wolters, M., and Coffey, P. (1990) (eds.), *The Netherlands and EC Membership Evaluated* (New York: St Martin's Press).

Wood, P. C. (1995), 'The Franco-German Relationship in the post-Maastricht Era', in C. Rhodes and Mazey (1995: 221–43).

Woolcock, S. (1991), *Market Access Issues in EC–US Relations: Trading Partners or Trading Blows?* (London: Royal Institute of International Affairs).

—— (1993), 'EC Trade Diplomacy', in Story (1993: 292–313).

—— (1994), *The Single European Market: Centralization or Competition among National Rules?* (London: Royal Institute of International Affairs).

—— (1996), 'Competition among Rules in the Single European Market', in W. Bratton, J. McCahery, S. Picciotto, and C. Scott (eds.), *International Regulatory Competition and Coordination: Perspectives on Economic Regulation in Europe and the United States* (Oxford: Clarendon Press), 289–321.

—— and Hodges, M. (1996), 'EU Policy in the Uruguay Round: The Story behind the Headlines', in H. Wallace and W. Wallace (1996: 301–24).

—— —— and Schreiber, K. (1991), *Britain, Germany and 1992: The Limits of Deregulation* (London: Royal Institute of International Affairs).

Woolley, J. (1994), 'Linking Political and Monetary Union: The Maastricht Agenda and German Domestic Politics', in Eichengreen and Frieden (1994: 67–86).

WTO (1995) (World Trade Organization), *Trade Policy Review: European Union 1995* (Geneva: WTO).

—— (1997), *Annual Report 1997* (Geneva: WTO).

Wynne, B., and Waterton, C. (1998), 'Public Information on the Environment: The Role of the European Environment Agency', in *British Environmental Policy and Europe: Politics and Policy in Transition* (London: Routledge), 119–28.

Young, A. R. (1995), 'Participation and Policy-Making in the European Community: Mediating between Contending Interests', paper presented at the Fourth Biennial International Conference of the European Community Studies Association, Charleston, SC, 11–14 May.

—— (1997), 'Consumption without Representation? Consumers in the Single Market', in H. Wallace and Young (1997: 206–35).

—— and Wallace, H. (2000), *Regulatory Politics in the Enlarging European Union: Weighing Civic and Producer Interests* (Manchester: Manchester University Press).

Zanders, P. (1994), 'Europese politiesamenwerking in een historisch perspektief', in Transpol (1994: 7–20).

Zielonka, J. (1998) (ed.), *Paradoxes of European Foreign Policy* (The Hague: Kluwer Law International).

Zito, A. R. (1995a), 'Integrating the Environment into the European Union: The History of the Controversial Carbon Tax', in C. Rhodes and Mazey (1995: 431–48).

—— (1995b), 'The Role of Technical Expertise and Institutional Innovation in EU Environment Policy', University of Pittsburgh Ph.D. thesis.

—— (1998), 'Comparing Environmental Policy-Making in Transnational Institutions', *Journal of European Public Policy*, 5/4: 671–90.

—— (2000), *Creating Environmental Policy in the European Union* (London: Macmillan).

Zuleeg, M. (1993), 'Die Zahlung von Ausgleichszulagen über die Binnengrenzen der europäischen Gemeinschaft', *Deutsche Rentenversicherung*, 2: 71–5.

Index